Ragnar Hanas, M.D.

INSULIN-DEPENDENT DIABETES

in Children, Adolescents and Adults

HOW TO BECOME AN EXPERT ON YOUR OWN DIABETES

For dosages and applications mentioned in this book, the reader can be assured that the author has taken great lenghts to ensure that the indications reflect the standard of knowledge at the time this work was completed. However, insulin needs and diabetes treatment must be individually tailored for each and every person with diabetes. Advice and recommendations in this book cannot be expected to be generally applicable in all situations and always need to be supplemented with individual assessment by a diabetes team. The author cannot accept any legal responsibility or liability for any errors or omissions, or the use of the material contained herein and the decisions based on such use. Neither will the author be liable for direct, indirect, special, incidental or consequential damages arising out of the use, or inability to use, the contents of this book.

The use of general descriptive names, trade names, trademarks, etc., in this publication, even if not specifically identified, does not imply that these names are not protected by the relevant laws and regulations. Actrapid, Insulatard, Monotard, Mixtard, Ultratard, Penset, Novolin and Velosulin insulins are trademarks of Novo Nordisk A/S. Humulin, Humutard, Humaject and Humalog insulins are trademarks of Eli-Lilly & Co. Isuhuman Infusat, Isuhuman Rapid, Isuhuman Basal and Isuhuman Comb insulins are trademarks of Hoechst AG. The indwelling catheter Insuflon is a trademark of Maersk Medical, Denmark and is distributed by Chronimed Inc., Minnetonka, Minnesota in the US.

Ask your Becton Dickinson representative in your home country how to obtain this book. Let me know your views and impressions of the contents so that we can together improve the treatment of diabetes.

Ragnar Hanas

M.D., Consultant Pediatrician
Department of Pediatrics
Uddevalla Hospital
S-451 80 Uddevalla
Sweden

Tel   +46-522-92000
Fax +46-522-93149
e-mail ragnar.hanas@bll.se

ISBN 91-630-6261-5

First edition in English 1998

Published by Piara HB, Uddevalla, Sweden
Printed by Studentlitteratur AB, Lund, Sweden

Supported by a medical grant from Becton Dickinson. The author's view on different issues is not necessarily the same as those of Becton Dickinson's.

To Pia and our children

You might very well feel that there is an overwhelming amount of knowledge you must take in, but nobody expects you to memorize the contents of this book. If you use it as a reference book and read a bit at a time the context will gradually be clearer.

The cover illustration shows how glucose enters into the cell with the help of insulin. See page 20 for further information.

Contents

Foreword

"If you want something well done, do it yourself" is a wise old saying, but of course you need to know how to do it as well. Having diabetes requires one to have a thorough understanding of the disease and it's management. As anyone living with diabetes knows, it is an illness that you have to live with 24 hours a day.

Traditionally physicians have decided insulin dosages and administration intervals and the patient took the insulin as prescribed, neither less, nor more. I now have more than ten years of experience doing quite the opposite, teaching the fundamentals of diabetes to start off with, and gradually delegating more and more of the daily responsibility of the diabetes care to the patient. It usually takes about a year before a patient has experienced most of the daily life situations that are affected by diabetes such as holidays, birthdays, parties, illness and

The diabetes clinic will often function as an information center where we pass on good ideas from one family to the other.

heavy exercise. As you feel more secure with yourself you will begin to accumulate your own experiences and discover things about your diabetes that we at the diabetes clinic will want to take part in. It is my impression that we often function as an information centre where we pass on suggestions and knowledge from one family to another.

Knowledge also changes with time. What was advisable 5 to 10 years ago is often not applicable now. In the past when informing families about new diabetes treatment strategies, I would often hear: "Well, we have done it like that for many years, but we didn't dare tell anyone". Nowadays we share knowledge and learning with each other instead.

This book deals with type 1 diabetes in children, adolescents and young adults. The treatment of type 2-diabetes is not covered at all. I describe methods of treating diabetes that are common in Sweden as well as in many other countries. Other methods may be employed at other centers. There are many ways to reach the goal, which is to find a way of treating your diabetes effectively.

The underlying theme of this book is: "If you want something done well, do it yourself". You are the only one that can be by your side 24 hours a day and one day you can be the greatest authority on your own diabetes. Learning to care for your diabetes from scratch, like learning anything else, is a matter of trial and error. And in the process, mistakes are inevitable. You learn something from every mistake and somehow the learning impact of your own mistakes is always greater than from the mistakes other people have made.

I have written this book keeping in mind the family with a member who has newly been diagnosed with diabetes. If you already have diabetes you will probably recognize many areas. Do not try to read the book from cover to cover or to memorize it. Use it as a reference book instead. The small exponents in the text indicate the references which are found at the end of the book. I have included many latin medical terms but the text is self-explanatory so you will not need to learn these terms to understand the meaning of the text.

You may find some parts of this book difficult to understand, especially on the first reading. Please don't let this discourage you. Put the book aside for a while. When you come back and read the text a second time, and when you learn more of the context of diabetes, it will all begin to fit together.

Remember that you can learn things in many different ways. We usually schedule lessons where we have a systematic approach to diabetes. However, the spontaneous conversation with a nurse, her intonation, her body language and glances also contain information. During the more formal lessons you will get the official views. However, an unofficial view is also available from the assistant nurse, fellow patients and others by watching their body language, pauses while talking, what is said and perhaps especially what is not said. This type of information will also be passed on by doctors in their every-day contact. Body language often makes a stronger impact than words and in the choice between official information and informal information the patient will often remember the informal information.[265]

If a member of the family has been in contact with diabetes earlier, perhaps through a relative or a work mate, they will often have a fairly good picture of what diabetes is like. It is very important to remember that this experience is not at all the same as having diabetes yourself or in your own family. The treatment potential is quite different for the person just having been diagnosed with diabetes compared to a person who has had diabetes for a number of years.

Often many of your first thoughts will concern the future and the difficult things that may await you. You will receive straight forward information from your diabetes team concerning complications that

CECILIA 8 YEARS

might arise in the future, why these complications arise and how to postpone them as long as possible or even avoid them. Our policy is to tell all there is to tell and not to exclude any information. Sometimes there is no straight answer to a question but we will tell you as much as we know.

During the first weeks we want you to get to know your child or yourself all over again. Your child (or you) now has diabetes and initially you will find things difficult, insecure and at times even a bit dangerous since you don't yet know how to tackle the different situations. But you will soon get to know your child/yourself in this new situation and you will gradually feel more secure with the variety of situations you are presented with in life.

"It is time to replace the old mistakes with more modern ones."

Grönköping's Weekly

"The ability to think differently today than yesterday is what separates the wise from the stubborn."

John Steinbeck

We must have a humble attitude in that what we today look upon as established knowledge may tomorrow turn out quite differently.

Introduction

Diabetes mellitus, most often just referred to as diabetes, has been known to mankind since ancient times. Diabetes means "flowing through" and mellitus means "sweet as honey". Diabetes is usually divided into type 1 and type 2. Egyptian hieroglyphic findings from 1550 BC. illustrate the symptoms of diabetes. Some data indicate that the type of diabetes depicted was type 2 and that type 1 diabetes is a relatively new disease, appearing within the last two centuries.[63]

Diabetes used to be diagnosed by tasting the urine. There was no real treatment except for alcohol which lowered the blood sugar level. Before insulin was discovered, diabetes was a disease with a deadly outcome. The first human to be treated with insulin was a 14 year-old boy, Leonard Thomson, in Canada in the year 1922. In Sweden the first insulin was administrated in 1923, among others to a 5 year-old boy who subsequently lived almost 70 years with his diabetes. Insulin was initially distributed as a powder or tablets which were mixed with water before being injected.

Type 1 diabetes (insulin-dependent diabetes, IDDM)

Type 1 diabetes is also called juvenile diabetes as the onset is usually before the age of 35. Type 1 diabetes is insulin-dependent, meaning that insulin therapy is required from the onset of the disease. In type 1 diabetes the insulin-producing cells of the pancreas are destroyed, eventually leading to a total loss of insulin production. Without insulin, glucose remains in the blood stream and the blood glucose level increases, especially after meal time. Glucose will then be passed out into the urine.

Type 2 diabetes (non insulin-dependent diabetes, NIDDM)

Type 2 diabetes is also called adult onset diabetes as the onset usually occurs after the age of 35 - 40.

In type 2 diabetes the ability to produce insulin is not totally abolished. The body displays an increased insulin resistance, which however can be improved by medication. Most often insulin therapy is not needed initially in type 2 diabetes. The tablets do not contain insulin, but act by increasing the sensitivity for insulin in the cells or by increasing the release of insulin from the pancreas. Type 2 diabetes is also called non insulin-dependent diabetes but approximately 10 % are treated with insulin in much the same way as those with type 1 diabetes are.

Some children and adolescents may have a rare form of type 2 diabetes (MODY) which is characterized by low insulin requirements and a strong heredity for diabetes.

Being overweight will make you more vulnerable to type 2 diabetes as your body in the long run will not be able to produce the large amounts of insulin necessary to keep the blood sugar normal. Japanese sumo wrestlers with a body weight of 200 - 260 kilos have an increased risk of type 2 diabetes when they stop their intensive training.

Insulin-dependent diabetes in children, adolescents and adults

How common is diabetes?

The number of individuals having diabetes varies greatly from country to country. In Europe and the USA it is estimated that 50 million people have type 1 or type 2 diabetes. The risk for a child to develop type 1 diabetes before adulthood is approximately 0.3 - 0.5 % in the Scandinavian countries, making type 1 diabetes the second most common chronic disease in childhood and adolescence, second only to asthma.[231]

In Sweden 350 - 400 children and adolescents in the age-group of 0 - 14 years of age are diagnosed with diabetes each year.[96] There is a slow but steady increase in this incidence (the number of cases diagnosed per year).[98] Finland has the highest incidence of childhood and adolescent diabetes in the world and Sweden comes in third after Sardinia. In Japan childhood and adolescent diabetes is very uncommon. Although 120 million people live in Japan (compared to Sweden's 8 million) the actual number of Japanese children and adolescents with diabetes does not exceed Sweden's. We don't know

Juvenile diabetes is most common in the Nordic countries. In spite of having 15 times the population of Sweden, Japan has the same number of children and adolescents with diabetes as Sweden.

why there is such a great difference between different parts of the world, but it depends at least partly on cultural and environmental differences. Diabetes is more common amongst Japanese immigrants living in Hawaii than in their relatives remaining in Japan. See also "What is diabetes caused by?" on page 221.

Can you catch diabetes?

Diabetes is not a communicable disease. For an adult this may be obvious. However, friends of a child with diabetes may often wonder about this. It is most important to inform all friends, both at home and at school of this. It is best to explain it to the whole class when returning to school. Tell them about diabetes and show them how injections and blood glucose tests are performed. Also tell them about the symptoms of hypoglycemia and what they can do to help. It is especially important for the teenager with a newly diagnosed diabetes to tell his/her friends. If you, for some reason, don't do this shortly after you are diagnosed there is a substantial risk that you will not tell them at all. Telling others about diabetes is a very important part of accepting your disease.

Did I get diabetes because I have eaten too much candy?

No! The amount of sweets you have eaten does not influence the risk of getting diabetes in adolescence or childhood. Remember to tell this to your child's friends as they often wonder if they also will get diabetes. Type 2 diabetes, however, can be provoked by having too much to eat or having too many sweets. Parents may often think: "If we only had done this or that our child would probably not have gotten diabetes". Stop badgering yourself. There is nothing you could have done differently to prevent your child from contracting diabetes.

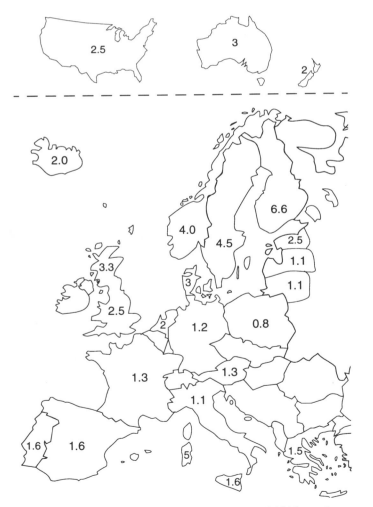

The map shows approximately how many of 1000 newborn children that will develop diabetes before the age of 15.[164,221]

The first time with diabetes

The treatment of diabetes involves lifelong medication with insulin, but also a lifelong adaptation of one's life style. Diabetes care entails both medical treatment and education. We want patients and parents to feel that they can assume responsibility of their treatment and have the possibility of influencing their life with diabetes. When your diabetes is manageable, life in the family will once again become manageable.

We want you to feel as secure as possible during your first days and weeks with diabetes. Feel free to express your views and wishes regarding the most suitable arrangements for you and your family.

At the onset of diabetes

In Sweden and many other countries,[35] newly diagnosed diabetes is usually treated in the hospital where patients stay 1 - 2 weeks on the ward. We have no given rules of how many days you must stay in the hospital. Some families stay one week while others find it difficult to go home before 3 weeks time have elapsed.

We usually give 1 or 2 days of intravenous insulin therapy (see page 55) to achieve a quick and effective normalization of the blood glucose level. Studies have shown that this can prolong the ability of the beta cells to produce insulin during the years to come [264,363] (see "Remission phase" on page 68).

We offer all children and adolescents to try indwelling catheters (see page 100) during the first 1 or 2 weeks of insulin injections to assure as painless a start as possible with injections. After a week or two they will try regular injections and can later choose which method they prefer.

The insulin requirement changes daily and initially there will be frequent changes of the insulin dosages. The first days you will need high doses of insulin which then are gradually reduced. You/your child will promptly feel much better and have a magnificent appetite. This is natural if you consider that most newly diagnosed patients have been insulin deficient for several weeks prior to the discovery of diabetes and have lost many kilos (or pounds) in weight. We usually let them have as much food as they want initially, regulating the

doses of insulin instead. The appetite is usually normalized after a few weeks.

During the first few days you will often experience a feeling of chaos and it is difficult to even comprehend that you/your child now has diabetes. It is important to have time to examine your feelings and to gradually adjust to the completely new situation that your family now is faced with. During our first discussions we mostly just listen, answer questions and then gradually move on to teaching about diabetes. Most things will be new and you will often find them difficult to understand from the beginning, but gradually things will fall into place. During the second week you will usually have

"When a problem is too large and seems unsolvable, don't forget that you can eat an elephant assuming it is cut it into small enough pieces".

Slavian saying

The first week is often chaotic and it is difficult to understand the connection between different facts. Try instead to concentrate on one piece of information at a time. During the second week your understanding will become much better and things begin to fit together.

Home again at last! Now it is time to tell your friends at home and at school or work that you have diabetes. Then they will know and need not ask when you do something they don't understand, such as taking a blood glucose test. Even if you are worried about telling them, it often feels better once it is done.

gained some understanding of how insulin and blood glucose affect each other. You will experience that in diabetes the blood glucose level often fluctuates and that even under close supervision it is difficult to have a perfect blood glucose level.

Parents often find that they are out of sync with each other when one parent has been on the ward or clinic more frequently than another. Not knowing or understanding what is going on is a difficult feeling and it is essential that both parents participate as much as possible in the daily care of the child. Check with your insurance company about which possibilities exist in this situation.

If you initially stay at the hospital you will usually be allowed day leave over the first weekend to try things out on your own. To feel secure in this situation you should know what to do if your blood glucose level falls too low (see "Treating hypoglycemia" on page 48). If you/your child has not experienced hypoglycemia with distinct symptoms we usually choose to provoke it by giving insulin as usual before a meal but by withholding food until the blood glucose level has decreased enough to feel symptoms.[273] Most often you will find that managing your diabetes at home is easier than you had anticipated.

In other countries and centers outpatient initiation of insulin therapy is more common.[77] This approach requires the 24-hour availability of a diabetes team to ensure a safe institution of insulin therapy. Still it may be difficult to administer the large doses of insulin needed initially.[35] In either approach it is essential to maintain daily contact with the diabetes team during the initial 1-2 weeks to provide basic understanding and self-confidence in insulin administration.

You will have time to meet a dietitian as well as a counsellor who can help you with practical issues like insurance policies (see page 197). Diabetes is an illness that can create many setbacks even in a normal family with a normal child upbringing. We usually let our families see a child psychologist to discuss such matters. If you run into problems later on it is much easier to seek help if you have previously established a contact.

In a family with a young child with diabetes the teaching will be primarily directed to the parents for obvious reasons. It is however important that later the child be given the opportunity to successively learn and take a greater responsibility for his/her diabetes, for example by attending a diabetes camp. A child in puberty or prepuberty should take an active part in his/her diabetes education from the start.

Our goal is that children with diabetes, regardless of age when diagnosed, will be able to take an independent responsibility for their diabetes before they enter puberty. The child will then identify diabetes as his/her own illness (not mother's or father's problem) and teenage rivalry will hopefully be directed into other areas (see also page 236).

"Give a man a fish and he will not go hungry that day. Teach him how to fish and he will not be hungry for the rest of his life."

Chinese saying

It is important that early on you get used to handling your own or your child's diabetes. If you understand "why and how", you will be better prepared to meet different situations in life in harmony with your diabetes.

At home

Clinical visits will initially be weekly, and thereafter at 2 - 3 week intervals. Eventually you will meet us every third month. At the visits we test your glycemic control during the last 2 - 3 months (HbA$_{1c}$, see page 86). It is important that you realize from the start that it is not possible to achieve perfect blood glucose levels every day. Everyone with diabetes has high blood glucose levels every now and then and with the methods of treatment available today this is inevitable. What is important is that your average blood glucose level is acceptable. More information on this follows further on.

Older teenagers often prefer to come alone to their visits or perhaps together with a friend or partner. When living in a steady relationship it is most important that your partner/spouse accompanies you to the clinic visits. You will often see the dietitian during team visits, but you can also establish a direct contact with him/her for further information. Once a year you will undergo a more thorough check-up including a physical examination. It is very important to follow the child's/adolescent's physical development. During puberty the body requires much more insulin (see page 67). It is important to know when to increase the doses. Several blood tests may be included in the yearly check-up (se page 205).

Can I carry on with my previous life style?

Diabetes is a chronic illness that will affect you every day for the rest of your life. It is easier to manage diabetes well if you have a life with regular habits and hours. If you are accustomed to a life style full of improvisations without any stable principles and habits you will find it more difficult to combine this with diabetes. Try to become friends with your diabetes (or at least not to be enemies)

We check your weight and height at every visit to make sure that you continue to grow like you did prior to having diabetes. If you don't get enough insulin you will lose weight and may even experience growth retardation. If, on the other hand, you get too much insulin (and food) you will gain too much weight.

since you can't escape it and there is no currently known cure.

It it most important that from the start you decide to carry on with your life in the fashion that you feel comfortable with. Don't let your diabetes dictate the type of life you should live.

It is common to think: "This or that, which I used to do before my diagnosis, can't be done now that I have diabetes". Most things are not only allowed, but can be performed very well. Nothing is absolutely forbidden, but you must think things through more carefully than you used to do in various situations. It is important to experiment and learn by trial and error. If you choose the life you want to live it is our job as diabetes professionals to tailor an insulin treatment suited to your needs.

"It is much easier to have a strong opinion if you don't know all the facts involved".

You and your family will find that many people you come in contact with may think that they know a great deal about diabetes. Often their knowledge is far from being in accordance with modern diabetes treatment. Be a bit sceptical when you hear generalized statements about diabetes, especially early on before you have your own knowledge to rely upon.

Keep a list of your questions to avoid problems recalling them when visiting us at the diabetes clinic.

How does a healthy body work?

It is important to understand how a healthy body works in order to understand how it changes when having diabetes. If you are not too familiar with medical terms or not interested in learning them, you can skip the terms in parentheses. You do not need to know them to understand the context.

The three most important constituents in our food are carbohydrates (sugar), fat and protein. When we eat, the digestion of starch (long chains of sugar) begins immediately in the mouth with the help of a special enzyme (saliva amylase). An enzyme is a protein compound that breaks the bonds, holding chemical together. The food is accumulated in the stomach, where it is mixed and degraded by the acidic gastric juice. The stomach will empty small portions at a time into the duodenum through the lower opening of the stomach (pylorus, see illustration on page 19 and 50).

When the food has entered the small intestine it will be further broken down by digestive enzymes from the pancreas and suspended in bile produced by the liver. If you eat sugar (like if you have hypoglycemia, see page 48) it cannot be absorbed into the blood until it has entered the small intestine. Glu-

As soon as you see food your mouth will water and your body will begin to prepare to digest it.

cose cannot be absorbed from the oral mucous membranes [166] or from the stomach. In this sense the emptying rate of the stomach will have a large impact of how quickly the sugar you eat enters the blood stream and increases your blood glucose level (see page 143).

The carbohydrates that we eat will be broken down into the simple sugars (mono-saccharides); glucose (dextrose, grape-sugar), fructose and galactose. Fructose must first be transformed into glucose in the liver before it can affect your blood glucose level. Food proteins are broken down into amino acids, and fat into very tiny bubbles (chylomicrones composed mainly of triglycerides). Simple sugars and proteins are absorbed directly into the blood while the fat bubbles are absorbed into the lymph system and enter the blood stream through the lymph vessels.

The venous blood draining the stomach and intestines will pass through the liver before reaching the rest of the body. A large amount of glucose will be absorbed by the liver with the help of insulin, and then stored in its reserve form as glycogen (see page 32). These stores can be used in-between meals, during the night, and when starving. Only glucose that is not absorbed by the liver can reach the peripheral blood stream, supplying the rest of the body with glucose. This glucose can be measured by a finger prick or venous tap.

The muscles can also store a certain amount of glucose as glycogen. Whereas the glycogen store in the liver can be used to raise the blood glucose level, the store in the muscles can only be used by the muscles during exercise. Your body's ability to

Phases in glucose metabolism

① **Storing at meals:**
During a meal and for the following 2 - 3 hours glucose from the meal will be used as fuel by the cells. At the same time the stores of glycogen (glucose in long chains, see picture on page 143) fat and protein are rebuilt.

② **Fasting in between meals**
After 3 - 5 hours the carbohydrate content of the meal is consumed and the blood glucose level starts to decrease. The glycogen stores in the liver will then be broken down to maintain the blood glucose level constant. The glucose produced in this way will mainly supply the brain while the body uses mainly free fatty acids from fat tissue as fuel.

> ## How insulin works
>
> ① Opens the door for glucose to enter the cells.
>
> ② Stimulates the storing of glucose in the liver (as glycogen).
>
> ③ Stimulates the development of fat from excess carbohydrates.
>
> ④ Stimulates the development of protein compounds in the body.

store glucose is very limited. The glycogen stores are only sufficient for 24 hours of fasting for an adult and 12 hours for a child.[367]

The glucose content of the blood is surprisingly constant during both day and night in a non-diabetic person (approximately 5 - 6 mmol/l). For an adult this blood glucose level corresponds to no more than approximately 2 lumps of sugar. When you consider this, it is not surprising that even a small amount of sugar, like some candy, can disturb the glucose balance in your body.

The smallest building blocks in the body are called cells. A cell needs glucose to function well. With the help of oxygen glucose is broken down into carbon dioxide, water and energy (see "A healthy cell" on page 20).

Insulin

Many of the different functions in your body are mediated by hormones. Hormones work like keys, "opening doors" to different functions in the body. The hormone insulin is produced in the pancreas in special types of cells called beta cells. The other very important function of the pancreas is to produce enzymes for food digestion. This part works quite well even in a person with diabetes. The beta cells are located in the Islets of Langerhans which also contain alpha cells producing the hormone glucagon (see picture on page 20).

Insulin is very important for the development of your body. Insulin is the key that "opens the door" for glucose to enter the cells. As soon as you see or smell food, signals are delivered to the beta cells to increase insulin production.[141] When the food has entered the stomach and intestine, other special hormones further signal the beta cells to continue an increase in insulin production.

The beta cells contain a "blood glucose meter" that registers when the blood glucose level increases, secreting an adequate amount of insulin into the blood stream. With food intake the insulin concentration in the blood will rapidly increase in a non-diabetic person to take care of the glucose coming from the food, transporting it into the cells. A non-diabetic person's blood glucose level will normally not rise more than 1 - 2 mmol/l after a meal.[141]

Insulin follows the blood stream to the different cells of your body, sticking to the cell surface in special insulin receptors and makes the cell wall permeable to glucose. Insulin stimulates certain proteins inside the cell to come to the cell surface, collect glucose and then release it inside the cell. The blood glucose level will be kept at a constant level in this way.

Certain cells do not require insulin to transport glucose into their interior. These cells will absorb insulin directly in proportion to the blood glucose level. Such insulin independent cells are found in the brain cells, nerve fibres, retina, kidneys, adrenals, cells in the blood vessels and the red blood cells. It may seem illogical that certain cells can absorb glucose without insulin. However, in a situation when there is not enough glucose in the body, the insulin production will be stopped, reserving the glucose for the most important organs.

All the organs in the body are built of cells like the bricks in a house. Each organ has special cells depending on it's function, e.g. kidney cells, liver cells or muscle cells.

If you have diabetes and a high blood glucose level, the cells not requiring insulin will absorb large amounts of glucose. In the long run this will be toxic to the cells, and these organs will be vulnerable to complications.

The body needs a small amount of insulin even in between meals and during the night to accommodate the glucose coming from the liver (see page 32). Approximately 40 - 50 % of the total insulin production/24 hours in a non-diabetic person is secreted in between meals.[56]

The excess of carbohydrate from a meal is transformed into fat and stored in the fat tissue. The excess of fat from a meal is stored in the same way. The ability to store fat in the body is almost unlimited. The proteins from the meal are used in the different tissues. There is no special form of storing amino acids. Breaking down amino acids to produce glucose (as when fasting for a longer time) will therefore imply breaking down the tissues of your body.

Your body will always think as if it was still non-diabetic

When you read about how your body functions with diabetes remember that it always "thinks" and reacts as if it still was non-diabetic, e.g. as if the insulin production was still working optimally. Your body will therefore not understand why things often go wrong when there is a deficiency of insulin. On the other hand your brain can assist by considering what the effects will be when the insulin production does not work anymore. It is therefore most important that you stop and think about why and how your body reacts as it does in certain situations and how you can influence this.

Your insulin doses will vary from day to day since you rarely live the same life every day. Earlier your beta cells would adjust for this automatically, but now it is up to you to find out how the days are different and how much insulin is needed in different situations.

What happens to the carbohydrates in the food?

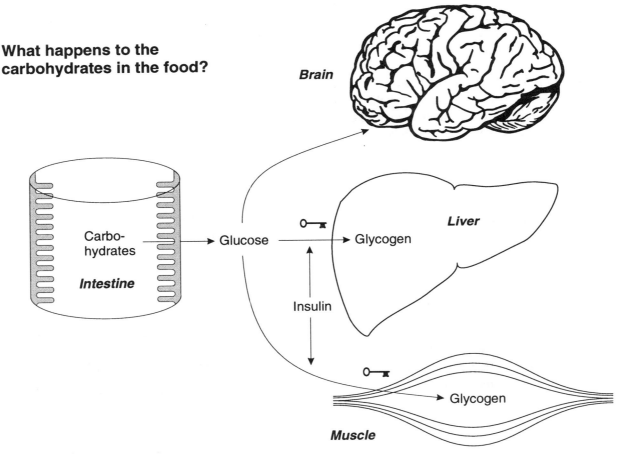

The complex carbohydrates in the food are broken down to simple sugars in the intestine. Glucose is absorbed into the blood stream and stored as glycogen in the liver and muscles. Insulin is needed to transport glucose into the cells of these organs. The brain cannot store glucose and is thereby dependent upon an even supply to function well. The nervous system and some other cells (like the eyes and kidneys) can take up glucose without the help of insulin. This is an advantage in the short run as the nervous system will not sustain a lack of glucose even in the absence of insulin. However, in the long run it is a disadvantage as the nervous system will be exposed to high glucose concentrations inside the cells when the blood glucose level is high.

The anatomy of your body

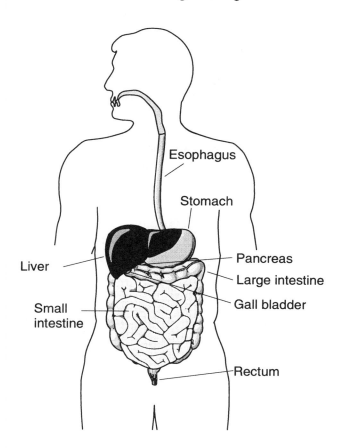

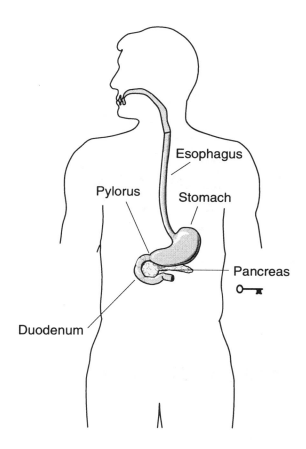

The food that you eat will pass the esophagus on its way down to the stomach. Glucose can not be absorbed into the blood until the food has passed the lower opening of the stomach (pylorus) and entered the intestine. It will there be digested by enzymes from the pancreas and the intestinal mucosa. The first part of the small intestine is called the duodenum and is 25 - 30 cm (10 - 12 inches) long. The small intestine is very folded and its length in an adult is 3 - 5 meters (9 - 15 feet). The food will then pass into the large intestine which is approximately 1½ meters (4 - 5 feet) long. The large intestine passes around the abdominal cavity before entering the rectum.

Your pancreas is about the size of the palm of your hand. It is located under the left rib cage in the back of the abdominal cavity, close to the stomach. The pancreas has two main functions: to produce enzymes which help digest food and to produce insulin which helps control blood sugar.

Pancreas

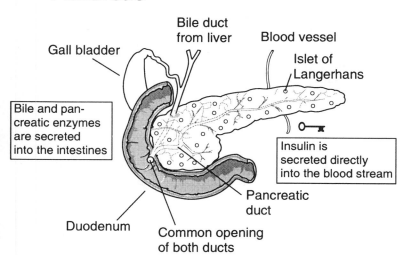

The digestive enzymes from the pancreas reach the intestine through the pancreatic duct. It drains into the duodenum together with the duct from the liver and gall bladder. There are approximately one million islets of Langerhans in the pancreas. Insulin produced in the beta cells of the islets is secreted directly into the small blood vessels passing through the pancreas.

Insulin-dependent diabetes in children, adolescents and adults © R. Hanas 1998

Islets of Langerhans

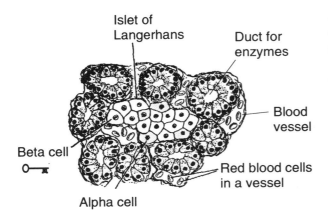

An islet of Langerhans, seen through a microscope, contains both beta cells producing insulin and alpha cells producing glucagon. Both hormones are secreted directly into the blood. The beta cells contain a kind of blood glucose meter. If the blood glucose is raised, insulin will be secreted. If it is lowered, the secretion of insulin is stopped. If it falls even lower, glucagon is secreted.

The islets are very small, only 0.1 mm (four thousands of an inch) in diameter. All the islets together contain approximately 200 units of insulin in an adult. The volume of all the islets combined is not more than a finger-tip.

Cellular metabolism

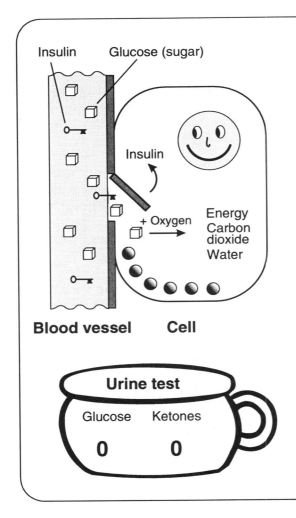

A healthy cell

Sugar in the food is absorbed from the intestine into the blood in the form of glucose (dextrose) and fructose. Glucose must enter the cells to be of any use to them in producing energy or for other metabolic processes. The hormone insulin is needed to "open the door", i.e. make the wall of the cell permeable to glucose. Inside the cell, glucose is metabolized with the help of oxygen into carbon dioxide, water and energy. Carbon dioxide is exchanged for oxygen in the lungs.

Energy is of vital importance to the cell and enables it to work well. Glucose is also stored in the form of glycogen in liver and muscle cells for future use. The brain is not capable of storing glucose as glycogen and is thereby dependent on an even and continuous supply of glucose from the blood.

Starvation

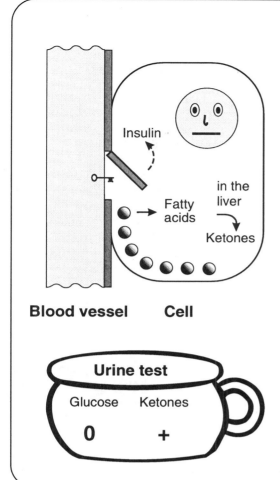

Blood vessel   Cell

When there is no food available there will be a lack of glucose in the blood. Opening the "cell door" with the help of insulin will then do no good. In a healthy person the production of insulin will be stopped almost completely when the blood glucose level decreases. The alpha cells in the pancreas recognize the lowered blood glucose level and secrete the hormone glucagon into the blood stream. Glucagon signals the liver cells to release glucose from the reserve supply of glycogen.

If the starvation continues the body will use the next reserve system for glucose supply. Fat is broken down into fatty acids and glycerol with the help of the stress hormone adrenaline. The fatty acids are transformed into ketones in the liver ("starvation ketones") and glycerol is changed into glucose. These reactions will take place when you are fasting or when you are too ill to eat, like when having gastroenteritis (stomach flu).

The cells of the body (except the brain) can burn fatty acids while the muscles and the brain can burn ketones. The cells will retrieve some energy from this but not as much as when glucose is available. If the body is starving for a longer period of time proteins will also be broken down and converted into glucose.

Diabetes and insulin deficiency

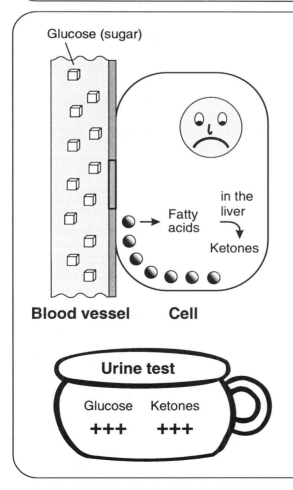

Blood vessel   Cell

Diabetes (type 1) is a deficiency disease where the hormone insulin is absent. This results in glucose not being able to enter the cells. The cells will then act exactly as in the starvation situation in the illustration above. Your body will try to raise your blood glucose to even higher levels since it believes that the reason for the lack of glucose inside the cells is a low glucose level in the blood (see "Your body will always think as if it was still non-diabetic" on page 18). The hormones adrenaline and glucagon (see page 32) will give signals to the liver to release glucose from the glycogen stores.

However, the starvation takes place in the midst of abundance. In the blood stream there is an excess of glucose being passed out into the urine. Inside the cells fatty acids are being produced which are then transformed into ketones in the liver ("diabetes ketones"). The ketones are also passed out into the urine. When insulin is supplied the cells can function properly again and this "vicious cycle" will be broken.

"Starvation ketones" and "diabetes ketones" are chemically identical but we often refer to them differently depending on how they originate (see page 79).

Insulin and blood glucose

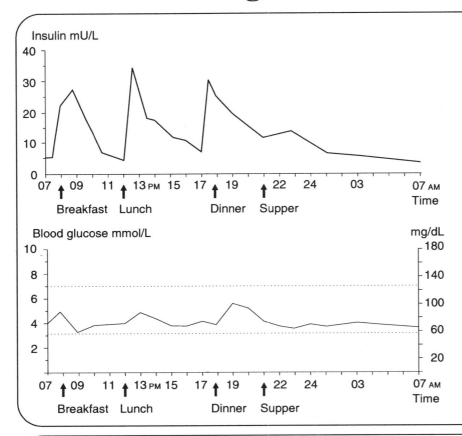

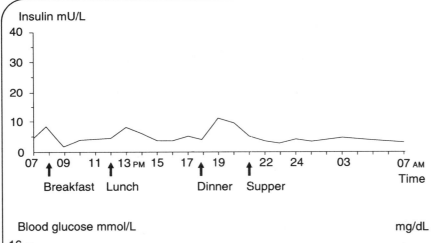

A healthy person

In a non-diabetic person the insulin concentration in the blood will rapidly increase after a meal.[307] When the glucose in the food is absorbed from the intestine and the blood glucose has returned to normal levels the insulin level will drop back to baseline once again. However, the insulin level will never approach zero, as a low level of basal insulin is needed to take care of the glucose coming from the reserve stores in the liver between meals and during the night.

The resultant blood glucose level will be very stable in a non-diabetic person as this graph illustrates.[276] The normal blood glucose level is between 3.3 and 7 mmol/L (60 - 125 mg/dL).

Diabetes

In a person with newly diagnosed type 1 diabetes the beta cells are unable to produce sufficient amounts of insulin. The insulin levels will be very low and are not in any way sufficient to take care of the glucose coming from a snack or meal.

The resultant blood glucose level will be very unstable and only occasionally within normal levels. Every time the blood glucose level is higher than the renal threshold (see page 78) glucose will be passed out into the urine.

Taking care of your diabetes

Goals for managing diabetes

The International Society of Pediatric and Adolescent Diabetes (ISPAD) has compiled recommended guidelines for the treatment of diabetes.[211] Other national and international programs for the treatment of diabetes in childhood and adolescents are the APEG Handbook on Childhood and Adolescent Diabetes from the Australasian Paediatric Endocrine Group,[364] The St. Vincent Declaration [84] and the American Diabetes Association's Clinical Practice Recommendations [14] to name a few.

Not having symptoms or disabilities due to diabetes is an obvious goal. Overall well-being and health will lessen the risk of long term complications. It is essential that all children grow and develop normally. To ensure this we closely follow weight and height development charts. Insulin treatment plans in the past unfortunately resulted in growth retardation for many children. During puberty an increased and more individually tailored insulin treatment plan is needed.

"My home is my castle", as the saying goes. Build yourself a castle of knowledge and motivation to make it possible to get along well with your diabetes.

with their friends and at the same time manage of their diabetes adequately. With maturation into adulthood, having a family and children becomes most important. In the long run it is an essential goal to prevent side effects and complications from diabetes.

How do you achieve these goals?

Traditionally there are three cornerstones of diabetes treatment: insulin, diet and exercise. Insulin is obvious as there is a lack of this hormone in your body. However, the other cornerstones in a modern diabetes treatment are questioned today, especially from a pediatric point of view. Diet is essential but a diabetes diet does not have to differ very much from an ordinary diet that all can benefit from. Exercise is recommended for everyone and will give you a good general condition. However, newer studies of diabetes and exercise do not show an improved glucose control.[417] If you have high blood glucose levels it is not a good idea to exercise. Exercise is therefore today not considered as a part of the actual diabetes treatment, although it is rec-

---

Goals of treatment

- ♠ No symptoms or discomfort in every-day life
- ♠ Good general well-being
- ♠ Normal growth and development
- ♠ Normal puberty and schooling
- ♠ Normal peer life and professional life
- ♠ Normal family life including possibilities of pregnancy
- ♠ Prevent long-term complications

Diabetes should not disturb school attendance. It is difficult to follow lessons when hypoglycemic. It causes concentration disturbances. During puberty peers will become more and more important and our goal is to teach teenagers how to be together

Traditional approach
♣ Insulin
♣ Exercise
♣ Diet

Diabetes today
Professor Johnny Ludvigsson, Sweden:
♥ Insulin
♥ Love
♥ Care

"It is no fun getting diabetes but you must be able to have fun even when having diabetes"

I would like to add a fourth cornerstone:

♥ Knowledge

Motivation of your own ➡ Self-care

If you want to manage well with diabetes you must:

① Become your own expert on diabetes.

② Have more knowledge on diabetes than the average doctor.

③ Accept your diabetes and learn to live with it.

ommended for more general reasons. See further the chapters on diet and physical exercise.

Dr. Johnny Ludvigsson (Professor in Pediatric Diabetology) in Sweden has re-defined the cornerstones of treatment as: insulin, love and care. These goals coincide well our clinic's view of diabetes treatment. Diabetes is a deficiency disease and it is natural to replace what is missing, i.e. insulin. Love and care are essential parts of every child's upbringing.

I would like to introduce a fourth cornerstone in the treatment of diabetes, namely knowledge. A Chinese saying goes "Give a man a fish and he will not go hungry that day. Teach him how to fish and he will not be hungry for the rest of his life...".

Becoming your own expert

Your own motivation is most essential for a good self treatment of diabetes. It is important that you know that the treatment is for your own sake, not for your parent's or your family's, and certainly not for your doctor or nurse. Your motivation could be to be as good (or better...) at football as you were before, to achieve good results on a school examination without having hypoglycemia, or to get a job with irregular working hours and to make it run smoothly. If you have diabetes you must become your own expert to handle the different situations of life in a satisfactory way.

One often encounters prejudice concerning diabetes. The modern method of treating diabetes has changed a great deal in recent years. Knowledge and information of this treatment is unfortunately not generally widespread. From this it follows that a person with diabetes must know a great deal about diabetes to be able to function well, in fact more knowledge than the average doctor! To obtain this knowledge you will have to ask questions and get information when things are not clear to you. Be sure to contact your diabetes team whenever you have questions on insulin dosages or other diabetes items. If you save the question until the next

visit, which is perhaps three months hence, you will probably have forgotten all about it.

Engaging yourself in your own diabetes care is of vital importance. Diabetes is an illness that you have to live with 24 hours a day. It is therefore very important to decide early on in the course of the disease if you are going to adjust your life to diabetes or decide what kind of life you want to live and then adjust your diabetes treatment to it. We emphasize that children and teenagers should take as active part as possible in their diabetes treatment from the start. We prefer that children have a good grasp of their diabetes by the time they reach puberty. This is important as so many other things occupy the mind of a teenager those years. If the child's mastery of the diabetes area is at least partly completed it will aid and not hinder his/her general liberation during puberty.

Can I take some time off from my diabetes?

Well, this is really not possible since your diabetes is there 24 hours a day. You will however benefit from differentiating between every-day life and having a good time. Most people (with or without diabetes) will allow themselves something extra

blood glucose than usual, but of course not so high that it affects your/your child's well-being.

It is better to have 15 "bad" and 350 "good" days without a bad conscience than 75 "half-bad" and 290 "good" days and a bad conscience. Many persons with diabetes choose to have a slightly higher blood glucose when they are about to do something important, e.g. an examination in school or an interview for a new job. And they are right. In certain situations it is much more important to avoid hypoglycemia than to have a perfect blood glucose level.

"To dare is to lose foothold for a short while — not to dare is to lose yourself."

Sören Kierkegaard, Danish philosopher 1813-55

It is not easy to take individual responsibility for your own diabetes. On the other hand you are the only one who can do it. Only you can be there 24 hours a day, and this is what it takes to make your diabetes function well both today and in the future.

Alternative treatments

Sometimes we encounter questions about alternative treatment methods. In Sweden it is forbidden to treat children under 8 years of age with so called "alternative medicine" according to the law of quackery. Many parents have told us that despite this they have been told of different forms of treatment for their child when they have consulted a homeopath. In Finland a 5 year old boy died in 1991 after his parents stopped giving him insulin and instead gave him different types of herbal- and steam baths. Both the parents and the person who initiated the alternative treatment were prosecuted for causing the death of the child.

when attending a party, even if they know that this little extra is not very healthy. If already an every-day life-style appropriate for diabetes you can also allow yourself to be a bit "more relaxed" with food when having a good time (see also "Party-time" on page 151).

If you go on vacation or a school trip it will be difficult to have the same routines as at home. The goal on these occasions should not be to have perfect glucose control. What is important is that you/your child feels well enough to participate in all activities. This may involve accepting a slightly higher

All children need love and care....

Hurrah, today is my birthday! Consider this day as a party, forget for a day to follow all routines and rules. The child/teenager must remember his/her birthdays and other special occasions as joyful and without every-day restrictions.

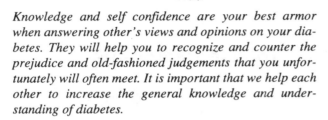

Knowledge and self confidence are your best armor when answering other's views and opinions on your diabetes. They will help you to recognize and counter the prejudice and old-fashioned judgements that you unfortunately will often meet. It is important that we help each other to increase the general knowledge and understanding of diabetes.

From the United Kingdom four cases have been reported where insulin doses have been decreased or stopped completely and different types of alternative treatment been given instead (prayers, healing, special diet and treatment with vitamins and trace elements). Three of these patients ended up with ketoacidosis and the fourth had high blood glucose levels and weight reduction.[160]

I have discussed this topic with parents on several occasions. In my opinion three issues are of special importance:

① We must have an open dialog with each other. If you as a parent or person with diabetes want to try an alternative treatment despite our recommendations, I believe it is better that it be done openly and that your doctor and diabetes nurse know about it.

② The child/adult with diabetes must definitely continue with insulin in unchanged doses and with other medical treatment, otherwise the person's health will be in serious danger.

③ The treatment must not in any way be dangerous or harmful to the patient.

Sometimes you may feel like this when everything you have planned goes wrong and your blood glucose level is much too high or low. It might then be a good idea to put all testing and adjustments aside for a week and just "take time off" to be able to start all over again later with new vigor. Check your blood glucose only to avoid hypoglycemia. Most things in life are learned this way, in "waves". As you get to know your/your child's diabetes better these moments of exasperation will occur less and less often.

DANIEL

High blood glucose levels

When the blood glucose level is high glucose will be excreted into the urine. The increased urine output at high blood glucose levels is caused by the extra fluid that is excreted together with glucose. Thirst and increased urinary output are often the first symptoms of diabetes. When you loose fluid the skin and mucous membranes will be dryer. Women may complain of itching in the genital area for this reason. The itching can also be caused by a fungal infection which is more common when the blood glucose level is high. The white blood cells in the body's defence against infection will work less effectively if the blood glucose level is higher than approximately 14 mmol/L (250 mg/dL).[27]

A temporarily high blood glucose level, e.g. after a large meal, may often pass unnoticed. Many will feel fine even with a blood glucose level of 16 - 18 mmol/L (290 - 325 mg/dL). You may be a little bit thirsty and somewhat tired but the symptoms are not at all as obvious as when the blood glucose level is low. However, if the high blood glucose

Beware of vomiting with diabetes. It is often the first sign of insulin deficiency. The child's well-being may quickly deteriorate when he/she can't drink. Contact your diabetes clinic or the hospital if you have the slightest doubts how to handle the situation.

level is caused by a lack of insulin you often will feel unwell when your blood glucose reaches as little as 12 - 15 mmol/L (215 - 270 mg/dL). ***It is the lack of insulin that makes you feel unwell, not the high blood glucose level as such.***

What happens in the body when there is a lack of insulin?

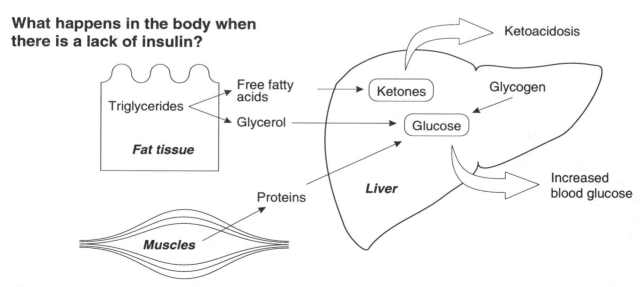

The reaction in a non-diabetic body when there is a lack of insulin are quite logical as long as you remember that the levels of insulin are low only when the blood glucose also is low. The body will then mobilize more energy to the blood. The levels of the counter-regulating hormones (adrenaline, glucagon, cortisone and growth hormone) increase and the production of both glucose and ketones increases. The ketones can be used as fuel by the brain in a situation of starvation. If the diabetes is untreated or undertreated a lack of insulin will occur at the same time as the blood glucose is high. However, the body will not "understand" this. Instead it will try to increase the blood's supply of energy in the same way as before having diabetes. The amounts of ketones in the blood will increase, and this can lead to ketoacidosis. The blood glucose level will be greatly increased even without eating anything.

Symptoms of insulin deficiency

These symptoms will develop more quickly if you have a larger proportion of short-acting insulin. If you use an insulin pump you are even more sensitive to insulin deficiency as the pump uses only short-acting insulin.

① **Production of ketones**

⮕ Nausea, vomiting

⮕ Tiredness

⮕ Abdominal pain

⮕ Heavy breathing, acetone odor

⮕ Pain in the chest or side, respiratory distress

⮕ Impaired consciousness

⮕ Diabetes coma

② **Depletion of energy stores, breakdown of muscles**

⮕ Weakness

⮕ Weight loss

⮕ Decreased growth (long-standing insulin deficiency)

Insulin deficiency

Insulin deficiency will result in a lack of glucose inside the cells (see figures on page 20). The ketones that are then produced can be used as fuel, but if produced in large amounts they will also have negative effects. In smaller children nausea and vomiting are often the first symptoms when the level of ketones in the blood increases. If you for example forget the bedtime insulin the child will often feel nauseous or vomit in the morning. *If a child with diabetes vomits one should always suspect a lack of insulin.* See the chapter on illness on page 176 for further information.

Remember that the blood glucose level will rise when you have a lack of insulin even if you don't eat. This is caused by an increased level of hormones sending signals to the liver to mobilize glucose (see "Counter-regulation" on page 31) as a response to the lack of glucose inside these cells. This is logical if you remember that before having

diabetes, there was a lack of glucose inside the cells only when the blood glucose level was low.

How to treat a high blood glucose level

A temporary high blood glucose does not require any emergency measures at all. Always check for ketones in the urine. The absence of urine ketones means that the cells are not starved (see "Ketones in the urine" on page 79). If you feel well, measure the blood glucose level once again before the next meal and if necessary add another 1 - 2 units of short acting insulin to the premeal dose if the blood glucose level is still high (see page 127 for further advice).

If the blood glucose level is high for several hours and there are ketones in the urine this indicates a lack of insulin (see page 80). If the amount of ketones increases (e.g. from 2+ to 3+) in spite of taking extra insulin you should always contact the hospital or your physician. If you have the slightest doubt or can't get in touch with someone experienced in diabetes you should seek medical help.

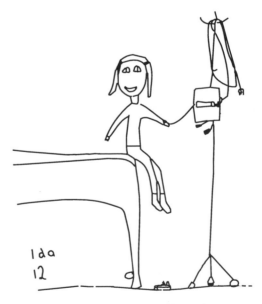

Most centers in Sweden have a routine of treating newly diagnosed diabetes with intravenous insulin the first 1 - 2 days even if the patient is not suffering from ketoacidosis. This is a safe and effective way of normalizing the high blood glucose, giving the insulin producing beta cells in the pancreas a chance to rest. It is thought to increase the beta cell restitution and the chance for sustained insulin production in pancreas (see "Remission phase" on page 68).[264,363] In other countries it is more common to initiate insulin therapy with subcutaneous or intramuscular injections.

Symptoms of high blood glucose

① Glucose in the urine
➡ Increased frequency of urination, also at night
➡ Large urine volumes

➡ Fluid losses
➡ Very thirsty, dry mouth,
➡ Dry skin, dry mucous membranes

➡ Energy deficit
② Weight loss, weakness
③ Blurred sight

Diabetic coma (ketoacidosis) can quickly develop into a lift threatening condition. This must be treated adequately in a hospital with intravenous fluid and insulin.

See also "What do I do if the blood glucose level is high?" on page 127.

When there is a lack of insulin the blood glucose level will be high and the urine tests will show ketones. After extra insulin has been given the interpretation of urine tests is more difficult. There are two types of ketones (beta-hydroxybutyric acid and acetoacetate) but only one type (acetoacetate) will show on the ketone sticks. Often both types of ketones are increased when there is a lack of insulin. When giving extra insulin further production of ketones is blocked. However, in the early phase of treatment there may be a paradoxical rise in ketones in the urine as beta-hydroxybutyric acid is transformed into acetoacetate, which will appear as an increase in ketones on the stick, although the total amount of ketones in the blood has decreased (see also page 81).

Ketoacidosis (diabetic coma)

Ketones are produced when there is a lack of insulin. An excess of ketones will make the blood acidic, causing ketoacidosis.[115] The body will try to get rid of the ketones by excreting them in the urine. Another way is to excrete ketones is in the form of acetone via exhalation through the lungs, causing a fruity odor on the breath. The breathing frequency will be increased (called Kussmaul breathing) to get rid of as much acetone as possible. Normally the muscle cells can use ketones as fuel. Insulin enhances this utilization.[5,217] When insulin is lacking the ketones will accumulate in the blood.

Diffuse abdominal pain and tenderness may be caused by ketoacidosis but an underlying abdominal problem should not be overlooked.[336] If you cannot increase the intake of fluid to compensate for increased urinary losses, you will become dehydrated. If this continues without treatment unconsciousness and coma will follow. Ketoacidosis is a life threatening condition that must be treated with intravenous fluid and insulin in an emergency facility.[252,336] In spite of adequate treatment there are still cases of death from diabetic coma, ranging from 2 - 5 % in developed countries and 6 - 24 % in developing countries.[252]

Ketoacidosis can occur at the onset of diabetes or if you are completely without insulin for 12 - 24

Causes of diabetic ketoacidosis (DKA):

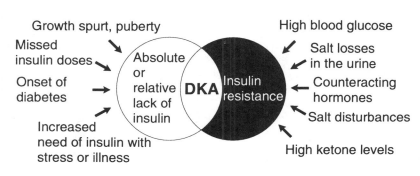

Growth spurt, puberty
Missed insulin doses
Onset of diabetes
Increased need of insulin with stress or illness

Absolute or relative lack of insulin

DKA

Insulin resistance

High blood glucose
Salt losses in the urine
Counteracting hormones
Salt disturbances
High ketone levels

Ketoacidosis is always caused by a relative or absolute deficiency of insulin. Relative insulin deficiency occurs for example if you have not increased the insulin doses when ill or febrile, or during the growth spurt of puberty. The increased blood glucose level as well as many other contributing factors result in increased insulin resistance (i.e. a decreased sensitivity for insulin, see page 69). Substantially increased doses of insulin are needed to achieve the same blood glucose lowering effect as earlier.

hours. It can also occur when you take your ordinary doses but your body needs more insulin, e.g. when having a febrile infection. The frequency of ketoacidosis at the onset of diabetes varies considerably between different countries.[35]

Insulin deficiency and ketoacidosis will develop more quickly if a smaller part of your daily insulin consists of intermediate- or long-acting insulin. The reason for this is that the insulin depot will be much smaller when using short-acting insulin compared to intermediate- or long acting insulin. See "Depot effect" on page 60. With an insulin pump the depot is very small since it delivers only short-acting insulin. One can therefore feel nauseous and vomit already after a night without insulin if the pump has stopped (see page 110). With the use of insulin lispro (Humalog, henceforth referred to as direct-acting insulin) in pumps the depot will be even smaller, resulting in still quicker symptoms of insulin deficiency if the delivery is interrupted (see page 119).

Why is my sight sometimes blurred?

Blurred sight can be a symptom of high blood glucose. This is caused by a different glucose content in the lens compared to that of the blood. The lens contains no blood vessels (if it did they would block the passage of light into the eye). Glucose from the blood must therefore be transported into the lens through the surrounding fluid (aqueous humous, see figure on page 209). This can cause the glucose level of the lens to be different from that of the blood when the blood glucose level is changing rapidly. If the glucose content of the lens is higher than that of the blood, the lens will try to absorb water, causing it to swell. The lens will then refract the light differently, causing a transient shortsightedness.

Symptoms of hypoglycemia are usually fairly easy to recognize. However, when the blood glucose level is high many persons will not have any symptoms at all. Try to train yourself in this. If you have an "autopilot" warning you when the blood glucose level is rising you will lessen the need for blood glucose testing. Thirst and excessive amounts of urine are symptoms arising when the blood glucose level increases above the renal threshold. Remember that this level can be different in different persons (see page 78). Other common symptoms are apathy and a sense of "slow motion". What bodily signs do you recognize when the blood glucose level is high?

The eye is not damaged by this phenomenon and vision often returns to normal within a few hours. It is like borrowing somebody else's glasses — you can focus but it is tiresome for your eyes. This type of vision disturbance will usually occur when the glucose level is quickly increasing or decreasing and has nothing to do with the eye complications that can occur after many years of diabetes. See also page 210.

Hypoglycemia

In the blood stream of an adult person there is normally about 5 g (1/5 ounce) of glucose (barely 2 lumps of sugar) circulating when fasting. At the same time the blood needs to deliver about 10 g (1/3 ounce) of glucose every hour to the tissues of the body.[2] If there is no supply of glucose to the blood there will be a deficiency of glucose in the blood within an hour.

Counter-regulation

In a healthy person the body will regulate the blood glucose within narrow boundaries, normally between approximately 3.3 and 7.0 mmol/L (60 - 125 mg/dL). When your blood glucose falls below 3.0 - 3.5 mmol/L (55 - 65 mg/dL) you will not feel well. When the blood glucose decreases all reactions in ýour body mobilize to give the brain access to the little glucose available. The body tries to mobilize available stores of glucose while the cells outside the brain will decrease their use of glucose. The brain is not able to store glucose rendering it dependent on an even and continuous supply of glucose from the blood. However, after a longer fasting state the brain can adapt to using other types of fuel, mainly ketones.

Besides having a hormone to lower the blood glucose (insulin), there are hormones in your body to raise it. The body reacts to low blood glucose by defense reactions, called counter-regulation. The autonomic nervous system cooperates with many different hormones to raise the blood glucose. This defense against hypoglycemia is very important to your body. The symptoms associated with hypoglycemia depend on the brain's response to a glucose deficit as well as to the effects resulting from the counteracting hormones.

Children are generally more sensitive to hypoglycemia than adults. In one study on healthy children and adolescents, hypoglycemic symptoms and adrenaline responses were evident at a blood glucose level of 3.8 mmol/L compared to 3.1 mmol/L (68 vs. 56 mg/dL) observed for adults.[218]

Usually the effects of insulin are opposite from those of the counteracting hormones. But sometimes their effects are cooperative, e.g. both insulin and growth hormone will build up the muscles.

It may be difficult to understand the biochemistry of the hormones and which hormone is doing what.

Where does the glucose in the blood come from?

① From the food

② From the breakdown of glucose stored as glycogen in the liver (called glycogenolysis)

③ From protein and fat used for production of glucose (called gluconeogenesis)

Counter-regulating hormones that increase the blood glucose

① Adrenaline ② Glucagon	Increases the blood glucose for 2 - 4 h. after hypoglycemia.[62]
② Cortisone ④ Growth hormone	The effect starts after 3 - 4 h. and lasts for 5 - 12 h. after hypoglycemia[62]

Effects of insulin

➠ Insulin is produced in the beta-cells in the pancreas.

① Decreases blood glucose by:
   ➠ increased uptake of glucose into the cells
   ➠ Increased storage of glucose as glycogen in liver and muscle
   ➠ Decreased production of glucose in the liver

② Counteracts the production of ketones in the liver. Stimulates utilization of ketones in the cells.

③ Increases the production of muscle protein.

④ Increases the production and decreases the breakdown of body fat.

Body reserves at fasting and hypoglycemia

① The liver store of glycogen is broken down to glucose.

② Fat is broken down to free fatty acids that can be used as fuel. Fatty acids can be transformed into ketones in the liver. Ketones can be used as fuel, mainly by the brain.

③ Proteins from the muscles are broken down to be used in the liver for production of glucose.

The figures on page 20 and 21 give you a good summary.

The liver

The liver functions as a bank for glucose. When times are good you deposit glucose in it and when times are bad you will have glucose to withdraw. The excess of glucose from a meal will be stored as a reserve in the liver and muscle cells in the form of glycogen (see illustration on page 143). Insulin is needed to transport the glucose into both liver and muscle cells.

The difference between liver and muscle cells is that liver cells can release glucose into the blood from the store of glycogen, whereas in muscle cells the glucose released from the glycogen stores can only be used as fuel inside the cell. An adult has about 100 - 120 g (3.5 - 4.2 ounces) of glucose stored in the liver.[217] The glycogen store can be broken down to glucose when the blood glucose is low (glycogenolysis) and can compensate for about 24 hours of fasting in an adult.[367] In children the glycogen stores are smaller and can compensate for a shorter time of fasting. A pre-school child has enough glucose for about 12 hours of fasting, a smaller child even shorter. A child has a relatively higher turnover of glucose in a resting state compared to an adult since the child's brain is larger in relation to body mass.

The liver can also produce glucose from fat and proteins to raise the blood glucose level (gluconeogenesis). The adult liver will produce about 6 g (1/5 ounce) of glucose per hour in between meals.[367] The majority of this glucose will be consumed by the brain which utilizes glucose without the help of insulin. A smaller child's liver will produce up to 6 times as much glucose counted per kg body weight. The liver of a 5 years old will produce as much glucose/hour as an adult. After a longer fasting (2 weeks or longer) the kidneys can also produce glucose in the same way as the liver does. [145]

A person with diabetes can also use the stores of glycogen when the blood glucose is low. If you have depleted your stores of glycogen, e.g. during a game of football when the body needs a lot of extra glucose, you will have less reserves to take care of a hypoglycemia episode occurring later in the evening or during the night. This implies an increased risk of hypoglycemia several hours after physical exercise (see page 167).

In a healthy person insulin is produced in the pancreas. Since the blood flow from the pancreas goes first to the liver, this organ will have the quickest and highest concentration of insulin. When insulin is injected it will enter a superficial blood vessel and pass the liver first after the blood has passed through the heart. Persons with diabetes will therefore have much lower insulin concentrations in the liver than non-diabetic individuals.

Glucagon

During the day you will feel hungry at intervals of about 4 hours, whereas during the night you can do without food for up to 8 - 10 hours. This is possible due to the breakdown of liver glycogen to glucose, mediated by the hormones glucagon and adrenaline. Small children who have smaller stores of glycogen, need to eat more frequently.

The glucagon production in the pancreas is not affected at the onset of diabetes. However, the abil-

The liver acts like a bank for glucose in your body. When times are good, i.e. during the hours after a meal, glucose will be deposited in the "liver bank" where it is stored as glycogen.

When times are bad, i.e. a couple of hours after the meal and during the night, glucose is withdrawn from the "liver bank" to maintain an adequate blood glucose level.

ity to secrete sufficient amounts of glucagon in response to hypoglycemia is usually already impaired after a few years of diabetes, even in children.[17,9] This is probably not a long-term complication but rather a adaptive effect when a person has had repeated episodes of hypoglycemia.[93] A person with a partly remaining insulin production seems to preserve the glucagon defense better.[93,9] Some data suggest that the glucagon defense can be at least partly restored if you succeed in avoiding hypoglycemia [143] (see "Hypoglycemic unawareness" on page 42).

The production of insulin will be decreased in the same manner in a healthy beta cell being exposed to high glucose levels during a period as short as 2 days.[251]

In a non-diabetic person the production of glucagon will be minimized when the blood glucose and insulin concentration rise following a meal. For a person with diabetes the glucagon production will not be minimized in the same way in spite of a rising blood glucose since injected insulin will be less concentrated when it reaches the glucagon producing alpha cells in the pancreas. In addition to the glucose coming from a meal, one will have an increase of glucose in the blood from the liver,

---

The effects of glucagon

➠ Glucagon is produced in the alpha-cells in the pancreas.

① Raises blood glucose by:
➠ Release of glucose from the glycogen stores in the liver.
➠ Activates the production of glucose from proteins.

② Stimulates the production of ketones in the liver.

---

both contributing to an increase in blood glucose after a meal.[119]

Glucagon injection

If a person with diabetes is unconscious or unable to eat or drink you can give an injection of glucagon to stimulate the breakdown of glycogen in the liver, thereby raising the blood glucose. Giving such an injection is easy to learn. It would be wise to make sure that if a teacher or leader can give this on a school outing or sports camp.

Glucagon is given as a subcutaneous injection in the same way as an insulin injection. If you are using an indwelling catheter (Insuflon) you should not use this for glucagon as you will have a risk of lessened effect if the catheter is not working properly. The dose of glucagon is 0.1 - 0.2 mg/10 kg (22 pounds) body weight.[93,10] The blood glucose raising effect starts within 10 min. and lasts for at least 30 - 60 min.[10] The effect will be just as good after a subcutaneous as an intramuscular injection, so it does not matter how deep you insert the needle.[10]

Give a glucagon injection if your child has a severe hypoglycemia associated with unconsciousness or convulsions. If he/she has not woken up within 10 - 15 minutes, call an ambulance. However, if the child is awake with a normal blood glucose when the ambulance arrives, you not need to go to the hospital.

It may be difficult to mix glucagon for the first time in an acute situation. Check the contents of the box and read through the instructions as soon as you bring them home. Indicate the dose to give on the syringe with a felt tip pen and you will not have to worry about this when you are stressed. Make a mark with a felt tip pen on the syringe of how much glucagon to give in case of an emergency. When the expiration date has passed and you have gotten a new box of glucagon you can use the old one for practicing the mixing and drawing up of glucagon. Write in your own words the directions for how to give glucagon on a small piece of paper and put in the kit.

The higher dose (0.2 mg/10 kg, 22 pounds) will give a slightly higher blood glucose rise but at the same time may increase the risk of side effects. [10]

All persons with diabetes using insulin should have glucagon available.[197] Check the expiration date! When the expiration date has passed and you have picked up a new injection kit from the pharmacy you can use the old one for practicing and demonstrating mixing procedures.

One should wait at least 30 min. after the injection before eating to avoid nausea and vomiting. These are relatively common side effects and they usually occur within 30 - 60 min. Large amounts of food following a glucagon injection should be avoided as this will increase the risk of nausea. A glucagon injection should not be repeated as it will only increase the risk of nausea without giving extra blood glucose raising effect.[10] If the blood glucose does not rise after an injection of glucagon this is probably due to depleted glycogen stores already, e.g. after heavy exercise or a recent hypoglycemic episode.

If you have to give glucagon, wait 10 - 15 minutes for the person to wake up. If still unconscious, call an ambulance. If the person with diabetes has revived, is feeling well and has a normal blood glucose when the ambulance arrives it is not always necessary to go to the hospital. If the blood glucose is still low the ambulance staff can give intravenous glucose.

Glucagon is counteracted by insulin. The concept is quite logical, seeing that non-diabetic persons will

Glucagon

➠ Every patient treated with insulin should have glucagon available.

➠ Indications: Severe hypoglycemia (unconscious/convulsions or cannot eat or drink by him-/ herself)

➠ Dose: 0.1 mg/10 kg (22 pounds) body weight (1mg/ml solution)

➠ Effect within 10 - 15 min.

➠ The effect lasts for 30 - 60 min. Eat something when you are feeling better to keep the blood glucose up until the next meal, but don't eat too much at once.

➠ Side effects: Nausea. Wait at least 30 min. before you eat to avoid this problem.

➠ Do *not* repeat the dose! One injection gives a sufficient level of glucagon in the blood.

➠ Loss of effect can be caused by:

Store of glycogen already depleted by	Glucagon counteracted by
1) Exercise	1) Alcohol
2) Recent hypoglycemia	2) High dose of
3) Decreased food intake,e.g. illness	insulin

➠ Always bring glucagon with you, e.g. when going on a picnic, a hiking trip, a boat tour or a trip abroad.

➠ Teach those that are close to you how to administer glucagon!

➠ You can never make a mistake when giving glucagon. It has the same effect whether injected in the subcutaneous tissue or into the muscle.

never have high concentrations of both hormones at the same time. Insulin is secreted when the blood glucose is high and glucagon when it is low. If hypoglycemia is caused by too large a dose of insulin, glucagon will have a poorer effect than if the low blood glucose is caused by not eating enough (see also "Too little food or too much insulin?" on page 45).

Many diabetic patients, especially children and adolescents, have encountered disturbing nausea after a difficult hypoglycemia, even if glucagon has

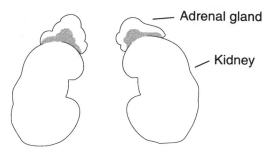

Adrenaline and cortisone are produced in the adrenal glands.

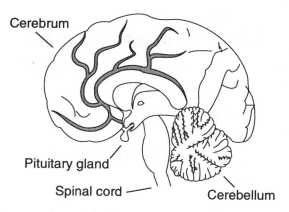

Cross-section of the brain. Growth hormone is produced in the pituitary gland.

not been injected. One explanation is that production of glucagon from their own pancreas also can result in nausea as a side effect.

Glucagon stimulates the transformation of fatty acids to ketones in the liver (see illustration on page 20). The fatty acids are formed from the breakdown of fat in the starving cells, caused by a lack of food or not enough insulin. The ketones contribute to nausea as a side effect after a glucagon injection. Ketones can easily be detected in the urine by self testing sticks. See also "After the hypoglycemia" on page 51.

At present, glucagon can only be given as an injection, but promising experiments have been conducted with glucagon as a nasal spray.[375]

Adrenaline

Adrenaline is a stress hormone that is secreted from the adrenal glands. It raises the blood glucose mainly by breaking down the glycogen stores in the liver. The concentration of adrenaline rises when the body is exposed to stress, fever and acidosis

(when your blood becomes acidic, e.g. diabetic ketoacidosis).[238] Adrenaline also decreases the cellular uptake of glucose which might seem strange at first glance. However, it does make sense if you consider that all the reactions in your body during hypoglycemia aim to reserve all available glucose for the brain.

Our bodies were originally designed for living in the Stone Age. When one ran into a polar bear or a mammoth the only alternatives were to fight or take to flight. In both situations extra fuel, in the form of glucose, was needed in the body. The problem with our present way of life is that adrenaline will be secreted even when getting excited in front of the TV when extra strength is not needed. With a well functioning insulin production a healthy person will easily take care of the extra glucose while a person with diabetes will have a raised blood glucose (see "Stress" on page 173).

When a person with diabetes has hypoglycemia adrenaline secretion can raise the blood glucose by stimulating the breakdown of the glycogen stores in the liver.[367] Adrenaline also stimulates the breakdown of body fat to fatty acids which can be converted into ketones in the liver. See illustration on page 21.

Effects of adrenaline

⇒ Adrenaline is produced in the adrenal glands

① Raises blood glucose by
- ⇒ Release of glucose from the glycogen stores in the liver
- ⇒ Activates the production of glucose from proteins
- ⇒ Reduced cellular uptake of glucose
- ⇒ Reduced production of insulin (in non-diabetic persons)

② Causes symptoms of hypoglycemia, such as shakiness and irritation.

③ Stimulates breakdown of body fat

Effects of cortisone

⇒ Cortisone is produced in the adrenal glands

① Raises blood glucose by
- ⇒ Reduced cellular uptake of glucose
- ⇒ Breakdown of proteins that can be used in the production of glucose in the liver

② Stimulates breakdown of body fat

The effects of growth hormone

⟹ Growth hormone is produced in the pituitary gland

① Stimulates growth

② Raises blood glucose by
➡ Reduced cellular uptake of glucose

③ Breaks down body fat

④ Increases muscular mass

⑤ Increased ability to take initiatives

Cortisone

Cortisone is another important stress hormone that affects the body metabolism in many ways. It increases the blood glucose by producing glucose from proteins (gluconeogenesis) and by decreasing the cellular uptake and usage of glucose. Cortisone also promotes the breakdown of body fat into fatty acids that can be converted into ketones.

Growth hormone

Growth hormone is produced in the pituitary gland, situated just under the brain. Some of the body's most important hormones are produced in this gland. The most important effect of growth hormone is to stimulate growth. It also has a blood glucose raising effect by counteracting insulin on the cell surface, thereby reducing the uptake of glucose into cells. In addition, growth hormone increases muscle tissue and ability to take initiatives and stimulates the breakdown of body fat.

During puberty, when the child is growing quickly, large amounts of growth hormone are secreted, thus requiring increased doses of insulin.[125] Growth hormone is released in high concentrations during the night which explains why teenagers often need very high doses of bedtime insulin. The blood glucose raising effect of growth hormone will start after 3 - 5 hours. This contributes to the problem of high morning blood glucose that is common for teenagers, especially if their HbA_{1c} is high.[62] Growth hormone will also stimulate the production of ketones, thereby increasing the risk of ketoacidosis in adolescence.[125].

Adolescents with diabetes have higher levels of growth hormones than healthy adolescents despite this they can have impaired growth if their glucose control is not acceptable. The reasons for this is that the effect of growth hormone in the body is mediated by the protein IGF-1. IGF-1 production in the liver is stimulated by insulin. Since the insulin concentration in the liver is lower in persons having diabetes (see page 33) the levels of IGF-1 will also be lower.[125]

Symptoms of hypoglycemia

Hypoglycemia means low blood glucose. Sometimes the same symptoms can be experienced when the blood glucose is not so low or even high (see "At which blood glucose level will I experience symptoms of hypoglycemia?" on page 40). It may be appropriate to refer to the symptoms of hypoglycemia as "sensations", implying the presence of symptoms but not really saying anything about the actual blood glucose level.

Different individuals experience different symptoms of hypoglycemia. However, the symptoms are usually the same from time to time for a given individual.[93] Especially when your diabetes is newly diagnosed you should check your blood glucose every time you have some symptoms or are feeling strange, to learn to recognize your individual reactions to hypoglycemia. When your diabetes is newly diagnosed it is important that the diabetes team at your hospital or outpatient clinic evaluate your own individual symptoms of hypoglycemia. If this does not occur spontaneously, hypoglycemia should be induced early on during the education of the newly diagnosed patient.[273] It is important that all family members be capable of treating hypoglycemia in a safe and effective manner.

Usually symptoms of hypoglycemia are divided into those of the body attempting to raise the blood glucose (autonomic and adrenergic symptoms) and

Hypoglycemic reactions

Hypoglycemic symptoms are usually divided into two types:

① Symptoms from the defense mechanism in your body attempting to raise the blood glucose (adrenergic and autonomic symptoms).

② Symptoms from the brain due to low blood glucose (neuroglycopenic symptoms).

Different types of hypoglycemia

① **Asymptomatic hypoglycemia**
Low blood glucose (< 3 mmol/L, 55 mg/dL), but without symptoms.

② **Moderate hypoglycemia**
Your body reacts with warning symptoms of hypoglycemia (autonomic symptoms)

③ **Hypoglycemia unawareness**
You experience symptoms from the brain (neuroglycopenic symptoms) without having had any autonomic warning symptoms beforehand. Persons observing you can clearly see that you are having symptoms.

④ **Severe hypoglycemia**
Severe symptoms of hypoglycemia disable you temporarily, requiring the assistance of another person to give you something to eat or a glucagon injection. Severe hypoglycemia can proceed to unconsciousness and convulsions.

Avoid situations where hypoglycemia might imply catastrophic consequences. This does not mean that it is impossible for a person with diabetes to practice risky sports, e.g. mountain climbing, paragliding or diving. In such cases you should be very well prepared, carefully consider possible situations that can arise and not practice the activity alone. See the section on diving on page 171 for more information.

those of the brain caused by a deficiency of glucose in the central nervous system (neuroglycopenic symptoms). See the key fact frames on page 38. A person having diabetes and faced with hypoglycemia will usually first notice bodily symptoms (e.g. shakiness, heart pounding) while observers often first notice the symptoms of the brain being affected (e.g. irritability, cognitive changes). The brain's reaction to hypoglycemia is usually triggered at a slightly lower blood glucose than the symptoms from the body.[93]

The brain is not impaired by a deficit of insulin since its cells do not require insulin for glucose uptake. On the other hand the brain is very sensitive to hypoglycemia and the bodily reactions therefore aim at avoiding hypoglycemia. The brain of children and adolescents will be affected with an impairment of mental flexibility, planning and decision-making, attention to detail and reaction-times at blood glucose concentrations of 2.8 - 3.2 mmol/L (50 - 58 mg/dL).[339] Adults seem to adjust slightly better to low blood glucose concentrations as they experience neuroglycopenic symptoms at lower blood glucose concentrations (2.5 - 2.8 mmol/L, 45 - 50 mg/dL).[84,93] This level does not seem to vary too much within the same individual. Changes in EEG (brain wave) activity will occur when the blood glucose falls below 2 mmol/L (35 mg/dL),[16]

and unconsciousness occurs at a blood glucose of approximately 1 mmol/L (20 mg/dL).[3]

It is possible to have a normal blood glucose and still have symptoms of hypoglycemia from the brain (neuroglycopenia). The hormonal defense has then raised the glucose level in the blood but there is a time lag before being passed into the brain.[362]

Hypoglycemia is often experienced as unpleasant, as losing control over your body. And that is exactly the case as the brain does not function well without glucose. Some people can become more irritable; others can look sick or sleepy. However, it is fortunately rare that one does something really dangerous or stupid, like hurting someone else. Traffic accidents with a bicycle or car can however be caused by an hypoglycemic event. Sometimes one does really strange things. One boy spread butter on a paper towel and tried to eat it. It is very important that your family and friends understand that when you are having a hypoglycemic reaction you are not quite in control and cannot help what you are doing.

Although a person with diabetes is aware of having symptoms of hypoglycemia he/she is often unable to eat or drink even if food is right in front of them. It might be difficult for a parent to understand that their diabetic child can react so peculiarly, but diabetic adults have described the feeling as follows: "You know you should drink the juice, but your body just does not obey the orders from the brain". If the blood glucose is lowered quickly, even if it stays in the normal range, it can provoke symptoms of hypoglycemia in certain people.

Symptoms of hypoglycemia from the brain

The blood glucose concentration at which your brain begins showing symptoms of dysfunction(neuroglycopenic symptoms) are triggered is lower than, and to a larger extent independent of, your recent blood glucose levels. [16,93]

➡ Weakness, dizziness

➡ Concentration difficulties

➡ Impaired short-term memory

➡ Slurred speech

➡ Feeling of warmth

➡ Unsteady gait, lack of coordination

➡ Headache

➡ Confusion

➡ Behavioral changes, poor judgement

➡ Double or blurred vision

➡ Disturbed color vision (especially red-green colors)

➡ Drowsiness

➡ Impaired consciousness

➡ Convulsions

Symptoms of hypoglycemia from the body

These symptoms (autonomic and adrenergic symptoms) are mediated both by adrenaline secretion and the autonomic nervous system and usually start at blood glucose concentrations less than 3 - 3.5 mmol/L (55 - 65 mg/dL). The threshold for triggering these symptoms will change depending on your recent blood glucose concentrations (the "blood glucose thermostat", see page 40).

➡ Trembling

➡ Anxiety

➡ Heart palpitations

➡ Throbbing pulse in the chest and abdomen

➡ Numbing of the lips, fingers and tongue

➡ Irritation

➡ Hunger, nausea

➡ Paleness

➡ Cold sweating

Severe hypoglycemia

Severe hypoglycemia is defined as a hypoglycemic reaction with low blood glucose (< 2.8 mmol/L, 50 mg/dL [432]) where the diabetic patient requires assistance or has been admitted to hospital. Most often the patient has impaired consciousness, is unconscious and/or has convulsions. In one year, 10 - 25 % of persons with IDDM will have a severe hypoglycemic episode at least once.[90] Every time this happens you should carefully check your insulin doses. If you cannot identify a clear reason for what happened (for example exercise or not enough food) you should decrease the "responsible" dose of insulin (see table on page 125). The anxiety over having a new severe hypoglycemia and the feeling

When the blood glucose quickly decreases one can have more intense hypoglycemic symptoms, especially if the HbA_{1c} is high.[290] In one study the blood glucose in a group of patients with an HbA_{1c} of 11 % was lowered from 18 to 9 mmol/L (325 - 160 mg/dL) using intravenous insulin.[127] These subjects showed the same type of increased cerebral blood flow that both non-diabetic and diabetic persons in good control have at a blood glucose of 2.0 mmol/L (35 mg/dL). However, in a group of children and adolescents with an HbA1c of 10.8 % on average no symptoms of hypoglycemia were noted when the blood glucose level was dropped from 21 mmol/L to 6 mmol/L (380 to 110 mg/dL).[165]

Symptoms of hypoglycemia in children and adolescents

Hypoglycemic symptoms in children and adolescents differ slightly from those experienced by adults in that behavior changes are more common. The table below is from a British study in which the parents of children and adolescents between the ages of 1.5 - 16 years were asked about their observations of hypoglycemic symptoms.[283]

Paleness	88 %
Sweating	77 %
Tearfulness	74 %
Irritability	73 %
Poor concentration	69 %
Argumentative	69 %
Hunger	69 %
Tiredness	67 %
Aggressive	64 %
Trembling	64 %
Weakness	64 %
Confusion	60 %
Dizziness	51 %
Headache	47 %
Abdominal pain	43 %
Naughty	40 %
Nausea	33 %
Slurred speech	29 %
Night mares	20 %
Blurred vision	19 %
Convulsions	16 %
Double vision	11 %
Bed wetting	10 %

"The glucostat"

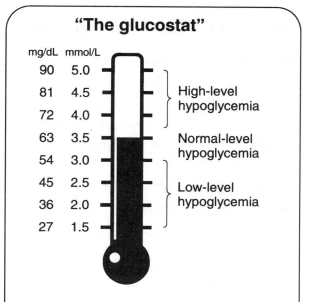

The blood glucose level at which you experience symptoms of hypoglycemia functions similar to a thermostat ("the glucostat"). Unfortunately this thermostat is adjusted up or down much too easily. When the blood glucose has been high for a couple of days you will have symptoms at a higher blood glucose level ("high-level hypoglycemia") and when it has been low for several days you will experience symptoms at a lower blood glucose level ("low-level hypoglycemia").

	Symptoms at mmol/L	mg/dL	Measure
High-level hypoglycemia	> 3.5-4	65-75	Wait with eating
Normal-level hypoglycemia	3.0-3.5	55-65	Eat something with glucose
Low-level hypoglycemia	< 3.0	< 55	Avoid all low blood glucose values

of not being able to trust one's body can be very troublesome. If you have recurrent severe hypoglycemias this problem might be managed by the use of an insulin pump.[194]

Convulsions

A very low blood glucose (close to 1 mmol/L, 20 mg/dL)) can trigger convulsions. Some very sensitive children can have muscle twitches when their blood glucose is close to 3.0 mmol/L (55 mg/dL).[268] These children are often conscious when the twitching starts. Some children can even talk and give eye contact at this time. Convulsions are usually not dangerous for the child but are, of course, very alarming for those observing. It may even appear that the child is dying. However, breathing

is seldom affected. Turn the child on the side (recovery position), after making sure that the airways are free. This is the safest position should the child vomit. Prepare glucagon and give an injection (for doses see page 36). Call an ambulance if the person does not wake up within 10 - 15 minutes.

You should always reconsider your insulin doses after a hypoglycemic incident accompanied by convulsions and lower the dose if there is not an identifiable cause for the blood glucose being so low at the time. Anti-convulsive medicine can be consid-

Why did I have a hypoglycemia?

➠ Less food than usual?

➠ Skipped a meal?

➠ Physical exercise?
The risk of hypoglycemia is increased during the rest of the day and also the night following heavy physical exercise.

➠ Too large a dose of insulin?

➠ New site of injection?
(e.g. from thigh to abdomen or to a site free of fat pads (lipohypertrophia)

➠ Recent hypoglycemia?
➠ glucose stores in liver depleted
➠ less warning symptoms of hypoglycemia (hypoglycemic unawareness)

➠ Very low HbA_{1c}?(increased risk of hypoglycemia unawareness)

➠ Alcohol intake?

Should I always eat when I feel hypoglycemic?

① Measure your blood glucose

② < 3 mmol/L (55 mg/dL) ➠ Eat something

③ 3 - 3.5 mmol/L (55 - 65 mg/dL)
➠ Eat something if your next meal is more than ½ - 1 hour off or if you know that your blood glucose is decreasing, e.g. after physical exercise.

④ > 3.5 - 4 mmol/L (65 - 75 mg/dL)
➠ You may be having hypoglycemic symptoms at too high a blood glucose level. Wait a short while and test yourself again. Don't eat until the blood glucose has fallen below 3.5 mmol/L (65 mg/dL), see point ③. See also the text on page 41 and 73.

ered as a preventive measure for children having convulsions at a blood glucose of 2.5 - 3.0 mmol/L (45 - 55 mg/dL), even if the child has a normal EEG (brain-wave). We had one teenager who sometimes had convulsions at a blood glucose of 3.3 - 3.5 mmol/L (60 - 65 mg/dL). After medication his threshold for hypoglycemic convulsions was lowered to 2.5 mmol/L (45 mg/dL). At this time he has ordinary hypoglycemic symptoms, enabling him to react appropriately.

Will the development of my child be affected by severe hypoglycemias?

It is not clear whether or how severe hypoglycemias affect the physical and intellectual development in children with IDDM. Glucose is the most important source of energy for the brain. When the blood glucose is low, the blood flow to the brain can be increased to allow a larger supply of glucose.[127]

Small children (under the age of 5) are more vulnerable to severe hypoglycemias with seizures because their nervous system is still developing.[45] Permanent neurological damage and EEG-changes have been described in some cases where the chil-

dren have had a severe hypoglycemia, rendering them unconscious.[369] One study of children and teenagers between the age of 10 - 19 years showed slightly poorer school results for those who developed diabetes early in life.[338] These data are however difficult to judge as the studies are done retrospectively. A Swedish study of adult patients in which the intensively treated group had an increased number of severe hypoglycemias showed no difference in cognitive function after 5 years of follow up.[328]

Children less than 2 years of age are especially vulnerable to hypoglycemia. Severe hypoglycemia should be avoided at any price in this age group, even if it means having a higher HbA_{1c}.[268]

At which blood glucose level will I experience symptoms of hypoglycemia?

In the brain there is a kind of blood glucose meter that will trigger defense reactions in your body to raise a low blood glucose. It works similar to a thermostat ("glucostat"), which is triggered at a certain blood glucose level. This reaction is greatly dependent on how your blood glucose has been during the last few days.[94,260] If the blood sugar has been high for some time symptoms of hypoglycemia and release of counter-regulating hormones will appear at a higher blood glucose level than usual.[64,114] With

It is difficult to determine if a child's development is affected by severe hypoglycemia. Single episodes will probably have no effect it but if the child has recurrent severe hypoglycemia during the first 2 - 3 years of life some studies indicate that school results will be less than optimal. If the child has had a severe hypoglycemia the insulin doses should always be adjusted to avoid another such episode. With young children one may have to accept a higher HbA_{1c} in some cases to avoid severe hypoglycemias.

a high HbA_{1c} it is not unusual to have symptoms of hypoglycemia already at a blood glucose of 4 - 5 mmol/L (70 - 90 mg/dL).[64,193,218] This type of reaction seems to be less pronounced in adults.[35]

When the "glucostat" adjusts to another blood glucose level this will mainly affect your bodily (autonomic) symptoms (mediated by adrenaline or the autonomic nervous system). The blood glucose level where the brain is affected (neuroglycopenic symptoms) is less influenced by recent blood glucose levels than the bodily symptoms,[16,17,93] possibly due to a preservation of normal glucose uptake into the brain despite a low blood glucose level.[65] Short-term memory is impaired when the blood glucose falls below approximately 3.0 mmol/L (55 mg/dL). In a study with poorer glycemic control with a higher HbA_{1c} (9.2 %) the short-term memory was affected already at 3.9 mmol/L (70 mg/dL).[193] See also page 73.

To decrease the blood glucose level at which symptoms of hypoglycemia appear you must restrain yourself from eating until the blood glucose is close to 3.0 mmol/L (55 mg/dL) despite having symptoms of hypoglycemia. Do whatever is required to avoid high blood glucose levels the following 1 - 2 weeks. The "glucostat" threshold will then change to a lower blood glucose level, normalizing the value at which your hypoglycemic sensations will appear (see also "Insulin sensitivity and resistance" on page 69).

The level at which you start experiencing symptoms of hypoglycemia will change depending on the frequency of hypoglycemias during the last few days. Make it a habit to measure your blood glucose when you have a hypoglycemia. If you usually have your hypoglycemias at 3.0 mmol/L ("normal-level hypoglycemia") and now have no symptoms until the blood glucose falls to 2.6 mmol/L ("low-level hypoglycemia") you have had too many low blood glucose values recently. On the other hand, if you have symptoms of hypoglycemia already at a blood glucose of 3.5 - 4.0 mmol/L ("high-level hypoglycemia") you have had too many high blood glucose values and your HbA_{1c} is probably rising (see also page 73).

The opposite applies if you have frequent hypoglycemias. The "glucostat" will then change so that the defense mechanisms of hypoglycemia will not start until the blood glucose falls below 3 mmol/L (55 mg/dL).[16,192] In one study the threshold for symptoms of hypoglycemia changed, being 0.3 - 0.5 mmol/L (5 - 9 mg/dL) lower after only 4 days with low blood glucose values (2.2 - 2.8 mmol/L, 40 - 50 mg/dL) during one or a couple of hours per day.[422]

In another study, a single episode of afternoon hypoglycemia (approximately 2.8 mmol/L, 50 mg/dL) caused less symptoms as well as a reduction of the hormonal defense when having a new hypoglycemia the following morning.[94] The patients also had an increased insulin sensitivity, i.e. the blood glucose was lower than the day before although the insulin level in the blood was the same.

Nighttime hypoglycemia with an average of 2.2 mmol/L (40 mg/dL) during 2 hours resulted in less bodily (adrenergic) symptoms as well as less brain (neuroglycopenic) symptoms when having a new hypoglycemia with the same blood glucose level the next day.[403]

Thresholds for reactions of hypoglycemia

	Non-diabetic persons	Diabetic HbA$_{1c}$ 9%	Diabetic HbA$_{1c}$ 5,2%
mmol/L			
Symptoms start at	3.3	3.3	2.0
Adrenaline response	3.2	3.2	2.3
EEG-changes	2.0	2.0	2.0
mg/dL			
Symptoms start at	60	60	36
Adrenaline response	58	58	41
EEG-changes	36	36	36

With a low HbA$_{1c}$ you will get bodily (adrenergic) hypoglycemic symptoms and adrenaline responses at much lower blood glucose values than if your HbA$_{1c}$ is high.[16] However, the blood glucose level at which your brain is affected is the same both whether you have a high or a low HbA$_{1c}$.

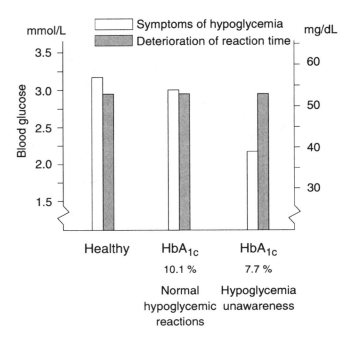

In a British study healthy persons were compared with 2 groups with IDDM having an HbA$_{1c}$ of 10.1 % and 7.7 % respectively.[277] Both diabetes groups had the same number of symptomatic hypoglycemias while in the group with lower HbA$_{1c}$ all had recorded at least 3 blood glucose readings of less than 3 mmol/L without symptoms of hypoglycemia (hypoglycemia unawareness) during the past 2 months. Most of them also had experienced one or more severe hypoglycemias (demanding help from another person) during the past 6 months.

In the group with hypoglycemic unawareness the patients had no symptoms of hypoglycemia until the blood glucose was lowered to 2.3 mmol/L (41 mg/dL). Despite this they had a deterioration in reaction time at the same blood glucose level (2.9 mmol/L, 52 mg/dL) as did the other groups. This means that if you have experienced hypoglycemic unawareness and drive a car with a blood glucose of 2.8 mmol/L (50 mg/dL) you may feel quite well but your reaction time will be impaired, and you will be a danger in traffic.

Coffee and Coca-Cola contain caffeine which may cause one to notice the symptoms of hypoglycemia at a little higher blood glucose levels than usual.[227]

Some drugs used for high blood pressure and premature labor (beta-blockers) can lessen your symptoms of hypoglycemia. Diabetic patients using beta-blockers should always check their blood glucose whenever unexpected sweating occurs as this may be the only symptom of a very low blood glucose, 2.8 mmol/L (50 mg/dL) or below.[193].

Hypoglycemic unawareness

Hypoglycemic unawareness is defined as a hypoglycemic episode without having had warning symptoms associated with decreasing blood glucose. If you have frequent hypoglycemias the threshold for symptom recognition will occur at a lower blood glucose level (see page 40). If the threshold for secreting counter-regulatory hormones falls below the blood glucose level where the brain reacts you will not have any bodily warning symptoms. You will subsequently not react in time (i.e. eat something) and the hypoglycemia can easily proceed to a severe hypoglycemia. Sometimes you will not even remember afterwards that you had hypoglycemia.

Hypoglycemic unawareness will increase the risk of severe hypoglycemia by 5 - 6 fold,[91] and is more common among those having severe hypoglycemias.[92] This implies that the brain is unable to adjust to recurrent hypoglycemia.[17]

If you have problems with hypoglycemic unawareness you should aim for a slightly higher mean blood glucose and above all avoid hypoglycemia below 3.5 - 4.0 mmol/L (65 - 75 mg/dL). In as little as 2 weeks time you will usually recognize symptoms of hypoglycemia more easily.[93,143] In one study the ability to recognize symptoms of hypoglycemia was improved after only 2 days of meticulous avoidance of blood glucose levels less

---

Two types of hypoglycemia.

① **Not enough food:**
Typical of this type is a hypoglycemia before a meal. The blood glucose is low and often the insulin level in the blood also is low. If you use multiple injections you will not take the insulin until shortly before the meal. Adrenaline and glucagon can therefore easily release glucose from the liver and you may very well get a rebound effect with high blood glucose lasting several hours after the hypoglycemia.

② **Too much insulin:**
Typical of this type is taking the insulin as usual but not eating enough (e.g. if you don't like the food). The blood glucose is low at the same time as the insulin level is increasing. The insulin will then counteract the production of glucose from the liver, resulting in a deeper hypoglycemia. The high insulin level will thus prevent the rebound phenomenon.

---

than 3.3 mmol/L (60 mg/dL).[260] By training yourself in recognizing subtle symptoms as your blood glucose is decreasing you will increase your chances of treating the hypoglycemia in time.[17] See also page 73 and 88.

Many patients with a long duration of diabetes will have a reduced adrenaline response to low blood glucose and thus have less warning symptoms from their autonomic nervous system. This contributes both to diminished symptoms and less effective counter-regulation when the blood glucose is decreasing.[17] The change from porcine (pork) and bovine (beef) insulin to human insulin has been associated with an increase in hypoglycemic unawareness. Although several studies have addressed this issue there has been no scientific evidence of such an increase.[17]

Symptoms of hypoglycemia at a high blood glucose level?

Some children will experience the same symptoms when the blood glucose is high as when it is low. Especially younger children will often have difficulties in discerning the two. They feel hungry or hollow in the stomach when their blood glucose is high because the cells are starving due to a lack of insulin (see figure at the bottom of page 21 and

"What do I do if the blood glucose level is high?" on page 127).

Rebound phenomenon

Your body will try to reverse hypoglycemia via defense reactions (see "Counter-regulation" on page 31). Often this counter-regulation will be a bit too effective and the blood glucose will rise to high levels during the hours following hypoglycemia. This is called a rebound phenomenon (posthypoglycemic hyperglycemia). During the hours of increased levels of the counter-regulatory hormones there will also be an insulin resistance (see page 69), e.g. higher doses of insulin than usual are needed to lower the blood glucose to normal levels (for example when taking an injection before you eat).

When having hypoglycemia it is common to eat too much. It is also common to decrease the next insulin dose, to avoid new hypoglycemias. Both these factors contribute to the rebound phenomenon, resulting in an even higher blood glucose.

The rebound phenomenon will only develop if the insulin level in the blood is low during the hours following a hypoglycemia,[62] (like when you have a hypoglycemia caused by exercise or skipping a snack). The insulin level after nighttime hypoglycemia will decrease when the insulin wanes as the night goes on. If, however, the hypoglycemia is caused by too large an insulin dose the high level of insulin will cause a diminished secretion of the counter-regulating hormones and the rebound phenomenon will therefore not occur.

Children are more prone to having rebound phenomena due to a more vigorous hormonal response to hypoglycemia than adults.[17] The defense mechanisms are also triggered at higher blood glucose levels than those of adults.[218] The rebound phenomena often lasts 12 hours or more in adults,[4] whereas with children the high blood glucose often lasts only a few hours (see the blood glucose graph page 44). Sometimes the rebound phenomenon can give a raised blood glucose spanning more than 24 hours.[335] As the hormones return to normal levels the blood glucose will also gradually normalize.

If you take an extra insulin injection when the blood glucose is high following a rebound phenomenon you may experience a very quick fall in blood glucose resulting in a new hypoglycemia. High sensitivity to insulin increases this tendency. You should therefore be careful with giving extra insulin after a rebound phenomenon. There are large inter-individual difference in the tendency for having rebound phenomena. If you are likely to have long-lasting rebound effects you can try increasing the insulin injection at the meal that follows hypoglycemia.[4]

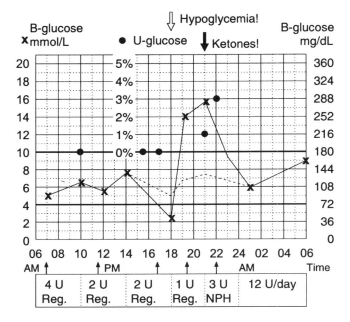

This 5 year old girl has recently been diagnosed with diabetes. She has a pronounced rebound phenomenon in the evening. Note the ketones in the urine after the hypoglycemia which are caused by her own production of glucagon (see also "Ketones in the urine" on page 79). The blood glucose may have followed the dashed line instead, if she had not experienced hypoglycemia and the resulting rebound effect.

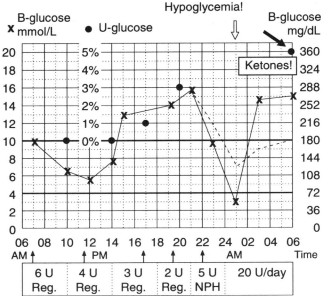

Nighttime hypoglycemia with rebound phenomenon. Without a blood glucose test at 1 AM it would appear as if this 6-year old girl had a high blood glucose all night long. An increase in the bedtime insulin would have led to an even lower blood glucose the next night (the Somogyi phenomenon). Note the presence of both ketones and glucose in the morning urine. Without the night-time hypoglycemia her blood glucose may have followed the dashed line.

Somogyi phenomenon

If the blood glucose is low at night you will often continue sleeping without noticing it. However, the secretion of counter-regulating hormones in your body can result in a rebound phenomena with a rise in blood glucose to high levels in the morning. If you haven't measured a low blood glucose value in the middle of the night you may believe that your bedtime insulin needs to be increased. A higher dose of bedtime insulin the next night will give an even lower blood glucose and a more intense rebound effect, resulting in an even higher blood glucose the following morning. You can easily end up in a viscous cycle. This type of nighttime rebound phenomenon is called the Somogyi phenomena after the chemist who first described it.[237,370]

If your morning blood glucose is sometimes low and sometimes high you may have problems with the Somogyi phenomenon. Some nights the blood glucose might be low enough to start the rebound phenomenon, causing the morning blood glucose to be high. Other nights the blood glucose will not be low enough to trigger the rebound phenomenon and the morning blood glucose will subsequently be lower (see blood glucose graphs on page 44).

The Somogyi phenomenon has been questioned throughout the years but consensus today is that it is mainly seen in patients using primarily short-acting insulin (multiple injections and insulin pumps) resulting in a small insulin depot.[62,89] These patients also have a higher than normal rise in blood glucose after breakfast following a night-time hypoglycemia.[237]

When using twice-daily injections the depot of intermediate-acting insulin will be larger (see page 60). Insulin can be released from this depot during the night, resulting in a level of insulin that is rarely low enough to trigger a rebound phenomenon.[62]

A urine test in the morning can be difficult to interpret in this situation. It will show both ketones (caused by a low blood glucose early in the night or by insulin deficiency later in the night when the blood glucose was high) and glucose (from the later part of the night). You will attain the same urine test result (ketones and glucose) if your blood glucose has been high all night without a hypoglycemia (see page 135).

Dawn phenomenon

The blood glucose will rise early in the morning because of the so called "dawn phenomenon"

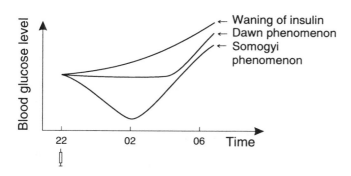

Different factors influence the blood glucose level during the night and in the morning. The dawn phenomenon depends on the nighttime secretion of growth hormone and the Somogyi phenomenon is a nighttime rebound phenomenon. The insulin waning effect depends on the pharmacological properties of the insulins available today.

which occurs in 80 - 100 % of patients with IDDM.[62] This effect is caused by an increased secretion of growth hormone raising the blood glucose late in the night and early in the morning.[4,61,125] The dawn effect will increase the morning blood glucose by approximately 1.5 - 2 mmol/L (25 - 35 mg/dL) compared to the blood glucose at midnight.[62] A high morning blood glucose is a common problem for growing children, especially during the later part of puberty when the growth spurt is at its peak.[125]

Too little food or too much insulin?

Both can result in a low blood glucose, but the body's way of handling the situation is different. The effect of glucagon on breaking down the stored glucose (glycogen) is counteracted by insulin. Insulin acts in the opposite direction, e.g. transports glucose into the liver cells to be stored as glycogen. From this it follows that the higher the insulin level, the more difficult it will be to release glucose from the liver. This means that a low blood glucose caused by a large insulin dose (e.g. if you

---

have taken extra insulin) will be more difficult to reverse than a low blood glucose due to inadequate food intake.

Nighttime hypoglycemia

Nighttime hypoglycemias are more common than most people tend to believe. Many studies have shown that as many as 30 % of both children and adults have nighttime hypoglycemias.[274] Often you will not awaken from slight symptoms of hypoglycemia, and this may open the way for them to develop into more severe ones. Symptoms of hypoglycemia may also be more difficult to recognize when you are lying down than when you are standing.[195]

The only way to know for sure if your blood glucose is low is to get up in the night and take a blood glucose test. Many children will wake up when hypoglycemic and tell their parents. Other times a parent will wake up to strange or unusual sounds. When the child is newly diagnosed with diabetes it is often a good idea to have the child sleep in a room close by with the doors opened. Smaller children often sleep in their parents' bedroom, at least for a period of time following diagnosis.

See page 131 and 76 for recommendations when to take nighttime tests depending on which bedtime insulin you use.

A nighttime hypoglycemia can be caused by too large a dose of bedtime insulin. Another cause is too high a dose of short-acting insulin prior to the evening meal which will result in a early night hypoglycemia. Nighttime hypoglycemia can also be caused by vigorous afternoon or evening exercise (see page 167).

If you are injecting short-acting insulin in the thigh before dinner or the evening meal the slow absorption of insulin can result in nighttime hypoglycemias.[183] If you inject the bedtime insulin perpendicular to the skin or without lifting a skin

---

Symptoms of nighttime hypoglycemia

➡ Nightmares

➡ Sweating (wet sheets)

➡ Headache in the morning

➡ Tired in the morning

---

fold you might easily be injecting intramuscularly. The insulin will then be absorbed quicker and you will risk a low blood glucose early in the night. [184]

A good basic rule to avoid nighttime hypoglycemias is to always have something extra to eat if the blood glucose is 6 mmol/L (110 mg/dL) or less before going to bed.[355] See also "Bedtime insulin" on page 130. Remember that an extra sandwich before going to bed is never a guarantee for avoiding nighttime hypoglycemias. If you have doubt the only way to know for sure is to get up in the middle of the night to check the blood glucose level.

You can also experiment with the evening meal to find something that gives a slower rise in blood glucose over a longer period of time. Try for instance high fiber bread with butter on it. Your stomach will empty slower, resulting in sustained glucose absorption.

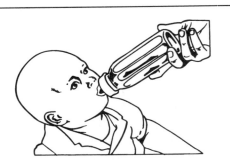

Corn flour mix when going to bed

Mix 2 tablespoons of corn flour with 1 dl (0.2 pints) of water. This mixture contains 14 g (½ ounce) of very slow-acting carbohydrates. It should be mixed cold and heated up as little as possible. Heat breaks down the cells of the corn flour and makes the carbohydrates more quick-acting.

If the child has a meal of formula at bedtime you can replace parts of it with corn flour mix. Begin with a small part and increase gradually it as the child accepts it. Try to lower the temperature a little each day and the child will often soon accept drinking the mixture at room-temperature.

If the child is less than 3 years old one might need to add pancreas enzymes to break down the corn starch. Ask your pediatrician about this.

For older persons, a corn starch bar with acceptable taste has been proven useful.

The most "long-acting" carbohydrate available for an evening meal is raw corn starch, which gives a rise in blood glucose over about 6 hours, thereby effectively preventing nighttime hypoglycemia. We give it to children with diseases other than diabetes who experience problems maintaining their blood glucose during the night. However, one drawback is the taste. It cannot be heated or prepared in any way or the carbohydrates will become more "short-acting". Younger children usually can get used to the taste of corn starch formula. For older persons, a corn starch bar has a more acceptable taste.

In a study among children and adolescents the number of hypoglycemic episodes (< 3.3 mmol/L, 60 mg/dL) at 2 AM and before breakfast were reduced from approximately 1/week to 0.3/week when 25 % - 50 % of the carbohydrates in the evening meal was given as uncooked cornstarch in milk.[224] Unheated cornstarch (0.3 g/kg, 2 grains/pound) given at the time of the bedtime injection during 4 weeks time increased the blood glucose level at 3 AM by, on average, 2 mmol/L (35 mg/dL) in adults with diabetes.[26] The number of nighttime hypoglycemias < 3.0 mmol/L (55 mg/dL) were reduced by 70 % without changing the overall glycemic control.

Another possibility worth trying, if you are having problems with nighttime hypoglycemias, is to eat ordinary (not "Light") potato chips (crisps) as an extra late snack before going to sleep. The manufacturing process and the high fat content result in the glucose from potato chips (crisps) being absorbed very slowly.[76] The blood glucose will still not have reached its peak after 3 hours (see graph on page 159). Twenty-five grams of potato chips have the same content of both fat (8 g, 0.3 ounces) and carbohydrates (15 g, 0.5 ounces) as a cheese sandwich. This is often an attractive alternative to minimize the risk of nighttime hypoglycemias for youngsters and teenagers actively engaged in sports.

☞ Make sure that the pens you use for daytime and night-time insulin are so different that you cannot accidentally take the wrong pen, even if it is completely dark.

☞ Beware of this also if you use disposable pens! You should not use disposable pens of the same brand for both daytime and night-time insulin due to the risk of taking the wrong type of insulin.

Will a low blood glucose in the night normalize even if the child does not wake up?

The long- or intermediate-acting insulin that you took in the afternoon or at bedtime will have lost most of its action in the morning and the blood glucose will rise even if the child does not wake up from a hypoglycemia. The body will also try to raise a low blood glucose by different defense mechanisms (counter-regulation, see "Rebound phenomenon" on page 43).

Can you die from hypoglycemia?

An increase of unexplained deaths in otherwise healthy persons with IDDM has been noted in recent years where they have been found dead in bed in the morning. In 1989, twenty-two such cases (aged 12 - 43 years) were recorded in England. [389]

Between the years 1977 - 1990, 2653 boys and 2341 girls were diagnosed with diabetes in Sweden. Nine of these (aged 15 - 23) were found dead in their beds. Hypoglycemia may be a possible cause as none had signs of alcohol in their blood. During the same period 7 children and adolescents died due to ketoacidosis. The total risk of dying was increased by 2 - 3 times for the children and adolescents with diabetes compared to non-diabetic peers. [348]

A possible explanation for the such nighttime deaths could be an erroneous injection of short-acting insulin at bedtime instead of the usual intermediate- or long-acting insulin. [174] Adolescents and young adults often have high doses of bedtime insulin and it is not uncommon to take the wrong insulin pen when administering the bedtime insulin. For example this happened twice to the same 13 year-old during one of our diabetes summer camps.

Adults with IDDM have died from hypoglycemia after drinking alcohol (which prevents the liver from producing glucose). They usually suffered from other diseases that worsened the stress that follows a hypoglycemic attack (e.g. some kind of heart disorder). [304,389]

Night-time hypoglycemias may be caused by:

⇒ The dose of short-acting insulin before the evening meal was too high (hypoglycemia early in the night).

⇒ The dose of bedtime insulin was too high (hypoglycemia around 2 AM or later with NPH-insulin).

⇒ Short-acting insulin before dinner or the evening meal was given in the thigh (hypoglycemia early in the night being caused by a slower absorption from the thigh).

⇒ Not enough to eat in the evening or an evening meal containing mostly "short-acting" foods being absorbed too quickly.

⇒ Exercise in the afternoon or evening without decreasing the dose of bedtime insulin.

⇒ Alcohol consumption in the evening.

Which dose of insulin contributed to the hypoglycemia?

① Multiple injection therapy

Pre-meal *short-acting* insulin and NPH-insulin at bedtime

Time of hypoglycemia	"Responsible" dose
Before lunch	Breakfast short-acting
In the afternoon	Lunch short-acting
In the evening	Dinner short-acting
Late evening/ before midnight	Evening meal short-acting
After midnight	Bedtime NPH-insulin

With *direct-acting* insulin the pre-meal dose will be "responsible" for hypoglycemia during 2 - 3 hours after the injection. After that the basal insulin is more likely to contribute to hypoglycemia.

② 2-dose treatment

Short-acting and NPH-insulin before both breakfast and dinner

Time of hypoglycemia	"Responsible" dose
Before lunch	Breakfast short-acting
In the afternoon	Breakfast NPH-insulin
Early evening	Dinner short-acting
Late evening / before midnight	Dinner NPH-insulin
After midnight	Dinner NPH-insulin

Insulin-dependent diabetes in children, adolescents and adults © R. Hanas 1998

Treating hypoglycemia

Ten grams of glucose will raise the blood glucose of an adult by about 2 mmol/L (35 mg/dL) after 15 min.[67,93] The blood glucose will rise over 45 - 60 minutes and then start to fall. Smaller children can be given a smaller amount of glucose. For instance 1.5 g of glucose/10 kg (10 grains/10 pounds) body weight will raise the blood glucose by approximately 2 mmol/L (35 mg/dL) (see table on page 49). It is important not to take too much glucose "just to be on the safe side" since the blood glucose will then rise too steeply (see "Rebound phenomenon" on page 43). If you tend to eat a lot when having hypoglycemias you will gain weight.

Remember that glucose in food can only be absorbed into the blood after passing from the stomach into the intestine. Glucose can not be absorbed from the oral mucous membranes [166] or the stomach. Glucose given rectally does not raise the blood glucose level in children [8] or adults.[22]

Practical instructions:

① Take a blood glucose test. The sensations of a hypoglycemic reaction do not necessarily imply that your blood glucose is actually low. If your symptoms are so intense that it is difficult to measure the blood glucose you should of course eat something containing glucose or sugar as soon as possible. If your blood glucose happens to be high, a little extra glucose will not make much of a difference. This will outweigh the risk of having a more severe hypoglycemia if you had not started reversing it without delay.

② If your blood glucose is low (less than 3 - 3.5 mmol/L, 55 - 65 mg/dL) have something sweet to eat, for example glucose tablets. Start with a lower dose according to the table on next page and wait 10 - 15 minutes for the glucose to have effect. If you don't feel better after 15 - 20 minutes and your blood glucose has not risen, you can take the same amount of glucose once again.

It is important to take something containing only sugar, e.g. glucose tablets or juice. Avoid food and drink containing fat (as chocolate, cookies, milk or chocolate milk) if you want a quick increase in blood glucose. Fat causes the stomach to empty slower and the glucose will then reach the blood stream later (see also "Fat" on page 145).

③ If the child is not unconscious but has difficulties chewing give glucose gel or honey.

④ If the child is unconscious or has convulsions, give a glucagon injection (for dosage, see page 36) and call for an ambulance! Never give an unconscious person food or drink because it might by mistake be inhaled and cause suffocation or subsequent pneumonia.

⑤ Refrain from physical exercise until all symptoms of hypoglycemia have vanished. Wait at least 15 minutes before you do anything that demands your full attention or a quick understanding, e.g. driving, operating a machine or taking an exam in school.

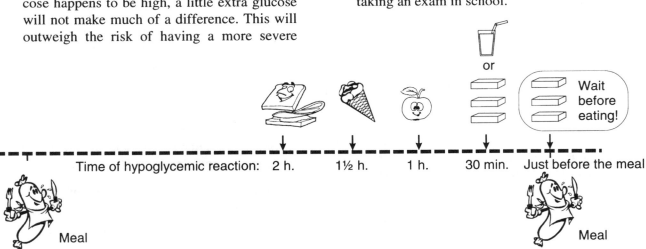

				or
				Wait before eating!

Time of hypoglycemic reaction: 2 h.   1½ h.   1 h.   30 min.   Just before the meal

Meal

Meal

It is important to consider the time span to your next meal when you have hypoglycemia. Don't eat more than you will need to manage until the next meal. It is all too easy to have too much to eat since it takes a while before the blood glucose rises and makes you feel better. If you have a hypoglycemic reaction when sitting with the meal in front of you it may take quite a while before you feel better again if you eat immediately. It is better to eat something with a higher sugar/glucose content (e.g. glucose tablets), wait 10 - 15 min. or until you feel better, and then enjoy your meal.

How many glucose tablets (3 g) are needed to treat hypoglycemia? [93]

Body weight		Rise in blood glucose	
		2 mmol/L	4 mmol/L
Kg	Pounds	35 mg/dL	70 mg/dL
10	22	½ tablet	1 tablet (3 g)
20	45	1 tablet (3 g)	2 tablets
30	65	1½ tablet	3 tablets
40	90	2 tablets	4 tablets
50	110	2½ tablets	5 tablets
60	125	3 tablets	6 tablets
70	155	3½ tablets	7 tablets
Glucose /10 kg		1.5 g	3 g
" /10 pounds		10 grains	20 grains

"Rule of thumb"

1 tablet (3 g) of glucose/10 kg (½ tablet/10 pounds) body weight will raise the blood glucose approximately 4 mmol/L (70 mg/dL), i.e. your blood glucose will be approximately 4 mmol/L higher after 15 - 30 min. than it would be without extra glucose. Most often an increase of 2 mmol/L (35 mg/dL) will be enough but if you have recently taken insulin and your blood glucose is falling, you may need more glucose.

⑥ Don't leave a child alone after a hypoglycemic reaction. If he/she is in school make sure a qualified person will receive him/her at home. Smaller children need someone to accompany them if the parents cannot come to the school.

⑦ If there is no apparent explanation for the hypoglycemia you should decrease the "responsible" dose of insulin the next day. See further the chapter on adjusting insulin, page 125.

Time table of hypoglycemia

The time interval between the hypoglycemia and your next meal will determine which response is appropriate.

① **Hypoglycemia just before your eat:**

Take glucose and wait 10 - 15 minutes before you start eating. If you eat directly, the food will mix with the glucose in the stomach. Since it normally takes about 20 minutes before solid food has been

How quickly does the sugar work?

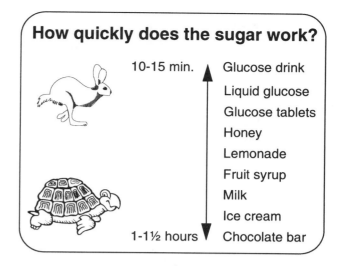

10-15 min. ↑	Glucose drink
	Liquid glucose
	Glucose tablets
	Honey
	Lemonade
	Fruit syrup
	Milk
	Ice cream
1-1½ hours ↓	Chocolate bar

digested (enough to be emptied into the intestines) an increase in your blood glucose will take at least as long time. Remember that the glucose in the food must reach the intestines before it can be absorbed into the blood.

② **Hypoglycemia 45 - 90 minutes before next meal:**

The same advice applies as in the previous example ① to reverse the hypoglycemia quickly. Afterwards you will need something to eat (like a fruit) to keep your blood glucose up until the next meal.

③ **Hypoglycemia 1 - 2 hours before next meal:**

Take glucose and wait 10 - 15 minutes before you eat anything else in order to quickly reverse the hypoglycemia. Since it will be a while until your next meal it is important to eat something that contains more "long-acting" carbohydrates. If the hypoglycemia develops slowly you can skip the glucose and have a glass of milk and/or a sandwich instead.

What should I do if I find someone with diabetes who is not feeling well?

In this situation you will most often not know the blood glucose and you may lose precious time trying to measure it. The best course of action is to give something containing sugar as quickly as possible and then to call for help. If the person is feeling ill from a high blood glucose the extra glucose will not have any adverse effects. It is not the high

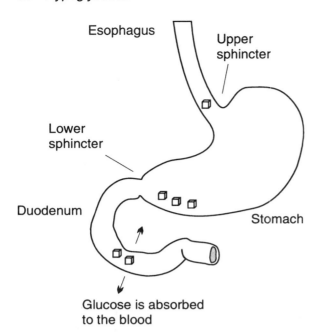

Esophagus

Upper sphincter

Lower sphincter

Duodenum

Stomach

Glucose is absorbed to the blood

Sugar must reach the intestine to be able to be absorbed into the blood stream and to raise your blood glucose. Glucose cannot be absorbed through the oral mucosa,[166] or from the stomach. The lower sphincter (pylorus) regulates the emptying of the stomach. Different factors influence how quickly the stomach empties (see page 143) and will thereby determine how quickly ingested glucose can be absorbed into the blood to correct a hypoglycemia.

blood glucose as such which causes you to feel ill, but the lack of insulin that causes the high blood sugar. If the blood glucose is low it is most important that the person in question get sugar as quickly as possible.

Glucose

Pure glucose has the quickest effect when correcting hypoglycemia. Glucose is available in tablets and gel form (HypoStop®, InstaGlucose®). It is important to think of glucose as a medication for hypoglycemia and not simply as a sweet. Anyone with diabetes should always have glucose handy and must know when he/she needs to take it. Friends must also know in which pocket he/she has the glucose tablets. A wrist bag to carry glucose in is practical for younger children.

Sports drink (like Gatorade®) contains pure glucose and gives a quick increase in blood glucose since glucose in liquid form passes the lower sphincter of the stomach (pylorus) quicker than in solid form (tablets). It also contains a small amount of salt which will accelerate the absorption of glucose. Juice contains mostly fructose, and it gives a slower

increase in blood glucose. A glass of juice containing 20 g (2/3 ounce) of carbohydrates gives a slower increase in blood glucose than glucose tablets containing the same amount of carbohydrates. Ordinary sugar is composed of both glucose and fructose (see illustration on page 143). It will therefore not give the same increase in blood glucose as the same amount of pure glucose.

It is of great importance that everyone understand why a child with diabetes must bring glucose tablets everywhere he/she goes. Those lacking understanding might otherwise think that the child is "cheating", eating the tablets as candy instead of taking it as a medication for hypoglycemia.

Fructose

Refined sugar contains half fructose and half glucose. Fructose has a sweeter taste than ordinary sugar. Fructose is absorbed more slowly from the intestine and is not as effective as glucose in raising the blood glucose level. [147]

Fructose does not affect the blood glucose directly. It is mainly taken up by the liver cells (without the help of insulin) where it is converted into glucose or triglycerides. A high intake of fructose will increase the body fat.[147] Fructose can also raise the blood glucose by stimulating glucose production in the liver.[147] Honey contains 35 - 40 % glucose and the same amount of fructose. Sorbitol, found in many sweets, is converted in the liver to fructose (see also page 153 and 154).

Sweets when hypoglycemic?

Candy containing only pure sugar (caramels, candy canes) will raise your blood glucose quickly. However, it is not recommended to exclusively give sweets when the child is having a hypoglycemia. Sometimes children provoke hypoglycemias to attain sweets. If the child has a "sweet tooth" and is suspected of "cheating", it might be a good idea to allow him/her some candy for a short period of time (a week or two). He/she does not have to pretend a hypoglycemia and the vicious cycle will resolve. It is best to reserve glucose tablets as "medicine" for low blood glucose. Medicine is not for treating your friends. If the child has sweets for treating hypoglycemia there is a certain risk that the child will offer them to his/her friends and may be without them when the blood glucose is low. One alternative is to only give sweets for hypoglycemia when the child is engaged in sports, e.g. riding or skiing.

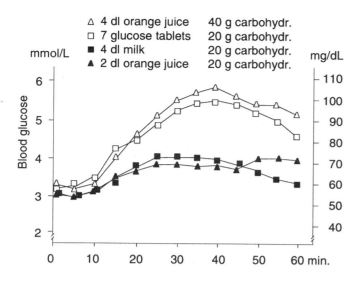

△ 4 dl orange juice	40 g carbohydr.
□ 7 glucose tablets	20 g carbohydr.
■ 4 dl milk	20 g carbohydr.
▲ 2 dl orange juice	20 g carbohydr.

The curves are averages from a study where 13 adults with type 1 diabetes were given different types of sugar to reverse a hypoglycemia.[67] Four dl (2/3 pint) of water was given with the glucose tablets. Milk contains fat and gives a slower blood glucose rise as fat leads to a slower gastric emptying.

Candy containing chocolate and chocolate bars raise the blood glucose very slowly and should not be used to treat hypoglycemia (see graph on page 159).

After the hypoglycemia

Often you will feel better within 10 - 15 minutes after you have eaten something containing glucose. However, it will often take one or two hours after the blood glucose has normalized before returning to a level of maximum performance again, necessary for example for an exam at school. In one study (of non-diabetic persons) hypoglycemias were provoked with insulin (blood glucose 2.4 mmol/L, 45 mg/dL, for 70 minutes). The reaction time was decreased for 1½ hour and only returned to normal 4 hours after the normalization of the blood glucose.[128] However, in one study cognitive functions (short-term memory, attention and concentration) were normal in the morning after a night with hypoglycemia (blood glucose < 2 mmol/L, < 36 mg/dL, for one hour).[37]

After a difficult hypoglycemia it is common to have a headache. Less common are transient neurological symptoms such as a temporary paralysis or difficulties of speech caused by some degree of cerebral edema (brain swelling). Contact your doctor if this happens.

If the child doesn't wake up, being fully conscious, within 15 - 30 min. after a severe hypoglycemia despite now having a normal blood glucose, he/she might have swelling of the brain (brain edema).[273] It may take many hours before the child is awake and normal again. This is an acute condition that requires immediate treatment at a hospital!

Sometimes you will feel nauseous or vomit after hypoglycemia, especially if the blood glucose has been low for some time. You will then often have ketones in the urine. Both ketones and nausea are caused by the hormone glucagon that is secreted from the pancreas during hypoglycemia. This is the same type of side effect that can be experienced after a glucagon injection. If the vomiting continues you should contact the hospital. Since the glucagon secretion from your own body usually diminishes after several years of diabetes, this reaction is more common if you have had diabetes for only a few years.

Can parents have hypoglycemic reactions?

As a parent it may be difficult to understand what low blood sugar really feels like. We encourage parents who are interested in experiencing hypoglycemia, assuming they are healthy, to try this by taking insulin under closely supervised conditions. We usually give 1 unit of short-acting insulin per 10 kilo body weight (0.5 units/10 pounds), rounded up to even units. If this does not give any symptoms at all one can repeat the procedure once again, increasing the dose with 2 units.

Give the injection between 2 meals (at 10 AM or 2 PM) without having a snack and measure blood glucose every ½ - 1 hour. After 1½ - 2 hours you will usually feel the full effects of the insulin. Stop the test when it is time for lunch or dinner. We usu-

A drink of juice can come in handy if the child has a hypoglycemia. It is easy to carry along and if the child does not want to eat anything it is often easier to give a sip of juice than to use glucose tablets or gel.

It will be difficult to achieve top results on an examination if you have or have had a hypoglycemic reaction recently. Usually it will take a couple of hours after a difficult hypoglycemia before you are back in top shape.

Always bring glucose tablets wherever you go. Older children can keep them in their pockets. Younger children may find some kind of small bag that can be attached to their wrist or belt useful. Make sure that your friends know where you have your glucose tablets in case f you need help finding them during a difficult hypoglycemic reaction.

ally do not put in an intravenous line when doing this but a nurse or doctor should assist in case they are needed. Some adults who try this will not actually have hypoglycemia. Instead they experience hormonal symptoms from the body working to raise the blood glucose, such as shakes, trembling or irritation. The hormones in your body are then working so effectively that the blood glucose never becomes low.

Remember! *You should only try this if you are in good health and after having discussed it with your doctor! Never try insulin at home or on your own!!*

Practice recognizing hypoglycemic symptoms!

Every time you measure a blood glucose lower than 3.5 mmol/L (65 mg/dL) you should ask yourself: "Exactly what symptoms caused me to take the blood test now?" "Did I experience any symptoms 10 or 20 minutes earlier that could have warned me that my blood glucose was falling?" If your blood glucose is below 3.0 mmol/L (55 mg/dL) and you have not experienced any symptoms you should always ask yourself: "Were there really no symptoms at all warning me that my blood glucose was low?" Ask your friends if they have noticed any change in your behavior that could have been caused by the low blood glucose.

Programs for training patients to better recognize subtle and variable clues while developing

hypoglycemia, including the use of simple cognitive tests, have been proven successful. To test for bodily symptoms stand up and walk around. Move your outstretched arm in a circle or hold a pen between your fingers to test for shakiness. To test for symptoms from your brain, repeat your mother's or brother's age and birthday, your friends' phone numbers or the combination of your bike lock.

Insulin treatment

The goal of all insulin treatment is to mimic the healthy pancreas' way of secreting insulin to the blood stream. Normally a small amount of insulin is constantly secreted during the day. After a meal a larger amount of insulin is secreted to take care of the glucose coming from the food.

Previously bovine (beef) and porcine (pork) insulin were used for all patients with diabetes. Nowadays mostly human insulin is used, i.e. insulin with a chemical structure identical to the insulin produced by the human pancreas. Human insulin is produced using gene technology or by semi-synthetic methods. Genetic engineering involves the insertion of human insulin-producing genes into a yeast cell or bacteria. In this way the yeast cells or bacteria are tricked into producing insulin instead of their own proteins.

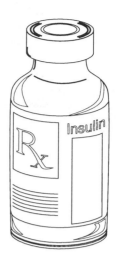

Regular short-acting insulin

Production of human insulin

① **Semisynthetic method:**

| Porcine insulin is changed enzymatically | Velosulin Hoechst insulin |

② **Biosynthetical DNA-technology method**

| Production from baker's yeast | Novo-Nordisk insulin except Velosulin |
| Production from coli-bacteria | Eli-Lilly insulin |

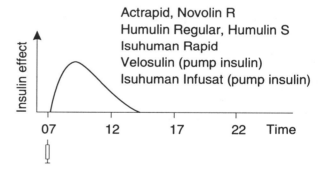

Actrapid, Novolin R
Humulin Regular, Humulin S
Isuhuman Rapid
Velosulin (pump insulin)
Isuhuman Infusat (pump insulin)

Regular short-acting insulin (also called soluble insulin) is given as a premeal bolus injection. It is also used to obtain a quick effect during times of hyperglycemia.

The listed brand names are examples of insulins. Ask your diabetes clinic to find out which insulins that are available in your home country.

Short-acting insulin is pure insulin without any additives and is a clear liquid. It doesn't require stirring or mixing before usage. Different additives are used to make the insulin more long-acting, thus making the insulin cloudy. The cloudy part of the contents will sediment in the bottle or cartridge, and must be resuspended by turning over or rolling (but not shaking) 10 - 20 times before use.

How to postpone the action of insulin

① **NPH insulin** — Bound to a protein from salmon (protamin)

② **Lente insulin** — Excess of free zinc.

Intermediate-acting insulin

Long-acting insulin

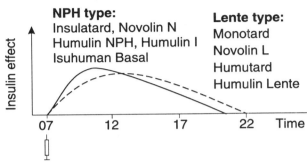

NPH type:
Insulatard, Novolin N
Humulin NPH, Humulin I
Isuhuman Basal

Lente type:
Monotard
Novolin L
Humutard
Humulin Lente

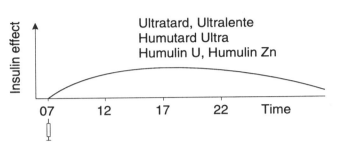

Ultratard, Ultralente
Humutard Ultra
Humulin U, Humulin Zn

Intermediate-acting insulin is used as basal insulin when injecting twice-daily and as bedtime-insulin when using multiple daily injections. There are two different types: NPH insulin (——) and Lente insulin (-----).

Long-acting insulin has effect during at least 24 hours. We use it mostly in combination with the direct-acting insulin analogue (Humalog). It is usually injected twice daily to give a basal insulin level in between meals and during the night.

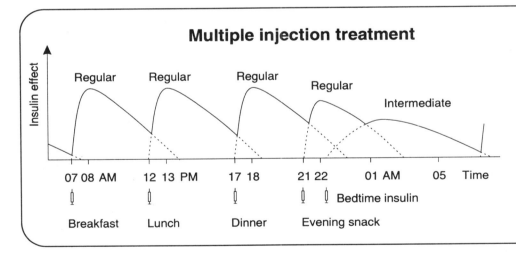

Multiple injection treatment

With 5 daily insulin doses (4 doses of short-acting insulin and 1 dose of intermediate-acting) the body's normal meal time insulin secretion is mimiced. The system is easy to understand as each insulin dose affects only one meal. Compare this insulin curve with the curve of a healthy person (top picture page 22).

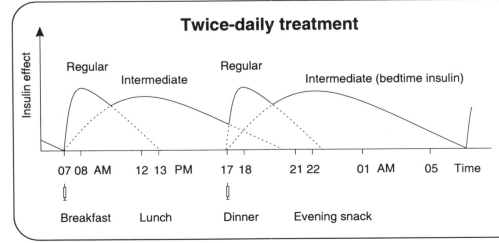

Twice-daily treatment

Before the introduction of the insulin pen in 1985 we mostly used twice-daily injections, mixing short-acting and intermediate-acting insulin. The advantage was fewer injections/day. The disadvantage however was difficulty in dosage adjustment due to changes in food intake or physical activity, or during intercurrent illness.

Intravenous insulin

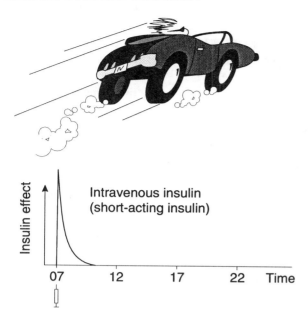

Short-acting insulin given intravenously has an extremely rapid action with a half life of only 4 minutes.

In intravenous insulin therapy the short-acting insulin is given directly into the blood stream. This treatment is given only in hospitals as an intravenous drip or in a motorized syringe. Since the half-time of insulin is very short, only about 4 min. [149], the blood glucose will increase sharply if the intravenous insulin is stopped. When using intravenous insulin one must check the blood glucose every hour (even during the night) to monitor the correct dosage.

We use this type of insulin treatment at the onset of diabetes as an early and intensive insulin treatment. In this phase it may prolong the honeymoon phase and might preserve part of the insulin production for some time.[363] Intravenous insulin is often used during surgery or a complicated gastroenteritis with prolonged vomiting. It is also a practical method for determining the insulin requirements/24 hours, for example when starting up a subcutaneous pump therapy program.

Pre-mixed insulin

Pre-mixed insulin is today available in cartridges for insulin pens in different proportions of short-acting and intermediate-acting insulin of NPH type (Mixtard, Humulin Mix and Isuhuman Comb). However, we do not use these insulins very often since the proportions of the two insulins can-

Direct-acting insulin (lispro)

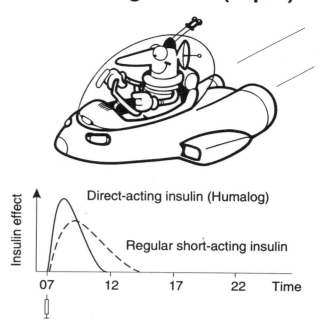

The new lispro insulin (Humalog, henceforth referred to as direct-acting insulin) has a much more rapid action than regular short-acting insulin. You can inject it just prior to a meal and still get a good insulin effect at the time when the glucose from the food reaches the blood stream. However, the insulin effect might wane too quickly, causing the blood glucose to rise before the next meal. Because of this, basal insulin (intermediate- or long-acting) is usually given twice daily (see page 137).

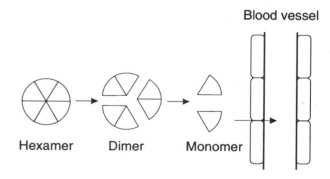

Insulin is always in the hexamer form when it is injected. It must then dissociate into dimers and monomers before it can pass between the cells of the blood vessel to enter the blood stream. The new direct-acting insulin (Humalog) dissolves much faster than regular short-acting insulin, thus making the time of action much faster.[206] Massage of the injection site can also enhance the dissociation, causing a faster absorption of the injected insulin.[258]

not be adjusted. If you change the dose you will get more or less of both types of insulin even if you only need more short-acting insulin, for example at meal-time.

A larger dose lasts longer

A larger insulin dose will give a stronger insulin effect which also lasts for a longer time.[179] An exception to this is the direct-acting insulin (Humalog) which has the same time span of action even when the dose is increased.

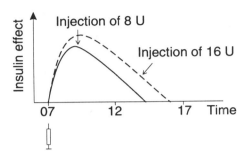

A larger insulin dose (dashed line) gives both a stronger and longer-lasting insulin effect.

Units

Insulin is administrated in units, abbreviated U (international units). One unit of insulin is defined as the amount of insulin that will lower the blood glucose of a healthy 2 kg (4.4 pounds) rabbit that has fasted for 24 hours to 2.5 mmol/L (45 mg/dL) within 5 hours.[334] Quite a complicated definition, don't you think? Also see "How much does insulin lower the blood glucose level?" on page 124.

Today the most common insulin concentration is 100 units/ml (U-100). In many countries other concentrations are used, mostly 40 U/ml (U-40).

For the smallest children we often use 40 U/ml for low doses (less than 2 - 3 units) to be able to adjust in half units. There is an insulin pen available for 40 units/ml with ½ units increments (Diesetronic®D-pen 40/0.5). It uses a cartridge that is filled from insulin bottles. Some standard pens for insulin 100 /ml can be used for giving ½ units.

Disposable syringes can be practical to use if you need to change the insulin dose in very small increments. Syringes for 30 units (100 U/ml) can be used for adjusting doses with an accuracy of ± 0.25 units in the interval between 2.5 and 3.5 units.[365] However, they may be difficult to use for very small doses of 0.5 - 1 unit. In one study, in which parents were supposed to deliver 1.0 units of insulin, the actual dose varied between 0.6 and 1.3 units.[74] The variability was even greater when the dose was administered by pediatric nurses. Syringes for U-100 insulin should not be used with U-40 insulin (risk of underdosage), nor should syringes for U-40 insulin be used with U-100 insulin (risk of overdosage).

Insulin units are counted in the same way regardless of the concentration. A weaker insulin will give a faster absorption.[154] Insulin of 40 U/ml gives approximately 20 % higher insulin levels 30 - 40 minutes after injection compared to the same number of units of 100 U/ml.[366] Patients should be advised that the onset of the insulin effect will often be faster when switching from 100 U/ml to 40 U/ml.

Twice-daily treatment

Twice-daily injections is the standard treatment for many patients with insulin dependent diabetes today. It has its advantages when the patient has a low total daily insulin requirement, as during the honeymoon phase, or if the patient, for various reasons, has difficulties in taking multiple injections. A twice-daily injection regimen usually results in a less flexible meal planning during the day. The afternoon dose of intermediate-acting insulin is often not large enough to cover the insulin requirements during the night, thus resulting in morning hyperglycemia. A large amount of intermediate-acting insulin daytime will increase the need of in between meal snacks.

Multiple injection treatment

Multiple injection treatment has been used since 1984 and the first insulin pen was introduced in 1985. Many studies have shown that one can obtain a better glycemic control with this regimen.[205] However, patients using multiple injection treatment will not always obtain a better HbA₁c [121,203], but will often experience positive psychosocial effects [204] as well as a freer life-style with greater flexibility in meal planning.[201] In studies more than 90 % of the patients have found multiple injections acceptable.[205] In the DCCT study (see page 216) the majority of patients on intensive treatment used multiple injections with syringes if not on insulin pumps. In 1987 we switched the patients in our clinic (aged 2 - 20 years) from twice-daily injections with syringes to multiple injection treatment with insulin pens. Only one patient was dissatisfied with this new regimen and switched back to twice-daily injections.

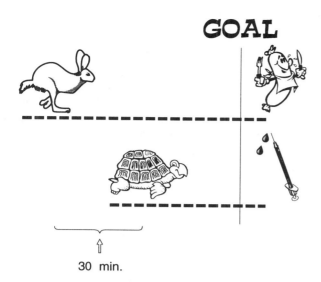

GOAL

Premeal injections

↑
30 min.

Since it takes 30 minutes for regular short-acting insulin to begin its action you must give the insulin a head start, otherwise the race will be very uneven. The carbohydrates from your meal will enter the blood stream first and give you a high blood glucose. The insulin will enter the blood stream later resulting in a risk of low blood glucose at snack-time and before the next meal. Taking the injection 30 minutes before the meal is most important at breakfast, however if you recognize these problems you should take the injection 30 minutes before all meals. The new direct-acting insulin (Humalog) has a very rapid action and can be given directly prior to the meal.

Today our policy is to use multiple injections already from the onset of diabetes with 4 - 5 injections of short-acting insulin as premeal boluses and an intermediate-acting insulin prior to bedtime. This regimen mimics the insulin secretion of a healthy pancreas better than a twice-daily regimen (se graphs on page 22 and 54).

In multiple injection treatment it is fairly easy for the person with diabetes and his/her family to understand which dose of insulin that affects a certain time of the day. This is quite essential since the goal of our diabetes education is that the patient and the family gradually assume increasing responsibility for their treatment, eventually becoming experts on their own diabetes.

Short-acting insulin (regular insulin) begins to act 15 - 30 minutes after a subcutaneous injection and begins its maximal effect after 1½ - 2 hours. The blood glucose lowering effect lasts for about 5 hours. This means that you should not wait more than 5 hours between your main meals and injections of regular insulin. Children and teenagers having a late evening meal will need a 4th injection of regular insulin, otherwise there will be a lack of insulin late at night before the bedtime injection has begun its action.

Remember that it takes 2 hours before the bedtime injection (of NPH type insulin) has any significant effect. This means that the time span between the last dose of regular insulin and the bedtime injection should not be more than 3 - 4 hours. If you for any reason prefer only 4 injections/day one alternative is to take a combination of short-acting and intermediate-acting insulin at the time of the evening meal. Mixing these insulins in one syringe or taking them as pre-mixed insulin is not an ideal method. If you inject in the thigh there is a risk of hypoglycemia early in the night from the short-acting component whereas if you inject in the abdomen there is a risk that the intermediate acting insulin will not last until morning.

There is no difference in effect between different brands of regular short-acting insulin. Direct-acting insulin (Humalog) gives a faster onset of action than regular short-acting insulin. The abdomen is the most common injection site for premeal injections (see page 93). If you take your regular premeal insulin in the thigh (or buttocks) you will probably need to add another 15 - 30 minutes to these time limits. The time limits given in this chapter refer to abdominal injections of regular short-acting insulin if not otherwise stated. If you use direct-acting insulin you must adjust the mentioned time intervals.

Your insulin depot from the bedtime injection will be almost gone in the morning. You should therefore give the morning injection of regular insulin at least 30 minutes before breakfast. Use a longer interval if your blood glucose is high and a shorter if it's low (see page 134).

When should I take my premeal insulin? (abdominal injections)

Meal	Regular short-acting insulin	Direct-acting insulin (Humalog)
Breakfast	At least 30 min. before	Just before the meal
Other meals	0 - 30 min. before (see text)	Just before the meal
Hypoglycemia at mealtime	Just before you eat	After the meal
High blood-glucose at mealtime	Wait 30 - 60 min. before eating	Wait 15 - 30 min before eating

Can I take my injection just prior to the meal?

To find out take the injection just prior to the meal and measure your blood glucose before and 1½ - 2 hours after the meal. The blood glucose should have risen 3 - 4 mmol/L (55 - 70 mg/dL) at the most. If it has risen more the effect of your regular insulin is too slow.

Try the same thing when you take your insulin 15 and 30 minutes before eating to find out which suits you the best. If the blood glucose is too high, even when you have taken the insulin 30 minutes before the meal, you will probably need a higher dose.

If you use the new direct-acting insulin (Humalog) it should be normally injected just prior to the meal.

Ideally regular short-acting insulin is administered 30 minutes before all meals since the blood glucose is not affected until 30 minutes after an injection. However, at lunchtime some of the short-acting breakfast insulin still remains in your body and the same holds true for the other meals. Because of this, the 30 minute insulin "head start" is not as essential with other meals as it is with breakfast.

Children using small doses and having a thin subcutaneous fat layer will absorb the insulin faster and rarely need to wait 30 minutes before they eat [268] (provided the premeal blood-glucose isn't high). Taking insulin 30 minutes before each meal can lead to a difficult schedule for younger children with many interruptions of their daily activities. We

therefore recommend younger children to take their insulin just prior to the meals (except breakfast). Some children will however absorb the insulin slowly and individual advice on this point is necessary. Older children and teenagers will rarely experience problems taking the insulin 30 minutes before mealtime.

If you inject regular insulin just before mealtime it is important that the food not be absorbed too quickly from the intestine. If so, the blood glucose will increase before the insulin reaches the blood stream. This can be achieved by drinking at the end of the meal. The gastric emptying rate will then be decreased, slowing the blood glucose response. Any fat content of the meal will also slow down the gastric emptying rate. For example ice cream made with milk products will give a slower rise in blood glucose than a popsicle. See the food chapter, page 141.

The blood glucose reading before the meal will indicate when it is appropriate to take the injection. If the blood glucose is high you should wait 45 - 60 minutes before eating. If you have a low blood glucose reading you should hold the injection until it is time to eat or wait 15 minutes at the most (see the table on page 125).

The new short-acting insulin analogue (Humalog) can be injected just before a meal and still give a good insulin effect at the time when glucose from the meal enters the blood stream. You must then

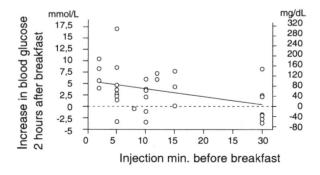

It is important to give the regular short-acting insulin 30 minutes before breakfast. In this study the blood glucose increased about 5 mmol/L (90 mg/dL) when the children took their insulin just prior to breakfast compared to less than 1 mmol/L (20 mg/dL) when taking insulin 30 minutes before the meal.[341]

adjust the above mentioned time tables. With a high blood glucose prior to the meal you can try waiting 15 - 30 minutes before eating. If you have a low blood glucose you can try holding the insulin until after you have eaten. Most often Humalog is combined with twice-daily injections of basal insulin (intermediate- or long-acting, see page 136).

Can I skip a meal?

A low level of insulin is needed in the blood even between meals to take care of the glucose produced by the liver. When using multiple injection treatment you must therefore take a low insulin dose even if you skip a meal. Half the ordinary insulin dose is usually enough, but you must try this out yourself. Intervals between meals and injections of regular insulin should not exceed 5 hours. Listen to your hunger signals and you will know when you must eat. You cannot skip a meal and also skip the snack a couple of hours later. If your blood glucose is low you must of course eat something.

If your blood glucose is above 15 mmol/L (270 mg/dL) you can try taking your ordinary dose and skip the meal or parts of it (does not apply to breakfast). Chewing gum or some vegetables might be a good alternative to relieve your feelings of hunger. Instead you can eat more at snack-time or at the next meal when the insulin has lowered the blood-glucose (also see "Temporary changes of insulin doses" on page 125).

Bedtime insulin

The bedtime insulin injection is the most difficult dose to adjust. Although we do not eat during the night the body needs a low level of insulin throughout the night to take care of the glucose being produced by the liver. Usually we give an intermediate acting insulin of NPH type at bedtime. An insulin with longer effect (Ultratard, Ultralente, Humulin U, Humutard Ultra) may be a better alternative for some teenagers.

The bedtime insulin covers 1/3 of your 24-hour day and is in that sense the insulin dose that affects your HbA$_{1c}$ the most. High blood glucose readings dur-

ing the night can give you a high HbA$_{1c}$ even if your glucose level during daytime is normal.

When should I take the bedtime insulin of NPH type?

It is important to take the injection at the same time every night on week days. If you change the time from day to day it will be more difficult to see a pattern in your blood glucose readings. Since the most common problem is to get the bedtime insulin to last until morning (see graphs on page 131) we recommend taking the bedtime injection as late as possible, i.e. shortly before your usual bedtime. There is no use sitting up late, waiting to take your insulin injection. 11 PM can be a practical time for adults, for older children 10 PM is usually more practical. Younger children must take their evening injection earlier. A better alternative is to give the bedtime insulin when the child is asleep, which is easily done if the child has an indwelling catheter (Insuflon).

The dose of NPH insulin (Insulatard, Humulin NPH, Isuhuman Basal) taken in the evening will take effect after 2 - 4 hours and will usually last during 8 - 9 hours of sleep. Lente insulins (Monotard, Humutard) are a bit more long acting and give

Can I change my meal times?

You can usually adjust your timetable for meals and injections with ± 1 hour. Just remember not to go over 5 hours between meals and injections of regular short-acting insulin if you don't use a basal insulin during the day. If you wait more than 5 hours between injections of regular insulin there is a risk of insulin deficiency.

maximal effect first after 4 - 5 hours. It is important to remember that smaller doses of insulin not only give less effect but also last for a shorter duration.

It is important to rotate the cartridge for insulin pens several times before injecting. The cartridge with NPH insulin contains a small glass ball that will help to mix the insulin crystals with the clear liquid.

When should I take the long-acting injection?

These Lente type insulins (Ultratard, Ultralente, Humulin U, Humutard Ultra) are made long-acting by binding the insulin to large crystals. They begin their action around 4 hours after the injection, give a peak effect after 8 - 18 hours and can still give some effect after 24 hours. Because of this very long action you should take the injection earlier in the evening, e.g. at the evening meal or often already at dinner-time. The timing is very individual and you will need to experiment to find out which suits you best. You should take at least 30 - 40 % of the total 24-hour insulin dose as long-acting insulin to get a good basal insulin effect. Remember that you also have an insulin effect into the next day with these long-acting insulins. With high doses of long-acting insulin it is optimal to divide the dose and take half in the morning and half before dinner or at the evening meal. If you use direct-acting insulin (Humalog) for premeal injections you will also need to divide the long-acting basal insulin into two injections.

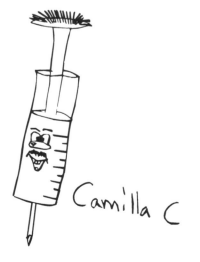

Since long-acting insulins act over more than 24 hours it is important not to change the dose more often than 1 - 2 times per week.

Lente insulins are not available in cartridges for insulin pens. The reason for this is that the insulin is in crystal form and the crystals will break if a glass ball is used in the cartridge for mixing.

Mixing insulins

Insulin of NPH type (Insulatard, Humulin NPH, Isuhuman Basal) can be mixed with both regular short-acting insulin and direct-acting insulin. If, however, you mix insulin of Lente type (Monotard, Humutard, Ultratard or similar) with short-acting insulin you will lose part of the short-acting effect. This is due to an excess of zinc in the Lente insulin that binds to the short-acting insulin and flattens the peak of action, making it more long-acting.[46,180] If you prepare the mixture from vials stored in the refrigerator [314] and if you inject directly after mixing in the syringe this problem seems to be less pronounced. If you use long-acting insulin (Ultratard, Ultralente, Humulin U, Humutard Ultra) together with short-acting insulin in a multiple injection treatment these should preferably be taken as separate injections. It is also not a good idea to use Lente insulins in indwelling catheters (Insuflon) for the same reason. However, direct-acting insulin (Humalog) seems to be an exception to this rule. Mixing Humalog and Ultralente did not change the peak action when injected within 5 minutes of mixing.[33]

Depot effect

If only intermediate- or long-acting insulin is used, a depot of insulin is formed in the subcutaneous fat tissue, corresponding to about 24 hours of insulin requirements.[52] The larger the share of intermediate- or long-acting insulin you use, the larger the depot will be. When using multiple injection treatment with regular short-acting insulin the depot will correspond to about 12 hours of insulin requirements.[52] When changing the dose of bedtime insulin the size of the insulin depot makes it necessary to allow for 2 - 5 days of adjustment before achieving a new equilibrium (see "Basic rules" on page 128).

The disadvantage of a large insulin depot is that the insulin effect will vary from day to day. The disadvantage of a small insulin depot is that little or no

Bubble pool
Not for
persons with
diabetes!

You may feel sad and disappointed when you see a sign like this, maybe even feel like you have the plague. The reason for the warning is that insulin will be absorbed faster when the skin is heated by the hot water. This might cause a hypoglycemia. If you are aware of this phenomena and have taken proper precautions you can take your bubble bath without worrying.

If you have a diabetic foot ulcer or nerve damage you should talk this over with your doctor or foot therapist before taking a bubble bath since hot water will soften the skin on your feet and increase the risk of infection.

extra insulin is stored in your body. The depot functions like a "spare tank" in that the extra insulin stored in your body can be used when needed. If your insulin needs are increased (e.g. when having an infection) or if you forget an insulin injection you are more susceptible to insulin deficiency (ketones in the urine, nausea or vomiting). With pump therapy only short-acting insulin is used resulting in a very small depot of insulin. If the insulin supply is stopped or blocked symptoms of insulin deficiency will develop within as little as 4 - 6 hours (see page 110).

How accurate is my insulin dose?

A correctly used insulin pen will give a very accurate insulin dose with an error of only a few percent. However, the effect of a given insulin dose also depends on a number of other factors. A variability of as much as 25 % in insulin effect may exist for the same dose given to an individual at the same site, whereas the variability approaches 50 % when the same dose is given to two different individuals.[179,192]

Factors influencing the insulin effect

① **Subcutaneous blood flow**
(increased blood flow will give a faster insulin absorption).

Increased by	Heat, e.g. sauna, bubble pool or fever.[179]
Decreased by	Cold, e.g. a cold bath.[41] Smoking (constriction of the blood vessels).[230,233] Dehydration.[179]

② Injection depth — Faster absorption after an intramuscular injection.[154,400]

③ Injection site See page 93 — An abdominal injection will be absorbed faster than a thigh injection. The absorption from the buttocks is slower that the abdomen but faster than the thigh.

④ Insulin antibodies — Can bind the insulin resulting in a slower and less predictable effect.

⑤ Exercise — Increases the absorption of short-acting insulin even after the exercise is ended, particularly if the injection is given intramuscularly.[152,233]

⑥ Massage of the injection site — Increased absorption, probably due to a faster breakdown of the insulin.[258]

⑦ Subcutaneous fat thickness — A thicker layer of subcutaneous fat gives a slower absorption of insulin.[188,366]

⑧ Injection in fat lumps (lipohypertrophies) — Slower [431] and more erratic absorption of insulin.

⑨ Concentration of the insulin. — 40 U/ml is absorbed faster than 100 U/ml.[154]

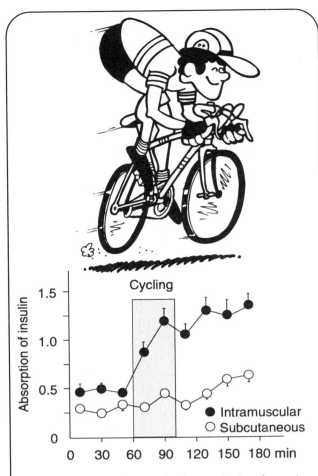

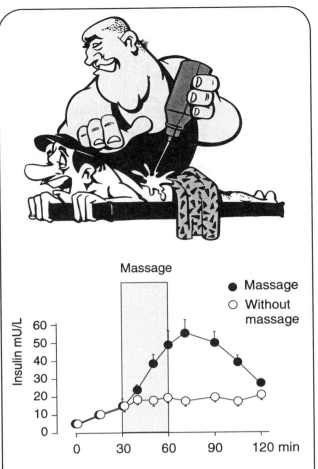

After an injection in your thigh muscle the absorption rate will increase considerably when you exert the muscles in your legs. The insulin (10 U) was given at 0 minutes. After an injection in the subcutaneous fat you will only see a slight increase in the absorption rate, probably due to the subcutaneous insulin depot being "massaged" by the moving muscles.[153]

Massaging the injection site will increase the absorption of insulin considerably.[258] The insulin (10 U) was given at 0 minutes. You can utilize this if you want a particularly rapid insulin effect, for example with a high blood glucose level with ketones in the urine. Give the injection site a thorough rubbing for 15 - 30 minutes and you will find that the effect of the insulin is much faster.

Insulin absorption

The absorption of insulin from the injection site can be influenced by a number of factors. Heat will increase the absorption. If the room temperature increases from 20° to 35° C the absorption of short-acting insulin will increase by 50 - 60 %.[233] A 85° C sauna bath will increase the absorption by as much as 110 %! In other words, there will be a risk of hypoglycemia if you inject short-acting insulin shortly before the sauna bath. A hot bath (42° C) in a bubble pool may double the insulin level in your blood while a cold bath (22° C) will decrease the absorption of insulin.[41] Massage of the injection site for 30 minutes gave higher insulin levels and lower blood glucose, both with short-acting,[258] and long-acting insulins.[41]

The skin temperature is also important. In a study the same insulin injection gave twice the concentration in blood after 45 minutes when a skin temperature of 37° C was compared to that of 30° C (same room temperature).[366] In the same study persons with thicker subcutaneous fat layer (10 mm) had lower insulin levels than those with a thin subcutaneous fat layer (2 mm). Also see "Where do I inject the insulin?" on page 92.

If the child won't finish his/her meal.

As a parent you are only too aware how much your child will eat of a certain dish. It is a good idea to

Sometimes it is difficult to know if a small child will finish a meal. It may then be better to give a smaller insulin dose before the meal to avoid the situation where you will have given a full dose of insulin and the child refuses to eat. An alternative, especially if you use direct-acting insulin (Humalog), is to give the injection after the meal. If the child has an indwelling catheter (Insuflon) it is easy to give half the insulin dose before the meal and then add a few units after, depending on how much the child eats.

read through the school menu in advance and discuss what he or she does not like and what can be eaten instead. Smaller children are especially unpredictable as to how much they will eat at the time when the insulin is given. If the child eats less than anticipated there will be a risk of hypoglycemia. It is not ideal to give insulin after the meal, but in this situation it might the best alternative, especially if you use direct-acting insulin (Humalog). You can also try giving insulin corresponding to a smaller meal first and then give the rest of the insulin if the child eats a normal sized meal after all. If the child uses an indwelling catheter (Insuflon) the extra injection does not create a problem.

A child with good glycemic control will often have a well balanced opinion of how much he or she needs to eat. If the blood glucose is high the child will not be as hungry as usual and will not need to eat as much. (see "Hungry or full?" on page 150).

You can compensate if the child has had more or less than usual to eat when it is time for the next snack. If the child has had a small lunch, schedule the snack a bit earlier and give the child a little more at that time (perhaps something extra tasty if his or her appetite has been bad).

If the child eats less while using twice-daily injections you should decrease the dose of short-acting

insulin (Actrapid, Humulin Regular, Humalog) but give the same dose of intermediate-acting insulin (Insulatard, Monotard, Humutard).

What should I do if I forgot to take my insulin?

You can try the following suggestions if you have had diabetes for some time and are well acquainted with how the insulin you inject works. *If you are even slightly unsure you should contact the hospital or diabetes clinic.*

① **Forgotten premeal injection**
(multiple injection treatment**)**

Take the same dose of regular short-acting or direct-acting insulin or decrease it by a unit or two, if you remember immediately after you have eaten. If an hour or 2 have lapsed you can try taking about half the dose of regular short-acting insulin or, even better, a dose of direct-acting insulin (Humalog). If a longer time has passed add a few units to your next meal injection, but not until you have measured your blood glucose level.

If you are out dancing remember that this is also exercise. Don't forget to eat something during the evening. Because of the exercise you will probably not need an extra meal injection, that is if you are not planning on staying up very late. You may also need to decrease your bedtime injection by 2 - 4 units to avoid hypoglycemia if you have been dancing a great deal.

② Forgotten bedtime injection
(multiple injection treatment)

If you wake up before 2 AM you can still take your bedtime insulin, but you should decrease the dose by 25 - 30 % or 1 - 2 units for every hour that has passed since the normal time of injection. If less than five hours remain before wakening, measure your blood glucose and take an injection of regular short-acting insulin (*not* Humalog). You can try a dose of regular insulin with half the number of units of your normal bedtime injection of intermediate-acting insulin. However, never inject more than one unit per 10 kg of body weight at one time.

If you wake up with high blood sugar, nausea and ketones in the urine you have symptoms of insulin deficiency. Take 0.1 U/kg (0.5 U/10 pounds) body weight of short-acting insulin (regular or even better Humalog) and measure your blood glucose again after 2 - 3 hours. If your glucose level does not decrease take another dose of 0.1 U/kg (0.5 U/10 pounds) body weight. **If you still are feeling sick or if you vomit you should immediately contact the hospital.**

③ Forgotten injection with twice-daily treatment

Take the same dose or decrease the regular short-acting part by 1 or 2 units if you remember immediately after having eaten. If your remember after an hour or two you can try decreasing the regular part to about half and the intermediate part by about 25 %. If you remember your injection even later, measure your blood glucose before the next meal and take only regular short-acting insulin at this meal.

If you have forgotten the afternoon injection and remembered in the evening you must take a smaller dose of intermediate acting insulin before going to bed. A little more than half should be enough but you must test this with blood glucose controls. You will probably also need an injection of short-acting insulin at your evening meal. Try the same dose (or a few units less) than the short-acting part of your afternoon injection. You should check your blood glucose at night to avoid hypoglycemia.

Can I sleep in on weekends?

Sure, you can sleep a while longer on weekends. One hour extra is rarely a problem and usually you can sleep in two hours as well. Some persons with diabetes who experience problems with high morning blood glucose (see page 133) will find it difficult to sleep longer since their glucose level may rapidly rise during the morning hours. In some families this is solved by parents giving an early morning injection. The child or teenager can then sleep in an hour while their blood-glucose starts to decrease before having breakfast.

If you stay up late at night and plan to sleep in late in the morning you should take your bedtime insulin when you go to bed. It will then last the duration of a normal nights sleep including the extra hours in the morning.

However, if you plan to have an early breakfast you should decrease the bedtime dose as the night will then be shorter than usual. Otherwise there is a risk of hypoglycemia when your breakfast insulin starts working.

If you stay awake very late (2 - 3 AM) you will need another injection of premeal insulin (and food) late at night. Remember not to give the injections of regular short-acting insulin more than five hours apart.

If you have a late breakfast your lunch will usually also be a little late since your are not as hungry at your normal lunchtime. In this way your whole day will be shifted and you will usually have no problem spreading your meals evenly over the day. Just remember that the time between the injections of regular short-acting insulin should not exceed five hours.

When switching between summertime and wintertime you need only adjust your watch. You do not need to gradually adjust the time for meals and insulin injections.

What if I stay awake all night?

Staying up all night is not common practice, but it is sometimes necessary when one is an adolescent or young adult. An 18 year old boy with diabetes worked as a travel guide and was required to stay awake all night in the bus on the way to a ski resort. Also during long flights one will often remain awake for a long time passing through time zones (see "Passing time zones" on page 204).

If you stay awake all night you should not take your bedtime insulin. Instead you inject regular insulin and eat every 4th or 5th hour. Adjust the dose according to how much you eat (compare the size of your meal with your usual lunch/dinner or evening meal). You should not use the amount of insulin taken at breakfast for comparison because more insulin is commonly needed for breakfast (see "Distribution of insulin doses" on page 123).

Birthday parties

It is very important for a child with diabetes to be able to take part in birthday parties or school parties without being embarrassed about having diabetes. In my opinion a person with diabetes should learn how to handle whatever food is served at a party instead of bringing their own "diabetes food". It is often a good idea to call before the party and arrange for something to drink with artificial sweet-

eners and request that there be not too many "goodies" served. At most parties the children receive a bag of candy at the end to take home, which suits the child with diabetes well.

Nowadays the food served at birthday parties is not as sweet as it used to be. Often there is just cake or ice cream on the menu and then perhaps hamburgers or hot dogs. Try giving an extra unit of insulin with the birthday cake.

Often children run around a lot at a party and it is quite possible that a child will manage very well without extra insulin. Check blood glucose and urine tests when the child comes home. Write the results down in a diary and you will be better prepared for the next party.

The best time for a party at the day care center is during snack time. Always make sure there is something to drink with artificial sweetener for children with diabetes. A good idea is to have a package of "light ice cream" in the refrigerator. The staff is usually very obliging for the small extra arrangements needed to accommodate a child with diabetes. Sometimes you might need to give an extra unit of insulin if, for example, a birthday cake is served (see above).

When going to an adult party many types of cookies, cakes and other sweet things are often served. The child will then need extra insulin to be able to pick and choose from all that is served. Try to find some kind of compromise here, for example only a few cookies or a little bit of cake (and if needed one or two units of insulin extra). It usually does not work out very well if you eat a lot of everything offered at a party. And do tell grandmother (who is only looking out for their grandchild's best) that so called "sugar free" cookies or "diabetes cookies" are not a very good alternative. They are not at all free from sugar and many children find them repugnant.

Of course the procedure will depend on how often you go to parties. Once in a while you can certainly make an exception and accept some sweets or a piece of cake when offered. But if you make exceptions every week they are not exceptions anymore and your HbA_{1c} will probably be affected.

Insulin at school or day-care centers

Sometimes it is difficult to get help with insulin injections at a day care center or to get the teacher to remind the child to take their insulin at school. The staff has no formal obligation to give injections when needed, but it is often possible to find a teacher or someone working in the school cafeteria who will help. At some larger schools where many pupils have diabetes they often meet at lunchtime, to eat together, and someone from the staff can help them if needed.

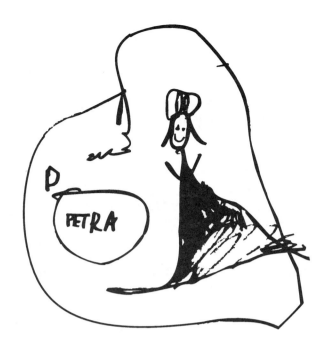

Sleeping away from home

Children truly enjoy staying over night at a friend's home. As a parent of a child with diabetes one is of course worried when faced with such a request. It is easy to assume an overprotective attitude if you don't feel secure about how to deal with this situation. It is important that the friend's parents are familiar with how and when a child should take his/her insulin and how to treat hypoglycemia. A good idea is to write down a list for the child with when and how much insulin should be taken depending on blood glucose measurements. Don't forget to leave your telephone number if you will be out for the night.

Insulin requirements

How much insulin does my body need?

A non-diabetic adult produces approximately 0.5 units of insulin/kg (0.23 units/pound) body weight every day.[4] This means 35 units/day for a 70 kg (155 pounds) adult. After the remission phase (usually within 1 - 3 years after the onset of diabetes) the insulin requirement for a growing child is rather constant, generally on the order of 0.7 - 1.0 units/kg/day (0.3 - 0.45 units/pound/day),[268,364] most frequently close to 1 unit/kg/day (0.45 units /pound). Sometimes only a few units less per day can result in quite a difference in HbA_{1c}. When sick you will usually need to increase the insulin doses, especially when you have a fever (see page 175).

Puberty and growth

During puberty when the growth rate is increased, larger doses of insulin are needed. Boys usually have their growth spurt around 14 years of age and girls around 12 years of age (one year prior to their first menstruation) but this depends on when they enter puberty. Boys usually require much higher doses during puberty, often as much as 1.4 - 1.6 units/kg/day (0.6 - 0.7 units/pound/day),[266] sometimes even more. Girls may also need to increase their doses to exceed 1 unit/kg/day during their growth spurt. After their first menstruation they grow at a slower rate and usually stop increasing in height within 2 years. At this time it is very important to lower the insulin doses (and food intake) to avoid "gaining width" instead.

Within some years after puberty the insulin requirement decreases to an adult level, usually 0.7 - 0.8 units/kg/day (0.3 - 0.35 units/pound/day). Try to get used to counting insulin requirements in units/day in different situations as well as considering the number of units in each injection.

Height and weight should be monitored regularly. Poor diabetes control, especially during early puberty, can retard the child's height development

During the growth spurt of puberty the insulin doses often need to be increased considerably.

and decrease the growth spurt during puberty.[125,424] Puberty may be delayed and girls may have irregular or missed menstruations.[125] Generally the HbA_{1c} will then be high but if there is both a lack of insulin and poor nutrition, HbA_{1c} might not be excessively high. It is therefore very important to consider both insulin and nutritional requirements in relation to the child's growth phase. Treatment with an insulin pump can considerably improve the growth velocity in poorly controlled diabetes by establishing a reliable supply of basal insulin.[374]

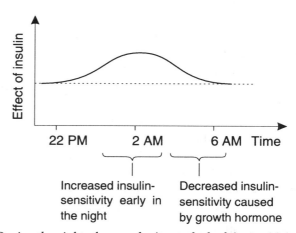

During the night when we don't eat, the body's sensitivity to insulin is increased. The secretion of growth hormone increases early in the night but the blood glucose raising effect will not appear for 3 - 5 hours.[62] Growing children have an increased level of growth hormone compared to adults which explains why the dawn phenomenon is more pronounced in children and adolescents. The levels of growth hormone are even higher during puberty. Patients with a poorer glucose control have further increased levels of growth hormone which further contributes to increased blood glucose levels in the morning and impaired growth (see page 36).[62]

Insulin requirements (after the remission phase)

☞ Pre-pubertal growth	0.7 - 1.0 U/kg/day, usually closer to 1 U/kg/day.
☞ Puberty	Boys 1.1 - 1.4 U/kg/day, sometimes even more. Girls 1.0 - 1.3 U/kg.
☞ After puberty	Girls: < 1 U/kg/day from a couple of years after the first menstruation.
	Boys: ~ 1 U/kg/day at 18 - 19 years of age, less after a couple of years.
	(1 kg = 2.2 pounds)

Remission phase

Large doses of insulin are required at the onset of diabetes. This is due to the body's decreased sensitivity for insulin caused by having high blood glucose levels during the weeks prior to diagnosis (about the same time that you were extra thirsty). The sensitivity for insulin will quickly increase after insulin treatment is initiated and within a week or so the insulin requirements will have decreased considerably.

When the blood glucose level has been normal for some time the beta cells will usually begin again to produce insulin, which contributes to decreased insulin doses. Often this production will increase considerably and, if the insulin doses can be lowered to 0.5 units/kg (0.23 units/pound) body weight or less, the child has entered the remission phase (also called honeymoon phase). The advantage of insulin coming from your own pancreas is that it is secreted in relation to the blood glucose level which facilitates your diabetes management.

Even a small production of insulin in the beta cells is sufficient to counteract the production of ketones. Insulin inhibits the breakdown of fats into fatty acids, which then can be transformed to ketones in the liver. Patients with a residual production of insulin for several years have a certain "protection" against ketoacidosis.[217] When faced with a difficult stress or an infection there will be a relative deficiency of insulin since the need for insulin increases considerably in such situations. The increased levels of cortisone and adrenaline result in an increased breakdown of fat into fatty acids and increased production of ketones.

The remission phase usually lasts 3 - 6 months, sometimes a year or longer. One usually has the lowest insulin requirements between 1 and 4 months after the onset of diabetes.[268] However, this varies from person to person. Some will not have a remission phase at all while others have it for over a year. After 2 - 4 years of insulin treatment most will not have any insulin production at all. If you had symptoms (thirst, large urine output, weight loss) during a brief period (1 - 2 weeks) before starting insulin treatment, your chance of entering the remission phase is higher. Younger children usually have a shorter remission phase. Intensive insulin treatment at the onset of diabetes is thought to give the beta cells an opportunity to rest and increase the chances that the insulin production later will suffice to enter the remission phase.[264,363] This is the reasoning behind the initial 1 - 2 days of intravenous insulin treatment that most pediatric centers in Sweden use at the onset of diabetes (see page 55).

During the remission phase the insulin doses can often be decreased considerably and the child may only require a few units a day. One might hope that the diabetes will disappear but this is never the case. With our present knowledge, there is no way of curing diabetes. The need for insulin is life-long and the remaining insulin production from the beta cells will slowly decrease. An infection will often trigger an increased need for insulin, causing the blood glucose levels to rise. Insulin doses must be increased accordingly. If you quickly adjust the doses according to the blood glucose readings there is a chance that the total insulin requirement per day will decrease again once the child has recovered.

When I refer to the remission phase I actually mean partial remission. A complete remission means needing no insulin at all for a shorter or longer period of time. We usually don't withdraw all the insulin although the insulin requirement may be very low.[35] An exception to this rule is when the child is experiencing hypoglycemia with even minute doses of 0.5 - 1 unit. The reason for not withdrawing insulin completely is that even small doses contribute to sustaining the beta cells and thereby increasing the chance of a longer remission phase.

Insulin requirements during the remission phase

During the remission phase insulin requirements are low, usually only a few units to a meal. Our policy is then to withdraw the lunch and evening meal

Insulin requirements/day

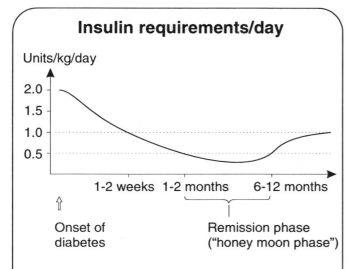

During the first 1 - 2 weeks after diagnosis usually large doses of insulin are needed as you have had high blood glucose levels for a sustained period of time, resulting in considerable insulin resistance in your body. The insulin requirements usually decrease significantly during the first months.

A growing child will often require close to 1 unit/kg body weight/day. If your child needs less than this, his/her pancreas is probably producing some insulin of its own. This is common during the first 6 - 12 months after the onset of diabetes. When you need less than 0.5 units/kg/day (0.23 units/pound/day) you have entered the remission phase ("honey moon phase").

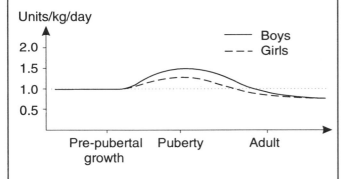

During puberty the teenager grows quickly and larger doses of insulin are needed. It is important to supply sufficient amounts during this time. Growth hormone is secreted predominantly during the night and you may need to increase the dose of bedtime insulin considerably. If you don't get enough insulin during puberty you may lose a few centimeters in final height. When you have reached your final height insulin needs to be decreased once again.

insulin doses, i.e. leave only 3 doses/day (short-acting for breakfast and dinner, and intermediate acting for bedtime). When the blood glucose level increases after lunch or after the evening meal it is

time to reinstate these other doses again. Another common policy is to give 2-dose treatment during the remission phase.

Direct-acting insulin (Humalog) can certainly be given as premeal bolus doses during the remission phase since the residual insulin production is sufficient for the basal needs in between meals. In an adult study the frequency of hypoglycemia after the meal decreased with this type of insulin treatment.[309]

Daily glucose testing is important during the remission phase to find out when to increase the insulin doses again. For younger children it is usually sufficient to start out with frequent urine testing. If you find glucose in the urine, take blood glucose tests before each meal to find out which of the doses needs to be increased and/or reinstated.

How much insulin does my pancreas produce?

It is not possible to directly measure the insulin produced in the pancreas since it is chemically identical to the insulin you inject. However, internal insulin production can be indirectly assessed by measuring C-peptide, a protein that is produced in equal measure with insulin in the pancreas but is not present in the insulin you inject (see page 220).

Insulin sensitivity and resistance

The body's insulin sensitivity is essential in determining how much the blood glucose level will be lowered by a given dose of insulin. One would think that the same dose of insulin would have the same effect on the blood glucose in any single individual, but unfortunately this is not the case. Certain factors increase insulin sensitivity while others decrease it (see key fact frame on page 70).

Insulin resistance implies that a higher insulin concentration in the blood is needed to obtain the same blood glucose lowering effect. One can also say that the insulin sensitivity is decreased. The decreased effect of insulin is caused by a restrained transport of glucose through the cellular wall when the blood glucose level is high.[243,429] The decreased uptake of glucose into the cells can also be caused by a constriction of the blood vessels, resulting in a decreased blood flow.[158] Insulin resistance will, in this sense, be a defence for the insulin sensitive cells

Think of your blood glucose level as similar to your body temperature, the blood glucose meter as a thermometer and the regulation of the blood glucose as a thermostat (the same type that radiators have to maintain an even temperature). When faced with insulin resistance, i.e. decreased sensitivity for insulin, it is like turning up the thermostat. Your blood glucose will be higher and more insulin than usual is needed to decrease it again. This is similar to having fever whereby your body's thermostat is raised, causing the temperature to increase.

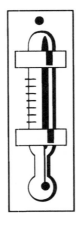

When you have recovered your body will reset the thermostat and your body temperature returns to normal. In the same way the "glucostat" resets to a normal insulin sensitivity when the blood glucose level has been normalized for a day or two.

that are prevented from taking up too much glucose.[430] These cells will not be exposed to glucose toxicity and will not be affected by the long-term complications of diabetes. The cells that are not dependent on insulin for their glucose uptake (e.g. the eyes, the kidneys and the nerves) will, on the other hand, have a high uptake of glucose, and are exposed to glucose toxicity leading to long term complications.

In one study the blood glucose level was held at 17 mmol/L (305 mg/dL) during part of the day and night, 15 hours in total.[144] The following day the patients had a decreased sensitivity for insulin. Another study showed that if the blood glucose level had been sustained between 13 - 20 mmol/L (220 - 360 mg/dL) during a 24 hour period the effect of a given insulin dose was decreased by as much as 15 - 20 %.[428]

After 44 hours with a blood glucose level of 15 mmol/L (270 mg/dL) the insulin effect decreased by 32 %.[150] In the same study it was found that admission to the hospital in itself resulted in a decreased insulin effect by 21 %, probably caused by concomitant illness, bed rest and temporary changes in life style. The effect seems to be due to a increased blood glucose level as such, since the levels of the blood glucose increasing hormones (adrenaline, cortisone and growth hormone) were not increased.

If the blood glucose level has been high only briefly (sometimes only a day), such as during an infection, your body will require higher insulin doses to achieve the same blood glucose lowering effect. A meal of a given size and composition will accordingly need a higher dose of insulin than usual. This increased insulin need may continue for a week or so after the infection has been cured if the blood glucose level has been high for a longer period of time.

Increased insulin resistance

A **Short-term factors**

① High blood glucose level for 12 - 24 hours [3,144,428]

② Rebound phenomenon (see page 43)

③ Infection with fever

④ Stress [291]

⑤ Surgery

⑥ Inactivity, bed rest [414]

⑦ Ketoacidosis

B **Long-term factors**

① Puberty

② Pregnancy (the later part of)

③ Weight gain, being overweight [19]

④ Smoking [23,133,296]

⑤ High blood pressure

⑥ Drugs, e.g. cortisone, contraceptive pills

⑦ Other diseases like toxic goiter, chronic urinary tract infection, dental root canal infection, pollen allergy [3]

Decreased insulin resistance

① Low blood glucose levels

② Weight loss

③ Physical exercise [417]

④ Breast-feeding

After some time with high insulin doses (and normal blood glucose levels) you will start experiencing hypoglycemia despite having unchanged insulin doses and unchanged amounts of food. The body's sensitivity for insulin will change when the blood glucose level is low, and the same insulin concentration in the blood will now lower the blood glucose more effectively,[91] resulting in a lower dose of insulin for the same meal. As you experience this you will learn to decrease your insulin doses slightly when your blood glucose levels have been normalized a day or two (or up to a week depending on individual differences), thus preventing hypoglycemia.

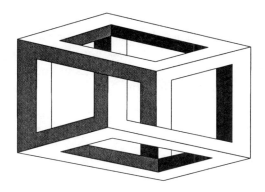

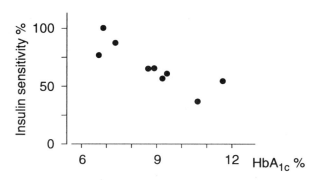

Sometimes you will find it quite frustrating to find the right insulin dose. It seems that no matter how you approach the problem there is no making heads or tails of your blood glucose measurements and insulin doses. It is common to seek the "ideal insulin dosage". Just imagine, finding this would ensure "smooth sailing" for a long time to come. Unfortunately this seldom is the case. Your insulin doses will often not be suitable for more than a couple of weeks at a time. After that, something in your daily life changes, the insulin sensitivity is affected and suddenly your doses are not appropriate anymore. This is, of course, very frustrating and difficult to understand. I think it is important not to have unrealistic expectations in the pursuit of the perfect insulin dosage. Just as every day life slightly differs from week to week and month to month, the insulin requirements will also change.

If you are unable to find a schedule that works it is often a good idea to keep exactly the same doses for a week. You will then be better equipped to see a pattern in your glucose readings and insulin doses. Contact your diabetes clinic for a discussion on how to proceed.

A vicious cycle may easily develop where a high blood glucose level can give an increased insulin resistance within 24 hours.[428] Insulin will then have less effect, you will have more problems in getting your blood glucose down to normal levels and your HbA$_{1c}$ will rise after some time with high blood glucose levels. The graph above shows that a high HbA$_{1c}$ implies that twice the amount of insulin is needed to obtain the same blood glucose lowering effect.[429]

Initially you must increase the insulin doses to exit this vicious cycle. However, in the long run the key issue is to become more "accurate in aiming" your insulin doses, not letting the blood glucose increase too much or too often again. Already after 1 - 2 weeks with lower blood glucose levels you will be able to decrease the insulin doses again. When using pump treatment for 3 - 6 months it was possible to decrease the insulin doses by 10 - 30 % when the insulin resistance had decreased after a period with lower blood glucose levels.[429]

Compare your blood glucose level with a thermostat that regulates the heating in a house. If the thermostat is adjusted to 20° C (68° F) more energy will be needed to maintain this temperature if the outside temperature is colder than usual. In the same way more insulin will be needed to keep the blood glucose at the same level when insulin resistance is high. If the blood glucose level has been low for a while the "thermostat" will adjust and you will start having hypoglycemia at a higher blood glucose than usual. If you have had very low blood glucose levels for some time the thermostat will readjust in the opposite direction and you will not experience hypoglycemia until the blood glucose level is very low (see also page 40 and 73).

Weight gain increases insulin resistance while weight loss decreases it. This is one of the reasons that it is difficult to maintain a normal blood glucose level if one is obese. Especially the male type of obesity ("apple fatness") will give an increased insulin resistance.[272] Other factors can contribute to

an increased or decreased insulin resistance (see key fact frame on page 70).

Increased levels of stress hormones (adrenaline, noradrenaline) will induce an insulin resistance that develops quickly, within 5 - 10 minutes.[272] Stress also causes cortisone release which will increase insulin resistance within hours.

During puberty there is an increased secretion of growth hormone which raises the blood glucose level. This causes an insulin resistance that contributes to the need for increased insulin doses during puberty. Smoking leads to an increased insulin resistance because nicotine decreases the uptake of glucose to the tissues of the body.[23] Regular exercise (at least every other day) leads to a decreased insulin resistance while inactivity (for instance caused by being bedridden) gives an increased resistance within days.[414]

Ideal insulin doses?

It is common to search for the ideal insulin doses but unfortunately this is not a realistic goal since insulin requirements vary according to activity, other illnesses, insulin resistance (see page 69) and other factors. Consider an analogy with body temperature. Your body strives to maintain a temperature around 37° C (99° F,) but this would be difficult if you always wore the same amount of clothing regardless of weather or temperature. Just as an outfit that is perfect one week can be much too warm the next a perfect insulin dosage will usually only remain ideal for a week or two before needing readjusting. Just as with your clothing you will need to make daily adjustments in your insulin doses to remain comfortable.

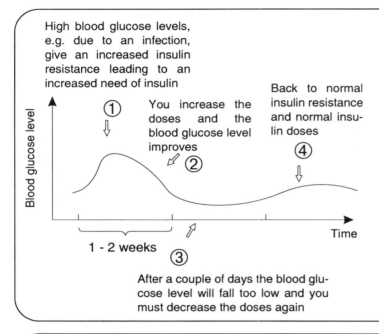

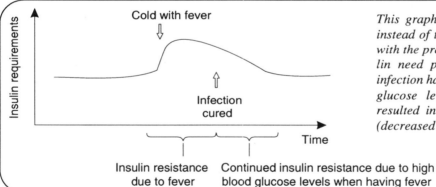

When the blood glucose level is increased for some reason (e.g. an infection) more insulin is needed depending on an increased resistance. If you continue with the same doses you will start having hypoglycemia after a period of time. The best strategy is to lower the doses as a prophylactic measure when the blood glucose begins to show many low readings. These "waves" of insulin resistance usually appear with an interval of a few weeks.

This graph shows the insulin requirements instead of the blood glucose level. Compare with the previous graph. The increased insulin need persists for some time after the infection has been cured since the high blood glucose level (caused by the fever) has resulted in an increased insulin resistance (decreased insulin sensitivity).

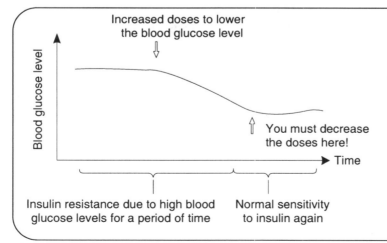

The same type of insulin resistance will arise if the blood glucose is high for a period of time due to other reasons, e.g. from not following the diet or eating too much candy. Even if you stop eating candy higher doses of insulin than usual are needed to bring the blood glucose to normal levels. To avoid hypoglycemia lower the doses once again when the blood glucose has been normal for 1 - 2 weeks. Otherwise there is a risk that you will start eating larger amounts again to avoid hypoglycemia and thereby gain weight, ending up in a vicious circle

Insulin-dependent diabetes in children, adolescents and adults   © R. Hanas 1998

Why do I notice hypoglycemia at different blood glucose levels?

The air balloon

I use an air balloon to illustrate the level variations where hypoglycemias are first noticed. The level of the balloon corresponds to your average blood glucose level during the day. The basket under the balloon corresponds to the blood glucose level where you first notice initial symptoms of hypoglycemia. With an average glucose level of 10 mmol/L (180 mg/dL) symptoms are usually noticed at approximately 3 mmol/L (55 mg/dL).

The HbA_{1c}-scale on the right corresponds to the average blood glucose over a 2 - 3 month period, which is presented on the left side of the scale. An average blood glucose of 10 mmol/L (180 mg/dL) will give an HbA_{1c} of approximately 8 % (DCCT comparable method, see page 86).

The illustrations on the next page shows what will happen when the blood glucose level changes. However, illustrating the level of hypoglycemia with only one basket is really a simplification. The level at which you recognize hypoglycemia will change but the level where clear thinking and reaction time is impaired is less dependent of your recent blood glucose levels.[277] This implies that while the body can adjust to a low blood glucose level, brain function cannot adjust as well. See also page 36.

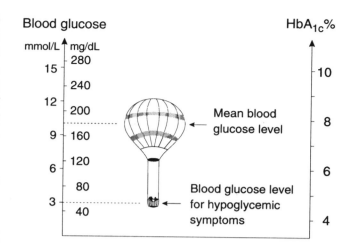

Bodily symptoms of hypoglycemia

Thinking ability and reaction time is impaired due to hypoglycemia in the brain

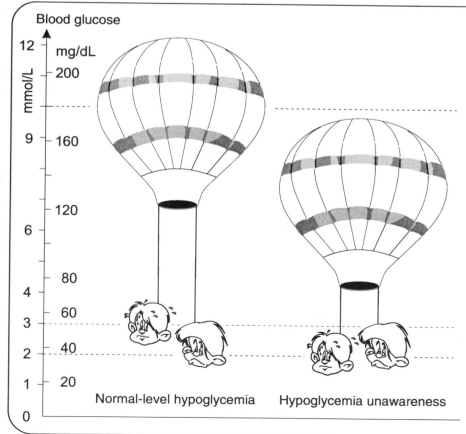

Normal-level hypoglycemia   Hypoglycemia unawareness

Normally you will notice bodily symptoms (like shakiness and cold-sweating) at slightly higher blood glucose levels than symptoms from the brain (like difficulties in concentrating). This enables you to continue to think clearly and to promptly take appropriate action.

If you have a low average blood glucose level and many low blood glucose values (less than 2.5 - 3.0 mmol/L, 45 -55 mg/dL) you will risk having hypoglycemic unawareness (see page 42). Hypoglycemia may then go unnoticed until the blood glucose level is so low that it affects the brain. You will have difficulties thinking clearly and your reaction time will be impaired. Bodily symptoms will occur first when the blood glucose is even lower, but you will then have difficulties to take appropriate action.

It is much better if you have bodily symptoms before the symptoms from the brain appear, warning you in time to do something about your low blood glucose level in an effective way.

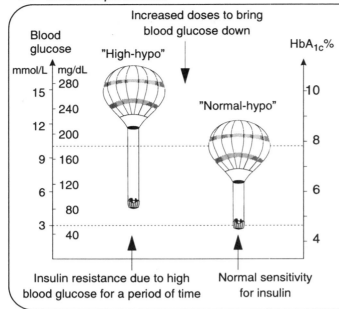

Insulin resistance due to high blood glucose for a period of time

Normal sensitivity for insulin

High blood glucose levels

If your blood glucose has been high for a period time the "glucostat" (see page 39) in your body will readjust and you will notice symptoms of hypoglycemia at higher blood glucose levels ("high-level hypoglycemia"). If you have had an average blood glucose level of 15 mmol/L (270 mg/dL) for a week or two (sometimes even shorter) you may very well notice symptoms of hypoglycemia already at the level of 4 - 5 mmol/L (70 - 90 mg/dL). When you increase the insulin doses the blood glucose level will fall. It is then very important to measure your blood glucose when you experience symptoms of hypoglycemia and not to eat until it comes close to 3 - 3.5 mmol/L (55 - 65 mg/dL). After 1 - 2 weeks of "suffering" you will have a normal sensitivity for insulin once again and recognize symptoms of hypoglycemia at a lower glucose level ("normal-level hypoglycemia").

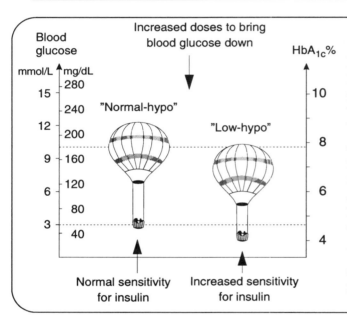

Normal sensitivity for insulin

Increased sensitivity for insulin

Low blood glucose levels

If you continue with the same doses the blood glucose level will fall even more after a week or two since the insulin sensitivity now increases (less insulin resistance). With a lower average blood glucose, the level where bodily symptoms of hypoglycemia appear will also decrease. If your average blood glucose level is 7 - 8 mmol/L (125 - 145 mg/dL) you will probably not notice symptoms of hypoglycemia until your glucose level falls as low as 2 - 2.5 mmol/L (35 - 45 mg/dL) ("low-level hypoglycemia"). The risk of having hypoglycemia unawareness will increase.

When the average blood glucose level decreases the sensitivity for insulin increases and you must lower the insulin doses to avoid hypoglycemic levels.

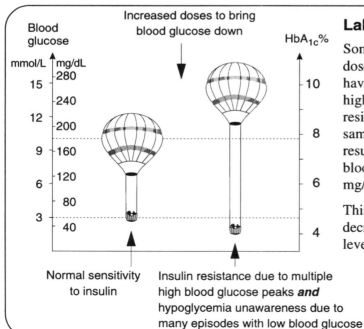

Normal sensitivity to insulin

Insulin resistance due to multiple high blood glucose peaks **and** hypoglycemia unawareness due to many episodes with low blood glucose

Labile blood glucose levels

Sometimes it may be difficult to manage the insulin doses in that when you increase them you will indeed have many low blood glucose readings but also many high values. The high values will give you an insulin resistance and a high HbA$_{1c}$. The low values will at the same time adapt your body to low blood glucose levels, resulting in a loss of warning symptoms until your blood glucose drops below 2 - 2.5 mmol/L (35 - 45 mg/dL).

This problem can be difficult to straighten out. Start by decreasing your insulin doses to avoid blood glucose levels less than 3 - 3.5 mmol/L (55 - 65 mg/dL). When your hypoglycemic symptoms start coming at levels of 3 - 3.5 mmol/L (55 - 65 mg/dL) again, you can carefully increase those doses that are needed to cut off the high blood glucose peaks.

Testing

"Everyone is a child when starting something new" is a Swedish saying that is very applicable when adjusting insulin dosages. It is difficult, if not impossible, to manage your diabetes without home testing. Trying it without testing like driving a car without a speedometer, fuel gauge, temperature gauge or mile gauge. Without these instruments your car may run for a short while, but you will probably end up in the wrong place or have a breakdown.

Tests can be divided into:

① Immediate tests   Tests that you take because you are interested in what your blood- or urine tests show at any given moment.

② Routine tests   Tests that you take regularly, helping you to make long-term adjustments in your insulin doses, eating habits and other activities.

③ Long-range testing   Tests that reflect your diabetes control over a long time (such as fructosamine and HbA_{1c}).

Measuring your blood glucose level is like checking the fuel gauge in your car. The difference is that you need not only to watch out for running out of gas (sugar) but for having too high a level as well.

How many tests should I take?

A   Urine tests

Although urine glucose testing is no longer recommended as the primary method of glucose monitoring,[12] the method has it's advantages in certain situations where blood glucose testing is difficult or impractical, provided that the level of renal threshold is known.

Three to four urine tests a day will give a very good indication of how the blood glucose has been during the whole day, provided that the child has a normal renal threshold level (see page 78). The correlation between home glucosuria (2 - 4 urine glucose tests/day) and HbA1c has been shown to be as good as that between blood glucose (profiles with 7 blood samples/day, 1 - 2 profiles/week) and HbA_{1c}.[185]

Measuring urine glucose is a "screening method" in that you can determine during which part of the day glucose is excreted and then check closer with blood glucose tests.

We recommend smaller children to take a urine test every time they go to the bathroom at home. If the child wears diapers you can usually squeeze them, forcing out a drop for the urine test. When the child grows older it becomes more difficult to get frequent urine tests and often you will have to be satisfied if the child takes a urine test every morning.

Time-table of testing

Test	Reflects the blood glucose during
Blood glucose	Minutes
Urine glucose	Hours
Fructosamine	2 - 3 weeks
HbA_{1c}	2 - 3 months

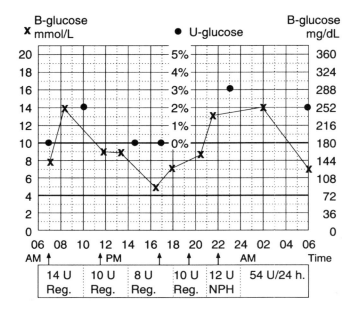 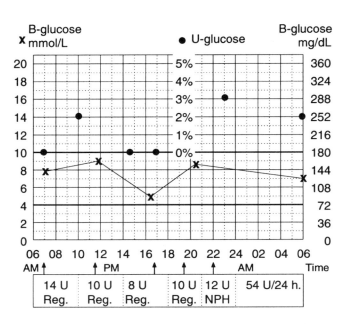

A 24-hour glucose profile can look like this when you take blood glucose tests before and 1½ hours after meals. It looks nice if you combine the individual readings with a line and it's also easier to read the chart. You will obtain more information if you test the urine for glucose and ketones frequently (including morning urine) the same day you perform the 24-hour glucose profile.

Remember that you will not know anything about your blood glucose levels in between the times when you have performed tests. This chart may appear quite nice... but it is the same day as the chart on the left, except with fewer readings. It is easy to fool yourself into believing that the lines also reflect the blood glucose levels in between the individual readings. Look at the urine tests. They show that glucose has been excreted into the urine which implies that the blood glucose must have been high somewhere in between the blood glucose assessments.

Ketones are only revealed in urine tests. It is therefore not possible to manage your diabetes effectively without urine testing.

B Blood tests

We recommend taking a 24-hour glucose profile every or every other week. You should then measure your blood glucose before and 1 - 1½ hours after each meal (including the evening meal) as well as once during the night, usually at 2 to 3 AM. We recommend this type of 24-hour glucose profile every second week even for smaller children. It is a good idea to take certain tests every day as a routine to help adjust your daily dosages. Testing on other occasions should serve to answer a specific question such as: "Is my child having a hypoglycemic reaction"? "Can he/she manage the night without eating something extra?", "How much insulin should I give in the morning?" Just taking tests without responding to the reading is of no value.

24-hour profile tests

Blood tests:

1) Before each meal
2) 1 - 1½ hour after each meal
3) One test during the night depending on which bedtime insulin you use:
   2 - 3 AM - NPH insulin
   (Insulatard, Humulin NPH, Isuhuman Basal)
   3 - 4 AM - Lente insulin
   (Monotard, Humutard)
   4 - 6 AM - Lente insulin
   (Ultratard, Ultralente)

Urine tests: Morning urine (glucose and ketones), if possible also at other times.

When should I take tests?

Two, sometimes up to 4 blood glucose tests/day are usually needed to gain the necessary information for the adjustment of insulin doses from day to day that is needed to obtain an acceptable diabetes control. More intense testing is needed in situations when you change your diet or other habits. After a while you will be more familiar with how much insulin is needed in different situations and you can then take fewer tests.

Insulin-dependent diabetes in children, adolescents and adults © R. Hanas 1998

You will need more frequent testing at times when your insulin requirements are changing, e.g. when being stressed, having an infection, participating in sports or going to parties. It is then a good idea to take a blood glucose test before each meal and if needed change the dose accordingly. To see which effect "quick-acting" carbohydrates (like candies) have on your blood glucose you should test it about 30 minutes after intake. With slower carbohydrates, like chocolate or ice cream, measure after 1 - 1½ hours and with a mixed meal 1 - 1½ hours after the meal is finished.

If you take only one blood glucose test a day

When using multiple injection therapy many families prefer to take a blood glucose test before the evening meal to decide which insulin dose is needed or how much to eat in order to achieve an adequate blood glucose when starting the night. You can otherwise take a test when it is time to give the bedtime insulin, changing this dose if needed or giving something extra to eat (see page 130).

If you take two tests daily

Take one test according to the text above and one test in the morning to be able to adjust the breakfast dose.

Good or bad tests?

It is common to refer to normal blood glucose readings as "good" and high readings as "bad". If the child often hears that the tests are bad he/she may after a while start looking upon himself/herself as bad. High blood glucose sounds more neutral and is a more adequate term. Tests are just a bit of information, not a quality of the child or adult with diabetes.

Diabetes or not?

In a non-diabetic body the blood glucose level will be regulated within close limits (normally between 3.3 and 7 mmol/L, 60 - 125 mg/dL) although our intake and expenditure of food is very different throughout the day. In the fasting state the blood glucose level is normally below 5.6 mmol/L (100 mg/dL). Higher values indicate that the person has an impaired ability to handle glucose (impaired glucose tolerance). A fasting blood glucose level higher than 6.7 mmol/L (120 mg/dL) (venous blood

Send your blood glucose charts by mail or facsimile to your diabetes clinic and we can discuss them over the telephone.

or capillary blood) on two occasions or a non-fasting value higher than 11.1 mmol/L (200 mg/dL) in capillary blood (10.0 mmol/L, 180 mg/dL, in venous blood) implies that a person has diabetes (WHO 1985 [382]). From 1998 the criteria for the diagnosis of diabetes will be changed to a fasting blood glucose of 6.1 mmol/L (110 mg/dL) or higher, which equals a fasting plasma glucose of 7.0 mmol/L (126 mg/dL).[15] For younger persons 5.6 mmol/L (100 mg/dL) is the upper limit for a normal fasting blood glucose.

Mmol/L and mg/dL			
mmol/L	mg/dL	mg/dL	mmol/L
1	18	20	1.1
2	36	40	2.2
3	54	60	3.3
4	72	80	4.4
5	90	100	5.6
6	108	120	6.7
7	126	140	7.8
8	144	160	8.9
9	162	180	10.0
10	180	200	11.1
12	216	220	12.2
14	252	250	13.9
16	288	300	16.7
18	324	350	19.4
20	360	400	22.2
22	396	450	25.0

Patient meters measure whole blood glucose levels while plasma glucose levels are used for diagnostic purposes. Plasma glucose is also used in many studies. Plasma glucose is approximately 15 % higher than blood glucose. In this book I have aimed at using blood glucose values as this is what patients measure.

It is not always easy to remain motivated to all the testing. Sometimes you need to find your own incentive or reward to make testing a little easier to carry out.

One should not rely on patient meters for diagnosis of diabetes. Sometimes your friends or relatives want to try their blood glucose on your meter. Encourage them to do that when the child with diabetes is watching. It usually helps to see others taking tests. How will the child otherwise dare doing something that an adult does not dare? But if the blood glucose reading is high you should not say that "you probably have diabetes". Instead ask the person to check their fasting blood glucose with their physician.

Are some things forbidden?

We often get the question whether you are allowed to do this or that when you have diabetes. The best answer is that nothing is really strictly forbidden. The important thing is to experiment to find out what each individual can and cannot do. It is important to encourage experiments with both food and insulin provided you follow up with glucose testing. The only thing you risk is a temporarily high or low blood glucose.

Always document in your logbook the results of your tests and what activity you were participating in. Next time you go for a pizza or to a party you will find your notes very valuable.

Urine tests

All urine that is produced in the kidneys will be mixed in the bladder. This means that when you measure urine glucose it will reflect an average blood glucose level since the last time you passed urine. It is also important to remember that urine glucose concentration is measured as a percent. This means that 5 % will represent much less glucose when you have small amounts of urine than if you have large amounts of urine with 5 % glucose. A negative glucose reading says nothing about how low the blood glucose is or has been, only that is has not been above the renal threshold since the last time you voided.

Renal threshold

The kidneys will try to reabsorb as much glucose as possible from the urine. When the blood glucose is above a certain level the kidneys' "glucose pump" is saturated and glucose will be passed out with the urine instead. The level where this happens is called the renal threshold and is usually between 8 - 10 mmol/L (145 - 180 mg/dL) in children,[268] and 7 - 12 mmol/L (125-215 mg/dL) in adults. The renal threshold will usually increase with age. Certain individuals have a very low renal threshold, down to 5 mmol/L (90 mg/dL), while others have a high threshold of up to 15 mmol/L (270 mg/dL). It is important to know your renal threshold when interpreting urine tests.

You can determine your renal threshold by taking blood glucose and passing urine once every 30 minutes. If there is glucose in the urine and your blood glucose is decreasing, your renal threshold will be the level at which the urine is negative for glucose.

Urine tests		
Glucose	**Ketones**	**Interpretation**
0	0	Good
+	0	Too much glucose (or more insulin needed)
+	+	Not enough insulin ("diabetes ketones")
0	+	Not enough food ("starvation ketones")

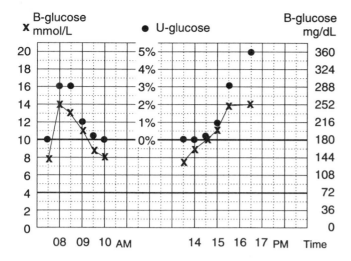

A good practice for younger children is to take a urine test every time they go to the bathroom.

You can determine your renal threshold by checking your blood glucose every 30 minutes, while watching for glucose to be shown in the urine. You can test this either as the blood glucose is going up or as it is going down. In this chart the test taken in the morning contained glucose until the blood glucose dropped to between 11 and 9 mmol/L (200 and 160 mg/dL). In the afternoon glucose was noted in the urine when the blood glucose rose from 9 to 10 mmol/L (160 - 180 mg/dL). This implies that this persons renal threshold is between 9 and 10 mmol/L.

If the blood glucose is increasing and your urine tests are negative for glucose, the renal threshold will be at a level where glucose first is noted in the urine (see chart). The renal threshold does not affect kidney function, but you will find it more difficult to use urine tests if you have a very high or very low renal threshold.

Ketones in the urine

Blood ketone testing is not available in most countries, thus one has to rely on urine tests for ketone determination. Positive ketone readings are found in normal individuals during fasting and in up to

30% of first morning specimens from pregnant women.[12]

It is most important to check urine tests for ketones when sick, vomiting or having nausea. Test sticks for both glucose and ketones are available (such as Keto-Diabur Test 5000® or Keto-Diastix®) and are only slightly more expensive. If you use these you will not need to ask yourself when to measure glucose and when to measure ketones in the urine.

Check the key fact frame how to interpret these tests. Start by looking for ketones. Ketones in the urine indicate that the cells are starving. The ketones that are produced when the body is starving or when there is a deficiency of insulin are chemically the same, but we often differentiate them as "starvation ketones" or "diabetes ketones" as they are produced in different situations. See also "Cellular metabolism" on page 20.

Ketones

➠ Can only be measured with urine tests

➠ Common symptoms: Hunger (!)
Nausea
Vomiting

☞ *Always check for ketones when you are not feeling well!!*

When should I check for ketones in my urine?

➠ When acutely ill, like a common cold with fever.

➠ When the blood glucose has been higher than 13 - 14 mmol/L (230 - 250 mg/dL) for more than a couple of hours.

➠ When having symptoms of insulin deficiency (nausea, vomiting, abdominal pain).

➠ Regularly during pregnancy (see page 187).

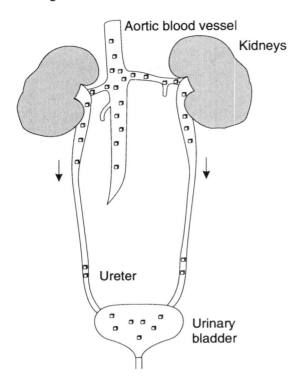

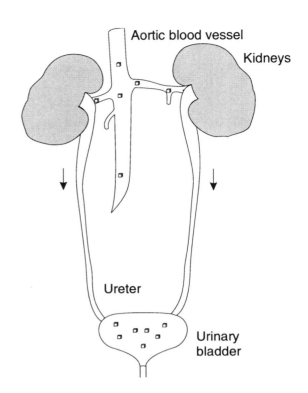

When the blood glucose level is higher than the renal threshold (usually 9 - 10 mmol/L, 160 - 180 mg/dL) glucose will appear in the urine. The urine from the kidneys is collected in the bladder before being voided.

When the blood glucose level has returned to normal values, glucose leakage from the kidneys will cease. However, glucose will still be present in the urine of the bladder from the period prior to this. When you take your next urine test you will find a high urine glucose, although your blood glucose will simultaneously check normal (see also charts page 135).

① Starvation ketones

Starvation ketones are produced when the blood glucose level is low. The urine glucose concentration will then also be low. The cells are starving due to a lack of glucose in the blood. This will be the case if you have too little to eat or throw up, for example when having gastroenteritis. If low blood glucose is caused by a high dose of insulin the production of ketones will be lower as insulin counteracts the transformation of fatty acids to ketones.

② Diabetes ketones

If you have a deficiency of insulin the available glucose will be in the wrong place, e.g. in the blood stream outside the cell instead of inside the cell. Both the blood glucose level and the urine glucose concentration will then be high.

High blood glucose level at the same time as ketones and high urine glucose concentration (3 - 5 %) always imply an insulin deficiency, as long as the urine test is taken during the day and that there has not been a recent hypoglycemia (see the blood glucose chart on page 44).

③ Ketones in the morning urine

The morning urine has been in the bladder for such a long time that it is difficult to say just when during the night that glucose or ketones entered the urine. A urine test will show both glucose and ketones if you first had a hypoglycemia early in the

---

Ketones in the urine during daytime?

Type of ketones	Treatment
Starvation ketones (only ketones)	Eat extra food. Take glucose if you have hypoglycemia.
Diabetes ketones? (glucose and ketones)	Take extra insulin (see page 127). Drink extra fluid (containing glucose if you find it difficult to eat). Contact the hospital if vomiting.

Sources of error when measuring ketones in the urine

False positive
(looks like ketones but there are none)

⇒ If you take certain drugs
(e.g. captopril - Capoten®)

⇒ Increased acetone level after ketosis or ketoacidosis (see text)

False negative
(ketones don't show but they are there)

⇒ The lid of the jar has been off too long.

⇒ The sticks are too old - discard the jar when expiry date is passed.

⇒ If you have eaten too much vitamin C (ascorbic acid)

It may be difficult to attain urine samples from modern diapers, which very effectively absorb the urine. The older type of diapers with plastic wrappings or cloth diapers are easier to squeeze a couple of drops out of.

night (giving ketones) and then a rebound effect in the morning (see page 43) with high blood glucose yielding glucose in the urine. The same results are seen if the blood glucose has been high all night and the cells have been starved due to an insulin deficiency (see chart on page 44). Ketone production during the night will often cause nausea in the morning when you wake up.

④ High amounts of ketones in the blood.

When having insulin deficiency you will not feel well. This is caused by the increased level of ketones and not by the high blood glucose level. If the production of ketones is high the blood becomes acidic. Passing ketones into the urine is the body's way of decreasing the excess level of ketones. After you have taken extra insulin there will be no further production of ketones. However, ketones will still continue to be passed into the urine for several hours and can sometimes be measured 1 - 2 days following ketoacidosis (see page 29).[115,163] The reason for this is that ketones are partly transformed into acetone which is stored in fat tissue. Acetone is slowly released to the blood and excreted via the lungs, giving the breath a fruity odor.[115] Acetone gives a false positive reaction on ketone sticks.

Vomiting and ketones

Always look upon a child with diabetes who is vomiting as having an insulin deficiency until the opposite has been proven! *Vomiting and diarrhea may be caused by a gastroenteritis, but vomiting alone may just as well be caused by ketones produced as a result of insulin deficiency.* The blood glucose level will then be high and you will find both glucose and ketones in the urine. It is important that you firmly stress this point if you for example contact a doctor while on vacation. Many times we have encountered that vomiting has been misinterpreted as gastroenteritis by medical personnel who then have given the erroneous advice to decrease the insulin dose when the child on the contrary needs more insulin. See also "Nausea and vomiting" on page 176.

Blood tests

When you take a blood test it will reflect your blood glucose level at that moment. However, the blood glucose can quickly go up or down and you may have quite a different reading 15 or 30 minutes later. Always check your blood glucose level when you are not feeling well so that you can avoid eating extra just to be on the safe side when suspecting hypoglycemia. This is especially important when you are recently diagnosed with diabetes and are not as familiar with the symptoms of hypoglycemia yet. Later on you will feel more confident with your symptoms of hypoglycemia. See also "Symptoms of hypoglycemia at a high blood glucose level?" on page 43.

Recognizing symptoms of high blood glucose is usually more difficult. Many teenagers seem to learn how their body reacts when their blood glucose is high. They will then possess a kind of "auto-pilot" making it possible to adjust insulin doses and food portions without as many blood tests. Always try to guess your blood glucose before checking it and you will eventually figure out how your body reacts when your blood glucose level is low or high.

Why should I take blood tests?

☞ **Advantages**

➠ Take a test instead of eating "just to be on the safe side".

➠ Learn the symptoms of hypoglycemia.

➠ Calculate your renal threshold.

➠ Find out when you need to change insulin doses, e.g. with infections, stress, physical exercise, or going to a party.

➠ The only way to know if you have night-time hypoglycemia.

➠ Blood glucose testing is necessary to get a good glycemic control and in the long run lessen the risk of complications as much as possible.

☞ **Disadvantages**

➠ Ketones don't show in blood glucose tests

➠ Pricking your finger can be painful.

Pricking a hole in children

Small children think of their body as a balloon. If you prick the balloon it will burst and the contents will pour out. The child often thinks: "If many blood tests are taken there will be no more blood in my body!" That is why bandages are so important,

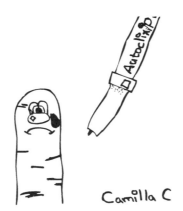

You can try to anesthetize the finger tip with a piece of ice before pricking it. A local anesthetic (EMLA®-creme) will not work on your finger tips as the skin is too thick. Sticking slightly on the side of the fingertip is preferable since it bleeds well and hurts less.

they stop the body contents from being poured out. It is important to raise this issue even if the child doesn't ask. Try to explain that we only take a tiny amount of blood for the test and that the body will quickly produce new blood again. The red blood cells are produced in the bone marrow and live for only about 120 days, which means that there is a continuous production of new red blood cells going on in the body.

How do I take blood tests?

Wash your hands with soap and water before taking a blood test. Apart from hygienic aspects there might be sugar on your fingers (e.g. from glucose tablets) giving a false high reading. Use warm water if your fingers are cold. Do not use alcohol for cleaning your hands as this will make the skin dry. The risk of an infection from a finger prick is minimal.

Many different finger-pricking devices are available for taking blood glucose tests. With some you can adjust the pricking depth by changing the cap. With one type (Softclix®) you can adjust the depth in 6 or 12 increments. Various lancets are somewhat different in size and cutting. Try different types to find out which suits you best. There are even lancets available that do not require a separate device to use them. From a hygienic standpoint you can use the same lancet for a day's blood tests assuming that your fingers are clean. However, the lancet will be slightly dulled every time you use it and the pricks might therefore be more painful with repeated usage.

If you prick the sides of your fingertips your sensitivity will be less affected, e.g. if you play piano or guitar. Don't use your thumbs and right index finger (or left if you are left-handed) for finger pricking. Sometimes you will feel pain the day after a finger prick and you need the sensation of touch more so in these fingers.

Blood glucose meters that utilize a photochemical method register how much light that is reflected. The advantage of this method is that you can compare the color shift of the stick to a color scale on the container if the meter does not function properly. Blood glucose meters using an electro-chemical method measure a weak electric current through the drop of blood. With this method no information of your blood glucose level is attainable if the meter does not work. However, these meters are often easier to use and have less sources of error, e.g. time limits when the sticks should be wiped off.

Most blood glucose meters have memories for storing test results and some even for insulin dosages, meals and other events. The stored information can be transferred to a computer to view, analyze and print. This may be a very useful tool for the diabetes team and for interested patients and parents as well.

Can you borrow somebody else's device for pricking your fingers?

There is a small risk of blood contamination whereby a small drop of blood can be left on the device. An epidemic of hepatitis B in a hospital ward was caused by using the same testing device (Autolet®) despite switching lancets between each test.[123]

Does the meter show the correct value?

The margin of error in a correctly used blood glucose meter is approximately 10 - 15 %. This means that with a blood glucose level of 20 mmol/L (360 mg/dL) the meter can show 2 - 3 mmol (35 - 55 mg/dL) above or below. However, at a blood glucose of 3 mmol/L (55 mg/dL) the error should not exceed 0.3 - 0.5 mmol/L (5 - 10 mg/dL). It is very important to apply enough blood to the stick. Too small a drop will give a false low reading. Don't rub the blood onto the stick. If you have sticks that should be wiped off it is very important that you do this exactly according to the instructions. If you have sugar on your fingers (e.g. after taking a glucose tablet) when you take the test this will cause a false high reading.

Lancets for blood glucose tests

Brand	Diameter of needle	Fits to device
B-D Microfine +	0.36 mm	Standard
Monolet	0.65 mm	Standard
Surelite	0.65 mm	Standard
Autolet	0.66 mm	Autolet
Unilet G Superlite	0.66 mm	Standard
Autoclix	0.80 mm	Standard
Softclix	0.80 mm	Softclix
Mini-lancet	0.80 mm	No device used

Standard = Glucolet, Monojector, Penlet II, Autoclix P, B-D Lancer

All lancets can be used for finger-pricking without using them in a device.

All the names mentioned above are ® or ™ of respective company. Other lancets may be available in your country.

Sources of error when measuring blood glucose

False high reading	False low reading
Dirt on window	Drop applied too late
Wiping too late	Finger too quickly removed
Not enough wiping	Not enough blood on the stick
Glucose on fingers	Water or saliva on finger

Regular use of the control stick or control solution provided with your meter for calibration is very important to get maintain reliable values.

Be sure to follow the instructions on timing in the owner's manual of the meter to avoid false readings. If you are about to purchase a new meter you should consider one that will start automatically when the drop of blood is applied as this will lessen the risk of a false reading. Ask your diabetes nurse for advice about which meters are available and their respective prices. Often you can get a discount price when buying a new meter if you submit your old one at the time of purchase.

Comparing different meters will often cause confusion since they may show different readings, e.g. 12 mmol/L (215 mg/dL) on one and 14 mmol/L (250 mg/dL) on the other. My advise is to stick to one meter that works well as the difference of one or two mmol/L is not that significant at high readings. Bring the meter with you at the clinical visits and ask your diabetes nurse to make a check with glucose control solution at regular intervals.

When hospitalized blood glucose tests are often drawn from an intravenous needle to lessen the

pain. In non-diabetic persons venous blood tested after a meal has about 10 % less glucose than capillary blood. This is logical if you remember that venous blood has delivered some of it's glucose contents to the tissues. However, in persons with diabetes the difference was only 0.1 mmol/L (2 mg/dL), probably explained by the lack of fine-tuned insulin release in response to the blood glucose level.[245]

If the child refuses to take a blood glucose test

It is difficult to force your own child to comply since the pricking hurts. It is also difficult to give general advice in this situation. If the child panics you should, in my opinion, take the blood glucose test only if this is absolutely necessary (which is most often not the case). You can instead let the child choose to take a urine test as this will also reveal some information. It is better to say: "We can then take the test a little bit later if that is what you want" (maybe the next day if you are taking a 24 hour profile), than "OK, you don't have to take the test". Remember that the goal is to get your child to accept blood glucose testing in the long run, not only for the time being.

If the child is not feeling well it is important to emphasize that after taking a blood glucose test you can do something to be able to alleviate their symptoms. If the child then realizes that he/she really feels better after testing and taking the necessary

---

Blood glucose meters

Brand	Range mmol/L	Range mg/dL	Memory
Accutrend Alpha	1.1 - 27.8	20 - 500	9
Accutrend mini	1.7 - 22.2	30 - 400	1
Accutrend GC	1.1 - 33.3	20 - 600	50
Accutrend sensor	0.6 - 33.3	10 - 600	100
ExacTech	2.2 - 25.0	40 - 450	1
Glucocard Memory 2	1.1 - 33.4	20 - 600	20
Glucometer Dex	0.6 - 33.3	10 - 600	100
Glucometer Esprit	0.6 - 33.3	10 - 600	100
Glucometer Elite	1.2 - 33.3	20 - 600	10
Glucometer GX	1.4 - 22.1	25 - 400	10
Glucometer II	2.0 - 22.0	35 - 400	
Glucometer 4	0.6 - 33.3	10 - 600	
*Gluco Touch	0 - 27.8	0 - 500	10
Glucotrend	0.6 - 33.3	10 - 600	10
*Hypoguard Supreme	2.2 - 27.7	40 - 500	14
MediSense Card	1.1 - 33.3	20 - 600	10
MediSense Pen	1.1 - 33.3	20 - 600	10
One Touch Basic	0.0 - 33.3	0 - 600	250
One Touch Profile	0.0 - 33.3	0 - 600	250
Precision QID	1.1 - 33.3	20 - 600	10
Super Glucocard II	1.1 - 33.3	20 - 600	20

*Test strips have a color comparison chart for use without a meter.

All the names mentioned above are ® or ™ of respective company. Other meters may be available in your country.

Which blood glucose level is optimal?

Try to attain blood glucose readings between 4.0 and 10.0 mmol/L (70 - 180 mg/dL).[84] If you have problems with hypoglycemic unawareness you should aim at a slightly higher blood glucose during a few weeks (see page 42).

Blood glucose	Before meal	1½ h. after meal
Ideal	4 - 6 mmol/L 70-110 mg/dL	5 - 8 mmol/L 90-140 mg/dL
Acceptable	6 - 8 mmol/L 110-145 mg/dL	8 - 10 mmol/L 145-180 mg/dL
Hypoglycemic unawareness	5 - 9 mmol/L 90-160 mg/dL	8 - 11 mmol/L 145-200mg/dL

A question of conscience: "Do you take the tests for your own sake or do you take them to have something to show your doctor or diabetes nurse / educator when you come to the clinic?

measures it will often be easier to take the test next time this happens.

If a small child has difficulties in seeing blood coming from his/her finger you can try pricking the ear lobe instead.

Does a high blood glucose level make you feel ill?

It is the increased level of ketones that makes you feel ill, not the high blood glucose level as such. If you have a high blood glucose and ketones in the urine you usually have nausea and feel bad (see "Symptoms of insulin deficiency" on page 28). However, if your blood glucose level has been high for some time but without ketones in the urine you will often feel quite well. Often you will not notice that your body is not working optimally but when your blood glucose has returned to normal levels

again you will clearly feel the difference: "Is this how alert I should really feel?" is a usual comment.

If your blood glucose level is normally below 10 mmol/L (180 mg/dL) you will more easily register when it increases. Even if you don't clearly real-ize recognize this yourself, somebody else, e.g. a teacher or friend, will certainly notice that you/your child are tired and uneasy when the blood glucose level is high.

Is it worth taking tests?

In a Belgian study of children and young adults with good blood glucose control (HbA_{1c} was 6.9 % on average) it was found that HbA_{1c} was affected both by the actual number of tests taken (on aver-age up to 77 tests/month) and the number of visits to the diabetes clinic (on average 6.6 vis-its/patient).[121] The patients taking 4 doses of insu-lin/day had a freer diet than those taking 2 doses/day but there was no difference in HbA_{1c} between the groups.

It is important to reflect on the reasons for your blood glucose values and, if necessary, to take action and change your insulin doses after having evaluated the tests. The blood glucose level will not improve by merely measuring it. Remember that the tests are for your own sake, not just to have something to show your diabetes nurse, educator or doctor. See also "Will a better blood glucose con-trol really lessen the risk of complications?" on page 215.

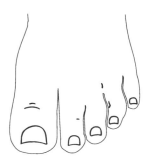

Taking blood glucose tests from your toes in the evening, during the night or in the morning will spare your finger tips. Children and adolescents with healthy feet can do this without any problems.[21] However, if you have reduced sensibility or foot lesions you should avoid tak-ing tests from the toes.

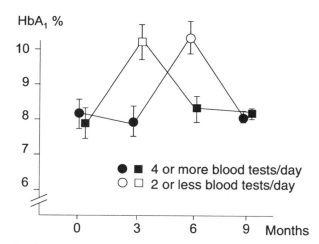

In this study 2 groups of patients took 2 or 4 blood glu-cose tests/day during 3-month periods. HbA_1 levels were monitored which give approximately 2 % higher values compared to HbA_{1c}. HbA_1 was significantly better in both groups when they were taking 4 tests/day. [354]

HbA$_{1c}$ is short for Hemoglobin, Adult and 1c being a subgroup when the test is analyzed. Hemoglobin binds and transports oxygen in the red blood cells. This test is based on red blood cells living for 120 days and then being destroyed in the spleen. The blood cells are continually produced in the bone marrow. During the red blood cell's life span more or less glucose is bound to its hemoglobin depending on how high or low the blood glucose level is.[399]

HbA$_{1c}$ is a measure of the percent of the hemoglobin in the red blood cells that has glucose bound to it. This reflects an average measurement of the blood glucose levels during the last 2 - 3 months.[261,386] The blood glucose levels from the week prior to testing will not be included in the reading as this fraction of HbA$_{1c}$ is not stable. If HbA$_{1c}$ is monitored at regular intervals (at least every 3 months) at the diabetes clinic this will provide a good summary of how your glycemic control has been throughout the year.

It is also important to remember that you measure an average of your blood glucose levels. You can get a good HbA$_{1c}$ reading with a combination of high and low blood glucose values. Most often you will feel better when your blood glucose level is more even. However, there is no scientific evidence that there will be more diabetes complications with an unstable blood glucose level than with even blood glucose readings assuming that HbA$_{1c}$ is the same. On the contrary, some recent data indicate that it might be the other way around (see page 217).[110]

It is more difficult to obtain a good HbA$_{1c}$ value during puberty since the secretion of growth hormone will raise the blood glucose levels.[125] During puberty you will often have an increase of HbA$_{1c}$ with up to 2 % (e.g. from 7 to 9 %) even if you are as careful with your diabetes as before puberty..

How should my HbA$_{1c}$ be?

It is difficult to state an interval within which your HbA$_{1c}$ should be because different laboratories have different reference values. Many laboratories, including the DCA-2000 desk top method that we use, have reference values with their methods at the same level as the DCCT reference laboratory.[108] With these methods an acceptable HbA$_{1c}$ is 7 - 8 %.[109] Other HPLC methods give quite different readings. In Sweden the readings are approximately 1 % lower,[270] resulting in a recommended HbA$_{1c}$ of 6 - 7 % while in Berlin the level is 1 % higher,[105] resulting in a recommended HbA$_{1c}$ of 8 - 9 %.

Many studies has shown that with a HbA$_{1c}$ of 7 - 8 % (DCCT-equivalent method) the risk of

---

HbA$_{1c}$

⟱ Glucose is bound to hemoglobin in the red blood cells

⟱ The level of HbA$_{1c}$ depends on the blood glucose levels during the life span of the blood cell.

⟱ A red blood cell lives for about 120 days

⟱ HbA$_{1c}$ reflects the average blood glucose during the last 2 - 3 months.

The red blood cells take up oxygen in the lungs and transport it to the cells. They take carbon dioxide from the cells back to the lungs.

HbA_{1c} and blood glucose

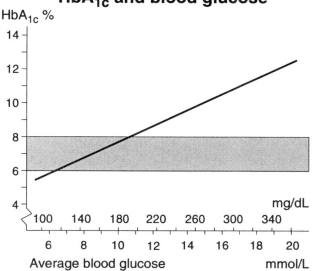

HbA_{1c} in different studies

HbA$_{1c}$ (average) %	6.0	8.0	10.0
Linköping, Sweden [59]	5.4	7.4	9.5
Stockholm, Sweden [329]	5.0	7.1	9.2
Oslo, Norway [103]	6.6	8.3	10.1
Steno, Denmark[146]	6.7	8.7	10.8
DCCT, USA [109]	6.3	8.4	10.5

Unfortunately HbA$_{1c}$-values are not the same when measured at different laboratories. Remember this when you compare your own HbA$_{1c}$ with the results of the studies on page 215. The table is from reference 240.

Your HbA$_{1c}$-value depends on the average blood glucose levels during the last 2 - 3 months. An 1 % increase in HbA$_{1c}$ means that you have had an average increase of approximately 2 mmol/L (35 mg/dL) in blood glucose levels compared to when your last test was taken. A simple equation to calculate the average blood glucose level is: [108]

Blood glucose (mmol/L) =
2 x HbA$_{1c}$ (%, DCCT-equivalent method) - 6

Blood glucose (mg/dL) =
36.5 x HbA$_{1c}$ (%, DCCT-equivalent method) - 105

Example: An HbA$_{1c}$ with a DCCT-equivalent method of 7.6 % corresponds to an average blood glucose of approximately 2 x 7.6 - 6 = 9.2 mmol/L while an HbA$_{1c}$ of 9.2 % corresponds to an average blood glucose level of 2 x 9.2 - 6 = 13.4 mmol/L.

The graph shows readings from the American DCCT study.[109] Aim at having your HbA$_{1c}$-value within the gray shaded area (6 - 8 % with DCCT-equivalent method). The graph is redrawn from reference 347.

long-term complications will decrease considerably.[109,330] If your HbA$_{1c}$ is above 9 % we feel that this is unfair to your body since we know that in the long run it will sustain damage from this (see "Will a better blood glucose control really lessen the risk of complications?" on page 215).

As of today there is no international standard for measuring HbA$_{1c}$ but a true reference laboratory method is under development.[198] A given blood test can have a values ranging from 8 to almost 15 % in different laboratories.[54] To know what your HbA$_{1c}$ value really means you should compare it with the results of one of the long-term studies (see page 215). The American Association for Clinical

Chemistry is developing a standardization allowing laboratories to relate their results to those of the DCCT and many laboratories already give their answers in DCCT-numbers. Denmark and Holland have decided to do the same and many other countries will probably follow, enabling centers and patients in different countries to compare their results. HbA$_{1c}$-methods calibrated to give the same values as the DCCT study are most useful since you directly can compare your own value with the results of the study. If you have 7 % with this method you know that the risk of long time complications is low while an HbA$_{1c}$ of 9 % is a warning signal that the risks are considerably increased.

After a visit to the diabetes clinic you may feel more motivated to "pull yourself together", obtaining lower blood glucose readings. However, after a few weeks this often falls to the back of your mind as other things of daily life regain importance. One must remember that it was not only the insulin treatment that was intensive in the DCCT study. HbA$_{1c}$ was taken at every visit with monthly intervals and telephone contacts were made in between the visits. Hence our routine of coming to the clinic every month to check HbA$_{1c}$ until it has come down below 8.5 - 9 %, preferably to 8 % or less.

Studies of adults have shown that persons with a lower HbA$_{1c}$ experience a better psychological well-being including less anxiety and depression, improved self-confidence and a better quality of life. [192]

The occurrence of severe hypoglycemia will limit how low HbA$_{1c}$ the individual patient can achieve. An HbA$_{1c}$ within the range for non-diabetic individuals usually means a high risk for severe hypoglycemia and/or hypoglycemic unawareness. In the DCCT study patients with low HbA_{1c} had a significantly higher risk for severe hypoglycemia. However, the risk decreased during the years of the study. At centers where intensive insulin treatment has been routinely implemented for a longer time the relationship between the HbA_{1c} value and severe hypoglycemia is not as pronounced.[301,405]

Does it pay off to check one's HbA_{1c}? For who's sake are we taking the HbA_{1c} test? Many patients may feel as if they are visiting a control station, when being examined by the diabetes team to see how well they have "behaved themselves". On the contrary we think that HbA_{1c} has it's greatest value for the individual with diabetes. When you see the reading you know if your living the last 3 months has been OK in achieving the average blood glucose level you want for the future. It may be difficult to manage this every time but I have often seen that for a teenager it is enough to state: "Oh, now my HbA_{1c} has increased again". I will have to do something about it. Without much more being said at the clinic, the HbA_{1c} value is considerably lower at the next visit.

When HbA_{1c} was introduced, 240 adults with diabetes measured it every third month without changing their diabetes treatment otherwise.[247] After 1 year the average HbA_{1c} value was unchanged but it turned out that those with very low values had increased them and vice versa.

How often should I check my HbA_{1c}?

HbA_{1c} should be checked regularly every 3rd month in all persons with insulin dependent diabetes. If it is high (> 8 - 9 % with DCCT-numbers or an equivalent method) this is not acceptable considering the risk of future complications. We then recommend checking HbA_{1c} every month until it has decreased to an acceptable level again.

If your blood glucose control is improving and your tests are showing lower readings it will take some time before this shows on your HbA_{1c}. Half the change will show after about one month and after two months ¾ of the change has taken place.[386] If you start with a very high HbA_{1c} (12 - 13%) it can be lowered by not more than 1 % every 10th day.[385]

How should my HbA_{1c} be?

	DCCT-method and equivalent
Normal value non-diabetes	4 - 6 %
HbA1c too low (high risk of severe hypoglycemia	< 6 %
Ideal diabetic glycemic control	6 - 7 %
Acceptable glycemic control	7 - 8 %
Needs improving	8 - 9 %
Not acceptable High risk of complications	> 9 %

There may be individual differences in the HbA_{1c} values that can be achieved. Discuss with your diabetes team what may be realistic for you.

Can HbA_{1c} be "too good"?

If you have a very low HbA_{1c} your average blood glucose will be too low resulting in a high risk of having serious hypoglycemia without any symptoms of warning ("hypoglycemic unawareness",

---

For how long does my blood glucose levels affect HbA_{1c}?

Your recent blood glucose readings affect HbA_{1c} much more than those from 2 - 3 months ago. However, your readings during the last week will not show on most methods since this fraction of HbA_{1c} is very changeable. Of a given HbA_{1c}-value the contribution of the blood glucose is (counting backwards): [386]

Day 1 - 6	very low
Day 7 - 30	50 %
Day 31 - 60	25 %
Day 61 - 90	15 %
Day 91 - 120	10 %

---

see page 42). In very young children (less than 2 years of age) the brain is still developing and repeated severe hypoglycemias with a very low blood glucose and convulsions can damage the brain (see page 40). In pre-school children avoiding severe hypoglycemia should have the highest priority and to avoid it a slightly higher HbA_{1c} may have to be accepted.

In a group of patients with an HbA_{1c} of 5.8 % (with a method giving lower readings than the DCCT) and hypoglycemia unawareness low blood glucose readings were carefully avoided and the patients aimed for a slightly higher average blood glucose.[143] Already after 2 weeks the patients recognized their hypoglycemias better. After 3 months the threshold for triggering the counter-regulatory hormones (the defence against low blood glucose, see page 31) had changed from 2.3 to 3.1 mmol/L (41 to 56 mg/dL). At the same time HbA_{1c} was raised to 6.9 %.

HbA_{1c} when travelling

Sometimes you will want to know your HbA_{1c} but for different reasons it may be difficult to visit a diabetes clinic. You can then put a few drops of blood on a filter paper and send to it the laboratory. This might be practical to do, for example if you are visiting another country for a longer period of time. It may be difficult to contact a local doctor who doesn't know you or your diabetes. If your diabetes is well controlled it is often sufficient to send a HbA_{1c} test every three months. Then call to discuss the result.

Sometimes you will want to take HbA_{1c} with shorter intervals (e.g. after a change in your insulin dose) and the travelling distance to your clinic might be a bit long. Ask your diabetes nurse or educator if "HbA_{1c} by mail" is available and how it works. If your clinic uses this method for routine testing make sure you have taken the test long enough in advance to have the results ready in time for the visit.

Fructosamine

Fructosamine is a method of measuring the amount of glucose that is bound to proteins in the blood. The value reflects the blood glucose during the last 2 - 3 weeks. Fructosamine can be good indicator during times of very short changes in glycemic control, such as when you start with a new method of

Send a HbA_{1c} test by mail to your diabetes clinic if you are away from home for a longer period of time.

treatment. However, if you only take a fructosamine test every 3rd month you will not get a representative measurement of your glycemic control over a longer period of time. It is therefore not recommended for routine testing of long-term glycemic control.[12]

A healthy non-diabetic body will automatically work the way it should. Before having diabetes your pancreas allocated insulin without you having to give it a thought. Now you must listen to your body's signals and administer insulin in a manner that is suitable for the different situations you are faced with.

Injection technique

Insulin can only affect the cells by binding to the receptors on the cell surface. Because of this, insulin will only have effect when it has entered the blood stream, regardless of how it is administered. Today the only practical method of administration is by injection. However, many research projects are exploring alternative ways of administration (see page 226).

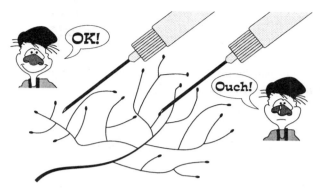

Nerve fibers look like thin branches of a tree. If you hit a nerve you will feel more pain than if you inject between the nerve fibers.

How do you get used to injections?

Taking an injection is never a pleasure. Instead it is a nuisance and causes pain, at least when you just start. But you can adapt to most things, at least if you are allowed to practise them at your own pace. To make the introduction of injections as painless as possible when you first are diagnosed with diabetes, we in our pediatric department offer every child and adolescent with newly diagnosed diabetes to try an indwelling catheter (Insuflon®, see page 100) for injections and take all blood glucose tests from an intravenous needle during the first week. You will then have plenty of time to practice injections into oranges or whatever practice is common at your clinic. Our next step is usually to practice injecting a nurse or parent before you are ready to try an ordinary injection on your own. A majority (75 - 80 %) of the children and adolescents choose to continue with ordinary injections, whereas the others continue with indwelling catheters for as long as they wish.

Mom and dad must also try injections

How do you teach yourself or your child to take or give insulin injections? For an adult it is very important to show the child that taking injections is not such a big deal. If mom and dad can overcome

their needle phobia the child will find it a lot easier to learn how to take injections. Let the child try injections and blood glucose testings on their parents (and perhaps also on a brave brother or sister or grandparent) as often as he/she wants to and show that it is not dangerous. Try to put yourself in the child's situation and think how it would appear if your parents didn't want to or were scared of taking injections – "Should I take several injections every day the rest of my life and yet my father doesn't want to take one? Daddy, who usually is so brave and dares to do just about anything.... Taking injections must be something terrible?!"

Don't tell younger children too far in advance when it's time for an injection or blood glucose test. Many children will become anxious if they know something unpleasant will happen too far in advance. Other children want to know exactly and in plenty of time what and when things will happen. Try to find out which suits your child best.

How do I inject with a minimum of pain?

Pain is generated by thin nerves and their endings. The nerves spread like the branches of a tree. If you directly hit a nerve it will result in increased pain. You can try by pressing the needle carefully against the skin and then feel where it hurts more and where it hurts less. Remember to hold the needle so that the sharp end of the needle will penetrate the skin (see top right picture). Certain areas on your abdomen and thighs will probably hurt less than

Try to find an injection site that hurts less by pressing the needle against your skin!

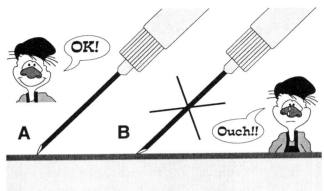

Look closely at the needle tip before pushing it through the skin. The tip of the needle is cut very sharp to pierce the skin with ease. If you prick the skin with the eye of the needle facing towards the skin (B) you will feel more pain than if you prick the skin with the sharp tip pointing towards the skin (A).

others. However, the disadvantage of always using the same places for injections is that you will easily develop fat pads (lipohypertrophy, see page 120). Insulin will be absorbed more slowly from such pads. If you insert the needle quickly with thrust you will feel less of the pricking. However, some prefer to push the needle slowly and carefully through the skin.

Where do I inject the insulin?

The recommendations for how to inject insulin has changed considerably during the years. With old (25 mm, 1 inch) needles it was natural to use a raised skinfold when injecting. When the 12-13 mm (½ inch) needles were introduced it was thought that a perpendicular injection would deposit the insulin within the subcutaneous (fatty) tissue. However, as mentioned below, there is a considerable risk for intramuscular injections with this technique, and the recommendation is now again to inject at an angle into a raised skinfold.[396]

Insulin should be given as subcutaneous injections. To avoid injecting into the muscle it is important to lift a skin fold with the thumb and index finger ("two-finger pinch-up") and insert the needle at a 45° angle (see illustration on page 94).[152,396] In a British study, the distance from the skin to the muscle was measured by ultrasonography and the conclusion was that most boys and some girls who used the perpendicular injection technique risked injecting intramuscularly, and at times even into the abdominal cavity.[368] In a French study, 31% of children who used a whole-hand skinfold with perpendicular injection technique performed the injection intramuscularly. The figure was as high as 50% in young slim boys.[323]

Wiggle the needle slightly before injecting. If the tip feels "stuck" you have probably reached the muscle. Withdraw the needle a little bit before injecting. You can also inject insulin in your buttocks where the layer of subcutaneous fat usually is

thick enough to insert the needle perpendicularly without lifting a skinfold. The speed of injection (varied between 3 and 30 seconds) does not affect how rapidly the insulin is absorbed according to a Danish study.[186]

There is usually not more pain when injecting into the muscle [183,427] but the insulin will be absorbed faster. The uptake of short-acting [152] and intermediate-acting [400] insulin is increased by at least 50 % from an intramuscular injection compared to a subcutaneous injection in the thigh. However, the insulin absorption is the same when comparing intramuscular and subcutaneous injections in the abdomen.[152]

In adults, insulin is absorbed more rapidly after a subcutaneous injection in the abdomen compared to an injection in the thigh and the blood glucose lowering effect is also increased [30,152] (see figures, page 93). The absorption from a subcutaneous injection in the abdomen is comparable to that of an intramuscular injection in the thigh.[152] This is caused by an increased blood flow in the subcutaneous fat in the abdomen compared to the thigh.[30] There are not many studies pertaining to children on this issue but the differences between the abdomen and thigh are probably less pronounced than for adults. The insulin uptake from the buttocks is quicker than from the thigh but not as quick as from the abdomen.[306] In some countries the upper and outer area of the arm is used for subcutaneous injections as well. This is not recommended in other countries (like Sweden) since the subcutaneous layer is very thin and it is difficult to lift a skin fold at the same time you inject at an angle of 45°. Injection through clothing is practiced by some patients for reasons of convenience and it seems that adverse skin reactions are exceptional.[148] However, it is more difficult to perform a proper skin-fold through clothing, thereby increasing the risk of an erroneous intramuscular injection.

The thicker the layer of subcutaneous fat the more the blood flow is decreased. This results in a slower absorption of insulin. In one study, short-acting insulin (8 units were injected into the abdomen) was absorbed twice as fast from a subcutaneous fat layer of 10 mm (3/8 inch) compared to 20 mm (3/4 inch).[188] The same result was found in patients using insulin pumps. You can take advantage of this phenomenon by injecting where the subcutaneous layer is thinner if you wish to have a quicker insulin effect. When injected above the umbilicus the absorption will be slightly quicker than when injected below or on the side of the umbilicus.[155]

The absorption of intermediate-acting insulin (NPH-insulin) is better balanced after a injection in the thigh and will give a lower insulin effect early in the night and a higher insulin effect later in the night compared to an abdominal injection.[184]

As insulin is absorbed more quickly from the abdomen than from the thigh we recommend giving the premeal doses of short-acting (or direct-acting) insulin in the abdomen and the bedtime injection of intermediate- or long-acting insulin in the thigh (or in the buttocks). We don't recommend changing the site of injection between the thigh and the abdomen from day to day as this will give you an irregular effect of the insulin.[29] A small child has a smaller area on the abdomen suitable for injections. Therefore we recommend using the buttocks for

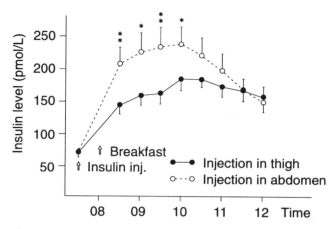

In an American study adults took the same dose of short-acting insulin before breakfast in the abdomen one day and in the thigh one day.[30] The injection in the abdomen gave both a faster onset of insulin action and a higher peak level of insulin in the blood.

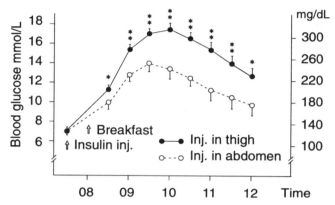

Blood glucose values from the same study as above. Because insulin enters the blood more quickly after an injection in the abdomen, this will cause the glucose content from breakfast to enter the cells more effectively, resulting in a lower blood glucose level.

short-acting insulin (and indwelling catheters) as well.

A small child using indwelling catheters for injecting short-acting insulin can try using this device for the bedtime insulin as well if it is of NPH-type. However, if you encounter problems with nighttime hypoglycemia or high blood glucose readings in the morning, it is better to give the bedtime insulin in the thigh as a separate injection (see also page 100).

Don't give short-acting insulin in the thigh late in the day. The slower uptake may result in hypoglycemia early in the night.[183]

We don't recommend giving extra short-acting insulin at bedtime to decrease a high blood glucose level, not even if you inject it in the abdomen. The effect of such a dose will overlap with the bedtime injection, risking a hypoglycemia at 2 - 3 AM.

Recommended injections sites

Direct-acting insulin (Humalog)	Abdomen
Short-acting insulin	Abdomen
Intermediate-acting insulin	Thigh or buttocks
Long-acting insulin	Thigh or buttocks

In children the buttocks may be used for injecting short- and direct-acting insulin to spread the injection sites and lessen the development of fat pads (lipohypertrophies). The buttocks may also be preferable for a pregnant woman with a distended abdomen.

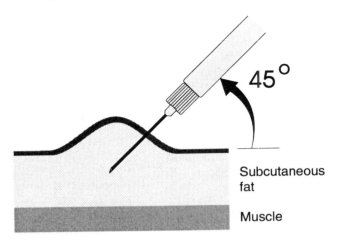

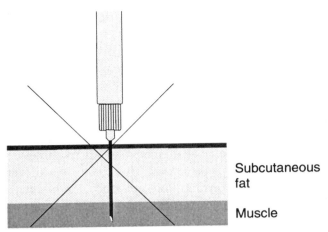

Lift a skinfold with your thumb and index finger ("two-finger pinch-up") and inject at a 45° angle from the skin. Wait 15 seconds before withdrawing the needle, then release the skinfold. When injecting into the buttocks the subcutaneous fat layer is usually thick enough to inject without lifting a skinfold.

If you inject at a 90° angle with a 12 - 13 mm needle there is a considerable risk of accidental intramuscular injection. This risk is substantial even with the shorter 8 mm needle if you inject in areas with a thin subcutaneous layer, such as the outside of the thigh, the upper arm or the lateral sides of the abdomen. Insulin from an intramuscular injection is absorbed more quickly into the bloodstream and you will sustain a stronger but shorter effect of the insulin dose. However, you can take advantage of this type of injection in the thigh if you want a quicker onset of insulin effect, or if you have problems with lipohypertrophies (see page 120).

However, when using direct-acting insulin (Humalog) you can administer an extra dose along with the bedtime insulin if the blood glucose level is high since the effect of this insulin will have waned before the onset of the intermediate-acting insulin effect. The absorption of insulin is affected by many other factors as well (see page 61).

If you inject with a perpendicular approach into the abdomen there is a considerable risk that you will inject the insulin directly into the abdominal cavity.[154]

Do I need to disinfect the skin?

You need not disinfect the skin with alcohol before injecting with an insulin pen or syringe. The risk of skin infection is negligible and alcohol disinfection often causes a stinging pain when inserting the needle.[282] Good hygiene and careful washing your hands are more important.

If you use an insulin pump or indwelling catheter you should wash the skin with chlorhexidine in alcohol or a similar disinfectant. Some skin disinfectants contain skin moisteners and may cause the adhesive to loosen more easily.

Storage of insulin

Insulin withstands room temperature well. According to manufacturers, 1 - 2 months at room temperature (not above 25° C, 77° F) will not diminish insulin's effectiveness. Insulin will lose only 10 % of its effect after more than one year at room temperature (if stored in darkness).[308] Using the same

insulin cartridge or bottle for up to 2 months is a safe routine and will minimize wasting.[42] Short-acting insulin is less stable than intermediate- and long-acting insulin. Check the expiration date on the bottle/cartridge. A practical routine is to have your insulin supply stored in the refrigerator (4 - 8° C, 39 - 46° F) and the bottle or cartridge that is currently in use stored at room temperature. However, if you mix Lente-type insulins (Monotard, Humutard, Ultratard, Ultralente) with short-acting insulin in the same syringe before injecting, the action profile will be more rapid when mixing insulin from refrigerated vials [314] (see page 60).

Don't put the insulin too close to the freezing compartment in the fridge as it cannot withstand temperatures below 2° C (36° F). When stored at temperatures above 25° C (77° F) insulin loses effect and above 35° C (95° F) it will be inactivated quickly. Don't expose insulin to strong light or heat, such as the sunlight in a car or the heat of a sauna. Short-acting insulin that has become cloudy or intermediate/long-acting insulin that has become flaky should be discarded.

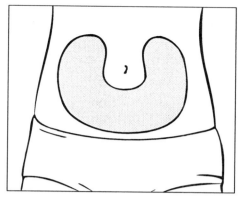

The abdomen is usually used for injections of short-acting and direct-acting insulin (Humalog). It will be absorbed slightly faster above the belly button compared to other areas of the abdomen.[155] Always use the same area for a given type of insulin, e.g. the abdomen (or buttocks for small children) for short-acting insulin and the thigh for bed-time insulin. It is important to vary the injection sites within each area to avoid the development of fat pads (lipohypertrophies, see page 120).

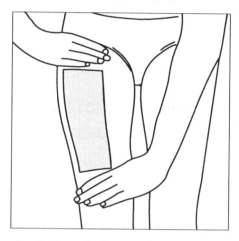

Put one hand above the knee and one below your groin. The area between your hands is suitable for injections in the thigh. Remember that insulin will be absorbed more slowly from the thigh than from the abdomen.

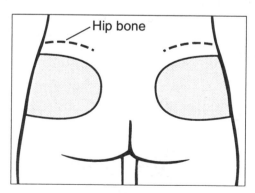

You can also use your buttocks for injections. Inject a few centimeters below the edge of the hip bone. The buttocks can be used for injections in small children who have a thin subcutaneous fat layer on the abdomen or a tendency of developing fat pads (lipohypertrophies). The absorption of insulin is slightly slower from the buttocks than from the abdomen. The illustrations are from reference[362].

Insulin is sensitive to heat and sunlight so don't leave it in the sun or a hot car.

Syringes

Disposable syringes have been used since the 1960's and are still the standard injection device in many countries. They are graded in units, and are available for U 100 insulin (100 units/ml) or U 40 (40 units/ml). Be careful, especially when traveling to countries using a different concentration of insulin, not to use U 40 insulin in a U 100 syringe or vice versa. Syringes are used when mixing two types of insulin into the same injection or for types of insulin that are not available in pen cartridges. In countries where pen injectors are not so common, syringes are used for multiple injections therapy (like the DCCT study in the USA). In many countries with lower economic standards, non-disposable glass syringes with needles needing manual sharpening are still used.

Injections with syringes

Cloudy insulin (intermediate and long-acting) needs to be mixed before use, which is done by turning or rolling the bottle 10 - 20 times. Don't shake the bottle! Short acting insulin doesn't need mixing before use. Start the injection by aspirating air into the syringe corresponding to the dose of

Different ways of administering insulin

♠	Syringes	1-3 injections/day
♠	Insulin pen	4-6 injections/day
♠	Insuflon®	Indwelling teflon catheter. Can be used if injection pain is a problem.
♠	Insulin pump	Delivers a basal rate over 24 hours and bolus doses at meal time
♠	Jet injector	Injection without a needle. A thin jet stream of insulin is shot through the skin.

insulin you will inject. Inject the air into the insulin bottle, turn it upside down and then aspirate the correct dose of insulin. Hold the syringe with the needle upwards, tap a couple of times on it and eject the air bubbles.

If you are using two types of insulin in the same syringe, start by injecting air into the bottle of intermediate acting insulin. Then inject air into the bottle of the short-acting insulin and aspirate the insulin as above mentioned. Carefully insert the needle into the bottle of intermediate-acting insulin and aspirate the correct dose (without injecting into the bottle). It is best to aspirate the insulins in this order as it matters less if a drop of short-acting insulin enters the bottle of intermediate-acting insulin than the other way around.

Pen injectors

A pen injector is a practical tool that is loaded with a cartridge of insulin for repeated injections. The standard cartridge contains 150 units (1.5 ml) but there are also pens for larger cartridges (3 ml = 300 units). Pen injectors will give a more accurate dosage compared to syringes, especially in the low doses.[132,205] Younger children will need a pen which can give one unit increments. Some pens can even be adjusted to half units. When you use a pen injector start by holding the pen with the needle upwards and eject 1-2 units into the air to ensure insulin flow (see also page 99). Insulin pens are usually made for insulin U 100 but there are pens available for U 40 as well (see page 56).

Disposable pens with 1.5 ml cartridges are also available (Penset®, Novolet®, Humaject®). These pens can only deliver an even number of units. If you adjust the pen for a dose of 7 units (in between 6 and 8 units) the pen will only deliver 6 units. Disposable pens are a practical alternative for carrying

Needles for insulin pens

Brand	Diameter of needle	Length
B-D Microfine +	0.25 mm	8 mm
NovoFine	0.30 mm	6 mm
B-D Microfine +	0.30 mm	8 mm
NovoFine	0.30 mm	8 mm
Omnican mini	0.30 mm	8 mm
Penfine	0.33 mm	8 mm
Penfine	0.33 mm	10 mm
Penfine	0.33 mm	12 mm
Omnican fine	0.33 mm	12 mm
B-D Microfine +	0.33 mm	13 mm
NovoFine	0.36 mm	12 mm
Optipen	0.36 mm	12 mm
Insuject	0.40 mm	13 mm

spare insulin, like when travelling. Make sure that you have an extra disposable insulin pen at school, at work, with your grandparents or in other places you often visit.

Why are all types of insulin not available for pens?

Intermediate- and long-acting insulin are cloudy and the bottle must be turned or rolled (not shaken!) 10-20 times before the insulin is injected. The pen cartridge contains a small glass marble that will help stir the insulin when the pen is turned. Lente-type insulins (e.g. Monotard, Ultratard, Humutard) are in crystal form and the crystals will break if a glass marble is present. For this reason the only types of insulin available in pen cartridges are short- and direct-acting insulins (which don't require stirring) and insulin of NPH-type (e.g. Insulatard, Humulin NPH, Isuhuman Basal).

A small syringe can be experienced as a huge, frightening thing by someone who is afraid of injections. Daniel made this drawing of his insulin syringe on one of the first days in the hospital.

Needle choice guidelines [377]

Patient sex and age	Body type	Needle recommended
Children < 12	All	8 mm
Males 12 - 18	All	8 mm
Females 12 - 18	Normal	8 mm
Females 12 - 18	Overweight	8 or 13 mm
Adult males	Normal	8 mm
Adult males	Overweight	8 or 13 mm
Adult females	Normal	8 or 13 mm
Adult females	Overweight	13 mm

All injections should be given with a lifted skinfold ("two-finger pinch-up") at a 45° angle regardless of the needle used, except for injections in the buttocks where perpendicular injections without pinch-up can be used.

Replacing pen needles

Manufacturers recommend only single-use of disposable needles and syringes. However, many patients reuse them for several injections. The risk of infected injection sites when reusing disposable needles seems to be negligible.[83,358] However, the injections may hurt more since the needle becomes blunted due to tip damage after repeated use [79] and the silicon lubricant wears off. There is also some evidence that reused needles with damaged tips cause an increased microtrauma when injecting, releasing certain growth factors that may lead to the development of fat pads.[378]

You must replace the needle of intermediate-acting insulin after every injection, because of the risk of leakage of fluid from the cartridge or air entry [205] (see below). The needle may also be blocked by insulin that has crystallized inside the barrel. Remove the needle directly after the injection and put the new one on prior to the next injection.

Eject a unit or two into the air with each new pen needle to make sure that the tip of the needle is filled with insulin.

What should I do if I take the wrong type of insulin?

Taking short-acting insulin instead of intermediate or long-acting insulin by mistake at bedtime is not uncommon. Don't worry, this is no catastrophe but

you will have problems with low blood glucose for a couple of hours and you will have a night with little sleep since you need to check your blood glucose frequently. You should have glucose and food close by. Start by checking your blood glucose values every hour, and even more often if the blood glucose falls below 6 mmol/L (110 mg/dL). Eat one or more extra meals during the night, preferably food rich in carbohydrates but with as little fat as possible (if you need to take dextrose to counter hypoglycemia, the effect will be much slower if you have a fat-rich meal in your stomach). Make sure that you are not home alone as you will need somebody awake and ready to help you throughout the night. If you are alone in this situation you must go to the hospital.

Remember that the effect of short-acting insulin usually diminishes after 5 hours (a little later if you have taken a dose larger than 10 units). Because of this you will probably need an extra dose of short-acting insulin 5-7 hours after the erroneous injection. In the morning you can take your breakfast insulin as usual, adjusting it according to your morning blood glucose reading.

If you happen to take a dose of intermediate-acting instead of short-acting insulin during the day it will not give you much of a blood glucose lowering effect for that meal but the effect will come some hours later. If you, for example, have taken intermediate-acting insulin for breakfast (on a multiple injection treatment) you can try taking a small dose of short-acting insulin or preferably direct-acting

Daniel 7

Daniel made this drawing before he was discharged from the hospital. The giant syringe is now a small insulin pen and on his stomach he has placed a small indwelling catheter. The initial fright of needles has been substituted by a more realistic view of the modern injection aids available today.

(roughly half your ordinary dose) to help take care of your breakfast. Measure your blood glucose before lunch and if it is high (more than 10 mmol/L, 180 mg/dL) take half your ordinary lunch dose.

Taking the wrong type of insulin will only be dangerous if you take short-acting insulin at bed-time without noticing it. If you are used to low blood glucose values your body might not give any warning symptoms until the blood glucose is dangerously low (see "Hypoglycemic unawareness" on page 42). This is one plausible explanation for the "dead in bed-syndrome" that has been discussed in recent literature.[389] See also "Can you die from hypoglycemia?" on page 47.

Different pens for daytime and nighttime insulin

It is easy to take the wrong pen injector by mistake if the pens for daytime and nighttime insulin are similar. *To avoid taking the wrong type of insulin we recommend that you always use two completely different pens for day- and bedtime insulin so that you can even feel the difference if it is completely dark. If you have experienced taking the wrong type of insulin once, you might consider having two different pens as a cheap life insurance.*

Air in the cartridge or syringe

When the cartridge warms up with the needle attached (e.g. when you carry it in an inner pocket), the liquid in the cartridge will expand and a few drops will leak out through the needle. When the temperature falls again, air will be sucked in. In one study the surrounding temperature was lowered from 27° to 15° C (81° to 59° F) which resulted in air corresponding to 4 units of insulin being sucked in.[78]

A special problem will occur with intermediate-acting insulin when the temperature is lowered. As the insulin is in the crystals that sink to the bottom of the cartridge, only the inactive solution will leak out through the needle. The result will be that the remaining insulin will become more potent, up to a concentration of 120 or 140 U/ml. If the pen is stored upside down the problem will be reversed. The insulin crystals will then be closest to the needle and leak out when the temperature increases

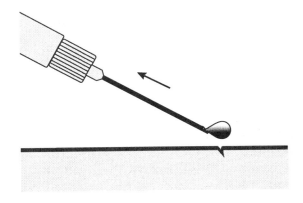

If there is air inside the pen cartridge you often experience a drop of liquid coming out from the needle-tip after your have withdrawn the needle from the skin.

and the liquid expands. The remaining insulin will then be diluted, perhaps to 80 or 90 U/ml.

The problem of altered concentration will not occur with short-acting insulin as the insulin is completely dissolved in the liquid. However, the air as such can cause problems of accuracy. You will have the least problems if you store the pen with the needle pointing upwards, for example in the pocket of your jacket.

Sometimes, by mistake, one injects a bubble of air from the syringe or cartridge along with the insulin. Subcutaneously placed air is quite harmless to the body and is quickly absorbed by the tissue. The problem is that you at the same time have missed a certain amount of insulin as it was displaced by air. You may need to take a unit or two extra to compensate for the air.

The same is true for air when using an insulin pump. Air injected through the tubing is completely harmless but you will have missed a certain amount or insulin at the same time which may cause problems.

A drop of insulin on the pen needle?

Sometimes a drop of insulin will leak from the tip of the needle after it is withdrawn from the skin. The drop contains ½ - 1 unit of insulin. This drop is caused by air in the cartridge which is compressed when you press the pen knob.[161] You can avoid the problem by waiting a little time for the air to expand (about 15 seconds) before withdrawing the pen needle. You can also remove the needle after each injection which will prevent air from being sucked into the cartridge. This problem will not occur when using syringes because you inject all the insulin.

Needle shortener

An ordinary 13 mm needle is sometimes too long, especially if you have a thin subcutaneous fat layer. Shorter 8 mm needles for insulin pens are now available in most countries. You should lift a skin fold even when injecting with a 8 mm (1/3 inch) needle. If you use an indwelling catheter (Insuflon®) you should always use 8 mm (1/3 inch) needles. A 13 mm (1/2 inch) risks penetrating the tubing, causing a leakage of insulin. You can otherwise cut the needle cover of a 13 mm (1/2 inch) needle and put it back again to shorten the needle if 8 mm needles are not available (see illustration on page 99).

What if I run out of insulin?

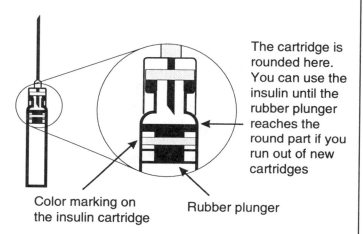

The cartridge is rounded here. You can use the insulin until the rubber plunger reaches the round part if you run out of new cartridges

Color marking on the insulin cartridge

Rubber plunger

There is a color marking on the cartridges indicating when it is time for replacement. When the rubber plunger reaches the upper end of the color marking there remains about 12 units of insulin. If you don't have a new cartridge available you can use the old one until the plunger reaches the part where the glass begins to round off. If you continue to use it until you cannot depress the pen mechanism any more, the final units will contain less insulin than expected.

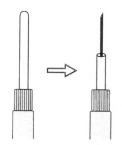

You can cut the needle cover in half and put it back again to make a 13 mm needle shorter.

You cannot use this method with NPH-insulin cartridges (Insulatard, Humulin NPH, Isuhuman Basal) as these contain a small glass marble for mixing the contents. If the rubber plunger is pushed beyond the color marking the marble cannot mix the contents properly.

Used needles and syringes

Discard used syringes, pen needles and finger pricking lancets in an empty jar or milk container so that no one will be pricked by mistake. There is a special cutter available for the removal of needle points (Safeclip®).

How to get rid of the air in the insulin cartridge.

When you replace the needle you can get rid of the air by doing the following:

① When the needle is removed, depress the pen mechanism a few times so that there is an increased pressure inside the cartridge. Tap on the cartridge to make the air rise.

② Slowly push the needle through the rubber membrane on the cartridge.

③ Air will leak out the moment the needle penetrates the rubber membrane. If you push the needle through the membrane too quickly an air pocket will remain in neck of the cartridge (see illustration).

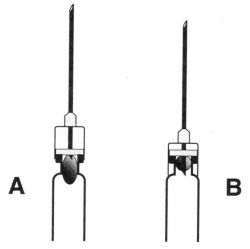

A   B

Push the needle slowly through the rubber membrane when you replace it to allow air to leak out (A). When the needle is pushed quickly all the way in, a small pocket of air is formed in the neck of the cartridge (B).

Injection aids

Indwelling catheters

Erik 7

If pain is a problem the injections can be given through an indwelling catheter (such as Insuflon®) instead of sticking the child's skin. The insulin is then injected through a rubber membrane.

Our present policy is to offer every child or adolescent newly diagnosed with diabetes to try indwelling catheters during their first week of subcutaneous injections. We take all the blood glucose tests from an intravenous cannula. These procedures ensure as little pain as possible at the onset of the child's life-long disease. Painless injections have made it less complicated for the family to cope with their crisis reaction and has facilitated their participation in the diabetes education program. After a week or so the child has had time to adjust psychologically and to learn technically the correct injection techniques and can then try regular injections. When discharged from the hospital the children have their free choice of method of injection. Seventy-five to eighty percent choose regular injections while the others continue with indwelling catheters for as long as they wish.

Using indwelling catheters will facilitate the use of multiple injection treatment for small children and will make it easier for those who are not used to

Tips for using indwelling catheters

➠ Use EMLA®-cream when inserting the catheter in small children and when new to the technique. Apply it for 1½ - 2 hours before insertion.

➠ Lift a skinfold and insert Insuflon at a 45° angle of (see figure on next page). Lift the skin with 3 or 4 fingers if the subcutaneous tissue is thin, as is likely to be the case in small children.

➠ Insert with a thrust and there will be less risk of "peel-back".

➠ Apply the adhesive end that covers the insertion site first. Never try to remove an adhesive that is already stuck to the skin.

➠ Insert the injection needle with the opening turned towards the skin and it will not get stuck on the plastic wall. Rotate the needle gently. See figure on page 102.

➠ Use an adhesive of stoma-type (such as Compeed®) if you experience itching or eczema from the enclosed adhesive.

➠ Use an 8 mm (1/3 inch) needle for both pens and syringes and there will be no risk of penetrating the teflon catheter by pushing the needle too far in.

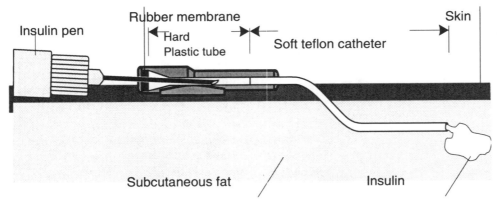

Insulin pen — Rubber membrane — Hard Plastic tube — Soft teflon catheter — Skin — Subcutaneous fat — Insulin

When using Insuflon you pierce a rubber membrane with the needle instead of the skin. The soft teflon catheter is placed subcutaneously and you inject the insulin through it. The catheter is replaced on average every 4ᵗ - 5ᵗʰ day. This can easily be done at home and if it hurts one can use local anesthetic cream (EMLA®) before replacement.

giving injections to give insulin, like grandparents, baby-sitters or day-care staff. It will also be easier to give an extra injection when needed since it will not imply more pain for the child. For example, sometimes it is difficult to know how much a small child will eat and it is then better to give half the insulin dose before the meal and perhaps give some extra insulin after the meal depending on how much the child actually eats.

We have not found that more children continue to use indwelling catheters when introducing them at the onset of diabetes, compared to our earlier policy which was to offer indwelling catheters only to those who had problems with injections. However, children using indwelling catheters are probably at less risk for needle-phobia if they are spared frightful injections during the initial period of their disease.

One study showed that in particular the younger patients using indwelling catheters and multiple injection treatment would have found this method more difficult to accept if indwelling catheters had not been available.[170]

Children and adolescents find that they can take injections without indwelling catheters after a shorter or longer period of time. Many, especially teenagers, use indwelling catheters on and off, often taking a break during the summer, when they prefer a nice suntan on their abdomen.

When should the catheter be replaced?

The average time between replacements is 4 - 5 days.[169] Some patients will be quite comfortable replacing it once a week while others may need replacement twice a week. Disinfection with alcohol is recommended before inserting the catheter to minimize the risk for infection.

Which insulin can be given in the catheter

Small children usually use the same indwelling catheter both for short-acting insulin at mealtimes and for bed-time insulin of NPH-type (e.g. Insulatard, Humulin NPH, Isuhuman Basal). However, if a longer action time of the bedtime insulin is desirable it is better to give it as a separate injection in

the thigh. Older children usually accept this without any problems. It is not advisable to mix insulins of Lente-type (e.g. Monotard, Humutard) with short-acting insulin to give in the catheter since part of the short-acting effect will vanish (see "Mixing insulins" on page 60). However, if the patient already is doing well mixing these types of insulin there should be no disadvantage giving them through an indwelling catheter.

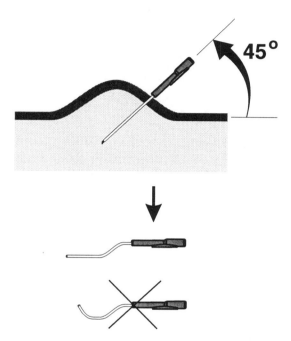

Aim with a 45° angle when inserting Insuflon or a pump needle/catheter. After removal you can check the catheter profile to see how it was inserted. A "fish-hook" appearance (lower picture) indicates that it was inserted too superficially.

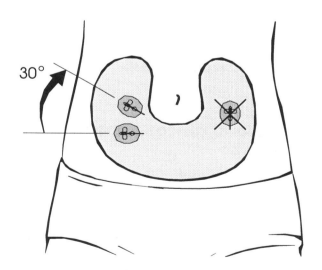

Use the shaded area of the abdomen for insertion of indwelling catheter. Insert it in a horizontal position or up to 30° from a horizontal line. Otherwise there is a risk of bending the catheter when you lean. If you have problems with lipohypertrophies ("fat pads") you can insert the indwelling catheters in the buttocks as well.

Dead space

The dead space of the catheter (the hollow inside that will be filled with insulin with the first injection) is half a unit of insulin in a clinical setting.

For most older children and adults 0.5 U more or less will not make any practical difference. Because 1 drop of insulin of 100 U/ml roughly equals one unit, there are small margins of error if the child's entire dose is only 1 or 2 units. With such small doses we use insulin of 40 U/ml. Many patients prefer to add one extra unit with the first injection after replacing an indwelling catheter. This is OK if they are aware that they will be getting an extra 0.5 U in this way.

When administering the bedtime insulin the catheter will already be filled with short-acting insulin. This will partly be exchanged for intermediate-acting insulin during the injection. Remaining in Insuflon will be a mixture of approximately 0.3 units of bedtime insulin and 0.2 units of short-acting insulin. In practice, these tiny amounts of insulin are usually insignificant.

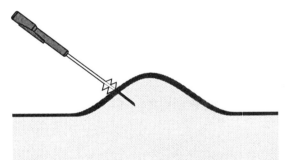

The catheter can peel backwards on the metal needle (called peel-back) if you penetrate the skin too slowly. This is a typical beginner's problem.

High blood glucose after a few days use?

Sometimes the blood-glucose level will rise after a few days use of an indwelling catheter. If this happens on a regular basis, there are often signs of lipohypertrophy present. We then instruct to replace the indwelling catheter at shorter intervals. X-ray studies of catheters have shown a delayed absorption in some cases of lipohypertrophy but normal in others.[171] The short- and long-term metabolic control were not altered when using Insuflon during a 2-month cross-over study.[172]

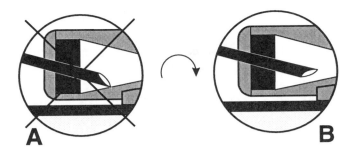

Insert the needle with the opening of the tip directed towards your skin and it will be easier (picture B). Wiggle the needle sideways and rotate it if it still gets stuck.

Studies of insulin pump users have shown both an unchanged insulin absorption during 5 days' use [307] and an increased absorption after 3 days' of using of the same injection site.[2] Studies from Finland with indwelling catheters show no change in insulin absorption during 5 days of use.[220] A Swedish study using radio-actively labelled insulin did not show any change in absorption during 4 days' use of indwelling catheters.[173]

Most patients will have impaired home test results from time to time without knowing the exact reason. This will, of course, also happen to patients using indwelling catheters. As a measure of caution we instruct patients to replace the catheter whenever this happens, although the catheter itself is usually not the cause of the increased blood glucose level.

Infection and redness

We have seen a very low frequency of infections requiring antibiotic treatment (1/140 patient months or 1/850 used catheters). Infection of the catheter canal in the subcutaneous tissue is recognized by redness and/or pain around the insertion site. If you have problems with redness or infections at the insertion site we recommend that you use chlorhexidine in alcohol (or similar disinfectant) for skin disinfection and hand washing. Don't use products containing a skin moistener since this causes the adhesive to come loose.

Redness and/or itching can be caused by an allergic reaction to the adhesive. Application of 1 % hydrocortisone cream usually helps. It the problem continues we have successfully used a stoma type adhesive (such as Compeed® or Duoderm®). Cut a hole for the catheter hood before applying it.

Problems with indwelling catheters?

Problem	Measure
Adhesive comes off	Wash off the EMLA®-cream carefully with water. Don't use disinfectant containing skin moistener. Let air dry before applying the adhesive. Warm the adhesive with a hand for a couple of minutes after you have applied it. Apply extra tape if needed.
Itching, eczema from adhesive	Apply Hydrocortisone cream. Use a stoma type adhesive (e.g. Compeed®).
Sticky rests of adhesive	Wipe off with medical benzine.
Infection/irritation at the injection site	Wash hands and skin with chlorhexidine in alcohol. Replace the catheter more frequently.
Leakage of insulin	Bent catheter? Replace it! Use 8 mm (1/3 inch) needles or a needle-shortener (see page 99).
Sore skin from plastic wings	Apply a piece of tape beneath the wings.
Scars in the skin from old catheters	Caused by an infection of the injection site. Replace Insuflon more frequently.

Itching can also be caused by perspiration in hot weather or during sports activities. The itching usually disappears when one stops sweating.

Hygiene is more important if you use an insulin pump or indwelling catheter. Always wash your hands before replacing the catheter. We recommend using chlorhexidine in alcohol for disinfection of the insertion site.

Automatic injector

An automatic injector will thrust the needle very quickly through the skin which lessens the pain. With one type (Injectomatic®, Inject-Ease®) the needle is pushed through the skin automatically, but you have to inject the insulin yourself. A similar device (PenMate™) is available for the pen injector NovoPen 3®. With the another type (Autoject®) the needle is pushed in and the insulin is injected automatically. The Diapen® both inserts the needle and injects the insulin automatically.

Jet injector

A jet injector uses very high pressure to form a thin jet stream (0.15 - 0.4 mm in diameter) of insulin that penetrates the skin. The insulin is absorbed quickly and the glycemic control can be as good as with an insulin pump.[80,205] The pain of a jet injector is comparable to that of an ordinary injection needle. Bleeding and delayed pain after the injection have been described.[202] A jet injector might be a good alternative for patients with pronounced needle-phobia.

RoBERT

An eight-year old boy made this drawing of himself using an indwelling catheter. Previously his father had to come home from work twice every day to help his mother hold him, while giving him his insulin injections.

Insulin pump

Our aim is to be able to offer all diabetic individuals an insulin treatment that is right for them. When multiple injection treatment does not give acceptable glycemic control we usually suggest an insulin pump. Many of our teenagers with brittle diabetes feel much better after the transition to pump therapy. More than 40 % of those in the intensive treatment group in the DCCT-study chose an insulin pump. There are 32.000 patients on insulin pumps in North America (1997).

Insulin pump therapy is more expensive than conventional syringe or pen therapy. Since insulin pumps are not subsidized in most countries they may be a financial burden. Ask your diabetes team how this can be solved in you community

Only short acting insulin is used in the insulin pump. Often short-acting insulin with special solvent is used to avoid blockage of the catheter (buffered insulin, Velosulin, Isuhuman Infusat). The action time and effect of this insulin is similar to ordinary short-acting insulin (e.g. Actrapid, Humulin Regular, Isuhuman Rapid). Today most catheters are made of a material with less risk of blockage, and ordinary short-acting insulin will

usually suffice.[372] Buffered U-40 insulin for smaller children is not available. We have had no problems with catheter blockage using regular short-acting 40 U/ml insulin in insulin pumps. Direct-acting insulin (Humalog) has also been tried with success in insulin pumps [433] (see page 119).

The insulin pump will deliver a steady basal rate of insulin 24 hours a day. Most modern pumps can be adjusted for different basal insulin rates during the day and night. Extra insulin is given with meals by pushing a button on the pump (bolus dose). The insulin is pumped through a thin tubing (catheter) that is connected to a metal needle or indwelling catheter placed subcutaneously.

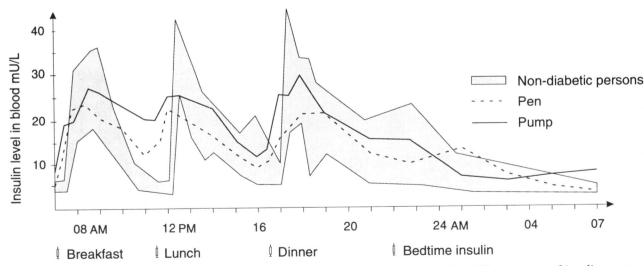

This figure is from a study where insulin levels in the blood were compared when using different types of insulin treatment.[305] The patients in this study used insulin pens with 3 premeal doses of short-acting insulin and one dose of bed time insulin. The graph shows that pump therapy resulted in higher insulin peaks after meals but also higher insulin levels between meals. Compare with the shaded area showing that the insulin level in non-diabetic individuals rises very steeply after a meal. In the early morning insulin pumps give higher insulin levels than multiple injections.

Advantages with insulin pump

➠ The basal rate will give you sufficient amounts of insulin in the early morning to avoid a high blood glucose level when you wake up.

➠ Certain individuals need a higher level of insulin between meals which the insulin pump can provide.

➠ The continuous supply of basal insulin will make you less dependent of the mandatory interval of not more than 5 hours between meals in multiple injection treatment.

➠ You always have your insulin with you and it is easier to take a bolus dose with the pump than to take an injection with a pen or syringe, especially if you don't feel like injecting when out with a group of people.

➠ If the pump can be programmed for different basal levels you will have the advantage of adjusting the pump for the differing needs of basal insulin during the day and night.

➠ The pump uses only short-acting insulin which ensures a more predictable insulin effect compared to intermediate- and long-acting insulin.

➠ Possibility of adjusting the premeal doses in 1/10th unit increments.

➠ The risk of severe hypoglycemia is usually reduced when using an insulin pump.

➠ A small insulin depot will decrease the risk for unpredictable release of insulin during physical exercise.

➠ During exercise a temporary basal rate can be used.

Disadvantages with insulin pump

➠ A small insulin depot will make you very sensitive to an interruption in the insulin supply, risking the rapid development of ketoacidosis.

➠ You must take more tests when using an insulin pump.

➠ The insulin pump will be connected to you 24 hours a day. Some feel that this makes them more tied up to their diabetes.

➠ The pump will be very obvious, for example when going to a public bath. Your diabetes will no longer be a secret disease. Often you will get curious questions about the pump, something that a person who has not fully accepted his/her diabetes fully might experience as uncomfortable.

➠ The pump's alarm will trigger every now and then and you might need to stop your activities to change the needle or tubing at an inconvenient time.

A common problem with pen injectors and syringes is that the insulin will not always give quite the same effect even if the dose is exactly the same. With an insulin pump the insulin will be deposited in the same site for several days and the absorption will be more even.[248] Insulin absorption after a premeal dose will be constant for at least 4 days provided that the needle is inserted in an area free of lipohypertrophies.[307]

The total insulin requirement per 24 hours usually decreases 15 - 20 % after starting with insulin pump treatment [57,103,374] and the glycemic control often improves, resulting in a lower HbA_{1c}.[57,103] Some patients (especially teenage girls) will gain weight when they start using an insulin pump if they don't decrease their food intake as their glycemic control improves. The extra glucose that was earlier lost with the urine will now remain in the body and be transformed into fat instead.

The risk of severe hypoglycemia usually decreases with pump treatment,[55,57,103] whereas the risk of ketoacidosis (diabetic coma) may increase according to some studies [103] while it decreases in others.[57] Ketoacidotic episodes usually occur early after initiating pump treatment when the patient is new to the method.[287] Some teenagers are frequently hospitalized due to ketoacidosis caused by interrupted insulin supply. Such episodes can drastically be reduced with an insulin pump that makes a continuous insulin supply possible.[49]

The basal rate

Approximately 40 - 50 % of the daily insulin requirement is given as the basal rate (often close to 1 U/hour for an adult person) and the rest as premeal bolus injections.[192] After a change in the basal rate it will take 2 - 3 hours before the blood glucose level is affected.[187] The basal insulin is absorbed

Insulin pump treatment will be easier if you: (adapted from [387])

➠ Are comfortable with the pump being constantly attached to your body and understand how it works

➠ Regularly check your blood glucose, at least 2 - 3 times daily (including morning and evening).

➠ Regularly perform urine tests for ketones: every morning, when ill or having nausea or when blood glucose is above 15 mmol/L (270 mg/dL).

➠ Recognize symptoms of low blood glucose. Always carry glucose tablets.

➠ Recognize early symptoms of ketoacidosis (diabetic coma). Always carry extra insulin and a pen or syringe to be able to treat this condition.

➠ Have frequent contact with a diabetic clinic.

➠ Persons living alone should have frequent contact with a close friend or relative.

Daytime basal rate

These guidelines apply to pumps with programmable basal rates. Make changes in basal rates in collaboration with your doctor and diabetes nurse.

It may often be appropriate to divide the hours of the day into different basal rate profiles where each contains a main meal. Measure the blood glucose level before the meal a couple of days in a row. Change the basal rate profile *preceding* the meal (first check that the preceding meal's bolus dose was set correctly):

Blood test before meal	Measure
< 5 mmol/L < 90 mg/dL	Decrease the basal rate by 0.1 U/hour.
> 8 - 10 mmol/L > 144 - 180 mg/dL	Increase the basal rate by 0.1 U/hour.

Another way of adjusting your daytime basal rate is to skip breakfast (and the prebreakfast bolus) and adjust the basal rate to keep the blood glucose level constant until lunch.[56] Repeat the procedure with the other meals during the day.

twice as rapidly if the person has a thin subcutaneous layer (less than 10 mm in a lifted skin fold) compared to a thicker subcutaneous fat layer (more than 20 mm).[189]

The body's insulin requirement is about 20 % lower between 1 - 3 AM compared to 5 - 7 AM.[62] If one uses a pump with the possibility of different basal rates you can administer a lower basal rate between 11 - 12 PM to 3 AM to avoid nighttime hypoglycemia.[62] If you have problems with high glucose readings in the morning you can try a slight increase in the basal rate (0.1 - 0.2 E/hour) between 3 and 7 AM.

The insulin sensitivity will increase when the blood glucose level has been lowered for some time (from a few days up to a week). To avoid hypoglycemia you should be prepared to decrease the basal rate (especially at night) when blood tests start to show lower readings.

The advice on basal rates in this chapter are written for a pump that can be adjusted for different basal rate levels throughout the day and night. With some pumps the basal rates are adjustable every hour and others can be set for different profiles for a longer

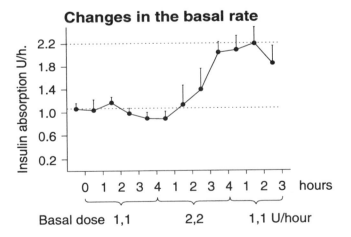

Changes in the basal rate

When you change the basal rate it will take 2 - 3 hours before any effect will appear, e.g. an increased absorption of insulin into the blood stream. The reason for this is that when you increase the basal rate, part of the insulin will stay in the subcutaneous tissue as an insulin depot. When you decrease the basal rate, the insulin from the depot will continue to be released and absorbed into the blood stream for another 2 - 3 hours until the depot has decreased in size. The graph is from reference [187].

Nighttime basal rate

Check your blood glucose levels during a night after an ordinary day when you have been feeling well and have not had extra exercise. Adjust the premeal bolus dose before the evening meal to reach a blood glucose level of about 7 - 8 mmol/L (126 - 144 mg/dL) at 10 - 11 PM.[62]

Blood test at 3 AM and in the morning	Measure
< 6 mmol/L < 108 mg/dL	Decrease the basal rate after midnight and/or early in the morning by 0.1 U/hour.
> 9 - 10 mmol/L > 162 - 180 mg/dL	Increase the basal rate after midnight and/or early in the morning by 0.1 U/hour.

If your pump cannot be adjusted for different basal rate profiles you should adjust it to fit the nighttime need of basal insulin to reach a blood glucose level of 6 - 7 mmol/L (110 - 125 mg/dL) at 3 AM. [62]

Make the changes in basal rates in collaboration with your doctor and diabetes nurse.

When should the basal profiles be changed? (adapted from [56])

You should not change the profiles of the basal rate too often. When you are used to the pump it may be practical to change the basal profiles once or twice in a month according to what your 24 hour blood glucose profiles show. Change the premeal bolus injections to adjust for temporary changes in diet or blood glucose readings. In the following situations it may be necessary to change the basal profiles:

⇒ Illness with fever and increased need of insulin.

⇒ Change in school or work activities with a new schedule or different physical activity.

⇒ Change in body weight with 5 - 10 % or more.

⇒ Pregnancy

⇒ Women may have different insulin needs during different phases of the menstrual cycle (see page 190).

⇒ Initiation of treatment with drugs that increase the need of insulin (such as cortisone).

⇒ Prolonged physical exercise (12 - 24 hours duration or more).

or shorter period of time. If you have a pump that can be programmed for only one basal rate you should adjust it according to your nighttime blood glucose values. You will then have to adjust the premeal bolus doses to fit the fixed basal rate.

Temporary change of the basal rate

On many pumps you can make temporary changes of the basal rate for one or several hours. This is

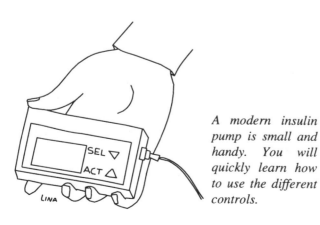

A modern insulin pump is small and handy. You will quickly learn how to use the different controls.

practical if, for example, you have problems with low blood glucose and repeated hypoglycemia for sustained periods despite extra food intake. It will usually help to decrease the basal rate or stop the pump completely for an hour or two. If your blood glucose is high at bedtime you can temporarily increase the basal rate by 0.1 - 0.2 U/hour for a couple of hours. If your blood glucose is low early in the night you can temporarily decrease the basal rate for a few hours. The temporary basal rate is very useful for prolonged exercise. For example, during a 5 hour bike ride, decrease the basal rate by 50 %. If you have exercised in the evening you should decrease the basal rate by 0.1 - 0.2 U/hour for the whole night.

Premeal bolus doses

Take a bolus dose 30 min before the meal when using regular insulin in the pump and just prior to the meal if using direct-acting insulin (Humalog).

Changing the basal rate

Since it takes 2 - 3 hours before a change in the basal rate will have effect, you must plan ahead.

① Change the dose 2 hours before you want it to have effect, e.g. increase from 3 AM if you want an increased insulin effect from 5 AM on.

② If you want to quickly increase the effect of the basal rate (e.g. if you are ill with fever) you should administer an extra dose of insulin of the same size as 2 hours of the basal rate. You will then quickly increase the insulin depot resulting in a quicker absorption of insulin into the blood.

③ If you want to quickly decrease the effect of the basal rate (e.g. if you are going to exercise) you should stop the basal rate for 2 hours and then start it again with a lower level. The insulin depot will then quickly decrease in size and the change in basal rate will soon have effect.

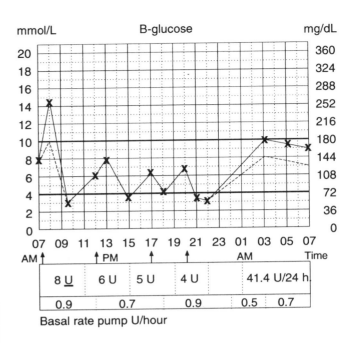

8 U	6 U	5 U	4 U	41.4 U/24 h.
0.9	0.7		0.9	0.5	0.7

Basal rate pump U/hour

Interpreting the 24-hour profile

It is best to take tests for a couple of days in a row to be sure that any one day was not just an exception. Start by looking at the evening meal since it determines what blood glucose you will have when going to bed. The dotted line shows what the blood glucose values might have been with the suggested changes.

Evening meal: The blood glucose after the meal is a bit low. Decrease the dose by 1 unit. Adjust the dose to have a blood glucose of about 8 mmol/L when you go to bed.

Night: Early in the night the basal rate needs to be increased slightly to 0.6 U/hour as the blood glucose is rising until 3 AM. The blood glucose level from 3 AM to 7 AM is stable so this rate does not need to be changed.

Breakfast: The blood glucose rises very quickly after breakfast. The insulin could have been given even earlier before breakfast to prevent the peak at 8 AM. An increased breakfast bolus dose or basal rate would increase the risk of hypoglycemia before lunch.

Lunch and dinner: No changes.

Don't change all doses at the same time as it can be difficult to see which change resulted in what. Let a few days go by between changes to make sure that the profiles look similar from day to day

However, the timing also depends on what your actual blood glucose level is (see page 125). Adjust the doses up or down in the same way as when on multiple injections. The breakfast dose is usually slightly larger than the other premeal bolus doses. Since the basal need of insulin between meals is now supplied via the pump your premeal bolus doses will be lower than when on multiple injections. You will probably need to decrease the size of extra insulin doses as well if, for example, you eat something extra.

You can calculate the amount of insulin needed for a given amount of carbohydrates by dividing the total amount of carbohydrates eaten during the day by the amount of insulin taken as a premeal bolus injections.[107] See example on page 109. Usually one unit will accommodate 10 - 15 grams of extra carbohydrate. If, for example, you eat ice-cream containing 26 g of carbohydrate, 2 units of extra insulin will probably be enough.

You will not be bound to maintaining an interval between meals (and insulin injections) of at most 5 hours as when on multiple injection treatment. The basal rate will probably make it possible to increase the time span between meals to 6 - 7 hours which might be an advantage if you have an irregular schedule.

Your should, however, be aware of eating and taking premeal bolus injections with intervals shorter than 5 hours as there will be a risk of overlapping insulin doses when using short-acting insulin in the pump. Try reducing the second premeal bolus by 1 or 2 units if the previous meal was only 3 - 4 hours earlier. You will not have this problem if you are using direct-acting insulin (Humalog) in the pump as the action profile of this insulin is considerably shorter.

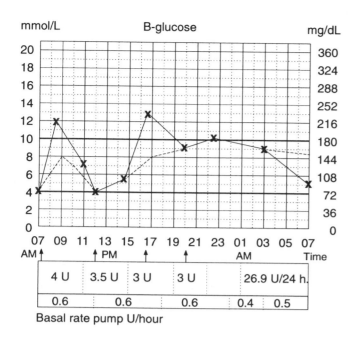

Basal rate pump U/hour

4 U	3.5 U	3 U	3 U		26.9 U/24 h.
0.6	0.6	0.6	0.4	0.5	

Basal rate pump U/hour

<table>
<tr><td colspan="3">How many carbohydrates will one unit of insulin accommodate?[107]</td></tr>
<tr><td>Example:</td><td>Carbohydrates (g)</td><td>Insulin units</td></tr>
<tr><td>Breakfast</td><td>60</td><td>6</td></tr>
<tr><td>Lunch</td><td>50</td><td>4</td></tr>
<tr><td>Dinner</td><td>55</td><td>5</td></tr>
<tr><td>Evening meal</td><td>35</td><td>3</td></tr>
<tr><td>Total</td><td>200</td><td>18</td></tr>
</table>

Quotient carbohydrates / insulin =11.1 gram/unit

In this example of a 12-year old boy (38 kg, 84 pounds) one unit of insulin will accommodate 11 grams of carbohydrates without changing the blood glucose level.

Interpreting the 24-hour profile

See the previous profile for general interpretation.

Evening meal: *No changes*

Night: *The blood glucose does not change early in the night. However, late at night it drops significantly, so reducing the basal rate to 0.7 U/hour is recommended.*

Breakfast: *The blood glucose rises quickly after breakfast and the dose should preferably be increased to 5 units. The basal rate is probably sufficient as the blood glucose is lowered at lunch again. However, when the breakfast bolus dose is increased to 5 units the basal rate might need to be decreased.*

Lunch: *The blood glucose two hours after the meal is only slightly increased indicating that the premeal bolus dose is correct. However, as the blood glucose rises prior to dinner, the basal rate could be increased to 0.7 U/hour.*

Dinner: *No changes.*

Change of insertion site

The most common site is the abdomen because the absorption of insulin is quickest here. With small children it is preferable to use the buttocks as well to be able to spread the injection sites, thereby decreasing the risk of lipohypertrophies (fat pads). You can also use the thigh or the upper arm but both sites can result in an increased absorption of insulin when exercising. There is also a greater risk of the needle catching on the clothing and being pulled out.

Individual advice is needed on how often the needle should be replaced. We recommend the use of a soft teflon catheter, such as Sof-set®, Clinisoft®, PL Comfort®, Disetronic®Tender or similar. Start by replacing it twice a week and then try to increase the number of days between replacements. You can often allow the needle to be in place for 4 - 5 days if your blood glucose readings are not raised. Smaller children usually need to replace it more often. The longer the catheter remains in one site, the greater the risk of developing lipohypertrophies (fat pads, see page 120) and infections. If you have problems with fat pads or redness of the skin you should replace the needle/catheter more frequently.

If the redness doesn't disappear quickly after replacing the needle you can accelerate healing by applying a dressing with warm soapy water for 20 minutes 4 times daily. You can also try an antibiotic ointment or hydrogen peroxide. If the redness increases or starts hurting, you might need antibiotic treatment. Contact your diabetes clinic or doctor.

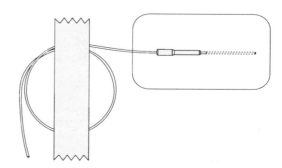

Put the tubing in a sling and fix it with some adhesive to minimize the risk of pulling the needle loose if the tubing is pulled or jerked.

When do I replace the parts?

Teflon catheter	Start by replacing it twice a week. If there are no problems try using it 4 - 5 days before replacement.
Metal needle	Replace every second day, more often if signs of irritation are noted.
Tubing	Replace the tubing at least every other time you replace the needle/catheter and when you replace the reservoir.
Insulin reservoir	Some pumps have prefilled reservoirs, others need to be filled. Do not reuse them as the silicon on the plunger wears off, resulting in "no delivery" alarms.

Problems with irritation or infection of the insertion site can be prevented by careful hand washing, disinfection and needle/catheter replacement every second or third day. Use chlorhexidine in alcohol or similar agent for hand-washing. Don't use products containing skin moisteners, since these may cause the adhesive to loosen more easily. If you are allergic to the adhesive, it can cause redness or itching (see page 102).

Insert the new needle or catheter before removing the old one. If you do it the other way around there is a greater risk that you will contaminate your hands on the old site, thereby increasing the risk of transferring bacteria to the new one. Insert the new needle/catheter at least 2 - 3 centimeters (one inch) away from the old one to avoid developing fat pads. The adhesive should not cover a previous injection site until it is completely healed. It is best to change sides on the abdomen (left/right) with each replacement.

If you have recurring problems with infected sites in spite of good hygienic routines, the bacteria might originate from you armpits or nostrils. Try washing your hands with a disinfection agent as well. If a culture reveals bacteria from the nasal cavity, antibiotic treatment may be necessary. Avoid inserting the needle in skin folds, close to the belly button or under the waist-line. Straighten your back before you apply the adhesive to avoid tight skin. Always check your blood glucose 3 - 4 hours after replacing the needle/catheter to make sure that it works properly.

Replacement of needle/catheter

➠ If you replace the needle/catheter before taking a premeal bolus it will be flushed clean from possible tissue rests by the larger volume of fluid.

➠ Avoid replacing your infusion set before bedtime as you will need to be awake for a couple of hours to see that it functions properly.

➠ Start by washing your hands with soap and water.

➠ Disinfect a skin area that is a little larger than the adhesive your are going to apply. Use chlorhexidine in alcohol or similar disinfectant. Use this for hand-washing as well if you have problems with skin infections.

➠ Be careful not to touch the sterile needle.

➠ Pinch a two-finger skin fold and insert the needle at a 45° angle (see ill. on page 101).

➠ Apply the adhesive carefully. If it sticks unevenly don't try to move it. There is a considerable risk of removing the needle at the same time if you try to move the adhesive.

➠ Withdraw the old needle after the insertion of the new one. Pull the adhesive from the side where the tip of the needle/catheter is located and it will come off more easily.

If you change to a new injection site in the evening you will find it more difficult to detect a blockage in the tubing which will cause the blood glucose to increase. Many pump users find it most convenient to replace the injection site when coming home from school or work. You will still have plenty of time to find out if something is wrong with the new injections site. If you replace the needle/catheter before taking a meal bolus dose the tubing will be flushed clean from possible tissue rests.

Insulin depot with a pump

The disadvantage of using an insulin pump is that the insulin depot will be very small, since only short-acting insulin is used If the insulin supply is interrupted you will quickly develop symptoms of insulin deficiency like high blood glucose, nausea and vomiting (see "Depot effect" on page 60). This will be important if the pump is blocked or if you

High blood glucose and ketones?

If the blood glucose is higher than 15 mmol/L (270 mg/dL) and you have ketones in the urine, this indicates a blocked insulin supply.

① Take 0.1 U/kg (0.5 units/10 pounds) body weight of short-acting insulin (or preferably direct-acting Humalog) with a pen or a syringe. Don't use the pump as you are not sure if it works well.

② Measure blood glucose every hour. If it doesn't decrease the insulin dose of 0.1 U/kg (0.5 units/10 pounds) body weight can be repeated (every 1 - 2 hours with Humalog, every 2 - 3 hours with regular short-acting insulin).

③ Check the pump by disconnecting the tubing and the needle. Activate a bolus dose. Insulin should immediately appear from the tubing. If it drops slowly you should give another bolus injection. If this dose also drops slowly it indicates a partially blocked tubing, e.g. caused by coagulated blood or crystallized insulin. Replace both the tubing and the needle.

④ Replace the needle/catheter if the tubing works well. Check for signs of redness in the skin and of moisture close to the injection site indicating insulin leakage.

Other causes of a lack in insulin delivery:

➠ The connector between the tubing and the insulin reservoir can be broken.

➠ Hole in the tubing.
A cat bite in the tubing resulted in leakage which lead to ketoacidosis for a teenage girl.

➠ Air in the tubing is not dangerous as such but will give you less insulin.

➠ Squeezed or bent tubing, e.g. by a belt or tight jeans, will take several hours before the pump's blockage alarm is triggered.

Causes of ketoacidosis

➠ Insulin delivery is interrupted, such as a crack in the connector or a loose needle.

➠ Increased insulin requirements caused by intercurrent illness without the insulin dose being increased, e.g. a cold with fever.

➠ Inflammation or infection at the injection site (redness or pus).

➠ Decreased insulin absorption, for example caused by inserting the needle into a fat pad (lipohypertrophy).

➠ Decreased insulin potency, as after it has been frozen or exposed to heat/sunlight.

their depot.[189] From this follows that thin individuals will be more sensitive to an interrupted basal rate since their insulin depot is smaller.

Ketoacidosis (diabetic coma)

A small insulin depot will result in early insulin deficiency symptoms if something goes wrong with the pump or the tubing. One night's interrupted insulin supply is enough to cause incipient ketoacidosis in the morning with symptoms of insulin deficiency such as nausea and vomiting. Be extra careful to check both blood glucose and ketones in the urine when you don't feel well.

If your blood glucose is above 15 mmol/L (270 mg/dL) and you have ketones in the urine you should take an extra dose (0.1 U/kg or 0.5 U/10 pounds body weight) of short-acting insulin (preferably direct-acting Humalog if available). The dose can be repeated after 2 - 3 hours if needed (1 - 2 hours with Humalog). Contact the hospital if you vomit or have nausea and are unable to drink.

Always use local anesthetic (EMLA®-cream) before replacing the needle/catheter when beginning with pump treatment with small children. Apply the cream 1½ - 2 hours ahead of time to get the full effect. Another alternative to lessen the pain is the Sof-serter™ for automatic insertion of the Sof-set® catheter.

intentionally turn it off, such as when sporting or swimming.

Thicker layers of subcutaneous fat will result in a larger insulin depot of the basal dose. In one study a basal rate of 1 U/h was used. The insulin depot for persons having a subcutaneous fat of 40 mm (1½ inch) was close to 6 U while those with less than 10 mm (1/3 inch) subcutaneous fat had only 1 U in

How many tests should I take when using an insulin pump?

➠ Blood glucose at least 2 - 3 times daily (including morning and before going to bed), preferably 4 - 5/day, especially if using Humalog in the pump.

➠ 24-hour profile every week or every other week with readings taken before and 1 - 1½ hour after each meal and at night.

➠ Before each meal when ill or not feeling well for some other reason.

➠ Urine tests:
Glucose and ketones every morning. Ketones when having nausea, during illness or when the blood glucose level is high (> 15 mmol/L, 270 mg/dL).

IMPORTANT!!

When using an insulin pump you have a greater risk of ketoacidosis since you have a very small insulin depot.

Always check blood glucose and urine tests (ketones) when you have nausea or vomit!!! If the amount of ketones increases (e.g. from 2+ to 3+) this means that the insulin deficiency is increasing. You must then contact the hospital to discuss what to do next!

Be aware that insulin deficiency leading to increased ketone production immediately shows up in the urine. If you take extra insulin the production of ketones will stop. However, the excretion of ketones in the urine will continue for many hours but you will see that the concentration stabilizes and then decreases as the hours pass.

If you are the least bit doubtful or cannot get hold of someone who knows insulin pumps well, you should take an injection of insulin by pen or syringe and then go to the emergency ward.

Always bring extra insulin wherever you go even if you are only going to be away from home for a couple of hours!

More frequent home testing

Since there is a greater risk of insulin deficiency with a pump you must be willing to take more blood glucose tests. A minimum is 2 - 3 tests a day including morning and late evening. You must also be careful to check urine tests every morning and when not feeling well (ketones are a sign of insulin deficiency). A 24-hour blood glucose profile with tests before and 1 - 1½ hours after each meal is needed every week or every second week to adjust your doses correctly. You should also take night-time tests when compiling a 24-hour profile (at 2 - 3 AM and if needed at 5 AM as well).

Use a logbook in which you clearly document the pump's basal rate. We find it best to use a logbook where every entry is written on a blood glucose chart. This will enable you to visually observe patterns in your blood glucose readings (see charts on page 108). Make it a habit to check the pump daily for the total number or units delivered/24 hours and record this in your logbook.

Disconnecting the pump

Sometimes you will want to disconnect the pump for one reason or another. Some needle/catheter sets allow you to disconnect the tubing or between the needle and the tubing by using a rubber membrane as a one way valve. Remember to save the needle's sterile casing so that you can put it back on again when you want to disconnect the tubing. Use

self-sticking Velcro® to fix it onto the pump's leather case. If you have a so called Luer connection between the tubing and needle/catheter you should fill it with insulin before connecting. It is easiest to have the pump deliver a bolus dose, letting the drops fall into the Luer connector.

Pump alarm

Insulin pumps seldom malfunction. If one does, it will stop. There is no risk that the pump will pulse or surge, giving you too much insulin. The pump alarm will go off when something is wrong, e.g. blocked tubing, an empty insulin container or low or flat batteries. Check the operating instructions to see what the different alarms stand for and how to respond to them.

Most pumps have an alarm that is triggered if you have not pushed any of the buttons after a certain number of hours. It may wake you up early in the morning if you didn't take your evening meal insu-

Causes of high blood glucose
(adapted from [372])

① **The pump**
Basal rate too low
The pump has triggered an alarm and shut itself off
Other pump trouble

② **Insulin reservoir**
Wrong position in the pump
Empty reservoir
Leakage in the connection with the tubing

③ **Tubing and needle/catheter**
Forgetting to fill the tubing when replacing
Leakage in connections
Adhesive and needle is loose
Air in the tubing
Blood in the tubing
Needle/catheter has been in place too long
The tubing was replaced in the evening without giving a bolus dose to build up the pressure.
Bent/squeezed tubing
Blocked needle/catheter

④ **Injection site**
Redness, irritation / infection
Fat pad at the injection site
Placement close to waist band

⑤ **Insulin**
Cloudy insulin
Expiration date passed
Exposed to heat / sunlight

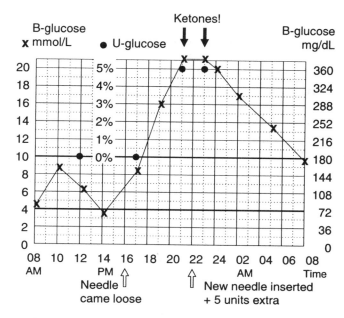

A few hours of interrupted insulin supply is sufficient to make the blood glucose rise quickly. The blood glucose will rise even if you don't eat because the liver will produce glucose when there is a lack of insulin (see page 32). When the blood glucose level was raised in the evening the patient was feeling nauseous. He checked for ketones and discovered that something was wrong. When he checked the needle it was loose and the insulin was not entering his body. He gave himself 5 extra units with a pen injector, replaced the needle and started the pump. The blood glucose level returned to normal during the night.

If the blood glucose rises quickly you should remove the needle/catheter. Give a bolus dose and see if insulin comes out from the tip. Bend the catheter and give another bolus dose. The pump should now give a blockage alarm. Check the tubing and connections for leakage. Replace the needle/catheter and check the blood glucose level frequently to make sure that it decreases. Take an extra injection (with a pen or syringe) of 0.1 U/kg (0.5 units/10 pounds) body weight if you have ketones in the urine and check your blood glucose once again after 1 - 2 hours. Repeat the dose if necessary.

lin or forgot to push one of the buttons before going to bed.

"No delivery alarm"

The pump alarm will be triggered if there is an increased resistance when pumping insulin. It cannot tell where that the blockage is in the system. It may be that the insulin reservoir is empty, the plunger may be sluggish or the tubing or needle blocked. The tubing can be bent or squeezed, for example by a belt buckle. If the "no delivery" alarm is triggered start by checking the tubing for bends or pinches. Then give the remainder of the premeal bolus. If no alarm is triggered, all is well now and you have received the intended amount of insulin. If the alarm goes off again the next step is to stretch

out and try careful massaging of the infusion port and catheter under the skin. If you haven't disconnected the tubing there is no need to take extra insulin other than the remaining premeal dose if the pump now works without alarm (assuming that the blood glucose level is not raised).

If the needle or tubing is blocked it may take several hours before the pressure has increased enough to trigger the alarm. During this time you will not have received any insulin. Find out how much is needed to trigger the pump alarm in your pump. It may also depend on which tubing you have and how long it is. test it by pushing the needle into a rubber cork or pinch the end of the catheter. If you

Stopped pump

Time that the pump has been stopped	Measure
< ½ - 1 hour	No extra insulin needed.
1 - 2 hours	Take an extra dose when you connect the pump corresponding to the basal rate you have missed.
2 - 4 hours	Take an extra dose before you disconnect the pump corresponding to the basal rate that you should have had during the missing 2 - 4 hours. Check your blood glucose when you connect the pump and take an extra bolus dose if needed.
> 4 hours	Dose before disconnecting as above. Using a pen injector or syringes, take extra short-acting insulin every 3 - 4 hours corresponding to the missed basal rate. Take the premeal bolus dose with the pen or syringe.

Occlusion alarm ("no delivery")?

① Check the tubing for bends and pinching. Try a careful massage of the infusion port and the catheter under the skin. If the alarm was triggered when taking a pre-meal bolus, take the remaining portion.

No alarm   → OK, no problems
Alarm   ↓

② Disconnect needle/catheter from tubing. Start a bolus dose with the pump.

No alarm   → Replace needle/catheter
Alarm   ↓

② Disconnect tubing from insulin reservoir. Start a bolus dose with the pump.

No alarm   → Replace tubing
Alarm   ↓

④ Remove the insulin reservoir from the pump and start a bolus dose.

No alarm   → Replace reservoir
Alarm   ↓

⑤ Something is wrong with the pump. Contact the pump dealer and deliver insulin with a pen or syringe.

then give a bolus dose you will see how many units are pushed into the tubing before the alarm is triggered.

If your pump for example has given 4.3 units of the meal bolus dose when the alarm goes off and you know that 2.6 units are needed to build up pressure to trigger the alarm, you will have only received 4.3 - 2.6 = 1.7 units of the bolus dose.

For smaller children we often use insulin of 40 U/ml. You must then remember that fewer units are needed before the alarm goes off since the fluid volume is larger. If 2.5 units of 100 U/ml are needed to trigger the alarm this will equal 1 unit of 40 U/ml.

Sometimes the pump will alarm for a block in the tubing even after you have replaced both the tubing and the needle. If this happens, remove the insulin reservoir from the pump. Then start the pump again. If the alarm still goes off, the problem is an internal one, e.g. motor problems. If the pump works well without the reservoir the reason may be that you have reused it. When doing so the silicon on the plunger wears off, and this may result in a "no delivery" alarm.

Leakage of insulin

The pump can't alarm if there is an insulin leakage. It will only trigger if the motor runs against resistance. Insulin can be disposed outside the injection site if the needle has been retracted. Often this can be only detected when you take a bolus dose. When the basal dose is running the amounts of insulin are so small that it can be difficult to pick up if there is a leakage.

The tubing connector on the pump end can crack, causing leakage, especially if you are too rough when connecting it. Feel the connector with your fingers. If there is a leakage you can often detect the smell of insulin.

Air in the tubing

When you connect the tubing to the pump there is always a risk of air entry, especially if you fill it with cold insulin. Air will come out of the solution when the temperature rises. Always make sure that

Problems with the pump?

Problem	Measure
Infection/irritation at the injection site	Wash hands and skin with chlorhexidine in alcohol. Replace needle/catheter more frequently.
Blocked needle or catheter	It can be bent or blocked by coagulation or insulin crystals. Replace it.
Blocked tubing	Can be caused by precipitation of insulin. Disconnect the needle and tubing and give a bolus dose. Replace if the alarm is triggered.
Blood in the tubing	Disconnect the tubing from the needle and give a bolus dose. The pump will then trigger the occlusion alarm if it is blocked.
Air in tubing?	See text on page 114.
White spots on the inner layer of the tubing	Many kinds of tubings are made of double plastic layers that can come apart, showing as white spots. This does not affect the function or the insulin.
Leakage of insulin at the insertion site	Has the needle/catheter come loose? Is there a bent catheter? Replace the needle/catheter.
Moisture under the adhesive	This indicates insulin leakage. Replace the needle/catheter.
Adhesive comes off	Wash the EMLA®- cream off carefully with water. Don't use disinfectant with skin moistener. Let the skin air dry before you apply the adhesive. Warm the adhesive with your hand after application. Apply extra tape if needed.
Itching, eczema from adhesive	Apply hydrocortisone cream. Use a stoma-type adhesive.
Sticky rests of adhesive	Wipe off with medical benzine.
Sore skin from plastic wings	Apply a piece of tape beneath the hard plastic.
Scars in the skin from old catheters	Caused by an infection of the insertion site. Replace needle/catheter more frequently.
Redness of the skin at the needle tip	Can be caused by insulin allergy. See page 121
Nothing works	Try running the pump with both insulin and tubing removed.

An insulin pump needs to be looked after, and tubing and batteries need to be replaced. When the alarm triggers you must know how to deal with it. You will be the "first line pump mechanic" and will probably find this easier if you are technically oriented. However, this is not a requirement.

the insulin is at room temperature before refilling the reservoir. Introducing air into the subcutaneous tissue is of no concern, but you will miss the corresponding amount of insulin. The alarm will not be triggered since the pump's microcomputer cannot tell the difference between air and insulin in the tubing.

If you see air in the tubing when you are about to take a meal bolus dose you can compensate with a little extra insulin. Five to seven cm (1 - 1½ inch) of air in the tubing usually correspond to 1 unit of insulin. To find out the exact dimension of your pump tubing give a bolus dose of 1 unit when replacing the tubing. Make a mark on the tubing with a felt tip pen corresponding to the insulin travels for that unit.

If the air in the tubing corresponds to more than ½ - 1 unit when the basal rate is running (e.g. between meals) it is best to disconnect the tubing from the needle in the skin. Give an extra bolus dose "into the air" to purge the air in the tubing and fill it with insulin once again.

Intercurrent illness and fever

When you are ill, especially with fever, your body will increase its insulin requirements, often by 25 % for each degree celsius of fever (see page

Insulin pump and illness

➠ Continue with your ordinary meal bolus doses, increasing them by 1 - 2 U if necessary.

➠ Increase the basal rate by 0.1 - 0.2 U/hour if the blood glucose continues to be high.

➠ Never discontinue the basal rate completely even if you have problems with hypoglycemia.

➠ Check your blood glucose every 2nd to 4th hour. Check for ketones in the urine frequently. Keep good records in your logbook.

➠ Take extra insulin (1 U/10 kg or 0.5 U/10 pounds body weight), preferably Humalog, if your blood glucose is high and you have ketones in the urine. Give another 1 U/10 kg (0.5 U/10 pounds) every 2nd hour until the blood glucose is below 10 mmol/L (180 mg/dL) and the level of ketones in the urine is decreasing.

➠ Give the extra insulin with a pen or syringe. The reason for the high blood glucose may be pump malfunction.

➠ Try to drink large amounts of fluids as this will increase the excretion of ketones and lessen the risk of dehydration. As long as there is glucose in the urine you will lose extra fluid. Drink glucose-free fluids when the blood glucose is above 10 - 12 mmol/L (180 - 215 mg/dL) and change to something containing glucose when the blood glucose is below this level. If you are nauseous, try to drink small volumes (a couple of mouthfuls) at a time.

Call the hospital

➠ the first time you become ill after having started with the pump.

➠ if you have nausea that prevents you from eating for more than 6 - 8 hours.

➠ if you have vomited more than once during a 4 - 6 hours period.

➠ if the blood glucose level has not been lowered or the ketones in the urine have not decreased after the second extra dose of insulin.

➠ if your general well-being is worsening.

➠ if you are in the least uncertain as to how to handle the situation.

Infusion sets with soft cannula

Brand	Length cm	inches
PL Comfort ®	60, 80, 110	24, 32, 43
Clinisoft ®	55, 80, 110	22, 32, 43
Sof-set ®	61, 107	24, 42
Disetronic ® Tender	30, 60, 80, 110	12, 24, 32, 43

For most tubes, 5 -7 cm (2 - 3 inches) contain approximately 1 unit of insulin. The Sof-set ® needle can be used with an automatic inserter (Sof-serter ™) that lessens the pain.

175). It is advisable to start by increasing the basal rate. Start by a 10 - 20 % increase when you notice that your blood glucose is rising. You will probably also need to increase the meal bolus doses according to your blood glucose readings. It is important that you test your glucose level before each meal when ill and preferably 1 - 1½ hours after the meal as well. Most often you will also need to check the blood glucose levels in the night.

Doses without the pump

It is very important that you always carry extra insulin wherever you go in case of pump malfunction. Check to see that the insulin has not expired. You should have written down what doses to begin with if you temporarily need to use a pen or syringes.

① **Use the old doses**
It is easiest to start with the same doses that you had when you used a pen injector or syringes, on the condition that you have written down the doses and that not too much time has elapsed since then, e.g. that you still have approximately the same insulin requirements.

② **Intermediate-acting insulin at bedtime**
Look at the pump doses. The breakfast dose with a pen will be the sum of the pump prebreakfast dose and the basal rate between breakfast and lunch. If you have a high basal rate (>1.5 - 2 U/hour) start by only counting 1 - 1.5 U/hour when calculating the dose with pen or syringes.

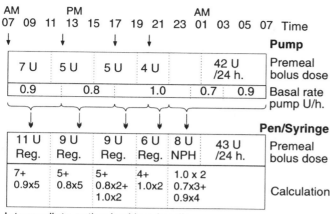

Intermediate-acting bedtime insulin

Sometimes you must use an insulin pen or syringes for a while, e.g. if something is wrong with the pump. You can calculate which dose to use if you add the meal bolus dose in the pump with the basal rate. You will probably need to increase the night dose since the pump is more effective, giving more insulin late at night and early in the morning than you would get from the intermediate acting bedtime insulin. Check with your diabetes nurse if you are unsure what doses you used previously when on multiple injections.

7 U	5 U	5 U	4 U	46 U/24 h.
12U UT		13U UT		

Long-acting basal insulin (Ultratard = UT)
Basal rate in pump 21 U+20% = 25U divided in 2 doses

Another alternative is to replace the basal rate in the pump with a long-acting insulin (Ultratard, Ultralente) given twice daily and continue using the same bolus doses (and the same type of insulin, short-acting or direct-acting) before meals as with the pump. You will probably need to increase the amount of basal insulin by 10 - 20 %.

The bedtime dose of intermediate-acting insulin (Insulatard, Humulin NPH, Isuhuman Basal) is calculated by adding the basal rates between 10 PM and 8 AM (see example on page 117). You can also use short-acting insulin (*not* Humalog) during the night, giving two doses, at 10 PM and 3 AM corresponding to the sum of the basal rates during the night.

③ **Long-acting basal insulin**
The most logical choice is to replace the basal dose in the pump with long-acting insulin (Ultratard, Ultralente) and to use the same bolus doses (and type of insulin) before meals as when using the pump. Take the total basal dose during 24 hours, add 10 - 20 % and divide into 2 equal doses that you take with breakfast and dinner (around 5 - 6 PM).

Being admitted to the hospital

If you are admitted to the hospital in an acute situation you will often find that there is no staff available who are familiar with the pump. If you have problems with the pump it is usually best to begin injecting insulin with a pen or syringes until the daytime staff arrives. If you vomit or have signs of ketoacidosis the best treatment is intravenous insulin (see page 55).

Physical exercise

When physical active you can disconnect the pump for 1 - 2 hours time without taking any extra insulin. If your exercise lasts longer than 2 hours you will probably be better off by keeping the pump connected and using the temporary basal rate. Try half the basal rate while exercising and for an hour or two following. You may need to lower the basal rate even more — but the only way to know for sure is to try it yourself.

If the time of exercise is within 1 - 3 hours after a meal you can try taking half the meal bolus dose or even skipping it if the exercise is particularly strenuous. However, you will then probably need to keep the pump connected to get the basal rate during the entire time of the exercise.[414]

Don't forget to refill your glucose storages after exercise (see page 167). After strenuous exercise (e.g. a ball game or skiing) you must decrease the basal rate by 0.1 - 0.2 U/hour during the night to avoid hypoglycemia. Try this out yourself and note the blood glucose tests in the logbook for future reference if faced with a similar situation.

Nighttime pump?

Some feel that the pump has obvious advantages during the night but that multiple injections are better during the day. If you look at the insulin level in the blood it will be slightly higher at night and especially early in the morning, when using a pump (see figure on page 104). This is an advantage. During the day, in between meals, the insulin level is slightly higher with a pump, which is not desirable since it will increase your need to eat snacks and that can contribute to a weight gain.

You should not hesitate to try connecting the pump in the evening, letting it stay in place during the night, and disconnecting it in the morning. During

In the winter when it's cold you must keep the pump close to your body. The tubing is very thin and no part of it must be outside the clothing, or it will easily freeze. It may be a bit awkward to take the bolus dose but since the insulin can't be allowed to freeze, you must protect it from low temperatures.

the day you can use a pen injector or syringes for premeal bolus doses. Talk to your diabetes doctor if this sounds appealing.

Is the pump disturbing?

You must carry your insulin pump 24 hours a day. "How do you sleep with it?" many ask. You will be surprised how quickly you get used to wearing the pump at night. Some people who lie quite still put the pump besides or under the pillow and wake up in the morning with it still there. Others, who are more restless, find it better to have the pump on a belt or in a pajama pocket. "What do you do with the pump when having intercourse?" was the first question my friends asked me, an 18 year old girl told us. It is easiest to disconnect it for a while if it is disturbing. Making love is also physical exercise and you might do quite well with a little less insulin for a while.

Will I gain weight when I start with the pump?

There is always a risk of gaining weight when your blood glucose improves since you lose less glucose into the urine. You should therefore try to reduce your calory intake when starting with a pump. If you have frequent hypoglycemias you will risk weight gain since you will frequently need to snack. If you start enjoying extra "freedom" like candy and chips you will also gain weight. Talk to your dietitian about how to find a way around these problems. It might be easier to lose weight without an increase in HbA_{1c} if you have an insulin pump because you can then decrease both your food intake and meal bolus doses but still have the basal rate to ensure your basal insulin requirements.

> ### When should I disconnect the pump?
>
> ⇒   In the bath tub
>
> ⇒   In a public bath or swimming pool
>
> ⇒   In a sauna or whirl pool
>
> ⇒   During an X-ray, Cat scan or MRI

Taking a bath or shower

Most pumps can stand some water but you must disconnect them when taking a bath. When taking a shower there is a shower protector to put over the pump, but many prefer to simply disconnect it for a short while. You should also disconnect the pump if you have a sauna since insulin can't take the heat. The heat in a sauna will cause previously injected insulin to be absorbed much more quickly (see page 62). There is a protective waterproof case available which can be used, for example on the beach.

Travel tips

Don't forget to adjust the pump's clock if you travel across time zones. Change the clock to the time of arrival when you get on the plane. Measure blood glucose before each meal and make necessary adjustments of the bolus dose. Always bring extra insulin and an insulin pen or syringes wherever you go. You may need a certificate for customs declaring that you need to wear an insulin pump. The pump does not usually trigger the metal detector at airports. See page 201 for further travel tips.

Pregnancy

Using an insulin pump is an excellent method to obtain blood glucose values close to those of a person without diabetes. With a close to normal blood glucose, the risk of complications during pregnancy decreases to the same levels as for non-diabetic women (see page 187). During the later part of pregnancy it might be difficult to have the pump needle on the distended abdomen. You can instead try the buttocks, the upper part of the thighs or the upper arm. There is an increased risk of ketoacidosis during pregnancy. You should check your blood glucose more often and also change tubing and needle more often (every day with metal needles and every other day with teflon catheters). Contact the hospital immediately if your blood glucose level is high and you have ketones in your urine. Adding a bedtime dose of intermediate-acting insulin (0.2 U/kg) in addition to the normal basal dose delivered by the pump has considerably deceased the risk of ketoacidosis.[278]

Humalog in the pump?

As direct-acting insulin (Humalog) acts more rapidly when taken prior to a meal and more closely mimics the non-diabetic insulin response, it seems logical to try it when using an insulin pump. In a Canadian study regular short-acting insulin and direct-acting insulin were used in insulin pumps during a 3 month double-blind cross-over study.[433] All bolus doses were given immediately before the meals. HbA$_{1c}$ was significantly lower (7.7 % compared to 8.0 %) when using direct-acting insulin but there was no difference in the frequency of hypoglycemia.

One problem when using insulin with an even shorter duration is that your body's depot of insulin will decrease considerably as well. This implies that insulin deficiency symptoms will arise quickly if the pump fails.

In a German study the pump was stopped in the morning in 7 patients.[312] A deterioration in control was defined as an increase in blood glucose of more than 8.3 mmol/L (150 mg/dL), an increase of more than 2.2 mmol/L (40 mg/dL) in 15 min., appearance of ketones in the urine or symptoms of insulin deficiency.

When the subjects used regular short-acting insulin the deterioration occurred at a mean of 386 min (range 135 - 510 min) while the mean was 251 min (range 45 - 380 min) when direct-acting insulin was used. In other words one can compare a pump stoppage of about 4 hours with direct-acting insulin compared to about 6 hours with regular short-acting insulin. However, notice that variability is great, meaning that the individual differences are considerable.

Some patients have already tested direct-acting insulin in their pumps and many like it. However, if you develop symptoms shortly after the pump stops you are probably better off using regular short-acting insulin.

When using direct-acting insulin in the pump you may need to lower the bolus doses since the bolus doses of regular insulin you previously used supplied part of the basal insulin, overlapping with the next meal as well. To compensate for this you may need to increase the basal rate instead.

The onset of action with a premeal bolus dose of Humalog may be to rapid in certain situations, like when eating a meal that digests slower (like pasta or pizza), or a longer dinner with may courses like when on conference. You can the try by taking the bolus dose after the meal. If you have a pump that can deliver the dose more slowly ("square wave bolus") this is an ideal solution in these situations. You can use it even if you have problems with gastroparesis (slower emptying of the stomach due to diabetic neuropathy, see page 212) (see the diet chapter on page 145 for further advice on the use of Humalog).

An insulin pump will enable you to fine tune your insulin doses and will give you more "horsepower under the hood" to take care of your diabetes. However, it will demand greater knowledge and attention to make it work well just like a stronger and faster car. If you use it correctly an insulin pump is a very good tool and a powerful support on your long diabetes journey.

Side effects of insulin treatment

Pain

If an injection is extra painful you have probably hit a nerve or a tactile organ (see ill. on page 91). If you can stand the pain you can readily inject the insulin, otherwise you must pierce the skin once again.

Insulin leakage

It is not uncommon for a drop of insulin to come out on the skin after withdrawing the needle. Two to three drops from a pen needle contains approximately one unit of insulin (100 U/ml). In one study on children and adolescents with diabetes 68% encountered leakage of insulin after injections during one week. Twenty-three percent of the injections were followed by leakage of up to 18% of injected dose (2 units of an intended dose of 11 units).[376] It may be difficult to avoid insulin leaking, but the risk is smaller if you lift a skin fold and inject at a 45° angle (even if you use an 8 mm needle). Try to inject more slowly. You can also try to withdraw the needle halfway and then wait 20 seconds before withdrawing it completely. Earlier the standard advise was to stretch the skin sideways when injecting to avoid this problem, but this is not a good idea because you instead risk an intramuscular injection.

Blocked needle

Sometimes the needle will be blocked when you inject long- or intermediate-acting insulin. This can be caused by the crystals in the insulin that aggregate. It seems to depend on how quickly you inject the insulin. Try injecting more slowly or even more rapidly. The risk increases when reusing the needles as remaining insulin may crystallize inside the needle barrel.

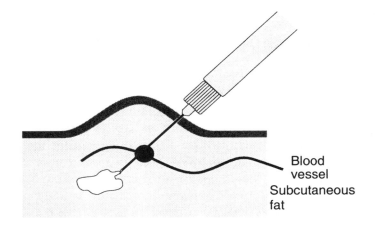

Blood vessel

Subcutaneous fat

If you penetrate a superficial blood vessel with the needle there may be a bleeding. A bleeding under the skin will feel like a small bubble, which is often bluish in color.

Bruises after injections

If you penetrate a superficial blood vessel in the subcutaneous fat a small bleeding may arise. The blood vessels in the subcutaneous fat however are so small that there is no risk that insulin will be injected directly into the vessel. It will feel like a small bubble under the skin that sometimes is bluish in color. Such a bleeding is quite harmless and is absorbed completely after some time.

Fat pads

Fat pads (lipohypertrophies) contain both fibrous and fat tissue.[397] They are caused by insulin's effect of stimulating growth of fat tissue. This is a common problem when you don't vary your injection sites frequently enough. A child usually wants to prick the skin where it hurts the least, resulting in injections too close together. It is important to carefully explain this and to help find a system for rotating the injections sites effectively. Younger children (less than 10 - 12 years of age) should have a parent helping them with 1 - 2 injections per day and then preferably inject at places that the child might have difficulties in reaching, such as the buttocks (see "Where do I inject the insulin?" on page 92).

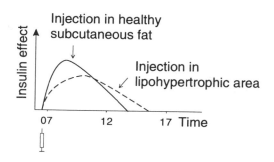

Insulin will be absorbed slower if you inject in an area with fat pads (lipohypertrophy).

Reusing needles causes blunting which increases the microtrauma of repeated injections. This may contribute to increased lipohypertrophy by build-up of fibrous tissue from the release of local growth factors.[378]

Injections in fat pads will usually result in a slower absorption of insulin.[242,431] An area with lipohypertrophy should be left alone for a couple of weeks. One way to accomplish this can be to use an indwelling catheter (Insuflon, see page 100) with which the injection sites can be actively rotated. Another way is to use a guide with a rotation scheme, designed with holes or sectors for different days of the week.[151]

Remember that insulin will have a quicker action of you inject it in an area free from lipohypertrophy. You may have to lower the dose to avoid hypoglycemia.

Redness after injections

Redness, sometimes with itching, that occurs immediately or within hours of an insulin injection can be due to an allergy towards the insulin or a preservative. This type of reaction will usually subside after some years as you continue with insulin treatment.[313] Inform your doctor if you have prob-

Insulin causes the subcutaneous tissue to grow if you often inject into the same spot. You will get a "fat pad" (lipohypertrophy) in the skin that feels and looks like a bump.

lems with redness after injections. There is a special skin test available to find out if you are allergic to the insulin or the preservative. There is often an increased level of insulin antibodies in the blood (see below) as well. If problem with redness continue, adding a small amount of cortisone to the insulin usually has a good effect.[262] A generalized allergic reaction after insulin injection is very rare.[81]

Allergy towards nickel in pen and syringe needles can cause redness after injections. The needles are covered with a layer of silicone lubricant. If you are allergic to nickel you should not use the needles more than once as the silicone layer wears off and the nickel will come in closer contact with the skin. Needles on syringes have a thicker silicone layer since they need to penetrate the rubber membrane of the bottle when drawing up insulin, thereby being more appropriate if you have a nickel allergy. You can take a skin test to see if you are allergic to nickel. You will usually react to nickel in other materials as well, for example ear-rings, belt buckles or wrist watches.

EMLA®-creme (a topical anesthetic used for venepuncture or when replacing indwelling catheters) can cause an allergic redness that looks very much like an allergy against the adhesive.

Insulin antibodies

The body will produce antibodies against foreign substances. Insulin antibodies with porcine and bovine insulin were common. With the use of human insulin it is not common to have high enough levels of antibodies to cause problems. Insulin antibodies work by binding insulin when there is a high level of free insulin, e.g. after a meal bolus injection.[17] When there is a low level of free insulin, e.g. during the night, they release insulin.[17] In this way the insulin concentration in your blood will be levelled off in an unfortunate manner. When you want a high level of insulin after a meal it will be lowered (resulting in high blood glucose) and when you want a low level in the blood during the night you will instead have too much insulin (resulting in hypoglycemia). One can say that with high levels of insulin antibodies you will produce long-acting insulin on your own.

One possible method to lessen these problems is to give a fairly large dose of short-acting insulin in the morning to "saturate" the insulin antibodies. During the day you give smaller and smaller doses of short-acting insulin prior to meals. At bedtime give only a small dose of insulin to lessen the risk of nighttime hypoglycemia.

Switching to direct-acting insulin (Humalog) substantially decreased the level of antibodies and problems with early morning hypoglycemia in a case report.[244] Apparently, the structural differences between regular short-acting and direct-acting insulin molecules prevented Humalog from binding to the human insulin antibodies.

You can measure how much of the total amount of insulin which is bound to antibodies with a blood test. Normally this level is approximately 6 % but we have seen values above 90 % in cases where the patient has had especially difficult problems. Insulin antibodies can be very troublesome but usually the negative effects will slowly subside after several years even if you have measurable levels of antibodies.

Lipoatrophy

Lipoatrophy is manifested as a cavity in the subcutaneous tissue. The reason for its development is somewhat unclear. Lipoatrophy usually does not appear in areas where you have given very frequent injections. It is instead believed to be an immunologic reaction towards insulin in which subcutaneous tissue is broken down.[313] Patients with lipoatrophy often have high levels of insulin antibodies. You can treat the cavities by injecting insulin along the edges. This will cause the formation of new "fat pads" and eventually the cavities will disappear.

Insulin edema

Sometimes you can get a local or generalized edema when you quickly improve the glycemic control. This is caused by a temporary accumulation of fluid in the body and usually subsides spontaneously over a period of days to weeks with continued good glycemic control.[364] In severe cases, ephedrine has been used successfully.[200]

Adjusting insulin doses

Distribution of insulin doses

When starting with subcutaneous injections at the onset of diabetes we mostly use a multiple injection treatment. The total dose is often as high as 1.5 - 2 units/kg/day (0.7 - 0.9 units/pound/day) the first days, but then quickly declines. Smaller children are more sensitive to insulin and usually need fewer units/kg. Insulin dosages are very individual and two children of the same age often need quite different doses.

Insulin is adjusted in relation to the carbohydrate content of the meal. Before breakfast higher doses of insulin are needed in relation to the size of the meal. This is due partly to increased levels of growth hormone (dawn phenomenon) and partly to waning of the bedtime insulin. Besides, breakfast usually contains a greater proportion of carbohydrates than the other meals (e.g. from juice, bread, cereals).

Multiple injection treatment

Meal	Type of insulin	% of 24 h. dose
Breakfast	Short-acting	20 - 25
Lunch	"	15 - 20
Dinner	"	15 - 20
Evening meal	"	10 - 15
Bedtime	NPH insulin	20 - 30

2-dose treatment

Meal	Type of insulin	% of 24 h. dose
Breakfast	Short-acting	20 - 25
	Intermediate-acting	35 - 40
Dinner	Short-acting	10 - 15
	Intermediate-acting	25 - 30

The predinner intermediate-acting insulin can be given with the evening meal or before bedtime if one prefers a 3-dose treatment.

Many things need to be balanced in your body to keep the blood glucose level steady. It isn't easy to make all the pieces fit and many times it is difficult to figure out what went wrong. One must accept that there is not always a good explanation for why the blood glucose level was high or low at a given time.

Increase the dose?

Decrease the dose?

How much does insulin lower the blood glucose level?

The actual blood glucose lowering effect of a given insulin dose depends on many factors; the meal size, the amount of insulin taken earlier in the day, the level of stress and so on. A dose of 0.1 unit/kg (0.5 units/10 pounds) body weight will give a maximal blood glucose lowering effect and extra doses in the home should never exceed this amount as it will only increase the risk of hypoglycemia after a couple of hours.

One unit of insulin given between meals will lower the blood glucose with about 1 mmol if you weigh 70 - 80 kg and about 2 mmol if you weigh 30 - 40 kg (20 mg/dL if you weigh 150 - 170 pounds and 35 mg/dL if you weigh 65 - 90 pounds). Another way of counting is to divide 1500 ("1500 Rule") by your daily insulin dose in units and you will have the blood glucose lowering effect of one unit in mg/dL.[116] Divide 83 by your daily insulin dose to find the answer in mmol/L (see key fact frame to the right). With Humalog it has been suggested to use 1800 (100 with mmol/L) instead as this insulin

How much does 1 unit lower the blood glucose level?

Units/24 hours	Short-acting Regular	Direct-acting Humalog
20	4.2 mmol/L	5.0 mmol/L
30	2.8 mmol/L	3.3 mmol/L
40	2.1 mmol/L	2.5 mmol/L
50	1.7 mmol/L	2.0 mmol/L
60	1.4 mmol/L	1.7 mmol/L
70	1.2 mmol/L	1.4 mmol/L
80	1.0 mmol/L	1.3 mmol/L
90	0.9 mmol/L	1.1 mmol/L

The figures are from the "1500 Rule" for regular short-acting insulin [107,116] (divide 1500 by daily insulin dose for mg/dL, 83 for mmol/L) and the "1800 Rule" for direct-acting Humalog [415] (divide 1800 by daily insulin dose for mg/dl, 100 for mmol/L).

You can try using this table if you for instance want to increase the premeal dose because of a high blood glucose reading. If your child usually takes 35 units/day and has a blood glucose of 12 mmol/L (before the meal, an extra dose of 2 units will lower the blood glucose level an additional 5 mmol/L. In the same way you can subtract units form the pre-meal dose if the blood glucose level is low.

Units/24 hours	Short-acting Regular	Direct-acting Humalog
20	75 mg/dL	90 mg/dL
30	50 mg/dL	60 mg/dL
40	38 mg/dL	45 mg/dL
50	30 mg/dL	36 mg/dL
60	25 mg/dL	30 mg/dL
70	21 mg/dL	26 mg/dL
80	19 mg/dL	23 mg/dL
90	17 mg/dL	20 mg/dL

Questions before taking insulin

① What is my blood glucose level?

② What am I going to eat? More or less food than usual, higher or lower sugar content in the meal?

③ What am I going to do after the meal? Physical activity, normal work or school, relaxation?

④ What happened last time I was in the same situation? Check your log book!

lowers the blood glucose level quicker.[415] See table on this page.

The instructions for adjusting insulin doses in this chapter are primarily applicable to multiple injection treatment even if many of the principals can be applied even when using 2- or 3-dose treatments. If you are in the remission phase (honeymoon phase) and produce insulin of your own, you should reduce the recommended doses (see page 138).

❶ Temporary changes of insulin doses

With temporary changes I mean changes that you do based upon your permanent everyday dosage. Don't "hunt" high blood glucose readings. If you change your permanent insulin doses on a daily basis according to the immediate blood glucose reading you will soon find it impossible to identify which dose actually does what. The blood glucose can swing up and down like a rollercoaster, resulting in many and often severe hypoglycemias without your understanding why.[36] Many times you know the reason for a temporary high or low blood glucose reading, but sometimes things go wrong without an obvious explanation. It is then best to wait until the next meal before taking extra insulin in order to see if the blood glucose is still high.

If I eat more or less than usual?

When you are accustomed to how the size of a meal relates to your individual insulin dose you are often able to determine the size of the meal by eye. If you

---

When does insulin have effect?

Dose	Effect when?
Direct-acting:	
Before meal	That meal
Short-acting:	
Before breakfast	Until lunch
Before lunch	Until dinner
Before dinner	Until the evening meal
Before evening meal	Until midnight
Intermediate-acting:	
At bedtime 10 PM (multiple inj. treatment)	During the night until breakfast
2-dose treatment: In the morning	Lunch and afternoon
Afternoon	Evening and night
Long-acting:	
At dinner-time	During the night and the morning thereafter
Morning	Afternoon, evening and part of the night

Temporary changes of the premeal insulin dose, e.g. when infected

1 - 2 E implies changing the dose by 1 unit for a child (premeal dose of < 10 U) and 2 units for a teenager or adult (premeal dose of > 10 U). The time schedule applies to regular short-acting insulin (not Humalog). It is modified from reference.[192]

Blood test before meal	Measure / Change in dose
< 3 mmol/L < 55 mg/dL	1) Take 10 g of glucose (1/3 ounce, 3 dextrose tablets) or 1 glass of sweet juice (see table on page 49). 2) Wait 10 - 15 min. before eating anything else to allow glucose to pass into the blood stream. 3) Take the insulin just prior to the meal. 4) The dose might need to be decreased by 1 - 2 units.
3 - 8 mmol/L 55-145 mg/dL	Take your ordinary dose
8 - 11 mmol/L 145 - 200 mg/dL	1) Increase the dose with 1 - 2 U or skip drinking milk with the meal. 2) Take the insulin at least 30 min. before you eat.
11 - 14 mmol/L 200 - 250 mg/dL	1) Increase the dose with 1 - 2 U or skip drinking milk. 2) Take the insulin at least 45 min. before you eat.
14 - 20 mmol/L 250 - 360 mg/dL	1) Increase the dose by 2 - 4 U and skip drinking milk. 2) Take the insulin 45 - 60 min. before you eat or wait until the blood glucose has been normalized before you eat.
> 20 mmol/L	1) Increase the dose by 0.1 U/kg (0.5 U/10 pounds) body weight. 2) Same as 14 - 20 mmol/L
Consider for a moment...	Is there any special reason for the blood glucose being high right now? Missed insulin dose? Other illness or fever? Have you eaten extra?
Ketones?	**Contact the diabetes clinic or emergency ward if the child vomits or if his/her general well-being is affected.**

---

eat a little more than you usually do you can take 1 - 2 units extra and if you eat a little less, decrease the dose by 1 - 2 units. Measure your blood glucose 1 - 1.5 hours after the meal to see if you estimated the dose adjustments correctly. Make a note in your logbook for future reference in case you are confronted with a similar situation later on.

A useful "rule of thumb" is that one unit of insulin takes care of approximately 0.1 gram of carbohydrates (one unit/10 g carbohydrate, 3 units/ounce). This applies if you eat something extra between meals which contains mainly glucose (such as cake or ice cream at a party). When eating a mixed meal many other factors influence the blood glucose response. See also page 143.

Physical exercise or relaxation?

If you will be exercising within a few hours after a meal you may need to eat a little extra or decrease your premeal dose by 1 - 2 units (see also the chapter on physical exercise, page 165). If you will be resting more than usual you may need to increase the dose by 1 - 2 units.

Changing the size of a meal to affect blood glucose

Another alternative is to change the size of the meal depending on the actual blood glucose level. If the blood glucose before the meal is increased (8 - 14 mmol/L, 145 - 250 mg/dL) you can drink water instead of milk with the meal or decrease the size of

How much should I change the dose at a time?

If you need to change the insulin dose, for instance when having an infection or while exercising, we recommend the following changes to start out with:

If your ordinary insulin dose is	Change by
1 - 3 units	½ unit
4 - 9 units	1 unit
> 10 units	2 units

Premeal doses (adults)

These suggestions for doses can be used by adults and teenagers after puberty.[34] You can try using the table if you want to regulate your blood glucose level closely for some days, e.g. when trying a new insulin or when ill.

Blood glucose		Units of regular short-acting insulin		
mmol/L	mg/dL	Breakfast	Lunch	Dinner
- 2	< 50	6	4	4
2 - 4.5	50 -100	7	5	5
4.5 - 7	101-150	8	6	6
7 - 9	151-200	9	7	7
9-11	201-250	10	8	8
11-14	251-300	11	9	9
14-18	301-400	12	10	10
> 18	> 400	13	11	11

the meal. If the blood glucose is more than 15 - 20 mmol/L (270 - 360 mg/dL) you can try taking insulin without eating at all. When the blood glucose comes down you can eat the meal or a large snack and then increase the size of the next meal as long as the blood glucose has gone down.

Skipping meals is not something you should do very often. It can be a temporary solution but you should always give afterthought to why your blood glucose was that high. Did you eat too much the hours before or was the previous insulin dose too small?

Your stomach will empty slower when your blood glucose level is high.[360] Because of this you may very well have food remaining in your stomach from the previous meal if your blood glucose level is high. Food will then continue to empty into the intestine (where glucose can be absorbed into the blood) although you have not eaten recently.

Liquids are emptied from the stomach more quickly than solid food.[402] Drink early in the course of the meal if your blood glucose is low. If it is high it is better to wait until the end of the meal before drinking as the stomach will then empty slower. See also "Emptying the stomach" on page 143.

You may feel hungry even if the blood glucose level is high. This is due to a lack of glucose inside the cells which signals hunger. If you eat as usual (without taking extra insulin) despite a high blood glucose level, your blood glucose will remain high.

If this continues for some time it will result in increased insulin resistance, e.g. a given insulin dose will be less effective than usual (see page 69).

N.B. Don't change the amounts of food to regulate your blood glucose level if you are ill.

When you are ill the high blood glucose level is usually caused by an increased need for insulin. You should then increase the insulin doses rather than decreasing food intake (see page 175).

What do I do if the blood glucose level is high?

① You are feeling quite well

A temporary high blood glucose level from time to time is impossible to avoid in every-day-life. A child or adult with diabetes normally does not feel unwell when this happens, nor does it affect long-term diabetes control.

Don't take extra insulin immediately — you will only risk hypoglycemia after a while. A temporary high glucose will usually come down without extra measures. Wait until the next meal and then increase the insulin dose by 1 - 2 units *if the blood glucose level still is high.* Another alternative is to have a little less to eat or to skip the snack.

② High blood glucose before a meal

Instead of increasing the insulin dose you can decrease the size of the meal. You are usually not as hungry when the blood glucose level is high (see "Hungry or full?" on page 150). Drink water instead of milk or juice. If the blood glucose is above 15 - 20 mmol/L (270 - 360 mg/dL) you can try administering the ordinary insulin dose without eating. Begin eating when the blood glucose has decreased to a normal level which usually coincides with snack-time.

③ High blood glucose when going to bed

There is always a risk of nighttime hypoglycemia when you give extra short-acting insulin before going to bed. If you need to give extra insulin in this situation it is better to give direct-acting insulin (Humalog), as the effect of this insulin has generally disappeared before the bedtime insulin has begun to act. If the blood glucose level is high (more than about 12 mmol/L) you can increase the

---

> ### Important
>
> *You should not adjust insulin doses in relation to food quantities "by eye" when ill - see the chapter on illness on page 175.*

dose of bedtime insulin by 1 - 2 units. Check your blood glucose at 2 - 3 AM a couple of times when changing the dose of bedtime insulin to make sure that you are not too high or too low at this time.

④ You are not feeling well (e.g. very hungry, nauseous or vomit)

Check a urine test: **The presence of ketones is a sign of insulin deficiency** (see page 79). If this is the case give an extra dose of short-acting insulin (0.1 U/kg, 0.5 U/10 pounds) to lower the blood glucose and block the production of ketones in the liver (see page 35). Extra insulin should not be administered more frequently than every 2nd or 3rd hour or there is a risk that the insulin effects will add up, resulting in hypoglycemia. If you have access to direct-acting insulin (Humalog) it is preferable to use it in this situation. The very rapid effect of this insulin means there is less risk of overlapping.

If the child is hungry it may be a good idea to give him/her some chewing gum in order to have something in their mouth until the insulin begins to work. Also give something to drink because the child will pass extra urine when the blood glucose is high.

> ### Why didn't my blood glucose turn out the way I expected it?
>
> ➡ Not the same amount of food as usual?
>
> ➡ Was the timing between the meal and the injection correct?
>
> ➡ Recent physical exertion? More exercise than usual?
>
> ➡ Feeling ill, a cold or a fever coming?
>
> ➡ Hypoglycemia with rebound phenomenon?
>
> ➡ Different injection technique than usual? Changed injection site (premeal injection in thigh)?
>
> ➡ Injection into muscle rather than fat?
>
> ➡ Injection in fat pad (lipohypertrophy)?

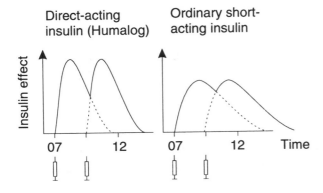

Direct-acting insulin (Humalog)   Ordinary short-acting insulin

Direct-acting insulin is preferred when the blood glucose level is high. You can give an extra dose at snack-time without risking dose overlapping and hypoglycemia, since much of the effect is gone after 2 - 3 hours. Compare with the right chart illustrating ordinary short-acting insulin.

⑤ **The blood glucose level is high at the same time of the day for several days in a row**

Take a blood test 1½ hours after the meal several days in a row:

   If it is > 10 mmol/L ➡ increase by 1 - 2 units.

Change the present premeal dose. It is however important to wait a couple of days between each dosage increase or it will be difficult to see which change led to what.

High blood glucose and ketones

If your blood glucose level repeatedly tests high (15 - 20 mmol/L, 270 - 360 mg/dL) and particularly if you have ketones in the urine (as a sign of insulin deficiency) you need extra insulin.

① Give 0.1 units/kg (0.5 units/10 pounds) of short-acting insulin or preferably direct-acting insulin (Humalog)

② Test the blood glucose level again after 2 - 3 hours.

③ Give another 0.1 units/kg (0.5 units/10 pounds) if the blood glucose level has not decreased.

Do not give short-acting insulin more often than every second hour or you will risk dose overlap, resulting in hypoglycemia after a couple of hours.

Contact your doctor or the hospital if the child vomits or you are the least unsure of how to manage the situation!

❷ Permanent changes of insulin doses

Aim for blood glucose values not below 4.0 mmol/L (70 mg/dL) and not above 10 mmol/L (180 mg/dL) when adjusting insulin doses. See page 84 for recommended levels before and after meals

Basic rules

① You cannot adjust insulin doses while having hypoglycemias. A high blood glucose level could be the result of a rebound phenomenon following a hypoglycemic episode. Begin by decreasing the doses to avoid hypoglycemia before attempting long-term adjustments.

② Symptoms of hypoglycemia should appear at a normal level, i.e. at 3.0 - 3.5 mmol/L (55 - 65 mg/dL). If they first appear when your blood glucose has fallen below 3.0 mmol/L (55 mg/dL) you should meticulously avoid all low blood glucose levels for the next 1 - 2 weeks to improve this situation. If you have hypoglycemic symptoms at levels above 4.0 mmol/L (70 mg/dL) you should wait to eat until the blood glucose has fallen below 3.2 - 3.5 mmol/L (60 - 65 mg/dL). You must "suffer" for 1 - 2 weeks until your symptoms appear at a lower blood glucose level (see pages 40 and 73).

③ Be sure that you eat your usual meal size when you are adjusting insulin doses.

④ Don't change more than one dose at a time. It is otherwise easy to end up in a vicious cycle where you don't know what has caused what. Change the doses by not more than 1 - 2 units at a time (see page 126).

⑤ Wait a couple of days between insulin changes to be able to see more clearly what the outcome is. There is always a depot of insulin in your body and it will take a couple of days before this has reached equilibrium (see "Depot effect" on page 60). Intermediate-acting insulin (e.g. Insulatard, Humatard, Isuhuman Basal) should not be changed more often than 1 - 2 times per week. When using long-acting insulin (Ultratard, Ultralente, Humulin U, Humutard Ultra) you should wait at least one week between dose changes.

⑥ Review blood glucose readings and insulin doses once a day when you have time to sit down and plan preliminary doses for the following day in the logbook. This will lessen the risk of making rash decisions.

⑦ Never take extra insulin on days when you are making adjustments in permanent doses. You will otherwise distort all the information pertaining to the ordinary doses. If you feel that you must administer extra insulin (as when ill) it is better to stop the blood glucose testing for the 24 hour profile. Start over again after a couple of days or a week when you are back to normal doses again.

⑧ For the same reason you should not eat anything extra if you measure a low blood glucose level, between 3 and 4 mmol/L (55 - 70 mg/dL), but feel well. This applies also to the 2 - 3 AM blood glucose test. You want to know the blood glucose values during a night with normal sleep, not when you have been eating. As you have no symptoms you would have slept on without eating if you had not taken the test.

⑨ If you don't understand why the blood glucose reading turned out the way it did, try keeping the same doses for another day or two. Often you will see the pattern better then.

⑩ Do not make large changes of the doses immediately. Change doses less than 10 U by 0.5 - 1 unit at a time and those more than 10 U by 2 units at a time.

Do like this in practice:

Register all blood glucose readings in your logbook, otherwise you can never make an adequate judgement. If you have difficulties remembering to write them down, an "electronic" logbook can be a good alternative. Many blood glucose meters have memories and can be connected to a computer for visualization. In an American study patients who recorded their blood glucose readings in a logbook had better HbA_{1c} values (7.1 % compared to 7.9 %) than those not recording their tests.[55]

Blood glucose before evening meal

When taking the pre-evening meal dose you should aim at having a blood glucose level between 8 - 10 mmol/L (145-180 mg/dL) prior to taking the bedtime dose.

Test before evening meal	Measure
< 5 mmol/L < 90 mg/dL	Decrease the dose by 1 - 2 units
>12-14 mmol/L > 215-250 mg/dL	Increase the dose by 1 - 2 units or eat less for the evening meal.
>18-20 mmol/L > 325-360 mg/dL	Give 1 - 2 units extra and eat less for the evening meal. You can also try taking your regular dose if you eat a very small meal (or skip the meal completely) but then you must check your blood glucose level again before going to bed.

In which order should I change the doses?
(multiple injection treatment)

① Lower the doses to avoid hypoglycemia. Then concentrate on one dose at a time for a couple of days.

② Start by adjusting the dose for the evening meal.

③ Then adjust the bedtime insulin dose

④ Then adjust the breakfast insulin dose

⑤ Then adjust the dose for lunch and dinner

① Low blood glucose levels

If you have a hypoglycemic reaction without an apparent reason (such as exercise or too little food) you should decrease the "responsible" insulin dose the following day (see table on page 47).

② Insulin for evening meal

During the day it is fairly easy to observe the child and see signs of hypoglycemia. At night however, it is much more difficult when everyone is asleep. One alternative is to take a blood glucose test before the parents go to bed, but everybody who has tried this knows that it is not much fun for anyone involved to wake up a child and try to persuade him/her to eat something at this time. A better solution is to try to aim for starting the night with a suitable blood glucose level by taking a blood glucose test before the evening meal and adjusting food and insulin dose thereafter. This system works especially well for younger children and for those going to bed fairly early, as long as they have not had too much physical exercise after the evening meal.

Two units/sandwich is usually an appropriate dose if you have a glass of milk along with the sandwiches for the evening meal.

Studies have shown that blood glucose levels less than 6 mmol/L (110 mg/dL) when going to bed increase the risk for nighttime hypoglycemia.[355] I recommend starting the night with a slightly higher blood glucose level, preferably 8 - 10 mmol/L (145 - 180 mg/dL). You will then have "more glucose to draw from" and you can give a higher dose of bedtime insulin without risk. A higher dose will give a longer duration and therefore has a better effect on the morning blood glucose level (see page 56).

③ Bedtime insulin

The night is long and high blood glucose levels during the night affect HbA_{1c} substantially. It is often difficult to succeed in having the bedtime insulin last until morning. A smaller dose will not only give less insulin effect, but will also last for a shorter period of time.

Many different factors contribute to a high blood glucose level in the morning. Modern insulins used for bedtime injections have their greatest effect early in the night. At the same time the body's insu-

---

Tests to take when adjusting the bedtime dose

The tests will be more representative if your day has been routine, without heavy physical exercise or hypoglycemia. The blood glucose level should be about 8 - 10 mmol/L (145-180 mg/dL) when you take the bedtime dose to ensure a "normal" night.

☞ Blood tests: Before evening meal
Evening at 10 PM
Night at 2 - 3 AM
Morning

☞ Urine tests: Morning (ketones?)

Getting up in the middle of the night to take a test is not much fun. Try to take tests during "normal" nights when you will obtain most information.

Blood glucose testing before bedtime insulin

Younger children will usually allow blood tests and injection of bedtime insulin to be done while they are asleep. On the other hand, giving food to a newly awakened child can be very tricky, especially when the blood glucose is low. It is often more practical to test before eating the evening meal. You can then adjust the amount of food and insulin dose to aim for an optimal blood glucose level to begin the night with.

Test before bedtime insulin		Measure
< 6 mmol/L < 110 mg/dL	⟶	Give a sandwich and milk
6 - 12 mmol/L 110 - 215 mg/dL	⟶	Give the ordinary dose
> 12 mmol/L > 215 mg/dL	⟶	Increase the bedtime dose by 1 - 2 U or give 1 - 2 U of Humalog

Avoid giving extra short-acting insulin (if the blood glucose level is high) along with the bedtime insulin as this increases the risk of a hypoglycemia early in the night. Direct-acting insulin (Humalog) is better in this situation as the peak effect is over before the action of the bedtime dose has begun.

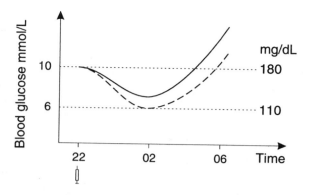

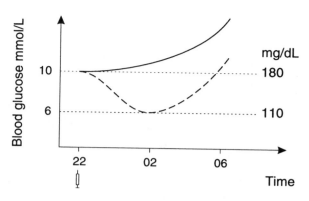

The blood glucose level during the night usually assumes a "hammock-like" curve when you use insulin of NPH type for bedtime injections (e.g. Insulatard, Humulin NPH, Isuhuman Basal). This insulin will have its greatest effect 4 - 5 hours after the injection. If you increase the dose, the morning blood glucose will be lower (dashed line) but the risk of nighttime hypoglycemia will increase. The blood glucose level at 2 AM should therefore be used as an indicator when adjusting the bedtime insulin dose.[62] Ideally you should aim for a blood glucose of about 10 mmol/L (180 mg/dL) when you take the bedtime insulin and then let it fall about 4 mmol/l (70 mg/dL) to reach 6 mmol/L (110 mg/dL) at 2 AM which usually is the lowest point during the night.

If the blood glucose level is below 7 - 8 mmol/L (125-145 mg/dL) when taking the bedtime insulin you should be prepared for problems with nighttime hypoglycemia with the same dose of bedtime insulin (it will still be lowered about 4 mmol/L (70 mg/dL). If you decrease the bedtime dose the morning blood glucose level will be higher. In this situation it is therefore better to eat something extra before going to bed.

lin sensitivity is increased between 12 PM and 2 AM compared to 6 - 8 AM,[62] (due to the nighttime secretion of growth hormone). Combined these factors result in an increased risk of hypoglycemia at 2 - 3 AM.

Later in the night the effect of the bedtime insulin decreases at the same time that the insulin sensitivity also decreases due to the dawn phenomenon (see page 44), causing the blood glucose to rise in the morning. Nighttime hypoglycemia followed by rebound phenomenon (so called Somogyi phenomenon) can further contribute to a high morning glucose (see charts on page 45 and 132).

In adults on multiple injection treatment the risk of nighttime hypoglycemia seems to follow a different pattern, probably due to a lower degree of hormonal activity. In one study [38] only 30 % of the nighttime hypoglycemia would have been detected at a 3 AM blood glucose test. In another study [406] 29% of the patients had nighttime hypoglycemia (< 3.0 mmol/L, 54 mg/dL) but none of these

A small difference in insulin dose can cause a large difference in the blood glucose level due to an either/or-effect. The insulin sensitivity increases (decreased insulin resistance) early in the night, causing the blood glucose to fall, but only if the blood glucose is within normal levels for non-diabetic persons, below about 7 mmol/L (125 mg/dL, dashed line). If the blood glucose increases early in the night, the insulin resistance will increase as well and the bedtime insulin dose will not be sufficient in lowering the blood glucose (solid line).

occurred between 1.30 and 3.30 AM This suggests a longer time to peak action of the bedtime insulin (of NPH type) which was taken at 11 PM. The con-

Nighttime blood glucose testing

Take a test when you expect the lowest values. This may differ from person to person. See page 76 for suggestions on times for testing.

① **Testing for a 24-hour chart**
If you have something to eat the entire night's blood glucose values will be affected and the chart will be difficult to interpret. Eat only if the blood glucose level is less than about 3 mmol/L (55 mg/dL) or you are/your child is not feeling well. If it is above 3 mmol/L (55 mg/dL) it is better to take another test ½ - 1 hour later to see in which direction the level is heading.

② **Testing because of actual risk of nighttime hypoglycemia**
If you/your child has not eaten well or has exercised more than usual during the afternoon/evening you should take precautions to avoid hypoglycemia during the night. Give something to eat if the blood glucose level is < 5 - 6 mmol/L (90-110 mg/dL) and you can sleep on safely.

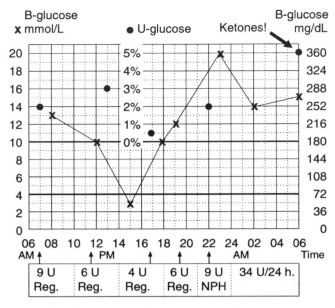

9 U Reg. | 6 U Reg. | 4 U Reg. | 6 U Reg. | 9 U NPH | 34 U/24 h.

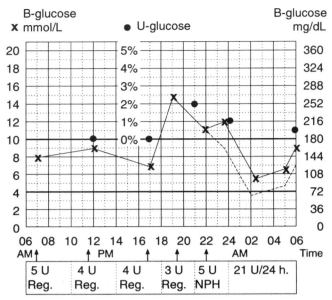

5 U Reg. | 4 U Reg. | 4 U Reg. | 3 U Reg. | 5 U NPH | 21 U/24 h.

The blood glucose level rises early in the night and is still high in the morning after a night with high values. With a large insulin dose for breakfast the blood glucose level will fall before lunch, but you will risk hypoglycemia in the afternoon.

Start by decreasing the lunch dose to avoid the afternoon hypoglycemia. Then increase the pre-evening meal insulin dose (or perhaps give less to eat), increase the bedtime insulin (remember to check the blood glucose at 02-03 AM!) and adjust the dose before breakfast when you have obtained a better blood glucose level during the night.

The dawn phenomenon (see page 44) contributes to a rising blood glucose level during the later part of the night. If you increase the insulin dose for bedtime you will have a lower morning blood glucose level (dashed line) but you will also increase the risk of a nighttime hypoglycemia. You must therefore check the blood glucose at 2-3 AM when adjusting the bedtime insulin dose. Compare with the graphs on the top of page 131.

clusion from this study was that early night hypoglycemia always is proceeded by a bedtime glucose reading of < 7.5 mmol/L (135 mg/dL) and that early morning hypoglycemia does not occur if the blood glucose level when wakening up is > 5.5 mmol/L (100 mg/dL).

If the blood glucose level early in the night is higher than in a non-diabetic person (about 7 mmol/L, 125 mg/dL) the blood glucose level as such will cause insulin sensitivity to decrease (increased insulin resistance). This will result in that the increased insulin sensitivity, which is present at a normal blood glucose level, will not occur.[62] This is an important part of the explanation why it is so difficult to adjust the bedtime insulin dose. You will have a sort of either/or-effect when it will be practically impossible to find "the correct" insulin dose.

Either...
If the insulin dose is high enough to bring the blood glucose down to about 7 mmol/L (125 mg/dL) or less early in the night the insulin sensitivity increases and there will be a risk of a nighttime hypoglycemia.

Or...
If the insulin dose is too small causing the blood glucose to increase above 7 mmol/L (125 mg/dL), the insulin sensitivity will decrease, and the blood glucose will be even higher later in the night and in the morning.

In practise the blood glucose level will vary a great deal from morning to morning due to this either/or-effect. The dawn phenomenon on the other hand is mostly constant from night to night. The variability in morning blood glucose despite the same insulin dose is caused by how quickly the injected dose of bedtime insulin is absorbed in combination with a waning insulin effect early in the morning.[62]

The only way to know for sure what the blood glucose level is in the middle of the night is to take a test. Take it at 2-3 AM if you use NPH insulin (e.g. Insulatard, Humulin NPH, Isuhuman Basal), at 3-4 AM when using intermediate-acting Lente insulin like Monotard or Humutard and at 4-6 AM when using long-acting Lente insulin (e.g. Ultratard, Ultralente, Humulin U).

The difficult, often impossible balance of bedtime insulin

Either...

You must increase the bedtime insulin dose to lower the blood glucose level in the morning.....

Or...

... but if you increase it too much the insulin sensitivity early in the night will increase when the blood glucose is lowered and there is a risk of hypoglycemia. This will happen not only if you increase the bedtime dose too much, but also if you forget to decrease the bedtime insulin when needed, e.g. after a game of football or when you have had less to eat for your evening meal than usual. See the text for a strategy to address this "either/or" dilemma.

How do I proceed?

Increase the night dose by 1 - 2 units at a time until the blood glucose level at 2 - 3 AM approaches 6 - 8 mmol/L (110 - 145 mg/dL). The blood glucose level should be at least 6 mmol/L (110 mg/dL) when you take the 2 - 3 AM test to avoid night time hypoglycemia. A level of 6 mmol/L as such is not disturbingly low but you should have some leeway as the blood glucose level another night might very well be 1 - 2 mmol/L (20 - 40 mg/dL) lower, even if you take the same insulin doses.

High blood glucose levels in the morning - what can I do?

The problem is that the bedtime insulin injection will often not last until morning. You must increase the dose to make it last longer (see page 56). To be able to do that without sustaining nighttime hypoglycemia you must start out the night with a slightly higher blood glucose than usual, tentatively 10 - 12 mmol/L (180 - 215 mg/dL). Try this:

① Lower the pre-evening meal dose until the blood glucose level is 10 - 12 mmol/L (180-215 mg/dL) at the time you take your bedtime insulin.

② Increase the bedtime insulin dose slowly. However, the blood glucose at 2 - 3 AM, should always be at least 6 mmol/L (110 mg/dL).

③ You might have to accept that the morning blood glucose level is still slightly high, assuming that you/the child feel(s) well and the HbA$_{1c}$ is acceptable.

④ You can also try using another insulin with a slightly longer (intermediate-acting lente: Monotard, Humutard) or much longer (long-acting lente: Ultratard, Ultralente, Humulin U, Humutard Ultra) duration. With intermediate lente the lowest blood glucose level will usually be somewhat later, often around 3 - 4 AM.
Long-acting lente is very long-acting and sometimes can give problems with hypoglycemia the next day, in the morning or even afternoon. Therefore it needs to be injected much earlier, preferably at the same time as the pre-dinner dose (at 4 - 5 PM), to have a good effect during the night. If the dose is large it is best to split it up into one dose before breakfast and one before dinner.

Try giving the bedtime insulin of NPH type (e.g. Insulatard, Humulin NPH, Isuhuman Basal) as late as possible to ensure that it lasts until morning. Giving it at 10 PM usually works well for most families. You must of course consider your family routines. It is not recommended that parents sit up at night, waiting for the time to give the bedtime insulin. If the child has an indwelling catheter (Insuflon, see page 100), one can easily give the bedtime insulin when he/she is asleep.

Blood glucose before lunch

The pre-breakfast dose of regular short-acting insulin dose is adjusted with the help of the test results before lunch. With direct-acting insulin you can use readings taken at snack-time.

Blood glucose	Measure
< 4 mmol/L < 70 mg/dL	Decrease the breakfast dose by 1 - 2 units
> 8 mmol/L > 145 mg/dL	Increase the breakfast dose by 1 - 2 units
> 12 - 20 mmol/L > 220-360 mg/dL	Think! Is there any special reason that the blood glucose level is high at this moment? Missed breakfast dose? Feeling ill?
Hypoglycemia between breakfast and lunch?	Decrease the breakfast dose by 1 - 2 units

You can get extra information by measuring the blood glucose level at the mid-morning snack (see glucose chart below).

When do I take the pre-breakfast insulin?

It is especially important to take the insulin some time before breakfast if you use ordinary short-acting insulin. This may be difficult to accomplish in a stressed morning routine. Measure your blood glucose first thing after waking up and adjust the time to eat. Use this schedule to start from when you experiment with finding your individual times:

Blood glucose level mmol/L mg/dL		Insulin at breakfast	
		Ordinary short-acting insulin	Direct-acting insulin
< 3	< 55	just before	after the meal
3-5	55-90	15 min. before	just before
5-8	90-145	30 min. before	just before
8-12	145-215	45 min. before	10 min. before
> 12	> 215	60 min. before	20 min. before

If you still have a high morning blood glucose level (more than 10 mmol/L, 180 mg/dL) you might need to try another bedtime insulin with a longer duration (e.g. Monotard/Humutard or Ultratard/Ultra Lente/Humulin U/Humutard Ultra). See key fact frame above. Discuss this with your doctor or diabetes nurse.

Blood glucose levels at night

If you are taking tests for a 24 hour profile to adjust permanent insulin doses, you should not eat anything if the blood glucose is above 3 mmol/l and you are not showing any hypoglycemic symptoms. The child would not have woken up if you had not taken the test and you are interested in how an ordinary night at home looks. Instead of eating, check the blood glucose once again after 1 - 2 hours and don't forget to check the morning blood glucose as well. This will be a tiresome night but you will learn a lot about how your child's diabetes works. Check also the urine for glucose and ketones in the morning to be able to compare with the blood glucose levels that you have measured during the night. Don't forget to register all tests in the logbook.

High blood glucose in the morning?

① Insufficient insulin effect late at night due to the dawn phenomenon (see page 44) or too low dose of bedtime insulin?

② Rebound phenomenon after nighttime hypoglycemia?

③ Too much to eat for the evening meal?

④ Too high blood glucose level in the evening?

⑤ Forgot to mix the bedtime insulin thoroughly?

Nighttime hypoglycemia

The first thing to do is to decrease the bedtime insulin dose. See page 45 for further instructions.

④ Insulin for breakfast

It is more difficult to obtain a good blood glucose level during the night than during the day. Ideally you want to start out the morning with a normal blood glucose level. Sometimes you will have to accept that the blood glucose level rises early in the morning as long as it can be lowered adequately before lunch and as long as HbA_{1c} is acceptable.

Morning tests

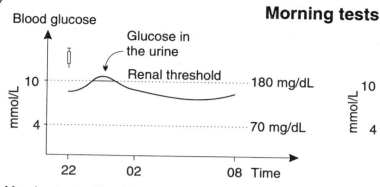

Morning tests: Blood glucose 8 mmol/L (145 mg/dL)
Urine glucose 0.1%
Ketones 0

When the blood glucose level rises above the renal threshold glucose passes into the urine. Since the blood glucose level is low in the morning you know that it has been higher earlier during the night. You must know your renal threshold to be able to interpret urine tests correctly (see page 78).

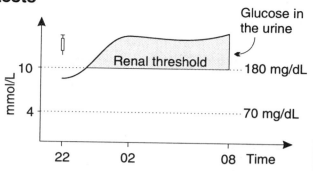

Morning tests: Blood glucose 14 mmol/L (250 mg/dL)
Urine glucose 5%
Ketones ++

The blood glucose level has been high during most of the night due to a lack of insulin and large amounts of glucose has passed into the urine. The ketones in the urine are caused by a lack of glucose inside the cells.

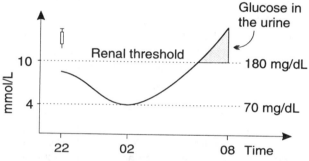

Morning tests: Blood glucose 14 mmol/L (250 mg/dL)
Urine glucose 0.5%
Ketones 0

The blood glucose level has been adequate during most of the night since the urine glucose concentration is low. Only blood glucose testing during the night can determine how low the blood glucose level actually has been What you do know from the urine test is that the blood glucose level only has been above the renal threshold for a short while since the urine glucose concentration is low.

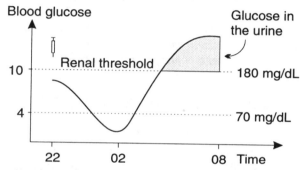

Morning tests: Blood glucose 14 mmol/L (250 mg/dL)
Urine glucose 5%
Ketones ++

There has been a rebound phenomenon after hypoglycemia in the night. Ketones were passed into the urine during the hypoglycemia (starvation ketones) and glucose was passed into the urine when the blood glucose level was high. The morning tests are exactly the same as in the example above. If you misread this, believing that the blood glucose has been high all night, you may very well increase the insulin dose instead. The blood glucose level would then fall even lower the following night, giving an even more pronounced rebound phenomenon. This type of reaction is called the Somogyi phenomenon (see page 44). The only way to distinguish it from the pattern above is to check a 2 - 3 AM blood glucose.

The insulin dose for breakfast generally needs to be slightly higher in relation to the size of the helpings as breakfast generally contains more carbohydrates than other meals (see "Distribution of insulin doses" on page 123). The breakfast injection usually contains the largest premeal dose of the day.

Just as all fingerprints are different all insulin dosages are different. It is not that strange if you think about it — we are all very different as individuals and insulin must be adjusted to fit the individual life-style.

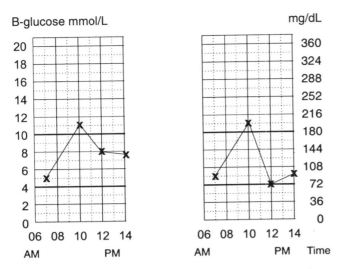

If your blood glucose readings look like the chart on the left you can try increasing the breakfast dose by 1 - 2 units. If the blood glucose level decreases before lunch like on the chart on the right you will have problems with hypoglycemia if you increase the prebreakfast insulin dose. It is better to take it earlier, i.e. 45 min. before breakfast, if you usually have a 30 min. interval. If you use direct-acting insulin you can try taking the injection 15 min. before instead of just prior to breakfast.

⑤ Insulin for lunch and dinner

Measure the blood glucose level before and 1½ hours after the meal. The same strategy is applicable both for lunch and dinner doses. If lunch at school is very early (10.30 to 11.00 AM) the dose can be divided into two, where one dose is taken with the early lunch and one with a larger snack in the afternoon.

Using direct-acting insulin (Humalog)

The action of this insulin will begin much quicker than regular short-acting insulin (see page 55). This means that you can administer it just before meals and still get a good insulin effect when the blood glucose starts rising, provided it is given as an abdominal injection. On the other hand, as the effect will wane as early as 2 - 3 hours after injection, there may be a lack of insulin before the next meal. Because of this you need to take an injection of intermediate-acting (e.g. Insulatard, Humulin NPH, Isuhuman Basal) or long-acting insulin (Ultratard, Ultralente, Humulin U, Humutard Ultra) in the morning to adequately cover your need for basal insulin between meals.

When more than 2 - 3 hours have passed since the previous meal, the liver will supply glucose to pre-

When can I use direct-acting insulin for premeal injections?

Since the effect of direct-acting insulin is too short to cover between meals you must have a basal insulin on board as well, i.e. another type of insulin that covers the basal need of insulin between meals. You can try using direct-acting insulin (Humalog) in the following situations:

⇒ If you take 2 injections of intermediate- or long-acting insulin as basal insulin (see page 137).

⇒ If you are in the remission phase (honeymoon phase) your pancreas will produce insulin on its own in amounts sufficient to cover the basal needs between meals.

⇒ If you use an insulin pump it will supply the basal insulin. If you use short-acting insulin in the pump and want to sleep half an hour longer in the morning you can take the pre-breakfast dose with direct-acting insulin in a pen or syringe just prior to eating. This is also a good alternative if the blood glucose before the meal is high.

⇒ If you have insulin antibodies (see page 121) you will produce your own long-acting insulin by binding insulin to the antibodies. You can therefore try replacing your regular short-acting insulin with direct-acting. The structure of this insulin is slightly different and it may give you less problems with antibodies and redness after insulin injections.

vent the blood glucose level from falling too low. A low basal level of insulin is needed to take care of this glucose. If there is no insulin available at all, the counter-regulatory hormones (adrenaline and glucagon, see page 31) will raise the blood glucose level by increasing the output of glucose from the liver even more.

Regular short-acting insulin, when used for premeal injections, covers both the carbohydrate content of the meal and the need for basal insulin until the next meal. When using direct-acting insulin the supply will only have a substantial effect for 2 - 3 hours after the meal. This leads to less need for snacks between main meals (see page 150).

Because of this you will probably have to decrease the size of the premeal doses by about 10 % when starting with Humalog.[309] With the same dose you will increase the risk of hypoglycemia within some hours after the meal, especially if it contained less carbohydrates and more fat, e.g. meat with fat sauce and pasta.[69] In a study where the premeal doses were freely adjusted the number of hypoglycemic reactions decreased by 11 % when injecting Humalog immediately before the meal compared to regular short-acting insulin 30 - 45 minutes before.[18]

You may need to reconsider the composition of some of your meals. Cereal with milk for breakfast will now be quite OK while food that is absorbed slowly like pasta or spaghetti (with a low glycemic index, see page 147), which before may have been covered well by regular short-acting insulin, may give you problems now. With direct-acting insulin the result may be a lowering of the blood glucose level within one hour after the meal, before the glucose in the food has been absorbed into the blood. If you start the meal by drinking something con-

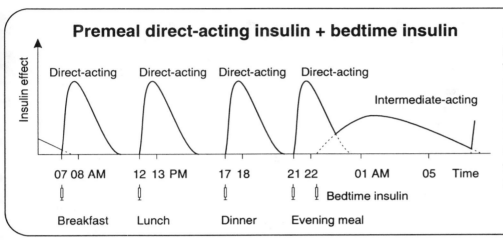

Premeal direct-acting insulin + bedtime insulin

If you replace the ordinary premeal short-acting insulin with direct-acting insulin (Humalog) you will have a better effect with that meal, but there will be a lack of insulin before the next meal as the direct-acting insulin will not last for more than 3 - 4 hours at the most.

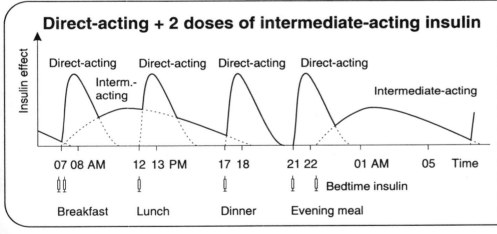

Direct-acting + 2 doses of intermediate-acting insulin

You can take a dose of intermediate-acting insulin (NPH type, e.g. Insulatard, Humulin NPH) for breakfast to attain a better insulin effect before lunch and dinner. It is, however, difficult to get this dose to last until the evening meal without risking too strong an insulin effect at lunch. A 3rd dose of intermediate-acting insulin at lunch may solve the problem.

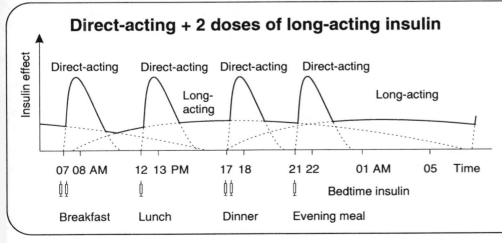

Direct-acting + 2 doses of long-acting insulin

With 2 doses of long-acting insulin/day (at breakfast and dinner) you will have a fairly even level of basal insulin in between meals. You must take the nighttime dose already around 5 PM for it to have its full effect during the night. The time span of long-acting insulin is very individual and you may need to vary the time when taking this dose.

taining glucose, such as a glass of milk or juice, the blood glucose may be prevented from falling. You may also take an injection of regular short-acting insulin with this type of meal while using direct-acting insulin for the other meals.

As the time action of direct-acting insulin is shorter you will need to rely more upon carbohydrates with a high glucose content (dextrose, honey, sugar) to treat hypoglycemia which may occur during the 2 - 3 hours after a meal, even if this happens at bed-time after the evening meal.

Humalog is well suited as an "emergency insulin" in a situation when you quickly need to lower a high blood glucose level, e.g. when you have nausea and ketones. You can take an extra injection at snack-time and still the effect of this dose will be mostly gone 2 hours later when it is time for your next meal. Do not administer more than 0.1 unit/kg (0.5 unit/10 pounds) body weight as an extra dose. If you give injections of regular short-acting insulin with 2 hour-intervals there is a great risk that the effects of the doses will overlap, risking hypoglycemia later on.

Holiday or weekday?

The amount of physical activity is often different when comparing school-days and work-days to week-ends. Often one sleeps in longer on week-ends and the meal schedule may be different. Due to these factors it is often appropriate to have different insulin doses during week-days and week-ends. Make notes in your logbook and try finding a schedule that works well for you.

Exercising or relaxing?

If you practice competitive sports or do hard physical training certain days or evenings you will probably need different doses of insulin, with less insulin for the evening meal and at bedtime on these days (see "Physical exercise" on page 165).

Experiment!

We encourage experimenting with the premeal injections in different situations. Try to avoid terms like permitted or forbidden. The point is to find out what is suitable just for you. Do remember to measure the blood glucose level and register your results in the logbook so that you know what you

Sometimes you may feel hunted by all tests and changes in insulin doses. If this applies to you, take a break for a week or two, taking blood glucose tests only when necessary to avoid hypoglycemia. Make sure that you (and your child) concentrate instead on having as good a time as possible. You can then come back to testing later on with new vigor.

are doing. The worst situation you can find yourself in after trying something new is hypoglycemia or a temporary high blood glucose level. Gradually you will get to know yourself better, finding out which insulin doses your pancreas would have supplied if it had worked as usual. There is a saying that goes: "You can only learn by your own mistakes". Remember that most lessons in life are learned by trial and error!

Insulin adjustments during the remission phase

A couple of weeks after your diabetes onset your insulin doses will probably have been lowered considerably and they will be lowered even further in the weeks to come. If you have a temporary high blood glucose level there is no reason to worry. Don't take extra insulin. Wait instead and check it again before the next meal — it probably will have normalized on its own.

In practise you can do as follows during the first weeks after diagnosis:

① **Hypoglycemia:**
The next day lower the "responsible" dose of insulin (see page 129) by one unit (2 if the dose is more than 10 units) if you or the child/teenager had hypoglycemia, with a blood glucose lower than 3.5 mmol/L (65 mg/dL), and you are not sure what the cause was (e.g. too little to eat or more exercise than usual).

② **Low blood glucose readings:**
Decrease the insulin in the same way as above if the blood glucose is 4 mmol (70 mg/dL) or less at the same time of the day for 2 days in a row (even if there are no symptoms of hypoglycemia).

③ **Hypoglycemia before a meal**
During the remission phase you may need to shorten the recommended interval between the injection and eating to 15 - 20 min when using regular short-acting insulin.[309] If you switch to Humalog it is advisable to decrease the dose by 10 % as the profile of this insulin more closely follows the blood glucose rise after a meal.[309]

When the daily insulin dose is less than 0.5 units/kg (0.2 units/pound) of body weight the individual has entered the remission phase (honeymoon phase, see page 68). The duration of this phase varies widely among individuals. It is important to immediately increase the insulin doses if the blood glucose level rises, e.g. when having an infection. Check blood glucose levels before each meal and increase the dose by one unit at a time (2 if the dose is more than 10 units) if you find that the blood glucose is 8 mmol/L (145 mg/dL) or higher and the child is eating well. You may have to increase to nearly double the dose very quickly (more than 1 unit/kg, 0.4 units/pound), during an illness accompanied by fever (see chapter on illness, page 175). Always give the diabetes clinic a call when your child is ill for the first time after being diagnosed with diabetes!

Everyone doesn't like physical exercise. Some people feel more like having a lazy time with a fishing rod. You must find your own style of life and it is our job, at the diabetes clinic, to help you find a way of adjusting the insulin doses to your life style.

"You must swim up-stream if you want to find the spring"

Iraqi saying

When you feel that you know the basics of your diabetes it is important to have the courage to explore new pathways.

During the remission phase you should take smaller doses of extra insulin if you eat something extra (e.g. ice cream or pizza) since you are producing some insulin of your own (see "How much insulin should I take extra?" on page 156).

An intensive insulin treatment during the remission phase increases the possibility for prolongation of it. High blood glucose levels seem to be harmful to the insulin producing beta cells. The insulin production is already decreased at a blood glucose level of 11 mmol/L (200 mg/dL) and at 28 mmol/L (305 mg/dL) one can see alterations inside the cells.[131] From this it follows that if your "aim" is better when adjusting the insulin treatment during the remission phase, the chances of a prolonged remission increase. It is important to regularly take blood- or urine tests even when you are/your child is feeling perfectly well, in order to be able to see when the dose needs to be raised to deal with an increasing blood glucose level. This is especially important when you have an infection with fever which often increases the need for insulin (see page 175).

Puberty

During the teen years and puberty, when the body is developing quickly, the need for insulin is increased and you will often need to increase the doses considerably. Girls grow fastest the year before their first menstruation, while boys have their growth spurt later on in puberty. During puberty the levels of growth hormone (see page 36) in the body increase. If you give too little insulin during the years of the growth spurt the final height will be one or more centimeters less than pre-

Land softly! Don't make too many or too large changes in insulin at a time or you will have difficulties finding out what caused what afterwards.

Younger children often run around a lot while playing and will thereby get a certain degree of exercise in a natural way. Glucose gel may come in handy when having hypoglycemia at the beach. Glucose tablets will easily become wet and sticky.

dicted.[125] In earlier years it was common for children with diabetes to be stunted in their growth, but today this is very rare (see also page 67).

Large doses of growth hormone are secreted into the blood stream at night during puberty, increasing the blood glucose level,[125] and thus requiring large doses of bedtime insulin. Non-diabetic individuals have increased levels of insulin in the blood to manage this.[125] One problem with having diabetes is that the pharmaceutical preparations of insulin we have today have their peak of action early in the night, as early as 2 - 3 AM, which implies that the blood glucose level will rise in the morning (see "Dawn phenomenon" on page 44).

You will often need to increase the bedtime insulin to very large doses. For example, NPH insulin (e.g. Insulatard, Humulin NPH, Isuhuman Basal) may have to be increased from 12 to 20 or 24 units within a short period, and may need to be increased further, up to 30 units, a couple of months later. One teenage girl using multiple injections treatment increased her bedtime dose of NPH insulin from 6 to 20 units within a year. One teenage boy increased his 24 hour dose from 1.2 units/kg to 1.7 units/kg (0.5 to 0.8 units/pound) during his growth spurt.

Increase the bedtime insulin by 2 units at a time until the blood glucose at 2 - 3 AM approaches 6 mmol/L (110 mg/dL, see page 131). Wait a few days before increasing the dose again to make certain that the effect is fully established. If your blood glucose level is still high in the morning, despite your 2 - 3 AM being 6 mmol/L, you may need to try another type of insulin for bedtime injections. Long-acting lente type insulins (Ultratard, Ultralente, Humulin U, Humutard Ultra) are suitable alternatives, or maybe even better is an insulin pump (see page 104). It will deliver sufficient amounts of insulin during the later part of the night.

In winter when snow falls most children will rush outside to play. One must often decrease the doses by a unit or two in the afternoon and at the evening meal to avoid hypoglycemia. If the children have been out playing for many hours it is advisable to lower the bedtime dose as well.

Diet

One must pay attention to the diet even if you don't have diabetes. But remember that food is not medicine. Food should look and taste good. Meals ought to be pleasurable, we should enjoy food and feel satisfied afterwards. If you look upon food as medicine an important part of life will be disturbed. Your dietitian will inform you about a diabetes diet and help you to plan a menu based upon the meal-times and routines that already exist in your family.

Glucose in the food can only be absorbed into the blood after it has passed into the intestines. It cannot be absorbed from the oral mucosa as earlier believed.[166] To reach the intestines the food must first pass through the lower opening of the stomach (pylorus, see illustration on page 19). The sphincter will only allow small pieces, a few mm in size, pass through.

Complex carbohydrates must first be broken down to simple sugars before they can be absorbed into the blood. The length of the carbohydrate chain does not seem to affect the absorption as much as earlier believed since cleavage is a fairly quick process. Simple carbohydrates are cleaved by enzymes in the intestinal mucosa while more complex carbohydrates and starch are first prepared by enzymes from the saliva and pancreas (amylase). Starch fibres cannot be cleaved into carbohydrates in the intestine. A new drug (acarbose, Glucobay®),

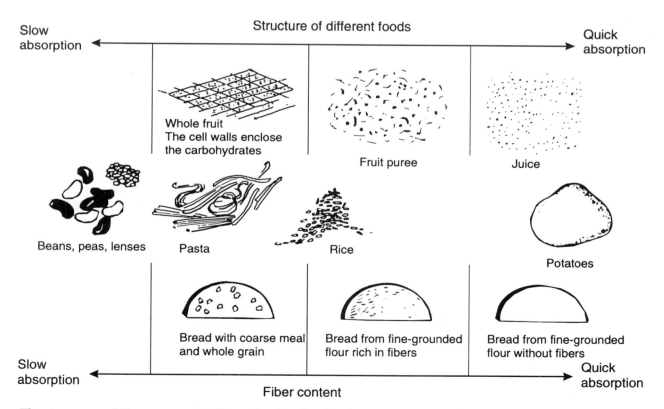

The structure and fiber content of different food-stuffs affect how quickly the carbohydrate content is absorbed. The illustration is from the book "Diet and diabetes" by the Swedish Diabetes Association, printed with permission.

Factors that increase the blood glucose level more *quickly*

① Heating:

Boiling and other types of heating will break down the starch in food.

② Preparing the food:

Polished rice will give a quicker rise in blood glucose than unpolished, mashed potatoes quicker than whole potatoes and grated carrots quicker than sliced.[395] Wheat-flour gives a higher blood glucose response when baked to bread than when used for pasta.[219]

③ Drinking with the food:

Drinking with the meal causes the stomach to empty quicker.[19] It is therefore best to only drink one glass along with the meal.

④ Glucose content:

Extra sugar along with a meal can give a rise in the blood glucose level, but not as pronounced as formerly believed. Particle size and cell structure in different food compounds give them different blood glucose responses in spite of their containing the same amount of carbohydrates.[19]

⑤ Salt content:

Salt in the food increases the absorption of glucose into the blood stream.[395]

Factors that increase the blood glucose level more *slowly*

① Size of bites:[327]

The larger the bites one swallows the longer the time it takes to digest the pieces in the stomach and intestine. Larger pieces also cause the stomach to empty more slowly.

② Gel-forming dietary fibers:

A high fiber content (as in rye bread) gives a slower rise in blood glucose by slowing down the emptying rate of the stomach and binding glucose in the intestine.

③ Fat content:

Fat in the food will retard the emptying of the stomach.[419]

④ Cell structure

Beans, peas and lenses retain their cell structure even after cooking. Whole fruits give a slower blood glucose response than peeled fruits and juice.[407]

⑤ Starch structure:

Boiled and mashed potatoes give a quicker blood glucose response (as fast as ordinary sugar) while rice and pasta give a slower blood glucose response.[407]

mainly used for type 2 diabetes, stops simple carbohydrates (disaccharides) from being cleaved by inhibiting the enzymes in the intestinal mucosa. This drug has lessened the risk of nighttime hypoglycemia in type 1 diabetes in a clinical trial.[284] In one study on patients with type 1 diabetes HbA_{1c} decreased on average 0.4 % when taking Glucobay® together with meals 3 times daily for 6 months.[199]

Formerly carbohydrates were divided into quick-acting and slow-acting, mainly depending on the size of the molecule. It is more accurate to speak of quick-acting and long-acting foods and to evaluate the composition, fibre content and preparation in order to determine the effect on the blood glucose level, rather than simply its content of pure sugar.[219,412] The term "glycemic index" is used to describe how the blood glucose level is affected by

different foods (see page 147). The glycemic index can be difficult to interpret since a mixed meal will affect the blood glucose level quite differently from the way its individual components do.[383]

Dietary fibre content and particle size seem to be of great importance according to recent studies.[19] The starch in vegetables is broken down more slowly than the starch in bread.[395] The starch in potatoes is quickly broken down to glucose. The starch from pasta products is broken down much more slowly even though it is made from white flour, which is low in fibers.[219]

The size of the food particles swallowed also influences the blood glucose response.[327] Industrial manufactured mashed potatoes contain a fine powder that is mixed with fluid. The glucose in mashed potatoes is absorbed just as quickly as a glucose solution.[407] Pasta and rice are swallowed in larger bites and must be digested before they can be

Carbohydrates

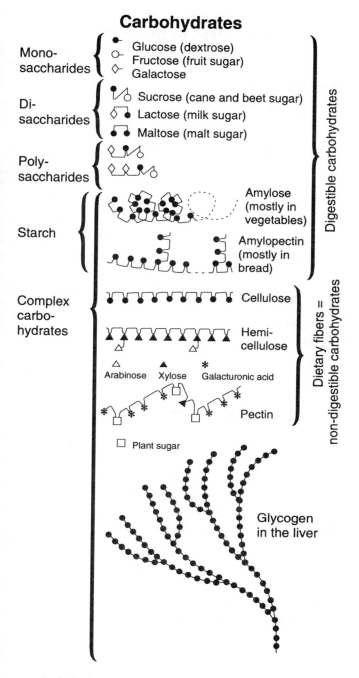

Carbohydrates important for metabolism in the body. Only mono-saccharides can be absorbed from the intestine. Di-saccharides and starch must first be broken down by digestive enzymes. Dietary fibers cannot be broken down to saccharides in the intestines. The glycogen store in the liver is composed of very long chains of glucose.

The amount of carbohydrate listed on a food label can be misleading as digestible and non-digestible carbohydrates are not separated. Non-digestible carbohydrates cannot be broken down in the intestines and will therefore not give a blood glucose response. The illustration is modified from reference [19].

A scale can be useful for weighing candy or chips to calculate the carbohydrate content. Otherwise we recommend estimating helpings and nutritional contents by eye,[412] after the initial learning period at the onset of diabetes.

absorbed. Likewise, a whole apple will give a slower rise in blood glucose than apple juice which contains smaller particles and is in a liquid form.

Heating decomposes starch, making sugar more accessible and faster to digest. Industrial food processing usually involves higher temperatures which gives food a quicker blood glucose rasing effect compared to home-cooked meals.[395] Industrial baby food and semi-manufactured food (sometimes used in schools) can raise the blood glucose more than comparable home-cooked meals.

Emptying the stomach

Everything that causes the stomach to release food into the intestines more slowly will also result in a slower increase of the blood glucose level.[19] From this it follows that the composition of the meal will be important, not only the amount of sugar it contains. Fat [419] and fibers [302] cause the stomach to empty more slowly while a beverage with the meal will make it empty more quickly.[402] A meal containing solid food (like pancakes) is emptied more slowly than liquid food (like soup).[402] Swallowing without chewing also causes a slower rise in blood glucose.[327] Extremely cold (4° C, 39° F) or hot (50° C, 122° F) food will slow down stomach emptying.

The emptying of the stomach is also affected by the blood glucose level. It is emptied more quickly if the blood glucose is low and more slowly if high. Both solid and liquid food are emptied from the stomach at twice the rate when the blood glucose is lowered from a normal level (4 - 7 mmol/L, 72 - 126 mg/dL) to a hypoglycemic level (1.6 - 2.2

mmol/L, 29 - 40 mg/dL).[359] Even small changes in blood glucose, within the normal ranges for non-diabetic persons, seem to affect the emptying rate. In one study in non-diabetic persons there was a 20 % decrease in the emptying rate when the blood glucose level was increased from 4 to 8 mmol/L (72 - 144 mg/dL).[360]

A high insulin level in the blood can also cause slower stomach emptying.[134] This is logical since the body (before the onset of diabetes) was used to having high levels of insulin only when the blood glucose was high as well. This reaction works against us when having diabetes. If one has a low blood glucose level due to a large dose of insulin one wants the stomach to empty as quickly as possible to allow the glucose to be absorbed into the blood.

Non-strenuous exercise will lead to unchanged or more rapid emptying of the stomach while physical exertion stops the stomach from emptying for 20 - 40 minutes after muscular activity is terminated.[68] A possible explanation for retarded emptying after physical exertion is an increased secretion of adrenaline and morphine-like hormones (endorphines).

Stomach emptying can be delayed in gastroenteritis.[31] This may contribute to the low blood glucose level that is often seen with gastroenteritis.

Sugar content in our food

From a nutritive point of view we do not require pure sugar at all. The liver can produce the 250 - 300 grams of glucose that an adult normally needs per day.

Carbohydrates in the food[19]

(the amounts of carbohydrates apply to adults):

Extra snack

(10 - 20 g of carbohydrate)

Only sweeteners without carbohydrates should be used, like aspartam (but not sorbitol). See page 154.

Ordinary snack

(20 - 40 g of carbohydrate)

A small amount of sugar, such as 1 - 1,5 g in a bun, is quite acceptable. Fructose and sorbitol have no advantages over sucrose (sugar). Cookies should be avoided as they have a high fat content. Ice cream sweetened with aspartam (light-ice cream) can replace milk with a snack.

Main meal

(50 - 70 g of carbohydrate)

It is important that the amount of carbohydrate be fairly constant from day to day although the type of carbohydrate matters less. A high content of fiber is essential. A dessert containing sugar is acceptable if the sugar content is included within the total carbohydrate amount. Fructose and sorbitol as parts of a meal have no advantages over sucrose.

In summary, a diabetes diet should be rich in fiber and low in fat (so should, by the way, everyone's diet be, diabetic or not). Dietary advice should stress the fat content and not, as is common today, the carbohydrate content.

It isn't easy to get the diabetes diet to work at all times. Many seem to think that "It can't be that difficult, since a diabetes diet is what we all should eat". Many persons act as "sugar-guards", reminding you as soon as you eat something sweet that you shouldn't, even if you have hypoglycemia. Try to explain that at times it can be both healthy and necessary to eat something sweet and you may avoid some of the glances and remarks.

Insulin-dependent diabetes in children, adolescents and adults   © R. Hanas 1998

How is the emptying of the stomach affected?

More quickly	More slowly
Small bites	Large bites
Liquid food	Solid food
Drink with food	Drink after food
	Fat food
	Food rich in fibers
	Extremely hot or cold food
Hypoglycemia	High blood glucose
	High level of insulin
	Smoking
	Gastroenteritis
Light exercise	Heavy exercise

carbohydrate content was the same for both types of meals.

Earlier it was the norm to decrease the carbohydrate content in the diabetes diet at all costs. The risk in doing this is that the fat content is usually increased instead and that such a diet is poorer than that of non-diabetic children.[383,412] It is much more important to eat regularly and to adjust the insulin dose according to appetite and size of helpings.

Fat

Small amounts of glucose along with a meal do not cause an increased rise in blood glucose according to several studies in which a small amount of starch has been exchanged for glucose at mealtime.[19] This means that you can add 5 grams (1/5 ounce) of sugar to a meal without risk, for example in the form of ketchup.[382] However, the sugar intake in between meals affects the blood glucose level much more. Your blood glucose level will be equally affected if you eat candy or white bread (without butter or something on it) in between meals.[157] The important factor is whether the snack contains fiber or fat (like chocolate-covered biscuits) which delay stomach emptying.

The recommendation to decrease the sugar content in food is based on more general factors:

① Sugar gives "empty calories", i.e. sugar gives only energy and contains no other nutrients. This energy will cause you to gain weight and to eat less of more healthy foods.

② Sugar is not healthy for your teeth.

In an American study where children took insulin twice daily there was no difference in their blood glucose charts when they had a diet with 2 % of the carbohydrates as pure glucose (in fruit and bread) compared to 10 % (in fruit and bread, cereal and toast with jelly for breakfast, chocolate chip cookies with lunch, chocolate for an afternoon snack and ice milk with dinner).[263] This may be surprising, but can be explained by the fact that all the meals also contained both fat and protein. The total

Fat has no direct effect on the blood glucose level. However, fat affects the blood glucose level indirectly by slowing the stomach's emptying rate.[419] When studying monkeys is has been found that the stomach empties portions of food through the lower sphincter with the same amount of energy every minute.[285] As fat yields more energy than carbohydrates the stomach is emptied more slowly when the fat content is high. A meal with a high fat content will therefore give a slower rise in the blood glucose level. The fat in the food must pass into the intestine before it can affect the emptying rate of the stomach.[419] If one starts the meal with something rich in fat the signal slowing down the emptying rate will reach the stomach more quickly. The possibility of eating some kind of fat that affects the emptying rate of the stomach but is not absorbed into the blood has been discussed. By doing this,

You can have ketchup with your food without problems if you use normal amounts. However, if you use ketchup as a sauce in large amounts the sugar content will be too high.

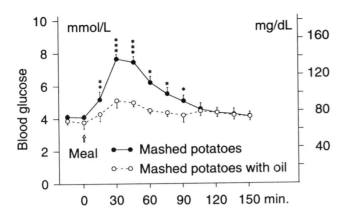

If the meal contains fat the emptying of the stomach will be delayed, causing the blood glucose to rise more slowly. In this study two helpings of mashed potatoes (50 grams of carbohydrate) was given with or without corn oil (approximately 30 ml, 2 tablespoonfuls). The study was done in non-diabetic adults who can quickly increase the amount of insulin in their blood.[419] Notice that the blood glucose level increased quickly despite this, already within 30 minutes, when the persons had mashed potatoes without oil.

persons with diabetes could utilize this positive effect (the slowed stomach's emptying rate), and at the same time avoid the influence of fat on heart and blood vessels.

If you eat a meal very rich in fat there may still be food remaining in the stomach when you are about to have your next meal. You will then need to decrease the food amount without changing the insulin dose to avoid an increase in blood glucose. When using direct-acting insulin (Humalog) there may be a risk of hypoglycemia shortly after a meal rich in fat. Try giving the injection after the meal instead.

The reason a person with diabetes should be careful with fat is that they have an increased risk of arteriosclerosis (see page 208). One should be particularly careful with saturated fat and so called trans-fatty acids. The softer the fat the better. Liquid margarine and oil do not contain any trans-fatty acids at all and also have a low content of saturated fatty acids. Choose a margarine that contains at least 25 % polyunsaturated fat. Light margarine is not recommended for the youngest children as they have an increased need for fat in their diet.

Ordinary margarine and butter contain only 3 % polyunsaturated fat. Cooking-oil (corn-oil, olive-oil or rape-oil) contain large amounts of polyunsaturated fat and are useful for frying. However, if the frying pan is very hot the polyunsaturated fat can be broken down. Some types of light-margarine cannot be used for frying.

It is the total amount fat over time that is important in the long run. You can cut down on fat during the week and then have a festive meal on the weekend with a delicious cream sauce.

Drinking with food

You can affect your blood glucose level considerably depending on what you drink along with your meals. Sweet drinks like fruit juice can be used to quickly raise the blood glucose when hypoglycemic. If the blood glucose level is high it is better to hold off on drinking until the end of the meal and then to drink water. If you want ice cream for dessert you can skip milk and drink water with the meal instead.

Milk

Many children drink milk along with their meals. Different types of milk have different fat contents. However, all types have the same amount of milk sugar (lactose, 5 grams/dl, 1 ounce/pound) and usually the same amounts of vitamins. A small child (3 years old or less) needs more fat in their diet and should drink whole milk. The type of milk most suitable also depends on how much the child drinks per day. Half a liter/day (1 pint) is recommendable for the calcium intake. If an older child drinks less than this it is probably better to choose whole milk.

Diet rules of thumb

➠ Eat meals and snacks at about the same time of the day every day.

➠ Plan meal times and contents with other daily activities in mind, i.e. physical exercise or sitting still in school/at work.

➠ Take extra insulin when needed, such as at parties or when having weekend candy.

➠ Eat fresh fruit as a snack rather than drinking fruit juice.

➠ Eat less at each meal if you have weight problems.

➠ Aim at a high fiber content in your diet.

Glycemic index

The glycemic index is an attempt to describe the blood glucose raising effect of different foods. A certain amount of carbohydrate is given (most often 50 g) and the area under the blood glucose curve is measured for 2 hours. White bread is the reference product with a glycemic index of 100. The glycemic index can be misleading if you want to know how the blood glucose level is affected during a shorter period of time, like ½ - 1 hour. The list is based on references 364 and 426.

High glycemic index

Glucose	138
Puffed rice	132
Honey	126
Corn Flakes	115
Jelly candy	112
Weetabix	109
Waffles	106
Water melon	101
White wheat bread (reference)	100
Oatmeal porridge	91 - 105
Mashed potatoes	98
Fanta	95
Raisins	93
Banana (with brown spots)	90
Sucrose (sugar)	89
Rye bread (wholemeal)	89

Average glycemic index

Potato (boiled)	80
Leaven bread	70 - 76
Banana (all yellow)	75
All bran	74
Chocolate	69
Rye bread (whole grain)	68
Pasta	60 - 70
Rice (parboiled, boiled 15 min)	68
Orange	59
Banana (with green spots)	59
Lactose (milk sugar)	57

Low glycemic index

Apple	53
Ice cream, yoghurt	52
Milk	45
Lentils (dried)	37
Kidney beans (dried)	43
Fructose (fruit sugar)	26
Soya beans (dried)	20

See reference [288] for an extensive list of foods.

The starch in vegetables is broken down more slowly than other types of starch. Vegetables also contain fibers which affect digestion positively, preventing constipation.

Formula (gruel)

Gruel is a flour mix formula, common for infant feeding especially in the Nordic countries. The glucose content of gruel is absorbed fairly quickly. With a multiple injection therapy the child will need short-acting insulin for every bottle of gruel (5 - 6 insulin doses/day). When using insulin of 40 U/ml one can adjust in half units to find the right dose. If the child drinks gruel at night a small dose of short-acting insulin can be given with this meal. Gruel will not maintain an elevated blood glucose level for any period of time during the night, but by adding a small amount of fat (30 ml, 2 table spoonfuls of oil or liquid margarine) the gruel will stay a little longer in the stomach (see "Fat" on page 145), giving a prolonged effect on the blood glucose level during the night. If the child has problems with nighttime hypoglycemia corn flour mix may help (see page 46).

If the child is breast-fed and takes full meals you can give insulin in the same way as described above for formula. However, if the child sips more frequently a 2-dose treatment may work better.

Dietary fibers

Fibers in the food are healthy in many ways. They help prevent constipation. Coarse rye bread with a high fiber content will satiate you for a much longer time than the same amount of white bread without fiber.

A high fiber content will also decrease the cholesterol level in the blood.[302] Adding fibers (guar) to a meal will cause the stomach to empty more slowly.[302] The fibers form a thin film on the intesti-

Potatoes

The carbohydrates in raw potatoes are absorbed slowly but boiling causes the cell walls to burst and the carbohydrates can thereby be absorbed more quickly from the intestines. The carbohydrates in mashed potatoes are absorbed as quickly as pure glucose. This can give a quick rise in blood glucose after the meal but may also result in hypoglycemia 2 - 3 hours later, since all the carbohydrates in the mashed potatoes have been absorbed during a fairly short time after the meal. If you change the surface of a potato (like when frying, deep frying, or letting them cool in the refrigerator to be used in potato salad) the glucose will be absorbed more slowly than if you eat it freshly boiled. The manufacturing process and the high fat content in potato chips (crisps) result in the glucose being absorbed very slowly [76] (see graph on page 159).

In an adult study chocolate cake was substituted for a baked potato without an increase in blood glucose levels.[317] However, if the chocolate cake was added to the baked potato the glucose level increased.

How quickly is the blood glucose increased?

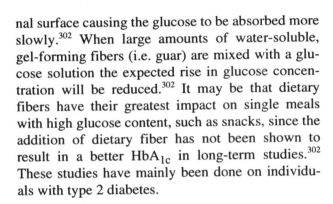

Puffed rice
Corn Flakes
Mashed potatoes
Boiled potatoes
White bread
Wholemeal bread
Rice
Pasta
Potato chips
Beans, lentils, peas

nal surface causing the glucose to be absorbed more slowly.[302] When large amounts of water-soluble, gel-forming fibers (i.e. guar) are mixed with a glucose solution the expected rise in glucose concentration will be reduced.[302] It may be that dietary fibers have their greatest impact on single meals with high glucose content, such as snacks, since the addition of dietary fiber has not been shown to result in a better HbA_{1c} in long-term studies.[302] These studies have mainly been done on individuals with type 2 diabetes.

Raw carrots and fiber enriched rye bread can be a good foundation if the meal otherwise contains mainly "quick-acting" carbohydrates. One can also utilize the "fiber effect" by offering a slice of coarse rye bread with margarine and cheese before the child eats his/her weekend candy. Both the fiber and fat content will help slow down the rise in blood glucose level.

Vegetables

You can eat freely from this food group (except potatoes) as the carbohydrate content is very low. Vegetables also contain healthy fibers. Put the vegetables on the table before the children come to eat and they will probably help themselves to them while waiting for the food to be served.

Bread

It was formerly stressed that persons with diabetes should eat unsweetened bread. Today we know that fibers in the bread cause the glucose to be absorbed more slowly. One can use ordinary recipes when baking bread and there is no need to omit sugar or experiment with alternative sweeteners. Half to one dl (3 - 6 tbs) of sugar or syrup for a dough made from 5 dl (1 pint) of liquid is quite acceptable when baking your own bread. After baking, only a small amount of sugar remains in the bread, and one rarely eats more than a few slices with each meal. It is more important to choose bread that is rich in fiber than to omit small amounts of sugar.

Pasta

Pasta gives a slow rise in blood glucose since it is prepared from crushed or cracked wheat, not wheat flour.[289] This makes pasta a suitable food for people with diabetes (and besides most children like pasta). When using direct-acting insulin (Humalog) the rise may even be too slow, resulting in a hypoglycemia within 30 - 60 minutes. In this case take the insulin after finishing the meal or use regular short-acting insulin when eating pasta (or beans like in chili con carne).

Meat and fish

Meat and fish do not contain carbohydrates and will therefore not increase your blood glucose level. Instead the protein content is high and sometimes the fat content as well. Products with little fat (cod fish, haddock, coal fish or very lean meat) can preferably be prepared with some extra fat (when frying, baking in a gratin-dish or with a sauce containing more fat). Otherwise you will risk having hypoglycemia after a couple of hours since the stomach is emptied much quicker if the meal is entirely free from fat. As the energy content of boiled fish is fairly low it may be a good idea to increase the size of the helping in order to avoid hypoglycemia.

Pizza

Pizza contains bread, meat or fish and vegetables, in other words a healthy meal. One problem if you have diabetes is that a pizza meal will usually be larger (more bread) than a usual dinner. The bread is baked hard which causes the carbohydrates to be absorbed more slowly. Cheese has a high fat content and this causes the stomach to empty more slowly. Try taking 1 - 2 extra units of insulin with the pizza or avoid eating the crust.

Salt

A high salt content in food can increase the uptake of glucose from the intestine. Salt in the form of sodium chloride will increase the blood pressure and can be a risk factor since diabetes in itself implies an increased risk of heart and vascular diseases (see page 208). Salt is also available as potassium chloride but is more expensive than common salt and tastes somewhat different. Sea-salt and herb-salt usually contain the same amount of sodium as table-salt.

Herbs

Herbs will not affect your blood glucose at all. Grill-herbs and soya may, however, contain a lot of salt. If the spicing is strong enough to make you drink extra your stomach may empty more rapidly, resulting in a quicker rise in the blood glucose level.

Fruit and berries

Fruits and berries have a high carbohydrate content (see table on page 152). The higher the fiber content the less the effect on the blood glucose level will be.

Meal times

Each family has its own routines and meal times that they have found comfortable. The dietitian usually starts out by considering these hours when adjusting your diabetes diet. If you use multiple

Common meal planning.

Time	Meal	Example of doses for a child weighing 33 kg (73 pounds)
7.30 AM	Breakfast	9 U Regular
11.30 AM	Lunch	6 U "
4.30 PM	Dinner	6 U "
8.30 PM	Evening meal	4 U (2U/sandwich)
9 - 10 PM		8 U bedtime insulin

Alternative meal planning.

Time	Meal	Example of doses for a child weighing 33 kg (73 pounds)
7.30 AM	Breakfast	9 U Regular
11.30 AM	Lunch	6 U "
3.00 PM	Snack	4 U (2U/sandwich)
7.00 PM	Dinner	6 U Regular
9 - 10 PM		8 U Bedtime insulin

injection treatment with regular short-acting insulin no more than 5 hours should elapse between the meals accompanied by insulin. When using direct-acting insulin (Humalog) it is less important to have strict meal times since you take basal insulin twice daily.

Snacks

Non-diabetic individuals have low insulin levels in between meals. As regular short-acting insulin lasts for 5 hours (and intermediate-acting for even longer, if using twice daily injections) a person with diabetes has a higher insulin concentration than non-diabetic individuals in between meals. This is why one needs to snack. Since the morning injection is usually larger than the lunch dose, a snack is more essential in the morning. A child in school will usually require a sandwich for mid-morning snack. However, if the school lunch is served early a fruit might do. In the afternoon a fruit will usually be sufficient as a snack.

If the blood glucose level is high a snack is not necessary. Try having half the snack if the blood glucose level is close to 10 mmol/L (180 mg/dL) and skip it completely if it is above that.

Some younger children (up to 9 - 10 years of age) need a larger afternoon snack when they come home from school. Many families find it better to give insulin with this snack and have dinner a little later. The evening meal is then omitted. Try giving the same amount of insulin with the afternoon snack which the child ate earlier with the evening meal (see the meal schedule above).

When using direct-acting insulin (Humalog) you will be less dependent on snacks in between meals since its action profile better matches the blood glucose rise after a meal. This results in a lower insulin level between meals.

Do I have to eat at the same time every day?

It is usually not a problem eating (and taking insulin) an hour earlier or later than usual. Just remember not to exceed 5 hours between the doses of ordinary short-acting insulin. If you use direct-acting insulin (Humalog) and twice daily basal insulin you will probably not have to be as strict about the hours between meals. You can try shifting meal-times by up to 2 hours.

Hungry or full?

A person with a well controlled diabetes can often rely on sensations of hunger or satiation. It is important to trust the child's feeling of appetite. If you continue to tell the child that he/she must eat more or less regardless of feelings of hunger, he/she will stop registering these feelings after a while. The child will usually not feel as hungry if the blood glucose level is high. Give the child time to reflect and build his/her own opinion about the size of meals. However, what and how much to drink along with the meal will usually require parental input.

Beware! If one has a lack of insulin and a badly regulated diabetes one may very well have feelings of hunger even when the blood glucose level is high (see page 43).

School

It is seldom a problem for a child to order a diabetes diet and snacks at school. The dietitian can speak to the staff if necessary. However, older children don't always want to have a diabetes diet at school. They might not find it as tasty or don't want to be different from their peers. Giving general advice in this situation is difficult. Some children and teenagers can manage well by adjusting their insulin dose to ordinary school meals while others find this more difficult.

It may be difficult to get school staff to understand that a child with diabetes will not always eat the same amounts of food. Some older children can certainly practise eating less when the blood glucose level is high (see "Changing the size of a meal to affect blood glucose" on page 126).

School lunches are best eaten at the same time every day, not too early since the time until the next insulin dose may be too long way off when using a multiple injection treatment. See the suggestions for meal schedules on page 150. The school will usually need to know well in advance what meal-times your child prefers, in order to be able to make the appropriate schedule adjustments.

When school mates buy candy a child with diabetes may find it difficult to resist. There is always a risk that he/she will instead "show off" by eating even more candy than the others. A compromise could be to buy a small amount of candy to have after lunch when the stomach is filled with food. At that time and under those conditions the blood glucose level will not be affected as much. Skipping lunch and buying candy instead, as some teenagers do, can be deleterious for those with diabetes.

Special "diabetic" food?

So called diabetic food (often found in health food stores) is not recommended for children with diabetes [364,412] and is not suitable for adults either. It is often both more expensive and has a higher energy content than similar normal food. Besides, many find the taste un-appetizing. It is much better to learn how to handle ordinary food when having diabetes.

"Fast food"

Many children, teenagers and adults like fast food, and it has become a fixture of modern life. As fast food often is high in fat content, it is not a good idea to base your diet on it. However, to eat fast food once in a while will not be problem, and after

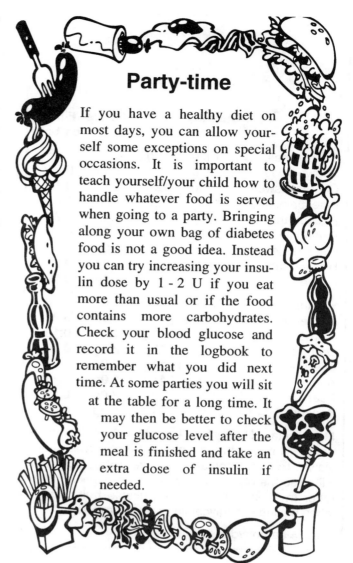

Party-time

If you have a healthy diet on most days, you can allow yourself some exceptions on special occasions. It is important to teach yourself/your child how to handle whatever food is served when going to a party. Bringing along your own bag of diabetes food is not a good idea. Instead you can try increasing your insulin dose by 1 - 2 U if you eat more than usual or if the food contains more carbohydrates. Check your blood glucose and record it in the logbook to remember what you did next time. At some parties you will sit at the table for a long time. It may then be better to check your glucose level after the meal is finished and take an extra dose of insulin if needed.

School menu

It may be a good idea to note your insulin doses on the school menu.
The child usually knows what he/she likes and when it doesn't taste as good.

Units	Food
5U	Spaghetti Bolognese
4U	Fish with rice
6U	Mashed potatoes and sausage
4U	Lasagne

Check with the school dietician to make sure that you have received the diabetes menu and not the ordinary menu!

Fruits

	Quantity	Carb.	Fibers	Fiber/carboh
Raspberries	100g	8g	3.7g	0.46
Strawberries	100g	10g	2.4g	0.24
Cherries, sweet	100g	12g	1.7g	0.13
Pineapple, fresh	100g	12g	1.2g	0.09
Redcurrant	100g	13g	3.4g	0.27
Pineapple, canned	100g	16g	1.0g	0.06
Blackberries	100g	16g	7.2g	0.46
Blackcurrant	100g	16g	4.9g	0.32
Grapes	100g	17g	1.6g	0.09
Raisins	1 tbs	8g	1.0g	0.12
Grapefruit	1 fruit	9g	2.0g	0.22
Plums	2 fruits	9g	1.2g	0.13
Orange	1 fruit	13g	2.0g	0.16
Kiwi fruits	2 fruits	14g	3.8g	0.27
Apple	1 fruit	14g	1.9g	0.13
Pear	1 fruit	16g	3.0g	0.19
Banana	1 fruit	21g	1.5g	0.07

More dietary fiber/gram (1 ounce = 28 g) carbohydrate will cause the glucose to be absorbed more slowly. Bananas contain very little dietary fiber and will raise the blood glucose level more quickly than other fruits. It is therefore a suitable fruit to take when having hypoglycemia or during exercise.

Carb. = carbohydrates

anemia which can show as tiredness. You should always discuss with your dietitian or doctor before changing your diet.

Different cultures

Families from different cultures and different religions often have quite different eating habits. The number of meals can be fewer and sometimes certain foods are excluded due to religious reasons (i.e. muslims not eating pork). The way of cooking is usually not the same. Lactose intolerance is more common among children from some countries. One should of course take the family's food habits in consideration when discussing diet issues with a person who has diabetes. With a multiple injection treatment and pre-meal injections there are usually no difficulties in adjusting the diabetes diet to fit family traditions.

a couple of times you will have found out what insulin doses are appropriate for your favorites.

Vegetarian diet

A pure vegetarian diet (vegan diet) may result in a disturbed balance between the amount of protein and carbohydrates in the diet since vegetarian nutrients contain much less protein than animal nutrients. A lactovegetarian diet includes milk and milk products resulting in a higher protein content. A strict vegetarian diet is not recommended for children due to the risk of a deficiency of protein, vitamins and minerals. Not eating meat, fish and eggs is not synonymous with being a vegetarian. In vegan or lactovegetarian diet the animal products are mostly replaced by products from leguminous plants. The intake of vitamin B_{12} will be cut in half when the vitamins in animal products are not replaced. This will lead to a considerable risk of

Sweeteners

Sugar free?

When manufacturers state that a product is sugar free, it does not always mean that is it completely devoid of sugar. It usually implies that no sugar is added, whereas the natural sugar from berries or fruits are still present. Sugar-free chocolate or ice cream can contain more calories than ordinary alternatives. They often contain sorbitol which eventually is transformed into glucose in the liver. Check the food label. Unfortunately manufacturers do not always state exactly how much of each ingredient that is added but the items are listed in descending order of amount.

Sweeteners

Sorbitol

Sorbitol is a natural component of plums, cherries and other fruits and berries. Chemically sorbitol belongs to the sugar alcohol category. Sorbitol and other sugar alcohols absorb water in the intestines and function as nourishment for intestinal bacteria. Large amounts of sorbitol can cause abdominal pains and diarrhea. The sweetness of sorbitol is about half of that of sugar. It is transformed into fructose when broken down.

Aspartam

Aspartam consists of two synthetic proteins, asparaginic acid and phenylalanine. It is nearly two hundred times sweeter than sugar and is used in such small amounts that the energy content is negligible. It can lose its sweetness through cooking and baking.

Saccharin

Saccharin is a synthetic product. It is many hundred times sweeter than sugar and contains no energy. It gives a slight metallic taste when heated above 70° C (158° F) and should therefore only be added after cooking.

Acesulfam K

This new sweetener is also many hundred times sweeter than sugar. It withstands heating well and can be used when baking. It is mixed with milk-sugar (lactose) but in amounts too small to give any significant amount of energy.

Cyclamate

Cyclamate is 30 times sweeter than sugar and is non-energetic. It can withstand cooking without giving an after-taste.

Sugarfree?

➡ Unsweetened	No compound with sweet taste has been added to the product. However, it can contain natural sugar (fruit sugar, milk sugar).
➡ Without sugar (saccharose)	Does not contain saccharose. However, it can contain natural sugar (fruit sugar, milk sugar).
➡ Unsugared Sweetened without sugar; No-added sugar	No sugar is added but it can contain natural sugar (fruit sugar, milk sugar) and artificial sweeteners.
➡ Sugarfree; Without sugar	Contains no type of sugar, either natural or added. Other sweeteners with or without energy may be added (but these should be on the label of contents).

Sweeteners without energy

Substance	Trade name	Common in
Aspartam	NutraSweet ®	Chewing gum Candy
	Canderel ®	Grains
	Result ®	Cubes
	Hermesetas Gold®	Cubes
	Dietorelle®	Candy
	Light ®	Light-drinks
Cyclamate } Saccharin }	Zucchettos® } Hermesetas® }	Cubes, liquid and grains
Saccharin	Solettes®	Cubes
Acesulfam K	Sweet'n Low®	Grains and cubes

Sweeteners with energy

Be careful with using these sweeteners as they contain energy (4 kcal/g). Don't use them at all if you have problems maintaining your weight.

Substance	Trade name	Common in
Fructose		Candy, pastry
Hydrolyzed starch syrup		Candy
Sugar alcohols		
Sorbitol	Sionon®	Grains
	Diabet ®	Grains
Xylitol		Candy
Mannitol		"
Isomaltose		"
Maltitol, Lactitol		Ice cream

Sugar alcohols affect the blood glucose level, but more slowly than sugars.

Fructose

Fructose is almost twice as sweet as sugar. Even if fructose does not affect your blood glucose level directly, it is transformed into glucose in the liver, and the calorie content can cause weight gain. Because of this fructose is not considered as a suitable sweetener for persons with diabetes in some countries. In other countries (such as Finland and Germany) many "diabetes products" containing fructose are sold (see also page 50).

Beverages

	Quantity	Carb.	Fat	Kcal
Low-fat milk	2 dl	10 g	1g	75
1.5%-fat milk	2 dl	10 g	3 g	96
3%-fat milk	2 dl	10 g	6 g	120
O'boy® (+milk)	2 dl	23 g	1.5 g	132
Juice	2 dl	20 g	-	100
D'Light ®	2 dl	6 g	-	24
Fun Light ®	2 dl	-	-	-
Lemonade	33 cl	30 g	-	120
Fanta Light ®	33 cl	2.5 g	-	10
Zingo Light ®	33 cl	2.5 g	-	10
Cola Light ®	2 dl	0 g	-	1
Cider Light ®	2 dl	0 g	-	30
(energy comes from the alcohol-content)				
Coffee	2 dl	0.3 g		2
Tea	2 dl	0 g		2
Herb tea	Can have a high sugar-content!			

20 cl = 2/3 fluid ounce, 28 g = 1 ounce
Carb. = carbohydrates

Light?

"Light" drinks are usually sweetened with aspartam and do not contain any sugar. These drinks are "unrestricted" when having diabetes. There are some exceptions from this rule such as Fanta Light ®, which contains some fructose, and Cider Light ®, which contains alcohol, giving it about the same carbohydrate content as milk.

When a food stuff is labeled "light" the situation is more complex. Usually these are not free from sugar in all cases. In some countries a food stuff may be called "light" if the sugar content is decreased by 25 %. However, this does not say anything about the initial and total sugar content! Products containing fat can be labeled "light" if the fat content has been decreased by at least 50 %. As the rules for labelling may vary from country to country you should check with your dietitian about what is applicable where you live.

Candy and ice cream

Sooner or later all children with diabetes will be tempted by their friends to treats like ice cream or candy. At home families often try to regulate this by allowing ice cream on certain occasions and sweets only on Saturdays. This is something all parents may find difficult to enforce, regardless of whether the child has diabetes or not. The obvious problem for a child with diabetes is that all these delicious things will also increase the blood glucose. This fact will often be the reason for your saying: "No, you cannot do that because you have diabetes".

When one says this, one often forgets that the answer would probably have been "No" even if the child did not have diabetes: "No, you will get cavities", "No, we cannot afford it", or "In our family we have candy only on Saturdays". The practical effect will be the same (no candy) but, for the child, the difference is important. If you always refer to the child having diabetes when saying "No!" the child will soon start hating the illness which lies behind all the limitations. The child will come to believe that if he/she only did not have diabetes all these things would have been possible.

What is in "unhealthy" stuff?

	Quantity/Weight		Carb.	Fat	Kcal
Peanuts		100g	15g	53g	630
Cheese doodles		28g	15g	9g	150
Potato crisps/chips		25g	15g	8g	130
Peanut rings	25g		15g	6g	120
Salt sticks	25 sticks	20g	15g	2g	80
Popcorn	5 dl	23g	15g	3g	110
Milk chocolate	6 squares	27g	15g	9g	150
Sugar-free milk chocolate		30g	15g	11g	170
Kitkat ®	1/2 cake	25g	15g		
Filled biscuits	2 pieces		15g	5g	105
Biscuits plain	5 pieces		15g	2g	90
Jelly beans	5 pieces	19g	15g	-	65
Toffee	4 pieces	17g	15g	3g	77
Candy canes	5 pieces		15g	-	60
Dextrose	3 lumps	9g	9g	-	36
Dietorelle ®	10 pieces		5-15g	1-2g	20-70
Chewing gum	1 package		10g	-	

1 ounce = 28g.

Carb. = carbohydrates

We don't want to ban candy from children (or adults) with diabetes, but we do not in any way want to say that it is unrestricted either. Our message is of course that you can have some candy or ice cream — but you must plan ahead. Just as most adults allow themselves a good time every now and then, we believe that children should be able to manage their insulin and diet in such a way that they can treat themselves to something sweet on occasion, without their blood glucose rising too high. It will be more fun to go to a party if one is

Read the list carefully! Fifteen grams of carbohydrate (½ ounce) corresponds to the contents of a sandwich. Which would you prefer? Four pieces of candy or ½ liter (1 pint) of popcorn? One kilo (2.2 pounds) of body fat can be produced from 7.000 kilocalories (kcal). Peanuts contain the most calories — you will gain almost 100 g of weight from eating 100 g of peanuts!

Try to choose chewy candy (such as wine gums) rather than candy with "free" sugar like candy canes. The gelatinous structure will cause the sugar to be absorbed more slowly, thereby affecting your blood glucose level less.

able to eat the same food as everyone else. However, just as adults won't feel well if partying every day, we emphasize to children that this is something you can do only on special occasions, but not every day.

How much insulin should I take extra?

One unit of insulin is usually enough for every 10 - 15 g (1/3 - 1/2 ounce) of extra carbohydrate,[107] i.e. sugar. If candy or ice cream is taken instead of a snack, count only the carbohydrate content which is in excess of that of your ordinary snack. You can take the insulin at the same time as you have the ice cream (ordinary ice cream, not a popsicle or ice lolly!) or chocolate but you should take it 30 minutes before having candy as this will affect your blood glucose more quickly. Direct-acting insulin (Humalog) has a better action profile for candy containing pure sugar, but may be too quick for treats containing fat, such as ice cream and chocolate bars.

The blood glucose level will of course not be perfect and this is not something we recommend you do on a daily basis — but it is a good method for special occasions. Remember that exceptions must be exceptions — if you do it every day it will become a habit and such a habit is not compatible with your diabetes.

The amount of extra insulin needed will depend on your total insulin requirement. If you are in puberty with a high total insulin dose (more than 1 U/kg/24 hours, 0.5 U/pounds/24 hours), you may need more than 1 U of insulin for every 10 g (1/3 ounce) of carbohydrate. If you are in the remission phase (low insulin requirements during the first 6 - 12 months after the onset of diabetes, see page 68) you should only take ¼ - ½ unit extra per 10 g (1/3 ounce) of extra carbohydrate. Your own insulin production will supply the rest. Measure the blood

Contents of some common ice creams

Corresponds to (whole milk)		Carb.	Fat	Kcal
Super Cornetto®	3 glasses	31 g	10 g	230
Cornetto® strawberry	2½ "	26 g	14 g	184
Mister Long®	2½ "		25 g	15 g	260
Magnum®, lolly	2½ "	24 g	25 g	300
Solero®	1½ "	18 g	6 g	133

Ice cream package (approximate figures)
		Carb.	Fat	Kcal
Light ½ lit. (1 pint)		45 g	12 g	275
Whole-fat ½ lit. (1 pint)		60-70 g	25-30 g	650

Popsicle (ice lolly)
(contains sugar = glasses of juice)
		Carb.	Fat	Kcal
Calippo®	1½ glass	24 g	0 g	114
Spirello®	1 glass	18 g	0 g	75

For comparison
	Carb.	Fat	Kcal
1 glass of 3 %-fat milk	10 g	6 g	120
1 sandwich with margarine and 2 slices of cheese	15 g	8 g	150

Carb. = carbohydrates

glucose level half an hour after the candy intake and experiment to find out what works well for you. If you use an insulin pump see page 109.

Ice cream

A summer without ice cream is no summer at all in the eyes of many children. Of course you can have ice cream even if you have diabetes. The usual advice applies: Think ahead and experiment to find out what is best for you. There are mainly two types of ice cream: popsicle (ice lolly) and "ordinary" ice cream made from of dairy products. Popsicles are like frozen fruit juice and affect the blood glucose level in the same way as juice except that it takes longer to lick a popsicle than to drink a glass of juice. Popsicles are quite suitable if you have hypoglycemia. You should then make sure it is an ordinary popsicle, and not a "light" type since the latter will not affect the blood glucose level at all.

When should I test my blood glucose level?

Candy, popsicle	After ½ hour
Ice cream, chocolate bar	After (1) - 1½ hour
Potato chips (crisps)	After 2 - 3 hours

Ice cream cones

Ice cream cones from a booth usually contain:

Soft ice cream   20 - 30 g of carbohydrate
Ice cream (3 scoops)   20 - 25 g   ”

"Ice cream test"

① Measure your blood glucose level at snack-time.

② Calculate the carbohydrate content of your snack in grams (one sandwich = 15 g, one glass of milk = 10 g, for fruit see table on page 152).
Decide which ice cream you want (not pop-sicles — they contain just frozen juice).

③ Calculate the carbohydrate content of the ice-cream.

④ Take one unit of extra insulin for every 10 g of excess carbohydrate in the ice-cream.

⑤ Decrease the dose by 1 - 2 U if the blood glucose level before the ice cream is less than 4 - 5 mmol/L or if you are about to exercise. Increase by 1 - 2 U if the blood glucose level is above 10 mmol/L.

⑥ If you are in the remission phase (honey moon phase, see page 68) you should only take ¼ or ½ of the above mentioned extra doses of insulin.

⑦ Measure your blood glucose level 1 - 1½ hour after you have finished the ice-cream to see if things worked out the way you expected.

⑧ Document what you did in your logbook and you will be better equipped the next time you feel like eating ice cream.

Remember that no child eats ice cream every day, with or without diabetes. Your parents decide this and the same rules should apply to you as to your non-diabetic siblings and friends.

Ice cream made from dairy products ("milk-type ice cream") contain fat that causes your stomach to empty more slowly. Thus the increase in blood glucose level will not be seen until 1 - 1½ hours after eating ice cream. From this it follows that dairy product ice cream is not suitable for reversing hypoglycemia, but can be a good alternative when playing football, an activity which requires extra sugar over a longer period of time. Dairy product ice cream goes well with regular short-acting insulin in the sense that the insulin will start working at about the same time as the ice cream starts raising the blood glucose level.

During our diabetes camps we do some experimenting with ice cream and caramels. The dietitian tells the children about the contents of different ice creams. We then have an "ice cream test" at snack-time. The children measure their blood glucose levels beforehand and then discuss with their leaders how to proceed in order to be able to have their favorite ice cream. If needed they will take an extra dose of insulin along with the ice cream. It may not be the best idea to have a large ice cream if your blood glucose level is 15 mmol/L (270 mg/dL) — but life is full of such situations and it is a good idea to know how to handle them. The children can have their choice of ice cream — but only if they take extra insulin. When we measure the blood glucose level 1 - 1½ hour after the ice cream the average level is lower than it was before eating the ice cream.

Saturday candy

How does one deal with weekend candy? My advice is to give the candy as part of a regular snack. Start by having a sandwich (preferably bread with a high fiber content) with margarine and a slice of cheese. The blood glucose level will then not be affected as much as both the fat and fiber content will slow down the emptying of the stomach.

Saturday candy

The child's usual afternoon snack:

2 sandwiches = 30 g carbohydrate

Saturday snack:

1 sandwich	= 15 g carboh.
20 - 30 g candy	≈ <u>15 g carboh.</u>
	30 g carboh.

15 - 20 g candy extra ≈ 10 g carboh. ➡ 1 U extra

(30 - 40g candy extra ≈ 20 g carboh. ➡ 2 U extra)

If the candy contains fat (e.g. chocolate) less extra insulin is needed since this produces a slower emptying of the stomach and thereby a slower rise in the blood-glucose level.

How much candy can the child have? You must try this out individually. A rule of the thumb is that more than half of the weight of candy is pure sugar. The carbohydrate content of a sandwich corresponds to approximately 20 - 30 g (1 ounce) of candy. Candy containing something besides sugar is better, such as milk chocolate or chocolate type sweets. Avoid caramels and other candies containing only pure sugar as these will increase your blood glucose level much more quickly.

A good way of having weekend candy is to take it during an afternoon walk in the woods, when riding or at a beach picnic. The children will then play around more, utilizing the extra calories that candy gives them.

What does the text on the candy mean?

Types of sugar	Fructose (fruit sugar) Lactose (milk sugar) Xylose
Sugar alcohols	Xylitol Mannitol Sorbitol
Hydrolyzed starch syrup	Lycasin
Rubber Arabicum	Jelly that makes the candy tough to chew
Gelatin	In foam candy. Dissolves in the stomach.

Candy stop?

It is not easy to manage diabetes when eating large amounts of candy as everyone who has tried can testify. And still many persons with diabetes do this. Outsiders observing teenagers at diabetes camp have commented: "We have never seen adolescents who crave candy as much as these". Such a situation is analogous to smoking — just cutting down doesn't work. You must totally refrain from candy, at least for some time. Unfortunately excessive candy eating must remain an exception for a person having diabetes. And if you do it every day it is not an exception any more...

Many families practice a system of" candy stop" as an alternative to weekend candy, both with and without diabetes in the family. The child will then receive money instead and often some kind of bonus if he/she can manage without candy for a half or whole year. This system works well for children who benefit from not having candy for other reasons as well, such as overweight. Adults can try giving themselves some kind of bonus, such as a new dress or a vacation, if they manage without candy for a longer period of time.

If you have weight problems you will find it difficult balancing candy and diabetes. If you eat candy containing fat this will affect your blood glucose less, but will cause you to gain weight. If you eat candy with less fat your blood glucose level will be affected more. A total candy stop is your only chance in this situation if you want to manage both your weight and your HbA_{1c}.

Licorice

Licorice contains a sweet compound called glycyrrhiza. Earlier licorice was used as a drug, for instance for treating stomach ulcers. Side effects of

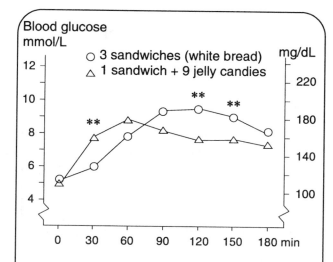

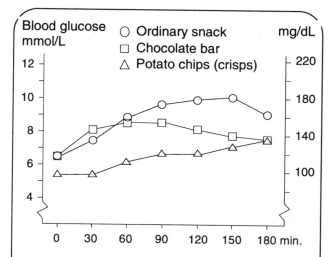

In a Swedish study 16 teenagers replaced 2 out of 3 sandwiches with jelly candies at snack time.[75] The blood glucose rise is slightly more rapid with jelly candies and sandwiches, but not at all as rapid as if they had eaten jelly candies alone. White bread contains almost no fibers but gives a larger volume compared to jelly candies alone, causing the stomach to empty more slowly. The fat in margarine and cheese also leads to a slower emptying of the stomach.

A sandwich made of bread rich in fiber, along with the jelly candies, would probably have made the blood glucose response even less pronounced. From this it follows that a good way to eat your Saturday candy is to eat it at snack-time. Begin with a sandwich and your blood glucose level will be less affected.

In another study different types of snacks with the same calorie-content were compared: 2½ slices of dark rye bread with cheese and an apple, a bar of milk chocolate (67 g, 2.3 ounces) and potato chips (crisps) (70 g, 2.5 ounces).[76] The ordinary snack containing slightly more carbohydrates gave the highest blood glucose rise while potato chips (crisps) gave the slowest rise. The bar of milk chocolate gave a slow rise making it unsuitable when hypoglycemic.

The fat in chocolate and potato chips (crisps) causes the stomach to empty more slowly and the increase in blood glucose level will thereby be slower. The food processing used in the manufacturing of chips causes the sugar to be less accessible to digesting enzymes, thereby being absorbed more slowly.

The message from the dietician Gunilla Cedermark who did these studies is not that we all should have chocolate and chips for snacks every day. Most children don't, even if they would very much like to... The difference is that saying "No!" to chips and bars of chocolate should be done on the same terms as it is for non-diabetic children. It is very important to avoid referring to diabetes more often than necessary when saying "No!".

A bar of chocolate is a good snack for children with diabetes when going on a hiking tour in the same way as for non-diabetic friends and siblings. During weekends you can replace the evening meal (or parts of it) with potato chips (crisps) together with the rest of your family and eat them with a good conscience.

a high licorice intake can be seen as swollen ankles, high blood pressure and salt disturbances. To be on the safe side one should not have more than 5 g (1/5 ounce) of licorice/day. The sugar content of licorice-candy is about the same as other types of candy.

Pastilles (small candy)

During our diabetes camp we exchange the apple of the afternoon snack (on the "Treasure hunt") for a box of pastilles (small candy) that contain jelly which makes them tougher to chew. Other pastilles which taste sweet and easily break into small pieces when chewing contain mostly pure sugar. Sugar-free pastilles usually contain sorbitol which is better for your teeth and raises the blood glucose level more slowly. We inform the children of these facts at the same time as they taste pastilles of various types to recognize the difference.

One box of sugar-free jelly-type pastilles (about 15 g, ½ ounce) has the same blood glucose raising effect as an apple or a pear. However, the contents of a box of sugar-type fruit pastilles gives the same effect as 6 lumps of dextrose (18 g, 2/3 ounce). If a

Which type of candy?

Pure sugar   **Jelly-type**   **Gelatinous**

Sugary   Jelly beans   Wine gum
sweets

6 tablets of
dextrose

Chew the tablets to feel the difference. The tougher they are, the longer time it takes the sugar to reach the blood stream and to affect your blood glucose level. If the pastilles are of the sugary type, one box (approximately 20 g, 2/3 ounce) contains the equivalent of 6 dextrose tablets while a box of the gelatinous type is equivalent to a fruit. Jelly-type tablets are somewhere in between. The longer time it takes for you to finish the box, the less it will affect your blood glucose level.

Different types of candy

	Quantity	Carb.	Fat	Kcal
Foam candy	100 g	83 g	0 g	350
Gelatinous candy	100 g	79 g	0 g	355
Caramels/ pastilles	100 g	97 g	0 g	400
Milk chocolate	100 g	54 g	33 g	570
Dark chocolate	100 g	60 g	32 g	560
Toffee	100 g	69 g	18 g	470

Carb. = carbohydrates

The contents are approximate as they vary from brand to brand. Chocolate with a high fat content will increase your blood glucose level more slowly. Gelatinous candy raises the blood glucose level more slowly than candy that is easy to chew.

The best time to eat candy is when physically active, when you have a low blood glucose level or together with a meal.

child chooses to eat one pastille of the jelly-type at a time during an afternoon it will not affect the blood glucose level at all. By saying this we don't mean that children should have pastilles every day. Weekend candy is a good rule for all children with or without diabetes. This situation should be the same as for families without diabetes, in that it is the parents who decide which rules that apply. The important thing is that a child with diabetes feel that he/she receives as far as possible equal treatment as their non-diabetic friends and siblings when it comes to candy.

These principals pertaining to ice cream and candy contain both freedom and responsibility. To be able to manage well one must practise and experiment. It is important to measure the blood glucose level both before and after trying something new. The blood glucose level will most often not be perfect the first time around, but after a couple of times you will get to know your body better. If the child demonstrates that he/she can handle such occasions in an acceptable manner it is OK — but if the child is careless one must withdraw all "Candy rights" for a while until the child has learned how to do things properly. The logbook is important — afterwards one can go back and determine what worked well and what did not.

Chewing gum

Chewing gum contains such small amounts of sugar (about 10 g, 1/3 ounce/package) that chewing one piece at a time over a couple of hours will not be a problem. If you chew in this way you can just as well use ordinary chewing gum as "sugar-free" from a diabetic point of view, but your dentist will of course recommend the latter. If you prefer chewing half a package at a time it is better to choose a brand with an artificial sweetener, like NutraSweet®.

Utilize the opportunity to eat your weekly candy ration when doing some physical exercise. One girl had her "Friday candy" every week while horse-riding and it did not affect her blood glucose level at all.

Weight control

Maintaining weight can be a big problem for many teenage girls even if they don't have diabetes. Many non-diabetic girls gain considerable weight the years following their first menstruation. They continue to eat the same amounts of food although they have stopped growing (normally a girl grows only 6 - 8 cm (2 - 3 inches) in total after their first menstruation). The difference for a girl with diabetes is that it is much more difficult to lose weight. It is therefore very important for teenage girls with diabetes to decrease both food intake and insulin doses after reaching their final height.

Being full or "stuffed"?

We often say that children should always eat enough to feel satisfied, but without differentiating between satiated and "stuffed". Feeling satisfied is not the same as eating as much as you want. Even younger children in their first years at school usually understand this reasoning and are often very motivated not go gain too much weight.

Of course it is unfair that some individuals can eat as much as they want while others gain weight by just looking at food. The reason for this is that our bodies work differently when it comes to taking care of energy and storing it. During the Stone Age it was very efficient to be able to store energy as fat when food was not available on a daily basis. Today this ability has instead become a disadvantage when the supply of food is unlimited.

Many children prefer to eat large helpings at every meal. This easily becomes a habit and the stomach will after a while become distended. There will be room for even more food before one feels full and satisfied. Stop eating when you begin to feel satisfied and wait for 10 - 15 minutes. Your feelings of hunger will then probably have disappeared although you have not eaten anymore. Vegetables will satisfy hunger without supplying carbohydrates or calories and are a good alternative if the child still wants more to eat.

Finishing up what is on the plate is something most parents are strict about. When trying to lose weight it can at times be difficult to know by sight how much you are going to eat. If you have weight problems, you should therefore ask permission to leave food on the plate if you find that you have taken too much and feel satisfied before you have finished.

Reducing weight

Losing weight can easily lead to a vicious circle when having diabetes. Taking insulin forces you to eat even if you are not hungry at the time. You cannot skip a meal as a non-diabetic person can. Instead you must try to decrease the amount of food and at the same time decrease the insulin doses. It is difficult to find the appropriate balance between insulin and food in this situation.

It may be difficult to know what to eat less of. Write down everything you eat during 3 days and record the exact quantities (include everything, food, drink, candy, ice cream and so on). Ask your dietitian to calculate the energy amounts and help you how to reduce the fat and calorie amounts.

If you decrease the amounts of food you will risk hypoglycemia, forcing you to eat in order to reverse it. Remember not to eat too much when having hypoglycemia. 10 grams (1/3 ounce) of sugar (3 pieces of dextrose, 2 for a younger child) is usually enough (see page 49). Then wait 10 - 15 min before eating anything else, even if you are still hungry, thus allowing the blood glucose level time to rise.

You should avoid losing weight too quickly. A slow and steady loss resulting from a change in habits is better than a quick loss caused by reducing your food intake to a minimum. A sufficient rate is usually 1 - 3 kg/month (2 - 6 pounds). It may not sound like much, but will result in many kilos in one year. Complete fasting can be dangerous for a person with diabetes and it is something I definitely discourage (see also page 164).

The little extras

A little extra food, candy or cookies every day will amount to quite a lot before the year is over. About 7000 kcal are needed to build up 1 kg (2.2 pounds) of fat in the body. An extra bun or a small sandwich each day (100 kcal) will cause you to put on 5 kilos of weight in one year! A small bag of peanuts (175 g, 6 ounces) *every week* will result in almost 8 kg (17 pounds) weight increase in one year!

Losing weight by having a high HbA$_{1c}$

Having a high blood glucose level will result in a loss of large amounts of glucose in the urine. You might say that you "eat for two" since you not only eat to cover your daily energy requirements but also for the glucose lost in the urine. When your HbA$_{1c}$ is between 9 and 10 % it is not unusual to lose glucose in the urine corresponding to 30 lumps of sugar in one day. The most I have seen is 205 g of glucose (7 ounces, 68 lumps of sugar) in the urine during 24 hours.

How do you count calories?

All food is made up of from different ingredients. Check the table of contents to calculate how many calories you will get.

Fat	9 kcal/g
Sugar	4 kcal/g
Protein	4 kcal/g
Alcohol	7 kcal/g
Sugar alcohol (in candy)	4 kcal/g

Having a high HbA$_{1c}$ can be an effective but dangerous way to lose weight. Many teenagers will deliberately skip insulin injections not to gain weight. In an American study 15 % of teenage girls with diabetes (but no boys) had used this method to diet.[320] You may win a few kilograms (pounds) temporarily, but the high blood glucose level that follows will increase the risk of long time complications. Instead of using this method, you should speak to your nurse at the diabetes clinic and he or she will try to help you find a safe way to control your weight.

Teenager, high HbA$_{1c}$ and overweight — what can I do?

Increasing the insulin doses will cause your body to use the glucose that was earlier lost in the urine and you will gain weight. Unfortunately this is the only way to do it because the high blood glucose level as such has induced an increased insulin resistance (see page 70). What you must do is to increase the insulin doses for a while (one or a few weeks) and then lower them as quickly as possible again. If you, at the same time, decrease food intake (talk to your dietitian!) you will have a good chance of succeeding.

Remember that if your blood glucose level has been high for some time you will have early symptoms

Calorie table

The following will give you 100 kcal		Activities which will spend 100 kcal	
Whipped cream	2 dl	Walking	
Sugar	4 lumps	slow	40 min.
Oil	2 teasp.	quick	15 min.
Mayonnaise	1 tbs	Bicycling	
Bun	1	normal	35 min.
Danish pastry	½	quick	10 min.
Chips	20 chips		
Peanuts	15g	Running	10 min.
Candy	8-10 pieces	Skating	25 min.
Chocolate	20g		
Snowball	1	Dancing	25 min.
Light beer	40 cl	Wood-	
Beer	25 cl	cutting	15 min.
White wine	10 cl		
Liquor	4.4 cl	Swimming	10 min.
Liqueur	2.8 cl		

28 g = 1 ounce, 10 cl ≈ 0.2 pints

How many lumps of sugar do I lose in the urine?

① Collect all urine for 24 hours. Start by voiding for example at 6 PM. (Do *not* collect that urine). Then collect all urine after that until 6 AM the next day (including the 6 AM urine). Mix all urine in a container.

② Note the total volume and leave a small sample at the laboratory. You will get an answer in mmol or grams of glucose.

③ mmol / 5.55 = grams of glucose
For ex. 459 mmol/day = 459 / 5.55 = 82.7 g/day.

④ 1 lump of sugar = 3 g
82.7 g/day = 82.7 / 3 = 27.5 lumps of sugar/day

⑤ 1 gram of glucose gives 4 kcal
82.7 g/day gives 82.7 x 4 = 330.8 kcal/day.

⑥ 7 000 kcal equals 1 kg of body fat.
330.8 kcal = 330.8 / 7 000 = 47g fat/day.

⑦ 47 g fat/day equals 47 x 365 = 17 kg fat in one year

Quick equation: 100 mmol of glucose in the urine/day equals 3.8 kg fat in one year (20 g of glucose equals 4.2 kg fat).

5.6 mmol = 1 g, 1 kg = 2.2 pounds

Exchange list

It is more important than one might imagine to choose an alternative with fewer calories. The table shows the difference (Diff.) between food stuffs in calories and weight gain.

If you replace	with	Diff. in kcal	Diff. in Weight
5 dl standard milk	5 dl low fat milk	120 kcal/day	6 kg /year
3 sandwiches with margarine and fat cheese	3 sandwiches with low-fat cheese but without margarine	205 kcal/day	10 kg /year
1 fried egg	1 boiled egg	40 kcal /day	2 kg /year
2 tbs mayonnaise	½ dl sour cream	155 kcal	1 kg/ 45 times
1 bar of chocolate	1 apple	235 kcal	1 kg/ 30 times
1 helping of french fries	1 helping of boiled potatoes	145 kcal	1 kg/ 50 times
1 bottle of beer	1 bottle of light-beer	45 kcal	1 kg/155 bottles)
1 bag of peanuts (175g)	5 dl of popcorn	1000 kcal	1½ kg/ 10 bags

1 dl ≈ 0.2 pints, 1 kg = 2.2 pounds

of hypoglycemia even at a low normal blood glucose level of 4 - 5 mmol/L (70 - 90 mg/dL).[64,193,218] You should therefore always take a blood glucose test when you feel hypoglycemic. Eat only if your glucose level is less than 3 - 3.5 mmol/L (55 - 65 mg/dL). If the blood glucose level is higher try to withstand eating despite symptoms. Your body is giving warning symptoms but remember that it believes that you want a higher blood glucose level as this has been the case for some time (see "At which blood glucose level will I experience symptoms of hypoglycemia?" on page 40). You must be prepared for a difficult time during the first 1 - 2 weeks but you will then experience warning symptoms at a lower blood glucose level. It is a good idea to have a friend or parent present when you practice this. You will need support and understanding from someone close to you to make it work.

One might sometimes feel the need for a guard by the refrigerator when you crave for something tasty...
One extra sandwich/day turns into 8 kg of extra fat in one year!

Does alcohol contain calories?

As a teenager or adult, you should be aware of the fact that alcohol contains quite a lot of calories (1 gram of alcohol gives 7 kcal, almost the same as 1 g of fat, which gives 9 kcal/g). A beer or a glass of wine per day will give 40 000 calories in one year that the body will transform into 5.8 kg (13 pounds) of fat! See also the table "Alcohol and calories" on page 184.

Eating disorders

Both anorexia and bulimia (binge eating) are symptoms of a weight phobia, in that the individual finds it impossible to eat without gaining weight. The body perception is always disturbed but the emotional disturbance is more important. A person with an eating disorder often has difficulties in understanding the seriousness of the problem and sees no reason to seek medical help. Eating disorders are more common amongst girls, but can occur in boys as well. Anorexia usually starts between 13 - 16 years of age, bulimia somewhat later.

Anorexia is defined as a weight loss of at least 15 % of the estimated normal weight for age or not being able to reach this weight at all. There is also an extreme fear of gaining weight and an erroneous perception of how the body appears (when looking into the mirror you experience yourself as fat although others think you are very slim). Food fixation is common, i.e. being interested in cooking for others but not eating anything oneself. A person with anorexia is usually quite physically active, often running many miles a day in an attempt to keep their weight down.

The starvation that a person with anorexia is going through can result in many bodily symptoms, such as headaches, lowered body temperature, increased body hair and irregular or disrupted menstruations. The psychological symptoms may include depression, feelings of insufficiency, sleeping disturbances and obsessions.

With bulimia one gorges large amounts of food, much more than a normal person can eat at one sitting. One loses control and cannot stop eating. Self-inflicted vomiting or laxatives are used to control the weight. These individuals are often very impulsive and may have difficulties with the regularity that their diabetes illness requires in order to be managed effectively.[332]

Eating disorders have both a hereditary and socio-cultural background and value changes of today's society play a significant roll. Family factors are also important. Certain sensitive individuals are more prone to have eating disorders.

Having an eating disorder is difficult. One often tries to manipulate the insulin when having anorexia or bulimia. It is not easy to find the right doses and one often has problems with low or high blood glucose levels. If you have anorexia or bulimia you definitely will need help. Tell one of us at the diabetes clinic or another adult in whom you have confidence so that we can refer you to a specialist in these problems.

In an American study eating disorder criteria were fulfilled in 9 % of 11 - 18 year old's, and were met with equal frequency amongst girls with diabetes.[320] Having diabetes and an eating disorder usually implies a bad blood glucose control and tendencies to manipulate insulin doses to control weight.[320,332,333]

Not eating enough causes low blood glucose levels and omitting insulin doses results in high blood glucose peaks. A person with diabetes cannot starve themselves the same way a non-diabetic can due to the hunger effect of insulin. It is much more dangerous for a teenager with diabetes to induce vomiting or purging. The body will be easily thrown off balance, especially if you change insulin doses up and down as well. Your condition can deteriorate to a dangerous level and hospitalization may be necessary. A high HbA_{1c} will also increase the risks for late complications from your diabetes in the future.

Anorexia and bulimia require long term psychiatric treatment Family therapy is the method of choice for teenage girls with a newly diagnosed anorexia. The treatment is usually provided in close collaboration between the pediatrician and a child psychiatrist/psychologist. Most people with these disorders will recover if they get the proper treatment.

Physical exercise

Physical exercise is healthy for everyone and a body in good general condition can withstand hardships better. However, exercise must be enjoyable and should not be something one is forced into. Younger children usually run around a lot while playing. Older children are very different. Some like sports or riding while others prefer to sit still with books, the television or a computer. We must adjust the insulin treatment to the individual and not the other way around.

Controlled studies have not been able to show a better diabetes control due to physical exercise.[382,417] Because of this fact, exercise is not considered as a treatment for diabetes. However, as with other children a child with diabetes should be encouraged to take part in some form of regular physical activity, even if it is only riding the bicycle to and from school. Regular physical exercise will decrease the risk of cardiovascular diseases. The pronounced lack of exercise and muscular activity that some teenage girls show seems to contribute to

an increased insulin resistance, a tendency to be overweight and worsened blood glucose control.[268]

When performing muscular work, the store of glucose in the muscles (muscle glycogen, approximately 400 g in an adult person) is utilized first. Secondly glucose from the blood and fatty acids (break-down products from fat) are used as fuel. Exercise lowers the blood glucose level by increasing glucose uptake into the muscle cells without increasing the amount of insulin needed. The reason for this is that more glucose is consumed in the muscles during exercise. After exercise, the muscles will have increased insulin sensitivity for 1 - 2 days [414] (see also "Insulin sensitivity and resistance" on page 69). This means that exercise four times/week will result in increased insulin sensitivity even between the training sessions and the total insulin dose can probably be lowered. Sometimes the increased insulin sensitivity does not begin until 4 - 6 hours after the exercise.[414]

When exercising the leg muscles insulin injected in the thigh will be absorbed somewhat more quickly from the subcutaneous tissue.[152] If you inject insulin deep enough to enter the muscle it will be absorbed much more quickly and you will risk having hypoglycemia (see page 62). *It is important to remember that exercise does not lower the blood glucose level at all if insulin is not present.* Glucose in the blood cannot enter the muscle cells without help of insulin.

The rate of glucose uptake into the muscles of an adult is approximately 8 - 12 g/hour (1/3 - 1/2 ounce/hour) when exercising at an ordinary rate and more than double with heavy exercise.[417] The levels of the hormones, adrenaline, glucagon and cortisone in the bloodstream increase during physical exercise. Glucose is released from the liver depot (liver glycogen, see page 32) and new glucose is produced in the liver from proteins. If the liver was unable to increase its glucose production the blood glucose level will decrease by about 0.1 mmol/L (2 mg/dL) per minute during exercise,

Exercise and effects on the blood glucose level

➠ Increased absorption of insulin from the injection site.

➠ Increases the consumption of glucose without increasing the need for insulin.

➠ BUT — insulin must be available or the muscle cells are not able to take up glucose!

➠ **Beware!** - Do not exercise when there is a lack of insulin (ketones in the urine and blood glucose above 15 - 16 mmol/L, 270 - 290 mg/dL). Take an extra insulin injection (2 - 4 units) and abstain from exercise until the blood glucose level has decreased (2 - 3 hours).

➠ Risk of hypoglycemia many hours afterwards (in the evening or night) since you have used the liver's store of glycogen during exercise.

How do insulin and exercise work together?

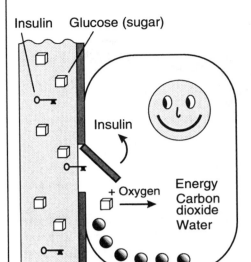

Insulin   Glucose (sugar)

Insulin

+ Oxygen

Energy
Carbon
dioxide
Water

Blood vessel   Cell

Sitting still

Insulin "opens the door" to the cell for glucose to enter. The size of your insulin dose decide how quickly your blood glucose level will fall. Your regular insulin doses during school or work days are adjusted for your normal physical activity.

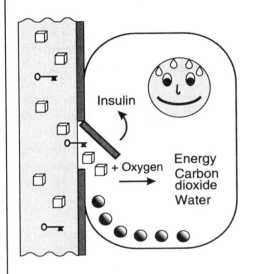

Insulin

+ Oxygen

Energy
Carbon
dioxide
Water

Physical exercise

If you play soccer or take part in some other type of intensive physical activity you will need to lower the insulin dose. Exercise will cause the same amount of insulin to keep the door open for a little longer, i.e. more glucose will be transported into the cell, and the blood glucose level can easily fall too low. Decrease the insulin dose slightly.

The effect of exercise will last for at least 8 - 10 hours which means that you should decrease your bedtime insulin as well (by 2 - 4 units) to avoid hypoglycemia after heavy exercise.

Exercise when there is a lack of insulin

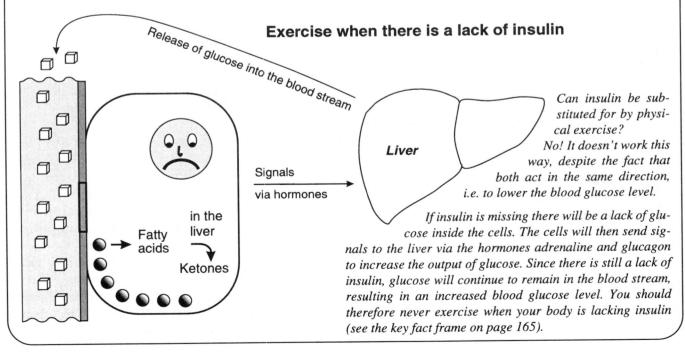

Release of glucose into the blood stream

Signals
via hormones

Liver

Fatty
acids

in the
liver

Ketones

Can insulin be substituted for by physical exercise?

No! It doesn't work this way, despite the fact that both act in the same direction, i.e. to lower the blood glucose level.

If insulin is missing there will be a lack of glucose inside the cells. The cells will then send signals to the liver via the hormones adrenaline and glucagon to increase the output of glucose. Since there is still a lack of insulin, glucose will continue to remain in the blood stream, resulting in an increased blood glucose level. You should therefore never exercise when your body is lacking insulin (see the key fact frame on page 165).

quickly resulting in hypoglycemia.[417] A high level of insulin in the blood counteracts the production of glucose in the liver and thereby increases the risk of hypoglycemia. In non-diabetic persons the level of insulin in the blood decreases during exercise.[417]

Can the blood glucose level increase from exercise?

Running will only lower your blood glucose level if insulin is available to "open the door" for glucose to enter the muscle cells. If there is a lack of insulin the blood glucose level will instead increase even more.

The blood glucose level will increase from exercise if there is a lack of insulin. The cells don't "understand" that there is plenty of glucose in the blood stream. On the contrary they act as if the body were starving (see fig. 2 and 3 on page 20). This is caused by the muscle cells having a lack of glucose following a period of exercise in the presence of insulin deficiency. The muscle glycogen is spent and due to insulin deficiency new glucose cannot enter the cells. Signals are sent to the liver to release more glucose from the liver's glycogen depot.

The signals to the liver are mediated by the hormones glucagon and adrenaline. The increased amount of glucose in the blood comes from both a breakdown of the liver's glycogen and a production of glucose in the liver. At the same time there will be a breakdown of fat to fatty acids which are transformed into ketones in the liver, resulting in a risk of developing ketoacidosis.[417]

When the blood glucose level is above 15 - 16 mmol/L (270 - 290 mg/dL), and there are ketones in the urine indicating a deficiency of insulin, exercise should be postponed. Running to lower a high blood glucose in this situation is not a good idea. It might even be dangerous.

Some friends of mine met a 45-year old man when starting out on a mountain hike. He asked them if he could accompany them as he was alone, and

they agreed. During the second day the man began having nausea, vomited and was very tired. He then told my friends that he had diabetes. He had been told that exercise lowers the blood glucose level and he thought that exercise might cure his diabetes. He had left all his insulin at home. One of my friends ran 20 km (13 miles) to the nearest telephone, and called for an helicopter. But when it reached the camping site the man was already dead. He died from a diabetes coma caused by a total lack of insulin. The insulin deficiency was worsened by the hard physical exercise.

This happened many years ago. Today knowledge is better and most persons with diabetes know that it is dangerous to not take insulin. In spite of this, episodes of serious ketoacidosis, caused by missed insulin injections, and requiring hospital treatment, are not uncommon. Many of these cases involve teenagers who do not realize how dangerous it can be to omit insulin injections.

With very heavy exertion, such as competitive sports, excessive amounts of adrenaline may be secreted, causing the blood glucose level to rise in spite of adequate insulin levels.[364]

Hypoglycemia after exercise

As the glycogen stores in the liver are depleted during heavy exercise there is a greatly increased risk of hypoglycemia several hours after the exercise. The muscles will have increased insulin sensitivity for at least another 8 - 10 hours, sometimes up to 18 hours after the exercise is finished. This means that there is a risk for hypoglycemia during the night

Riding your bicycle to and from school will give you some exercise every day. It is easier to find suitable insulin doses when exercising daily than if you sit still one day and do a lot of exercise the next.

> ***One can never replace insulin with exercise!***
> When exercising the need of insulin will be lower but if you exercise without enough insulin in your body the blood glucose level will rise.

after a game. The first thing to do is to try to refill the glycogen stores in liver and muscles, i.e. eat during and after the exercise. Count on an additional need of 10 - 15 grams (1/3 - 1/2 ounce) of carbohydrate (15 - 30 grams, 1/2 - 1 ounce, for an adult) for every 30 minutes of exercise after the initial 30 minutes. [414]

In an American study teenagers consumed a sports drink (Gatorade®, 6.5 % sucrose/glucose) corresponding to 1.3 grams of carbohydrate/10 kg body weight (5 grains/10 pounds) and exercised for 10 minutes.[390] In spite of this the blood glucose level fell by 4 - 5 mmol/L after 90 min. The boys performed the same test for 2 days and there was a clear similarity between the glucose lowering effect of exercise for each person during the testing. You might find it valuable to experiment with different amounts of carbohydrate during a game and then to consume the same amount of extra carbohydrate every time you play. If you start exercising within one hour of your insulin injection the absorption will be increased and you will probably need to further increase your carbohydrate intake while in action.[390]

Remember that it takes more than one meal to refill the glycogen stores in the liver and muscles after heavy physical exertion. This means that even if you have eaten a hardy meal after the game you may encounter hypoglycemia later in the day or evening since the glycogen stores have not had time to be refilled completely. If you play both in the morning and afternoon you are more susceptible to hypoglycemia during the afternoon game for the same reason.

In practise this often implies a need for extra food with the evening meal if the child has played a game after dinner. The child's appetite is usually a good indicator of how much is enough. Most often, the bedtime insulin dose should be decreased as well to avoid nighttime hypoglycemia (by 1 - 2 units for a younger child, 2 - 4 units for a teenager) and/or at the evening meal (by 1 - 2 units).

Physical education

Children and teenagers with diabetes can and should take part in physical education (P.E.) to the same extent as non-diabetic youngsters. To minimize the risk of hypoglycemia such activities should be placed during the first (or possibly the second) class in the morning or alternatively the first (or possibly the second) class after lunch. The

---

Physical exercise — rules

① Plan ahead so that you have eaten and taken your premeal insulin 1 - 2 hours before the exercise. You will otherwise risk having the greatest blood glucose lowering effect when starting your exercise.

② Take both a blood and urine test before starting the exercise. If the blood glucose is below 5 - 6 mmol/L (90 - 110 mg/dL) you should eat something before starting.[417] If you have ketones in the urine (but no glucose), showing that your cells are starving, you should wait until the blood glucose has increased before starting.

If the blood glucose is above 15 - 16 mmol/L (270 - 290 mg/dL) you should take extra insulin before starting the exercise. If you also have ketones in the urine exercise is forbidden for 1 - 2 hours until the insulin has had its effect.

③ Eat extra during exercise if it lasts longer than 30 minutes. Depending on your body size ½ - 1 banana (10 - 20 g of glucose) is usually suitable. Find out what suits you best. Take blood tests when exercising and note them in your logbook for future reference.

Check a urine test after exercise. Ketones without glucose means that you should have eaten more (starvation ketones). You need to empty your bladder before exercising in order to be able to interpret this correctly.

④ Decrease the insulin doses following exercise (evening premeal by 1 - 2 units and bedtime dose by 2 - 4 units).

⑤ Decrease the insulin doses prior to exercise as well, if necessary (especially with heavy exercise).

⑥ If you exercise to lose weight it is important to lower the premeal dose instead of eating extra after the exercise.

---

second class after lunch is not as suitable for younger children since they usually play during the lunch break as well. Arrange for the child to have an extra snack before the physical education if needed. Talk to the physical education teacher about the schedule well in advance to ensure that suitable arrangements are made.

Tips for heavy exercise

4 PM **Dinner.**
Ordinary insulin dose.
(Lower before competitive sport)
Make sure you have taken the premeal dose at least 1 hour before the game.
Take a blood test:

< 6 mmol/L   Eat extra carbohydrates
< 110 mg/dL

6 - 10 mmol/L OK to start
110 - 180 mg/dL

11-15 mmol/L Go ahead but take a blood glucose
180-270   test again after 1 hour. If the level is
mg/dL   decreasing there is insulin available and it is OK to continue. If the level is increasing there is a lack of insulin and you should stop exercising and take extra insulin.

>16 mmol/L Check for ketones in the urine.
> 270 mg/dL If positive take about 0.1 unit/kg (0.05 unit/pound) body weight of short-acting (or preferably direct-acting) insulin and wait 1 - 2 hours for it to have an effect.

5 PM **Game.**
½ (-1) banana just before the game.
Repeat at half-time

8 PM **Evening meal.**
Eat more than usual. You can try taking your ordinary dose but usually one will need to decrease it by 1 - 2 units.

10 PM **Bedtime insulin.**
Always lower the dose by 2 - 4 units or sometimes even more.
Always give the bedtime insulin in the thigh or buttocks!

Insulin doses: You often need to decrease the premeal dose before the game and/or with the evening meal when performing elite level sports. Find what suits you best - there are no universal solutions.

Rule of thumb: For every 30 min. of heavy exercise you will need about 10 - 15 g (1/3 - 1/2 ounce) of extra carbohydrate (15 - 30 g, 1/2 - 1 ounce, for an adult). Take half as "quick-acting" carbohydrates (like juice, sports drink) and half as slower carbohydrates (like a chocolate bar) or eat ½ - 1 banana (about 20 g, 2/3 ounces, of carbohydrate).

Hypoglycemia: Make sure that your coach and team-mates know how to help you if needed. Always carry dextrose in a pocket!

The blood glucose lowering effect of exercise will last for at least 8 - 10 hours.
Always lower the bedtime dose by 2 - 4 units after heavy exertion, such as a game of handball or soccer.

Due to the risk of hypoglycemia a child with diabetes should always be together with a friend (who knows how to help) when on outings such as nature walks, cross country running, swimming or on a school trip.

Camps and ski trips

When physically active for a longer period of time, as when on a ski trip or at a football camp, you will have an increased insulin sensitivity after 1 - 2 days which will probably call for substantially lower insulin doses (decreased by 30 % or sometimes even 50 %). You must increase your food intake to compensate for the increased energy output. One is generally hungrier after having been active all day. The increased insulin sensitivity will continue for at least a couple of days after returning home. Check your blood glucose levels and you will see when it is time to increase the insulin doses again.

Top level competitive sports

You can certainly take part in competitive sports even if you have diabetes. However, one should be careful with strenuous physical exercise if you have pronounced complications from the eyes, kidneys or nervous system as it will increase the risk of high blood pressure or skin wounds.[417] There are many successful sportsmen and -women with diabetes playing on international teams or at a professional level. Having a normal blood glucose level is essential to achieve maximum performance. You may need to decrease the insulin dose prior to the physical exercise, for example a football or soccer game. Remember that it takes several hours after a difficult hypoglycemia to return to a level of maximum performance. Check your blood glucose level frequently to find out how your body reacts in different situations during training and competition. It is easier to plan food intake and insulin doses for the training sessions if they take place at regular times.

The best time to begin exercising is 1 - 2 hours after a meal (when on multiple daily injections). During the first hour after an insulin injection the level of insulin in the blood increases quickly. If you were to exercise during this time, insulin would be absorbed even quicker (especially if you have injected in the thigh) and you will risk having hypoglycemia. You should therefore avoid injecting premeal doses in the thigh before exercising. Wait preferably one hour after the injection before you start intensive muscle work (warming up should be OK). If you must start within one hour you may need to decrease the premeal dose. If you have problems with nighttime hypoglycemia following evening training sessions it may be better to reschedule them to the afternoon.[417] Avoid strenuous training sessions when alone as you may need the help of a friend if you have a difficult or severe hypoglycemia.

If you use an insulin pump try taking the premeal dose as usual (or perhaps 1 - 2 units less) and disconnect the pump during the time of exercise (but not for more than 1 - 2 hours). Another alternative is to try skipping the premeal injection before exercising, and keeping the pump connected with the basal rate running during the exercise.

At competitions the situation is slightly different even though you perform the same physical work as when training. The stress will increase your blood glucose level (by increasing the liver output of glucose) with the help of adrenaline. This usually reduces the risk of hypoglycemia and the need for extra carbohydrates during a competition compared to a training session. On the other hand you will have an even greater need of eating extra afterwards to refill the glycogen stores in the liver and muscles. If you encounter increased blood glucose levels at the start of the competition you can try taking the insulin dose less than an hour before.

The effect of stress will often reveal itself early on during a competition. It is usually short-lived, often lasting only 10 or 20 minutes.[362] Different individuals react differently and you should find out how you react, for example by testing your blood glucose level during the first break of the game (as the professional soccer player Gary Mabbut does, see page 243).

One study of teenagers with diabetes showed that those with higher HbA_{1c} had poorer physical work capacity.[32] This means that if you want to achieve top performance you must also have an optimal HbA_{1c}. Competitive athletes risk decreasing their insulin too much in an attempt to avoid hypoglycemia, thus resulting in higher HbA_{1c}'s compared to those doing moderate physical exercise.[234] Although physical training enhances insulin sensitivity, it improves HbA_{1c} levels only if blood glucose is carefully monitored.

Marathon run!?

When performing heavy physical activity for an entire day you may need to lower your insulin doses considerably, (often 25% and sometimes even 50 %). You will need extra energy, glucose and fluid at regular intervals (approximately 40 g carbohydrate/hour). When performing prolonged physical work (many hours) it is best to try to gradually increase the time of activity by 1 - 2 hours each day. If you use an insulin pump or take basal insulin twice daily (2-dose treatment or 2 injections of intermediate/long-acting insulin using multiple daily injections) you will probably need to lower the basal dose. You may need short-acting or direct-acting insulin more frequently (every 2nd - 4th hour) together with extra energy in the form of quick carbohydrates.

How much energy is spent per hour? (adults)

⇒	Slow walking	100 - 200 kcal
⇒	Bicycling (leisure)	250 - 300 kcal
⇒	Table tennis, golf, tennis (doubles)	300 - 350 kcal
⇒	Dancing	300 - 400 kcal
⇒	Gymnastics	300 - 400 kcal
⇒	Tennis (singles)	400 - 500 kcal
⇒	Work-out	approximately 500 kcal
⇒	Jogging, downhill skiing, soccer	500 - 600 kcal
⇒	Swimming	approximately 600 kcal
⇒	Cross-country skiing	800 - 1000 kcal

It is possible to dive when having diabetes. You must be extra careful to avoid hypoglycemia as this can be very dangerous when under water. However, it is not justifiable from a medical standpoint to have a standard diving certificate. Diving with an instructor or two diving mates is always advisable.

One father took a very long distance canoeing trip with his two sons, covering the entire coast line of Sweden (more than 2000 km, 1250 miles). One of the boys was 15 years old, and had diabetes. He managed the whole trip without severe hypoglycemia. Discuss with your doctor how to plan insulin doses, food intake and glucose testing before attempting such extreme situations.

Anabolic steroids

Anabolic steroids are unfortunately used by many sportsmen in spite of all the warnings from the medical profession, not to mention the risk of being discovered in a doping control. How do anabolic steroids affect your diabetes? In non-diabetic persons anabolic steroids have caused disturbed glucose metabolism due to a decreased insulin effect (increased insulin resistance). Anabolic steroids will probably increase the insulin resistance also in persons with diabetes, but this has not yet been studied. In the long run there is also a risk of hormonal changes and some reports indicate problems with impotence. The long-term effects of anabolic steroids are not very well understood today.

Diving

Diving is a fascinating sport and places great demands on the persons performing it. Things that are easily done on shore (like opening a package of dextrose) may be very difficult to do in the water even if symptoms of hypoglycemia are absent. Diving with diabetes has often been discussed and there are different opinions on this issue.

Olle Sandelin, Swedish diving physician: [344]
— A declaration of health for a normal diving cer-

Tips when diving

➡ To be able to experience obvious symptoms of hypoglycemia below 4 mmol/L (70 mg/dL) on the day of diving you must carefully avoid having any readings below 4 - 5 mmol/L (70 - 90 mg/dL) 1 - 2 weeks prior to the dive.

➡ ***Never*** dive if you have hypoglycemic unawareness or if you have had any readings below 3.0 mmol/L (55 mg/dL) within 24 hours of the dive (otherwise your hypoglycemic warning symptoms will be inadequate, see page 42).

➡ Don't drink alcohol within 24 hours of the dive.

➡ Eat more carbohydrate than usual the day of the dive.

➡ Dive after a meal. Start diving at the earliest 60 min. after the premeal insulin dose. Try decreasing the dose by 1 - 2 units. The blood glucose level should be at least 8, preferably 10 mmol/L (145 - 180 mg/dL) when you start diving. Eat extra carbohydrates just before the dive.

➡ Have 2 packages of glucose in the pockets of your wet suit and practice taking them out in and under water. Glucagon for injection should be readily available in the boat and on the shore.

➡ Always dive with a friend who is capable of giving you adequate help (such as glucose under water) if you have hypoglycemia.

➡ Decide on a signal in advance to indicate when you begin to feel hypoglycemic.

➡ Measure your blood glucose after the dive and take extra food or insulin. If you deliberately have a slightly higher blood glucose level when diving you can take some extra insulin if it is still high after the dive. Otherwise your HbA_{1c} will be negatively affected if you dive often. Be aware of the risk for hypoglycemia after heavy exertion and use only small doses of extra insulin.

➡ Remember that diving illness ("the bends") and hypoglycemia give similar symptoms.

➡ All members of the diving team must be informed that you have diabetes.

See reference [129] and [239] for further advice.

tificate is not at all possible when it comes to diabetic individuals treated with insulin. Persons with diabetes should dive with an instructor or with a so called handicap certificate which is only valid when accompanied by two persons instead of one, which is the usual requirement.

Consulting physician Bengt Pergel from the Swedish Marine: [255]
— An ordinary diving certificate should not be issued to a person with diabetes out of consideration for both the diver and the person she/he is diving with. If a person diving has diabetes it is essential that everyone in the diving team know about it.

— When it comes to the physical examination the doctor issuing the certificate must be able to verify that the person doesn't have an increased risk of hypoglycemia when doing the heavy physical work associated with diving. This may be a difficult decision even for a qualified diabetologist. It is virtually impossible to adjust blood glucose levels while diving and it is very difficult even when swimming at the surface.

— If a diver counts on having glucose available their life jacket pocket he/she has probably never been diving in rapid water or a rough sea.

— In conclusion certain individuals with diabetes should be able to dive, but only in a group where everybody is informed about the disease and knows how to treat hypoglycemia.

It becomes somewhat of a "vicious cycle" when diving with diabetes. To be able to dive you must have a well controlled diabetes and an optimal HbA_{1c}. On the other hand this will imply an increased risk of developing hypoglycemia and if so you should not dive.

My advice is as follows:
You must have a well controlled diabetes without complications and an optimal HbA_{1c} (less than 7 - 8 %) to minimize the risk of feeling unwell due to an insulin deficit when diving. We now also know that the blood glucose level at which you will have hypoglycemia depends on your average blood glucose level during the previous 1 - 2 weeks as well as the number of recent low blood glucose readings (see "At which blood glucose level will I experience symptoms of hypoglycemia?" on page 40). If you do not have hypoglycemic symptoms until the blood glucose level falls below 3 - 3.5 mmol/L (55 - 65 mg/dL) you will have much too little leeway before the brain is affected by a lack of glucose during a dive.

You should start 2 weeks prior to the dive by slightly increasing your average blood glucose level. Even more important is to avoid blood glucose readings below 4 - 5 mmol/L, (70 - 90 mg/dL) as this will raise the threshold of your bodily symptoms, enabling you to appreciate hypoglycemia earlier. When diving you must be able to clearly recognize symptoms of blood glucose levels below 4 mmol/L (70 mg/dL). If you have so called hypoglycemic unawareness (see page 42) with blood glucose levels less than 3 mmol/L (55 mg/dL), without symptoms, *your life will be in danger* while diving!

You should eat extra carbohydrates before diving just as you would before a strenuous physical exercise to keep your blood glucose level reasonably high (around 10 - 12 mmol/L, 180 - 215 mg/dL) in order to, as far as possible, prevent hypoglycemia under water. Cold water increases the body's energy consumption!

Be careful not to decrease your premeal insulin dose by more than 1 - 2 units in spite of extra physical exercise or work. It is better to eat extra. If your blood glucose level is high due to an insulin deficit you will not feel well and diving will be dangerous to your life. Also check for urinary ketones before diving (see page 80). The message here is that it is much better to have a high glucose level because of eating too much rather than due to too little insulin.

Hypoglycemia in or under water is the greatest problem when diving with diabetes. Getting dextrose out of a pocket can be difficult enough even at the surface. To do it under water while experiencing hypoglycemia may be close to impossible, as your symptoms make things even more difficult. Practice finding dextrose both in and under water.

Stress

Stress and psychological strain affect your body and will at times increase the blood glucose level via the effect of different hormones.

When the body is exposed to stress the adrenal glands secrete the hormone adrenaline which in turn increases the output of glucose from the liver. To explain this you must understand our Stone Age inhabitants. Most often stress for them was associated with danger, for example an attacking bear, and the alternatives were to stay and fight or to run away as quickly as possible. Extra fuel in the form of increased glucose in the blood is needed for both these responses. Different persons are more or less sensitive to these reactions in their bodies.

Your body is built to withstand the strenuous life of a Stone Age man. In a stress situation large amounts of adrenaline are secreted to help prepare the body for fight against or flight away from the danger.

Today the same stress reaction can occur in front of the TV when watching something exciting but you will not benefit from the increased blood glucose level. A non-diabetic person will automatically release insulin from pancreas to restore the glucose balance. In theory it is possible for a person with diabetes to take extra insulin in this situation. In practice this is often difficult to accomplish since it is difficult to evaluate one's stress level, and besides the stress will be different from day to day. My advice is to be careful when treating high blood glucose caused by stress with extra insulin.

In one study, adults with diabetes performed a stress test for 20 minutes causing the blood glucose level to rise after one hour. It continued to be elevated by about 2 mmol/L (35 mg/dL) for another 5 hours.[291] The blood pressure was increased as well and the stress induced an insulin resistance (see page 69) via increased levels of the hormones adrenaline, cortisone and growth hormone. Patients that had an insulin production of their own had less influence on their blood glucose level.

Studies of heart attack victims have shown that so called positive stress is not dangerous. Positive stress is defined as having a lot to do, but it is self inflicted and one can influence one's own situation. The type of stress that increases the risk for having a heart attack is when one cannot influence the situation, such as when having problems at work or at home within the family, like a divorce. Similar situations may contribute to an increased blood glucose level as well. We had a little boy who sustained a high blood glucose level whenever an intravenous needle was inserted. His blood glucose level remained elevated for several days in spite of increased insulin doses. The needle bothered him and as soon as it was removed his blood glucose normalized and the insulin doses could be decreased again. In one study of adolescents, higher

A divorce is always stressful for a child. If the parents cannot cooperate and instead use the child as a "tug of war" rope, his/her situation will become very difficult. The child will feel bad in every sense and the blood glucose level and HbA$_{1c}$ will increase as a result.

Stress

➠ Stress that cannot be influenced (like problems in the family or at work) affects your diabetes the most.

➠ Adrenaline (stress hormone) gives

① Increased blood glucose level by:
   A) Release of glucose from the liver
   B) Decreased uptake of glucose in the muscles

② Ketones by:
   Breakdown of fat into fatty acids that are transformed into ketones in the liver. [238]

---

blood glucose levels were found after negative stress.[178]

Blood glucose readings taken at the hospital are often higher than those taken at home. This is also the case for blood pressure measurements, so called "white coat hypertension". In persons with diabetes, elevated blood glucose levels have been observed both in out-[70] and in-patient [172] settings.

Everyday stress factors can cause a higher HbA_{1c}.[87] If you increase your insulin doses you may end up in a vicious cycle when the stress temporarily decreases, resulting in lower blood glucose levels. A rebound phenomenon following hypoglycemia may raise the blood glucose levels again and lead you to think that the insulin doses need to be increased even more [335] (see page 43).

In one study it was found that persons with higher HbA_{1c} levels reported poorer life quality and more anxiety and depression.[280] When the HbA_{1c} value was increased or decreased during the scope of the study, the scores for life quality, anxiety and depression changed accordingly. These results suggest that you will feel better with a better HbA_{1c}. However, another interpretation is that it is easier to obtain a good HbA_{1c} when you feel well.

One study showed that stress causes a higher HbA_{1c} but only for individuals who handle the stress in an ineffective way.[321] Anger, impatience and anxiety were examples of ineffective coping mechanisms. Stoicism (not reacting emotionally in stressing situations), pragmatism (handling stress in a problem-oriented way) and denial (disregarding the stress and thereby not letting it affect you) were

effective coping mechanisms. However, denial has, in earlier studies, been correlated to impaired blood glucose control [321] which might be explained by the fact that a problem must first be recognized before being solved. To initially accept a chronic disease but then not let it affect your daily life may be an effective form of denial.

Since the daily management of diabetes involves such a great deal of practical applications it is probably necessary to control one's feelings in order to be more problem-focused.[394]

The parent's stress reactions are very important for the childs psychological adjustment to diabetes. Metabolic control is better in families where the mother and, in particular, the child have initial injection anxiety and protest, but less generalized distress.[394] This implies that distress in itself makes adaptation more difficult. Families who focus their emotional upset on the disease's practical problems utilize problem-solving coping strategies.

Negative stress, i.e. when one cannot change the stressful situation, such as when having problems at work or at home within the family, may contribute to an increased blood glucose level.

Fever and sick days

If you have an infection, especially with fever, the secretion of blood glucose raising hormones (mostly cortisone and glucagon [413]) is increased, effectively increasing your insulin requirements. However, it is common to eat less and rest more when ill. These factors usually balance out. The basic rule is therefore not to decrease the insulin doses despite a decreased food intake. Start by taking your usual dose. Measure the blood glucose level before each meal and adjust the dose before eating. If your blood glucose level is above 10 mmol/L (180 mg/dL) you can increase by one unit at a time (2 units if your premeal dose is larger than 10 units) until your readings are better.

With temperatures above 38° C (100.4° F) a 25 % dose increase is often needed. Sometimes up to a 50 % increase of the total dose over 24 hours is needed when the fever is above 39° C (102.2° F).[268] If you use a 2-dose treatment it is often difficult to meet the changing insulin needs when ill. It is probably best to temporarily change to 4 or 5 doses per day during the illness. An alternative is to give extra doses of short-acting insulin when needed at meal-time.

During the remission phase (honeymoon phase, see pages 68 and 138) the insulin doses often need to be increased considerably while ill. A child will usually need up to 1 U/kg/24 hours (1U/2.2 pounds), sometimes more. The rapid increase in need for insulin is due to the fact that your own pancreas no longer contributes substantial amounts of insulin.

Good glycemic control increases the body's defense against infections. Document your blood glucose, urine glucose, and ketone readings as well as insulin doses in your logbook and contact your diabetes clinic or the hospital if you are in the least unsure of your child's condition or how to handle the situation.

Illness and need of insulin

➠ Fever increases the need for insulin.

➠ **But** — decreased appetite and food intake decrease the need for insulin.

➠ **Thus** — you will probably have at least the same need for insulin/24 hours as usual.

➠ **Most often** there is an increased need for insulin when febrile (up to 25 - 50 % more insulin).

➠ **But** — there is often a decreased need for insulin when one has gastroenteritis with vomiting *and* diarrhea.

➠ There is a **risk of ketoacidosis** caused by insulin deficiency. Check for ketones in the urine!

Feeling ill or well

① **Feeling well**

➠ Start out with your need for food and your appetite.

➠ Adjust your insulin dose in relation to the size of the meal.

➠ Aim at not letting the blood glucose level rise too much.

② **Feeling ill**

➠ Start out from your need of insulin.

➠ Take your usual insulin dose to begin with (unless you have diarrhea!) and make sure that you can eat enough to supply the insulin with carbohydrates "to work with".

➠ Aim at not letting the blood glucose level fall too low by drinking something containing sugar if needed.

Diabetes and illness

(Adapted from [364])

① **Treat the current illness**
The reason for the child's illness must be diagnosed and treated in the same way as in non-diabetic children.

② **Symptomatic treatment**
When there is fever or headache paracetamol/acetaminophen (Alvedon®, Curadon®, Panodil®, Tylenol®) can be given to relieve symptoms. The child will feel better and often have a better appetite.

③ **Staying home from school**
One should be more liberal about letting a sick child with diabetes stay at home since his/her blood glucose level is affected by the infection.

④ **Fluid balance**
It is important to drink plenty of liquids when febrile, especially when you have a high blood glucose level (> 12 - 15 mmol/l, 215 - 270 mg/dL) since you will have larger urine volumes than usual. The risk of dehydration may quickly increase if the child is vomiting or has diarrhea.

④ **Nutrition**
It is important that the child gets insulin, sugar and nourishment. Serve something that the child likes and is likely to eat.

How do different illnesses affect blood glucose? (Adapted from [364])

① **Not much influence at all**
Illnesses that do not significantly affect your general condition usually do not affect your insulin requirements either. Examples are common colds without fever and chickenpox with few symptoms (in children).

② **Low blood glucose levels**
These illnesses are characterized by difficulties in retaining nutrients due to nausea, vomiting or/and diarrhea. Examples are gastroenteritis or a viral infection with abdominal pain.

③ **High blood glucose levels**
Most illnesses that give obvious distress and fever will increase the blood glucose levels, thereby increasing the need for insulin. Examples are colds with fever, otitis (inflammation of the ear), urinary infection with fever or pneumonia.

If the child does not feel like eating regular meals you should still try to convince him/her to eat regular amounts of carbohydrates by offering food that the child likes, such as ice cream or fruit soup.

Nausea and vomiting

For a child with diabetes nausea and vomiting are often the first signs of insulin deficiency. This is why it is always important to check both blood and urine tests when these symptoms appear. If the blood glucose level is high and there are ketones in the urine, the nausea is probably caused by insulin deficiency. A relative insulin deficiency may have developed even though you have taken your usual doses, if your insulin requirements have increased due to an intercurrent illness.

If, on the other hand, the blood glucose level is low the nausea is probably caused by the illness itself.

The increased insulin requirements during illness (e.g. a cold with fever) usually last for a few days, but sometimes they can last up to a week after recovery. This is due to the increased blood glucose level which in turn gives rise to increased insulin resistance (see page 69). Sometimes there are increased insulin requirements during the incubation period a few days prior to the onset of the illness.

Write down all insulin doses and test results in your logbook and you will find it easier to adjust insulin doses and food intake next time you are faced with same situation.

IMPORTANT!! *Do not adjust insulin doses "by eye" when ill!*

Insulin treatment during sick days (except gastroenteritis)

➡ Always start out by taking your usual dose (except when you have gastroenteritis).

➡ Check your blood glucose before each meal and in between when needed. Check ketones in the urine regularly.

➡ Adjust insulin doses according to the results of the blood tests. Increase the pre-meal doses by 1 - 2 units when needed (see text for guidelines).

➡ Give extra short-acting insulin (or preferably direct-acting Humalog) 0.1 unit/kg (0.5 units/10 pounds) body weight if the blood glucose is more than 15 - 16 mmol/L and you have ketones in the urine. Repeat the dose if the blood glucose level has not decreased after 2 - 3 hours.

➡ Never give more than 0.1 unit/kg (0.5 units/10 pounds) extra in a single dose. A larger dose will increase the risk of hypoglycemia considerably.

➡ Contact your diabetes clinic or the hospital when vomiting or if your/your child's general condition is affected.

Insulin and gastroenteritis

Make sure that it really is gastroenteritis:

➡ Vomiting *and* diarrhea

➡ Low blood glucose levels

➡ Ketones *but not* glucose in the urine

① Always call the hospital if it is the first time your child has gastroenteritis after contracting diabetes or if you are in the least unsure of what to do. If the child is vomiting often you should go to the hospital. We often treat with intravenous fluids and insulin in this situation.

② Give a drink containing real sugar *(not Light-drinks!)* in small and frequent portions (several sips every 10 - 15 min.) when the child is nauseous or vomiting. Suitable beverages are juice, tea with sugar and oral rehydration solution. Write down how much fluid the child has taken.

③ Measure blood glucose every other hour (every hour if at risk for hypoglycemia) and check the urine for glucose and ketones every time the child urinates.

④ Lower the insulin doses if needed. Ketones but not glucose in the urine are starvation ketones, indicating that more sugar is needed. There will be a balance between how much the child can eat and how much the insulin should be lowered. Low blood glucose levels will increase the insulin sensitivity (decreased insulin resistance, see page 69) and the doses usually need to be lowered by 20 - 30 %, sometimes even more.

If the child uses a 2-dose treatment start by decreasing the short-acting insulin which at times may even be omitted. The intermediate-acting insulin may need to be decreased as well.

⑤ Begin with solid food as soon as the vomiting improves or stops.

Ketones (but not glucose) may still be present in the urine as a sign of a lack of food (carbohydrates) when the child has no appetite.

If you have nausea when ill, and if you eat less, it is important that the food you do eat contain something sweet, both to give your body nourishment and to lessen the risk of hypoglycemia. The nausea will usually get worse if you drink large amounts of liquid at one sitting. It is better to drink small amounts frequently, for example a couple of sips every 10 minutes. Oral rehydration solution (ORS), available at the pharmacy, is very useful in this situation. However, older children may not accept the taste (since it is quite salty). Try adding some juice to improve its taste. *If the child vomits and cannot retain liquids you should contact the diabetes clinic or emergency ward!*

It is very important to give insulin, even if you cannot eat regular meals. Give something sweet to drink, so that the blood glucose level will not fall. *Make sure that the drink contains real sugar.*

Children usually like juice or fruit soups and will eat them without problems. Light-drinks should not be used at all in this situation.

When should I go to the hospital?
Adapted from [364]

➠ Voluminous or repeated vomiting

➠ Increasing amounts of ketones in the urine or labored breathing

➠ The blood glucose levels continue to be high despite extra insulin

➠ The child is confused or his/her general well-being is affected

➠ The underlying condition is unclear

➠ Severe or unusual abdominal pain

➠ The child is young (< 2 - 3 years) or has another disease besides diabetes

➠ Exhausted patents/relatives, for example due to repeated nighttime wakenings

➠ Always call if you are in the least unsure of how to manage the situation

Vomiting but no diarrhea?!?

Beware! Remember that nausea and vomiting often are symptoms of insulin deficiency!

When vomiting without diarrhea one should always suspect insulin deficiency. You will then have high blood glucose levels and ketones in the urine. See also "Insulin deficiency" on page 28 and "Ketones in the urine" on page 79.

Gastroenteritis

Gastroenteritis is an infection in the intestinal tract, most often causing both vomiting and diarrhea. Very little nourishment will stay in your body and there are generally problems with low blood glucose levels. Gastroenteritis is therefore an exception to the rule that the insulin need will increase when ill. A slower emptying of the stomach [31] contributes to a low blood glucose level when having gastroenteritis. One may need to lower the insulin doses by 20 - 30 % or more to avoid hypoglycemia.

Remember to drink plenty of fluids but take small sips at a time as long as you are vomiting. When the vomiting stops you can start with ordinary food. At present we don't recommend the diet that used to be after gastroenteritis (like boiled fish, rice, toast

etc.). It is better to eat what you like. The post-gastroenteritis diet often implied problems obtaining enough glucose and calories. The only exception is milk for small children. If diarrheas continue to be a problem one should exclude milk and milk products for one or more weeks.

Beware that vomiting can very well be a symptom of insulin deficiency which should be treated with increased insulin doses.

You should therefore check both urine and blood tests if you/your child has nausea or is vomiting. If you have a lack of insulin, your blood glucose level will be high and the urine test will show high readings both for glucose and ketones. Contact your diabetes doctor or nurse concerning the results before changing any doses if you are unsure about how to interpret them.

A cold with fever increases your insulin requirements, often up to 25 %, sometimes even up to 50 %. Begin by increasing all your doses by 1 - 2 units if your blood glucose levels are high. Increase further if needed, depending on results from to blood glucose and urine ketone testings.

Remember to check both blood glucose and ketones in the urine when ill!

Wound healing

One often hears that when a person with diabetes gets hurt they will heal more slowly and because of this regular foot therapy is needed. This is all true for a person who has had diabetes for many years and is beginning to suffer complications in the form of reduced circulation and reduced sensibility in the feet and toes (see also page 212). However, wounds and injuries in a child with diabetes will heal just as well as in a non-diabetic child if you take care of the wound carefully in order to avoid infections.

However, the infectious defence will not work as well if the diabetes is uncontrolled with a high

Take care of small wounds and poor friends... (Swedish saying)

☞ Wash the wound with soap and water.

☞ Apply a clean, dry dressing.

☞ Signs of infection? ➡ see a doctor!

① Pain / throbbing from the wound after the first 1 - 2 days.

② Increasing redness of the skin.

③ Red streak in the skin going from the wound towards the trunk (infection of the lymph vessel)

④ Painful nodule in the groin or armpit (infected or inflamed lymph node).

⑤ Fever

blood glucose, causing an increased susceptibility for infections.[246]

Surgery

Even when undergoing a minor surgical operation, a person with diabetes should be taken care of in the hospital. If the patient needs general anesthesia outpatient surgery should be avoided. The operation should be performed as early in the day as possible. During operations with general anesthesia it is advisable to give insulin intravenously (see page 55).[223,322] This system is very easy to adjust and will give you an appropriate blood glucose level during the operation and recovery phase. When you can eat and drink again you can return to your usual type of insulin administration.

During surgery it is advisable to administer insulin intravenously. It is a convenient and safe way to obtain a stable blood glucose level without risking hypoglycemia.

If your child is admitted to a pediatric surgical ward contact should be made with a pediatrician to discuss appropriate insulin treatment. As parents of a child with diabetes, you should express your own views on the treatment. Remember that your knowledge of a child with diabetes is usually much better than that of the staff on a surgical ward.

Teeth

Children with diabetes do not normally have an increased frequency of caries (cavities). On the contrary, they often have less cavities than children of the same age. One may be surprised that they have any cavities at all since they eat less candy

Even if you eat less candy than your friends there is a risk of cavities. This is caused by the saliva containing glucose when your blood glucose level is high. Don't forget to brush your teeth at least twice daily.

than their friends. However, an excretion of glucose in the saliva when the blood glucose level is high may contribute to cavities. The saliva does not normally contain glucose but if the blood glucose level is above a certain threshold, increased amounts of glucose will be found in the saliva. In this sense a person with very high or labile blood glucose level has a higher risk of caries.

Gingivitis is an inflammation in the gums caused by bacteria accumulating in the tooth sockets. The bacterial deposits on the teeth will harden into calculus. The gum will redden and bleed when brushing your teeth. Gingivitis and parodontal disease are slightly more common amongst those with diabetes. This is more common when the blood glucose level is high. People with diabetes may have a more rapid progression and more serious damage than in non-diabetic persons. If you see your dentist regularly you can ask for advice about your dental hygiene to avoid damage. Tell your dentist that you have diabetes!

Vaccinations

Children with diabetes should have the same vaccinations as other children. See page 201 concerning vaccinations when travelling abroad.

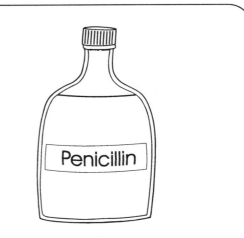

Does the medicine contain sugar?

Check the label for a list of the contents. Many antibiotics contain saccharose (sugar) while other drugs can be mixed with lactose (milk sugar), fructose (fruit sugar) or sorbitol.

Smoking

Everyone knows that it is unhealthy to smoke. Still a lot of people smoke. Strangely enough we are not too concerned about this from a moral point of view. However, many persons with diabetes feel that people around them often act as "candy police". If a person with diabetes stands in line to buy some candy, everybody who knows him/her stares and thinks that "he/she is not allowed to do that". Many will even make a comment in a manner that will hurt the individual's feelings. On the other hand, if a smoker is standing in the same line to buy cigarettes nobody will say anything in spite of the fact that smoking can cause just as many health problems as candy-eating in a person with diabetes.

Persons with diabetes smoke with the same frequency as other people. Smoking implies a substantially increased risk for lung cancer, chronic bronchitis and cardiovascular diseases like arteriosclerosis. Having diabetes will in itself imply an increased risk for cardiovascular diseases like arteriosclerosis, heart attacks and stroke. In diabetes the risks are additive. If you imagine diabetes as an act of balance on a slack rope, smoking will be like trying to do the same endeavor with a bandage over your eyes. Many studies in adults confirm that the risk of premature death for a person with diabetes who smokes is the double that of a person with diabetes who does not smoke.[296]

At the 1994 World Congress on Tobacco it was established that every second smoker will die from a disease that is connected with smoking. Smoking was called the greatest epidemic of the 20th century causing more deaths than both the plague and AIDS. A 14-year old who has begun smoking should be treated like a contagious tuberculosis patient considering the risk that he/she can entice other teenagers to start smoking!

Nicotine from smoking affects the blood glucose level by contracting the blood vessels, resulting in a slower absorption of insulin from the injection site.[230,233] Nicotine will also cause an increased insulin resistance [23,133] (a poorer blood glucose lowering effect of a given dose of insulin), which will make your diabetes more difficult to manage (see also page 69). The risk of acquiring type 2 diabetes is twice as large for a smoking person, especially for women.[296]

When smoking one will also inhale carbon dioxide which strongly binds to hemoglobin in the red blood cells, preventing oxygen from binding to the same sites. The amount of red blood cells will increase to compensate for this. Scientific studies show that smoking, for a person with diabetes, will

"A 14-year old smoker is about as contagious as a patient with tuberculosis, when you consider the risk that he/she can entice other adolescents to start smoking" (message at the 1994 World Congress on Tobacco).

You will stay in much better shape if you quit smoking!

increase the risk for renal failure, visual impairment, foot ulcers, leg amputations and heart attacks.[295,296,349]

Passive smoking

Even passive smoking will damage your health. It has been shown that children absorb nicotine into their blood-stream at twice the rate of adults when smoking passively. Smaller children are even more sensitive. Children of smoking parents also have increased levels of lead and cadmium in their blood. To smoke under the kitchen fan does not keep the smoke from spreading into the house. Somebody once said that: "It is about as effective as urinating in a corner of a swimming pool."

Passive smoking is dangerous to your health. Small children are often exposed to passive smoking by their parents. One woman who never had smoked acquired a mortal type of lung cancer that only smokers get. It was established that she had acquired her cancer because people were smoking in the room where she worked.

How do you quit smoking?

The easiest way is to never start. Most smokers have started in their teens. It is difficult to withstand the "peer pressure" but it can save many years of your life.

It may be difficult to quit smoking on your own. We can help you at the diabetes clinic with advice and nicotine chewing gum or nicotine patches that may be of help. However, without motivation of your own you can never quit smoking!

There is a risk that you will gain some weight when you quit smoking. Contact your dietitian if you want to prevent this.

Snuff

In Sweden 30 % of all men under the age of 30 use snuff and it is common in other countries as well. Nicotine from snuff is absorbed through the oral

It is never too late to quit smoking. For every day without a cigarette the deleterious effects of tobacco in your body decrease.

mucous membranes as quickly as with an intravenous injection. Just as for smokers, nicotine has strong effects on your heart, blood vessels and blood pressure. The addiction to nicotine is just as strong as for cocaine or heroin.

It it still not very well known how snuffing affects diabetes. Since nicotine will produce increased insulin resistance, snuffers (who have a higher level of nicotine in their blood than even smokers) should be expected to have problems with their diabetes control. From a study of construction workers using snuff it was concluded that snuffers, when compared to smokers, more frequently have high blood pressure, which is a risk factor for kidney damage if you have diabetes.[140]

It is just as difficult, if not more difficult, to quit snuffing as it is to quit smoking. It may be easier to accept snuffing from a medical point of view since it doesn't expose anyone else to smoke and the risk of lung cancer. Snuffing is thought to cause cancer in the oral cavity, but this is not yet proven.

Can you die from smoking?

Statistics presented at the 1994 World Congress on Tobacco [58] estimated that out of 1.000 20-year old habitual smokers

⇒ 1 will be murdered

⇒ 6 will die in traffic accidents

⇒ 250 will die in middle age from smoking-related diseases.

⇒ 250 will die in older age from smoking-related diseases.

Alcohol

We do not recommend a total ban on drinking alcohol if you have diabetes. However, it is important to know how alcohol works and that you take it easy, i.e. not drinking until you to get drunk. If you are not yet of lawful age your parents always have the final say when it comes to drinking or not. The age when you are allowed to buy alcohol differs from country to country. We at the diabetes clinic can neither allow you to do something, nor forbid it. We can only tell you how things work and what you should be especially aware of.

The liver is blocked

Alcohol counteracts the ability of the liver to produce new glucose (called gluconeogenesis) by keeping the enzymes occupied with the breakdown of alcohol. The liver can still release glucose from the glycogen store (see page 32) but when this is depleted you will have hypoglycemia. The concentration of cortisone and growth hormone in the blood will decrease after the intake of alcohol.[25] Both hormones have an enhancing effect on the blood glucose level that appears 3 - 4 hours after they are released into the blood (see page 31). This explains why you have an increased risk of hypoglycemia many hours after alcohol intake. The liver's ability to produce free fatty acids will also be impaired.[25] These biological factors cooperate to considerably increase the risk of hypoglycemia after drinking alcohol.

It is a well known fact that alcohol blocks the production of glucose in the liver. This is the background for the old tradition to have a cocktail before eating. The alcohol will block the liver, the blood glucose level will be lowered slightly, causing an increased appetite.

There is a risk when having diabetes that the blood glucose level will fall too low. This effect of alcohol will last the entire time it takes the liver to break down the alcohol in your body. The liver will break down 0.1 g (1.5 grains) of pure alcohol/kg body weight and per hour. If you weigh for example 70 kg (155 pounds) it will take one hour to break down the alcohol in a bottle of light beer, two hours for 4 cl of liquor and 10 hours to break down the alcohol in a bottle of wine. Therefore, if you drink in the evening you will have a risk of hypoglycemia all night and also part of the next day.

Why is it dangerous to be drunk when having diabetes?

When you have diabetes you must be able to think clearly in many situations, like taking your insulin at the right time and right amount and being aware of not feeling well from a lack of insulin or hypoglycemia. When drunk you cannot do this just as you cannot drive a car in a safe way after alcohol use. Severe hypoglycemia after the intake of alcohol has caused death in young persons with diabetes.

Recent studies show that alcohol's role in causing hypoglycemia depends to a greater extent on the diminished ability to detect hypoglycemia than on restraining the liver's ability of producing glucose.[156]

In a study, adults with diabetes were given alcohol along with a meal (4 cl of vodka as an aperitif, ½ a bottle of wine along with the food and 4 cl of cognac with the coffee) corresponding to 1 g of alcohol/kg (34 grains/pound) body weight.[235] It takes about 10 hours to break down this considerable amount of alcohol for an adult. The alcohol concentration in the blood reached a maximum of approximately 1 ‰ (22 mmol/L). Repeated blood glucose readings until the next morning at 10 AM were close to identical with the control day when the same persons ingested corresponding amounts of mineral water. None had symptoms of hypoglycemia but the fasting blood glucose level was on

It is not dangerous for an adult person with diabetes to drink a glass or two but if you drink too much you will find it difficult to think clearly...

> *"Never go to bed alone if you have been drinking enough to be influenced by the alcohol."*

An adult with diabetes can drink moderate amounts of alcohol if he/she eats food at the same time. 1 - 2 glasses of wine or 6 - 8 cl (1/5 - 1/4 fluid ounce) of liquor along with food will not increase the risk for hypoglycemia the following night.[66]

average 0.7 mmol/L (13 mg/dL) lower the morning after alcohol intake.

Basic rules

Always eat something at the same time that you drink alcohol. Remember that it must be "long-acting" carbohydrates as the risk of hypoglycemia extends into the next day. Alcohol containing sugar (like liqueur) will cause an initially high blood glucose level for a short time and after that a risk for hypoglycemia. A glass of beer contains about the same amount of carbohydrates as a glass of milk.

What do you do if you've had too much to drink?

Eat extra food the last thing you do before going to bed. You can eat potato crisps (chips) in this situation as they give a slow increase in blood glucose over several hours (see page 46). The blood glucose level should not be less than 10 mmol/L (180 mg/dL) when going to bed. Decrease the dose of bed-time insulin by 2 - 4 units to avoid hypoglycemia. Don't go to bed alone - if you have severe hypoglycemia during the night you will need someone to help you. If you come home very late, make sure to wake your mother or father and inform them about your condition. It may in fact be your life insurance even if it is embarrassing. Be sure to eat a steady breakfast as soon as you wake up the next morning.

It is important to remember that glucagon has a poorer effect in raising the blood glucose level if you have used alcohol. This is because alcohol counteracts glucagon's ability to increase the production of glucose in the liver.

Alcohol and calories

Drink	Alcohol content	Kcal	Carboh.
1 bottle, 33 cl (1 fluid ounce)			
Light beer	1.8%	96	13
Beer	2.8%	112	14
Strong beer	4.5%	149	11
1 glass, 15 cl (1/2 fluid ounce)			
Red wine	9.9%	114	3.5
White wine, dry	9.5%	99	0.7
White wine, sweet	10.7%	147	8.9
6 cl (1/5 fluid ounce)			
Sherry	16%	91	6
4 cl (1/7 fluid ounce)			
Vodka	32%	88	0
Whisky	32%	88	0
Punch	20%	104	12
Liqueur	19%	134	21

(Data from the National Swedish Food Administration)

If you have a severe hypoglycemia after drinking alcohol the person finding you may most likely assume that the problem is that you are drunk. It is very important that you bear something very obvious that indicates that you have diabetes, such as an ID-card or a necklace/bracelet.

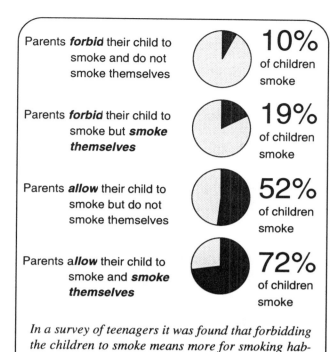

Parents *forbid* their child to smoke and do not smoke themselves — **10%** of children smoke

Parents *forbid* their child to smoke but *smoke themselves* — **19%** of children smoke

Parents *allow* their child to smoke but do not smoke themselves — **52%** of children smoke

Parents a*llow* their child to smoke and *smoke themselves* — **72%** of children smoke

In a survey of teenagers it was found that forbidding the children to smoke means more for smoking habits than if their parents smoke or not.[1]

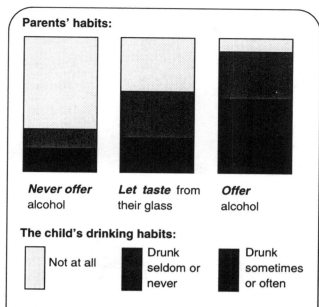

Parents' habits:

Never offer alcohol — **Let taste** from their glass — **Offer** alcohol

The child's drinking habits:

Not at all | Drunk seldom or never | Drunk sometimes or often

The same pattern was found concerning alcohol habits.[279] "Forbidden fruit is sweetest" does not seem to be the case. Instead it is important that parents are very clear in their attitudes of what is allowed and what is not.

Can you drink at home?

Many assume that "stolen pleasures are the sweetest", i.e. that it is better for teenagers to try alcohol at home under parental supervision than to sneak a drink on the side. However, studies have shown that more children start drinking alcohol if you have a permissive attitude towards trying alcohol in the home. A total prohibition of alcohol for the teenager seems to have a better preventative effect than the conception that it is advisable to test at home.[279] The same is true for smoking.[1] Whether or not parents allowed testing in the home had a greater impact in these studies than if the parents drank alcohol or smoked themselves.

Narcotics

Narcotics affect the brain and nervous systems and will make it much more difficult to manage your diabetes with a high risk of both hypoglycemia (when not eating enough) and ketoacidosis (diabetic coma) when you have not taken enough insulin or missed your doses. Narcotics are rapidly addictive and you will have great difficulty quitting without help. With diabetes you must realize that it is completely wrong from a medical standpoint and very risky to use or even try all types of narcotics.

Remember that we at the diabetes clinic can neither give you permission nor prohibit you to drink alcohol. This question must be raised with your parents. What we can do is to tell you how alcohol affects your body if you have diabetes and what special risks can occur.

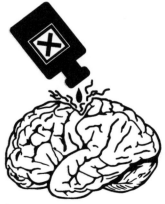

Narcotics work as poison for your brain and will quickly cause an addiction.

Malin 10

Pregnancy

One of the first things a girl with diabetes and her family will ask is if she can have babies. Pregnant exerts a certain strain on every woman but there is no reason to discourage a women with diabetes from having children. Their risk of developing diabetes complications later in life is not affected by pregnancy.[43] However, eye- and kidney damage may be accelerated by pregnancy. If the mother has kidney damage from her diabetes the risk of fetal growth retardation and spontaneous abortion will also increase considerably.[44]

Of the children born in Sweden, 0.2 - 0.3 % have a mother with type 1 diabetes.[44] About 1/10 as many have mothers with type 2 diabetes and 1 - 3 % have a temporary form of diabetes during pregnancy (gestational diabetes).[44] The symptoms of diabetes usually disappear after giving birth but these women have an increased risk (approximately 40 % within 20 years) of acquiring type 2 diabetes later in life.[88]

If the mother's blood glucose level is high there is a risk that the fetus will be affected. A high blood glucose level early in pregnancy (during the first 8 weeks) seems to give an increased risk of congenital malformations, about 2 - 3 times the 1.6 % risk that is present in all pregnancies.[44,315] If the mother has diabetes complications the risk of congenital malformations will increase further.[310] Half of these malformations are not compatible with life. These studies were done on women with type 1 diabetes. With gestational diabetes the risk for congenital malformations is not increased.[44] The risk for malformations is not increased if it is only the father that has type 1 diabetes.

If the woman has good glycemic control at conception and during early pregnancy there is no increased risk for malformations or spontaneous abortion.[112,175,229] The risk increases with a HbA_{1c} above 9 % and is very great (close to a 25 % risk!) when the HbA_{1c} is above 11 %.[315] It is therefore very important that your pregnancy be planned and that your HbA_{1c} be below 8 % before the pregnancy.[310] However, it is important to point out that although one's HbA_{1c} may be high during preg-

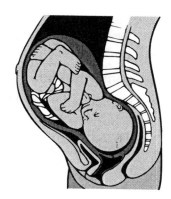

Decide to achieve a good HbA_{1c} before getting pregnant and your child will have a better start when growing and developing.

nancy there will usually not be congenital malformations. A high HbA_{1c} value is therefore not enough basis for recommending abortion.[315] Fifty percent of all women with a high HbA_{1c} (above 10 %) have quite normal pregnancies.[44]

One should wait with pregnancy until after the teens as a teenage pregnancy brings about increased medical risks both for the baby (premature birth, complications in the new-born) and the mother (anemia, toxemia).

Short periods of hypoglycemia are not dangerous to the fetus.[310] However, severe hypoglycemia with convulsions or unconsciousness can be dangerous.[315] Low blood glucose levels can give increased nausea and vomiting during pregnancy.[124] Nausea may make it difficult to eat regular meals, resulting in hypoglycemia. A vicious cycle may easily develop. The use of an insulin pump can be one effective way of minimizing these problems.

Insulin requirements may decrease early in pregnancy, especially if the woman has problems with nausea. It will thereafter rise steadily, close to full-term (36 - 38 weeks), often to twice the level it was prior to the pregnancy.[124,315] The increased insulin requirement is partly caused by weight gain during pregnancy but also by hormones excreted from the placenta, which counteract the blood glucose lowering effect of insulin. Normally a woman will gain 11 - 12 kg (24 - 26 pounds) during pregnancy but there are large individual variations.

Diabetes and pregnancy — risks for the fetus

① **Early in pregnancy**

➡ Increased risk of congenital malformations if the HbA_{1c} is increased, especially if higher than 9 - 11 %.

② **Complications at delivery**

➡ The baby will have the same blood glucose levels as the mother since glucose can freely pass through the placenta. An increased amount of glucose to the infant will lead to increased growth of the fetus, since it can produce insulin of its own.

➡ The infant will be large in size and there is a risk of having a difficult delivery.

➡ The infant will risk developing hypoglycemia the first days of life as he/she will continue to produce considerable amounts of insulin.

Insulin requirements during pregnancy [124]

	U/kg	U/pounds
Before pregnancy	0.6	0.27
Week 6 - 18	0.7	0.32
Week 18 - 26	0.8	0.36
Week 26 - 36	0.9	0.41
Week 36 - delivery	1.0	0.45
During delivery	Very low	
After delivery	Below 0.6	Below 0.27
Breast-feeding	Further decrease of insulin need	

The fetus continuously consumes a large part of the mother's glucose which may increase the need for snacks during the day and increase the risk of night-time hypoglycemia.[124]

If the mother has an increased blood glucose level this will be delivered to the child since the glucose in the mother's blood will easily pass through the placenta into the blood of the fetus. The fetus' own pancreas can produce insulin to take care of the extra sugar. However, insulin cannot pass back to the mother through the placenta. If the blood glucose level is high during a large part of the pregnancy, the fetus will have an increased growth, and will have gained excess weight by the time it is born. This may complicate the delivery.

In spite of a good HbA_{1c} during pregnancy the child may have gained excess weight when born. The blood glucose level after meals seems to be most significant according to a study.[85] The recommendation was to aim for a blood glucose level of approximately 7.3 mmol/L (130 mg/dL) one hour after the meal in this study. With lower levels there was a certain risk for the fetus to have, in place of weight gain, a slight growth retardation at the time of birth.

Blood glucose levels should be as normal as possible during labor and childbirth as high blood glucose levels in the unborn baby causes increased insulin production. This leads to decreased ability to withstand the partial lack of oxygen that even a normal delivery entails.[43] When the umbilical chord is cut the high insulin production will continue, causing a low blood glucose level. The child of a diabetic mother is therefore carefully monitored with extra blood glucose tests and if needed dextrose is given intravenously. The child will also receive extra food early on, before the mother's breast milk production has begun.

The woman's daily insulin requirement decreases quickly after childbirth. While breast-feeding the mother usually needs to decrease her insulin doses to levels lower than before pregnancy to avoid hypoglycemia. After a few weeks or months the insulin doses will usually be back to the same levels as before the pregnancy.

Maternal care

Pregnant women with diabetes are usually very highly motivated and will also receive closer attention from the maternity care unit. Tell us at the diabetes clinic as soon as possible if you suspect that you are pregnant. We can help you with a pregnancy test (so called chorionic gonadotropin test) which will give a reliable result within a couple of days after missing a period.

A general consensus is that it is a full time job to be pregnant if you have diabetes. This means that it takes quite a deal of work to maintain a normal blood glucose level during pregnancy. The goal is for HbA$_{1c}$ during pregnancy to be within the normal range for the individual laboratory. Treatment with an insulin pump may be an effective way to achieve this.

During the later part of pregnancy it is often it more difficult to recognize symptoms of hypoglycemia as the threshold for developing symptoms will be lowered because of frequent low blood glucose levels [337] (see "Hypoglycemic unawareness" on page 42). The HbA$_{1c}$ value for non-diabetic women is approximately 1 % lower at the end of pregnancy which is the reason for aiming for a HbA$_{1c}$ close to 6 % (upper limit for non-diabetic persons) during the later part of pregnancy.[176]

During pregnancy ketone production during periods of insulin deficiency is increased, increasing the risk for ketoacidosis.[43] Ketoacidosis during pregnancy is very dangerous with a highly increased risk of fetal death.[124,292] You should therefore check for ketones in the urine regularly, especially if you have nausea or an infection with fever. Some doctors recommend urine testing every morning to make sure you do not have "starvation ketones" from inadequate carbohydrate intake in the evening.

If you use an insulin pump you will have an increased risk of ketoacidosis due to a small insulin depot (see page 110). If the pump needle fails during the night you will have high blood glucose levels in the morning and ketones in the urine. One method of avoiding this is to give a bedtime injection of intermediate-acting insulin (0.2 U/kg) in addition to the normal basal dose delivered by the pump.[278]

Nearly every woman has thoughts during pregnancy about something being wrong with her child. However, most women with diabetes have a quite normal pregnancy and the child will be born healthy. If you have a low HbA$_{1c}$ before and during pregnancy the risks for your child are approximately the same as if you didn't have diabetes.

The renal threshold is usually lowered in pregnant women, causing an increased excretion of glucose in the urine. Urine tests for glucose are therefore not reliable.

How will the child develop?

Children of women with diabetes were normally developed at the age of 5 in a Swedish study.[43] The height and weight were also found to be normal in another study.[43] In an Australian study the children were followed to the age of 3 years.[361] Children of mothers having low HbA$_{1c}$ readings had a normal development while children of mothers with high HbA$_{1c}$ values during pregnancy had a delayed language development and a smaller head circumference.

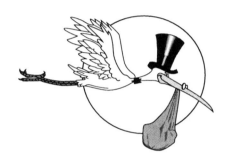

Will the child have diabetes?

If you have diabetes you may wonder: "Should I have a baby when there is an increased risk of the child getting diabetes?" In one study 3 % of the children of diabetic mothers acquired diabetes by the age of 10 - 13 years.[316] Although we believe that half the factors contributing to diabetes are inherited, only about every 10th child with newly onset diabetes has a parent or a sibling with diabetes.[96] This means that the hereditary disposition for acquiring diabetes is very common, at least 40 % according to certain studies.[97] From this it follows that we do not in any way discourage a person with diabetes from having children. See also "Heredity" on page 222.

Some choose adoption instead. They do this because of both the increased risk for the child acquiring diabetes and the increased risk of going through a pregnancy with diabetes, especially if diabetes complications are present (see also page 197).

It appears that the risk for a child of acquiring diabetes decreases as the age of the mother increases.

If a mother has diabetes and is older than 25 when she gives birth, the risk to the child of developing diabetes later in life is not significantly increased compared to non-diabetic mothers.[416] Another study showed that 8.9 % of children born to fathers with diabetes, but only 3.4 % of children born to mothers with diabetes acquired the disease before the age of 20.[50] If the mother was 8 years or younger when she contracted diabetes, the risk for the child was considerably higher, 13.9 %, in this study.

Menstruations

Sometimes poorly controlled diabetes can lead to irregular or missed periods, thus making it difficult to get pregnant. Women with average diabetes control have the same probability of getting pregnant as non-diabetic women.[43] If you suspect problems with infertility contact us at the diabetes clinic and we can help you with a referral to a gynecologist.

Is the need for insulin changed during menstruations?

Many women have noticed that their blood glucose level increases the days before the menstruation.[4,271] During the first couple of days of menstruation however, the level may fall, leading to hypoglycemia. If you notice that you have this type of problem, check your blood glucose level especially carefully the days close to menstruation. You can then make adjustments with higher insulin doses the days before menstruation, and a little lower during the days that follow.

Sexuality

A teenage boy or girl with diabetes will function just like his/her friends of the same age in sexual

With diabetes it is extra important that your pregnancy be planned. Tell us at the diabetes clinic if you need contraceptives and we will help you with referral to a gynecologist.

relations. The only difference is that it is extra important to use contraceptives to avoid an unwanted pregnancy. Remember that you may encounter hypoglycemia after having intercourse — making love can be heavy exercise. Some will not function well sexually if their blood glucose level is high, but can improve if this is corrected.[28]

Impotence may be a complication of diabetes, which some men who have had diabetes for many years will encounter. This can be caused by a combination of premature arteriosclerosis and a lessened intensity in nervous response caused by disturbances in the autonomic nervous system (see page 213). Just as for non-diabetic persons the explanation for impotence is often psychological. If you have morning erections this indicates a psychological reason for your impotence.[28]

Temporary disturbances of erection are something that all men encounter once in a while. The problem for a person with diabetes is that a temporary erectile disturbance is immediately attributed to diabetes. A vicious cycle may arise with negative expectations and the fear of continued failure. Talk to your diabetes doctor or nurse to straighten things out.

If the impotence is a complication of diabetes there are good chances of getting effective treatment. Part of the treatment is to lessen other risk factors such as alcohol, tobacco and drugs (like certain drugs for blood pressure).

Contraceptive methods

Condom	The only contraceptive that protects against sexually transmitted disease.
Ordinary pills	Sometimes result in a slight increase in blood glucose levels
Minipills	Risk of spotting. Less margin for error when forgetting to take tablets.
Depot injection	Affects metabolic control. Often troublesome side-effects.
Implant	Same as depot injection but easy to remove if side-effects are not acceptable.
Diaphragm + spermicidal jelly	Not so easy to use. Risk of itching as side-effect.
Intrauterine device (IUDs, spiral)	Risk of pelvic infection is low but an IUD is not recommended before the first pregnancy.
"Day-after" pills	For "emergency" situations. Needs to be taken within 72 hours.

Which contraceptive should I choose? [43]

① Pills (not minipills) for teenagers.

② Spiral (IUD) for women who have been pregnant.

③ Using a condom is always a good alternative and besides, it is the only way of protecting yourself from sexually transmitted diseases. Always use a condom in a temporary relationship.

Contraceptives

Formerly minipills were often recommended to women with diabetes. However, these increase the risk of spotting and have a narrower time margin for taking the pills (not more than 30 hours between pills). Combined contraceptives ("ordinary" pills) are more effective in preventing pregnancy. They contain 2 types of female sex hormones. Estrogen prevents the egg from developing and being released from the ovary. Progesterone prevents the sperm from passing through the mucous of the neck of womb (cervix). Minipills contain only progesterone. The use of oral contraceptives does not result in an increased risk of later complications from the eyes or kidneys.[159]

Combined contraceptive pills were previously considered to slightly raise the blood glucose level but recent studies show no adverse affects on glucose control.[318] If the glycemic control is different during the week without pills one can wait longer before interrupting, that is take pills for 3 months without interruption.[6] Today we recommend combined pills with a low estrogen content to begin with. Combined pills are not advisable if you smoke (due to an increased risk of thrombosis and heart attack), if you have a high blood pressure or complications from your eyes or kidneys.[6]

An intrauterine device (IUDs, spiral) is a safe contraceptive for women with diabetes according to recent studies.[228] Problems with infections or spotting are no more common than for non-diabetic women. However, they are not recommended if you have irregular or heavy menstruations. As there is an increased risk of womb and ovary infections (and thereby a risk of becoming infertile) intrauterine devices are not recommended for women who

Poor diabetes control with a high HbA_{1c} will increase the risk of impotence.[353] In the same way as with other complications (see page 207) the problems may be halted or regress if they are discovered early, and the diabetes treatment is changed, normalizing the blood glucose level.

Female sexuality is less affected by diabetes.[28] One problem that may be encountered as a late complication is dry vaginal mucous membranes, which can be troublesome when having intercourse. A pharmacy can give you advice of a suitable lubricant if you have this type of problem.

**Morning-after methods
Only for "emergency" use!**

① **Pills**

➡ Two pills taken within 72 hours after an unprotected intercourse and 2 pills after another 12 hours. Only special pills with high hormonal contents can be used.

➡ Contact a doctor or youth clinic as soon as possible. You need a gynecological exam within 3 - 4 weeks to discuss what contraceptive to continue with.

② **Inserting a spiral**

➡ Should be inserted within 72 hours, at the very latest within 5 days.

➡ Recommended only for women who have been pregnant.

---

have never been pregnant. However, for a woman with diabetes complications from the eyes or kidneys, intrauterine devices may be a good alternative to contraceptive pills. [228]

Depot injections or implantations contain the same hormone (progesterone) as minipills. However, they will give a higher hormone concentration and affect the blood glucose level more than mini pills. Common side-effects are nausea, increased appetite or irritability, all of which make it more difficult to control the blood glucose levels. The contraceptive depot injection is not considered suitable for women with diabetes as the effects of one injection last for many months.

A contraceptive implant contains the same hormone as a depot injection. It is implanted under the skin using local anesthesia. The advantage is that it can immediately be removed if the woman experiences serious side-effects and is, in this case, more suitable for a woman with diabetes than the depot injection.

Remember that most contraceptive methods only prevent unwanted pregnancy. It is as important to protect oneself against sexually transmitted diseases. It is not uncommon for these to diminish a woman's fertility. A condom is the only contraceptive that offers a full protection from sexually transmitted diseases. Discuss with your doctor which type of contraceptive is suitable for you. Depending

of local routines and regional practices, your doctor can give you a prescription or refer you to a gynecologist for further advice. Young women using oral contraceptives should have an annual gynecological check up.

Forgotten the pill?

If you discover that you have forgotten to take your contraceptive tablet within 48 hours you should take an extra tablet when you realize this. [6] If more than 48 hours have passed (more than 30 hours with mini pills) you will have no protection and you must use another method, such as condoms, during the next week. [6] If you forget this you must take a pregnancy test.

"Morning-after pills"

"Morning-after pills" are available in most countries for emergency situations, that is if you have had an unprotected intercourse between day 8 and 18 (counting with 28 days between menstruations, and day 1 being the first day of the menstruation). [162] The risk of getting pregnant after an unprotected intercourse is 6 - 7 % and at the time of ovulation as high as 20 - 30 %. [20] With "morning-after pills" this risk is decreased to 1 - 3 %.

This type of medication prevents the fertilized egg from implanting in the membranes of the uterus. The tablets must be taken at the very latest 72 hours after the intercourse, [162] which is why you should get in touch with your diabetes clinic, a youth clinic or a gynecologist as soon as possible. Contact the hospital if this happens during the weekend. In some areas "morning-after pills" are available also after office hours.

Insulin-dependent diabetes in children, adolescents and adults © R. Hanas 1998

Social issues

School

When you return to school again after the onset of diabetes, it is important to tell your friends about your diabetes and what to do if you have a hypoglycemia. It is a good idea for the diabetes nurse to come to class and talk about diabetes, inviting all teachers who deal with the child, including the physical education teacher or shop teacher. Invite the diabetes nurse to come to school again when you begin a new class or change to a new school.

Teachers usually have a good understanding of a child or teenager with diabetes. However, sometimes it may be difficult for them to know if something the child does or some behavior (like tiredness or irritation) is due to a low blood glucose level or something else. It is important for the child to be able to measure blood glucose values at school when necessary. Some parents have the impression that the school and teachers take diabetes more seriously after the child has had a serious hypoglycemic reaction at school.

Hypoglycemia will affect your school results, not only when the blood glucose level is low, but also up to 3 - 4 hours after is has been normalized. In a study in children and adolescents between the ages of 11 - 18 years, a significant decline in mental efficiency was found at blood glucose levels of 2.9 - 3.2 mmol/L (55 - 60 mg/dL). This was most

evident in measures of mental flexibility, planning, decision making, attention to detail, and rapid responding.[339]

Always make sure that you have something extra to eat during an examination. Many prefer to have a little higher blood glucose level during examinations to avoid hypoglycemia.

You should feel free to measure your blood glucose if you experience difficulties in concentrating during an examination. You will then know if you need to eat something extra. It may also be important to be able to show a low blood glucose reading to your teacher, if you feel that your results from the examination are not as good as they should be, and you want to retest. Sometimes we might need to write a medical certificate on this issue. (See also page 52, 150 and 168 concerning low blood glucose levels, food and physical education in school.)

Diabetes and school

☞ Make sure that your teachers and friends know where you have your dextrose tablets and when you need to take them.

☞ It is equally important that all of your classmates know and understand why you need to eat sugar from time to time and why your school lunch may sometimes be different.

☞ The school nurse should be able to assist you in measuring your blood glucose level if needed.

Don't send a child from school alone without checking that someone is at home. If the child experiences hypoglycemia on its way home and nobody is there to help it may easily develop into severe hypoglycemia.

School routines

It is desirable that school routines be adjusted to fit the needs of a child with diabetes:

➠ The staff needs to have sufficient background knowledge of diabetes and must be aware of the fact that diabetes in childhood is not at all the same disease as diabetes (type 2) in adults and the elderly.

➠ Friends must understand why the you may have to eat a fruit or a sandwich during class and why special food may be necessary at lunch (ones which many may find more tasty than the regular food).

➠ Understand what hypoglycemia is and how to treat it properly.

➠ Don't send a child with diabetes home from school earlier than expected (and especially not after a hypoglycemic episode) without first checking that someone is at home who can take care of him/her.

➠ Understand that the child can have poorer results on exams due to hypoglycemia. The child/teenager should have the possibility of re-doing the test as it is difficult to obtain full concentration for several hours after hypoglycemia.

Day-care centers

A child with diabetes attending a day-care center will need more time and attention than non-diabetic children of the same age. In some communities, children with diabetes can be counted as two in the accounting, giving the staff more time for the child. The rules and regulations differ from country to country.

In most countries, the staff of a day-care center or a baby-sitter has no formal obligation to help with blood glucose testing. However, you will usually find someone interested enough who will help, at least if the child is not feeling well. In many places the staff will also give insulin. This may be easier to do if the child has an injection aid, such as an indwelling catheter (see page 100). Sometimes it may be appropriate to have glucagon available if the staff knows how and when to give it.

The baby-sitter or day-care staff will benefit from accompanying the family to a clinical visit, or the

➠ Understand that the diabetes expert closest at hand is the child/teenager and his/her parents.

➠ Permanent meal hours should be established, with lunch as close to noon as possible.

➠ The food served must be appropriate for a child with diabetes. However, if not eaten it will not do any good for the blood glucose level at all. One must respect that a child with diabetes does not have the same choice as his/her peers to go hungry if he/she doesn't find the food appetizing. An alternative outside the regular menu must be available at times. As a parent it is often a good idea to check the school menu together with the child in advance.

➠ Free snacks should be available as well something to eat when having hypoglycemia.

➠ Physical education should be scheduled as the first or second lesson in the morning or the first or second lesson after lunch. Don't start with heavy physical exercise until one hour after an insulin injection (see also page 168).

➠ Report schedule changes to the parents well ahead, such as visiting a public swimming pool or a games day. Understand the need for frequent bath room visits when the blood glucose level is high.

➠ Facilitate the testing of blood and urine in an undisturbed environment when needed, as well as the possibility of testing blood glucose during lessons.

➠ Possibility of taking the lunch dose of insulin undisturbed.

➠ Help with testing, injections and hypoglycemic reactions according to the age of the child.

➠ Settle with school staff on how much help the child/teenager needs, such as being reminded to take insulin doses or blood tests.

➠ Organize a parent-teacher conference when needed, inviting the diabetes nurse or doctor to attend.

➠ Staff can come to the diabetes clinic along with the child to increase their knowledge of diabetes.

➠ Give realistic vocational guiding.

Policemen, firemen and pilots are examples of professions where it may be dangerous for your own or other peoples' lives if you have a severe hypoglycemia.

diabetes nurse may visit the child and tell the others about his/her diabetes (see also page 66).

Choice of profession

Almost all professions are open to people with diabetes. As for everyone else, it is important that you first and foremost think about what you would like to do. However, considering the risk of hypoglycemia you should avoid professions where your own or other peoples' lives depend on you functioning perfectly in all situations. Professions that includes some type of physical work or at least some degree of mobility have the advantage of giving you regular exercise.

Usually you can adjust insulin doses to fit with most working schedules, even when irregular hours are included. When working night shift or if there are frequent changes in one's work schedule and meals, this may be more difficult to accomplish. Shift work has been shown to increase the level of triglycerides in non-diabetic persons. In diabetic persons this may imply an increased risk of heart disease.[232]

The risk of having hypoglycemia will hinder someone with diabetes from becoming a policeman, pilot, or steward, and in most countries also driving a bus, taxi or train. Professional diving or working at high altitudes is usually discouraged. The rules will vary in different countries. Examine the possibility of trying out different occupations to find out how well you can cope with your diabetes in different situations. People with diabetes should be individually considered for employment based on the

requirements of the specific job. The American Diabetes Association states that: "Any person with diabetes should be eligible for any employment for which he/she is otherwise qualified".

Military service

In most countries you will automatically be exempted from mandatory military service if you have diabetes. In some countries certain limited services are allowed, such as office work. Tell your doctor when you are drafted to obtain a medical certificate. Your diabetes clinic and the military authorities can give you further information.

Driver's license

Most countries will allow people with diabetes who are taking insulin and are free of complications to obtain a driver's license. However, regulations, restrictions and the need for a medical review vary considerably from country to country. Your diabetes clinic or Diabetes Association can tell you exactly what is applicable in your country.

Traffic and diabetes

The risk of hypoglycemia is obvious when driving a car. Drivers with diabetes are generally not more prone to accidents than other drivers according to most studies.[93] However, there are case reports of serious accidents due to hypoglycemia.[117] If you don't experience hypoglycemic symptoms at low blood glucose levels (hypoglycemia unawareness) you are not fit to drive. Even if you feel quite capable of driving at a blood glucose level of 2.6 mmol/L (45 mg/dL) your reaction time will be impaired. This has been shown to occur below the

To consider in traffic:

① Check your blood glucose level before being seated behind the wheel. It should be at least 4 - 5 mmol/L (75 - 90 mg/dL) when you set out. **Even if you feel quite well, the blood glucose level must never fall below 3.0 mmol/L (55 mg/dL) to avoid impairment in reaction time and thinking capacity** [277] **(see figure on page 42).**

② Don't start out on a drive or a bicycle trip if you have not eaten recently.

③ Always bring along extra food and carry dextrose in your pocket or the glove compartment of the car.

④ Always pull over if you have hypoglycemia and wait until you feel better before continuing. Remember that your thinking and judgement will not be fully recovered until several hours later.

⑤ Be extra careful when the risk of hypoglycemia is increased, like after a sports event or when you recently have adjusted your insulin doses.

⑥ Alcohol increases the risk of hypoglycemia as well as making you unfit for driving. Make it a habit to never drive a car or motorcycle when you have been drinking.

⑦ Changes in your blood glucose level can result in transient blurred vision.

⑧ Refrain from driving for a week or so if you make major changes in your insulin regimen (such as changing from 2 to 4 or 5 doses/day) until you find out how the new treatment affects you.

⑨ No matter how good a driver you are with a normal blood glucose level, you are never a safe driver if you have hypoglycemic unawareness (no warning symptoms until the blood glucose level is very low). See page 42 how to treat this problem.

Licence for driving heavy trucks

No restrictions	Certain restrictions	Not allowed
Argentina	Australia	Belgium
Brasilia	Austria	Canada
Finland	Chile	Greece
Japan	Israel	Italy
Libya	New Zealand	Mexico
Puerto Rico	Great Britain	Poland
Tanzania	Sweden	Romania
Thailand		USA

The rules for people with diabetes regarding driving trucks heavier than 3500 kg vary considerably between countries.[117] USA and Canada are heading for less restrictions while the European Community is doing the opposite. If a person who already has a truck licence contracts diabetes the license will be suspended in 8 countries, restricted in 7, and in 6 will continue to be free of restrictions.

In an American study subjects with diabetes were tested in a driving simulator.[86] They were not told their blood glucose readings (a blind study). At a blood glucose level of 3.6 mmol/L (65 mg/dL) only 8 % showed impaired driving while at 2.6 mmol/L (45 mg/dL) 35 % drove more slowly, and had steering difficulties (more swerving, spinning, time over mid-line, and time off road). Only half of them were aware of their impaired ability. When the same investigations were re-done 3 months later the results were similar in that the same individuals had impaired driving at lower blood glucose levels.[326]

There are many situations in which one must be 100 % alert when driving a car. Never drive with a blood glucose level below 3.5 mmol/L (60 mg/dL) even if you feel ever so well!

level of approximately 2.8 mmol/L (50 mg/dL).[277] (See page 42 for further information on how to treat this phenomenon, which is caused by your body becoming accustomed to low blood glucose levels.)

Insulin-dependent diabetes in children, adolescents and adults © R. Hanas 1998

You may need to appeal if your health insurance conditions change after being diagnosed with diabetes.

Adoption

Some countries have restrictions on adoption by a parent with diabetes. This is due to apprehensions about diabetes complications rendering it more difficult to take care of an adopted child. In some countries these regulations are being liberalized. The country of origin may also have some restrictions concerning diabetes.

Child care allowance

In some countries a special allowance is available for parents of a child with diabetes to compensate for the extra time and commitment that is involved in diabetes care. As these regulations may differ from time to time the current status is best obtained from your diabetes clinic. Special rules may also apply to health care insurance when you stay home with your child because of illness.

Insurance policy

Insurance policy for people with diabetes may differ considerably from country to country and between insurance companies as well. If you have health insurance when the child contracts diabetes you may receive a one-time reimbursement or a monthly allowance from the insurance company. It can be difficult for a person with diabetes to get

health or life insurance although some companies may have special regulations, which allow enrollment for a higher premium. Check with your insurance company or Diabetes Association.

Diabetes ID

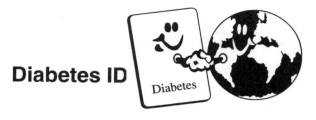

When travelling abroad it is often practical to have some kind of identification showing that you have diabetes and that you need to carry insulin and accessories. Insulin companies and Diabetes Associations often have special cards with text in different languages explaining what help you need if you have a hypoglycemic reaction.

It is a good idea to always carry something on your person showing that you have diabetes, such as a special necklace or bracelet (Medic-Alert® or something similar). It is not uncommon for a person with diabetes to be mistaken for drunk when in fact he/she is hypoglycemic. Even if you have only had a little to drink, people noticing the smell of alcohol, will often pass by without helping.

Sponsor family

Many things about diabetes are difficult to learn from a book or from the staff at the diabetes clinic. It is not the same as real life since most of us do not have diabetes or children with diabetes. Many clinics have a system for finding a sponsor family with a child of the same age, preferably living close by. They can give you valuable tips and information on practical ways of handling different situations such as school, birthday parties, travel and so forth. The sponsorship system may be just as valuable for an adult with diabetes.

The Diabetes Association

In nearly every country there is a Diabetes Association protecting the interests of people with diabetes. Local chapters are present in most towns. Find out if there is a special section for children and adolescents in your area. We strongly recommend joining the Diabetes Association. You will receive valuable information including a newspaper or journal.

Most diabetes associations have journals where you can read news on diabetes research and many other helpful articles. We encourage your becoming a member of your local diabetes association.

The International Diabetes Federation

The International Diabetes Federation (IDF) is open to members of all countries. It promotes diabetes interests in many different areas. An international conference is organized every 3rd year. The 1994 conference was in Kobe, Japan, the 1997 in Helsinki, Finland, and the conference year 2000 will be held in Mexico. You can obtain further information about IDF from the Diabetes Association or on Internet.

The St. Vincent Declaration

The St. Vincent Declaration (SVD) originated in 1989 when the European region of the IDF met with representatives of almost all European government health departments, the National Diabetes Associations and a broad multidiciplinary base of health care professionals from throughout Europe. Later meetings have expanded to countries outside of Europe, including Central Asia and the recent Declaration of the Americas has taken its central themes from the St. Vincent Declaration.

The SVD emphasizes the recognition of diabetic problems and the necessity of making available resources for solutions at national, regional and local levels. Specific target areas are: detection and control of diabetes, self-care, prevention, care of children, promoting independency and self sufficiency, access to health care, tackling discrimination against people with diabetes, reducing blindness, kidney-disease, amputation, heart disease, stroke and complications of pregnancy, setting up special diabetes registers and promoting international collaboration.

Diabetes camps

Participating in a diabetes camp will increase self-confidence by establishing friendships with other children with diabetes who have to abide by the same rules concerning insulin, diet and testing. The program varies from camp to camp but the majority of diabetes camps emphasize improving your ability to manage diabetes on your own. In small groups the children will learn about correct injection technique, testing methodology, diet, physiology and other issues on diabetes. For teaching physiology we use Bodylink® from Boehringer-Mannheim. It is an interactive tool that children and adolescents enjoy very much. It was developed by Dr. Martin Sulway from Australia.

It is more fun to take insulin and see what your blood glucose level does when your friends are doing the same. If a child has difficulties taking insulin or testing he/she will quickly learn all about this from peers at a diabetes camp. The children are often relieved to find that their friends at the camp already know what diabetes is. They do not need to explain what hypoglycemia is or why they take injections and so on, as is often the situation at home.

Many will meet new friends with whom they will keep in touch for years to come. At our camp for prepubertal children we emphasize the ability to manage diabetes independently. If they can handle diabetes on their own during puberty they will be helped in their struggle for independence and hopefully diabetes will not play too large a role in the family's conflicts associated with puberty (see also page 236).

Camping will also increase self-confidence in one's ability to manage without mother and father, especially for a child who is perhaps away from home for the first time ever, for more than a night or two. For parents it can often be relieving to be on their own, knowing that their child with diabetes is being taken care of by professional staff.

Diabetes and Internet

An increasing amount of information on diabetes is available on the Internet. Both medical companies and institutions have homepages displaying information and news. Use one of the search services to find the type of information you are looking for.

One thing is very important to remember when reading information on the Internet. Most of it is not reviewed by health care professionals and it may often only be the opinion of the person writing it. However, if you judge the information somewhat critically, you will find much of interest about diabetes.

When does one become an adult?

This may be difficult to tell as most of us carry part of our childhood with us throughout our lives. Practise and regulations of when diabetes care is transformed from pediatric to adult units differ between countries. It also differs between centers depending

At diabetes camp the children will meet friends with the same disease who understand what living with diabetes is like. Our aim is to have fun together but also to prepare the children for a life with diabetes by increasing their knowledge and ability to manage on their own.

Insulin-dependent diabetes in children, adolescents and adults © R. Hanas 1998

on local interests. At our clinic the adolescents usually start seeing an internist at the time when they move away from home, somewhere between 18 and 20 years of age. Systems of transferal vary. One common procedure is for the pediatrician to join the teenager for his/her first visit to the internist. Another is for the diabetes nurse from the adult team to join the last visit before transferal. Many centers also have special group sessions where both pediatric and adult staff are represented.

Reimbursed accessories

In most countries insulin is available free of charge for patients with diabetes. Often syringes, pen injectors and needles are reimbursed as well. Other accessories such as indwelling catheters are reimbursed in some countries, others not. Often the patient has to pay for blood glucose meters while the sticks for testing are reimbursed. Sometimes the companies producing the meters will provide them free of charge at the onset of diabetes. Insulin pumps and accessories for these are often not reimbursed, but may be available through various insurance companies or under special conditions.

Diabetes and Internet

Associations

International Diabetes Federation (IDF) www.idf.org
International Society for Pediatric and Adolescent Diabetes (ISPAD)www.ispad.org
American Diabetes Association (ADA) www.diabetes.org/default.html
Diabetes UK www.diabetic.org.uk/

Companies with diabetes interest

Becton Dickinson www.bd.com
Boehringer-Mannheim www.boehringer-mannheim.com/
Chronimed www.chronimed.com
Disetronic www.disetronic.com (http://www.disetronic.ch)
Eli Lilly www.lilly.com/diabetes (only for US residents)
Hoechst www.hoechst.com
LifeScan www.LifeScan.com/lshome/homels.html
Medi-Ject www.mediject.com/
MiniMed www.MINIMED.COM/
Novo Nordisk www.novo.dk

Patient information

Children with Diabetes www.castleweb.com/diabetes/index.htm
Patient Information Documents on Diabetes www.niddk.nih.gov/diabetesdocs.html
Understanding Insulin-Dependent Diabetes bcn.boulder.co.us/health/chn/diabetes/
    by Peter Chase typeIdiabbook/content.html
Diabetes Monitor www.mdcc.com
On-line Resources for Diabetics by Rick Mendoza www.cruzio.com/~mendosa/faq.htm
The Diabetic Data Centre by Ian Preece www.demon.co.uk/diabetic/
International Diabetes Institute, Australia www.idi.org.au/frameset1.htm
Diving and Diabetes www.cru.uea.ac.uk/ukdiving/medicine/diabetes.htm

Beware that the information on the Internet often is not reviewed by health care professionals and may often only be the opinion of the person writing it.

Travel tips

Travelling is an important part of life for many and you should not avoid this activity just because of your diabetes. If you think things over and plan the trip ahead, no destination or means of travel is impossible. However, you must be able to measure your blood glucose during the trip, and to adjust insulin doses according to temporary conditions to manage well.

More frequent blood glucose testing will be necessary. You could be high from sitting still on the plane or eating food with more carbohydrates than usual. All the excitement visiting a new city or country may also increase your blood glucose.

Remember to always bring spare insulin, at least 2 - 3 times the amount you expect to use. Keep insulin and pens/syringes in you hand luggage but make sure that you have an extra set in another bag if you are mugged. Don't put the insulin in the check in-luggage as there is a risk of freezing temperature in the airplane luggage container at high altitudes. The X-ray in security controls will not affect the insulin. It is important to have some kind of ID showing that you have diabetes but most often you will not need to show it to the customs officer.

Usually you will have no problem obtaining insulin from a pharmacy abroad if you can prove that you have diabetes. Bring a card where your doses, concentration and brand of insulin are documented. It may be difficult to store the insulin in a refrigerator all the time, but usually it will not be wasted during a short trip, as long as you avoid temperatures above 25° C (77° F). Remember that it can be extremely hot (up to 50° C, 120° F) in a closed car

Remember that you are never more than a phone call away from the diabetes clinic when on vacation or a business trip

on a sunny day. Bring a thermos and cool it with ice before putting insulin into it during hot days. Remember that insulin is absorbed more quickly from the injection site if you are very warm and that this can result in unexpected hypoglycemia (see also page 61).

Insulin completely loses its effect if frozen. You cannot leave it in the car when on a skiing tour. Keep the insulin bottles or the pen injector in an inner pocket if it is below freezing outside. Damaged insulin will often turn cloudy or floccular, sometimes with a brownish discolor. Some blood glucose sticks can give too high a reading when it is very hot outside and too low a reading when it is very cold.

Remember that some countries use other concentrations of insulin, mostly 40 U/ml. If you use insulin of 100 U/ml in syringes designed for 40 U/ml or vice versa, you will be in trouble. The insulin concentration appropriate for each syringe is clearly printed on the side of the syringe. If you run out of insulin it is probably better to buy both insulin and syringes for 40 U/ml if 100 U/ml is not available. You can continue taking your usual doses when counting in units. The units are the same and will give just about the same insulin effect with both 40 U/ml and 100 U/ml. The only difference is that insulin of 40 U/ml may give a slightly quicker onset of action. (See also "Units" on page 56.)

Make sure that you have dextrose and glucagon when travelling, sailing or hiking. With glucagon you can treat a serious hypoglycemia even if you are a long way from a hospital. Make sure that your friends know how and when dextrose and glucagon should be used.

Vaccinations

There are no special restrictions for vaccinations or gamma globulin due to diabetes. However, it is more important for a person with diabetes to actually get the recommended vaccinations, since ill-

Remember that insulin cannot with-stand heat and sun-shine as well as you can... The trunk of a car or bus will be too hot for the insulin in the summer and too cold in the winter.

ness will mean more difficult consequences with problems of diabetes control. It is a good idea to have the vaccinations well ahead of the trip, as some cause an episode of fever that can affect the blood glucose for a few days after the shot.

Ill while abroad?

Remember to bring documents concerning your health insurance so that you receive compensation if you fall ill abroad. Check the conditions to find out if your health insurance only covers acute illness or if it will take care of any deterioration of your diabetes as well.

> ### Avoid the following in hot climate
>
> Tap water (even when brushing your teeth)
> Ice
> Milk, cream, mayonnaise
> Ice cream, baked goods
> Diluted juice
> Cold buffets
> Food kept warm for a long time
> Shellfish
> Salad,   vegetables or unpeeled fruit rinsed
>   in water
> Raw food
> Chicken
> Steamed rice
>
> **Other advice:**[425]
> Wash your hands often
> The food should be freshly prepared and
>   piping hot
> Drink only bottled, carbonated fluids.
> Beer, wine, coffee and tea are also safe.

Always say that you have diabetes when you need to see a doctor abroad. If you become ill while in countries outside of Western Europe and the USA you should, if possible, try to avoid surgical intervention, blood transfusions and injections. If you need medication, ask for tablets instead of injections. If possible, also avoid dental treatment as there is a risk of acquiring a blood infection.

Travelers' diarrhea

Prophylactic antibiotic treatment aimed at avoiding travellers' diarrhea is a controversial subject. Since a person with diabetes will have problems with blood glucose levels and insulin adjustment when ill one should be able to be more liberal when prescribing prophylactic treatment for tourist diarrhea.[73] It can be given during a short trip (3 - 4 weeks or less) to high risk areas (Africa, Asia or Latin America) with a 70 - 90 % protective effect.[381] The risk of a diarrheal infection is otherwise 25 - 35 %. On a longer trip antibiotics should be given only if you have diarrhea. It is best to bring the antibiotics with you. Avoid buying them locally as you will not know exactly what you will get, thereby increasing the risk of side-effects.

Considering the risks of gastroenteritis you should avoid drinking water if it is not quite clean. Avoid all tap water (even frozen, i.e. ice cubes!). Bottled

---

> ### Insulin U-40
>
> Countries that use U-40 insulin (40 U/ml) as of 1994.[222]
>
> | | |
> |---|---|
> | France | Austria |
> | Italy | Spain |
> | Czechia | Slovakia |
> | Poland | Hungary |
> | Russia | Turkey |
> | Morocco | Tunisia |
> | Algeria | Kenya |
> | Nigeria | Egypt |
> | Syria | China |
> | Japan | Korea |
> | Germany (some regions) | |
>
> Blood glucose is measured in mmol/L in some countries and mg/dL in others (see page 77 for conversion table).
>
> 1 mmol/L = 18 mg/dL   100 mg/dL = 5.6 mmol/L

Oral rehydration solution

Oral rehydration fluid can be found at many pharmacies, both at home and abroad. You can also mix your own rehydration solution. Remember that the water you use must be pure! Buy bottled water if you are in doubt.

☞ 1 liter pure water
½ teaspoon of salt
8 dextrose tablets (3 g each)
or 2 tablespoonfuls of ordinary sugar

A camel can survive many days in the desert without drinking thanks to its humps. With diabetes you will be more sensitive to dehydration. Be sure to always drink plenty of fluids when you are in a hot climate, especially if you have problems with diarrhea or vomiting. If you have problems with vomiting or nausea you should drink often but only a few sips at a time. (See the chapter on illness page 175.)

water (Coca cola, Fanta or similar) is usually safe. Rehydration solution is a good alternative if you are nauseous or vomiting (see "Nausea and vomiting" on page 176).

If you travel under primitive conditions the water is best disinfected by boiling it briefly or by using water purifying tablets (Chlorine®, Puritabs®, Aqua Care® or similar).[425]

Diabetes equipment you may need on the trip

✈ Extra insulin in separate hand luggage

✈ Extra insulin pen and/or syringes (pre-filled pens are handy for this)

✈ Test strips for blood + meter

✈ Test strips for urine ketones

✈ Thermometer for refrigerator

✈ ID indicating that you have diabetes

✈ Dextrose/glucose tablets and gel

✈ Glucagon

✈ Fever thermometer

✈ Oral rehydration solution

✈ Tel. and fax. number of your diabetes clinic at home

✈ Insurance papers

Always take glucagon wherever you go and you will have your own emergency treatment handy.

Travel pharmacy

✈ Glucagon

✈ Fever depressing drugs: Paracetamol/acetaminophen or salicylic acid (adults only)

✈ Nose drops

✈ Imodium®(loperamid) for diarrhea, (above 12 years age)
Give if:≥ 4 loose stools/day or
≥ 2 loose stools/day and fever.
Dose: 2 tabl. initially, thereafter 1 tablet after each diarrhea.
Not more than 8 tablets/day for 3 days.
See a doctor if your general condition is affected, your symptoms worsen or if you do not improve within 3 days.[381]

✈ Oral rehydration solution
Powder or tablets (Resorb® or similar)

✈ Antibiotics for diarrhea when travelling to Southern Europe, Asia, Africa or Latin America:

Lexinor® (norfloxacin)
Not for children younger than 12 years old or for pregnant women.
Dose: 200 mg twice daily for prophylactic use or 400 mg twice daily for 3 days when having acute diarrhea.[381]

Eusaprim®(trimethoprim + sulphamethoxazol) or similar for children younger than 12 years old.

If you do not drink enough when outdoors in a hot climate you will risk dehydration. This causes the insulin to be absorbed more slowly.[179] When you later drink properly, more insulin will be absorbed and you will risk having serious hypoglycemia. A high blood glucose level above the renal threshold (see page 78) will also cause you to lose extra fluids due to an increased urine output.

Passing time zones

When you travel to other continents there will be a time difference. When going westwards the day will be longer, and when travelling eastwards it will be shorter. Calculate your insulin dose by increasing or decreasing it by 2 - 4 % for every hour of time shift.[222,345] It is better to adjust your insulin doses to the food being served on board than to order special diabetes food as this may not be as tasty. Due to the pressure differences in the cabin air bubbles easily accumulate in the pen cartridges. To avoid this remove the needle immediately after each injection. If air bubbles are present, be sure to get rid of them before taking injections after you have landed (see page 99). It is common to feel a bit weary before adjusting to the new time zone (called jet-lag) and it will take a couple of days before you feel back to normal and your sleeping pattern returns to normal.

Multiple injection treatment

Use short-acting insulin and eat every 4th to 5th hour during the trip. If you fly westwards take one or two extra doses. If you fly eastwards you will need fewer doses. Take your usual bedtime insulin in the evening when you arrive at your destination (at the "new" bedtime). It is important to check your blood glucose before every meal when improvising like this. If you sleep for many hours on the plane you can try taking a small dose of bedtime insulin. However, if you sleep less than 5 hours, it will probably be easier to adjust to the new time zone if you stick to short-acting insulin during the night (see also "What if I stay awake all night?" on page 65).

2-dose treatment

If you use a 2-dose treatment it may be difficult to adjust to a shorter or longer day. You will probably be better off if you temporarily change to premeal injections 3 - 4 times daily while travelling. You should have tested this regime well in advance to know what doses are needed with different types of meals.

If you use a 2-dose treatment and travel westwards (longer day) take extra premeal insulin doses on the plane and take your usual afternoon dose when you arrive, adjusting it to the nighttime at the destination. If you travel eastwards (shorter day) take a dose of short-acting insulin for the late evening meal on the plane. Don't take bedtime insulin. Instead take a dose of short-acting insulin with breakfast on the plane, preferably not more than 5 hours after the evening meal injection. If more than 5 hours elapse you will need another small dose of short-acting insulin. Take your usual dose of short-acting insulin with breakfast but decrease the intermediate portion by 20 - 40 %.[222]

Passing time zones
(adapted from [222])

☞ **Multiple daily injections**

✈ Going west (longer day):
- ➡ Extra doses of short-acting insulin with 1 - 2 meals
- ➡ Usual dose of bedtime insulin adjusted to the "new" night.

✈ Going east (shorter day):
- ➡ Decrease number of meals.
- ➡ Usual dose of bedtime insulin adjusted to the "new" night.

☞ **2-dose treatment**

✈ Going west (longer day):
- ➡ Extra doses of short-acting insulin with 1 - 2 meals
- ➡ Usual dose of bedtime insulin adjusted to the "new" night.

✈ Going east (shorter day):
Nighttime flight:
- ➡ Take only short-acting insulin with dinner.
- ➡ Short-acting insulin with the evening meal on the plane.
- ➡ Reduce the breakfast intermediate-acting insulin by 3 - 5 % per time shift hour.[345]

Daytime flight:
- ➡ Usual insulin dose with breakfast
- ➡ Reduce the intermediate-acting insulin with dinner on the plane by 3 - 5 % per time shift hour.[345]

Associated diseases

Some diseases are more common if you have diabetes. Celiac disease and hypothyroidism are examples of so called autoimmune diseases (see page 221) where the immune system is involved. Because diabetes is in part a hereditary disease it is also more common both for the person with diabetes and other family members to have other autoimmune diseases. Both hypothyroidism and celiac disease can be difficult to detect. Regular controls with blood tests are therefore a part of annual checkups. If they are taken at the time of diabetes onset one may have increased levels due to a general activation of the immunological defence. It is therefore better to wait about one year after the onset of diabetes before these tests are taken.

Celiac disease

Celiac disease (intolerance for gluten in wheat, oats, rye and barley) is ten times more common in children and adults with diabetes. Studies have shown that 3 - 4 % of all children with diabetes have this disease as well. If you have untreated celiac disease the bowel mucosa is damaged. The absorption of food is poorer, and as a result blood glucose levels after meals are seldom high. The insulin requirement is often low and hypoglycemia is commonly encountered. Often persons with this disease have no further symptoms, but some have diffuse abdominal complaints, constipation or diarrhea. The treatment for celiac disease is to avoid all food containing gluten.

Thyroid diseases

The thyroid gland can be damaged by auto antibodies which lead to a decreased production of thyroid hormones (called hypothyroidism). Your body will try to compensate for this by increasing the size of the thyroid gland (goiter). Thyroid hormones regulate the metabolism in the body and if there is a deficiency one will be tired, lethargic, cold intolerant and have problems with constipation. However, there are often no symptoms at all. The total insulin

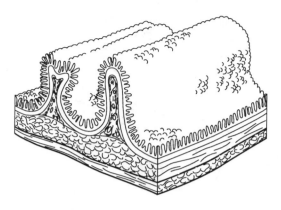

The bowel mucosa is arranged in narrow pleats with small projections that look like fingers (called villi). In this way the absorptive surface of the intestine increases to as much as 200 square meters (250 square yards). In celiac disease these villi are destroyed and the surface that can absorb nourishment decreases considerably, down to as little as 2 square meters (2.5 square yards).

need may be low and hypoglycemia is a common problem.

Hypothyroidism is a hormone deficiency disease just like diabetes but the treatment is much simpler, consisting of 1 - 2 tablets per day containing thyroid hormone. Your body will use the supplied hormone when it is needed.

Toxic goiter (hyperthyroidism, increased production of thyroid hormone) is also more common amongst persons with diabetes. Frequent symptoms are weight loss, feelings of warmth and diarrhea.

Skin diseases

When the blood glucose level is high, fluid losses in the urine may cause itchiness from dry skin.

Irregular red-brownish skin lesions, 2 - 10 mm (1/10 - 1/2 inch) in size, may appear on the lower part of the leg and are called shin spots. Sometimes they even appear on the forearm or thighs. The cause is unclear but they can develop after an accidental trauma such as bumping the leg on the edge of a table. This type of skin lesion is fairly common, especially in men, and usually arises after the age of 30.

Another diabetic skin lesion found in approximately 0.3 % of persons with diabetes is necrobiosis lipoidica diabeticorum. This shows as round or

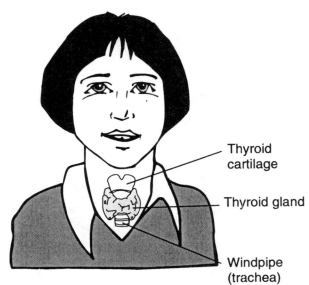

Thyroid cartilage

Thyroid gland

Windpipe (trachea)

The thyroid gland is located in front of the windpipe and is normally not visible. When the gland cannot produce enough hormone it will increase in size, making it clearly visible (called goiter). Goiter can also be caused by an overproduction of hormones but is then referred to as toxic goiter.

Diseases that can lead to a decreased need of insulin

Cortisone deficiency:

A low cortisone production in the adrenal glands decreases the blood glucose level. This can be caused by a disease in the glands (adrenal insufficiency, Addison's disease) or disturbed function of the pituitary gland.

Growth hormone deficiency:

Low production of growth hormone (pituitary insufficiency) decreases the blood glucose level.

Gluten intolerance:

Intolerance of gluten (celiac disease) causes reduced food absorption from the intestine.

Deficiency of thyroid hormone:

Low production of thyroid hormone (hypothyroidism) causes a slower metabolism in the body.

Renal insufficiency:

Renal insufficiency causes a decreased degradation and excretion of insulin.

---

irregular red-brownish lesions with very thin skin, and sometimes ulcers. Lesions are usually located on the front of the lower part of the leg but can also be found on the feet, arms, hands, face or scalp.[212] The lesions usually appear at the age of 30 to 40 years but can arise already in the teens.[313] They grow slowly over many years and are not affected by blood glucose control. The cause is unknown but some data indicate an autoimmune origin.[313] There is no known effective treatment but one can try applying a stoma-type bandage (such as Compeed®). Skin transplants have been used successfully in more difficult cases.

Adults with diabetes can develop blisters on their fingers or toes that look similar to burns, but the underlying skin is not irritated.[212] Usually they will dry within a week or so, but can lead to ulcers that heal slowly. The treatment of choice is to prick the blisters with a sterile needle and then apply a dry bandage.

As far as we know none of these skin lesions are correlated with glycemic control and HbA$_{1c}$. Acanthosis nigricans is a skin disorder characterized by hyperpigmentation and insulin resistance.

Infections

The white blood cells that help defend the body against infections work less efficiently if the blood glucose level is above 14 mmol/L (250 mg/dL), and this increases risk for infection.[27] There is an increased risk of urinary tract infections and skin infections with poor glycemic control.[246,313] From this it follows that the blood glucose level should be as close to normal as possible when fighting off an infection.

Fungal infections

Genital itching caused by fungal infections is more common in women and teenage girls with diabetes after puberty. The fungus thrives better when the blood glucose level is high. Itching may be very intense and there may be a whitish flaky discharge. Fungal infections often arise during treatment with antibiotics that disturb the normal genital bacterial flora, and are more common with higher blood glucose levels.[111] The treatment of choice is an antifungal agent and improved blood glucose control.[313]

Men can have the same type of fungal infection under the foreskin. Fungal infections in children can appear as cracks in the corner of the mouth, or lesions in the cuticle or between the fingers.[313]

Complications

It may be distressing to think ahead about how things will turn out in the future. Many have relatives or friends who have had diabetes for several years. Someone might tell you about a person with diabetes who has had all kinds of complications. It is important to remember that the diabetes complications we see today are caused by 30 - 40 years of diabetes with the type of diabetes treatment available during that time. The result may be discouraging with serious complications from eyes, kidneys, feet and nerves. These individuals may have had a shorter life span due to kidney damage or cardiovascular diseases.

At present approximately 2 % of all persons with diabetes in Sweden are blind,[113] a figure which is six times the risk of a non-diabetic person.[232] It is however very important to know that the prognosis for a person contracting diabetes today is not at all the same. Insulin treatment is much better and the possibilities of both preventing and treating eye complications have improved considerably in most countries.

It may be very difficult to know how much one should tell children about complications. Teenagers understand more and want to know about their situation. We feel it is important that "all the cards are on the table", so you know what type of complications can occur in the long run and what the risks are. It is important to know the facts, but it is not something you need to talk about on a daily basis.

A 13-year old girl believed that candy as such (and not the high blood glucose level that can follow) caused blindness. No wonder she was in agony whenever she ate something sweet and still she just could not resist doing it...

During teaching sessions on complications in diabetes I always encourage the child or teenager to sit in although I do not force anyone to listen. Younger children need to know as much as they can understand, but perhaps not too many details. But I will ask a question every now and then to see how interested he/she is in what we are talking about. If the child wants to go and play after a while it is an indication that the subject no longer is interesting.

At home I believe that one should raise the topic of complications in a careful way every once in a while, preferably when the child/teenager (or adult) with diabetes is in the mood for talking. Many children and teenagers contemplate these questions in silence. They don't want to raise the issue with mother or father in fear of hurting their feelings. During our diabetes camp we have group discussions on the dangers associated with diabetes and most children reveal that they on some occasion have thought about such issues.

Threats of kidney damage or blindness if the child/teenager does not do what you tell them will not get either of you anywhere. On the contrary, such threats will generate feelings of hopelessness, like "drawing a blank in the lottery of life". I have all too often met children who have told me that their parents have said "Don't eat candy because it will make you blind!" Such statements will only cause anguish since children cannot understand the time perspective. Try instead to explain and motivate the child to consider when and how much candy is OK to eat.

Diabetes is such a common disease that if we do not tell our children about complications when they are old enough to understand, then someone else will. Sooner or later someone (with the best intentions) will say: "Poor child, your diabetes will someday make you blind...". I want the child to know the real facts and be able to answer: "That is how things used to be, but now there are much better ways to treat diabetes!".

We don't know for certain the reasons behind side effects and complications after many years of diabetes. However, we do know that they are caused by high blood glucose levels, and that high HbA$_{1c}$ values and a long duration of diabetes will increase the risk for complications. Different persons are more or less susceptible to develop these complications.

It was previously believed that the years before puberty were not significant when it came to the risk of developing complications. However, it has been clearly shown that 10 or 20 years of diabetes for someone contracting the disease before puberty means the same risk for eye complications as 10 or 20 years for a person contracting diabetes after puberty.[120,286]

In some patients signs of incipient complications can be found on close examination after 10 - 20 years of diabetes. Usually there will not be practical problems until after 20 - 30 years of the disease. Some who have had their diabetes for 60 years are still without signs of complications.

In the following text, different complications of diabetes are described rather briefly. See the literature list on page 264 for further information.

❶ Large blood vessels

Cardiovascular diseases are more common amongst persons with diabetes and the large blood vessels (in your body) are at greater risk of developing arteriosclerosis (hardening, narrowing and eventually blocking of the blood vessels). The increased risk for arteriosclerosis and cardiovascular diseases is thought to be caused in part by the high blood glucose level. Another contributing factor is hyperinsulinism (high level of insulin in the blood) which is common between meals when having diabetes.[141] With intermediate or long-acting insulin during the day (2-dose treatment) you will have higher insulin levels between meals than if you were to use short-acting or direct-acting insulin for premeal injections (multiple injection treatment).

A better glycemic control will retard the progression of early arteriosclerosis in persons with type 1 diabetes.[213]

Complications

① Large blood vessels: Arteriosclerosis
    Cardiovascular disease

② Small blood vessels: Eyes, kidneys, nerves

The increased risk of cardiovascular diseases is the reason that we recommend a reduction in dietary fat. Fat has no direct effect on the blood glucose level other than causing the stomach to empty more slowly (see page 145).

❷ Small blood vessels

Sustained periods with high blood glucose levels will lead to glucose being accumulated into the cells in the walls of the blood vessels, causing these vessels to become more brittle.[346] The cells mainly afflicted by such glucose toxicity are those not requiring insulin for glucose transport, i.e. the eyes, kidneys, nerves and blood vessels. As glucose can freely pass into these cells they will always be exposed to high glucose concentrations when the blood glucose level is high.

The red blood cells are stiffened in persons with diabetes since glucose binds to a protein in the cell wall. The stiffened cells will have difficulties passing through the finest capillaries resulting in a lack of oxygen delivery to the tissues.[293] Decreased blood glucose levels are of great importance for the red blood cells. Normal blood glucose levels for 24 hours restored the stiffness back to normal.[293]

Heart and vascular diseases
Diagnosis

① Blood pressure controls.

② Examination of pulses in feet and lower legs with a doppler device.

③ Analysis of cholesterol and triglycerides.

Treatment

The same advice is given to all persons with an increased risk of cardiovascular diseases, regardless of whether they have diabetes or not.

① Quit smoking

② Avoid excess weight

③ Avoid stress

④ Don't drink too much alcohol

⑤ Treat high blood pressure

⑥ The diet should be rich in fiber and low in fat.

⑦ Increase the amount of physical exercise or physiotherapy

A Eyes

Brittle capillaries can give rise to small protuberances called microaneurysms (see illustration on page 210). These are considered background lesions and do not affect the sight. It is important to realize that this type of early lesions can regress if the blood glucose control is improved. On the other hand, if you continue to have a high HbA$_{1c}$ the process of eye changes will continue, and there may be a progress of the lesions on the retina with formation of new blood vessels. These new blood vessels are brittle and can easily rupture and result in diminished vision. Most often the blood will be absorbed and the sight restored. Large or repeated bleedings that are left untreated can result in permanent visual impairment and, in the worst case, blindness. Impaired color or night vision can be a result of neurological damage caused by diabetes. Smoking will increase the risk of impaired vision.[295]

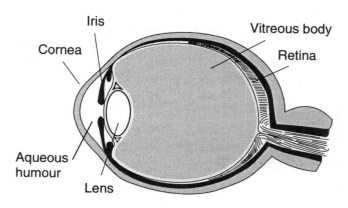

The eye seen in cross-section. Eye damage is first noted in the retina. At check-ups the retina is photographed (called fundal photography) and an eye specialist will have a close look at the pictures.

Treatment

As of today, the vast majority of people with 15 - 20 years of diabetes have some kind of retinal changes, half of which need laser treatment.[13,382] In an Australian study some degree of retinopathy was present in 28 % of a group of 178 children and adolescents aged 10 - 14 years with a diabetes duration of 4 - 10 years. In a group of 193 older adolescents aged 15 - 22, retinopathy was present in 52 %.[120] In a Swedish study 14.5 % of patients aged 8 - 25 years had retinopathy.[226] Of 1000 persons with diabetes, one will sustain serious visual impairment (visual acuity 0.1 or less) each year but blindness due to diabetes is today very rare in countries where modern treatment methods are available.[356]

The most important treatment is a good blood glucose control. This can reverse early changes of the retina. If you have established eye damage you may experience some additional impairment if you improve your metabolic control too quickly (as when starting with an insulin pump). It is important to know that studies have shown that this is a temporary impairment.[177] If you continue with the same good glycemic control the eye changes will reverse. If you have established eye damage you should therefore try to improve the blood glucose control slowly, over several weeks time, to avoid further visual impairment.

Many feel that blindness is the worst thing that can happen if you have diabetes. You may worry about this after having eaten too much candy. However, it may be difficult to raise the question with mom or dad (or your spouse) since they are also worried.

If you contract diabetes today and have a good HbA$_{1c}$ during the years to come there is a very little risk of becoming blind. This is due to the much better methods of treatment that have been developed during recent years, both for diabetes and for eye damage.

Try to talk about this at home even if it is difficult. It is important that you know all the facts and that you realize that you can influence the course of events yourself. Many adults have seen what has happened to persons with diabetes earlier, like friends at work or at home, and find it difficult to believe that the same prognosis does not apply to a person contracting diabetes today.

Laser is an effective form of treatment which can spare the sight and sometimes even improve it. Some eye lesions are operable. We inform our newly diagnosed children and teenagers that the risk of becoming blind is very small as we today have better methods both for treating diabetes and avoiding possible eye damage.

Eye damage — Diagnosis

Eye examination
(preferably fundus photography):

① Initially at diagnosis of diabetes.[106,364]

③ Annually after 2 - 5 years of diabetes (5 years in prepubertal children) [13,364] or from the age of 10 years.[226]

③ To obtain a driving licence in many countries.

Treatment

① Good glucose control

② Stop smoking [295]

③ Laser treatment

④ Surgery

To be able to discover changes as early as possible, all persons with diabetes should be given an eye examination annually after 2 years of diabetes (after 5 years of diabetes for those who are prepubertal).[364] In addition you will need an examination when applying for a driver's license. The most sensitive type of examination is a photography of the retina (fundus photography). Before taking the photograph, eye drops will be applied in order to dilate the pupils, so that a larger part of the retina can be seen on the photo. The retina can also be examined with a special instrument (called ophthalmoscope).

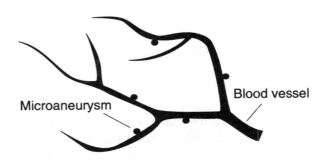

After many years of high blood glucose levels the blood vessels of the retina will become brittle and small "bubbles" can form (called microaneurysms). They do not affect your vision but can be seen on a photograph of the retina.

Disturbed vision at unstable blood glucose levels

Blurred vision for a couple of hours is a common symptom of unstable blood glucose levels. It is not in any way dangerous for your vision or affiliated with future visual impairment. Unstable blood glucose can also cause disturbances in color vision (see also page 30).

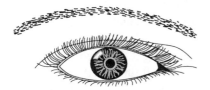

Temporarily blurred vision when blood glucose levels are high does not result in any permanent eye damage.

Sometimes the disturbed vision can continue for several weeks. This is caused by glucose being stored as sorbitol in the lens, disturbing the fluid distribution. This will temporarily affect the optic properties of the lens, making you shortsighted. However, if you have prolonged periods of increased blood glucose levels there is a certain risk that permanent clouding will occur (cataract). This may be the case if a child has had symptoms for a long time before diagnosis.[106] Cataract surgery can be performed with good results.

Glasses

Your blood glucose levels should be stable when trying out new glasses to prevent your vision from being affected by temporary changes in blood glucose. After the onset of diabetes it may take 2 - 3 months of normal blood glucose levels before the lens has returned to its usual shape.[113] It is therefore not a good idea to get glasses or replace them during this time.

Contact lenses

Persons with diabetes can use contact lenses. However, one should avoid long-term lenses (that are replaced every second or third week) as the protecting cell layer of the cornea is somewhat more brittle in diabetes.[82]

B Kidneys

In the kidneys the blood vessels are formed into small clusters where waste products in the blood are filtered into the urine. Damage to the walls of these blood vessels cause an increased leakage of protein into the urine. This protein can be detected in the urine even at a very low concentration (called microalbuminuria). If the leakage continues one is at risk of developing high blood pressure and a constant leakage of protein into the urine (proteinuria). This may occur after 10 - 30 years of diabetes and leads to uremia (urine poisoning, the body cannot get rid of its waste products), and the need for dialysis within 7 - 10 years if left untreated.[39] Only about 1/3 of all persons with diabetes will develop microalbuminuria and its associated risk of permanent kidney damage.[39,382] Good diabetes control decreases the risk of kidney damage, but we still not know why more than half of all persons with diabetes are not at all are susceptible to kidney damage.

Microalbuminuria is defined as 20 - 200 µg/min or 30 - 300 mg/24 hours in 2 out of 3 consecutive tests [39,84] taken within 2 - 3 months. Overnight

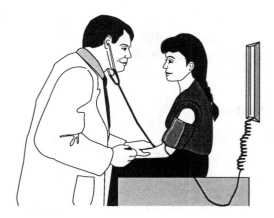

Control of blood pressure is very important to prevent and reduce kidney damage. We check your blood pressure regularly at the visits.

microalbuminuria can be measured as a concentration test (such as Micral-test®, cut-off 20 mg/l) or as timed sample (cut-off 20 µg/min).[84] Proteinuria can have other causes than diabetes as well.

In one study in adults the risk of progression with established kidney damage was increased in those with an increased diastolic blood pressure above 80 mm Hg.[297] In another study 53 of those smoking, 33 of those who had smoked previously, but only 11 % of those not smoking had a progression of their kidney damage within one year's time.[349]

Kidney damage — Diagnosis

① Measure blood pressure at every visit.

② Check for micro-albuminuria (small amounts of protein in the urine) annually after 2 years of diabetes (after 5 years for prepubertal children), and at every visit when it is already present.[364]

③ Measure kidney function when needed.

Treatment

① Good glycemic control (HbA_{1c})

② Quit smoking

③ Treatment of microalbuminuria with ACE-inhibitors

④ Treatment of blood pressure above 130/80 [39,297] or 95th percentile for age [364]

⑤ Treatment of urinary tract infections.

⑥ Reduction of protein and salt in diet

⑦ Dialysis

⑧ Transplantation

How do you collect an overnight sample for microalbuminuria?

① Urinate just before going to bed. Do not save this sample.

② Void the first thing in the morning and save this urine. Take a sample of it.

③ If you go to the bathroom during the night you should save this urine and mix it with the morning urine before taking the sample.

④ If you are collecting a timed sample note the exact time when you voided before going to bed and in the morning. Note the total amount of urine as well.

⑤ If the test shows microalbuminuria make sure that you have not done any extra physical activity during the day proceeding the retest as this may release small amounts of albumin into the urine.

Difficulties in completely emptying the bladder may be caused by diabetes. A person who has had diabetes for many years should therefore empty the bladder often and thoroughly.

Treatment

Just as with eye lesions the most important treatment is tight insulin and blood glucose control since an early discovered microalbuminuria can be reversed by lowering the blood glucose level. It is equally important to treat an increased blood pressure early on.

Treatment of albuminuria with a special type of anti-hypertensive drugs (ACE inhibitors) have shown good results even if the patient has a normal blood pressure. This is recommended as routine treatment as soon as permanent microalbuminuria is discovered.[39,408] However, ACE-inhibitors should not be used during pregnancy since they can cause damage to the fetus. One study showed that the risk of microalbuminuria progressing into manifest kidney damage decreased from 21.9 to 7.2 % when treated with ACE inhibitors.[409]

The progression of renal disease can successfully be slowed by a reduction in dietary protein.[311] Renal failure can be treated with dialysis or kidney transplantation.

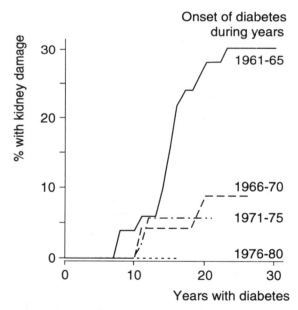

A study from Sweden shows that the risk of developing kidney damage (albuminuria) has decreased considerably in recent years.[59] Thirty percent of those contracting diabetes before the age of 15 (between the years 1961 - 65) developed kidney damage after 25 years of diabetes. Less than 10 % of those who contracted diabetes from 1966 and onwards have developed kidney damage.

c Nerves

Your body's small nerve fibers can be affected after many years of diabetes. The blood vessels supplying the nerve fibers can be damaged resulting in a decreased supply of oxygen.[391] This causes damage to the nerves' insulatory covering (myelin sheath) and ultimately results in poorer nerve impulses. Sensation decreases and there can be accompanying numbing or tingling primarily in the feet, fingers or lower parts of the legs. Later on a more general sensation loss can occur, starting from the toes and spreading upwards. Pain in the hands and shoulders can even be caused by nerve damage.

If you have a decreased blood flow in the small skin capillaries as well as decreased sensation this means that you will not feel the pain from small wounds and healing will be retarded. Decreased feet perspiration can cause the skin to be dry and to crack. With inadequate foot care small wounds will enlarge. If untreated this may lead to ulcers, gangrene, in the worst case amputation. If you have trouble with decreased sensation you should avoid sports that involve the risk of foot damage (blisters, cuts) such as running, football, or soccer.

If you step on a nail or splinter there is always a risk of wound infection. If you have nerve damage with diminished sensation the risk of infection increases as you may be unaware of the wound. Impaired pain sensation often implies that a person with diabetes will seek medical care later for such a wound (9 days after the trauma compared to 5 days for a non-diabetic person in one study[249]). The infection will then have had time to spread and the risk for complication, i.e. tissue or bone infection, is increased. In the above mentioned study 35 % of the persons with diabetes had an infection compared to 13 % of non-diabetic persons. Note-worthy is that 42 % of persons with diabetes had injured themselves bare-footed compared to 19 % of non-diabetic persons.

The part of our nervous system that is self-regulatory (uncontrollable by will power) is called the autonomic nervous system. This can also be damaged by diabetes but will yield different symptoms. These include disturbed perspiration, diarrhea, constipation, impotence (see page 190) or delayed emptying of the stomach. In later years a new type of drug has been tested for treating nerve damage (aldose reductace inhibitors).

The autonomic nervous system

Different organs can manifest damage to the autonomic nervous system after many years of diabetes (modified from ref. [379]).

Organ	Problem
Heart	Dizziness when standing up
Blood vessels	Impaired physical work capacity
Esophagus	Difficulties swallowing
Stomach	Vomiting,
	Slow emptying of the stomach
Intestines	Nighttime diarrhea, constipation
Rectum	Incontinence.
Urine bladder	Difficulties emptying the bladder
	Frequent voiding
Penis	Erection disturbance
	Ejaculation backwards into the bladder (can result in infertility)
Vagina	Dry mucous membranes
Sweat glands	Profuse sweating in the face and neck after eating hot food, spices or cheddar cheese. No sweating in feet, legs and trunk
Skin	Increased skin temperature
Pupils	Small pupils

Delayed stomach emptying can lead to hypoglycemia 1 or 2 hours after a meal. At that time the insulin level will be at its highest when using premeal injections. However, when the peaks of glucose from the meal are delayed the timing with premeal insulin injections will not match. One can instead try taking insulin after rather than before the meal. Other symptoms of delayed stomach emptying are an early feeling of satiety and a feeling of the stomach being filled up or distended. The emptying rate of the stomach can be examined by a special type of X-ray (scintigraphy). A decreased HbA_{1c} with the avoidance of high blood glucose levels can lead to a reduction of these types of symptoms. One should try to exclude everything that decreases the emptying rate of the stomach (fat, fibers, very cold or very hot food, see page 143). A drug that speeds up stomach contractions (cisaprid, Prepulsid®) has been tried with good success.

Nerve damage — Diagnosis

1. Test of vibratory sense (tuning-fork)
2. Tests with special instruments

Treatment

1. Improved glycemic control
2. Foot care, good shoes that don't hurt
3. Treatment of foot ulcers
4. Oxygen treatment in pressurized chambers can be tried if ulcers are slow in healing
5. Drug treatment — still mostly experimental (aldose reductace inhibitors)

Treatment

As for the other complications of diabetes the most important treatment for nerve damage is improved diabetes control. Good foot care is also important. If the skin lesions are slow in healing oxygen treatment in a pressurized chamber is an effective treatment.[142]

Children with diabetes have healthy feet and don't need special foot care. Ordinary hygiene is quite enough. Foot baths can be relieving for tired, healthy feet and there are no restrictions for children and adolescents with diabetes in this case. It is only if you already have nerve damage that foot baths with massage should be avoided. If you are in doubt about this ask your doctor.

Foot care if you have nerve damage

1. Don't walk barefooted.
2. Inspect your feet daily or twice daily.
3. Use shoes that don't hurt.
4. See a doctor as soon as possible if you see redness, callous growth, blisters, ingrown toenails or signs of infection.
5. Regular foot care at the diabetes clinic.

Slow emptying of the stomach
Diagnosis [24]

① Typical symptoms:
  Hypoglycemia 1 hour after a meal
  Early feeling of satiety (no more hunger)
  Feeling of being full
  Distended stomach

② Special X-ray (scintigraphy)

Treatment

① Improved glycemic control.

② Change in diet: Less fiber
  Less fat
  Small but frequent meals
  Temperature of food.
  not <4° or > 40°C
  (not <39 or >104° F)

③ Take insulin injection after food

④ Drug treatment (cisaprid)

Tobias 9 years

Will a better blood glucose control really lessen the risk of complications?

It may feel quite tiresome to constantly try to achieve a good blood glucose level. Many, including teenagers, have remarked that they are pessimistic about its benefits: "Things will go to pot regardless of what I do..."

However, the scientific evidence is very convincing that good glycemic control will pay off in the form of postponing and preventing complications. Still, to completely avoid all types of diabetes complications in the long run seems close to impossible despite today's methods of treatment. It is quite clear that a person with a higher HbA_{1c} has considerably greater risk of having early and more severe complications. Of course there are always exceptions. Some will have complications in spite of meticulous control while others, who have never "managed well" are spared of complications. This may seem very unfair, but it can also be of some comfort to a person with complications since there is no guarantee that, if he/she had achieved a better blood glucose level, the problems would have been avoided.

An unusual example comes from Kuwait, where a person with kidney disease (without diabetes) received a kidney donated from a person with diabetes who was killed in a traffic accident. The kidney had been severely damaged by diabetes but there was no other kidney was suitable for him. The transplanted kidney now was exposed to perfect glucose control since he did not have diabetes. After 2 years new tests were performed on the transplanted kidney and now the diabetes lesions were gone!

The Oslo study

Knut Dahl-Jörgensen and collaborators in Oslo performed a long-time study comparing 2-dose treat-

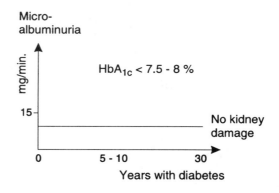

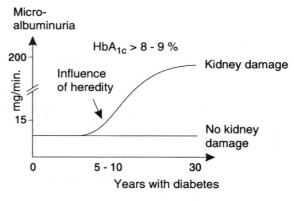

In the same Norwegian study it was shown that kidney damage will only developed in persons with a high HbA_{1c}. But not all persons with diabetes are susceptible to kidney damage as there seems to be a hereditary "sensitivity". With an average HbA_{1c} below 7.5 - 8 % you will probably not develop kidney damage even if you have such hereditary "sensitivity".

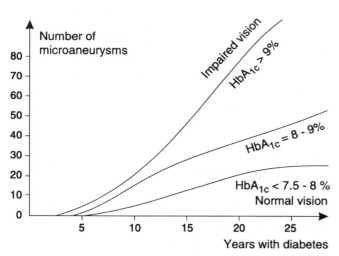

This graph is from a Norwegian study showing how the number of microaneurysms increase considerably with increased average HbA_{1c} for many years.[177] With a lower HbA_{1c} the changes will probably not be severe enough to affect your vision. The HbA_{1c}-levels in this study are approximately the same as in the DCCT-study (see page 87).

ment, multiple daily treatment and pump treatment.[177] This study showed clearly that the risk for complications decreased as the HbA_{1c} was lowered.

The Stockholm study

A Swedish study performed by Per Reichard showed that good glucose control pays off.[329] Two groups with diabetes were followed for 8 years, one with HbA_{1c} 7.1 % and the other with a level of 8.5 % (equals to 8.4 vs. 9.8 in DCCT-numbers, i.e. the HbA_{1c}-levels in this study were 1.3 % lower than in the DCCT-study). The risk of kidney damage, nerve damage and progression of eye damage decreased with lower blood glucose levels. In the group with higher HbA_{1c} levels, 27 patients developed eye damage, and 9 patients kidney damage, while in the group with lower HbA_{1c} levels only 12 patients developed eye damage and only one had kidney damage.

— Due to different hereditary predisposition some people will develop complications at an HbA_{1c} of 9 - 9.5 % while others have it at an HbA_{1c} of 13 %. Unfortunately this is very unfair, and we do not know why it is the case. With an HbA_{1c} less than 9 % serious kidney damage is avoided while one must have an even lower HbA_{1c} to avoid eye damage. Under a level of 7 % the risk of serious complications are minimized according to Per Reichard.[330]

The DCCT study

A recent American study clearly shows that a lower HbA_{1c} will decrease the development of complications.[109] Over a period of 9 years, 1441 persons with diabetes spanning the age range of 13 - 39 years were compared. They were divided into 2 groups, one with an average HbA_{1c} of 7 % (intensive treatment using insulin pumps (42% at the end of the study) or multiple daily injections, mostly with syringes) and one with a level of 9 % (conventional treatment with 1 or 2 doses/day).

The insulin treatment was not the only factor that differed between the two groups. In the intensive treatment group blood glucose was measured 4 times daily and the doses of insulin adjusted if needed. Clinical visits were scheduled once a month with telephone contacts in between on at least a weekly and often daily basis. HbA_{1c} was measured every month. The aim was specifically to

Many believe that complications strike randomly among those having diabetes. Others feel that it does not matter if you "manage well", complications will arise anyway. The truth is that modern research has clearly shown that the degree of long-term complications depends directly upon the blood glucose levels over the years that you have had diabetes.

attain low blood glucose readings (3.9 - 6.7 mmol/L, 70 - 120 mg/dL, before meals) and an HbA_{1c} of 6 %, at the highest. In the group using 1 - 2 doses per day the goal of treatment was to feel well including the absence of symptoms from high or low blood glucose levels. Clinical visits were scheduled every third months, blood tests were taken when needed and regular education was given at the visits. HbA_{1c} values were taken but the results were not revealed to this group.

In the group with lower HbA_{1c} the risk of developing eye damage was lowered by 76 %, early kidney damage (microalbuminuria) by 39 %, severe kidney damage (albuminuria) by 54 % and nerve damage by 60 %. The risk of severe hypoglycemia (requiring help from another person) increased by 2 - 3 fold in the intensive treated group. Neuropsychological tests did not show any permanent damage from the hypoglycemic incidents. However, the individuals in the group with intensive insulin treatment gained more weight (in average 4.6 kg, 10.1 pounds, more). There was a 46 % reduction in vaginal infections in the intensive treatment group, but no differences in the rates of other infections.[111]

Another way of presenting the data is that intensive treatment will give a patient 7.7 additional years of sight, 5.8 years of renal function, 6.0 years of limb preservation, and 5.3 additional years of life. In summary, each 10 % fall in HbA_{1c} (for example from 9.0 to 8.1 %) decreases complications by 50 %.

Endogenous insulin production was better sustained in the intensive treatment group (measured

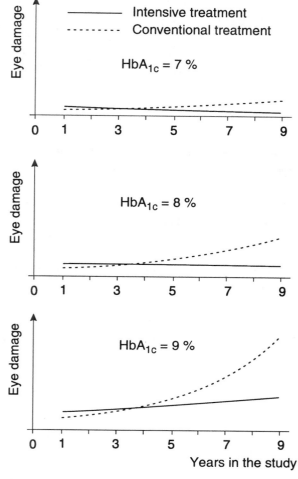

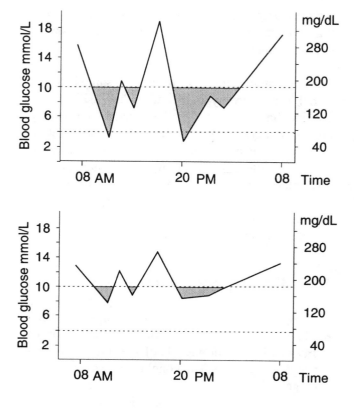

Patients in the DCCT-study with the same HbA_{1c} but different types of insulin treatment were compared.[110] Somewhat surprisingly there was a clear difference, i.e. a considerably increased risk of visual impairment when on conventional treatment (1 - 2 doses/day) compared to intensive treatment. With 1 - 2 doses/day the average HbA_{1c} must be reduced to 7 % to avoid visual impairment while in the intensive treatment group (pump or multiple injections) HbA_{1c} was above 8 % before impaired vision was observed. The figures are redrawn from reference.[110]

Many parents ask us if it is healthy for the blood glucose level to swing up and down throughout the day as often happens when multiple injections or insulin pump treatments are used to maintain an optimal HbA_{1c} value. The graphs above imply that there may be some further factor besides HbA_{1c} that affects the development of complications. A possible explanation is that with swinging blood glucose levels there are longer periods of normal glucose levels (top figure to the right), compared to when the glucose levels are slightly above 10 mmol/L (180 mg/dL) for the greater part of the day (bottom figure to the right), although HbA_{1c} remains the same. It may be that one should not be so concerned about the number of high blood glucose values (which increase the risk of complications) but instead look at the number of normal or low blood glucose levels (which decrease it).

Both charts give roughly the same average blood glucose level over the 24 hour period (approximately 10 mmol/L, 180 mg/dL, corresponding to an HbA_{1c} of 8 % with DCCT comparable methods). It may be that a blood glucose level of 18 mmol/L (320 mg/dL) is not much worse than 12 mmol/L (215 mg/dL). What is important may instead be the time that the blood glucose level is below a certain limit, such as 10 mmol/L (180 mg/dL, the grey shading in the figure). During this time there are not any abnormal amounts of glucose transported into the cells that are independent of insulin-mediated glucose transport. These cells are the ones which are susceptible to long-term complications (the eyes, kidneys, blood vessels, nerve fibers). Since the periods of "toxic glucose levels" within the cells will be shorter this may explain why complications develop more slowly. Future research will shed further light on these issues.

by level of maintained C-peptide) which, in turn, allowed for better metabolic control, less frequent hypoglycemia and fewer long-term complications. These observations emphasize the importance of implementing intensive treatment already during the first years of diabetes.[373]

In the group of adolescents between the ages 13 - 17 years those with 1 - 2 doses had an HbA_{1c} of 9.8 % and those with intensive treatment, 8.1 %. After 8 years the group with intensive treatment had 53 % less eye complications and 10 % less kidney complications. The overall conclusion was that the decreased risk of long-term complications more than compensates for the increased risk of severe hypoglycemia.

European studies have not shown the same increase in risk for severe hypoglycemia when using intensive insulin treatment.[351,357] The reason for this may lie in that there is a longer tradition of use of intensive treatment in Europe and that patients eventually learn, at least in part, how to avoid dangerously low blood glucose values. The frequency of hypoglycemia in the DCCT study decreased slightly towards the end of the study,[111] an observation that supports this hypothesis.

The Berlin eye study

In Berlin 346 persons with diabetes, aged between 8 - 35 years, were studied with a special type of X-ray displaying the vessels of the retina (fluorescence angiography). The conclusion was that if the average HbA_{1c} was lower during the previous years, the retinal vessel changes developed later.[105]

Average HbA_{1c}	Years before eye changes
< 8 %	25
8 - 9 %	16
9 - 10 %	13
> 10 %	12

The HbA_{1c}-levels with the method used in Berlin are approximately 1 % higher than in the DCCT-study.

Every percentage lowering of HbA_{1c} means a decreased risk of eye lesions. With an HbA_{1c} above 9 % the risk of eye damage increased considerably.

What HbA_{1c} is it possible to achieve in a diabetes clinic?

The Hvidøre Study Group on Childhood diabetes collected data from 2,873 children and adolescents from 18 countries in Europe, Japan and North America.[294] The patients took part in the routine care program which at all centers had a multidiciplinary approach involving pediatric diabetologists. All tests for HbA_{1c} were analyzed at a central laboratory.

The average HbA_{1c} was 8.6 % (DCCT-equivalent 8.3 %). However, the average HbA_{1c} among the centers varied significantly, both between and within countries, from 7.6 % to 10.2 %. Of the children who had had diabetes for 2 years or longer, 34 % had an HbA_{1c} below 8 % (7.7 % DCCT equivalent). HbA_{1c} increased with age, reaching a maximum at 16 - 17 years.

In Sweden every child with diabetes is referred to center with a pediatric diabetologist. At the Pediatric Department in Uddevalla we give service to 80 children and adolescents with diabetes aged 2 to 20 years. Our average HbA_{1c} is at present 7.8 % (DCCT-equivalent method). We emphasize intensive diabetes treatment in the same sense as was done in the DCCT study, i.e. more than simply the insulin treatment is intensive. We also include a close and frequent patient contact aiming at good quality of life while still stressing the short- and long-term advantages of good glycemic control.

Research

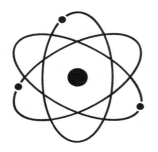

Huge efforts are put into diabetes research around the world and more than 5000 scientific studies are published yearly. A large part of this is basic research, trying to elucidate what causes diabetes and why different things take place in the body when having diabetes. Even if you hear of new methods in diabetes treatment from newspapers and TV you must remember that it usually takes several years before such methods become available outside the research clinics.

Research projects

- ⚛ Artificial pancreas implants.
- ⚛ Blood glucose meter that measures without blood specimens.
- ⚛ Subcutaneous insulin pump with continous monitoring of blood glucose levels (sensor).
- ⚛ Transplantation of pancreas or islets.
- ⚛ Alternative (noninvasive) methods of delivering insulin.
- ⚛ Immune modulation at the onset of diabetes.
- ⚛ Treating white blood cells with light at the onset of diabetes (photo-pheresis).
- ⚛ Adding C-peptide to insulin.
- ⚛ Drugs (nicotinamide) for prophylaxis of persons at risk of contracting diabetes.

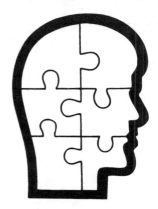

Implantable insulin pump

Insulin pumps for implantation in the abdominal cavity are being used by some but this method is still mostly at a research level.

Refilling of insulin in such pumps is done by inserting a syringe through the skin into the rubber membrane of the pump. Premeal bolus doses are given by using a small transmitter. Insulin from the pump is injected into the abdominal cavity (intraperitoneal) and is quickly absorbed into the blood stream. Contrary to what one may think, the risk of hypoglycemia decreases with this type of insulin treatment.[298] This is because the insulin administered in this way first passes through the liver before reaching the other parts of the body just as the insulin secreted from a non-diabetic pancreas does.

Another research project is an artificial pancreas which can be connected to a blood vessel. This device both measures blood glucose levels and injects insulin directly into the blood stream. This approach is still a very complicated one which is at present only found in a research laboratory.

Blood glucose meters

The possibility of measuring one's blood glucose at home has brought a revolution in diabetes treatment. We are now waiting for the next generation of blood glucose meters which can measure without obtaining a blood sample. One possibility is a infra-red ray of light (the "dream beam"). Another is to measure the glucose content directly through the skin with an electro-osmotic method (Glucowatch®).

Glucose sensor

A device that can measure the blood glucose levels continuously over a longer period of time is called a glucose sensor. So far such a device has only been shown to give reliable readings for a couple of days or a week's time. One type of sensor is implanted into the subcutaneous fat. Glucose is measured either by an electrical current or by a special method called microdialysis.[60] With this type of device we should be able to measure nighttime blood glucose levels without difficulties and thereby gain a better understanding of how to adjust bedtime doses.

C-peptide

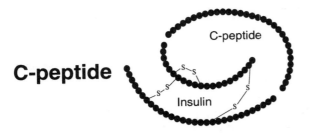

Bring newspaper clippings to the clinic when you have read something interesting, such as diabetes research, so we can discuss it together. We both may learn something!

When insulin is produced in a non-diabetic pancreas C-peptide (connecting peptide) is produced as well. Early data suggested that C-peptide was of no use in the body but recently positive effects on metabolism have been shown in the form of a decreased HbA_{1c}. During a month's treatment with C-peptide, leakage of protein into the urine decreased and capillary function in the retina improved.[215] C-peptide stimulates the uptake of glucose into the muscle cells and thereby improves the effect of insulin (decreased insulin resistance). Nerve function in patients with diabetes-related nerve damage is improved as well.[216] It is possible that in the future C-peptide will be given along with insulin.

Vaccination

Vaccinations have been proposed as one of the causes of diabetes. Some children have contracted diabetes shortly after vaccination against measles, mumps and German measles at the age of 18 months. However, scientific studies have not been able to show a correlation between vaccination and the onset of diabetes. On the contrary, it appears that vaccination against measles results in a slightly lower risk of contracting diabetes.[51] BCG-vaccination (against tuberculosis) has been proposed to have a protective effect but this has not been confirmed in studies.

Vaccination against diabetes would obviously be the ideal solution. Unfortunately this is not possible today. If a virus could be identified that triggers diabetes it might be possible to vaccinate against it. If cow milk protein plays a part in the cause of dia-

betes a vaccine could perhaps prevent the onset of diabetes.[139]

Research exploring the possibilities of blocking the autoimmune reaction that causes diabetes are being performed. One project is T-cells vaccination which means vaccination with antibodies that block the cells in the immune system (T lymphocytes) that trigger the attack on the beta cells. Experiments with this technique have been attempted with rheumatic diseases but have not yet been tested on diabetes.

Salicylic acid

Salicylic acid (aspirin), a component of many over the counter painkillers), has been used in trials to lessen the risk of cardiovascular disease as a long-term complication. The current policy is to use it only for patients with type 1 diabetes and established cardiovascular disease, but not for prophylactic use.[126] For patients with type 2 diabetes it has been used prophylactically for the prevention of cardiovascular disease, and some doctors believe that all type 2 patients without specific contraindications should be on aspirin.

What is diabetes caused by?

As of today we do not know what causes type 1 diabetes. However, we do know that it is not caused by eating too much candy. A common view is that about 60 - 70 % of type 1 diabetes is caused by non-hereditary factors, i.e. risk factors due to life-style habits, infections or being exposed to environmental factors.[97] But it is still unclear what those factors, infections or exposures are.

Many parents feel that: "If we had only done this or that our child would probably not have contracted the disease." It is important to realize that diabetes was not caused by something that you or your family could have avoided.

An autoimmune disease

Part of the explanation for the abnormal reaction of the body's immune defence is hereditary. Certain markers that can be measured in the blood are present in almost all children and adolescents with diabetes (such as HLA-antigens on chromosome number 6). However, these markers are also present in 20 - 60 % of persons not having diabetes.[97] Certain gene components have a protective effect in that a person who has them will not contract diabetes.

A viral disease is believed to induce antibodies that, in addition to killing the virus, crossreact with and damage the insulin producing beta cells in the pan-

Possible causes of diabetes

① One inherits a sensitivity for acquiring diabetes.

② A viral disease can trigger the onset of diabetes.

③ If the mother has certain viral infections during pregnancy the child may have an increased risk of diabetes.

④ Impaired insulin production in the beta cells of the pancreas can be found several years before the onset of diabetes.

⑤ Drinking cow's milk during pregnancy or the first year of life may be of importance.

⑥ Fathers eating smoked mutton (contains nitrose-amines) at the time of conception has been found to be a risk factor in Iceland.[181] High dietary intake of nitrite and nitrate has also been shown to be a risk factor. [95]

⑦ Overweight is of importance but only for the development of type 2 diabetes.

⑧ Psychological stress, such as severe life events, have been found to occur more often both during the first 2 years of life [393] and during the year before the onset of diabetes.[209,331] They are not believed to be the cause of the disease,[7] but may increase the risk by affecting the autoimmune process. [393]

⑨ A very good hygienic standard during infancy may lead to the immune defense not being "trained" correctly.[236]

⑩ ???????????????

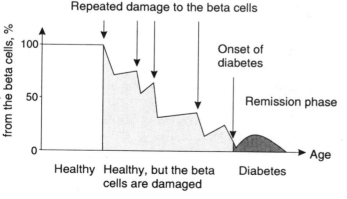

Repeated damage to the beta cells

Onset of diabetes

Remission phase

Age

Insulin production from the beta cells, %

Healthy   Healthy, but the beta cells are damaged   Diabetes

It is believed that the first attack on the beta cells in the pancreas (that produce insulin) takes place many years before a person shows symptoms of diabetes. At the onset of diabetes 80 - 90 % of the beta cells have been damaged. The illustration is from reference [231].

creas. As the damage is caused by a defect in one's own immune system, diabetes is considered an autoimmune disease.

The beta cells will usually partly recover after some time, but if the initial attack is repeated several times, insulin production will decrease enough to raise the blood glucose level. Antibodies directed against the insulin producing islets of Langerhans in the pancreas (ICA, islet cell antibodies), can be detected several years prior to the onset of diabetes, and are an early sign of cell damage. However, school classes are not screened for these antibodies since there is at present no way of preventing the onset of diabetes, even if you know the risks in advance. The antibodies can even disappear spontaneously without the child contracting diabetes.

Environmental factors that trigger the disease process may start early in life, many years before the onset of diabetes.[254] A low groundwater content of zinc, which may reflect long-term exposure through drinking water, was in one study associated with later development of diabetes. Another fact that points to an early influence is that an increased risk for diabetes has been correlated to the time and place of birth.[102] An explanation for the different ages of the diabetes onset may be that the rate of insulin production decline, once the disease process has started, is quite variable from one patient to another.

Sometimes children living close to each other contract diabetes at the same time which may indicate that viral infections trigger the onset.[343] One theory is that diabetes and other auto-immune diseases are caused by so called slow viruses, i.e. a virus that can reside in the body for many years, while avoiding detection and destruction by the immune system.[63]

The risk of contracting diabetes is very different in different countries (see "How common is diabetes?" on page 12). The reason for this is unclear but there are many proposed theories.

In countries with lower hygienic standards and more infections in the environment the immune system is activated to a greater degree at an earlier age. This has been shown to decrease the risk of contracting diabetes in animal studies.[236]

If a mother has German measles during pregnancy the risk for the child to contract diabetes is 20 %.[254] If the mother has other types of virus infections (enterovirus) during pregnancy the child will have an increased risk of developing diabetes later in life.[99,207]

Coffee-drinking during pregnancy has been correlated to (but not causative of) contracting diabetes.[398] Finland has the highest incidence of type 1 diabetes in the world and the highest coffee-consumption as well. Another risk factor is an increased height gain, seen in boys mainly, several years prior to the onset of diabetes.[53,325] Weight gain and obesity, on the other hand are not risk factors for contracting type 1 diabetes.[53] However, children who later contracted diabetes had a quicker weight gain early in life (before 2 - 2.5 years of age) according to one study.[214] No difference was found

When one identical twin has type 1 diabetes the risk for the other twin doing so was 53 % in a Danish study.[241] This indicates that roughly half the explanation for acquiring diabetes is inherited and the other half is dependent on environmental factors. The risk for diabetes in nonidentical twins was 11 % in this study.

in height or weight at birth in children who later developed diabetes.

Heredity

Only 13 % of children and adolescents who contract diabetes have a parent or sibling with diabetes.[96] The risk of contracting diabetes by age 30 for first-degree relatives (brother/sister or parent/child) is between 3 and 10 %.[122] The risk for contracting diabetes for a child of a person with diabetes is about 2 % if the mother has diabetes and about 6 % if the father has diabetes.[122] See also "Will the child have diabetes?" on page 189. Studies on identical twins have shown that the risk for the other twin to contract diabetes is in excess of 50 %.[241]

Environmental factors affect the individual, causing the risk for contracting diabetes to change in families that have emigrated. Asian children living in Great Britain and children from the Samoan Islands living in New Zealand have a higher risk of acquiring diabetes than children in their home countries.[404] Most of the population of Iceland originate from Norway and have the same type of hereditary disposition. Despite this the risk for contracting diabetes in Iceland is only between 1/3 and half of that in Norway.[182] This difference is thought to be caused by differences in environment and climate. However, Iceland and parts of Norway are located on the same latitude and have the same average temperature.

It is more common to contract diabetes during the winter months and during the years of puberty. However, climate and puberty are hardly the causes of diabetes. On the other hand they may very well be triggering factors as both growth spurt and cold weather increase the body's insulin requirements.[254]

Cow's milk

The number of new cases of diabetes per year (incidence) in different countries coincides well with the consumption of cow's milk.[104] Increased levels of antibodies against cow's milk have been found in children who have contracted diabetes.[100,350] In the Samoa Islands where children do not drink milk at all, there is essentially no childhood diabetes. Sardinia has about the same risk of diabetes as the Nordic countries. The consumption of milk is not as high as in Finland but on the other hand it is much higher than the rest of Italy.[145]

In rat studies it has been shown that whey protein from cow's milk increases the risk of contracting diabetes.[136] When rats were fed with soya formula instead of milk they did not get diabetes. It seems that only certain types of cows (our ordinary milk cow) have the protein components which affect the risk of contracting diabetes. Breast-feeding as such does not seem to affect the risk of diabetes,[342] but the time when the child is first introduced to cow's milk seems to be of importance.[410,404] However, there are traces of cow's milk in breast milk and even children who have been fully breast-fed have antibodies against cow's milk.[384] This might explain why even children who have been breast-fed for a long time still can acquire diabetes. In an Australian study, children who contracted diabetes after the age of 9 had ingested more milk the year prior to the onset of diabetes when compared to other children of the same age.[404]

Since it is not yet proven that cow's milk causes diabetes most authorities do not at present recommend any changes in infant diet.[269,352] However, The American Academy of Pediatrics recommends avoidance of cow's milk during the first year of life

Some studies indicate an increased risk of acquiring diabetes if a child is not breast-fed at all or for only 3 months or less.[404] Other studies indicate that it may not be the short breast-feeding as such but the child's early introduction to cow's milk that increases the risk for diabetes. However, there are not enough data available today to disadvise from milk drinking during pregnancy or early infancy.[352]

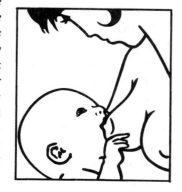

in families with a strong history of type 1 diabetes, particularly if a sibling has diabetes. [11]

Finland is planning a long term study including siblings of children with diabetes, where cow's milk is excluded from the diet during the first 9 months of life. The results are expected at the turn of the century.[231]

Climate

There is a higher risk for diabetes in northern countries. In Sweden there is also a tendency of an even greater risk in the northern parts of the country. Diabetes onset is more common during the winter. A cold climate increases the need for insulin which in turn increases the risk of triggering the onset of diabetes. Fewer hours of sunlight will lead to an increased risk of diabetes through the turn-over of calcium and a decreased production of vitamin D.[98]

Blocking the immune process

At the onset of diabetes 10 - 20% of the beta cells are still preserved (see illustration on page 221). If it would be possible to stop the autoimmune attack on these cells it might be possible to preserve a certain insulin production for a long time, thereby prolonging the honeymoon phase (see "Remission phase" on page 68).

Immune treatment

Immune-modulation in the form of cytotoxic drugs has been tried at the onset of diabetes. Cyclosporin A is a compound that has been used successfully and has even made it possible to stop using insulin for some time.

In a study of 188 patients with new onset diabetes 25 % managed without insulin after one year of cyclosporin treatment compared to 10 % of those who had not received cyclosporin.[392]

However, when you stop the cyclosporin treatment the insulin production will always decrease again. Cyclosporin can give serious side effects such as kidney damage and is therefore not used as a routine treatment at the present time. The International Study Group of Pediatric and Adolescent Diabetes (ISPAD) has stated that cyclosporin has no place in

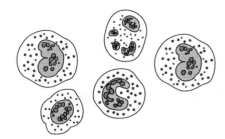

The white blood cells are the "soldiers" in your body's defense against bacteria and virus infections. When contracting diabetes there is an erroneous reaction from the immune defence resulting in an attack on the insulin producing beta cells. With immune-modulating treatment we try to influence this process.

the treatment of diabetes in children except for clinical trials addressing questions that cannot be answered in adults.[210]

Light treatment

Experiments are being conducted where the white blood cells are treated with ultraviolet light at the onset of diabetes (called photo-pheresis). The aim is to make it easier for the immune defence to recognize the cells that are causing damage to the beta cells.[267]

Diazoxid

At the onset of diabetes the immune defence attacks with antibodies directed against a special protein (called GAD) in the beta cell. When insulin treatment is started the beta cells do not need to work as hard and therefore the production of the protein that triggers the antibodies decreases as well, leading to a less intense immune attack. This is believed to be part of the mechanism behind the "honeymoon phase".

Diazoxid is a compound that potently blocks the activity of the beta cells, thereby decreasing insulin production. The production of the protein (GAD) that is attacked by the antibodies decreases as well, therefor decreasing the damage to the beta cells. When the treatment with diazoxid is stopped after a couple of months the hope is that the immune defence will not react as strongly anymore. A Swedish study in adults has shown a higher residual production of insulin one year after the onset of diabetes in a group with newly onset diabetes that was treated with diazoxid for 3 months.[48]

Nicotinamide

Nicotinamide is a type of vitamin B (niacin) that is thought to lessen the risk of contracting diabetes by protecting the beta cells from attack by the immune system. In New Zealand this substance has been given to siblings of children with newly onset diabetes for a couple of years time, thereby preventing them from acquiring diabetes.[138] It has also been given to school classes, resulting in a 60 - 70 % reduced risk of contracting diabetes.[137]

The ENDIT study is an ongoing study for parents and siblings of children with diabetes. Nicotinamide is given to those with a high risk of contracting diabetes indicated by a blood test. The study is done with a so called double blind technique, i.e. half of the patients are treated with nicotinamide and half with placebo (non-active tablets). Neither patients nor doctors know who gets what. After 5 years the code will be broken and we will then know if nicotinamide has had any effect. It may seem strange that half of the persons get inactive medication but this is the only way to do the study scientifically to see if is nicotinamide has a protective effect. It is common to use double blind technique when the effect of new drugs is tested.

Nicotinamide has been tried at the onset of diabetes to preserve the beta cell function. Only patients older than 15 years of age had a certain effect in that the C-peptide levels did not decrease as much after 12 months. This indicates a better preservation of insulin production.[324] Nicotinamide has also been tried on a group of patients with a diabetes duration of 1 - 5 years and a certain residual production of insulin. The group receiving nicotinamide had a better HbA_{1c} and a higher C-peptide level which indicates an improved beta cell production of insulin.[401]

Transplantation

❶ Pancreas

Pancreas transplantations have been performed for more than 20 years. Today it is possible to receive a pancreas transplant if you need a new kidney. Kidney transplants are today done on a routine basis. About 700 solitary pancreas transplantations are done each year.[275] If the transplantation works well there is no need for further insulin injections. One can eat a normal diet and the HbA_{1c} normalizes.

Problems can arise after transplantation due to rejection of the transplant (the immune defence does not like "foreign" things in your body but tries to reject them). After one year about 70 % of the pancreas transplants function well when a kidney is transplanted at the same time. However, the results of transplanting only the pancreas are not satisfying. The reason for this is that the rejection of pancreas is more difficult to discover than a rejection of the kidney. This means that when a kidney transplant is threatened by rejection, medication can be started early, thereby protecting the pancreas transplant as well. Another problem is the damage of the tissues of the host by digestive enzymes from the pancreas transplant.

After a transplantation several drugs are needed, among others cortisone, which counteracts the rejection. Cortisone increases the blood glucose level which leads to a complicated situation. Drugs used to prevent rejection (called cytotoxic agents or immune-modulating drugs) can also result in numerous side effects, some of them being serious.

The beta cells in the new pancreas are susceptible to attack by the immune defence, causing diabetes to come back again, especially if the transplant comes from an identical twin.[254] This is, however, effectively prevented by the immune-modulating drugs that are given to prevent rejection reactions.[380]

Even if all problems with rejection were solved pancreas transplantation can never be the method of choice for routine treatment of diabetes because of the limited availability of human pancreas for transplantation.

❷ Islet transplantation

The islets of Langerhans (see illustration on page 20) that contain insulin producing beta cells and can be extracted from the pancreas of pigs. These islets can be injected into the blood stream in a human and will then produce a certain amount of insulin. This method is still in the research stage and only a couple of hundred persons with diabetes around the world have tried it.

About 20 - 25 % of patients receiving new islets have been able to manage without insulin for more than a week's time and some 10 % of patients have had a substantial insulin production for up to 6 - 12 months time.[275] The problem is that antibodies and rejection reactions can strike these islets as well. Methods where the islets are put into small tubes or encapsulated with a plastic film have been tried to prevent the antibodies from attacking the islets. [371]

Experiments have been conducted where cells are manipulated genetically to produce insulin.[299] The thought is very appealing because if some of your own cells would be able to produce insulin there would be no rejection problems.

More than 5000 articles on diabetes research are produced yearly. Many small advances have resulted but so far no one has been able to solve the question of why one acquires diabetes or how to cure it. However, there is reason for an optimistic view for the future. There have been discussions on how some of the body's own cells (preliminary stages of the beta cells) could be manipulated with gene technology to start producing insulin.

Other ways of administering insulin

Nasal spray

Insulin given as nasal spray is absorbed quicker through the mucosa in the nasal cavity than when injected subcutaneously. Many studies have been performed on humans but it is still doubtful if this can become a clinical reality. Problems may arise with the insulin absorption in allergic subjects or when one has a cold. We do not know how insulin can effect the nasal mucosa in the long run. Twenty times more insulin was needed for intranasal administration compared to injections in one study.[191] However, 7 of the 31 patients interrupted the study prematurely due to problems with high or low blood glucose levels. HbA$_{1c}$ increased slightly in this study, from 7.1 to 8.1 %.

Tablets

The problem with insulin in tablets is that it is degraded by the acid in the stomach. This can be solved by encapsulating the insulin tablets in order to release insulin first after the tablets reach the intestines. Insulin can then be absorbed into the blood, but this is a slow process with a risk of an irregular insulin effect. One advantage is that insulin which is absorbed into the blood from the intestines passes the liver before it enters the general blood circulation just as insulin that is produced in a healthy pancreas. Insulin in tablets is extremely long-acting and one single dose can work for up to one week which may cause dosage difficulties.

Insulin as suppositories

Insulin is absorbed from the rectum when administered as suppositories. Due to poor absorption, more than 10 times the ordinary dose is needed to obtain a substantial blood glucose lowering effect.[190]

Inhalation of insulin

Experiments with administering insulin as an aerosol spray (in the same way as persons with asthma take their drugs) has been tried successfully. Insulin is quickly absorbed through the thin mucosa. In children insulin has been given by the help of a so called nebulizer that transforms the liquid into a mist which can be inhaled. One problem is that it may take quite some time (15 - 20 minutes) to take one dose.

Alternative insulin administrations	
⇒ Nasal spray	Quick effect, good for premeal injections
⇒ Oral insulin (tablets)	Slow effect, good for basal insulin
⇒ Suppositories	Quick effect but large doses are needed
⇒ Aerosol for inhalation	Quick effect but difficult to administer
⇒ Chemically bound insulin	Released only at high blood glucose levels. Technically difficult
⇒ Altered insulin structure	Quicker or slower action
⇒ C-peptide	Produced in the human pancreas but not included in today's insulin

Chemical alteration of the insulin molecule

Changing the composition of the insulin molecule can result in both more short-acting and more long-acting insulin. Normally insulin molecules stick together in groups of six (so called hexamer, see page 55). These bindings must be broken before the insulin can be absorbed into the blood. If the insulin molecules could be injected in a solution of single molecules (monomeric insulin) the action would be much quicker. Another advantage would be obtaining a normalization of insulin levels between meals, lessening the need of snacks.[141]

By switching the order of protein building blocks in the insulin molecule the problems of hexamer formation has decreased considerably. The new direct-acting insulin analogue (Lispro or Humalog, see page 55) gives a very rapid insulin effect.[118,206] It was introduced to the market around the world in 1996 and is today used by many persons with diabetes, both children and adults.

Psychology

Onset of diabetes

It is always a difficult situation for the whole family when a child, teenager or adult contracts a chronic disease. Adjusting to a new life is difficult and takes time. Most people go through the same stages when faced with crisis. Professor Johnny Ludvigsson describes the different phases of crisis:[265]

❶ Shock phase

During the shock phase it is difficult to think clearly. Thoughts will whirl around in your head. Everything seems unrealistic. This can't be happening to us, this can't be true. Is this a dream or is it reality? It is common to experience the surroundings in a kind of haze. One cannot take in information. One sees the doctor, observes his/her posture, mimic, eyes, and understands the gravity of the situation. One listens for hope, consolation, belief in the future, but shuts out all details of the disease, its course and treatment, all connections and mechanisms. One wants to ask questions but finds it difficult holding thoughts in place, to see a way out. The doctor should listen, the nurse should listen, everybody should LISTEN to my inner thoughts of what is most important right now.

❷ Reaction phase

A reaction of sorrow with tears, sleeplessness, aggressiveness and bitterness will also take time. Consolation is important but should be honest, not hearty and unrealistic. "You need not feel sad"

"You cannot stop the birds of sorrow from flying over your head — but you can stop them from building a nest there."

Chinese saying

seems false and "You should not be sad" feels like a punch in the face. Why shouldn't one feel sad? Everybody has the right to be sad in this situation. It is only natural to feel sorrow, bitterness and disappointment. One grieves over the healthy person who once was and life seems unfair. It is always unfair when someone is stricken by a severe disease, but the sorrow will eventually fade away. You will feel better. You have had no part in contracting the disease, it is not your fault. We must have the strength to listen, dare to have an eye contact, allow grief and fear.

❸ Repair phase

After some time one will enter the repair phase. We must be able to do something about this disease. Now knowledge is needed. What do you do if the blood glucose level falls too low? How do you give these dreaded injections? Not until it is done can one breathe a little easier. The worst part is over. Now we can learn more about insulin, testing, diet, and hypoglycemia. Systematically, a little bit at a time, we can absorb facts and rebuild things again.

❹ Reorientation phase

It takes a long time before a crises continues on to the reorientation phase, and a different but acceptable life where diabetes is an important part but by

---

The different phases of crisis

① Shock phase
② Reaction phase
③ Repair phase
④ Reorienting phase

---

no means everything. Those around you will at times have difficulties in understanding that it takes time to go through the different phases of a crises, but this is inevitable when someone in a family contracts diabetes. Sure, it is unfair, the treatment can be difficult, life is changed, you might be afraid of dying or being different from others. But there will still be Saturday afternoons, song, laughter, dancing, good food, school/work, picnics, vacations and friends. Life will never be the same again but it can be exciting and enjoyable although the premises have changed.

Some will come to a stand still in their grief, not being able to move on, and will then require professional help. A continued denial will inhibit one from absorbing knowledge and adjusting life to fit together with diabetes.

Regardless of whether a crisis is caused by the death of someone near and dear, a divorce, contracting diabetes or something else, there will always remain a memory of what happened, much like a scar. But when you have worked yourself through the crisis and accepted what has happened, it will be like looking at a wound that has completely healed: you can see the scar but you are for the most part unaware of its existence.

"You cannot teach a person anything — just help him or her to find it within themselves."

Galilei 1564 - 1642

When a newborn comes to a family, some parents may feel like he/she is like a ticking bomb. One never knows when the baby will start crying, dirty their diaper or get hungry. As time elapses one will learn and become more secure in the new role as a parent. One may feel the same way when a child has just contracted diabetes. Earlier you knew what was ahead. Now you don't know anything at all. How does the child react when hypoglycemic? What can we do together now? How can we manage this or that when our child has diabetes? But in the same way as when the child was a baby you will soon get to know him/her again in this new situation.

Diabetes rules or family rules?

Diabetes can be a "thorn in the side" in different ways depending on how old the child is. When you discuss rules at home it is important to consider what is actually motivated by the child having diabetes, and what is a part of a normal upbringing. If you often refer to diabetes when it comes to rules and prohibitions the child or teenager will come to hate his/her diabetes since it puts an end to so many nice things. However, if you think about it, most rules and methods of upbringing are motivated by other factors and hold true just as much for a child with diabetes as for his/her non-diabetic brothers or sisters or friends.

Your own attitude is a very important part of the diabetes treatment. Those who hate their illness will soon begin fighting against it.

Most children are only allowed candy on special occasions, such as Saturday candy. The child, on the other hand, would like to have candy every day if only it were allowed. This type of discussion goes on in every family. However, if a child has diabetes it is very convenient just to refer to the effect on the blood glucose level when saying "No" to candy. I often argue that it is very important to return to normal rules between children and parents as soon as possible and to refer to diabetes as little as possible when it comes to child upbringing and setting limits. In the long run it is important to be on as friendly terms as possible with your diabetes. If many rules and prohibitions are due to diabetes it will have the opposite effect in that one will soon start hating the disease.

One must actively explain to younger children that rules or limitations regarding for example food or candy are not caused by the child's diabetes. They would have applied anyway, even if the child was non-diabetic. The child will otherwise associate that all prohibitions are caused by diabetes.

Remember that there were both rules and limitations in the child's life even before diabetes entered the scene. With diabetes there are many restrictions, resulting in a lot of "not this and not that's". Try instead to encourage the things that the child can do, which still includes most parts of every day life. Give encouragement and praise, well-deserved praise, as a child with diabetes has to do many things on a daily bases that most adults would not do voluntarily. Praise the child when he/she takes

We must cooperate on equal terms when you come to see us at the diabetes clinic. If a visit feels like "a trip to the principal's office" it is completely wrong.

blood tests, and give them credit for taking injections many times daily (would you as a parent want to do that?). Encourage the child when he/she chooses to eat in a way appropriate for diabetes, show you appreciation when the child does not eat candy behind your back (how many parents have not taken out their own candy from the cupboard when the children have gone to bed?). With praise and encouragement everything runs much more smoothly.

Even as a parent you will naturally need encouragement, praise and "positive reinforcement" when coming to the diabetes clinic. If you feel like you are "going to the principal's office" it is completely wrong. You don't come to us to pass or fail a test. Instead we must be able to cooperate and in the best

"We learn by our own mistakes", as the saying goes. But does one always have to invent the wheel again? You can learn a lot by discussing with other parents or peers who have diabetes. They can give you tips about things in your daily life that we at the diabetes clinic are less familiar with, since most of us don't live with diabetes at home.

way possible help you with your diabetes or that of your child.

How far would a football team advance without encouragement and praise? The child or adult with diabetes needs a coach to pep them up, assess their abilities and potential, and adjust their diabetes training thereafter. Give the person with diabetes recognition of how difficult things are — most often it is much more difficult for the child to manage his/her life with diabetes well than it is for a mother or father to quit smoking... On the other hand, one should not make too big a deal of praise and encouragement at times when everything is going smoothly. Overprotecting a child with diabetes comes much too easily. Sympathy is fine but pity is of little help.

Yin and yang are conceptions in the Chinese philosophy for two principals that are in balance and harmony. Try to see your diabetes as a part of yourself which can melt into balance and harmony with the rest of your personality.

To make friends with your diabetes

Diabetes is an illness which is present 24 hours a day. One must, in some way, make friends with it, or at least avoid being enemies with it. If one hates it, it is difficult to continue life without being negatively affected by the illness. Three common ways of looking at your diabetes are as follows:

① **To completely ignore your diabetes, eat what you like and only take enough insulin to avoid feeling bad at that moment.**

Many teenagers will end up in this phase for a shorter or longer period of time, and some will never be able to leave it, which illustrates that they hate their illness. If you have this attitude when you enter adulthood there is a risk that you will never change it. Try instead to see the end of the teenage years as an opportunity during which you dare and can do something about your life-style and your diabetes.

② **To be absorbed and obsessed by diabetes and to live only to take care of the illness as well as possible.**

"Regulating illness" or "regulopathy" is the term used when you give up your ordinary life and your goals for the future. Initially both parents and caregivers at the clinic are under the impression that everything is going along very well. However, if the efforts to obtain a perfect glucose level prevent you from enjoying social activities, parties, being with friends or staying overnight with friends or at camps, things have gone too far. It is then time to turn the clock backwards, allowing yourself to start living life again.

If your diabetes is too strictly regulated it will often result in having many episodes of hypoglycemia (and often hypoglycemia unawareness, see page 42) which is not healthy for your body.

③ **Making diabetes a natural part of your life.**

This is easier said than done, as everyone knows who has tried. But it is possible to accept your illness without letting it take control of your life completely. If taking insulin becomes like brushing your teeth, something you do daily without really thinking about it but that you would absolutely not want to be without, then you have come a long way

How do you go about making diabetes a part of your daily life? Learn from your friends, observe others with diabetes and you will find someone who has an attitude worth learning from. Just as one in the old days had a period of apprenticeship when learning a profession one may perhaps need

One may feel like this many times. It is difficult to live with diabetes, often very difficult. But if you hate your diabetes it is difficult making friends with it... It is important not to let diabetes take control. Decide instead yourself what kind of life you would want to live and we will help you adjust your treatment according to your wishes.

to "be apprenticed" to someone who manages their diabetes in a good way.

Not an easy disease to have in the family

Different persons will feel differently about what is most difficult about diabetes. For a small child the injections are often the most difficult part. Older children and teenagers often find the need to be punctual, and explaining diabetes to others the most bothersome part. Adults often find the diet and weight control the most difficult part.

"Treatment of insulin dependent diabetes — art or science?" was the title of a lecture by the British pediatrician Robert Tattersall from Nottingham. He described what happens in a family when a child contracts diabetes:

— A good recipe of how to put the "thumb screws" on someone is to let a family member, preferably a child, contract a chronic disease.

— The disease should have an unclear cause but with a hereditary component so that one is forced to check the family tree to find a "scapegoat", Robert Tattersall continues. The treatment should be an important part of the disease, time consuming and preferably painful.

It may be a good idea to be apprenticed to someone who has had diabetes for many years and has had time to learn how to live with it in a good way.

— To further put pressure on the family the management of the disease should affect the life of the rest of the family. Self control and self management should be important components.

— The future outlook completes the picture. Terrible results of an unwise life style can be indicated perhaps by being placed in a waiting room together with amputated persons with diabetes. If there is an uncertainty among the health staff about the goal of treatment this will lead to contradictory information which of course will make the situation even worse, if possible. Don't forget that a family where someone has contracted diabetes will be exactly in this situation, was the massage from Professor Tattersall.

Diabetes is an invisible handicap, and can't be seen from the outside. It may sometimes feel better if nobody knows. However, both you and your friends will be better off in the long run if you let everyone know. If you for instance have hypoglycemia, everyone will understand what is going on and what to do. Many persons with diabetes have described how it was both embarrassing and troublesome when exposing their diabetes for the first time when they had hypoglycemia and needed help.

Being a relative or friend of someone with diabetes

People close to you only want what is best for you but it is not always perceived in this way. It is important to know what kind of help the person with diabetes wants and what he/she can manage on his/her own. At the same time a child or a teenager must understand how much their parents need to know about their every day life, for them to feel secure and confident. Over protection develops easily and the child or teenager can then react by wanting to manage too much by themselves or rebel by cheating with candy. Try to be as open as possible about each others' needs in the family. A "family council" where you put aside time to sit down together, can be an ideal forum to discuss how to come to agreement on different subjects within the family.

Friends need to know how they can help, otherwise they may turn into "candy policemen" who, with the best of intensions, will tell that this or that is not healthy to eat. It becomes a balance between saying: "I don't care about your diabetes, it is your problem" and "Are you really going to eat that cookie?". It is a good idea to talk things over and decide upon "how much or how little" help and support you want from those close to you.

Family and friends must also have the necessary knowledge about diabetes to be able to help and understand. How to treat hypoglycemia is an obvious example and one should also be able to give an injection of glucagon. The more they know the more help you can receive from your friends. Try to explain what you are doing and why. Explain how insulin works, how exercise works, why you sometimes can eat sugar and sometimes not.

TIGER

Teaching something to someone is not the same as the other person learning it ...

My earliest memory of diabetes is when I was 8 years old. The girl living next door was my age and had diabetes. The only thing I knew about it was that she was not allowed to eat sugar. But I also observed sugar lumps in her pocket that she would eat from time to time. I had difficulties understanding this and I thought she was cheating since nobody explained to me why she did it.

Tell your friends?

Many do not want to expose their diabetes since it is not visible from the outside. At the same time it is evident that you have not accepted your diabetes if you do not want to tell your friends. It is important that your friends know why you might not feel well and what they can do about it. It is best to tell everybody as soon as possible after you have been diagnosed with diabetes. Then it is done with and things will not feel so strange anymore. It is much worse to walk around wondering to yourself if this or that person knows about your diabetes...

How do you change life style?

Many have asked themselves this question. It is not easy to persuade someone that they have to change their habits to feel better. Persuasion may not even be the optimal way of getting a person to do what is best for his/her health. And what is really best for one's health from the patient's own perspective?

Elisabeth Arborelius, Ph.D. in Psychology, has studied how to change people's life habits.[72]

You may drift away from your friends if they do not understand why you at times must do certain things. Try to make diabetes a natural part of your life by telling friends at school or work about it. It is important that they know what to do if you need help, like when you have a difficult hypoglycemic episode.

— It is all about concentrating the information on behavior instead of knowledge. It is not always true hat knowledge will affect attitudes which in turn will affect behavior. We assume that human beings are rational but they are not, she claims. Something that is disadvantageous for your health from an objective point of view does not necessarily need to be experienced as such by the patient.

— I once heard a nurse say: "I am not a fanatic, but I see no reasons why people should smoke!" Of course she was right if she disregarded the patient's point of view. If the objective is to change behavior, the patient must have the opportunity to explain the advantages and disadvantages he/she will experience by changing the habits.

— We have come to believe that the balance between an individual's experienced advantages and disadvantages is of great importance in whether or not that person will change his/her behavior. If the disadvantages seem to outweigh the advantages it will not help that there is a threat of poorer health, the patient will not change his/her living habits anyway.

Daddies, are they needed?

In a Swedish study different factors, characterizing families where the children had a good or bad diabetic adjustment (high/low HbA_{1c} and psychological adjustment to disease) were investigated.[340] In families with poorer adjustment the fathers were more impulsive and dependent. The children were also more impulsive. In families with good adjustment the fathers were more independent and could thereby better support the mother and the child in coping with the diabetes. Boys especially will find it easier to identify with their father and be inspired to take a greater responsibility for their disorder.

It is difficult to generalize from a single study. However, from a clinical point of view it is clear that we see that things work best in families where both mother and father are engaged with the child and his/her diabetes. It is always better to be two and to be able to discuss how different situations can be managed. If the father is not involved, but lets the mother take care of diabetes, we have seen that boys especially will have problems in their teens. It is important that fathers be with their child as much as possible at the time of diagnosis and that both parents be allowed to take an active part in the diabetes management from the very beginning.

Diabetes in different developmental ages

The psychological effect of diabetes in the family is different at different ages and depends very much on the child's development and basic needs for that age. Naturally one will often feel unsure of how to handle specific situations as a parent. Sometimes one may need expert help to continue and a child psychologist can be very helpful. We usually let all children and adolescents see our psychologist at least once during the initial period of diabetes. It is always easier to reestablish contact if needed, when have met face to face.

Marianne Helgesson who is a psychologist at the Department of Pediatrics in Linköping, Sweden, lectures on psychology and diabetes in individuals at different ages. [256]

— It is not always easy to become three persons in a marriage. The first crack between spouses often appears when the first child is born. Discussions and disputes begin to focus on how to dispose one's time, something that earlier had been less of a issue.

— It will become a question of balance as to how much time and care one should devote to the child, to one's partner and to oneself. The parents must come to an agreement on how work at home should be divided, and of whether one of them or both will be able to pursue a career.

— Child raising is for the most part a repetition of how you were brought up yourself, since this is the only model you are familiar with. But usually there are two parents, both with their own upbringing behind them. Conflicts are inevitable and the result will be a combination of both parent's previous experiences.

— However, if the child has a chronic illness there is usually a lack of role models and one may feel insecure as a parent. The balance between dependency and responsibility is difficult to establish and the question arises as to how much to help the child without being overprotective.

Infants
(0 - 1½ years)

This period is characterized by a so called symbiosis, at first between mother and child and later on also between father and child. During this time it is very important that the parent subordinates his/her own needs in favor of the child's as it does not have any ability to give priority to the parent's needs. When the child is able to move around on its own, after one year of age, it will begin to explore the world.

Risks with diabetes

Diabetes at this age will inevitably bring stress into the family. If one has difficulties handling this without feeling tense and uncertain towards the child, it will be difficult to convey security and confidence to the child. Security and confidence will very much be a question of food and diabetes. The child does not understand why he/she must eat when not being hungry and vice versa and there is a considerable risk of feeding problems at this age.

The child needs to feel that both parents display trust and confidence in various situations, and for obvious reasons this may be difficult if the child has diabetes. Over-protection may lead to the child anxiously staying by his/her parents' side instead of orientating outwards towards the world beyond. The child cannot understand injections and blood-testing, which will give rise to a lot of pain, anger and anxiety. One cannot explain why it is necessary to hurt the child. Most often it is better to get it out of the way as quickly as possible, and then comfort the child.

Toddlers
(1½ - 3 years)

During this time the child will explore the world more actively. Around the age of 2 the child will often take a step "backwards", becoming more attached to the mother again. This is quite normal and is not due to inappropriate parental attitudes towards the child.

The "obstinate age" (the age of practising one's own free will) begins between 2 to 3 years of age. The child will first test the parents' and then his/her own ability to set limits. All children will show quite a lot of anger and frustration during this time. The child must experience his/her own limitations and this is not always pleasurable. It is important that parents engage in such "battles of will" as it is through these that the child will learn how to stand up for something, to compromise and to give in.

Risks with diabetes

It is difficult to know whether or not anger is caused by a low blood glucose level. Should one give the child something to eat every time he/she is angry? It may be difficult to take a blood test every time. A child with diabetes will have more limitations than other children due to injections, meal times and testing. There is always a tendency with a chronic illness that one will want to compensate for the restrictions caused by the illness by letting the child decide about everything else. In doing this one shows pity for the child and becomes less effective in setting limits in other areas. The child will become insecure and disorderly, and will continuously test the limits in order to provoke a parental reaction. However, if the parents do not have enough strength to deal with such aggressiveness the child may shut him/herself in and become passive and insecure, with a low feeling of self confidence. As a parent one will need understanding since things may be difficult, but also encouragement that children with diabetes, as much as anyone else, need a normal upbringing.

A fear of strange environments (such as the hospital) is often greater than the fear of injections. Some children at this age will become hysterical just by being held by force. Try to give injections and take blood tests in as secure an environment as possible.

Pre-school children
(3 - 6 years)

The child at this age begins to understand more about the outside world and will be conscious of the fact that one's body can cause both desire and pain. The child will role play and have a very rich imaginative life.

During this period the differentiation of sex roles takes place. The child wants to imitate the parent of the same sex and falls in love, wanting to marry the parent of the opposite sex. A child of 4 - 5 years of age will often be "the king of existence", knowing and being able to do everything, especially knowing what he/she wants and does not want. The child discovers a feeling of power when he/she discovers how to control others. A six year old is usually more obliging to the parent's demands and views.

The child will begin to develop a conscience, thinking about crime and punishment in a "primitive way" in terms of "an eye for an eye and a tooth for

It is difficult enough to find time for everything as an ordinary parent of small children. A parent of a child with diabetes would need more than 2 arms to manage blood glucose testing, injections, meal planning and all the other adjustments of daily life that come along with a diabetic child.

Plant the tree of knowledge early within children. Children who have grown up with diabetes find it easier to manage during puberty compared to those contracting diabetes in prepubertal or pubertal years. When children grow up they will be trained by their parents to take responsibility for themselves. The goal should be that they will be able to take responsibility for their diabetes before entering puberty.

Stealing candy from the cupboard when mon or dad are not watching is not uncommon for a pre-school child. One must avoid overdramatizing this — even children who do not have diabetes will do it. I think it is important that the result not be a total ban on candy. It is often more practical to give some extra candy once in a while, perhaps with the afternoon snack for 1 - 2 weeks, and give some extra insulin as well (see page 156). Explain that you are making an exception and that we expect the child to be able to chose wisely on candy as he/she grows older. The child will usually get over the candy craving after a while.

a tooth". He/she will be aware of the borders of the body. Bandages have a magic ability to restore and heal. See also "Pricking a hole in children" on page 82.

Risks with diabetes

The child may believe that he/she has contracted diabetes as a punishment for doing something wrong or that a blood glucose test is a punishment. This must be brought up and into the open with the child even if he/she does not ask about it. It is even common for adults to ask themselves "What have I done to deserve this?" when something unpleasant or unfortunate occurs. One tries to find a logical connection between things that have happened.

The child can be limited in exploring the surroundings due to the parent's fear of hypoglycemia. It may be difficult to give insulin and take tests if the child refuses to cooperate. He/she will have definite views on what to eat and what not to eat. It may be very difficult to know in advance how much of a meal the child will eat. Try letting the child decide upon some other details of daily life instead.

Don't tell the child too long in advance about injections, testing or other unpleasant things. The fantasy can easily enlarge this to unrealistic proportions.

There is even a risk that the child might think that their diabetes may be connected with their gender. If the child does not understand why one gets diabetes a girl may experience that it would be better to be a boy since her brother does not have diabetes (or vice versa).

"Consider what the restrictions may cost in terms of development before you say no ..."

Marianne Helgesson

Junior level children

Starting school may be an extra stress even for children without diabetes. Many children find it difficult to adjust in the beginning. School children are occupied with understanding and exploring the world. They like to take things apart and understand how everything works. They will also be interested in understanding how their diabetes works. Friends become increasingly important and it is important to do similar things. The experience of time is developing and the child likes to keep track of how long something takes, such as running an errand.

Risks with diabetes

The fear of the unknown is still there even if the child seems interested in things. It is important to adapt the information to the age of the child. "Normalize", i.e. tell the child that it is quite normal and fully understandable ("Other children would feel the same way") to feel the way he/she does in different situations, such as taking an injection or a blood test. Keeping track of time will often help, for instance when administering an injection.

Food at school does not taste the same as at home, and sometimes the child will not eat it at all. It may be difficult to find someone at school who is able and willing to help the child take insulin at lunch. At first you may feel very insecure — what happens if my child has hypoglycemia at school? Try to make it possible for one parent to be available by telephone and come to school if needed, especially in the beginning. It is important that the staff at school know how to take care of hypoglycemia. They will often take the child's diabetes more seriously after seeing overt symptoms of hypoglycemia.

Intermediate level children

This part of life is referred to as the latency phase in psychological terms. Children are usually very receptive for all types of education, including diabetes. They want to expand their views but at the same time have learned to stay within the limits their parents have set. During this time a social role is developed: "Can I partake?", "Will I be accepted? One will also compete with peers as to "who it the greatest, best and most beautiful". Peers become more and more important. Children will benefit by meeting others with diabetes in the same age group with whom they can identify, for instance at a diabetes camp. Encouragement is important at this age as children need confirmation that they have done things correctly.

Risks with diabetes

All children will ponder about their role in life during this period. At the age of 9 or 10 a child with a chronic disease will usually start to reflect upon and react to their illness in a way that he/she has not experienced earlier. "Why did this happen to me?" is a common question. There will often be a time when the child experiences everything that has to do with diabetes as difficult and strenuous. For the first time the child understands that having diabetes

means having it for the rest of one's life. It takes some time before the child accepts this.

During this time it is important to talk frequently to the child about what diabetes entails and try to help the child to accept the disease. Show that you as a parent also feel concerned and confirm that life with diabetes is both difficult and unfair. The child usually passes through this phase after a while but will, on occasion, need help from a psychologist or counsellor to continue.

As the child is very receptive to learning without defying his/her parents' authority it is important to make diabetes management a natural part of the child's life during the years prior to puberty. If the child is secure in managing his/her diabetes already before puberty there will be less risk of diabetes complicating the liberation process.

Puberty

During this period the teenager should begin the development of an adult identity, having independent and on equal standing with other adults. The increasing independency is fragile which is why teenagers strongly defend their integrity.

Being a good parent for a toddler is not the same as being a good parent for a teenager. The important, but difficult issue is to adjust the demands to the child's age in order to promote maturity. Children of all ages need lots of love, but it must be adapted to the age of the child. "Toddler love" to a teenager is experienced as overprotection and prevents liberation.

Insulin-dependent diabetes in children, adolescents and adults © R. Hanas 1998

Friends are very important in the teenage years. When you start coming to the clinic without your parents it is a good idea to bring a buddy or girl/boyfriend instead.

In a way earlier stages of development are repeated. A teenager will often vacillate between being a child and being grown up. It is very important to realize that one has the chance to "redo" what has been missed during earlier phases of development. Many parents look upon the teenage period with horror. If you instead look upon puberty as a "dress rehearsal" of the childhood and adolescent years prior to entering adulthood one may see things a bit more positively.

Friends are very important as it is only natural to want to be able to do the same things as everyone else. A teenager prefers to go out in the evening to have a hamburger or pizza with his/her friends, instead of staying at home to eat the usual evening meal. It is important that teens are given both the freedom and responsibility to experiment with insulin doses on such occasions. The teenager is very interested in his/her own body, especially during early adolescence, and is well aware that it is his/her own property. They want to be well informed about how diabetes affects their body. At the same time they are often shy about exposing their body and, in this sense, are not at all as open-minded as one might expect.

We encourage older teenagers to come to some of the visits without their mother or father. An alternative is to let the parent enter the room at the end of the consultation and then only raise issues that the teenager has consented to. It is important that the teenager realize that our professional secrecy also applies to parents. If a teenager wants to raise personal issues he/she should be able to do so in confidence.

Teenagers often bring a buddy or a boyfriend/girlfriend to the visits. They appreciate someone's support but feel too old to bring their mother or father.

It may be a difficult for a parent to know just how much one should and may interact in the teenager's diabetes. It will be difficult to maintain adequate knowledge as you take less and less part of the daily diabetes activities including clinical visits.

The teenager prefers to manage without his/her parents input but at the same time will want them to be informed. One 18 year old girl said: "Of course I want them to know how to manage my diabetes — who else can jump in and help me if I fail?"

"Teenagers are impossible to raise, but it doesn't matter as long as parents do not stop trying"
Ackerman

Risks with diabetes

The teenage years are a difficult period in which to contract diabetes. The teenager is not mature enough to take responsibility for his/her diabetes but finds it hard to let his/her parents do it. If the child is younger at the onset of diabetes it is easier for the parents to take full control and then to gradually let go as the child matures. Children who contract diabetes early in life will therefore often have better diabetes control during the years of puberty than those contracting it in the early teens.

The liberation process will be more difficult for a teenager with diabetes. They feel that they will never quite become an adult and will never get to decide completely over their own body. Just when it is time to cut the umbilical cord it is securely retied again. And besides, their body will be inspected at regular clinical visits.

Of course a teenager with diabetes is concerned about the future. One will ponder about choice of profession, how to find a partner, having children, complications of diabetes and so on. It is quite natural to become depressed about these things if one looks upon the future negatively. It is not uncommon to have existential thoughts in general, but one should be aware of the fact that suicidal thoughts may be present as well.

The teenager wants to take injections in an adult way, that is to say without emotion. He/she hates it if this is not manageable and he/she is forced to be "little" again (regress to an earlier age), with crying or inability to take the injection alone. It is just as important to "normalize" for teens as it is for younger children, that is to reassure them that many adults also find injections difficult. By accepting the teenager's behavior their self confidence will be affected in a positive direction.

Remember that being a good parent to a teenager is not the same as being a good parent to a younger child. Inappropriate adjustment by the teen to diabetes has been found to correlate with inappropriate adjustment of the parents to the child's increasing need for independence during the years prior to puberty.

Many teenagers manifest so called risk behavior in that they like to do things that are slightly (or very) risky to test their ability. This is often more pronounced in boys than in girls. If this is the case try connecting this behavior with the diabetes treatment and encourage experimenting with insulin dosages for example. There may very well be an element of risk included (such as how to dose insulin when staying up all night) but it is equally important that there be a "protective network" in the form of friends or adults whom the teenager can trust if something goes wrong.

A serious type of risk behavior is forgetting or skipping insulin injections. In an American interview study 25 % of the teenagers (11 - 19 years of age) stated that they had missed one or more insulin injections during the last 10 days, mainly due to forgetfulness.[418] Twenty-nine percent missed taking blood glucose tests which had been previously agreed upon and 29 % had entered a lower blood glucose reading in the logbook than was actually registered. The adolescents who had missed insulin injections had a higher HbA_{1c} value. When missing insulin doses blood glucose levels will start swinging and the diabetes will become difficult to regulate.

If a teenager has control over his/her diabetes other subjects can be brought up in the liberation process.

Let the teenager practise as much as possible on his/her own. However, it is equally important to discuss afterwards how things went and why.

Anders Carlberg, a youth leader in Stockholm was interviewed at a conference.[257] "How do you become an adult in today's society?"

— Liberation is necessary but terribly difficult, according to Anders Carlberg. One should not expect things to be learned without pain because they never are and they aren't supposed to either. Kids have to break out, it is the only way. Parents will never cut the umbilical chord voluntarily, adolescents have to chop it off!

— In the interplay between children and parents, negotiation and agreement are available methods. If the child/teenager says that he/she wants to assume the responsibility for something let them give it a try. Parents naturally always want to know where their children are. If the child/teenager has diabetes this is even more important. It is therefore a good idea to come to agreement about having contact at certain times.

A tip from one parent is to make sure that the child always has telephone money and a bus card. Today a pager or cellular telephone may be a practical and popular way of keeping in touch with a diabetic child or teenager.

Healthy siblings

Being a healthy brother or sister to a child with a chronic disease can be difficult at times. Siblings often see many of the "advantages" that the ill child has, not to mention all the increased attention from the parents. At the same time it is difficult for a

---

What to do about a teenager?

① Don't be too understanding during early puberty. Setting limits is another way of showing that you care.

② One may have to accept that certain things take precedence over diabetes for a year or two.

③ Try to argue about things other than diabetes when "fighting" in the family.

Insulin-dependent diabetes in children, adolescents and adults   © R. Hanas 1998

As a teenager you want to spend time with your friends. It is important that your diabetes not stop you from doing this. Practise taking responsibility on how to adjust your insulin doses and meal times so that they will fit with the type of life you want to live.

brother or sister to understand the situation of the child with diabetes completely. They will need help to answer some questions even if they don't bring them up by themselves:

— Is it my fault that my brother/sister has contracted diabetes?

— Is it contagious? Will I get it as well?

— Who will take care of me when my parents are busy with my brother's/sister's diabetes?

It is important to listen to the healthy sibling and accept that he/she can sometimes feel that "It is difficult to be the one not ill". As a parent it is easy to say: "You should be grateful that you are healthy" or "Would you want to take his/her place...". Often it will be enough just to confirm the non-diabetic child's feeling by saying: "I understand that it can be difficult at times".

Take it seriously when a sibling complains about a headache for instance or abdominal pains even if you as a parent have the impression that it is not so serious. The brother or sister may benefit from seeing a doctor of his/her own.

You can give the healthy sibling some extra attention. For example, the two of you could do something together on your own. It will not matter much what you do. Being alone with a parent is always something special. Take the opportunity to eat something tasty together and keep it "a secret" from the other family members. Do something else secretly together with the child with diabetes, like visiting a special playground, or, if the child is older, a theatre or exhibition. The purpose of keep-

ing it "a secret" is to avoid envy between the siblings (regardless of whether they have diabetes or not).

It is difficult for a sibling to always hear that he/she cannot eat this or that because their brother/sister has diabetes and must not be tempted. One method, practiced in most families, is to allow it to be eaten when the child with diabetes is not at home. As the child with diabetes gets older he/she must become accustomed to not having the same conditions as everyone else. Children with other diseases or problems (such as celiac disease, allergy, overweight) must learn that they cannot eat like their friends. Try to find something else that is desirable for the child with diabetes tin order to o avoid unfair treatment within the family. The goal is that as the child gets older he/she be able to withstand temptation on their own, for instance at school.

When the healthy brother or sister has their birthday party one should make an exception and let him/her completely decide what the treats should be. The child with diabetes can take some extra insulin that day in order to be able to join the party.

As brothers and sisters grow older a strong feeling of friendship usually develops. With older teenagers with diabetes we often see how such a relationship can help them to take the step towards adulthood, assuming responsibility for their diabetes, for example in situations where parents are caught up in a divorce conflict or are too overprotective, leading to difficulties in letting a maturing teenager take over responsibility and control.

Divorced families

More and more children do not live together with both parents. In larger cities as many as 1/4 of all children and teenagers live with only one biologic parent. Divorced parents often have difficulties communicating and the children will end up delivering messages between them.

When a child contracts a chronic illness great demands are put on the parents to both cooperate and trust each other. If the parents are divorced the best approach is for both to obtain the same information from the very onset of diabetes. If they have new partners they too will need information. There may be a tense situation between the parents, but for the child it is always best if the adults in both families are on speaking terms and cooperate with regards to the child's diabetes as much as possible.

Brittle diabetes

Brittle diabetes can be caused by many different factors. It is defined as a diabetes that is so difficult to control "that life is constantly being disrupted by episodes of high or low blood glucose levels, whatever their case".[388] In spite of great efforts from everyone the swinging blood glucose levels continue. The reasons may be purely organic (such as insulin antibodies, decreased insulin sensitivity, puberty, delayed emptying of the stomach, missed insulin doses, incorrect injection technique) but also psychological where chronic stress (as in a divorce situation) may create a high or swinging blood glucose level.

With brittle diabetes one often has very large insulin doses, even if the sensitivity for intravenously administered insulin is normal.[217] Ketones may be produced even when the levels of counter regulatory hormones are normal, and these patients will often have ketoacidosis.[217]

Sometimes a person with diabetes deliberately manipulates the insulin doses for various reasons, creating widely varying blood glucose levels. One ends up in a vicious cycle which is difficult both to understand and break. Afterwards, when looking back at this behavior, people often find it hard to believe that they really did this. If you think about it as a temporary coping response when the world is difficult to live in, it is not all that strange. Most adults have done things in their younger years that they are not all that proud of.

What is worrying is if the manipulative behavior continues, leading to deteriorated glucose control with many episodes of hypoglycemia and/or ketoacidosis. If you recognize yourself in this you definitely need help to straighten things out. The most important starting point is "to put the cards on the table" by beginning to enter correct readings in your logbook, taking insulin doses regularly, and noting in your logbook when you miss one. Otherwise we have no way of knowing what is going on in your body and, and because of this, may give you quite incorrect advice. For example, if you have missed doses frequently, leading to many high readings, I would in general advise you to increase the dose. However, if you take this higher dose you may end up with a severe hypoglycemia.

It may not be necessary at this point to actually state that you have been manipulating — we all find it difficult "to lose face" and the most important thing is to get a new start. Just one little wish:

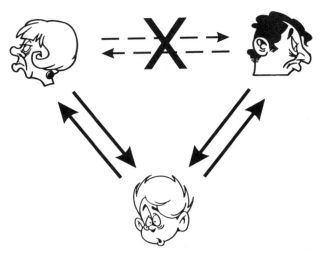

If the parents cannot agree, such as after a divorce, there is a risk that the child will act as a "messenger" between them. "Tell daddy that..." or "Ask mummy about...". This is a role that will put the child in an awkward situation, causing distress and ultimately a high HbA$_{1c}$ value.

If you sometimes (perhaps many years later) do tell your doctor or nurse what really happened we will have a better chance of finding clues and helping someone else in your situation to get out of the vicious cycle.

Occasionally sexual abuse from an adult in the child's or teenager's close surroundings, sometimes even by their father, can be the reason for a "brittle diabetes".[300] Remember that if something like this happens it is never the child's or teenager's fault. Sexual abuse is always the fault of the adult and it is illegal. Something like this is very difficult to think about and even more difficult to reveal to someone. However, if you recognize yourself when reading this you must confide in someone that you trust. This is the only way to make it stop, the only way to start over again and to have the opportunity to once again feel pure and intact.

All of us at the diabetes clinic are sworn to professional secrecy which means that everything you tell us stays between us. We are under professional and legal obligation to guard every secret disclosed. Another alternative may be to speak to a priest or counsellor whom you trust.

Needle-phobia

Phobia for injections and blood tests will manifest differently at different ages. Injection aids (such as indwelling catheters, see page 100), can help many children take injections, though blood tests today are impossible to avoid. If you "get stuck" in these matters it is important to see a psychologist as quickly as possible to prevent the needle-phobia from becoming a permanent problem for your child (or teenager/adult) and family. See also page 84 and 91.

Topical anesthetic cream (EMLA®) will effectively relieve pain and can be used for venous blood tests. It can be used for insulin injections on isolated occasions but in practise it is impossible to use for every insulin injection. The creme does not work on the finger tips as the skin is too thick there.

When questioning children about how they feel about injections they often wonder why adults look so happy when they prick children. "Do they enjoy pricking children?" It is easy to misinterpret an adult's smile, which is meant to comfort the child, as something else.

Needle-phobia — general advice:
(adopted from Marianne Helgesson)

① Parents' attitudes to pricking are very important. You must feel that the prick is necessary yourself, otherwise you can never convey this to the child. If you, as a parent, have a needle-phobia of your own, it will be difficult to prick your child.

② The child must know exactly what is going to happen and why. Many children (even older ones) may believe that the injection or blood test is a punishment for something done wrong. You must clearly state that the pricking is necessary, and not because anyone has behaved badly. Remember that the person pricking is not "being mean". He/she is only doing what has to be done.

③ Be honest about the pain. A prick can be painful, no matter how much we would like it not to be.

④ Indicate the acceptable limits of protest, such as: "You can cry if you feel like it, but you must not pull your hand away."

⑤ Offer realistic choices. They lessen the child's feeling of being a victim. But do not offer to wait with the injection as you cannot do that. The child will only remember that he/she was tricked and things will be even more difficult the next time around.

⑥ Suggest diverting activities, such as choosing a bandage.

⑦ The phase of persuasion should be short. When dealing with smaller children it is best to hold them firmly, do the pricking, and then comfort. If the pricking takes time the child's suffering will be prolonged. Use a firm grip if you must hold the child, so that the pricking is fast.

⑧ Don't smile to encourage. The child may believe that you are laughing.

⑨ **Afterwards**: Comfort, praise, and talk to the child. To draw or play what has been difficult often helps. Stay with the child when playing in order to be able to correct misunderstandings and help the child get over it.

Well-known persons with diabetes

People with diabetes can be found in most professions. You probably know prominent people with diabetes in you home town or country. Below are some examples of how successful people cope with their diabetes:

Per Zetterberg

Pär Zetterberg from Sweden is a professional soccer player in Belgium. He contracted diabetes at the age of 19 and at the time believed that his career was over. Today his opinion is that his general condition is better than before having diabetes. He likes to talk about his diabetes and is both an idol and role model for many adolescents. His advise to adolescents with diabetes interested in sports is: "Accept the disease! It will not stop you and you can do the same things as everyone else, including sports at top level." [135]

Bret Michaels

Bret Michaels from the USA is a singer in the rock group Poison. He has had diabetes from the age of 6.[281] Today he says: "I accept having diabetes. Besides I try to live my life as normally as possible. It is like everything else you accept — you must know the rules. Of course you break them at times, but you must know them before you can break them". He can practise for hours to reach musical perfection but tries almost as hard to manage his diabetes. He takes blood glucose tests 6 - 10 times per day, "I must always know my actual blood glucose level as my working schedule is so irregular".

His appearance shocks many adults. This is what he wants to say to an adolescent who has just had the message of acquiring diabetes:

— It is difficult. You have already lived part of your life and suddenly you will be stricken by this disease. OK, sit down, cry, hit the sand bag, hit the door, crush a window or make a hole in the wall - whatever is needed to make that day pass. Then

realize that you have diabetes and start taking care of yourself.

For young people he recommends a life without anxiety:

— Some young people with diabetes whom I meet are so scared. I want to tell them that there is nothing wrong with being scared, but you can't live a life of fear. One just can't say "Help - I have diabetes, I can't do anything". I want children to be taught to be prepared rather than scared.

— It is like this: go out and take hold of life and do your best. Just take care of yourself and always be prepared, wherever you go, whatever you do, partying or otherwise. Check that your friends know that you have diabetes, tell them what symptoms they need to learn to recognize and exactly what to do if you don't look well or act abnormal. Remember that you are worth something to yourself and your friends. If they are the type of people you can't tell that you have diabetes, or if they are such that will not help you, then they are not your friends!

— I always carry dextrose. No matter where I am I check that someone knows how to help me if I have a hypoglycemic reaction.

— Otherwise my opinion is that young persons with diabetes should continue to do what all adolescents do - ride skateboard or motorbike, play basketball or whatever they like.

Pontus Johansson

Pontus Johansson from Sweden has won 5 national gold medals in baseball. He acquired diabetes after having won his first gold. In his opinion diabetes has never been an impediment to vigorous training as long as he takes care of himself and eats regularly.[423]

Jan Lindblad

Jan Lindblad from Sweden was a very famous nature photographer who travelled around the world and often lived in very primitive and strenuous circumstances during his journeys.

Gary Mabbut

Gary Mabbut is a professional soccer player and has played many international matches for England. He contracted diabetes when he was 17 1/2 years old.[71] The doctor gave his parents the following advise: "Let the boy try a suitable regimen, let him continue his previous life and we will see what happens". And things went quite well! Gary takes 4 injections per day.

— A match day starts with a blood glucose test, insulin injection and then breakfast. I have now learned in detail what signals the tests give and from that I find out how much I can eat for lunch. Before warming up I take another test to find out how much sports drink I need before first half. The same procedure takes place in the break before second half. If the match goes into over-time a few tablets of dextrose is enough to take me through it.

If I follow this schedule I feel certain that nothing will happen.

When giving advise to young people with diabetes Gary is candid:

— Live as usual but keep an eye on insulin and meal times. Don't let the disease control you. Get control of it instead with the help of regular hours. No matter if it is about sports, studying or working you have the same great chances as others without diabetes. You make your own possibilities!

Lotta Mossberg

Lotta Mossberg is a TV-reporter who contracted diabetes while expecting her second child. She tells that she now is more humble towards life.[259] "Earlier I thought I was Superwoman" she says. When other journalists skip their meals during times of stress she will take her insulin and take time to eat.

— There are advantages and disadvantages to having to calm down for a while, says Lotta. Although I feel a little different it undoubtedly gives me a certain perspective on the situation in the outside world.

Lotta uses a multiple injection regimen with 3 - 4 doses of short-acting insulin and one bedtime dose. She compares her diabetes to having had a third child who demands constant attention. When she read that the risk of complications is higher for smokers she put her cigarettes aside. She checks her blood glucose often when she works and especially before broadcasting. It is important to be alert and not to feel sluggish due to high blood glucose levels or hypoglycemia while broadcasting.

The somewhat improvised living situation in her family has now changed. Lotta shops from a list every week. Nowadays she cooks all the food herself since it is easiest: "You need discipline for this but I am good at that."

— Comments from people are sometimes delivered with too much pity, and sometimes without enough understanding. I have learned to ignore them and just take care of my diabetes. At the same time I think: If they only KNEW how tough it is never to be able to release command of the disease!

— At the same time you don't want too much pity. After all, you can feel quite well although you have diabetes.

At last

Having diabetes in the family will naturally bring about many difficult situations. The child/teenager will balance between dependence and independence. The problem for a parent is to give enough support without being overprotective.

Having a member with a chronic disease puts extra demands on the family with a risk of marital conflicts. It is difficult to find enough time, time for the child and his/her diabetes, time for oneself and time to have an adult relationship with your spouse, not only parenting. Try to remember that it is frequently difficult to be a parent (or child/teenager) in a family in general as well. Always try to consider how you would have handled a certain situation if the child/teenager (or you/your spouse) had not had diabetes.

Land ahead! As an adult one will often continue with the same attitude towards diabetes as one had when leaving the teens. But don't forget that "today is the first day of the rest of your life". It is never too late to decide to do something radically about your diabetes if you have high HbA_{1c} values. Every percent's decrease in HbA_{1c} will result in a substantially lower risk of complications in the future!

Acknowledgments

I am greatly indebted to Pia for loving support and for sharing my interests as a diabetes nurse, to the children and teenagers with diabetes and their parents who have contributed with experiences, tips, knowledge and drawings, to my diabetes nurses Elsie Johansson, Kristin Lundqvist, Ann-Sofie Karttunen and Catarina Andreasson for continued confidence and enthusiasm, to my colleagues, collaborators and friends in Sweden and within ISPAD (International Society of Pediatric and Adolescent Diabetes) for joining me in increased efforts of intensive diabetes treatment and to Mats Bergryd for believing in the idea of writing a comprehensive diabetes manual for patients and parents. Without you there would have been no book.

I deeply appreciate the comments from Professor Johnny Ludvigsson, Dr. Jan Åman and Dr. Otto Westphal in writing the first Swedish edition. My sincere thanks to Maggie Andersson for quick and efficient typing of the English edition, to Graham Walker for initial support, to Dr. Jody Miller for proof-reading, to Linda Fredrickson, RN, for valuable comments and to Dr. Kenneth Strauss for enthusiastic and continued support in proof-reading and finalizing the book.

Ostrich strategy, i.e. not caring about diabetes and not taking any responsibility, is among the most dangerous things a person with diabetes can do. We can contribute with knowledge, tips and advise — but living with your diabetes must be done on your own...

"If you become a teacher, by your pupils you will be taught."

Hammerstein, Rogers 1951 [168]

I wish to express my gratitude to the following authors and medical journals (© owners) who kindly gave me permission to print their illustrations (the full credit line is in the reference list on page 253):

Acta Paediatrica Scandinavia
(Scandinavian University Press):
Cedermark et al 1990 (p. 159)
Dahlqvist et al. 1982 (p. 29)

Archives of Diseases in Childhood
(BMJ Publishing Group):
Sackey et al. 1994 (p. 58)

Clinical Science (The Biochemical Society and Medical Research Society):
Welch et al. 1987 (p. 146)

Diabetes/ Metabolism Reviews
(John Wiley & Sons Ltd.):
Olsson et al. 1988 (pp. 22, 104)

Diabetologia (Springer-Verlag GmbH & Co. KG):
Malherbe et al. 1969 (p. 22)
Maran et al. 1995 (p. 42)

Diabetes (American Diabetes Association):
Santiago 1993 (page 87)
The DCCT Study Group 1995 (p. 217)

Diabetes Care (American Diabetes Association):
Bantle et al. 1993 (p. 93)
Frid et al. 1988 (p. 62)
Hildebrandt et al 1986 (p. 106)
Linde 1986 (p. 62)
McCrimmon et al 1995 (p. 39)
Schiffrin et al. 1982 (p. 85)

Diabetic Medicine (John Wiley & Sons Ltd):
Hanssen et al. 1992 (p. 215)

Endocrine Reviews
(The Endocrine Society):
Yki-Järvinen 1992 (p. 71)

European Journal of Pediatrics
(Springer-Verlag GmbH & Co. KG):
Cedermark et al . 1993 (p. 159)

JAMA (American Medical Association):
Brodows et al. 1984 (p.51)

New England Journal of Medicine
(Massachusetts Medical Society):
Bojestig et al. 1994 (p. 212)

Nordic Medicine (Nordisk Medicin):
Knip 1992 (p. 221

Scandinavian Journal of Nutrition
(The Swedish Nutrition Foundation):
Andersson et al. 1986 (p. 143)

I am also thankful to the following authors and medical journals (© owners) for letting me adapt their tables for use in the book:

APEG handbook on childhood and adolescent diabetes (Australian Pediatric Endocrine Group):
Silink M. 1996 (p.178)

Diabetes Reviews International (Macmillan):
Kassianos G. 1992 (p. 204)

Diabetes Care (American Diabetes Association):
Kullberg 1996 (p. 87)
Skyler J. 1990 (p. 125)

The book: Diabetes.
SPRI and Swedish Medical Society 1989:
Berg K. (p. 194)
Sundkvist G. (p. 216)

The Insulin Pump Therapy Book (MiniMed):
Tanenberg RJ, Bode BW, Davidson PC, Sonnenberg GE (pp. 106, 107, 109, 113)

Special thanks to Diabetes, the official journal of the Swedish Diabetes Association, for letting me print quotations from their journal.

Drawings are reproduced with the permission of the individual artist. Comic strips are reproduced with the permission of the respective vendor. The clip art is published with permission from the following vendors (© owners):
3 G Graphics Inc., BeeLine ArtProfile, Corel Corporation, Image Club Graphics Inc., One Mile Up Inc. and Totem Graphics Inc. LifeART Images Copyright © 1989-1997 by TechPool Studios Inc. USA.

When using multiple injections or an insulin pump you will have increased freedom — but only if you take the responsibility that goes with it. One should not confuse this with an "anything goes" mentality where everything is allowed. It is a question of volume as well — exceptions must be exceptions. If you make the exception every day it becomes a habit instead.

It is important to remember that it is not your blood glucose level today or tomorrow that counts in the long run, but your average blood glucose level over a long period of time to come, years and tens of years. As a parent (or teenager/adult with diabetes) you need to make some exceptions to learn and get used to the guidelines you should continue with in the future.

Camilla is today a teenager using an insulin pump. She is in the midst of puberty with an HbA_{1c} of 6 - 7 %. She has strong support from her parents when she chooses to make exceptions, but also clear limits on how much and how many exceptions she can allow herself. In my opinion this is a very good start of a long life together with diabetes. Thank you Camilla, for all the observations and good points about living with diabetes that you have given me throughout the years.

Glossary

<   Less than
>   More than
≥   Equal to or more than
≤   Equal to or less than

28   The references where the text is taken from are shown as small, superscript numbers. See page 253.

Units

Weight
1 kg (kilogram   =   2.2 pounds
1 gram   =   15.4 grains=0.035 ounces

Length
1 cm (centimeter)= 0.4 inches
1 inch   =   2.54 cm

Capacity
1 liter   =   1.76 pints = 0.22 UK gallons
1 dl (deciliter) =   1/10 liter

Temperature
° F = (9/5 x °C) + 32

Time
14   =   2 PM
02   =   2 AM

A

ACE-inhibitors
Drugs that inhibit an *enzyme* (angiotensin converting enzyme) in the kidneys that increases the blood pressure.

Acesulfam K
Sweetener that does not provide any energy.

Acetone
Is produced when there is an excess of *ketones* in the blood. Acetone odor on the breath is present when the level of ketones is raised.

Acidosis
Shifting of the pH in the blood towards being acidic.

Adrenaline
Stress hormone from the *adrenal glands* that increases the blood glucose level.

Adrenal glands
Small organs placed above the kidneys that produce many hormones.

Adrenergic symptoms
Bodily symptoms of hypoglycemia caused mainly by adrenaline.

Albuminuria
A larger amount of albumin in the urine than the traces of albumin found with *microalbuminuria*. A sign of permanent kidney damage.

Aldose reductace inhibitors
Drugs that can affect nerve damage caused by diabetes.

Alpha cells
Cells in the *Islets of Langerhans* of the pancreas that produce the hormone *glucagon*.

Amino acid
Protein building blocks

Amnesia
Loss of memory

Amylase
An enzyme that is produced in the saliva and the pancreas. Amylase breaks down the starch in the food.

Antibiotics
Drugs that kill bacteria. Penicillin is one type of antibiotic.

Antibody
Produced by the *immune defence* to destroy virus and bacteria.

Anorexia
Self-starving disease.

Arteriosclerosis
Hardening, narrowing and eventually blocking of the blood vessels.

Aspartam
Sweetener that does not provide any energy.

Autoimmune
Sometimes things go wrong with the *immune defence* and the cells of your own body are attacked.

Autonomic nervous system
The "independent" part of the nervous system that is operated without one having give it a thought, like breathing and the movements of the intestines.

B

Basal insulin
Insulin that covers the body's need for a low level of insulin between meals and during the night. This insulin is given as *intermediate-* or *long-acting insulin* or in a pump.

Basal rate
With an *insulin pump* a low dose of basal insulin is infused every hour of the day and night.

Beta cells
Cells in the *Islets of Langerhans* of the pancreas that produce the hormone *insulin.*

Blood glucose
The level of *glucose* in the blood. Is measured in mmol/L (SI-units) or mg/dL (mg%). (For conversion table see page 77.)

Brittle diabetes
Diabetes with very unstable blood glucose (rapid swings up and down) that prevents the person from living a normal life.

Bulimia
Illness with binge eating, i.e sometimes eating huge amounts of food followed by purge (induced) vomiting or use of laxatives.

C

Capillary blood
The capillaries are the very fine blood vessels between arteries and veins where the blood delivers oxygen to the tissues. Blood tests from fingers contain capillary blood.

Carbohydrate
All compounds that are made up of different types of sugar, such as cane and beet sugar, grape sugar, syrup, starch, cellulose.

Cataract
Clouding of the lens in the eye.

Cellulose
Glucose molecules in long chains, present in all plants. Cannot be broken down in the intestines.

Chylomicrones
Small drops of fat that are being transported from the blood into the lymph drainage system.

Cyclosporin A
A *cytotoxic drug* that has been used to stop the immune process at the onset of diabetes

Celiac disease
Illness where the person cannot tolerate *gluten,* a substrate found in wheat, oats, barley and rye.

Coma
Unconsciousness. Can in persons with diabetes occur when the blood glucose is very low (*insulin coma*) or very high (*diabetic, hyperglycemic coma*).

C-peptide
"Connecting peptide", a protein produced together with insulin in the *beta cells*. By measuring C-peptide the residual insulin production of the pancreas can be estimated.

Cortisone
Stress hormone that is produced in the adrenal gland.

Counterregulation
The body's defense against levels of blood glucose that are too low. The excretion of the counter-regulating hormones (glucagon, adrenaline, growth hormone and cortisone) increases when the blood glucose level falls too low.

CSII
Continous subcutaneous insulin infusion, treatment with insulin pump.

Cyclamate
Sweetener that does not provide any energy.

Cytotoxic drugs
Drugs that affect the ability of cells to divide. Often used for cancer therapy.

D

Dawn phenomenon
The growth hormone level rises during the night, causing the blood glucose level to rise early in the morning.

Depot effect
Part of the insulin that is injected is stored in the fat tissue as a depot (a "spare tank" of insulin). The longer the action of the insulin the larger the depot is.

Dextrose
Pure glucose

Diabetic coma
Ketoacidos that has led to unconsciousness.

Diabetes ketones
Ketones that are produced when the cells in the body are starving due to a lack of insulin. The blood glucose level is high. See *ketones*.

Dialysis
The process of extracting harmful substances from the blood when the kidneys do not work properly. See *uremia*.

DNA
The genetic code inside the chromosomes is made of DNA.

Double-blind study
Technique to perform a study where neither the patient nor the investigator know who is treated with which type of medication or intervention.

E

EEG
Electroencephalography ("brain-wave"), a method for measuring the very weak electrical currents in the brain.

EMLA
Cream that anesthetizes or numbs the skin.

Enzyme
Protein compound that cleaves chemical bonds.

F

Fasting blood glucose
Blood glucose test taken before eating in the morning. In a non-diabetic person it is normally not higher than 5.6 mmol/L (100 mg/dL).

Fat pad
See *lipohypertrophy*.

Fatty acids
Is produced when fat is broken down in the body.

Fluorescein angiography
Special type of X-ray technique to visualize the retinal blood vessels in the back of the eye.

Fructosamine
Blood test that measures how much glucose that is bound to proteins in the blood. Gives a measure of the average blood glucose level during the last 2-3 weeks.

Fructose
Fruit sugar

G

Gastroparesis
Slower stomach emptying caused by diabetes complications (*neuropathy*).

Galactose
Sugar molecule. *Lactose* consists of galactose and *glucose*.

Gestational diabetes
Diabetes discovered during pregnancy. The symptoms usually disappear after childbirth but the woman has an increased risk to acquire diabetes later on in life.

Glucagon
Hormone that raises the blood glucose level. It is produced in the *alpha cells* in the *Islets of Langerhans of the pancreas*.

Gluconeogenesis
Production of sugar (*glucose*) in the liver.

Glucose
Simple carbohydrate, *dextrose*, grape sugar, corn sugar.

Glucose tolerance test
Test to diagnosis early stages of diabetes. Tells how much the blood glucose level rises after orally ingested (OGTT) or intravenously given (IVTT) glucose.

Gluten
Compound that makes the dough sticky. Found in wheat, oats, rye and barley.

Glycemic index
A method to classify *carbohydrates* and foods according to how they affect the blood glucose level.

Glycogen
Glucose is stored as glycogen in the liver and muscles. The glucose molecules are connected in long chains. See illustration on page 143.

Glycogenolysis
The breakdown of the *glycogen* store in liver or muscles.

Glycosylated hemoglobin
See *HbA$_{1c}$*.

Goiter
Enlarged thyroid gland.

Grape sugar
Glucose

Growth hormone
Hormone that is produced in the pituitary gland. Increased growth is the most important effect. Increases the blood glucose level.

H

HbA$_{1c}$
Blood test that measures how much glucose bound to red blood cells. Gives a measure of the average blood glucose level during the last 2-3 months.

HLA-antigens
Genetic markers on chromosome 6 that are of importance when transplanting organs and for studying the heredity of different diseases.

Honeymoon phase
See *remission phase*.

Hormone
Protein compound that is produced in one of the glands in the body and that attains its target organ or tissue through the blood.

Hyperglycemia
High blood glucose level.

Hyperinsulinism
High level of insulin in the blood.

Hyperthyroidism
Excessively elevated levels of thyroid hormone in the blood. The thyroid gland is enlarged (toxic goiter).

Hypoglycemia
Too low a level of blood glucose. Usually defined as a blood glucose level below 3-3.5 mmol/L (55-65 mg/dL).

Hypophysis
See *pituitary gland*.

Hypothyroidism
Too low a level of thyroid hormone in the blood. The thyroid gland is often enlarged (goiter).

I

ICA
Islet cell antibodies. Antibodies directed against the *Islets of Langerhans*. Indicates an attack of the immune defense on the islets.

IDDM
Insulin dependent diabetes mellitus, type 1 diabetes.

Immune defence
The defence in the body against foreign substances, such as bacteria and virus.

Implantable insulin pump
Insulin pump that is implanted under the skin in the subcutaneous tissue. Infuses insulin through a thin tubing into the abdominal (intra-peritoneal) cavity.

Incidence
The number of diagnosed cases per year of a particular disease.

Incubation time
The time between when you have been infected with a contagious disease and when you show the first symptoms of the disease.

Insulin
Hormone produced in the pancreas' *beta cells*. Lowers the blood glucose level by "opening the door" of the cells.

Insulin antibodies
Antibodies in the blood that bind insulin. The insulin that is bound has no function, but can be released at a later time when the concentration of insulin in the blood is lower (like during the night).

Insulin coma
Unconsciousness caused by severe *hypoglycemia*.

Insulin depot
See *depot effect*

Insulin pump
Insulin is infused into the *subcutaneous* tissue through a thin tubing continuously during day and night. Premeal doses are taken by pressing buttons on the pump.

Insulin receptor
Structure on the cell surface that insulin binds to. Initiates the signal that makes the cell membrane permeable to glucose.

Insulin resistance
Decreased insulin sensitivity. A higher level of insulin than normal is needed to obtain the same blood glucose lowering effect.

Intermediate-acting insulin
Insulin that has an effective time action of 8-12 hours, corresponding to a normal night.

Intramuscular injection
Injection into a muscle.

Intraperitoneal delivery of insulin
Insulin is administered into the abdominal (intra-peritoneal) cavity where it is absorbed into the blood stream that leads to the liver.

Intravenous injection
Injection directly into a vein.

Islets of Langerhans
Small islets in the pancreas with cells that produce insulin (*beta cells*) and glucagon (*alpha cells*).

J

Jet injector
Injection without a needle. A thin jet of liquid is propelled using a very high pressure and penetrates the skin.

Jet-lag
Tiredness after long-distance flights when the day gets longer or shorter.

Juvenile diabetes
Diabetes in childhood and adolescence.

K

Ketoacidosis
The blood turns acidic from a high level of *ketones* when there is a deficiency of insulin. Can develop into *diabetic coma*.

Ketones

Fat is broken down to fatty acids when the cells are starving due to a lack of *glucose*. The fatty acids are transformed into ketones in the liver. This can occur when there is a lack of insulin ("high blood glucose, diabetes ketones") or when there is a lack of food (low blood glucose, "starvation ketones").

Ketosis

Increased amounts of ketones in the blood.

Kg

Kilogram, unit of weight. 1 kg = 2.2 pounds.

L

Lactose

Milk sugar.

Langerhans

The scientist that discovered the *Islets of Langerhans* in 1869.

Latency phase

Psychological term for describing the years before puberty.

Lente insulin

Insulin made *intermediate-* or *long-acting* with a mixture of zinc.

Lipoatrophy

Cavity in the *subcutaneous* tissue that can be caused by an immunologic reaction towards insulin.

Lipohypertrophy

Tissue build-up ("fat pad") that develops when you inject many times into the same area.

Long-acting insulin

Insulin with a very long time action, up to 28 hours. Long-acting insulin is of *lente*-type.

M

Microalbuminuria

Small amounts of protein in the urine. The first sign of kidney damage (*nephropathy*) caused by many years of high blood glucose levels. Microalbuminuria is reversible if the blood glucose control is improved.

Microaneurysm

Small protuberances on the retinal blood vessels (see illustration on page 210). The first sign of eye damage caused by many years of high blood glucose levels. Microaneurysms are reversible if the blood glucose control is improved.

Microangiopathy

Diabetes complications in the small blood vessels (eyes, kidneys, nerves).

Macroangiopathy

Diabetes complications in the large blood vessels (arteriosclerosis, cardiovascular disease).

MODY

Maturity onset diabetes of the young. A special kind of type 2 diabetes that can be found in children and adolescents.

Monocomponent insulin

Purified porcine (pig) insulin. Gives less problems with antibody formation than older types of insulin.

Multiple injection treatment

Treatment with injections of *short-* or *direct-acting insulin* before meals and *intermediate-* or *long-acting insulin* to cover the night. When using direct-acting insulin for meals you will need *basal insulin* in the day as well.

N

Nasal insulin

Insulin in aerosol form that is given in the nose.

Necrobiosis lipoidica diabeticorum

A special type of skin lesion that can be seen in persons with diabetes.

Nephropathy

Kidney damage caused by many years of high blood glucose levels.

Neuroglucopenic symptoms

Symptoms of brain dysfunction caused by a low blood glucose level.

Neuropathy

Kidney damage caused by many years of high blood glucose levels.

NIDDM

Non-insulin dependent diabetes mellitus, type 2 diabetes.

Nicotinamide

A vitamin B compound that has been shown to lower the risk of acquiring diabetes in some studies.

NPH insulin

Insulin made *intermediate-acting* by adding a protein (protamin).

P

Pancreas

An organ in the abdominal cavity that produces digestive *enzymes* (released into the intestines) and different *hormones* (released directly into the blood).

Pituitary gland

Small gland situated in the brain where many of the most important hormones in the body are produced.

Premeal injection
Injection with *short- or direct-acting insulin* prior to a meal.

Prevalence
The total number of existing cases of a disease at a given time.

Prospective study
A study that investigates what happens from now and onwards when giving a certain treatment. This is the best method of conducting a study of the effect of a new treatment.

Protamin
A protein from salmon that is added to protract the action time of insulin. *NPH insulin* is based on this method.

Proteinuria
Protein in the urine due to permanent kidney damage (*nephropathy*) from having high blood glucose levels for many years.

Pylorus
The lower sphincter (opening) of the stomach into the small intestine.

R

Rebound phenomenon
After a hypoglycemia the blood glucose level may rise to high levels. This is caused both by the secretion of counteracting hormones (see *counterregulation*) and by eating too much when feeling hypoglycemic.

Regression
Psychological term to describe when a person temporarily regresses to an earlier stage of psychological development. An independent teenager who is hospitalized will often become more dependent and react as if he/she was several years younger.

Remission phase
Also called honeymoon phase. The need of insulin will often be lowered during the months after the onset of diabetes due to an increase of the residual insulin production in your pancreas.

Renal threshold
If the blood glucose level is above this level glucose will show up in the urine when you test it.

Retinopathy
Eye damage caused by many years of high blood glucose levels.

Retrospective study
A study that investigates what happened when a certain treatment was given by looking backwards in time at treated individuals. Compare with *prospective* study.

S

Saccharin
Sweetener that does not provide any energy

Sensor
Device to measure blood glucose continuously.

Short-acting insulin
Soluble insulin without additives.

Somogyi phenomenon
A special type of nighttime rebound phenomenon with high blood glucose level in the morning.

Sorbitol
Sweetener that gives energy.

Starch
Complex *carbohydrates* found for example in potatoes, corn, rice and wheat.

Starvation ketones
Ketones that are produced when the cells starve due to a low blood glucose level. Caused by not eating enough food containing *carbohydrates*.

Subcutaneous
In the fat tissue under the skin.

Sucrose
Cane or beet sugar, brown sugar, table sugar, powdered sugar, invert sugar, saccharose.

T

Transplantation
When a new organ is implanted in the body by surgery.

Type 1 diabetes
Insulin-dependent diabetes (IDDM). Diabetes that needs to be treated with insulin from the onset. Is caused by the pancreas not producing insulin.

Type 2 diabetes
Non insulin-dependent diabetes (NIDDM). Diabetes that initially can be treated with diet and oral drugs. Is caused by an increased resistance to the insulin produced by the pancreas.

U

U
Short for international units of insulin

Uremia
Urine poisoning when the body cannot get rid of its waste products. End stage of *nephropathy*.

V

Venous blood test
Test taken by puncturing a blood vessel (vein).

References

1) Aarø LE. Hauknes R, Berglund E-L. Smoking among Norwegian schoolchildren 1975-1980. II. The influence of the social environment. Scand J Psychology 1981;22:297-309.

2) Adamsson U, Lins PE. Hormonal counterregulation of hypoglycemia in insulin treated diabetics. Lakartidningen 1985;40:3369-70.

3) Adamsson U. Hypoglycemia. In the book: Diabetes. SPRI and Swedish Medical Society 1989: 238-47.

4) Adamsson U, Lins P-E. Clinical views on insulin resistance in type 1-diabetes. In the book: Agardh C-D, Berne C, Östman J. Diabetes. Almqvist & Wiksell, Stockholm 1992: 142-50.

5) Adrogué H, Eknoyan G, Suki W. Diabetic ketoacidosis: Role of the kidney in the acid-base homeostasis re-evaluated. Kidney International 1984;25:591-98.

6) Ahlqvist et al. Contraception. Recommendations from a group of experts. Lakartidningen 40/1993;90:3456-64.

7) Åkerblom HK. Aetiological factors in type 1 diabetes. Nord Med 1992;107:204-6,230.

8) Åman J, Wranne L. Treatment of hypoglycemia in Diabetes: Failure of absorption of glucose through rectal mucosa. Acta Ped Scand 1984;73:560-61.

9) Åman J, Wranne L. Hypoglycemia in childhood diabetes: I. Clinical signs and hormonal counterregulation. Acta Ped Scand 1988;77:542-7.

10) Åman J, Wranne L. Hypoglycemia in childhood diabetes: II. Effect of subcutaneous or intramuscular injection of different doses of glucagon. Acta Ped Scand 1988;77:548-53.

11) American Academy of Pediatrics, Work group on cow's milk protein and diabetes mellitus. Infant feeding practices and their possible relationship to the etiology of diabetes mellitus (RE9430). Pediatrics 1994/5;94:752-54.

12) American Diabetes Association: Tests of glycemia in diabetes. Clinical Practice Recommendations 1997. Diabetes Care 1997;20:Suppl 1.

13) American Diabetes Association: Screening for diabetic retinopathy. Clinical Practice Recommendations 1997. Diabetes Care 1997;20:Suppl 1.

14) American Diabetes Association: Clinical Practice Recommendations 1997. Diabetes Care 1997;20:Suppl 1.

15) American Diabetes Association: Report of the expert committe on the diagnosis and classification of diabetes mellitus. Diabetes Care 1997;20:1183-97.

16) Amiel SA, Pottinger RC, Archibald HR, Chusney G. Effect of antecedent glucose control on cerebral function during hypoglycaemia. Diabetes Care 1991;14: 109-118.

17) Amiel S. Gale E. Physiological responses to hypoglycemia. Counterregulation and cognitive function. Diabetes Care 1993;16, suppl 3:48-55.

18) Anderson JH, Brunelle RL, Koivisto VA, Pfützner A, Trautmann ME, Vignati L, DiMarchi R et al. Reduction of postprandial hyoerglycemia and frequency of hypoglycemia in IDDM patients on insulin-analog treatment. Diabetes 1997;46:265-70.

19) Andersson H, Asp N-G, Hallmans G. Diet and diabetes. Scand J Nutrition 1986;30:78-90.

20) Anzén B, Zetterström J. Postcoital contraception, a forgotten and unused resource? Lakartidningen 1992;89:2948-2950.

21) Apelqvist, J. Personal communication 1996.

22) Attvall S, Lager I, Smith U. Rectal glucose administration cannot be used to treat hypoglycemia. Diabetes Care 1985;8:412-13.

23) Attvall S, Fowelin J, Lager I, Schenck H, Smith U. Smoking induces insulin resistance - a potential link with the insulin resistance syndrome. J Intern Med 1993;233:327-32.

24) Attvall S, Abrahamsson H, Schvarcz E, Berne C Gastric emptying is important for the patients with diabetes Lakartidningen 1995 ;92(45):4166-72.

25) Avogaro A, Beltramello P, Gnudi L, Maran A, Valerio A, Miola M, Marin N, Crepaldi C, Confortin L, Costa F, Macdonald I, Tiengo A. Alcohol intake impairs glucose counterregulation during acute insulin-induced hypoglycemia in IDDM patients. Diabetes 1993;42:1626-34.

26) Axelsen M, Wesslau C, Lönnroth P, Smith U. Reduced number of hypoglycemic events at night by bedtime cornstarch supplement in intensively treated IDDM subjects. Eur J Endocrin 1997;136:Suppl 1, Abstract # 3.

27) Bagdade JD, Root RK, Bulger RJ. Impaired leukocyte function in patients with poorly controlled diabetes. Diabetes 1974;23:9-15.

28) Bancroft J. Sexual problems in diabetes. Diabetes Reviews International 1995;3:2-5.

29) Bantle JP, Weber MS, Rao SMS, Chattopadhyay MK, Robertson RP. Rotation of the anatomic regions used for insulin injections and day-to-day variability of plasma glucose in type 1 diabetic subjects. JAMA 1990;263:1802-6.

30) Bantle JP, Neal L, Frankamp LM. Effects of the anatomical region used for insulin injections on glycemia in type 1 diabetes subjects. Diabetes Care 12/1993;16:1592-97.

31) Bardhan PK, Salam MA, Molla AM. Gastric emptying of liquid in children suffering from acute rotavirus gastroenteritis. Gut 1992;33:26-29.

32) Barkai L, Peja M. Impaired work capacity in diabetic children with autonomic dysfunction. Lecture, ISPAD, Atami, Japan 1994.

33) Bastyr III EJ, Holcombe JH, Anderson JH, Clore JN. Mixing insulin lispro and ultralente insulin. Diabetes Care 1997;20:1047-8.

34) Beaser R. Fine-tuning insulin therapy. Postgraduate Medicine 1992;91/4.

35) Becker DJ. Management of insulin-dependent diabetes mellitus in children and adolescents. Curr Opinion Ped 1991;3:710-23.

36) Beer SF, Lawson C, Watkins PJ. Neurosis induced by home monitoring of blood glucose concentrations. BMJ;298:362.

37) Bendtson I, Gade J, Theilgaard A, Binder C. Cognitive function in Type 1 (insulin-dependent) diabetic patients after nocturnal hypoglycemia. Diabetologia 1992;35:898-903.

38) Bendtson I, Kverneland A, Pramming S, Binder C. Incidence of nocturnal hypoglycemia in insulin-dependent diabetic patients on intensive therapy. Acta Med Scand 1988;223:453-548.

39) Bennett PH, Haffner S, Kasiske BL, Keane WF, Mogensen CE, Parving HH, Steffes MW, Striker GE. Screening and management of microalbuminuria in patients with diabetes mellitus: Recommendations to the Scientific Advisory Board of the National Kidney Foundation from an Ad Hoc Committee of the Concil on Diabetes Mellitus of the National Kidney Foundation. Am J Kidney Dis 1995;25:107-12.

40) Berg Kelly K. Living with diabetes. In the book: Diabetes. SPRI and Swedish Medical Society 1989: 285-90.

41) Berger M, Cüppers J, Hegner H, Jörgens V, Berchthold P, Absorption kinetics and biologic effects of subcutaneously injected insulin preparations. Diabetes Care 1982;5:77-91.

42) Berne C, Eriksson G, Maherzi A, Persson G. Unaccetable waste of insulin - time for new guidelines? Lakartidningen 4/1990;87:188.

43) Berne C, Hansson, Persson B. Pregnancy and diabetes. In the book: Diabetes. SPRI and Swedish Medical Society 1989: 119-134.

44) Berne C, Persson B. Pregnancy. In the book: Agardh C-D, Berne C, Östman J. Diabetes. Almqvist & Wiksell, Stockholm, 1992: 226-41.

45) Biessels GJ, Kappele AC, Bravenboer B, Erkelens DW, Gispen WH. Cerebral function in diabetes mellitus. Diabetologia 1994;37:643-50.

46) Binder C, Lauritzen T, Faber O, Pramming S. Insulin pharmacokinetics. Diabetes Care 1984;7:188-199.

47) Birke G (Ed.) Drug Handbook. Swedish Pharmaceutical Company 1991-92, p 324.

48) Björk E, Berne C, Kämpe O, Wibell L, Oskarsson P, Karlsson FA. Diazoxide treatment at onset preserves residual insulin secretion in adults with autoimmune diabetes. Diabetes 1996;45:1427-30.

49) Blackett PR. Insulin pump treatment for recurrent ketoacidosis in adloescence. Diabetes Care 1995;18:881-2.

50) Bleich D, Polak M, Eisenbarth GS, Jackson RA. Decreased risk of type 1 diabetes in offspring of mothers who aquire diabetes during adrenarchy. Diabetes 1993;42:1433-39.

51) Blom L, Nystöm L, Dahlquist G. The Swedish childhood diabetes study. Vaccinations and infections as risk determinants for diabetes in childhood. Diabetologia 1991;34/3:176-81.

52) Blohmé G. Insulin treatment - possibilities and limitations. Swedish Diabetes Association, Booklet no. 6, 1987.

53) Blom L, Persson LÅ, Dahlquist G. A high linear growth is associated with an increased risk of childhood diabetes mellitus. Diabetologia 1992;35:528-33.

54) Bloomgarden ZT. American Diabetes Association Postgraduate Course, 1996: Monitoring glucose, defining diabetes, and treating obesity. Diabetes Care 1996;19:676-79.

55) Bode B, Steed D, Davidson P. Long-term pump use and SMBG in 205 patients. Diabetes 1994;43 (Suppl 1):220A.

56) Bode BW. Establishing & Veryfying Basal Rates. In the book: Fredrickson L (Ed). The Insulin Pump Therapy Book. Insights from the experts. MiniMed, Los Angeles 1995.

57) Bode BW, Steed RD, Davidson PC. Reduction in severe hypoglycemia with long-term continuous subcutaneous insulin infusion in type 1 diabetes. Diabetes Care 1996;19:324-27.

58) Boëthius G, Gilljam H. Out of 1000 youngsters who smoke today 500 will die from smoking. Is further documentation

necessary? Lakartidningen 119;92:375.

59) Bojestig M, Arnqvist H, Hermansson G, Karlberg B, Ludvigsson J. Declining incidence of nephropathy in insulin-dependent diabetes mellitus. New Engl J of Medicine 1994;330:15-18.

60) Bolinder J, Hagström-Toft E, Ungerstedt U, Arner P. Self-monitoring of blood glucose in type 1 diabetic patients: Comparison with continous microdialysis measurements of glucose in subcutaneous adipose tissue during ordinary life conditions. Diabetes Care 1997;20:64-70.

61) Bolli GB, De Feo P, De Cosmo S et al. Demonstration of a dawn phenomenon in normal human volunteers. Diabetes 12/1984;33:1150-3.

62) Bolli G, Fanelli C, Periello G, De Feo P. Nocturnal blood glucose control in type 1 diabetes mellitus. Diabetes Care 1993;16:suppl 3, 71-89.

63) Bottazo, GF. On the honey disease. Diabetes 1993;42:778-800.

64) Boyle PJ, Schwartz NS, Shah SD, Clutter WE, Cryer PE. Plasma glucose concentrations at the onset of hypoglycemic symtoms in patients with poorly controlled diabetes and in nondiabetes. N Engl J Med 1988;318:1487-92.

65) Boyle PJ, Kempers SF, O'Connor AM, Nagy RJ. Brain glucose uptake and unawareness of hypoglycemia in patients with insulin-dependent diabetes mellitus. N Engl J Med 1995;333:1726-31.

66) Brackenridge BP, Reed JH. Counting carbohydrates - the key to proper bolusing. In the book: Fredrickson L (Ed). The Insulin Pump Therapy Book. Insights from the experts. MiniMed, Los Angeles 1995.

67) Brodows G, Williams C, Amatruda J. Treatment of insulin reactions in diabetics. JAMA 24/1984;252:3378-3381.

68) Brown B. The effects of exercise on gastric emptying. Motility 1995/31:4-6.

69) Burge MK, Castillo KR, Schade DS. Meal composition is a determinant of Lispro-induced hypoglycemia in IDDM. Diabetes Care 1997;20/2:152-55.

70) Campbell LV, Ashwell SM, Borkman M, Chrisholm DJ. White coat hyperglycemia: disparity between diabetes clinic and home blood glucose concentrations. BMJ 1992;305:1194-6.

71) Carlsson O. Against all odds. Diabetes (Swed. Diab. Ass.) 3/1994:30-31.

72) Carpelan C. Why don't they change life-style? Diabetes (Swed. Diab. Ass.) 3/93:34

73) Cars O, Uhnoo I, Linglöf T, Svenungsson B, Burman L. Self administration of antibiotics in traveller's diarrhea. Advantages are not in balance with the risk. Lakartidningen 36/1990;87:2751-52.

74) Casella SJ, Mongilio MK, Plotnick LP, Hesterberg MP, Long CA. Accuracy and precision of low-dose insulin administration. Pediatrics 1993;91/6:1155-57.

75) Cedermark G. Selenius M. Tullus K. The postprandial blood glucose response to sucrose/glucose intake in a mixed snack in diabetic teenagers. Acta Pediatr Scand 1990;79: 473-474.

76) Cedermark G. Selenius M. Tullus K. Glycaemic effect and satiating capacity of potato chips and milk chocolate bar as snacks in teenagers with diabetes. Eur J Pediatr 1993;152:635-39.

77) Chase HP, Crews KR, Garg S, Crews MJ, Cruickshanks KJ, Klingensmith G, Gay E, Hamman, RF. Outpatient management vs in-hospital management of children with new-onset diabetes. Clinical Ped 1990;29:450-56.

78) Chantelau E, Heinemann L, Ross D. Air bubbles in insulin pens. Lancet 1989;336:387-88.

79) Chantelau E, Lee DM, Hemmann DM, Zipfel U, Echterhoff S. What makes insulin injections painful? BMJ 1991;303:26-7.

80) Chiasson, J L. Ducros, F. Poliquin-Hamet, M. Lopez, D. Lecavalier, L. Hamet, P. Continous subcutaneous insulin infusion (Mill-Hill Infuser) versus multiple injections (Medi-Jector) in the treatment of insulindependent diabetes mellitus and the effect of metabolic control on microangiopathy. Diabetes Care 1984 ;4: 331-37.

81) Chng HH, Leong KP, Loh. Primary systemic allergy to human insulin: recurrence of generalized urticaria after successful desensitization. Allergy 1995;50/12:984-87.

82) Christiansson J. The diabetic eye. Swedish Diabetes Association, Booklet no. 1, 1992.

83) Chlup R, Marsálek E, Bruns W. A prospective study of multiple use of disposable syringes and needles in intensified insulin therapy. Diabet Med 1990;7:624-7.

84) Consensus Guidelines for the Management of Insulindependent (Type 1) Diabetes. Implementing the S:t Vincent Declaration. European IDDM Policy Group, Medicom Europe BV, Bussum, The Netherlands 1993.

85) Combs CA, Gavin AL, Gunderson E, Main EK, Kitzmiller JL. Relationship of fetal macrosomia to maternal postprandial glucose control during pregnancy. Diabetes Care 1992;15:1251-57.

86) Cox DJ. Gonder-Frederick L, Clarke W. Driving decrements in type 1 diabetes during moderate hypoglycemia. Diabetes 1993;42:239-43.

87) Cox D, Taylor A, Nowdeek G, Holley-Wilcox P, Pohl SN. The relationship betwecn psychological stress and insulindependent diabetic blood glucose control: preliminary investigations. Health Psychol 1994;3:63-75.

88) Coustan DR. Gestational Diabetes. Diabetes Care 1993;16 (Suppl 3):8-15.

89) Cryer P, Gerich J. Hypoglycemia in insulin-dependent diabetes mellitus. In the book: Rifkin H, Porte D. Diabetes Mellitus, Theory and Practice. Elsevier 1990:526-46.

90) Cryer P. Iatrogenic hypoglycemia as a cause of hypoglycemia-associated autonomic failure in IDDM. A vicious cycle. Diabetes 1992;41:255-60.

91) Cryer P. Perspectives in Diabetes. Hypoglycemia begets hypoglycemia in IDDM. Diabetes 1993;42:1691-93.

92) Cryer PE. Hypoglycemia unawareness in IDDM. Diabetes Care 1993;16, suppl 3:40-47.

93) Cryer P, Fisher J, Shamoon H. Hypoglycemia. Diabetes Care 1994;17:734-55.

94) Dagogo-Jack S, Craft S, Cryer P. Hypoglycemia-associated autonomic failure in insulin-dependent diabetes mellitus. J Clin Invest. 1993;91:819-28.

95) Dahlquist G, Blom L, Persson LÅ, Sandström A, Wall S. Dietary factors and the risk of developing insulin dependent diabetes in childhood. BMJ 1990;300:1302-6.

96) Dahlquist G, Blom L, Holmgren G, Hägglöf B, Wall S. Epidemiology of diabetes in Swedish children 0-l4 years of age. A six year prospective study. Diabetologia 1985; 28:802-8.

97) Dahlquist G. Epidemiology of type 1-diabetes. In the book: Agardh C-D, Berne C, Östman J. Diabetes. Almqvist & Wiksell, Stockholm 1992:50-55.

98) Dahlquist GG, Mustonen LR. Clinical onset characteristics of familial versus nonfamilial cases in a large population-based cohort of childhood-onset diabetes patients. Diabetes Care, 1995;18/6,:852-4.

99) Dahlquist G, Frisk G, Ivarsson SA, Svanberg L, Forsgren M, Diderholm H. Indications that maternal coxsachie B virus infection during pregnancy is a risk factor for child-

hood-onset IDDM. Diabetologia 1995;38:1371-73.

100) Dahlquist G, Savilahti E, Landin-Olsson M. An increased level of antibodies to β-lactoglobulin is a risk determinant for early-onset type-I (insulin dependent) diabetes mellitus independently of islet cell antibodies and early introduction of cow´s milk. Diabetologia 1992;35:980-84.

101) Dahlquist G, Frisk G, Ivarsson SA et al. Indications that maternal Coxsackie B virus infection during pregnancy is a risk factor for childhood-onset IDDM. Diabetologia 1995;38:1371-3.

102) Dahlquist GG, Kallen BAJ. Time-space clustering of date at birth in childhood-onset diabetes. Diabetes Care 1996;19:328-32.

103) Dahl-Jørgensen K, Brinchmann-Hansen O, Hanssen K, Ganes T, Kierulf P, Smeland E. Effect of near normoglycaemia for two years on progression of early diabetic retinopathy, nephropathy and neuropathy: the Oslo study. BMJ 1986; 293: 1195-9.

104) Dahl-Jørgensen K, Joner G, Hanssen KF. Relationship between cow´s milk consumption and incidence of IDDM in childhood. Diabetes Care 1991;14:1081-83.

105) Danne T, Weber B, Hartmann R, Enders I, Burger W, Hovener G. Long-term glycemic control has a nonlinear association to the frequency of background retinopathy in adolescents with diabetes. Diabetes Care 1994;17:1390-96.

106) Datta V, Swift PG, Woodruff GH, Harris RF. Metabolic cataracts in newly diagnosed diabetes. Arch Dis Child 1997;76:118-120.

107) Davidson PC. Bolus & Supplemental Insulin. In the book: Fredrickson L (Ed). The Insulin Pump Therapy Book. Insights from the experts. MiniMed, Los Angeles 1995.

108) The DCCT Research group. Diabetes control and complications study (DCCT): Results of feasibility study. Diabetes Care 1987;10:1-19.

109) The DCCT Research Group. The effect of intensive treatment of diabetes on the development and progression of long-term complications in insulin-dependent diabetes mellitus. N Engl J Med 1993;329:977-986.

110) The DCCT Research Group. The relationship of glycemic exposure (HbA$_{1c}$) to the risk of development and progression of retinopathy in the Diabetes Control and Complications Trial. Diabetes 1995;44:968-83.

111) The DCCT Research Group. Adverse events and their association with treatment regimens in the Diabetes Control and Complications Trial. Diabetes Care 1995;18:1415-27.

112) The DCCT Study Group. Pregnancy outcomes in the Diabetes Control And Complications Trial. Am J Obstet 1996;174/4;1343-53.

113) Dedorsson I, Eye complications. In the book: Diabetes. SPRI and Swedish Medical Society 1989:135 - 42.

114) DeFronzo RA, Hendler R, Christensen N. Stimulation of counterregulatory hormonal response in diabetic man by a fall in glucose concentration. Diabetes 1980;29:125-131.

115) DeFronzo RA, Matsuda M, Barret EJ. Diabetic ketoacidosis. A combined metabolic-nephrologic approach to therapy. Diabetes Reviews 1994;2:209-38.

116) Denker P, Leonard D, DiMarco P, Maleski P. An easy sliding scale formula. Diabes Care 1995;18:278.

117) DiaMond Project Group on Social Issues. Global regulations on diabetics treated witn insulin and their operation of commercial motor vehicles. BMJ 1993;307:250-53.

118) DiMarchi RD. New structural design of insulin for clinical use. Lecture, IDF, Kobe, Japan 1994.

119) Dinneen S, Alzaid D, Rizza. Failure of glucagon suppression contributes to postprandial hyperglycemia in IDDM.

Diabetologia 1995;38:337-43.

120) Donaghue KC, King J, Fung ATW, Chan A, Hing S, Howard NJ, Fairchild J, Silink M. The effect of prepubertal diabetes duration on diabetes microvascular complications in early and late adolescence. Diabetes Care 1997;20:77-80.

121) Dorchy H. What level of HbA$_{1c}$ can be achieved in young patients beyond the honeymoon period? Diabetes Care 1993;16:1311-13.

122) Dorman JS, O'Leary LA, Koehler AN. Epidemiology of childhood diabetes. In the book: Childhood and adolescent diabetes. Chapman & Hall Medical, London 1995.

123) Douvin C, Zinelabine H, Wirquin V, Perlemuter C, Dhumeaux D. An outbreak of hepatitis B in an endocrinology unit traced to an capillary-blood-sampling device. N Engl J Med 1991;322:57.

124) Drexler AJ. Pump therapy in preconception and pregnancy. In the book: Fredrickson L (Ed). The Insulin Pump Therapy Book. Insights from the experts. MiniMed, Los Angeles 1995.

125) Dunger DB, Edge JA. Diabetes and endocrine changes of puberty. Pract Diab Internat 1995;12:63-66.

126) Early Treatment Diabetic Retinopathy Study Group: Aspirin effects on mortality and morbidity in patients with diabetes mellitus. JAMA 1992;268:1292-300.

127) Eckert B, Ryding E, Agardh CD. The cerebral vascular response to a rapid decrease in blood glucose to values above normal in poorly controlled type 1 (insulin-dependent) diabetes mellitus. Diabetes Res Clin Pract, 1995; 27/3:221-7.

128) Eckert B, Rosén I, Stenberg G, Agardh CD. The recovery of brain function after hypoglycemia in normal man. Abstract 161, EASD Prag 1992.

129) Edge C. Diving and diabetes. UK Sports Diving Medical Committee. http://www.cru.uea.ac.uk/ukdiving/medicine/diabetes.htm

130) Editorial. Insulin pen: mightier than the syringe? Lancet 1989;336:307-8.

131) Eizirik D. Damage and repair in human islet cells. Diabetes in the XXI century; Part II. 1995:21-22.

132) Ekholm L, Björk E, Åman J. Insulin pens have the best precision when injecting small dosages of insulin. Lakartidningen 22/1991;88:2050.

133) Eliasson B, Attvall S, Taskinen MR, Smith U The insulin resistance syndrome in smokers is related to smoking habits.. Arterioscler Thromb, 1994 Dec, 14:12, 1946-50.

134) Eliasson B, Björnsson E, Urbanavicius V, Andersson H, Fowelin J, Attvall S, Abrahamsson H, Smith U. Hyperinsulinemia impairs gastrointestinal motility and slows carbohydrate absorption. Diabetologia 1995;38:79-85.

135) Eliasson E. "Disabled" makes successful professional career. Diabetes (Swed. Diab. Ass.) 6/1992:30-1.

136) Elliott RB, Martin JB. Dietary protein: A trigger of insulin-dependent diabetes in the BB rat? Diabetologia 1984;26:297-9.

137) Elliott RB, Pilcher CC. Prevention of diabetes in normal school children. Diab Res Clin Pract 1991;14, suppl 1:85.

138) Elliott RB, Chase HP. Prevention or delay of Type I (insulin-dependent) diabetes mellitus in children using nicotinamide. Diabetologia 1991;34:362-5.

139) Elliott RB. Lecture, ISPAD Annual Meeting, Greece 1993.

140) Ernström U. High price for a pinch of snuff. Diabetes (Swed. Diab. Ass.) 4/91:32-33.

141) Escalante D, Davidson J, Garber A. Maximizing glycemic control. How to achieve normal glycemia while minimizing hyperinsulinemia in insulin-requiring patients with diabetes mellitus. Clinical Diabetes Jan/Feb 1993:3-6.

142) Faglia E, Favales F, Aldeghi A et al. Adjunctive systemic hyperbaric oxygen therapy in treatment of severe prevalently ischemic diabetic foot ulcer: a randomized study. Diabetes Care 1996;19/12:1338-43.

143) Fanelli CG, Epifano L, Rambotti AM, Pampanelli S, DiVincenzo A, Modarelli F, Lepore M, Annibale B, Ciofetta M, Bottini P, Porcellati F, Scionti L, Santeusanio F, Brunetti P, Bolli GB. Meticulous prevention of hypoglycemia nomalizes the glycemic thresholds and magnitude of most neuroendocrine responses to, symptoms of and cognitive function during hypoglycemia in intensively treated patients with short-term IDDM. Diabetes 1993;42:1683-89.

144) Fanelli C, Pampanelli S, CalderoneS, Lepore M, Annibale B, Compagnucci P, Brunetti P, Bolli GB. Effects of recent, short-term hyperglycemia on responses to hypoglycemia in humans. Relevance to the pathogenesis of hypoglycemia unawareness and hyperglycemia-induced insulin resistance. Diabetes 1995;44:513-19.

145) Fava D, Leslie D, Pozzilli P. Relationship between dairy product consumption and incidence of IDDM in childhood in Italy. Diabetes Care 1994;17:1488-90.

146) Feldt-Rasmussen B, Mathiesen ER, Jensen T, Lauritzen T, Deckert T. Effect of improved metabolic control on loss of kidney function in type 1 (insulin-dependent) diabetic patients: an update of the Steno studies. Diabetologia 1991;34:164-70.

147) Felig P, Bergman M. Integrated physiology of carbohydrate metabolism. In the book: Rifkin H, Porte D. Diabetes Mellitus, Theory and Practice. Elsevier 1990:51-60.

148) Fleming DR, Jacober SJ, Vanderberg MA, Fitzgerald JT, Grunberger G. The safety of injecting through clothing. Diabetes Care 1997;20:244-47.

149) Fort P, Waters S, Lifshitz F. Low-dose insulin infusion in the treatment of diabetic ketoacidosis: Bolus versus no bolus. Journal of Pediatrics 1980;96:36-40.

150) Fowelin J, Attvall S, v Schenck H, Bengtsson BÅ, Smith U, Lager I. Effect of prolonged hyperglycemia on growth hormone levels and insulin sensitivity in Insulin-dependent diabetes mellitus. Metabolism 1993;42:387-94.

151) Franzén I, Ludvigsson J. Specific instructions gave reduction of lipomas and improved metabolic control in diabetic children. Diabetologia 1997;40 (Suppl 1):A615, Abstract # 2421.

152) Frid A, Gunnarsson R, Günther P, Linde B. Effects of accidental intramuscular injections on insulin absorption in IDDM. Diabetes Care 1988;11:41-45.

153) Frid A, Östman J, Linde B. Hypoglycemia risk during exercise after intramuscular injection of insulin in thigh in IDDM. Diabetes Care 1990;13:473-77.

154) Frid A. Injection and absorption of insulin. Thesis, Lund, Sweden 1992.

155) Frid A, Linde B. Intraregional differences in the absorption of unmodified insulin from the abdominal wall. Diabetic Med 1992;9:236-39.

156) Fritsche A, Schnauder G, Eggstein M, Schmülling RM. Blood glucose perception (BGP) in type 1 diabetic patients during exercise and after consumption of alcohol. Abstract 582, EASD 1993.

157) Frost G. Is carbohydrate a complex problem? Pract Diab Internat 1995;12:160-63.

158) Ganrot PO. Insulin resistance syndrome: posiible key role of blood flow in resting muscle. Diabetologia 1993;36:876-79.

159) Garg SK, Chase PH, Marshall G, Hoops SL, Holmes DL,

Jackson WE. Oral contraceptives and renal and retinal complications in young women with insulindependent diabetes mellitus. J Am Med Assoc. 1994;271:1099-102.

160) Gill GV, Redmond S, Garratt F, Paisey R. Diabetes and alternative medicine: cause for concern. Diabetic Med. 1994;11:210-13.

161) Ginsburg BH, Parkes JL, Sparacino C. The kinetics of insulin administration by insulin pens. Horm Metab Research 1994;26:584-87.

162) Glasier A, Thong KJ, Dewar M, Mackie M, Baird DT. Mifepristone (RU 486) compared with high-dose estrogen and progesteron for emergency postcoital contraception. N Engl J Med 1992;327:1041-4.

163) Goldstein DE, Little RR, Lorenz RA, Malone JI, Nathan D, Peterson CM. Tests of glycemia in diabetes. Diabetes Care 1995;18:896-909.

164) Green A, Gale EAM, Patterson CC, the EURODIAB ACE Study Group. Incidence of childhood-onset insulin-dependent diabetes mellitus: the EURODIAB ACE Study. Lancet 1992;339:905-909.

165) Gscwend S, Ryan C, Atchinson J, Arslanian S, Becker D. Effects of acute hyperglycemia on mental efficiency and counterregulatory hormones in adolescents with insulin-dependent diabetes mellitus. J Pediatrics 1995;126:178-184.

166) Gunning R, Garber A. Bioactivity of Instant Glucose - Failure of absorption through oral mucosa. JAMA 1978;240:1611-12.

167) Haglund B, Ryckenberg K, Selenius O, Dahlquist G. Evidence of a relationship between childhood-onset type 1 diabetes and low groundwater concentration of zinc. Diabetes Care 1996;19:873-75.

168) Hammerstein O, Rogers R. The King and I. Williams music, Hel Leonard Publications, Milwaukee 1951.

169) Hanas R, Ludvigsson J. Side effects and indwelling times of subcutaneous catheters for insulin injections: A new device for injecting insulin with a minimum of pain in the treatment of insulin-dependent diabetes mellitus. Diabetes Res Clin Pract 1990; 10:73-83.

170) Hanas R, Ludvigsson J. Experience of pain from insulin injections and needle-phobia in young patients with IDDM. Practical Diabetes 1997;14:95-99.

171) Hanas R, Ludvigsson J, Stanke C-G, Östberg H. X-ray appearance of the indwelling catheter when using Insuflon for insulin injections. Abstracts of the 17th Annual Meeting of ISGD, Hormone Research 1991; 35:58.

172) Hanas R, Ludvigsson J. Metabolic control is not altered when using indwelling catheters for insulin injections. Diabetes Care 1994;17:716-18.

173) Hanas, R. Carlsson S, Frid A, Ludvigsson J. Unchanged insulin absorption after 4 days' use of subcutaneous indwelling catheters for insulin injectons. Diabetes Care 1997;20:487-90.

174) Hanas R. Dead-in-bed syndrome in diabetes mellitus and hypoglycemic unawareness. Lancet 1997;350:492-3 (letter).

175) Hanson U, Persson B, Thunell S. Relationship between haemoglobin Alc in early type 1 (insulin-dependent) diabetic pregnancy and the occurrence of spontaneous abortion and fetal malformation in Sweden. Diabetologia l990;33:100-4.

176) Hanssen KF. Pregnancy in insulin-dependent diabetis. Nord Med 8-9/1992;107:211-12.

177) Hanssen KF, Bangstad HJ, Brinchmann-Hansen O, Dahl-Jørgensen K. Blood glucose control and diabetic microvascular complications. Long term effects of near-normoglycaemia. Diabetic Medicine 1992;9:697-705.

178) Hansson SL, Pichert JW. Perceived stress and diabetes control in adolescents. Health Psychol 1986;5:439-52.

179) Haycock P. Insulin Absorption: Understanding the Variables. Clinical Diabetes Sept/Oct 1986:98-118.

180) Heine RJ, Bilo HJG, Fonk T, Van der Veen EA, Van der Meer J. Absorption kinetics and action profiles of mixtures of short- and intermediate acting insulins. Diabetologia 1984; 27:558-62.

181) Helgasson T, Jobnasson MR, Evidence for a food additive as cause of ketosis-prone diabetes. Lancet 1981;11:716-20.

182) Helgasson T, Danielsen R, Thorsson AV. Incidence and prevalence of Type 1 (insulin-dependent) diabetes mellitus in Icelandic children 1970-89. Diabetologia 1992;35:880-3.

183) Henriksen JE, Djurhuus MS, Vaag A, Thye-Rønn P, Knudsen D, Hother-Nielsen O, Beck-Nielsen H. Impact of injection sites for soluble insulin on glycaemic control in Type 1 (insulin-dependent) diabetic patients treated with a multiple insulin injection regimen. Diabetologia 1993;36:752-58.

184) Henriksen JE, Vaag A, Ramsgaard Hansen I, Lauritzen M, Djurhuus MS, Beck-Nielsen H. Absorption of NPH (Isophane) insulin in resting diabetic patients: evidence for subcutaneous injection on the thigh as the preferred site. Diabetic Medicine 1991;8:453-57.

185) Hermansson, G., Ludvigsson, J. and Larsson, Y. (1986) Home blood glucose monitoring in diabetic children and adolescents. Acta Paediatr Scand 75, 98-105.

186) Hildebrandt P, Sestoft L, Nielson RL. The absorption of subcutaneously injected short-acting soluble insulin:influence of injection-technique and concentration. Diabetes Care 1983;6:459-62.

187) Hildebrandt P, Birch K. Subcutaneous insulin infusion: Change in basal rate infusion has no immediate effect on insulin absorption rate. Diabetes Care 1986;9:561-64.

188) Hildebrandt P. Skinfold thickness, local subcutaneous blood flow and insulin absorption in diabetic patients. Acta Physiol Scand. 1991;143 (Suppl. 603):41-45.

189) Hildebrandt P, Vaag A. Local skin-fold thickness as a clinical predictor of depot size during basal rate infusion. Diabetes Care 1993;16:1-3.

190) Hildebrandt R, Ilius U, Schliack V. Effect of insulin suppositories in type 1 diabetic patients (preliminary communication). Exp Clin Endocrinol 1984;83(2):168-72.

191) Hilsted J, Madsbad S, Hvidberg AM, Rasmussen MH, Krarup T, Ipsen H, Hansen B, Pedersen M, Djurup R, Oxenbøll. Intranasal insulin therapy: The clinical realities. Diabetologia 1995;38:680-84.

192) Hirsch IB, Farkas-Hirsch R, Skyler JS. Intensive insulin therapy for treatment of type 1 diabetes. Diabetes Care 12/1990;13:1265-1283.

193) Hirsch IB, Boyle PJ, Craft S, Cryer PE. Higher glycemic thresholds for symptoms during b-adrenergic blockade in IDDM. Diabetes 1991;40:1177-88.

194) Hirsch IB, Farkas-Hirsch R, Cryer PE. Continuous subcutaneous insulin infusion for the treatment of diabetic patients with hypoglycemia unawareness. Diab Nutr Metab 1991;4:41-43.

195) Hirsch IB, Heller SR, Cryer PE. Increased symptoms of hypoglycaemia in the standing position in insulin-dependent diabetes mellitus. Clinical Science 1991;80:583-86.

196) Hirsch IB, Paauw DS, Brunzell J. Inpatient management of adults with diabetes. Diabetes Care 1995;18:870-78.

197) Hirsch IB, Polonsky WH. Hypoglycemia and its prevention. In the book: Fredrickson L (Ed). The Insulin Pump Therapy Book. Insights from the experts. MiniMed, Los Angeles 1995.

198) Hoelzel W, Miedema K. Development of a reference system for the international standardization of HbA1c/Glycohemoglobin determinations. J Internat Fed Clin Chem 1996;9:62-67.

199) Hollander P, Pi-Sunyer X, Conif R. Acarbose in the treatment of type 1 diabetes. Diabetes Care 1995;20:248-253.

200) Hopkins DFC, Cotton, SJ, Williams G. Effective treatment of insulin-induced edema using ephedrine. Diabetes Care 1993;16:1026-28.

201) Houtzagers CMGJ, van der Velde EA. Multiple daily insulin injections: a multicentre study on acceptability and efficacy. Neth J Med 1988; 33:16-25.

202) Houtzagers CMGJ, Visser AP, Berntzen PA, Heine RJ, van der Veen EA. The Medi-Jector II: Effiacy and acceptability in insulin dependent diabetic patient with and without needle-phobia. Diabet Med 1988;5:135-8.

203) Houtzagers CMGJ, Berntzen PA, van der Stap H, et al. Efficacy and acceptance of two intensified conventional insulin therapy regimens: a long-term crossover comparison. Diabetic Med 1989; 6:416-21.

204) Houtzagers CMGJ, Visser AP, Berntzen PA, et al. Multiple daily insulin injections improve self-confidence. Diabetic Med 1989; 6:512-519.

205) Houtzagers CMGJ. Subcutaneous insulin delivery: Present status. Diabetic Med 1989;6:754-61.

206) Howey DC, Bowsher RR, Brunelle RL,Woodworth JR. [Lys(B28,Pro(B29)]-human insulin: a rapidly absorbed analogue of human insulin. Diabetes 1994;43:396-402.

207) Hyoety H, Hiltunen M, Knip M, Laakkonen M, Uaehaesalo P, Karjalainen J, Koskela P, Roivainen M, Lenikki P; Hovi T et al. A prospective study of the role of coxsackie B and other enterovirus infections in the pathogenesis of IDDM. Diabetes 1995;16:652-7.

208) Hyllienmark L, Ludvigsson J. Insulin pump - a realistic alternative for treatment of diabetes in children and adolescents. Lakartidningen 13/1992;89:1057-62.

209) Hägglöf B, Blom L, Dahlquist G, Lönnberg G, Sahlin B. The Swedish Childhood Diabetes Study: Indications of severe psychological stress as a risc factor for type 1 (insulin-dependent) diabetes mellitus in childhood. Diabetologia 1991;34:579-83.

210) International Study Group for Diabetes in Children (now ISPAD). Position statement, Diabetes in the Young 1989.

211) International Society of Pediatric and Adolescent Diabetes (ISPAD) and International Diabetes Federation (European Region). Laron Z (Ed). Consensus guidelines for the management of insulin-dependent (type 1) diabetes mellitus in childhood and adolescence. Tel Aviv: Freund Publishing House Ltd, 1995.

212) Jelinek J. Skin disorders associated with diabetes mellitus. In the book: Rifkin H, Porte D. Diabetes Mellitus, Theory and Practice. Elsevier 1990:838-49.

213) Jensen-Urstadt KJ, Reichard PG, Rosfors JS et al. Early atherosclerosis is retarded by improved long-term blood glucose control in patients with IDDM. Diabetes 1996;45/9:1253-8.

214) Johansson C, Samuelsson U, Ludvigsson J. A high weight gain early in life is associated with an increased risk of Type 1 (insulin-dependent) diabetes mellitus. Diabetologia 1994;37:91-94.

215) Johansson BL, Kernell A, Sjoeberg S, Wahren J. Influence of combined C-peptide and insulin administration on renal function and metabolic control in diabetes type 1. J Clin. Endocrinol. Metab. 1993;77:976-81.

216) Johansson BL, Fernqvist-Forbes E, Kernell A, Wahren J. Combined C-peptide and insulin treatment improves renal and nerve functions in IDDM patients. Abstract 19, EASD Stockholm 1995.

217) Johnston DG, Alberti KGMM. Hormonal control of ketone body metabolism in the normal and diabetic state. Clin Endocrin Met 1982;11:329-361.

218) Jones TW, Boulware SD, Kraemer DT, Caprio S, Sherwin RS, Tamborlane WV. Independent effects of youth and poor diabetes control on responses to hypoglycemia in children. Diabetes 1991;40:358-63.

219) Karlander S, Efendic S. Rapid and slow carbohydrates in the diabetic diet - time for a reevaluation? Lakartidningen 39/1984;81:3463-64.

220) Käär ML, Mäenpää J, Knip M. Insulin administration via a subcutaneous catheter. Diabetes Care 1993;16:1412-13.

221) Karvonen M, Toumilehto J, Libman I, LaPorte R. A reviw of the recent epidemiological data on the worldwide incidence of type 1 (insulin-dependent) diabetes mellitus. Diabetologia 1993;36:883-92.

222) Kassianos G. Some aspects of diabetes and travel. Diabetes Reviews International 2/1992;3:11-13.

223) Kaufman FR, Devgan S, Roe TF, Costin G. Perioperative management with prolonged intravenous insulin infusion versus subcutaneous insulin in children with type 1 diabetes mellitus. J Diabetes Complications 1996;10/1: 6-11.

224) Kaufman FR, Devgan S. Use of uncooked cornstarch to avert nocturnal hypoglycemia in children and adolescents with type 1 diabetes. J Diabetes Complications 1996;10/2:84-7.

225) Kemp P, Staberg B. Smoking reduces insulin absorption from subcutaneous tissue. BMJ 1982;284:237.

226) Kernell A, Dedorsson I, Johansson B, Wickström CP, Ludvigsson J, Tuvemo T, Neiderud J, Sjöström K, Malmgren K, Kanulf P, Mellvig L, Gjötterberg M, Sule J, Persson LÅ, Larsson LI, Åman J, Dahlquist G. Prevalence of diabetic retinopathy in children and adolescents with IDDM. A population-based study. Diabetologia 1997;40:307-10.

227) Kerr D, Sherwin RS, Pavalkis F, Fayad PB. Effect of caffeine on the recognition of and responses to hypoglycemia in humans. Ann Intern Med 1993;119:799-804.

228) Kimmerle R, Weiss R, Berger M, Kurz K. Effectiveness, safety, and acceptance of a copper intrauterine device (CU Safe 300) in type 1 diabetic women. Diabetes Care 1993;16:1227-30.

229) Kitzmiller JL, Gavin LA, Gin GD, Jovanovic-Peterson L, Main EK, Zigrang WD. Preconception care of diabetes. Glycemic contol prevents congenital anomalies. JAMA 1991;265:731-36.

230) Klemp P, Staberg B. Smoking reduces insulin absorption from subcutaneous tissue. BMJ 1982;284:237.

231) Knip M. Prevention of Childhood type 1 diabetes. Nord Med 8-9/1992;107:207-210.

232) Knutsson A. Diabetes in the professional life . In the book: Diabetes. SPRI and Swedish Medical Society 1989:291-296.

233) Koivisto VA. Various influences on insulin absorption. Neth J Med 1985;28 suppl 1:25-28.

234) Koivisto VA. Exercise for IDDM. Lecture IDF, Kobe, Japan 1994.

235) Koivisto VA, Haapa E, Tulokas S, Pelkonen R, Toivonen M. Alcohol with a meal has no adverse effect on postprandial glucose homeostasis in diabetic patients. Diabetes Care 12/1993;16:1612-14.

236) Kolb H, Elliot RB. Increasing incidence of IDDM a consequence of improving hygiene? Diabetologia 1994;37:729.

237) Kollind M. Lins P-E. Adamsson U. The man behind the phenomenon. Michael Somogyi and blood glucose regulation in unstable diabetes. A controversial hypothesis still

discussed. Lakartidningen 10/1991;88:878-879.

238) Krane E. Diabetic Ketoacidosis. Biochemistry, physiology, treatment and prevention. Ped Clin North Am 4/1987;34:935-60.

239) Kruger D, Owen S, Whitehouse F. Scuba Diving and diabetes. Practical guidelines. Diabetes Care 1995;18:1074.

240) Kullberg CE, Bergström A, Dinesen B, Larsson L, Little RR, Goldstein DE, Arnqvist HJ. Comparisons of studies on diabetic complications hampederd by differences in GHb measurements. Diabetes Care 1996;7:726-29.

241) Kyvik KO, Gren A, Beck-Nilsen H. Concordance rates of insulin dependent diabetes mellitus: A population based study of young Danish twins. BMJ 1995;311:913-17.

242) Kølendorf K, Bojsen J, Deckert T. Clinical factors influencing the absorption of 125 I-NPH insulin in diabetic patients. Horm Metabol Res 1983;15:274-8.

243) Lager I. Metabolic disturbances in diabetes. In the book: Agardh C-D, Berne C, Östman J. Diabetes. Almqvist & Wiksell, Stockholm 1992:205-25.

244) Lahtela JT, Knip M, Paul R, Antonen J, Salmi J. Severe antibody-mediated insulin resistance: Sucessful treatment with the insulin analog Lispro. Diabetes Care 1997;20:71-73.

245) Landin-Olsson M, Öhlin AC, Agardh CD. Blood glucose: influence of different methods for analysis and procedures for sampling. Pract Diab 1997;14:47-50.

246) Larkin J. Typical infections in diabetes and their treatment. In the book: Pharmacology of Diabetes. Walter de Greyter, Berlin 1991:325-42.

247) Larsen ML, Hørder M, Mogensen EF. Effect of long-term monitoring of glycosylated Hemoglobin levels in insulin-dependent IDDM. N Engl J Med 1990;323:1021-25

248) Lauritzen T, Pramming S, Deckert T, Binder C. Pharmacokinetics of continous subcutaneous insulin infusion. Diabetologia 1983;24:326-29.

249) Lavery LA, Harkless LB, Walker SC, Felder-Johnson K. Infected puncture wounds in diabetic and nondiabetic adults. Diabetes Care 1995;18:1588-1591.

250) Lawler-Heavner J, Cruickshanks KJ, Hay WW, Gay EC, Hamman RF. Birth size and risk of IDDM. Diabetes Res Clin Pract 1994;24:153-9.

251) Leahy JL, Cooper HE, Deal DA, Weir GC. Chronic hyperglycemia is associated with impaired glucose influence on insulin secretion. A study in normal rats using chronic in vivo glucose infusions. J Clin Invest 1986;77:908-15.

252) Lebovitz HE. Diabetic ketoacidosis. Lancet 1995;345:767-71.

253) Lernmark Å, Sundkvist G. Etiology of type 1-diabetes. In the book: Agardh C-D, Berne C, Östman J. Diabetes. Almqvist & Wiksell, Stockholm 1992:56-64.

254) Leslie RD, Elliot RB. Early environmental events as a cause of IDDM. Diabetes 1994;43:843-50.

255) Lindberg A-S. Diving into the depth of prejudice - or ignorance? Diabetes (Swed. Diab. Ass.) 2/1990:22-25.

256) Lindberg A-S. Even children with diabetes need an upbringing. Diabetes (Swed. Diab. Ass.)2/1993:14-15.

257) Lindberg A-S. Adolescents breaking up. One must chop the umbilical cord. Diabetes (Swed. Diab. Ass.) 6/1993:18-20.

258) Linde B. Dissociation of insulin absorption and blood flow during massage of a subcutaneous injection site. Diabetes Care 1986;9:570-74.

259) Lindström L. How Superwoman became the "Practical Pig". Diabetes 5/1991:4-5.

260) Lingenfelser T, Renn W, Buettner U, Kaschel R, Martin J, Jakober B, Tobis M. Improvement of impaired counterreg-ulatory hormone response and symtom perception by short-term avoidance of hypoglycemia in IDDM. Diabetes Care 1995;18:321-5.

261) Little RR, Goldstein DE. Measurements of glycated haemoglobin and other circulating glycated proteins. In the book: Research Methodologies in Human Diabetes. Walter de Greyter, Berlin 1994.

262) Loeb J, Herold K, Barton K, Robinson L, Jaspan J. Systematic approach to diagnosis and managment of biphasic insulin allergy with local anti-inflammatory agents. Diabetes Care 6/1989;12:421-23.

263) Loghmani E, Rickard K, Washburne L, Vandagriff J, Fineberg N, Golden M. Glycemic response to sucrose-containing mixed meals in diets of children with insulin dependent diabetes mellitus. J Pediatrics 1991;119:531-537.

264) Ludvigsson J, Heding LG, Larsson Y, Leander E. C-peptide in juvenile diabetics beyond the postinitial remission period. Acta Pædiatr Scand 1977;66:177-84.

265) Ludvigsson J. Insulin, love and care. Diabetes (Swed. Diab. Ass.) 5/1987:24-27.

266) Ludvigsson J, Hermansson G, Häger A, Kernell A, Nordenskjöld K. Adequate substitution of insulin deficiency is a base in the treatment of diabetes in young people. Lakartidningen 22/1988;85:2004-08.

267) Ludvigsson J, Lennholm B. An internationally unique study in Linkoping. Photopheresis against newly diagnosed diabetes type 1 . Lakartidingen 28-29/1992;89:2451-2454.

268) Ludvigsson J, Tuvemo T. Diabetes in children. In the book Agardh C-D, Berne C, Östman J. Diabetes. Almqvist & Wiksell, Stockholm 1992:205-25.

269) Ludvigsson J. Is diabetes in children caused by cow's milk? Lakartidningen 16/1993;90:1529-1531.

270) Ludvigsson J. Measurement of HbA_{1c} with a rapid method. Improved handling of patients with diabetes. Lakartidningen 21/1994;91:2135-36.

271) Lunt H, Brown JLJ. Self-reported changes in capillary glucose and insulin requirements during the menstrual cycle. Diabetic Med 1996;13/6:525-30.

272) Lönnroth P. Insulin's effects. In the book: Agardh C-D, Berne C, Östman J. Diabetes. Almqvist & Wiksell, Stockholm 1992:29-37.

273) MacCuish AC. Treatment of hypoglycemia. In the book: Frier B, Fisher M. Hypoglycemia and diabetes: Clinical and Physiological aspects. Edward Arnold, London 1993:212-21.

274) Macfarlane PE, Walters M, Stutchfield P. A prospective study of symtomatic hypoglycemia in childhood diabetes. Diabetic Med 1989;6:627-30.

275) Madsbad S, Dejgaard A. Highlights of the 29th EASD meeting, Istanbul 6-9 September 1993. NovoCare.

276) Malherbe C, de Gasparo M, de Hertogh R, Hoet J: Circadian variations of blood sugar and plasma insulin. Diabetologia 1969;5:397-404.

277) Maran A, Lomas J, Macdonald IA, Amiel SA. Lack of preservation of higher brain function during hypoglycemia in patients with intensively-treated IDDM. Diabetologia 1995;38:1412-18.

278) Marcus AO, Fernandez MP. Insulin pump therapy. Postgraduate Medicine 1996;99/3:125-32.

279) Marklund U. Drugs and Influence. Pupil analysis as starting-point for drug education. Thesis, Göteborg Studies in Educational Science 42, 1983. Göteborgs University, Dept. of Pedagogics, Sweden

280) Mazze RS, Lucido D, Shamoon H. Psychological and social correlates of glycemic control. Diabetes Care 1984;7:360-66. Se [291]

281) Mazur M. Rock star Bret Michaels is in love with ... life, music and his health. Diabetes (Swed. Diab. Ass.) 1/1990:10-13.

282) McCarthy JA, Covarrubias B, Sink P. Is the traditional alcohol wipe necessary before an insulin injection. Diabetes care 1993;16/1:402.

283) McCrimmon RJ, Gold AE, Deary IJ, Kelnar CJH, Frier BM. Symtoms of hypoglycemia in children with IDDM. Diabetes Care 1995;18:858-61.

284) McCullough D, Kurtz A, Tattersall R. A new approach to the treatment of nocturnal hypoglycemia using alpha-glucosidase inhibition. Diabetes Care 5/1993;6:483-87.

285) McHugh PR, Moran TH. Calories and gastric emptying: a regulatory capacity with implications for feeding. Am J Physiology 1979;236:R254-60.

286) McNally PG, Raymond NT, Swift PGF, Hearnshaw JR, Burden AC. Does the prepubertal duration of diabetes influence the onset of microvascular complications? Diab Med 1993;10:906-8.

287) Mecklenburg RS, Benson EA, Benson)W, Fredlund PN, Cuinn T, Metz RJ, Nielsen RL, Sannar CA. Acute complications associated with insulin infusion pump therapy. Report of experience with 161 patients. JAMA 1984;252:3265-69.

288) Mendoza R. On-line Resources for Diabetics. Glycemic Index Lists. 1997 (http://www.mendosa.com/gilists.htm)

289) Mendoza R. The GI factor. 1997 (http://www.mendosa.com/gifactor.htm)

290) Mitrakou A, Platanisiotis D, Partheniou C, Kytelis E, Livadas S, Raptis SA. Glucose fall from hyper- to normoglycemia triggers norepinephrine seretion in type 1 diabetes. Abstract 575, EASD Istanbul 1993.

291) Moberg E, Kollind M, Lins P-E, Adamsson U. Acute mental stress impairs insulin sensitivity in IDDM patients. Diabetologia 1994;37:247-251.

292) Montoro MN, Myers VP, Mestman JH, Xu Y, Anderson BG, Golde SH. Outcome of pregnancy in diabetic ketoacidosis. Am J Perinatology 1993;10:17-20.

293) Morain WD, Colen BC. Wound healing in diabetes. Clin Plast Surg 1990;17:493-501.

294) Mortensen HB, Hougaard P and the Hvidøre Study Group on Childhood Diabetes. Comparison of metabolic control in a cross-sectional study of 2,873 children and adolescents with IDDM from 18 countries. Diabetes Care 1997;20:714-720.

295) Moss SE, Klein R, Klein BE. Ten-year incidence of visual loss in a diabetic population. Ophthalmology 1994;106:1061-70.

296) Mühlhauser I. Cigarette smoking and diabetes: An update. Diabetes 1994;11:336-43.

297) Mulec H, Blohmé G, Grände B, Björck S. The effect on metabolic control on rate of decline in renal function in insulin dependent diabetes mellitus with overt diabetic nephropathy.

298) Nathan DM, Dunn FL, Bruch J et al. Postprandial insulin profiles with implantable pump therapy may explain decreased frequency of severe hypoglycemia, compared with intensive subcutanous regimens, in insulin-dependent diabetes mellitus patients. Am J Med 1996;100/4:412-17.

299) Newgard C. Cellular engineering and gene therapy for insulin replacement in diabetes. Diabetes 1994;43:341-350.

300) Newton RW, Greene SA. Diabetes in the adolescent. In the book: Kelnar CJH (Ed). Childhood and adolescent diabetes. Chapman & Hall 1995:367-74.

301) Nordfeldt S, Ludvigsson J. Severe hypoglycemia in chil-dren with IDDM. A prospective population study, 1992-94. Diabetes Care 1997;20:497-503.

302) Nutall F. Dietary fibers in the management of Diabetes. Diabetes 1993;42:503-508.

303) Nyström L, Dahlquist G, Rewers M, Wall S. The Swedish childhood diabetes study. An analysis of the temporal variation in diabetes incidence 1978-87. Int J Epidemiol 1990;19:141-46.

304) Nyström, Ostman J, Wall S, Wibell L. Mortality of all incident cases of diabetes mellitus in Sweden diagnosed 1983-87 at age 15-34 years. Diabetes incidence Study in Sweden (DISS) Group. Diabetic Med. 1992;9:422-7.

305) Olsson PO, Arnqvist HJ, Von Schenck HV. Free insulin profiles during intensive treatment with biosynthetic human insulin. Diabete & Metabolisme 1988;14(3):253-8.

306) Olsson PO. Insulin treatment. In the book: Diabetes. SPRI and Swedish Medical Society 1989:226-32.

307) Olsson PO, Arnqvist H, Asplund J. No pharmacokinetic effect of retaining the infusion site up to four days during continuous subcutaneous insulin infusion therapy. Diabet Med 6/1993;10:477-80.

308) Östman J, Andersson D. Diabetes mellitus. In the book: Drugs. Swedish Pharmaceutical Company 1993-94:474.

309) Pampanelli S, Torlone E, Lalli C, Sindaco PD, Ciofetta M, Lepore M, Bartocci L, Brunetti P, Bolli GB. Improved postprandial metabolic control after subcutaneous injection of a short-acting insulin analog in IDDM of short duration with residual pancreatic β-cell function. Diabetes Care 1995;18(11)1452-59.

310) Pedersen M. Lecture EASD 1993. In: Madsbad S, Dejgaard A. Highlights of the 29th EASD meeting, Istanbul 6-9 September 1993. NovoCare.

311) Pedrini MT, Levey AS, Lau J et al. The effect of dietary protein restriction on the progression of diabetic and nondiabetic renal diseases: a meta-analysis. Ann Intern Med 1996;124/7:627-32.

312) Pein M, Hinselmann C, Pfutzner A, Dreyer M. Catheter disconnection in type 1 diabetic patients treated with CSII. Comparison of insulin Lispro and human regular insulin. Diabetologia 1996;39 (Suppl 1): Abstract # 847.

313) Perez M, Kohn S. Cutaneous manifestations of diabetes mellitus. J Amer Acad Derm 1994;30:519-531.

314) Periello G, Torlone E, Di Santo S, Fanwelli C, De Feo P, Santeusanio F, brunett P, Bolli GB. Effect of storage temperature of insulin on pharmacokinetics and pharmacodynamics of insulin mixtures injected subcutaneously in subjects with type 1 (insulin-dependent) diabetes mellitus. Diabetologia 1988;31/11:811-15.

315) Persson B, Hansson U. Diabetes and pregnancy. Swedish Diabetes Association, Booklet no. 5, 1987.

316) Persson B. Long term morbidity in infants of diabetic mothers. Acta Endocrinol 1986;suppl 1:156.

317) Peters AL, Davidson MB, Eisenberg K. Effect of isocaloric substitution of chocolate cake for potato in type 1 diabetic patients. Diabetic Care 1990:888-92. (Becker ref 39)

318) Petersen KR, Skouby SO, Vedel PV, Haaber AB. Hormonal contraception in women with IDDM. Diabetes Care 1995;18(6):800-806.

319) Peto R, Lopez AD, Boreham J, Thun M, Heath C Jr. Mortality from smoking in developed countries 1950-2000: indirect estimates from national vital statistics. Oxford: Oxford University Press, 1994.

320) Peveler R, Boller I, Fairburn C, Dunger D. Eating disorders in adolescents with IDDM. Diabetes Care 10/1992;15:1356-60.

321) Peyrot MF, Pichert JW. Stress buffering and glycemic con-

trol. Diabetes Care 1992;7:842-846.

322) Pezzarossa A, Taddei F, Cimicchi MC, Rossini E, Contini S, Bonora, Gnudi A, Uggeri E. Perioperative management of diabetic subjects. Subcutaneous versus intravenous insulin administration during glucose-potassioum infusion. Diabetes Care 1988;11/1:52-58.

323) Polak M, Beregszaszi M, Belarbi N, Benali K, Czernichow P, Tubiana-Rufi N. Subcutaneous or intramuscular injections of insulin in children; Are we injecting where we think we are? Diabetes Care 1996;19:1434-36.

324) Pozzilli P, Visalli N. Signore A et al. Double blind trial of nicotinamid in recent-onset IDDM (the IMDIAB III study). Diabetologia 1995;38:848-52.

325) Price DE, Burden AC. Growth of children before onset of diabetes. Diabetes Care 1992; 15:1393-95.

326) Quillian WC, Cox DJ, Gonder-Frederick LA, Driesen NR, ClarkeWL. Reliability of driving performance during moderate hypoglycemia in adults with IDDM. Diabetes Care 1994;17:1367-68.

327) Read NW, Welch IM, Austen CJ. Barnish C et al. Swallowing food without chewing; a simple way to reduce postprandial glycemia. Br J Nutrition 1986;55:43-7.

328) Reichard P, Britz A, Rosenqvist U. Intensified conventional insulin treatment and neuropsychological impairment. Br Med J 1991;303:1439-42.

329) Reichard P, Nilsson B-Y, Rosenqvist U. The effect of long-term intensified insulin treatment on the development of microvascular complications of diabetes mellitus. N Engl J Med 1993;329:304-309.

330) Reichard P. Are there any glycemic thresholds for the serious microvascular diabetic complications? J Diab Compl 1995;9:25-30.

331) Robinson N, Lloyd CE, Fuller J, Yateman NA. Psychosocial factors and the onset of type 1 diabetes. Diabetic Med 1989;6:53-8.

332) Rodin G, Craven J, Littlefield C, Murray M, Daneman D. Eating disorders and intentional undertreatment in adolescent females with diabetes. Psychosomatics 1991;32:171-6.

333) Rodin GM, Danman D. Eating disorders and IDDM. Diabetes Care 1992;15:1402-12.

334) Rosell & Davidsson. Pharmacological Principles. 3:e edition: 320, Tandläkarförlaget, Sweden.

335) Rosenbloom A, Beverly P, Giordano RN: Chronic overtreatment with insulin in children and: Am J Dis Child 1977;131:881-885.

336) Rosenbloom A, Hanas R. Diabetic Ketoacidosis (DKA): Treatment Guidelines. Clin Ped 1996;35:261-266.

337) Rosenn BM, Miodovnik M, Khoury JC, Siddiqi TA. Counterregulatory hormonal responses to hypoglycemia during pregnancy. Obstet Gynecol 1996;87/4:568-74.

338) Ryan C, Yega A, Drash A. Cognitive deficits in adolescents who developed diabetes early in life. Pediatrics 1985;75:921-927.

339) Ryan CM, Atchison J, Puczynski SS et al. Mild hypoglycemia associated with deterioration of mental efficiency in children with insulin-dependent diabetes mellitus. J. Pediatr.1990;117:32-38.

340) Rydén O, Nevander L, Johnsson P, Westbom L, Sjöblad S. Diabetic Children and Their Parents: Personality Correlates of Metabolic Control. Acta Paediatr Scand 1990;79:1204-1.

341) Sackey AH, Jefferson IG. Interval between insulin injection and breakfast in diabetes. Arch Dis Child 1994;71:248-50.

342) Samuelsson U, Johansson C, Ludvigsson J. Breast-feeding seems to play a marginal role in the prevention of IDDM. Diabetes Res. Clin. Pract 3/1993;3:203-10.

343) Samuelsson U, Johansson C, Carstensen J, Ludvigsson J. Space-time clustering in insulin dependent diabetes mellitus (IDDM) in south-east Sweden. Int. J Epidemiol. 1994;23:138-142.

344) Sandelin O, Rogberg N. Diving into the depth of prejudice. The Diving Journal 4/1989:28-29.

345) Sane T, Koivisto VA, Nikkanen P, Pelkonen R. Adjustment of insulin doses of diabetic patients during long distance flights. BMJ 1990;301:421-22.

346) Sank A, Wei D, Reid J, Ertl D, Nimni M, Weaver F, Yellin A, Tuan TL. Human endothelial cells are defective in diabetic vascular disease. J Surg Res 1994;57:647-53.

347) Santiago J. Lessons from the Diabetes Control and Complications Trial. Diabetes 1993;42:1549-1554.

348) Sartor G, Dahlquist G. Short-term mortality in childhood onset insulin-dependent diabetes mellitus: a high frequency of unexpected deaths in bed. Diabet Med 1995;12:607-11.

349) Sawicki P, Didjurgeit U, Mühlhauser I, Bender R, Heinemann L, Berger M. Smoking is associated with progression of diabetic nephropathy. Diabetes Care 1994;17:126-131.

350) Savilahti E, Åkerblom HK, Tainio V-M, Koskimies S. Children with newly diagnosed insulin dependent diabetes mellitus have increased levels of cow's milk antibodies. Diabetes Res 1988;7:137-40.

351) Schattenberg S, Bott U, Overmann H, Wagener W, Mühlhauser I, Bender R, Berger M. Translation of intensified insulin therapy into routine diabetes care: Lowering HbA1c without increase in the risk of sever hypoglycemia. Abstract no 64, EASD, Stockhom 1995.

352) Schatz DA, Maclaren NK. Cow's milk and insulin-dependent diabetes. Innocent until proven guilty. JAMA 1996;276(8):647-8.

353) Schiavi RC, Stimmel BB, Mandeli J, Rayfield EJ. Diabetes mellitus and male sexual function: a controlled study. Diabetologia 1993;36:745-751.

354) Schiffrin A, Belmonte M: Multiple daily self-glucose monitoring: it´s essential role in long-term glucose control in insulin-dependent patients treated with pump and multiple subcutaneous injections. Diabetes Care 1982; 5:479-84.

355) Schiffrin A, Suissa S. Predicting nocturnal hypoglycemia in patients with type 1 diabetes treated with continous insulin infusion. Am J Med 1987;82:1127-32.

356) Scherstén B et al. A consensus document: vision-threatening retinal changes in diabetes. Lakartidningen 51-51/1991;88:4475-4478.

357) von Schütz W, Fuchs S, Stephan S, Lange K, Heiming R, Hürter P. Incidence of severe hypoglycemia under conventional and intensive insulin therapy in diabetic children and adolescents. Abstract no 66, EASD -94.

358) Schuler G, Peltz K, Kerp L. Is the reuse of needles for insulin injection systems associated with a higher risk cutaneous complications? Diabetes Res Clin Pract 1992;16/3:209-12.

359) Schvarcz E, Palmér M, Åman J, Lindqvist B, Beckman K-W. Hypoglycemia increases the gastric emptying rate in patients with type-1 diabetes mellitus. Diabetic Med 1993;10:660-63.

360) Schwarcz E, Palmér M, Åman J, Horowitz M, Berne C. Physiological hyperglycemia slows gastic emptying in normal subjects. Abstract no 116, EASD, Stockholm 1995.

361) Sells CJ, Robinson NM, Brown Z, Knopp RH. Long-term developmental follw-up of infants of diabetic mothers. J Pediatr. 1994;125:1,S9-17.

362) Sjöblad (Ed). Consensus guidelines for the treatment of

childhood and adolescent diabetes. Swedish Pediatric Association 1996.

363) Shah S, Malone J, Simpson N. A randomized trial of intensive insulin therapy in newly diagnosed insulin-dependent diabetes mellitus. N Engl J Med 1989; 320:550-4.

364) Silink M (Ed.). APEG handbook on childhood and adolescent diabetes. Australian Pediatric Endocrine Group 1996.

365) Silva SR, Clark L, Goodman SN, Plotnick LP. Can caretakers of children with IDDM accurately measure small insulin doses and dose changes? Diabetes Care 1996;19:56-59.

366) Sindelka G, Heinemann L, Berger M, Frenck W, Chantelau E. Effect of insulin concentration, subcutaneous fat thickness and skin temperature on subcutaneous insulin absorption in healthy subjects. Diabetologia 1994;37:377-80.

367) Sjöblad S. Hypoglycemia in children. Paedriaticus 1988;18:90-101.

368) Smith CP, Sargent MA, Wilson BPM, Price DA. Subcutaneous or intramuscular insulin injections. Arch Dis Childhood 1991;66:879-82.

369) Soltész G, Ascádi G. Association between diabetes, severe hypoglycemia and electroencephalographic abnormalities. Arch Dis Child. 1989;64:992-96.

370) Somogyi M. Insulin as a cause of extreme hyperglycemia and instability. Weekly Bulletin of the St Louis Medical Society 1938;32:498-510.

371) Soon-Shiong P, Heintz RE, Meredith N, Yao QX, Zheng T, Murphy M, Moloney MK, Schmehl M, Harris M et al. Insulin independence in a type-1 diabetic patient after encapsulated islet transplantation. Lancet 1994;343:950-51.

372) Sonnenberg GE, Fredrickson L. DKA Prevention. In the book: Fredrickson L (Ed). The Insulin Pump Therapy Book. Insights from the experts. MiniMed, Los Angeles 1995.

373) Steffes M, Tamborlane W, Becker D, Palmer J. The effect of intensive diabetes treatment on residual betacell function in the Diabetes Control and Complications Trial (DCCCT). Diabetes 1996; :Suppl 2; 18A (abstract # 59).

374) Steindel BS, Roe TR, Costin G, Carlson M, Kaufman FR. Continous subcutaneous insulin infusion (CSII) in children and adolescents with chronic poorly controlled type 1 diabetes mellitus. Diabetes Research and Clinical Practise 1995;27:199-204.

375) Stenninger E, Åman J. Intranasal glucagon treatment relieves hypoglycemia with Type 1 (insulin-dependent) diabetes mellitus. Diabetologia 1993;36:931-35.

376) Stewart NL, Darlow BA. Insulin loss at the injection site in children with type 1 diabetes mellitus. Diabetic Medicine 1994;11:802-05.

377) Strauss K. Guidelines for using short insulin needles. Becton-Dickinson 1996.

378) Strauss K. Insulin delivery devices and correct injection techniques. Becton-Dickinson 1997.

379) Sundkvist G. Autonomic neuropathy. In the book: Diabetes. SPRI and Swedish Medical Society 1989. Svensk Medicin nr 14:159-70.

380) Sutherland D, Moudry-Munns K, Elick B. Pancreas Transplantation. In the book: Rifkin H, Porte D. Diabetes Mellitus, Theory and Practice. Elsevier 1990:869-79.

381) Svenungsson B, Jertborn M, Wiström J. Prophylaxix and therapy of travelers' diarrea. Nord Med 11/1992;107:272-73.

382) Swedish National Board of Health and Welfare. Recommendations from an expert meeting: Treatment of insulin-dependent diabetes mellitus. Lakartidningen 42/1989;86:3585-3589.

383) Swift PGF, Waldron S, Glass S. A child with diabetes: distress, discrepancies and dietetic debate. Pract Diab Internat 1995;12:59-62.

384) Tainio VM, Savilahti E, Arjomaa P, Salmenperä L, Perheentupa J, Siimes MA. Plasma antibodies to cow's milk are increased by early weaning and consumption of unmodified milk, but production of plasma IgA and IgM cows milk antibodies is stimulated even during exclusive breast feeding. Acta Paediatr Scand 1988;77:807-11.

385) Tahara Y. Shima K. Response to Chantelau and Rech. Diabetes Care 1994;17:345.

386) Tahara Y, Shima K. Kinetics of HbA1c, glycated albumin, and fructosamine and analysis of their weight functions aganst preceding plasma glucose levels. Diabetes Care 1995;18:440-47.

387) Tanenberg RJ. Candidate Selection. In the book: Fredrickson L (Ed). The Insulin Pump Therapy Book. Insights from the experts. MiniMed, Los Angeles 1995.

388) Tattersall RB. Endocrinol Metab 1977;6:403-419.

389) Tattersall RB, Gill GV. Unexplained death of type-1 diabetic patients. Diabetic Med. 1991;8:49-58.

390) Temple MYM, Riddell MC, Bar-Or O. The reliability and repeatability of the blood glucose response to prolonged exercise in adolescent boys with IDDM. Diabetes Care 1995;18:326-332.

391) Tesfye S, Malik R, Ward JD. Vascular factors in diabetic neuropathy. Diabetologia 1994;37:847-54.

392) The Canadian-European Randomized Control Trial Group. Cyclosporin-induced remission of IDDM after early intervention: association of 1 year of cyclosporin treatment with enhanced insulin secretion. Diabetes 1988; 37:1574-82.

393) Thernlund GM, Dahlquist G, Hansson K, Ivarsson SA, Ludvigsson J, Sjöblad S, Hägglöf B. Psychological stress and the onset of IDDM in children. Diabetes Care 1995;18:/10:1323-29.

394) Thernlund G, Dahlquist G, Hägglöf B, Ivarsson SA, Lernmark B, Ludvigsson J, Sjöblad S. Psychological reactions at the onset of insulin-dependent diabetes in children and later adjustment and metabolic control. Act Pediatr 1996;85:947-53.

395) Thorburn A, Brand J, Truswell S: The glycaemic index of foods: The Medical Journal of Australia, 1986;144:580-82.

396) Thow J, Home P. Insulin injection technique. BMJ 1990;301:3-4.

397) Thow JC, Johnson AB, Marsden S, Taylor R, Home PD. Morphology of palpably abnormal injection sites and effects on absorption of isophane (NPH) insulin. Diabetic medicine 1990;7:795-99.

398) Tuomilehto J, Tuomilehto-Wolf E, Virtala E, LaPorte RE: Coffee consumption as trigger for insulin-dependent diabetes mellitus in childhood. BMJ 1990;300:642-43.

399) Tuvemo T, Wibell L, Wålinder O. Hemoglobin A$_1$ - a new method for diabetes control. Lakartidningen 1980;77:2790-94.

400) Vaag A, Handberg A, Lauritzen M, Henriksen JE, Damgaard Pedersen K, Beck-Nielsen H. Variation in absorption of NPH insulin due to intramuscular injection. Diabetes Care 1990;13:74-76.

401) Vague P, Picq R, Bernal M et al. Effect of nicotinamide treatment on the residual insulin secretion in type-I (insulin-dependent) diabetic patients. Diabetologia 1989;32:316-21.

402) Valenzuela GA, McCallum R. Etiology and diagnosis of gastroparesis:An introduction. Motility 1988;1:10-14.

403) Veneman T. Mitrakou A. Mokan M. Cryer P, Gerich J. Induction of hypoglycemia unawareness by asymptomatic nocturnal hypoglycemia. Diabetes 1993;42:1233-37.

404) Verge CF, Simpson JM, Howard NJ, Mackerras D, Irwig L, Silink M. Environmental factors in IDDM. Diabetes Care 1994;17:1381-89.

405) Verotti A, Chiarelli F, Blasetti A, Bruni E, Morgese G. Severe hypoglycemia in insulin-dependent diabetic children treated by multiple injection regimen. Acta Diabetol 1996;33/1:53-57.

406) Vervoort G, Goldschmidt HMG, van Doorn LG. Nocturnal blood glucose profiles in patients with type 1 diabetes mellitus on multiple (>1) daily insulin injectionregimes. Diab Med 1996;13:794-99.

407) Vessby B, Gustafsson IB. Diet treatmeny. In the book: Diabetes. SPRI and Swedish Medical Society 1989:206-214.

408) Viberti G. Mogensen CE. Groop LC. Pauls JF. Effect of captopril on progression to clinical proteinuria in patients with insulin-dependent diabetes mellitus and microalbuminuria. European Microalbuminuria Captopril Study Group. JAMA 1994;271:275-79.

409) Viberti et al, The Microalbuminuria Captopril Study Group. Captopril reduces the risk of nephropathy in IDDM patients with microalbuminuria. Diabetologia 1996;39:587-93.

410) Virtanen SM, Räsänen L, Aro A, Ylönen K, Sippola H, Lounamaa R. Toumilehto J, Åkerblom HK. Feeding in infancy and the risk of type 1 diabetes mellitus in Finnish children. Diabetic Medicine 1992;9:815-19.

411) Virtanen SM, Saukkonen T, Savilahti E, Ylönen K, Räsänen L, Aro A, Knip M, Toumilehto J, Åkerblom HK and the Childhood in Diabetes in Finland Study Group. Diet, cow´s milk protein antibodies and the risk of IDDM in Finnish children. Diabetologia 1994;37:381-87.

412) Waldron S. Childhood diabetes - current dietary management. Current Pediatrics 1993;3:138-41.

413) Walker M, Marshall SM, Alberti KGMM. Clinical aspects of diabetic ketoacidosis. Diabetes/Metabolism Reviews 1989;5:651-63.

414) Wallberg-Henriksson H, Wahren J. Exercise. In the book: Agardh C-D, Berne C, Östman J. Diabetes. Almqvist & Wiksell, Stockholm 1992:97-107.

415) Walsh PA, Roberts R. Changing to Humalog? What you need to know on a pump. Diabetes Services 1997 (http://Diabetesnet.com/hmlgpmp.html).

416) Warram J, Martin BC, Krolewski AS. Risk of IDDM in children of diabetic mothers decreases with increasing maternal age at pregnancy. Diabetes 1991;40:1679-1684.

417) Wasserman D, Zinman B. Exercise in individuals with IDDM. Diabetes Care 1994;17:924-37.

418) Weissberg-Benchell J, Glasgow A, Tynan D, Wirtz P, Turek J, Ward J. Adolescent diabetes management and mismanagement. Diabetes Care 1995;18:77-82.

419) Welch IM, Bruce C, Hill SE, Read NW. Duodenial and ileal lipid suppresses postprandial blood glucose ind insulin responses in man: possible implications for the dietary management of diabetes mellitus. Clinical Science 1987;72:209-16.

420) Wibell L. Hyperglycemia and ketoacidosis. In the book: Agardh C-D, Berne C, Östman J. Diabetes. Almqvist & Wiksell, Stockholm 1992:169-181.

421) Wibell L. Surgery. In the book: Agardh C-D, Berne C, Östman J. Diabetes. Almqvist & Wiksell, Stockholm 1992:182-193.

422) Widom B, Simonson DC. Intermittent hypoglycemia impairs glucose counter-regulation. Diabetes 1992;41:1597-602.

423) Wikström H, Johansson P. Five gold medals in a row. Diabetes (Swed. Diab. Ass.) 6/1993:8-9.

424) Wise JE, Kolb EL, Sauder SE. Effect of glycemic control on growth velocity in children with IDDM. Diabetes Care 1992;15:826-30.

425) Wittesjö B, Stenström TA, Eitrem R, Rombo L. Every other traveller abroad risks diarrhea. Water and food are the most common sources of infection. Lakartidningen 1995;92:865-67.

426) Wolever TMS. The Glycemic index. In the book: Bourne GH (ed). Aspects of some vitamins, minerals and enzymes in health and disease. World Rev Nutr Diet. Basel, Karger 1990;62:120-85.

427) Wynne HA, Brown PM Sönksen PM. Acceptability and effectiveness of self-administered intramuscular insulin in juvenile-onset diabetes. Practical Diabetes 1985;2:32-33.

428) Yki-Järvinen H, Helve E, Koivisto VA. Hyperglycemia decreases glucose uptake in type 1 diabetes. Diabetes 1987;36:892-96.

429) Yki-Järvinen H. Glucose toxicity. Endocrine Reviews 1992;13:414-431.

430) Yki-Järvinen H. Glucose toxicity - its pros and cons. Nord Med 1996;111:80-3.

431) Young RJ, Hannan WJ, Frier BM, Steel JM, Duncan LJP. Diabetic lipohypertrophy delays insulin absorption. Diabetes Care 1984; 7:479-80.

432) Zinman B. Insulin regimens and strategies for IDDM. Diabetes Care 1993;16, suppl 3:24-8.

433) Zinman B, Tildesley H, Chiasson JL, Tsui E, Strack TR. Insulin Lispro in CSII: Results of a double-blind, crossover study. Diabetes 1997;46:440-43.

Further reading about diabetes

➠ American Diabetes Association. Complete Guide to Diabetes.

➠ American Diabetes Association. 101 tips for staying healthy with diabetes.

➠ Beaser RS (Joslin Diabetes Center). Outsmarting Diabetes: A Dynamic Approach for Reducing the Effects of Insulin-Dependent diabetes.

➠ Betschart J. It's Time to Learn About Diabetes: A Workbook on Diabetes for Children.

➠ Betschart J, Thom S. In Control: A guide for Teens with Diabetes.

➠ Brackenridge BP, Dolinar RO. Diabetes 101: A Pure and Simple Guide for People Who Use Insulin.

➠ Brand Miller JB, Foster-Powell K, Colagiuri S. The G.I. Factor: The Glycaemic Index Solution. Hodder Headline Australian Pty Limited, 1996.

➠ Brannan D. Life to the Fullest.

➠ Chase P. Understanding Insulin-Dependent Diabetes.

➠ Consensus Guidelines for the Management of Insulin-dependent (Type 1) Diabetes. Implementing the St. Vincent Declaration.

➠ Consensus guidelines for the management of insulin-dependent (type 1) diabetes mellitus in childhood and adolescence. ISPAD and International Diabetes Federation (European Region) 1995.

➠ Estridge B, Davies J. So your child has diabetes.

➠ Estridge B, Davies J. Diabetes and your teenager.

➠ Estridge B, Davies J. Pregnancy and Diabetes.

➠ Feste C. The physician within.

➠ Fredrickson L (Ed). The insulin Pump Therapy Book. Insights from the experts. MiniMed, Los Angeles 1995.

➠ Hillson R. Diabetes: the complete guide.

➠ Hirsch I. How to get great diabetes care.

➠ Jovanic-Peterson L, Stone MB. Managing Your Gestational Diabetes: A Guide for You and Your Baby's Good Health.

➠ Lowe L. Arsham G. Diabetes: A Guide to Living Well.

➠ North J. Teenage diabetes.

➠ Sönksen P, Fox C, Judd S. Diabetes at your fingertips.

➠ Wysocki T. The ten keys to helping your child grow up with diabetes.

Index

First published in Great Britain in 2019 by Wren & Rook

ISBN: 978 1526361868

E-book ISBN: 978 1526361875

10 9 8 7 6 5 4 3

Wren & Rook
An imprint of
Hachette Children's Group
Part of Hodder & Stoughton
Carmelite House
50 Victoria Embankment
London EC4Y 0DZ

An Hachette UK Company
www.hachette.co.uk
www.hachettechildrens.co.uk

Medical Consultant: Dr Max Pemberton

Publishing Director: Debbie Foy
Senior Editor: Laura Horsley
Art Director: Laura Hambleton
Designed by Thy Bui

Printed in England

bryony gordon

YOU GOT THIS

wren
&rook

contents

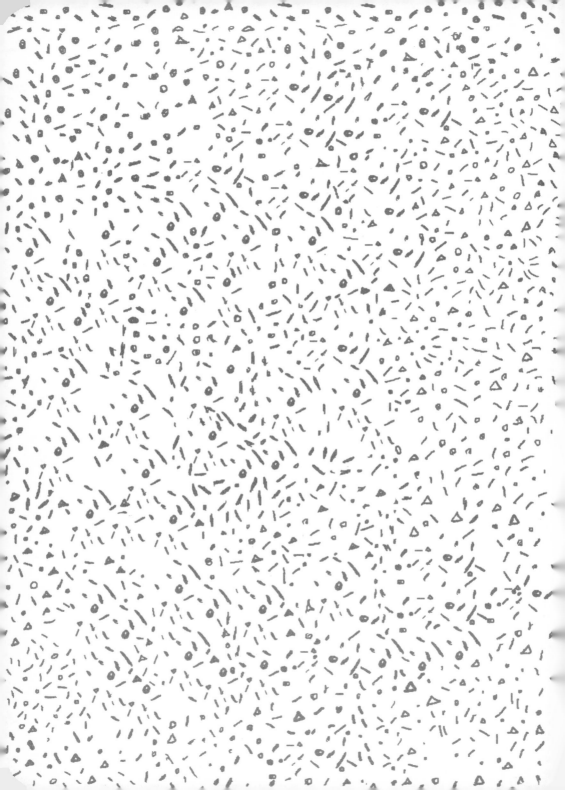

For Edie

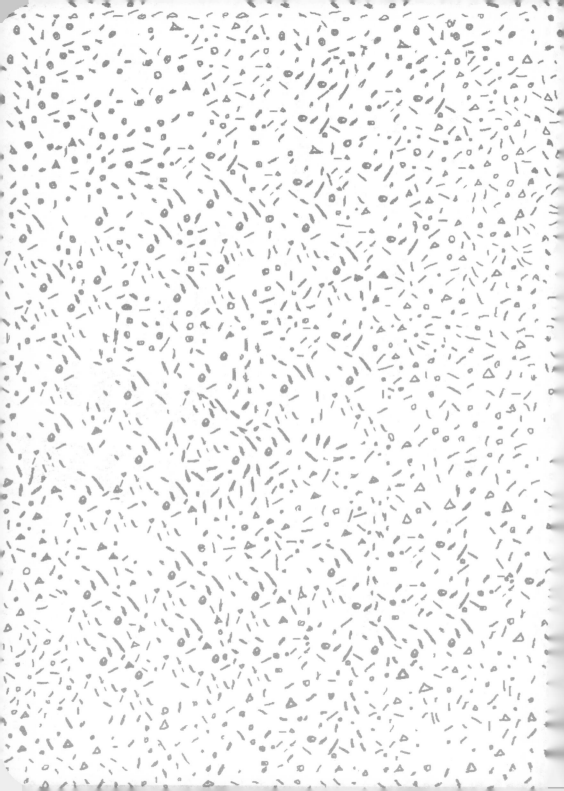

Introduction

What Do You Want To Be When You Grow Up?

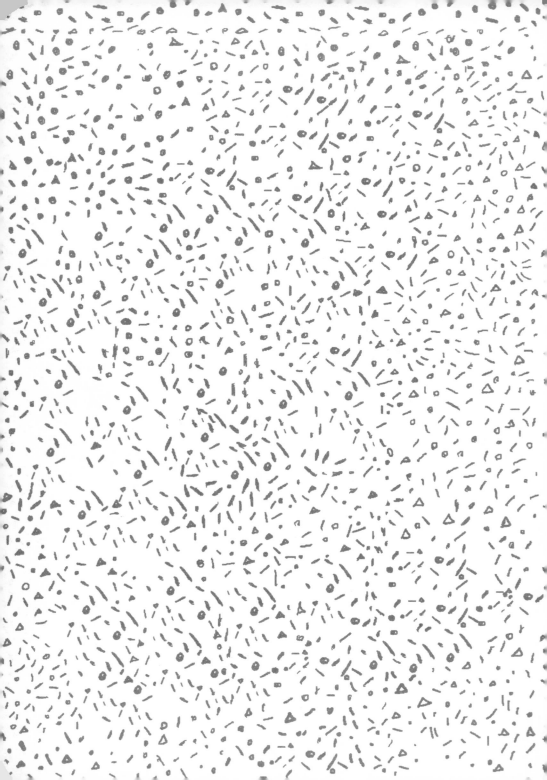

Hello, you.

Magnificent, marvellous, magical you.

Yes, you. You with all the insecurities. You with the head full of dreams that feel as if they will never ever be anything more than that.

You.

I have something to tell you, and I would like you to listen carefully.

Are you ready?

OK.

Here goes.

(You can imagine me clearing my throat right about now.)

You … are perfect.

You are brilliant.

You are neither too little, nor too much.

You are just right.

You are more than just right.

You are a total joy. You are glorious. You are great. You make me feel excited about the future. About all the possibility in your life. You make me want to be with you, just for a minute, to embrace you and let you know that everything is going to be OK. That everything is going to be better than OK, even if at times it might seem like the opposite is true. And I know this might be hard to believe, because when we are young – and actually, when we are old – we are not taught to see ourselves as everything we need to be. Instead, we are often told to pipe down, to be quiet, to watch out, to conform. We are asked silly, tedious questions, such as 'what do you want to be when you grow up?', as if you were a caterpillar waiting to turn into a beautiful butterfly and not a fully formed human trying to make their way in the world.

When I was young(er), I had plenty of answers to the question 'what do you want to be when you grow up?' – though almost all of them were designed to please the asker and then shut them up, so that I could get back to thinking about why I only had one eyebrow instead of two, and what exactly I was going to do about it. 'When I grow up,' I would confidently reply, 'I want to be a marine biologist/astronaut/lawyer/Arsenal player/ writer [delete as inappropriate].' I wanted to be all these things at once, if possible, so that people would gasp at my brilliance every time I walked into a room. But the thing I really wanted to be more than anything else? Well, I could answer that, immediately: I wanted to be a little less like me.

This yearning to be someone else was what fired me up on a daily basis. It was at the heart of almost everything I did. It was there as I desperately tried to make my handwriting look more like Isabel's in lower sixth (if only mine was as expressive and cool), and it was there every time I dyed the mousey roots of my hair (if only it was more like Madonna's). It was there every time I walked into a party I didn't think I was worthy of being invited to, wearing heels that made the balls of my feet burn and a dress that made my whole body feel painfully self-conscious (if only my hips didn't have that unsightly bump in them as they melded with my thunder thighs). It was there as I revised for exams (if only I was more clever like Alexandra who always won all the school prizes!) and it was there every time I was interviewed for a job or went on a date (if only I was more funny like Reese Witherspoon!). It was there every time I looked in the mirror. Why couldn't I be someone else, someone better, someone more glorious, someone like … I dunno, some imaginary female figure I had dreamt up with the help of toxic advertising billboards and Hollywood movies.

I wanted to unzip my scaly skin and slither into someone else's far smoother body; I wanted to have my brain replaced with one that wasn't so riddled with insecurities. This never struck me as anything out of the ordinary, because it wasn't. I just accepted it as the norm, one of those irritating facts of life, like mad parents and annoying siblings or people wanging on about Brexit. 'My name is Bryony, and I don't actually like myself' was not a particularly radical statement to be making, given that everybody around me seemed to be making it too. This was the cultural status quo: we were women, so we had been born with two X chromosomes, and into those two X chromosomes the DNA had been written that said we should always be yearning for someone else's DNA. I grew up in a world where nobody spoke about mental illness, where differences were disparaged rather than delighted in. Conformity was the thing that never, ever seemed to go out of fashion (unlike me). The media only ever really celebrated one type of body (thin), one type of skin (white), one type of sexuality (straight) and one type of emotion (happy). I could tick one of the boxes – my skin was white – but on the others, things were a little more complicated.

All around me people seemed to be putting themselves down, saying how much better their life would be if they could just lose five pounds, afford some new jeans and enjoy going to the gym. All around me were people who appeared to see compliments as the enemy – if one came near them, they had to set fire to it, then stamp on it and make sure it was dead. I would hear a girl compliment a friend on a dress, and this compliment would inevitably be beaten down, until it looked more like an insult. 'Oh, this old thing? It actually cost 50p at Primark and every time I wear it the sleeves dig into my sweaty armpits. It's a nightmare, really.' It never seemed to occur to anyone to just say 'thanks'. As a child I absorbed this, just as everybody else did. It was not the done thing to accept yourself as you were – if you did this, you were in danger of being perceived as arrogant, or up yourself, or self-obsessed. Instead, I had to aspire to be something other than myself. Aspiration was sold to me as a good thing – to aspire to something was positive, to want to be better was admirable. But the problem I always found was that aspiring to be something else often came at the expense of being myself.

Me, myself and I – we were not good enough. We were worse than not good enough – we were broken and in desperate need of fixing. Or at least, that was what I had come to believe. At 12, I developed a crippling form of Obsessive Compulsive Disorder that meant I washed my hands obsessively and felt unable to touch my family in case I gave them an incurable illness. I had to chant phrases to keep the people I loved alive. My head told me again and again I was the worst person in the world – it was like living with a jukebox in my brain that was stuck on one particularly hateful song. I would have done anything to change it. I fought hard against me – so hard that I made myself ill. I developed alopecia, and my hair began falling out in big patches. I started to vomit up my food in an attempt to change the way I looked. My early life was one long struggle against being me – and if my story sounds extreme, I should tell you now that it isn't. If I have learnt anything in the last few years, it is that my story is far from unusual.

Where did this desire to be someone else get me? Into all sorts of trouble, that's where. Entire oceans of trouble, filled with zillions of anxiety-inducing incidents I won't go into here because if I did your parents would almost certainly take this book off you and throw it onto a funeral pyre, before locking you away until you are 43. You are just going to have to trust me when I say that I was very, very badly behaved, until about … ooh, two years ago, when I wound up in rehab. Which I can categorically state was not somewhere I had planned to be when I grew up. Nope. This was not part of the plan when my well-meaning careers teacher asked me, aged 13, what I saw in my future.

Over the next three months of recovery I would discover that almost all of my problems in life stemmed from not wanting to be me when I grew up. Not wanting to be me when I grew up was at the heart of every dumb decision I ever made. I didn't want to be me so badly and I was fighting so hard with me, that I almost destroyed me.

But when I really sat down and thought about it, I realised that all of the things that I had ended up being celebrated for, all of the things that I had been truly successful in: well they were through being me. *Mad Girl*, a book in which I exposed my mental illness, had been a number one bestseller; I had been nominated for book awards for it, and I still get messages every day from people thanking me for it. Prince Harry had wanted to tell me about his mental health because I had been honest about my own – being me had, in the end, got me the biggest scoop of my career. Mental Health Mates, a walking group I set up that has now spread around the globe, had come from a desperate desire to just be me with other people who desperately wanted to just be them. And when, just 90 days after going into rehab, I was allowed out to be handed a Making A Difference award by Stephen Fry on behalf of the mental health charity Mind, I realised I was getting that award for being me. It took my breath away. All those decades trying desperately to be someone else, when all along being me was the thing that people most liked about me. Who knew?!

And in the end, it turned out that being me was much easier than not being me. It involved far less energy than trying to be someone else. Once you want to be yourself, I suddenly realised, all the other stuff – careers, relationships, monobrows – quickly get sorted.

As I curled up in that chair and sobbed, the counsellor asked me my age. It seemed to me a curious question. 'I'm 37,' I wept.

'No, I'm not asking you how old you are,' he said, gently. 'I'm asking how old you feel.'

Well that was very different. For a moment I stopped sobbing, and realised that on my left hand, I was rubbing my thumb with my index finger, something I used to do when I was feeling anxious as a child. The nail of my right thumb, meanwhile, rested at the front of my teeth, where I bit down on it – again something I had done when I was younger. And I realised then that I felt about 12. That, in my desperation to be something – anything – else when I grew up, I hadn't actually grown up at all. I had spent decades suspended in time, in many ways, refusing to nurture the stuff that made me … well, me. Now I wanted to race ahead and be fearlessly, unashamedly me.

And so, I find myself writing this book containing all the life lessons I wish someone had told me when I was younger, which I am only really learning now. I do not want to appear patronising or condescending, especially as I have made such a hash of being a grown-up over the years, and many of you could probably give me some pretty salient life advice (spoiler alert: most adults, your parents included, still don't know what they want to be when they grow up, and are basically making it all up as they go along, wondering when they're going to be found out – not least by you, their clever, wise offspring who seem so much more grown-up than they were at your age). And I know how irritating it can be when people try to give you advice on how to live your life. I know, because I was once a teenager too. This is really just my advice on how to live your life as you. And I'm writing it as much for me as I am for you – for the teenage girl in me, who needed someone to hold her hand and tell her she was just fine as she was.

For the teenage girl in all of us, who was never told that the most powerful thing she could be when she grew up was herself.

One

You Are Incomparable

Nothing compares to you.

Seriously, nothing.

I know that might be difficult to believe in a world that seems hell bent on lining you up against your friends and pointing out who has the best skin/hair/clothes/whatever, as if life were some sort of comparison parade. But it's true. Nothing compares to you, and nothing compares to your best friend, and nothing compares even to your worst enemy, I'm afraid. Nothing compares to *anyone*, truth be told. We are all completely unique, fully formed individuals, and to try and compare one person's individuality to another person's individuality is to undermine the very process that makes us so individual in the first place.

Let me tell you: the very fact you are here, right now, is absolutely miraculous. To discover just how true this is, you are going to have to think about your parents having sex. Yes, I know. It's gross. But if you can manage to dwell on it for even a minute or two, you will be rewarded with the knowledge of just how special you are.

I remember, when I was an adolescent, that I was forever being warned about the danger of teenage pregnancy: sometimes it seemed to me that I only had to look at a boy and I was at risk of getting up the duff. (This is no exaggeration. At the age of 12, I developed an obsessive and horrible paranoia that I had somehow become pregnant, having blanked out the event that had led to it. For months, I waited anxiously for my belly to grow and become hard – it never did, though instead of realising I was being ridiculous, I decided that I instead had another problem, namely that I had contracted something from the sexual encounter that never was. But that's a whole other book.)

Anyway, I was led to believe that becoming pregnant was inevitable, and that I must avoid looking at boys at all costs, at least until I was about 30. Later, when I was 30, I discovered through friends and much reading of the *Daily Mail* that getting pregnant was a little more complicated than that, and that later in life many people in fact find it quite hard. Indeed, the majority of couples trying for a baby have to wait over a year before they so much as set eyes on a positive pregnancy test; miscarriages, though not talked about, are surprisingly common.

I'm not suggesting for a minute that you go out there and have unprotected sex – indeed, I'm not suggesting for a minute that you go out there and have sex at all (believe me, there's plenty of time for that when you're older, and know what you want, and are able to vocalise it). And though some couples find it hard to conceive, some couples get pregnant the first and only time they have sex – there's absolutely no point in taking a risk to see which camp you fall into. All I'm saying is that you are a lot more extraordinary and magical then you have been led to believe. Because the likelihood of you existing, as you are, right now, is really, really tiny. It is so tiny that there is genuinely more chance of the dinosaurs being brought back to life, or England winning the World Cup. So tiny, that a couple of years ago a doctor called Ali Binazir came up with the odds of you existing as approximately one in $10^{2,685,000}$. That's 10 with 2,685,000 noughts after it. I mean, the chances of you existing are practically zero. You truly are one of a kind.

For a start, your parents have to meet. Then ... well, I have about as much interest in going into the details of 'then' as you do. If all has gone to plan, which we must assume it has, millions of your father's sperm are now hoping to make their way to your mother's egg – which, by the way, is only ready and waiting in the fallopian tube during a short window of each calendar month. Only one sperm can hit the jackpot, and to do this, it has to swim *upstream* (tiring), for the sperm equivalent of an Ironman (very tiring). Along the way, the woman's body is doing an incredible job of killing off the weakest sperm. Natural acids are released to put an end to the most pathetic sperm and then the ones that do get through the opening of the woman's cervix will have to navigate though a thick wall of mucous – this is a bit like you or me trying to punch our way into the next-door neighbour's house via the bedroom wall. Once the sperm has made it to the cervix, it has a choice of whether to take the left tube or the right tube. Only one tube will contain a mature egg each month and the egg, we must remember, is not there more often than it is. And because this egg is so damn rare, it is protected in the tube by a load of finger-like structures that push the egg down and the sperm back. There are also lots of white blood cells in front of the egg, protecting it like bouncers outside a nightclub. So, you see, the chances of you being conceived are really quite small. Had there been ever so slightly different conditions – your parents decided to get it on 30 seconds earlier, or later – a different sperm might have made it to the egg, and then you wouldn't exist. You would be someone else entirely. So sure, you didn't ask to be born – but the fact that you were is kind of cool, wouldn't you agree?

Something out there in the cosmos really, really wants you to be here. And it wants you to look exactly as you do.

Not like that reality TV star. Not like some Instagram influencer with zillions of followers. Not like your best friend, or a girl in the year above. It wants you to look like YOU.

Because you are perfect.

You have beaten all the odds.

You, my dear, are meant to be you.

top trumps:
your friendship group
edition

Imagine the scene: You are at your friend's house, idly scrolling through YouTube and Snapchat, when your mate suggests something really radical and old-fashioned: she suggests playing a game. A *parlour* game, as my granny used to call them, the kind your parents insist on after they've had one too many drinks at Christmas. A card game. Top Trumps to be precise. But not just any old version of Top Trumps – your friend has created a special version of this game. And what's special about it, what makes it stand out from the tedious 'parlour' games your parents seem so fond of when they are several sheets to the wind, is that *you guys are the cards!*

Yep, forget Top Trumps: the Harry Potter edition (an absolute classic, I am sure you will agree). Forget Top Trumps: the Candy Crush edition (I have checked and this actually does exist). Forget Top Trumps: Creatures of the Deep edition (my personal favourite). This … well this is Top Trumps: Your Friendship Group edition. Every girl in your gang has their own card on which they are marked in a number of categories:

- Hipness (based entirely on whether or not you have yet been allowed to get your ears pierced)

- Skin Quality (better hope you don't have acne)

- Social Media Influence (hope you've been accumulating those followers and managed some pretty impressive streaks on Snapchat)

- Your Netflix and Chillability (have you yet kissed anyone? Your gran's forehead does not count)

- Academic Power (Jesus, as well as all that, do I have to be top of the class *too*?)

- And finally, Make-up Bag (as in, do you even have one, and if so, how much glitter is in it?)

With a mixture of horror and curiosity, you decide to play the game. How bad can it be, after all? It's just a dumb card game, the kind of thing thousands of people play every day. And you're kind of interested to see how you score in all the categories because … well, because you're human.

Dealing out the cards, you are impressed that your friend has managed to create one for every girl in your class, and even some from other classes, too. This must have taken her *ages* to do. You get your cards into a neat pile, and you start to play. Oh my goodness, it is awful. It is worse than awful. It is *heinous*. It doesn't matter that you score highly on hipness on account of the fact you have your ears pierced – there is always one category, often more, where others get higher scores. Even the Queen Bee of your social group (for there is always one) loses out on the Academic Power category, because there's that absolute brain box in your year who is already being pitched as a candidate for Oxbridge. With shame coursing through your body and feelings of inferiority threatening to overwhelm your head (if there was a category for Douchebaggery, you are sure you would triumph in it), you carry on playing, but your heart isn't it. In truth, you'd rather be playing hopscotch on the M25. You'd rather be playing dollies with a three-year-old. You'd rather be playing *Assassin's Creed* with your loser of a brother. You'd rather be playing anything other than this awful, soul-destroying game of comparison with your friends.

The above scenario may seem far-fetched, but in truth we don't need our very own special edition of Top Trumps to play the game of comparison with our friends. We are doing it almost every waking minute. Look at her shoes, his bag, that girl's hair. Gawp at the holidays she gets to go on, compared to your week in a camper van in Cornwall. (Girlfriend: I am with you in that camper van. That was where I spent my childhood, and now adulthood with a child. It's not that bad, I promise. One day you might even come to like it.) Life is one big game of comparison for *all* of us, played out in our heads each and every day, often without us even realising we are doing it. This is a shame, a damn shame, because comparison is the thief of joy. You could quote me on that, but I didn't come up with it. Theodore Roosevelt, the 26th President of the United States of America, did. It's a pretty revolutionary quote, but unfortunately I didn't properly hear it until I was in my late thirties, by which point I had turned comparison into one of my specialist subjects, along with the early music of the Spice Girls.

I guess I didn't hear it over the deafening noise made by the cogs in my brain, as they whirred into action, frantically comparing elements of my body, mind and life to everyone else's. Here is a small (very small) selection of the things that I thought fit to compare on an almost daily basis during my teens. There are plenty more, but this book has a word count, and I don't want to use it all up in the first chapter.

my daily comparisons

❋ *The unruly eyebrows that made me look like Liam Gallagher with the beautifully shaped arches of Claire in English class.*

❋ *The giant birthmark on the top of my right thigh and the silvery stretch marks around it with the unblemished legs of women in magazines, whose legs appear unblemished in part due to computer wizardry.*

❋ The endless school reports
  stating I had 'potential' with
  everyone else's ability to excel at
  something, even if it is woodwork.

❋ My mousey hair and spotty skin
  with my younger sister's effortless
  ringlets and freckles, which made
  her look like Strawberry Shortcake,
  or some other similarly cute
  cartoon character.

❋ How fat Dr Martens boots made
  my legs look, with how thin they
  seemed to make everybody – and
  I mean **everybody** – else's look.

the comparison conspiracy

If you are prepared to look hard enough, you will always find yourself lacking. In fact, even if you are not prepared to look hard enough, you will find yourself lacking. That's because the world is often set up so that you find yourself lacking. It *wants* you to find yourself lacking. It wants you to compare yourself to others, because if you do this, you might buy the make-up and the clothes that they wear, or sign up to the lifestyle that they lead – and this is the way that most fashion and beauty businesses make lots of money.

The simple truth is that if we are happy in ourselves, and see everyone else as unique individuals doing their own thing rather than trying to be like the people we see online or in magazines or on billboards, we won't tend to spend hours of our time trying to copy their hair and make-up styles, or blow our pocket money on things we don't really want but feel we must have. We won't buy stuff to make ourselves feel complete, or in the hope that it will make us look acceptable to so-and-so. Buying stuff is not a bad thing, by the way. I love buying stuff every now and then. I have literally just this minute returned from buying: a gold skirt; a purple coat; some pink hair dye. But buying stuff because you think it's kind of cool, and because

you think you're kind of cool, and so *obviously* you and ⟨
are a match made in heaven ... well, that's one thing. Buying
stuff because everyone else has it and you will not be complete
or worthy until you have it too is something else entirely. It is
falling for the comparison conspiracy.

And this is something us girls tend to do more than boys. Take,
for example, my recent shopping list, and then compare it to
that of my husband.

Mine:

* Lipstick that I saw on Suki Waterhouse on Instagram

* More pink hair dye (I will never, ever grow up)

* Dry shampoo (why waste perfectly good time washing
  your hair when you could instead use it for an extra ten
  minutes in bed?)

* Carmex lip balm (you can never have too much Carmex
  lip balm)

* Some nice new stationery from Paperchase (so that I
  feel like I am fitting in even when I am working)

* Yoga mat (mostly for decoration in corner of living
  room, rather than for actual yoga)

* A mini cactus (because: mini cactuses)

My husband:

Some deodorant

That's it.

Which brings me to the most important part of the comparison conspiracy. No, not that it stinks and is in desperate need of some anti-perspirant. What I am actually talking about is its most fundamental purpose: to keep us sisters down. Roosevelt may have come up with the "thief of joy" quote, but he could never have known the full horror of comparison given that he was a man. I know blokes also get a bum deal nowadays and I don't want to turn this into some sort of comparison competition, as that would involve … well, comparison. All genders are welcome here: male, female, and everything in between. But I think it is important to acknowledge that for girls, the comparison conspiracy is particularly engrained, passed down from generation to generation in a way that has made it so normal, most of us barely even notice it is a thing.

In fact, women are constantly being pitted against each other: in the papers, in the news, on TV and online …

BLONDES VS BRUNETTES.

CURVY VS SKINNY.

Meghan vs Kate.

IS CARDI B THE NEW NICKI MINAJ?

Why skirts are in, and dresses are out.

Who wore it best?

My head hurts already …

And whether we like it or not, this has the effect of making us compete with one another in our everyday life. I think it's interesting that there is no real male equivalent to the film *Mean Girls*. I do not think this is because the female species is inherently bitchy and gossipy, while blokes are all chilled out and never see each other as a threat. I think it's because women have historically been *cast* as bitchy. We live in a patriarchal society, which means historically men have held primary power and authority in politics, business and the home. As a result, women have often felt undermined, undervalued and without a voice. We have felt that we have constantly had to vie for attention in what little room we have been given. The Sisterhood is stronger together, and yet due to the douchebaggery of a bunch of old dudes who have probably been dead for years, it is often kept apart.

This happens in all sort of ways, so that while we now accept that there is space for way more than one woman in a high-powered job, for example, this doesn't always get played out in reality. The first female presidential candidate was still beaten by a man who admitted to grabbing women by the genitalia. The Fawcett Society, which is a charity that campaigns for gender equality, found in 2018 – 100 years since women got the vote – that women still face obstacles at every stage of trying to get into parliament. After all, out of the 650 MPs currently sitting in the Houses of Parliament, only 208 are women. Outside Westminster, girls may beat boys in exams at school, but that is not always reflected in professional employment: almost 90 per cent of women work for companies that pay them less than their male colleagues. Women still have to fight twice as hard as men for success, and for the right to be treated humanely (I haven't even got into how sexual harassment in the workplace is predominantly a problem that females face). And this can often leave us feeling fearful that someone better is going to come along and take our place – which ultimately means we end up fighting and competing with one another. That is what is at the crux of comparison. That is what drives it. Because it makes us feel rubbish. Because it keeps us down.

But it's time to say scrap that – to strengthen our female bonds, pull other women up the ranks with us, and be happy in who we are. We need to remember that bitchiness is really only the result of centuries of being put down by men, in an effort to keep us in place. Because if we are all busy fighting each other, even if this fight is only in our heads and we would really rather not be having it at all, we don't have much energy left over to fight the real losers who threaten us: the patriarchy.

(Note: not all men are members of the patriarchy. Just the nasty ones with the kind of outdated views that would make even your grandparents' wince.)

All of this comparing and despairing is what many of us have been conditioned to do since early childhood by asking ourselves questions like who is the *best* behaved; who is your friend's *favourite*; who has done the *greatest* homework or handstand? And with social media, it's only got worse. The ability to size up who has the most followers and likes makes us all feel inadequate, like we aren't worthy of anything. (Stop that: you are.) It's like being a prey animal in the wilderness, constantly having to be on the lookout for predators. Except that the predator is not actually a predator at all. The predator has been conditioned to feel just as threatened by you, most likely. Believe it or not, the predator is actually your greatest ally. And by joining up with her, you – yes, YOU – can change the system for good.

There has never
been a better time to
be a girl, to rise up
and cast aside the
Instagram filters and
the false billboard
advertising, to stop
comparing yourselves,
and instead
start celebrating
yourselves.

You guys have the future in your glitter-painted hands.

But here's the really incredible thing about the comparison conspiracy, the thing that will blow your mind, and even better, blow the whole damn notion behind the comparison conspiracy apart. All along, people have been comparing themselves to *you*. Uh-uh. Don't shake your head and tell me I'm wrong. I'm perfectly happy to admit I've been wrong about many things during my years on this earth – my first boyfriend for example, and most of the ones that followed him – but on this, I will not back down. While you've been sitting there quietly but catastrophically listing all the ways in which you are inferior to your mates, those mates have been sitting there quietly but catastrophically listing all the ways in which they are inferior to you. Oh yes, they have.

I know this to be true because I have spent most of my life comparing myself to other people and finding myself lacking – and then, when my book *Mad Girl* came out, I received about a million messages (well, 10 or 15) from old school friends telling me that they couldn't believe that I felt like that, because they had always thought *I* was the cool one who had it all together. Me, cool and all together? I mean, I grew up with a crippling mental illness that made me wash my hands until they bled and silvery marks all over my boobs which seemed to have grown too soon, but sure, I was cool and had it all together. Hahaha. Hahahahahahaha.

Unbeknownst to us, we had all been sitting there writing ourselves off against each other, playing that imaginary game of Top Trumps with each other, when all along we were each individually great as we were. If we'd just opened up about our insecurities, we would have discovered that we were not alone in them, and in discovering we were not alone in them, we might have paused and questioned why it was so normal for us to feel so inadequate. We might have discovered that the grass is *not* greener on the other side. We might have realised that it is greener where you water it. And then we might have watered our own grass, instead of using all our valuable, life-giving H^{2}0 on someone else's.

set yourself free

So, how do you escape the comparison conspiracy? You do it by ...

Realising there is nothing to compare in the first place.

Listen to me when I say: exam grades, social media followers and items of clothing are not real reflections of your brilliance as a human being. They are passing, fleeting ... they are things you will barely think about or remember in the years to come. Yes, one of your mates might regularly get more likes on Instagram, and yes, someone in your class might be a whizz at maths while you struggle to do quadratic equations. But I can tell you now that I have never ever had to do a quadratic equation as an adult. And what do social media likes matter, if in real life you have deep, close friendships that you treasure with people you enjoy spending time with? Just one of those friendships is worth a zillion likes – it will be there for you when times get tough, and stand by you when the chips are down.

Remembering that nobody is better than anybody else.

You are just as valid and important a human being as Michelle Obama or Meghan Markle or Selena Gomez. Always, always keep in mind that you have things other people want. In fact, I am here to tell you that you have something that Michelle Obama, Meghan Markle and Selena Gomez want – which is the ability to go out with your friends and not be stalked by weirdos and the paparazzi. See, Selena Gomez is jealous of you. Yes, you.

Focusing on what you do have, rather than what you don't.

It could be: your health; a roof over your head; an ability to remain calm when all around you people are losing their heads; an awesome friend; a sibling you actually get on with; a teacher you can talk to; the book in your hands right now.

Taking negatives, and turning them into positives.

You may hate your curly hair, but there are people who long for curly hair and spend hundreds of pounds on curling tongs to get the look you have naturally – and by people, I mean me. If you hate being short, remember that the tall girl in your class would kill to be your height (she feels gangly); if you hate being tall, remember that the short girl in your class would kill to be your height (she feels dumpy).

Playing the gratefuls.

If you've got to play a game, play a game I concocted with my daughter called 'The Gratefuls'. Every night before bed we list three things we are grateful for from our day, no matter how bad that day has been. You'd be surprised how much lightness you can find in the dark.

Taking compliments.

Do not turn them into insults. Simply smile, say thank you, and move on.

Being proud of your achievements, however small they might seem to be.

Sometimes, just getting out of bed in the morning is a reason to pat yourself on the back. Don't take the things you have done well at, and then squash them under the suffocating weight of all the things you have failed at. Don't, once you have managed to get yourself out of bed, beat yourself up for not doing it sooner. That is pointless and harmful to your self-esteem. And your self-esteem is everything – it is the thing that will make you feel good about yourself even when your parents are behaving like dictators and your best friend is being basic and ghosting you on WhatsApp. (This. Has. Happened. To. All. Of. Us.)

Remembering that a little bit of self-doubt is healthy.

It keeps us in check and holds us accountable to ourselves. What is *not* healthy is when the doubt takes over and invades everything, like the emotional equivalent of the 'Baby Shark' – then it is really something more like self-loathing. (And please don't hate me for putting that song in your head. You have my permission to briefly put down this book and listen to your favourite playlist in order to cleanse your soul of any lingering Doo-Doo-Doo-Do-Do-Dos.) Anyway, the goal is not to be rid of self-doubt – it is accepting that, like the 'Baby Shark' song, it will sometimes get stuck in your head, just as it does to absolutely everyone. Don't nurture it, so that it's the only thing that you can hear. Use it to your advantage – let it propel you forward to those better songs in your playlist, that are *way* more fun to listen to.

Instead of aspiring to be like someone else, trying to be **inspired** by them.

When you aspire to be like someone, you can be so bowled over by them that you forget the good bits of yourself. But if you are inspired by them, you can take the quality you admire and then find it in yourself. The difference is small, but crucial.

Trying not to talk in bests and favourites when discussing people.

I know this is hard, because the concept of a best friend is one we are brought up with. And it is, of course, lovely to have a best friend, a favourite friend – one of the most wonderful feelings in the world. The problem is, it sort of implies that some people are better than others, which isn't true. (I know, I know. There's a really nasty person in your class and it is really stretching the realms of possibility to say that you and your mates aren't better than them – and when I say 'really stretching', I mean right into the kind of dark realms that can only be found in episodes of *Stranger Things*. But I promise you this person has goodness in them, somewhere.)

When I was at school, it felt like I was permanently moving up and down the friendship charts – these were, and probably still are, like a particularly brutal version of the iTunes charts. Being replaced as a best friend made me feel like I wasn't good enough. But I was – and you are, too. All this change in chart position really means is that, for the time being at least, someone feels their personality is better matched to another person's. You haven't done anything wrong. It is entirely the other person's problem, not yours.

Thinking of yourself as a delicious chocolate.

Just because somebody can't eat you anymore, it doesn't mean that you are no longer delicious – it just means that maybe they've got a diagnosis of diabetes, or for whatever reason, they are denying themselves sugar. Who wants to be friends with someone who denies themselves sugar *anyway*?! This person sounds like they're experiencing a total fun famine. You, meanwhile, are still a delicious chocolate.

Accepting yourself in all your strange, peculiar glory.

Do not edit yourself. Do not make yourself smaller, larger, quieter or louder. Be you. Do not hide your light, or try to turn it into something like a floodlight when it is more of a bedside lamp. Remember both serve very important, but different, purposes, and both are sorely needed. You cannot read in bed without a lamp. You can't watch Taylor Swift without a floodlight. Both reading and Taylor Swift are awesome – just in different ways.

Remember that perfection does not exist. Every human is flawed. The most perfect human is the one who learns to embrace those flaws.

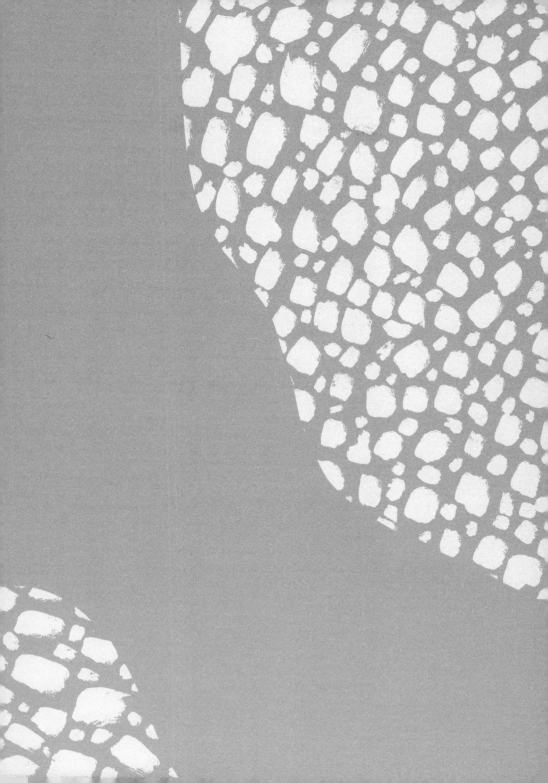

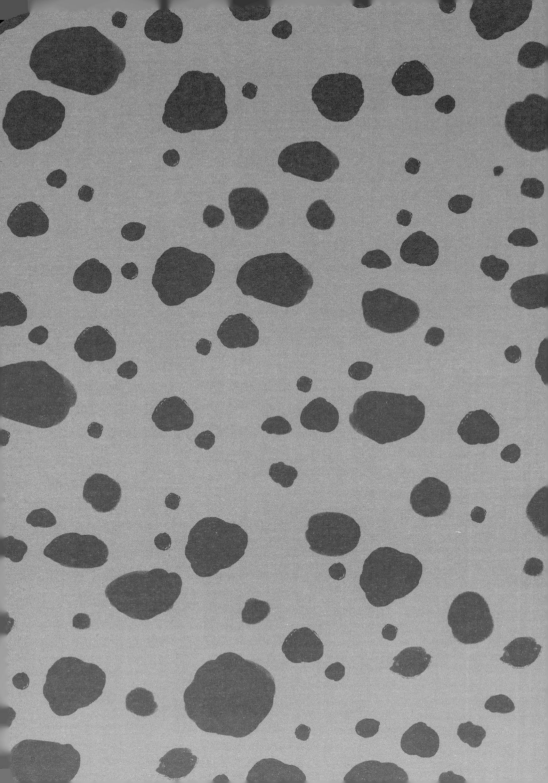

Two

You Are Changing. That's Cool. Go With It

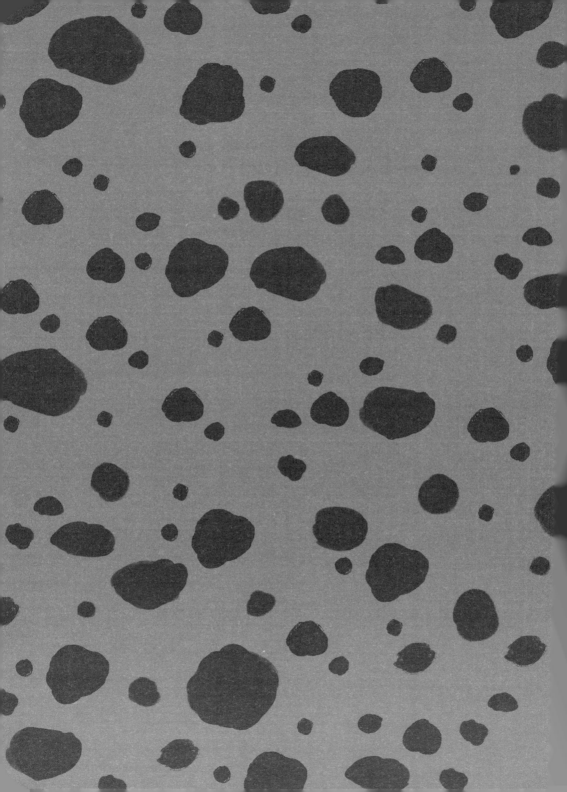

The hormones, when they come, can feel like an ambush.

One minute, life is all fairy lights and loveliness, the next it's ARR
RRRRRRRRRRRRRRRRRRRRRRGGGGGGGGGGGHHHHHHHHHHHH
HHHHHHHHHH.

I mean, really.
ARRRRRGGGHHHHHHHHHHHHHHHHHHHH.

And just for good measure: $%^&*£%^^^^^^^^^^!

Who touched my freaking fairy lights? (I have written 'freaking',
when you know as well as I do that I wanted to write something
far, far ruder.)

Why is everyone always messing with my fairy lights?

CAN YOU NOT ALL JUST LEAVE ME AND MY FAIRY LIGHTS THE
HELL ALONE?

The joys of puberty! You spend what feels like the whole of your
childhood wanting to be an adult – thinking wistfully about
buying your first bra, and being able to nod in sympathy with
your girlfriends when one of them mentions period pains –
and then BAM! Suddenly you are bleeding every month, your

breasts feel like they're punch bags, and your mood can go from chilled to ABSOLUTELY FURIOUS within about 60 seconds. What's that all about? Even the word 'puberty' is enough to make you cringe. Why couldn't they have called it something else, something like … I dunno, FunTimery? Sure, it would have absolutely no bearing on the process that takes place, but it might stop everyone wincing whenever a teacher or parent pipes up about it, as they seem to do on an almost daily basis, as if were a topic of casual conversation like the weather. The whole process is stressful enough as it is, but they had to go and make it *sound* mortifying, like a curly hair sprouting out of somewhere it clearly shouldn't be sprouting. Puberty is about as appealing a word to say as 'panties', or 'moist'. And how can we even begin to feel positive about it when just the word itself makes you want to vomit?

I was not ready for puberty. Then again, who is? You can read all the guidebooks in the world but it still comes as something of a shock when it is actually taking place. Puberty just seems to happen, over night. It has no set start date. And this is part of what makes it so anxiety inducing – there is every possibility that you and your friends could go through it months and months apart, so that you can't even hold each other's hands as your hormones take hold. It's a bit like waiting to see if your name is drawn for the Hunger Games, only instead of having a doom-laden fixed date for when it might happen that you can at least try and prepare for, you are aware that it could occur at any given moment, from when you are eating lunch in the canteen to swimming with your mates at the local pool.

And then, to add an extra layer of stress on to proceedings, your parents act as if this whole thing is *your* fault, as if you have *asked* to feel like a moody, sweaty, misery box with a hairy top lip. I mean, what is the evolutionary point of giving you – a girl – a moustache? Is it to provide you with something to twiddle with, a sort of hairy version of a fidget spinner?

When I went through puberty, I was perhaps different to many girls in that I refused to acknowledge what was happening to me. The whole concept of it was simply too mindboggling for me to even comprehend. And it wasn't hard to maintain an eyes wide shut approach to adolescence, because it wasn't as if anyone else was rushing to explain it to me. Admittedly my mother did like to tell me I was going through puberty all the time – I couldn't do anything from the age of 11 without her interpreting it as the work of my hormones. 'Oh look, Bryony's slammed her bedroom door, she must be going through puberty,' she would say, or 'Oh look, Bryony is eating chocolate, she must be going through puberty.' I couldn't *breathe* without her telling me it was a sign I was going through puberty. I suppose this might have been bearable if she had actually bothered to explain what it entailed, other than me being 'difficult'. Still, I suspect that even with Google at my fingertips to provide me with information, I would have felt alone – because puberty can make you feel like you're the only person in the world going through this stuff even if you've sat through all the stunningly awkward sex ed classes at school. You become Peter Parker after he was bitten by a radioactive spider, except your superpowers seem to include the ability to feel really, really stressed out about the slightest thing, and thinking that you smell a little bit gross.

In our house, this sense of awkward isolation meant that it felt as if I was forever being told off for being 'difficult'. And I suppose I was 'difficult' – but no more than the average teenager being pulled along by a sudden tsunami of hormones. Puberty can be 'difficult' – and sometimes, the reactions of the people around us can make it seem damn near impossible. Even today, my mum and dad will sometimes refer to my childhood in two parts: pre-puberty and post-puberty. The first part a delightful dream of an experience and the second a complete nightmare. I know what they are *trying* to say. They're trying to say that adolescence can make things a little complicated for parents (why is it always about them?). Yet what I still hear is that I somehow did it wrong, that I went into my chrysalis and when I emerged I wasn't the beautiful butterfly that they had been expecting. Instead, I was a moth.

But let me tell you something: moths are pretty cool too. Sturdier. Drawn to light. Have good taste in clothes (if the state of some of the moth-eaten frocks in my wardrobe is anything to go by). It's OK to be a moth, really it is. In fact, take it from this moth: I think I'm having a way better time than those butterflies who have to go to sleep when the sun goes down. BORING!

I don't have a magic wand that will help you go through this whole thing promptly and painlessly. And even if I did, I am not sure I would wave it – because puberty is not something to be waved away or sped up. It is something precious that needs to be handled as such – it is a time when you should treat yourself like the Queen that you are. It's an opportunity for self-care, an excuse to look after yourself. You might wonder how any of the things that are happening to you could in anyway be described as 'special'. And I get that. But puberty is a bit like like tidying a bedroom. At some point it's going to have to happen, whether you like it or not – and fighting against it is only going to make it a hell of a lot harder. So let's breakdown the process, and make it a whole lot less scary for you.

the main event: blood

Your periods are the biggest thing when it comes to puberty – the main event – so let's talk about them, and let's not be afraid to talk about them LOUDLY. Because even though roughly half of the population will have them, we are still expected to whisper about menstruation, or not speak of it at all, as if it were something to be ashamed of and not an integral biological process which forms the very basis of life.

Recently, I went into a branch of a popular high-street pharmacy to buy some tampons. I searched the aisles for these most vital of products, only to find them hidden at the back of the store in a section that had been delicately named 'monthly care', presumably because the phrase 'period' or 'products to help manage bleeding from the vagina' were deemed too upsetting for the men coming in to buy the Viagra advertised extravagantly in the window (I mean, talk about *priorities*).

And these euphemisms aren't just in pharmacies. They're everywhere. How many times have you heard your menstrual cycle referred to as …

THE
BLOB

Shark Week

The painters
being in

A VISIT FROM
AUNT FLO

CODE RED

Flying the
red flag

And my absolute favourite:

Surfing the
Crimson Wave

I mean, who comes up with this stuff?

Sure, I can see *why* our periods are sometimes referred to in this gross euphemistic way – because the emotional and physical pain that sometimes comes as part and parcel of a period can seem like a great injustice bestowed on you for simply having been born a girl. But I don't think any of us, female *or* male, are helped by these silly hush-hush references to a totally mind-blowing natural process without which none of us would exist. Instead, we should be celebrating our periods and all the amazing things the female body is capable of achieving.

After all, we bleed approximately five days a month but still manage to …

▶ Run marathons

▶ And countries

▶ And major companies

▶ Climb mountains

▶ Play football

▶ And just about everything else, actually

It might also seem unfair to you that boys don't get periods – but we don't have penises to contend with, which I imagine can be quite unwieldy. I've heard about wet dreams, and they don't sound fun, or in any way life-affirming. And I dare you to say the following to a boy: 'Imagine if bloody bits of your body fell out of you once every 28 days!' Wait for their face to cloud over with fear. They cannot even DEAL with the idea. And do you know what? Their lives are poorer for it. That's because periods make us strong.

Periods give us lion hearts.

The idea that they somehow make us weak or flaky is not just insulting – it's untrue. There's a particularly ridiculous episode of *South Park* in which a schoolteacher announces that he never trusts anything that bleeds for five days and doesn't die – but us girls know that if something doesn't kill us, it'll only make us stronger.

Oh yes.

period myths and truths

So while we're reclaiming periods, let's also bust some myths and celebrate some truths about our cycles:

There will be blood.

Before I had a period, I somehow managed to form the impression that I would end up weeing blood every month. I suppose it's difficult to demonstrate exactly what happens, which probably explains why, until recently, a clear blue liquid was used to represent menstrual blood in adverts for sanitary products. With depictions like that, it's no wonder I didn't have a clue what was going to happen to me. At school, the information was similarly random. I remember being told that I'd lose two teaspoons of blood every month – as if menstruation was a lovely afternoon round at your gran's with scones and jam. But as it turned out, this wasn't quite true. I didn't produce two teaspoons of liquid that looked blue – it varied from month to month. Everybody's 'flow' is different and some months there is lots of blood, so much so that you will actually feel it coming out of you. Nice, huh. And then sometimes there will be so little that you might wonder if you have actually had a period. To make matters even more confusing, you can also miss periods due to stress –

a throwback to the dark ages when your body would protect you from reproducing if times were difficult. So while we are now unlikely to encounter Vikings and savages on our travels, our periods can be influenced by other stressful situations like exams, relationships and schoolwork.

Accidents will happen.

I remember going on a half-term holiday to Yorkshire, staying in a cottage that had soft furnishings so chintzy and elaborate that I felt I was going to ruin them simply by sitting on them. And guess what? I did! Standing up after a long game of Monopoly one afternoon, I realised I had leaked through onto the cushions. I was absolutely mortified.

But really, this happens all the time. I'm a woman, I bleed – and sometimes I accidentally bleed on my chair. In fact, it seems to happen to me at least twice a year, *still*, despite having had my period now for a quarter of a century. You'd think I'd learn, but bodies have … well, minds of their own, and sometimes there is just no predicting a period so heavy that your bathroom ends up looking like a crime scene. I have leaked onto clothes several times, having to tie jumpers around my waist in an attempt at concealment, and I used to sneak my bed sheets down to the wash and put them on a 90-degree cycle to hide the stains.

But there are times when you simply *can't* hide the blood, and feeling humiliated by it is not going to help you.

Bleeding is something that happens to all of us. It's a thing that biologically has to happen, so let it happen, and if sometimes it happens a bit more than you would like it to, know that there is absolutely nothing to be ashamed of.

I am making it sound scary again – but I promise you, it's fine. You will live to fight another day, and learn not to wear white jeans or a pale denim skirt when you are on your period. Period.

Tampons are not terrifying.

Due to the popularity of myths and legends, you may have heard that you can lose your virginity to a tampon (not true), catch a deadly disease from it (Toxic Shock Syndrome is a thing, but an exceptionally rare thing), or lose one in your body (no, your vagina may be a thing of boundless beauty, but it is not an endless canal).

Tampons are your friends. Not literally, of course (that would be disturbing). What I mean is that they are there to help you and they are much easier to insert than you think. When you first try using them, start with 'regular' or 'lite' applicator tampons to make the process super easy (you'll notice that for some reason, most tampon manufacturers cannot spell the word 'light'). It's a bit like learning to ride a bike, only much easier, and with less possibility of grazing your knees.

Once you're finished, don't flush any part of a tampon down the loo – always dispose of in a sanitary bin. Flushing tampons might seem like the easiest thing to do – but the applicators will always bob back up the surface of the toilet (awkward, especially if you end up having to fish it back out of the loo to dispose of it), and everything that does make it down the pipes ends up in the ocean. Meaning that, inadvertently at least, just by trying to dispose of a sanitary product, we can be harming the planet we live on (it is super-tough gig, being a girl). So either wrap used tampons and towels in toilet paper to throw in the bin, or carry sanitary disposal bags in your rucksack to make life easier.

And do not be embarrassed if those sanitary disposal bags, or any tampons, roll out of your rucksack. You are a female. You have periods. Anyone who sniggers at that really needs to grow the hell up.

You have choices. So many choices!

If men got periods, there would be a whole world of gadgets out there to help get them through that time of the month. Jeremy Clarkson would present a prime-time show testing the products out and entire magazines would be dedicated to the nifty devices blokes had come up with to soak up the blood. There's no way that humanity would have put a man on the moon and invented the iPhone, while some boxes of sanitary pads and tampons hidden at the back of the chemist are the height of technology when it comes to menstruation.

Thankfully, though, times are changing. We are becoming less squeamish about periods and women are feeling more empowered, realising that menstruating is part of life and not a 'curse'. This means that companies are upping their game, using their imaginations, and coming up with an increasing number of alternatives to pads and tampons. You can now buy pants called Thinx that actually absorb the blood – you just chuck 'em in the washing machine at the end of the day and go about your business without worrying that you are destroying the planet with single-use plastic pollution simply because you were born female. Revolutionary, huh?

Then there are Mooncups, which have been about for a while. Oh, how we howled with laughter when adverts for these started appearing on the back of toilet doors up and down the country in the early noughties. Mooncups! Really! They sounded like the kind of thing a fairy had to insert into your vagina – thanks, but no thanks. Yet as we become more aware of issues like pollution, waste and the cost of having to buy sanitary products every month, they have actually become very popular. You simply insert the Mooncup and empty it when it's full. You can keep reusing them each month and they even go in the dishwasher – just make sure your mum and dad don't mistake it for a measuring cup and put it away in one of the kitchen cupboards.

You are perfectly entitled to fight for the right to menstruate in peace.

The Pink Protest, a group of awesome activists committed to ending period poverty experienced by girls and women who cannot afford menstruation products, was founded by a group of young women in their twenties. Scarlett Curtis, Grace Campbell, Honey Ross and Alice Skinner wanted to create a community that would empower other girls to use feminism as a way of gaining peace of mind about their bodies, and so the Pink Protest was born. Some of their work has been alongside Amika George, who founded the #FreePeriods movement that campaigns for free menstrual products for schoolgirls from low-income families, and change has been happening! Scottish schools now offer free sanitary products to students and English schools will follow soon. Then there's Gabby Edlin, who created the charity Bloody Good Period to provide refugees and asylum seekers with sanitary protection. And this is all the work of young women who are paving the way for change.

You don't have to set up a national campaign, but if you find that the facilities in your school are lacking – the sanitary bins are gross, for example, or don't actually exist at all – then you are perfectly within your right to shout about it. Find an understanding teacher and express your concerns or speak to your friends or parents about it. They'll get it. In 2017, there was a global outcry when a school in New Zealand refused to let a ten-year-old girl who had started her periods back into the building unless her parents donated a sanitary bin for her to use in the toilets. Furthermore, they actually suggested that her mum and dad put her on the contraceptive pill so she could 'manage' her periods. And as I was writing this book, it was reported that an 11-year-old in Bristol had been refused access to the toilet by a male teacher during lessons, and subsequently bled through her clothes. This is why we all benefit from talking about periods loudly, rather than in a hushed voice – because it destroys the idea that periods are shameful. Periods are not bad. They are something to be proud of, a rite of passage as you kick ass from a girl into a woman.

Periods can be something to look forward to!

Don't laugh. It's *true*! I know, I know, periods are meant to be difficult. The narrative that surrounds them is one of misery and suffering. There's the rollercoaster of emotions that is pre-menstrual syndrome, and I haven't even got on to the cramps. You never hear anyone talking about what a wonderful period they are having – but perhaps we should try and do this more often. Reframe the way you see periods, so that they feel like something to celebrate rather than endure. This doesn't mean ignoring the cramps and the crabbiness. It just means taking time out to appreciate and treat yourself as they happen – have a bath, lock yourself in your room reading, enjoy the fact you can legitimately refuse to talk to your parents (just grunt 'I'm on my period' at them), that kind of thing. There are also heaps and heaps of period subscription boxes out there, some as cheap as a box of tampons in Boots, that will arrive each month containing sanitary protection and treats.

'That time of the month' can be a euphemism for the time when you totally get to bliss out and look after yourself.

You can respect your hormones.

For most of my life, I have written off genuine feelings of anger and sadness as 'just my hormones'. This anger and sadness was real and happening – and yet I discounted my feelings because they happened to be happening at the same time that my period was due. For a woman, 'being hormonal' is basically code for everyone to discount how that woman is feeling because it is not convenient for the rest of the world.

Well sod THAT.

Look, hormones are not just anything. Hormones are powerful chemical messengers that control most of your major bodily functions. To write off the specifically female ones is completely daft. It's not just daft: it's essentially discounting the way a woman might feel for an average of three months of each year – for that is roughly how long you will be dealing with PMS and periods. If you find that you are having hormonal rages, don't fret. This is perfectly normal – you are, after all, having to get to grips with some of the most powerful chemicals known to womankind, and that takes some wrestling with. So no, you are not 'just' being hormonal. You are being human. You are being you. You have every right to feel angry, or sad, or any other emotion. And it's about time everyone stopped ignoring those emotions 'just' because you happen to be female.

Your menstrual cycle is an opportunity to listen to your body.

To track your body's natural cycle try a period app like Glow: I downloaded this for free and it's great for reminding me of when my PMS is going to hit so that I can plan to up my self-care during that time. For you this might mean avoiding hanging out with a friend who is particularly spiky or gossipy; or it might mean explaining to your mum that for a couple of days, you are going to be hanging in your room having 'you' time, and that she shouldn't worry about that.

Eat what you feel your body needs. If you feel like pigging out in the days running up to your period, then pig the hell out! The world won't spin off its axis. You don't have to feel guilty. Just see it as the trade off for PMS and cramps. As in 'I have to bleed once a month for up to a week, so don't mind me if I prepare myself with this giant tub of ice cream. Got a problem with it? Then why don't YOU try having my period for me!' Don't be hard on yourself.

Buy a punch bag or go for a run. Sometimes you might experience yourself feeling a fit of rage for no reason and this is basically your mind's way of processing this massive thing that is happening to you. I know someone who bought boxing gloves and pads to help her channel this.

Respect your body. It knows what it is doing, even if at times it might seem like it's *completely* malfunctioning. Think of the 'hormonal' events as something similar to the frustration you felt when you were learning to tie your shoelaces or play an instrument. It's all a bit higgledy-piggledy at first, but eventually your body will get the hang of things.

the supporting acts: hair, skin and smell

If you think of puberty as the Glastonbury Festival, then your menstrual cycle is Beyoncé, headlining the Pyramid Stage, having first been warmed up by a ton of supporting acts, all making a hell of a lot of noise and vying for your attention on other stages: the growth of body hair; the beginnings of body odour; the development of super oily skin and in some cases, acne. Of course, if you dream of going to Glastonbury, it might be difficult to equate the trial that is puberty to the world's most famous music festival. But if, like me, you are horrified by the thought of camping, mud, and not being able to use proper toilets for five days, then you will totally get this metaphor. Because, much like Glastonbury, puberty sometimes feels like something you've just got to get through. (When you are older, remind me to tell you my Glastonbury story. It involves, in no particular order: a lot of cider, a Winnebago, viral conjunctivitis.)

The big supporting acts, the ones that seemed to feature heavily in my very own festival of puberty, are detailed here.

skin

When you're really little you don't think much about your skin. It's there to be grazed, bruised or covered in plasters and transfers moonlighting as tattoos. But other than that, its sole purpose is to protect your insides from the outside.

As you become a teenager, you will probably suddenly become very conscious of your skin. It gets greasy and spotty. It can feel like every bit of bacteria in the northern hemisphere has invited itself to a party taking place on your face, as if your skin were some sort of reception venue, and not … well, the thing that everybody looks at the whole time. I used to squeeze my spots (PLEASE DON'T DO THIS), and when I wasn't squeezing them I was spending any spare money on potions and lotions that promised to get rid of them. In fact, they just made my skin tingle and burn and become red and inflamed.

But here's the thing: nobody is paying the slightest bit of attention to what's happening on your face. The way we perceive things is very different to the way other people perceive them.

So, you may think:

My skin looks like the moon

While everyone else thinks:

Absolutely nothing. (They're too busy worrying about their own skin.)

That spot party on your face is *literally* only going on in your own head, while everyone else is trying to quieten down the party that is going on in theirs. Also, try to remember that your spots look big because you are looking at them in a mirror that is approximately 2mm away from your face – and absolutely *nobody* else is. Even if somebody does notice a spot on your face, I can guarantee you that within fractions of a second, they will have started thinking about something else. Like the spot coming up on *their* face.

Of course, spots can be sore, irritating and knock your confidence, but seeing as they are already taking up space on your face, do you really want them to also take up space in your brain?

Here are some of my tips for owning spots, instead of letting them own you:

▶ *Leave your skin the hell alone. Do not prod it with something that looked as if it was last used in the Middle Ages to lance boils, and don't pick at it with your hands.*

▶ *Don't use harsh scrubs with chemicals that you could probably strip paint with.*

▶ *I would avoid peels, or anything that contains ingredients you might use to poison a mortal enemy with. Face masks are fine. Face masks are fun. What is not is anything that includes the word 'dermabrasion'.*

▶ *Remember that you have perfect skin. It is there, all over your body, doing what it is supposed to. Most celebrities and influencers have been filtered so that they appear not to have pores. But they do. If they didn't have pores, their skin would simultaneously dry out and then puff up like a grotesque water balloon, because pores both lubricate the skin and allow it to sweat so we can regulate our temperatures. Pores may not please fashion and magazine editors or people with trillions of Instagram followers. But without them, all those people would basically be dead.*

▶ *Skin is **supposed** to be bumpy, lumpy and textured. That's its **job**. And there is not a single spot that has lasted forever. Yes, acne can scar. But believe me, everyone is too busy focusing on their own perfectly imperfect flaws to notice yours. We all have things about our bodies that we don't like, but don't let those things define you.*

body odour

What's that smell? It's you. It really is. I hate to be the one to break it to you, but … all human beings can smell a bit weird. It's one of the few downsides of growing up – other than having to pay bills – and even some grown-ups don't see it as a downside. *Some* grown-ups like it. Honestly, I once had a boyfriend who preferred it when I didn't wash. Reader, he didn't last long.

I remember, when I was 12, being quite sure that the odour I could permanently smell was coming from someone else, because previously I had only noticed this pungent aroma on me after I walked past a kebab shop. But lo, like with many teenagers going through puberty, it was me developing BO. At first I was horrified. But now I realise that EVERY. SINGLE. PERSON. ON. THE. PLANET. SMELLS.

Once again, my perception of my body as a teenager was very different to everyone else's.

So while I was thinking:

> **OH MY GOD I STINK, I'M GROSS, I WANT TO DOUSE MYSELF IN BOTTLES OF MY MUM'S PERFUME**

My friends were thinking:

> **OH MY GOD, I STINK, I'M GROSS, AND HANG ON, WHY DOES BRYONY SMELL LIKE SHE'S JUST BATHED IN CHANEL NO. 5?**

This one's a brief supporting act, that is easily improved:

* *Body odour is caused by bacteria on the skin breaking down sweat and is largely linked to the apocrine glands in the groin and armpits – which means these parts of your body can start to smell more than, say, your leg. So, wash yourself with anti-bacterial soap and clean your clothes regularly. Be sure that you are removing the smell, and not just masking it (this is a rookie error that most people make at first)*

* *Invest in some deodorant that you apply every day*

* *And, er, that's it!*

hair

Our bodies are completely covered in hair. That's right girls, even your body, right now. And though this is mostly very fine hair, as you get older it will become thicker on your armpits, legs and your pubic area. This is really normal. There are about a million evolutionary reasons why pubic hair and armpit hair exist: to protect us from dirt, and for cooling and insulation purposes, and so on and so on. There is only one reason why you should get rid of it: apparently, it doesn't look 'sexy' … because obviously, this is the most important thing in the world. (Insert eye-rolling emoji here.) Now, I do shave my armpits and legs – like many women – but I feel really strongly that nobody should feel embarrassed by what the universe has given them, and that you shouldn't feel you have to remove every bit of hair on your body that isn't on your head.

I'm not an expert on hair removal – but what I do know is that almost all of it involves pain and irritation. Shaving can lead to you accidentally hacking bits of your ankle off. Lasering is apparently a thing, but I'm not so sure my armpit hair is such a problem that I need to employ the same techniques to deal with it that Darth Vader uses when he fancies destroying a planet. Leave hair removal cream on for too long, and your skin will thank you by burning wildly and leaving you with angry red welts. Waxing is a whole world of pain that I do not want to get involved with – I've had to give birth, and that was quite enough for me. Other things to be mindful of are: ingrown hairs; regrowth; the ridiculous expense involved.

My view on hair removal is that it should not take up more of your headspace or time than, say, deciding what you're going to watch on Netflix this weekend. I briefly pluck my eyebrows every few days, Veet off my moustache when it has reached Mario levels of lavishness, shave my legs and armpits every few days in the shower, and live by the motto that if you love me, then you can love my bush, too. I don't worry about offending anyone when I go for a swim, because what are they doing looking at my inner thighs anyway? Honestly. The state of some people!

the playlist of puberty

(Curated by me, in an attempt to make this whole thing seem a little less gross.)

For when you get your period:

'BAD BLOOD'
by Taylor Swift

'BLEEDING LOVE'
by Leona Lewis

For when you are suddenly experiencing feelings down there:

'I TOUCH MYSELF'
by Divinyls

'TEENAGE DREAM'
by Katy Perry

For when you start to smell weird and sprout strange hair and your skin seems to be covered in spots:

'SMELLS LIKE TEEN SPIRIT'
by Nirvana

'TEENAGE DIRTBAG'
by Wheatus
(the Girls Aloud version is also ace)

'FLUORESCENT ADOLESCENT'
by Arctic Monkeys

Three

You Are A Person With Wants And Needs. Don't Be Ashamed Of Them!

Like most people, I discovered masturbation before I even knew what masturbation was.

I was 11 years old and the world seemed a dull, dull place. My sister, who was two years younger than me, always wanted me to play Sylvanian Families – this despite the fact that when I agreed, I would visit an earthquake on her sweet, Sylvanian village. Whereas once we had been great friends, happily pulling each other's hair and stealing each other's toys, now I felt I had outgrown her. What did she think I was? Some sort of child? Yep, these were the dull days, just before my mother announced the vomit-inducing news that she was pregnant with our baby brother – which seemed to me to be the equivalent of shouting to the world that

SHE HAD RECENTLY HAD SEX WITH MY DAD, URGHHHH.

For now, my only real sources of excitement came from discussing New Kids on the Block and *The Simpsons* with my best friend Katie.

And having my first sexual awakening while swimming at the local leisure centre, obviously.

I mean, I didn't *know* at the time that what I was actually doing was making myself orgasm. As I think we've established by now, I didn't know anything about my body, other than that it existed. It sometimes seems to me to be a minor miracle that, sent out into the world in a state of such ignorance, I managed to make myself orgasm at all. But as Jeff Goldblum so eloquently puts it in *Jurassic Park* (a classic of my teenage years): life finds a way. Life *always* finds a way.

(This would probably be a good place for my mum and dad to stop reading, if indeed they actually made the mistake of starting in the first place.)

So there we were on our weekly excursion to the local pool, the local pool being, in suburban London circa 1991, about the only place to go other than Laser Quest at the Trocadero, which was *way* too expensive. This was what passed for 'family' time Chez Gordon – a trip to Brentford Fountain Leisure Centre, followed by a ten-pence pack of Walker's Salt & Shake (look it up). No phones to fiddle on, no selfies to take, no Snapchat streaks to start, no 3D movies to go and watch. Just us, and a slightly decrepit, dirty leisure centre that only occasionally bothered to turn on its slides and wave machine.

I remember, one day, moping in the pool on the edge, feeling terribly put out by the lack of glamour and glitz in my boring, 11-year-old life. I imagined my friends, doing exciting things together that I hadn't been invited to … visiting Chessington World of Adventures, perhaps, or if they were really lucky, Thorpe Park. I thought about the girls in my class who had already been allowed to have their ears pierced, and the fact that Amy Brown was pretty enough to snag the cutest boy in class, Sam Sharland … not that I would admit he was cute. I thought about how unfair it was that I wasn't allowed on my Gameboy for longer than half an hour a day – and then I accidentally passed over a jet, and I stopped thinking about anything at all.

Unbeknownst to me, my life changed that afternoon at Brentford Fountain Leisure Centre. In one accidental move, I discovered something incredible: and that was the power to feel blissfully ecstatic, hidden somewhere near my noo-noo. I had never felt anything like it before: not playing my Gameboy, not eating ice cream, not trying the delicious fries that were being sold by this new fangled fast-food restaurant called Burger King. Suddenly, our weekly visits to Brentford Fountain Leisure Centre didn't seem so bad after all.

I would sit there on the jet, minding my own business, letting the world go by as I inhabited my own, infinitely more pleasurable one. It makes me blush now to think of myself

masturbating in a public swimming bath, something which would surely get me arrested today. But back then I had nothing more than an inkling that what I was doing was naughty. I honestly thought nobody would notice. To the casual passer-by, I was just a young girl looking a little catatonic at the local swimming pool on a Sunday afternoon. Nothing to see here, people! But secretly, I was exploring what seemed like the most miraculous way to pass the time.

After a while, I discovered that I could create the same feeling in the privacy of my own bedroom, by lying on my front and putting my hand between my legs. How glorious life could be! I decided that whatever it was I had discovered, I was going to try and do it as much as possible. Sometimes this was easy, while other times I had to be clever about it. One weekend we went to stay with family friends, and while everyone went for a walk, I stayed behind so that I could masturbate furiously on the floor of the guest bathroom, with the door locked.

Reader, it was wonderful.

Until, suddenly, it wasn't.

shame dies when it is exposed to light

I can't pinpoint the exact moment that I started to see what I was doing as shameful. Probably it was when I went through puberty proper, and started to feel completely at odds with my body. All I know is that it would be about another 25 years before I masturbated in such a liberated way again (though I'd never be so liberated that I did it in public, you will be glad to hear), during which time I thought all manner of terrible, harmful, untrue things about myself.

I thought I was a bit of a pervert. Sometimes, I wondered if my relentless quest for orgasms made me somehow evil. Sure, it was normal for boys to always be seeking pleasure. But girls? From the music videos and movies I watched, and the magazine features I secretly read, it seemed that our one purpose was to *provide* that pleasure.

I WAS SO, SO WRONG.

I was, like most teenagers, preoccupied with seeming normal and fitting in. I wanted to be the good girl, the compliant one, the person that everybody liked. But at the same time, I felt as if I had this secret life – one where, when the lights went

out, I would lie in my bedroom trying to give myself multiple orgasms, like some sort of Primark porn star. My friends and I would giggle about snogging at school, this act we had heard about but most of us had never actually done, but giggling about snogging seemed pretty innocent compared to the filthy thoughts that went through my head every time I found myself alone in my room. My family weren't religious, but if they had been, I probably would have taken myself to the local Catholic church and confessed all my sins: the fantasises that seemed to involve licking and touching and and and ... well, *everything* really. I was so ashamed of these thoughts. I was so ashamed of *myself*.

I felt like I was carrying a terrible secret around, a burden. I felt shame when I thought about Jordan Knight from New Kids on the Block, and all the things I wanted to do to him. I felt shame when I thought about Jordan Knight from New Kids on the Block, and all the things I wanted him to do to *me*. I felt shame that sometimes I would think about women and boobs, and that I once sneaked a copy of the *Sun* into my room where I touched myself looking at a Page 3 girl. I felt so much shame, I thought somedays I might explode with it.

And as I got older, I carried this shame with me like an invisible 'friend' – or, more realistically, an invisible enemy. Wherever I went, there it was, taunting me, tormenting me, *making me feel*

like a bad person, so that I would do anything to appear good. Even things I didn't really *want* to do.

Sadly I felt shame that I was only having sex with myself, so when I was 16, I had sex with an older boy who was a total douchebag, on the floor of his sitting room, with the Olympics opening ceremony on in the background. Later, I confided in a friend, who told a friend, and pretty soon everyone knew. And because I was not deemed cool enough, he told everyone I was lying.

I felt shame then, and for a long time afterwards – I doubted everything I knew about sex, which really wasn't very much: just how to make myself orgasm, but crucially, not how to make anyone *else* orgasm. And as I navigated my way through my teenage years, all that mattered to me was my ability to give other people pleasure, so much so that I never, ever thought about what gave me pleasure, unless I was alone in my own room.

I also felt shame when, in my late teens, I fooled around with a female friend one night. I wasn't sure that was what I was supposed to do. And I didn't understand what it meant. Did this mean I was a lesbian? But I was sure I liked boys! Maybe I was just obsessed with sex?

And so, I soon developed a technique that involved hiding all my shames by burying them under new shames and fear. As coping mechanisms go, it wasn't very successful. But eventually, after decades of it, I realised I had to shake myself free of the shame and stop being so hard on myself. I came to see that shame was the most toxic of emotions, the thing that keeps us all isolated and alone. I knew that if I didn't rid myself of shame, I would never truly be myself.

Like a vampire, or a Gremlin, shame dies when you expose it to the light. It blisters and pops and withers and expires, destroyed by the beautiful brightness of being, never to be seen again.

a masturbation marathon

If only I could tell that to 11-year-old me, about to embark on her orgasmathon. 'Dude! Do not be ashamed of something perfectly normal!' I would shout. 'Because that's what masturbation is – as normal and healthy as a big old super food salad! You're not hurting anybody! You're not a serial killer! Kick that shame into the long grass, and then masturbate in it to your heart's content! Then again, perhaps keep it to the privacy of your own bedroom, as opposed to public swimming pools …'

Masturbation is nothing to feel guilty about. It's super fun, and relaxing, and an awesome way to get to know your body! Also, everybody does it. I mean, *everybody*. Even the people who say they don't. They're only saying that because, like me back in my adolescence, they're embarrassed about it. And sure, being embarrassed by masturbation is a totally normal reaction to have when you are a teenager, or about to become one. But you don't need to carry that embarrassment around, and wear it like a rucksack. You can let the embarrassment go, and masturbate happily without feeling like a freak. You might not want to discuss the act of pleasuring yourself with your mates – I get that – but don't feel bad while you are actually going about the act.

There is no right or wrong way to masturbate – all that matters is the attitude you have as you go about it. Because with a positive approach, masturbation can actually be really helpful, and empowering. It can be a vital life tool, even. If you are able to own your feelings and desires, you will be able to communicate them better when you are older. So when you start messing around with boys (or girls, or perhaps even both), you will be able to tell them what you want. But most importantly, you will be able to tell them what you *don't* want. You won't end up consenting to things you don't actually like the sound of, as I sometimes did. You will be confident enough in your own mind (and body) to say no, not that, not now, not ever. And if the person you are saying no to refuses to take no for an answer, then you can call the police on their grotesque, criminal arse, knowing that you have done absolutely nothing wrong, and that you have absolutely nothing to feel ashamed about.

It's only as I have become a mental health advocate – and found myself talking to heaps and heaps of people about heaps and heaps of deeply personal things – that I have come to realise that everything I felt sexually was perfectly normal. That exploring your sexuality *is* perfectly normal, as long as it is legal. That I didn't need to feel shame. That I am not the only person who sometimes masturbates furiously – I'm just another

person who sometimes masturbates furiously (and wishes now that they could masturbate *more* furiously, but finds they can't due to all the demands on their time). That desire and want is not just normal – it is actually essential for the survival of the human race. (How else would we end up reproducing?) Without it, the majority of us wouldn't exist at all.

So the next time you start to feel shame because you have a funny feeling down there, remember that this is simply your body doing its biological thing. It is absolutely **nothing** to be embarrassed about.

So here are the other things I would like to tell 11-year-old me as she embarked on her masturbation marathon, and began to experience the surreal twilight world of sexual and romantic feelings ...

Crushes can be overwhelming.

Desire isn't something you can just switch off at a moment's notice. Is it any wonder that when we first experience them, it can feel as if our world has changed completely – like in *The Wizard of Oz*, when everything goes from black and white to glorious technicolour? Except that just like in *The Wizard of Oz*, with its bright green witches and flying monkeys, this glorious technicolour can sometimes feel frightening, too, as if nothing will ever be the same again.

I remember my first proper crush, on a boy called Dominic, and how very, very important and transformational it felt at the time. It seemed inconceivable to me that I would ever feel the way I felt about Dominic about anyone else again. I simply couldn't imagine it. And I'm not going to undermine your first crush by telling you that you absolutely *will* feel that way about someone else again and again and again, or by admitting that I still get crushes on people *to this day*. Your feelings are not any less valid just because you happen to be experiencing them for the first time. I am not going to tell you how to feel – and know now that you must never, ever let anyone else do this to you. (If someone tells you how you should be feeling, do feel free to ask

who made them director and cast you in their movie, and how much they are planning to pay you.) So instead what I am going to do is advise you to sit with this weird new sensation, shove on a guided meditation on an app like Calm, and tell yourself that you are in charge of this crush, as opposed to this crush being in charge of you.

Nobody else's pleasure is worth sacrificing yours.

When I first started hanging out with boys, in a non-forced-to-sit-next-to-each-other-in-class way, I almost permanently felt like I was on some sort of runaway train that had pulled out of the station and could not be stopped. I mean, I definitely wanted to do all that kissing and touching, but I wasn't sure I wanted to do them at the pace we were going. I wanted to be able to look up the train timetable, and work out the best moment for me to board. And for some reason I didn't feel I could say any of this. Once I got on, would there be an emergency switch so I could hop back off again?

But listen, in this day and age, with health and safety regulations and what-not, there is *always* an emergency off switch. Always, always. Any person who refuses to engage it is not someone you should be riding on a train with. If something doesn't feel right, then at that moment, it is wrong for you – and that's not just OK, it is absolutely awesome. You are not wrong to feel this way. You are not wrong to feel any way. You wouldn't dream of letting your parents tell you how to feel

about something, so why should it be any different with a friend or potential love interest? This is advice you can apply to every area of your life, not just romantic and sexual relationships – choosing which subjects to study at GCSE, for example. So often, we are told about the power of saying 'yes' to everything, of grabbing the bull by the horns and embracing life in all the ways it presents itself to you. But there is power in saying 'no', too. Real power. Listening to your gut instinct, and then going with it, will always be the right thing for you to do. If you don't want to kiss someone, or fool around with them, or send them a picture that you'd really rather not take, then don't. And if that person doesn't respect that, then maybe you shouldn't be giving any of your respect to *them*.

Know that you do not have to rush into anything, but if you do, that's OK too.

It just makes you one of the billions of people who have been overcome with that incredibly powerful, evolutionarily essential emotional desire. So don't feel dirty, or bad, or wrong. You are not 'easy', or any of those other gross descriptions applied to girls but never to boys. But you do need to go easy on yourself.

You are earthly, and lovely, and following your feelings.

Bodies are really, really funny. All bodies. Every body.

We all fart, burp, make strange sounds, let off peculiar smells. Life is nothing like a porn clip – thank *God*. You may, when you are older, watch porn, and that is nothing to be ashamed of. But don't use it as a blueprint for matters of an intimate nature, any more than you would use an *Avengers* film as a blueprint for trying to achieve world peace. The point is, it's not real. You are. And your realness is what makes you so glorious.

Nobody else can ever shame you, no matter how hard they try.

When I think back to the experience I had after I lost my virginity, I don't feel shame any more. I just feel sad that I ever felt shame in the first place. I wish I had been kind to myself, instead of allowing this boy's toxic mentality to poison my own brain, making me feel both mad and bad.

I wish I had known that when people try to shame you, what they are really trying to do is make *themselves* feel better. That gossip is just a way of deflecting their own issues that make them feel uncomfortable. If someone is being nasty about you, it's usually just a twisted way of being less nasty about themselves. This doesn't make being publicly shamed any less painful, but it does give you the power to deal with that pain. It allows you to own the shame, and to voice how you feel about it. And once you have taken ownership of the shame, it no longer has ownership of you. The moment you stop trying to hide it and ignore it is the moment it stops eating away at you.

Because shame cannot live in the open.

And shame, my darling girl, is no match for your sass.

Four

You Are A Miracle

You are a miracle.

A total, bloody miracle.

No, really, it's true. There may be more than seven and a half billion people on the planet, but only one of them is you. Even if you happen to be an identical twin, you are still a distinct person in yourself – you have your own brain and think independently of your sibling. And the very fact that you exist? Well, as I explained in the very first chapter, with that mortifying drill down into the time your parents conceived you, that is a miracle in itself.

But there are other miracles too, like your living, functioning body, the one that has taken you from that moment in the fallopian tubes to right now, reading this book. I mean, *woah*. Woah. Just think about that for a moment, because truly, it is mind-blowing. And while we take the skin we live in for granted, our skin in itself is incredible. Each square inch of it contains about 650 sweat glands, 36 heat sensors and more than 1,000 nerve endings. We are each made up of around 100 trillion cells, all of which started from one, back when your father's sperm won the jackpot and melded with your mother's egg. Our heart beats about 100,000 times a day and over 35 million times a year; it will pump approximately 2,000 gallons of blood through your body over a 24-hour period. Your lungs allow you to take around 25,000 breaths a day, without even thinking. Our eyes can take in more information than the largest telescope known to man. Your stomach will create a new lining every four days. Right now, your liver and kidneys are doing a pretty good job of cleaning your blood. And even when we feel like rubbish because we have come down with a fever, that fever is there in order to burn up the viruses and bacteria that put us in danger. A fever is your body's way of telling you to get some rest. Awesome, right? And every night your body rebuilds and repairs itself through sleep, which also serves to improve our memory and synthesise hormones.

Your body is incredible.

Your body is not to die for – it is to live for.

Your body is an absolute miracle.

So, shall we start celebrating it, instead of trying to find things that are wrong with it?

Of course, it can be hard to love your body especially when it's changing so much. I was what was termed an 'early developer'. Even writing those words now has made me shudder involuntarily. I hate that term, just as I am sure some people loathe the term 'late developer'. Why does nobody ever seem to develop at the right time? And what *is* the right time, exactly? It certainly wasn't in the last year of primary school, when all I really cared about was playing my Gameboy. (A Gameboy was a sort of prehistoric version of a smartphone, without any of the smartphone capabilities. So not really a smart phone at all. It was a not-so-little console on which you could play games like Tetris and Zelda and Super Mario Bros and … um, that's about it really. It blew my tiny, pre-social-media mind.) But I digress. I remember the absolute horror of my changing body during the last year of primary school. It appeared to be rebelling against me. I suddenly smelled different. The nipples on my chest expanded. All that stopped me from screaming 'I DON'T KNOW WHAT IS HAPPENING TO ME' was the fear that, like the boys in my class, my voice was going to drop down several octaves. And sex education was absolutely terrible, in fact, it was worse than terrible, because it was non-existent. *And* we had no internet, which meant we couldn't even Google what was happening to us. We were just expected to keep quiet and ride it out, in

the hope that it would soon stop, and we could all get back to beating Bowser on our Gameboys.

So, given that I was never taught about my body, you won't be surprised when I tell you that nobody ever taught me to appreciate my body. Honestly, it was like living in the Middle Ages. They hadn't even invented the Spice Girls yet. If we learned anything about our bodies, then it was to dislike them. I suspect the same might be true for you, even now with the invention of smartphones and social media. In fact, *especially* now with the invention of smartphones and social media. I'm not saying that a teacher has stood up in front of you in a classroom and said, 'Morning, girls. Just to let you know that today we will be learning about the four processes of erosion, the themes of social advancement in *Great Expectations*, and the most efficient ways to tear yourself apart through self-loathing.' Or at least I hope not. No. You are taught to question your body by the filters that exist on your smartphone, to make you look 'better', even though you are perfect just as you are. You have been taught to question your body by simply existing and living in a world where television shows and adverts and movies show us varying versions of the same, perfect woman: slim, pretty, mostly white. The problem is that there are many kinds of women on the planet, and while the slim, pretty, mostly white one is perfectly valid, so are all the others, who don't get as much representation in the mainstream media. The result of this is that if you don't happen to be a slim, pretty, mostly white

human, you don't feel like you fit in. And even if you *are* a slim, pretty, mostly white woman, the chances are you won't think you are slim or pretty enough.

I spend quite a lot of my time being asked to appear at events about body confidence, largely because I am large(r) and – quite radically it would seem – do not appear to be overly bothered by my size. (Believe me when I say that it took a *long* time to get to this place of self-acceptance.) I ran the London Marathon in my underwear and I post pictures on Instagram of myself in my underwear without filters. Indeed, I think I would genuinely be much happier if I could wander around in my underwear – it's when you try and doll me up in a tight dress and a sky-high pair of heels that I begin to feel self-conscious. For this, I am often described by people as 'brave', as if I am going into Syria and single-handedly fighting ISIS, rather than simply accepting myself as I am. When I did the marathon, it amazed me how many women ran up to me and told me how much they admired what I was doing, because they hated their bodies – their bodies they were running 26.2 miles with, by the way. I mean, *hello*. Your body is doing an incredible thing and *still* you want to put a downer on it? Enough already!

I get it, of course. For most of my life I would rather have gone out in a pantomime cow costume than show the world any of my flesh. I suffered with bulimia, an eating disorder in which I alternately starved myself, then binged and purged. It was

a miserable existence of vomit, pain and eventually adult acne. Initially, throwing up my meals seemed really, really smart, because it meant I got to eat food without ever properly digesting it. I now know this is not true at all – in fact, with bulimia, you are more likely to absorb the calories of the food you have eaten than the nutrients. And then there were the burst blood vessels on my face, and the spots. I could not see the untold damage to my insides. In my twenties, I lost a tooth because all the stomach acid in my mouth was wearing away at my enamel. And yet still, I could never be too slim. Slim was the wondercure I had been sold and I would stop at nothing to get it – not even the systematic wearing down of my body, and my mind. The quest for a perfection that did not even exist haunted me for every step of my teens and twenties. Obviously this is no way to live your life – in fact, it can be an exceptionally damaging way to live your life. I thought I was ugly and grotesque, though I now see I was neither of those things. In fact, I was quite lovely. Scrap that – I *am* quite lovely.

And so are you.

Every time I appear on one of these body confidence panels, I hope it will be my last. Not because I dislike preaching body positivity to people – but because I dislike the fact I still *need* to preach body positivity to people. Sometimes, it can feel as if it is a rite of passage to find all the things you don't like about your body, and then set about on a loveless lifetime quest to fix these

things that are perfectly fine as they are. The thought of actually *liking* your body, the thing that keeps you alive and flourishing … well that is absolutely revolutionary, apparently.

I am here to tell you it shouldn't be. I am here to tell you that liking your body is one of the loveliest things you can do for yourself.

social media - argh!!

Of course, while I grew up with airbrushed images in magazines, what I didn't have was the ability to airbrush myself. When I appeared in photos, I looked like me. I had lumps, bumps and textures. The camera truly didn't lie. But now – well now we don't even have to look at real pictures of ourselves. We can filter and Photoshop to our heart's content, until we end up looking like avatars. We can watch make-up tutorials that will help us to shade and highlight our faces until they literally don't look anything like our faces – until they look like one-dimensional magazine ads, devoid of pores or spots or lines or any of the things that make us human.

My question to you is: *WHAT'S SO WRONG WITH THE REAL VERSION OF YOURSELF?* You may be able to list to me a zillion things, but I'm going to throw them back to you.

WORRIED ABOUT SILVERY STRETCH MARKS? Don't be – they are proof that your body is growing, as it should be when you are young. (The opposite of growing is … well, dying.)

NOT TOO FOND OF YOUR NOSE? Well you'd be in a real pickle if you didn't have it.

UPSET ABOUT THE SHAPE OF YOUR ARMS OR LEGS? Just think how amazing your limbs are to dance around with, and eat with.

DON'T LIKE YOUR THIGHS? Remember, you wouldn't be able to walk without them. Which would kind of suck.

Remember that most of the images you see are also not real, even if at first they appear to be. People like Kim Kardashian have filtered all the humanity out of themselves by the time their photos have been uploaded onto Instagram. Some of the images you see there and in magazines are no more real than Japanese Manga cartoons. They are computer-generated versions of the people they purport to be. And you may say to me, 'But what about the Victoria's Secret models on the runway? *They're* real.' And yeah, they are. But I was once flown to New York to report on that show, complete with backstage access, and let me tell you – these girls were not leading lives any of us would recognise. In the weeks and months leading up to the show, they had been on the kind of strenuous exercise regime that would make an Olympian blush. So yeah, they're real ... but they're by no means *normal*. Snapping a selfie and wondering why you don't look like Gigi Hadid is like going out for a run and wondering why you weren't as fast as Usain Bolt.

Trying to look like someone else is a pointless exercise and a total waste of your time. Trying to make yourself thinner, curvier, smoother, brighter – at the end of it all, if there even is an end to it all, you will still look like you. And if you don't like you, it will never, ever be good enough. There will always be something else you need to do, some other diet you need to go on, some procedure you have to save up for. And for what, exactly? For a ridiculous ideal presented in the media that nobody will ever attain, not even the idealised people being presented in the media, because they have been idealised by way of a ton of Photoshopping and airbrushing.

And if pictures of models and glamour girls make you feel bad, then stop looking at them. This can be hard, but in terms of social media, you can take matters into your own hands.

Unfollow anyone whose feed makes you feel 'less than'; choose people who are unapologetically themselves. And if you can, take regular social media breaks and tune in to the real world, where you will see real people in all their varied glory.

disordered eating

I hope that if you're reading this book, you love your body already, whatever size, shape or blemishes it may have, and that you feel confident just the way you are. I hope you know that your worth is not defined by some numbers on a set of scales. And I hope you can see that your value does not live and die according to the smoothness of your skin, the perkiness of your boobs, the fullness of your lips. The way you look is predetermined by that impossibly random genetic process that I have tried my best to explain at the beginning of this book: it really doesn't have any bearing on how successful you are going to be as a human, given that you have had nothing to do with it. It might sound unbearably cheesy (remember, I like cheese), but you really are perfect just the way you are.

It can be really hard to break free from feelings of negativity about your body, partly because they are so engrained in our society, and partly because one of the first ways we learn to exert control over things is by refusing to eat food. Think about it. Look at any toddler, spitting out their broccoli, refusing their peas, throwing some fish fingers on the floor. They are not just showing their distaste at the meal they have been given: they are trying to create some authority in a world that gives them none. From the very beginning, one of the easiest ways to exert some self-control is by not putting food in our mouths. And so, it's no wonder that when we are older, and feeling sad or depressed or frustrated – or perhaps all three – not putting food in our mouths can also seem like an effective way to take back control – even if, actually, the very opposite is true. Even with all the work I have done on myself, I still know that if I am feeling really low, then it can first manifest itself in the way I feel about my body. If I catch myself staring in the mirror and analysing, I know that I have to pull myself back and take a look at whatever it is that might be stressing me out in life. It's usually not my weight at all. It's usually something else entirely.

I wish someone had also told me how hard it is to untangle yourself from an unhealthy relationship with food. Remember that there are no 'good' or 'bad' foods; just that some foods when eaten excessively are unhealthy.

You are eating one slice of cake, not cyanide, so there's no need to give yourself a hard time about it. Cake is brilliant. Cake is lovely. Without it, the world would be a poorer place. So enjoy that cake. Revel in it. Truly, it is not going to kill you.

And if you find that you are bingeing on food or – at the opposite end of the spectrum – restricting it, try to talk to someone about how you feel … and how that bingeing or starving *makes* you feel. That person could be a friend, a doctor, a trusted teacher or maybe even your mum (I bet you she knows *exactly* what you are talking about). Remember that eating past the point of comfort, or being too scared to eat at all, does not make you a bad person. It just makes you a person – one who has been brought up with the same weird lessons about food as everybody else.

your wonderful, miraculous body

I'm going to jot down for you a few of the things I wish I had been told way back when – little things you can remind yourself of whenever you feel doubts creep in about your wonderful, miraculous body. Indeed, if you only read these tips and then go no further in the book, I will be happy with that (though be warned that you will totally miss all the fun bits).

- You are not obliged to find something you dislike about your body.

- And you should not feel guilty if there is something you like.

- If anybody uses the term 'puppy fat' in front of you, feel free to file them in a folder marked 'douchebag'. I do wish this phrase had never been invented, and that grown-ups would quit using it. To have your body compared to that of a dog is neither cute nor comforting. It has all the subtlety of a wrecking ball – and at a time when you are probably feeling a teensy bit sensitive due to all the changes going on. Your body is not something to grow out of. You do not have to lose bits of you to matter. I am here to tell you that right now, whatever your shape or size, YOU MATTER!

- If someone doesn't like the way you look, if someone tells you that you need to lose weight, then the thing you have to do is lose the weight of them. You are perfect and brilliant just as you are. No diet or cosmetic surgery will improve you, because there is nothing to improve on.

- Try not to put a filter on a selfie. When you add a touch of Clarendon or Amaro to your pictures, you are only doing yourself a disservice. You are setting yourself up so that every single picture you see of yourself will make you wince, as opposed to just the 1 in every 20.

- Look at different body types. It really helps on the quest to self-acceptance. In 2018 there was an almighty hoo-ha over the decision by *Cosmopolitan* magazine to put the plus-size model Tess Holliday on its cover. Tess is a size 26, and the usual crowd of old fogeys were up in arms, wanging on about how using overweight models was just as bad as using underweight ones, because it promoted obesity. I waded into the row on Twitter (always something of a risk) and received a message from a woman telling me that she would be just as appalled if her daughter said she wanted to look like Tess Holliday as if she had told her she wanted to look like Kate Moss. I explained that the whole point of putting people like Tess Holliday on magazine covers, and making other body types visible, was so that her daughter didn't want to look like anyone. It was so that her daughter grew up wanting to look like herself. Remember this. The best person you should want to look like is you, and seeing a variety of shapes, sizes and skin tones in your social media feeds will help you immeasurably in your journey to get to that place.

Smile. It's miserable how few people smile in pictures nowadays. I remember when I was a teenager, everybody gently ribbed Victoria Beckham for her permanent pout. But she was the exception, not the rule. Now *nobody* smiles in photos, because apparently smiling gives you lines and you look more like a model if your eyes are hollow and your mouth is half open like a fish. Can we please bring back smiling? When I see someone on Instagram with a grin on their face it is a sweet, sweet balm for my soul. Here's a tip: If someone points a camera in your face and it doesn't make you smile, maybe don't let them take your picture.

- Don't wait until you are older to see how beautiful you are now.

- Try not to use 'you look like you've lost weight' as a compliment. It feeds into the notion that a person's worth is found only in their appearance, and it isn't. Also, I've found that people tend to lose weight in times of crisis – heartbreak, bereavement, illness, and so on and so on. Complimenting someone on their weight loss is not always a good idea.

- Appreciate your body – the legs that allow you to go places, the stomach that digests delicious food. Your brain, which is the most precious organ of all, the only one that cannot be transplanted or replaced – this is the bit of your body that you should want to improve most of all, be it through the books that you read or the people who you tend to spend time with or the places you choose to go.

Don't feel that you are taking up space – and I mean emotionally as well as physically. Own the zone you are in. Truly occupy it. Never forget that you absolutely deserve to be there. Do not apologise for existing – if someone pushes past you or shoves you out the way, don't say sorry, as I have always done. You have absolutely nothing to be sorry for.

Remember that, unless there are some pretty wild advances in science, you only get one body. That it exists at all is kind of incredible. Be proud of it. Nurture it. Look after it. Love it like it loves you. Do that, and you will find that the miracles are never ending.

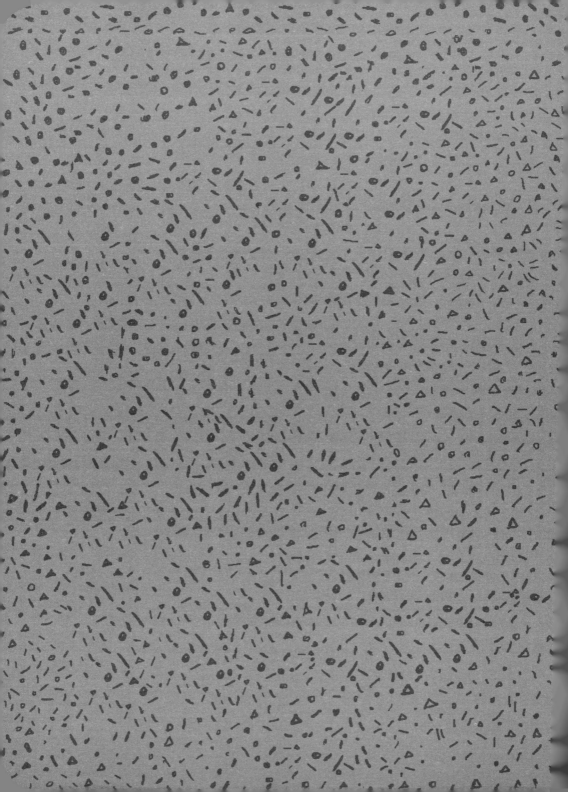

Five

You Are Stronger Than You Think

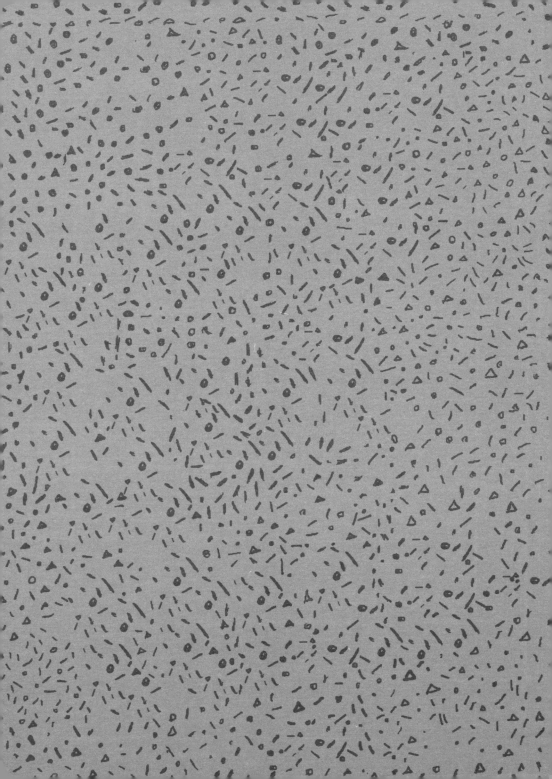

One of the most brilliant things about being human is all of the unique, amazing things we can do with our bodies that other species can't.

We can sing, dance, cook, read, write, love, play Twister. (The last is my favourite thing to do as a human.) But I once knew a girl who always thought about what she couldn't do. She couldn't do a handstand – her gymnastics teacher said she didn't have the strength or right kind of body to do one, whatever *that* meant. She couldn't make the netball A-team. She couldn't even make the netball B-team, in fact – and her school was so small that there was no C-team.

She couldn't run cross-country because even the words made her feel breathless and she definitely couldn't swim, cartwheel or roller-skate, even though those were the things she used to love doing. And as she got older, she felt acutely self-conscious in the changing room – the place where her body could often embarrass her with a nipple escaping there or a quick glimpse of an armpit sprouting hair. Not to forget the massive gym knickers which were always, always getting stuck up her bum, making her want to disappear up the crack they seemed to gravitate to.

She started to feel awkward and 'other'. She worried about other people, her school friends, who seemed to carry themselves with such grace and style, who didn't seem to get a stabbing pain in their boobs every time they so much as broke into a light jog. Was she having a *heart attack*? She thought her friends might snigger and judge as she dropped dead on the playing fields. It didn't matter that this never, ever happened – just the prospect of it was enough to leave her skin flushed and her heart racing. So, she made up excuses to get out of games, told lies, invented vague health conditions that she hoped nobody would ever question. She hated doing games, but she also hated *not* doing games, because it made her feel like a fraud. Her friends asked her why she always seemed to have a headache on a Tuesday morning – they teased her, because they knew. They knew she was making it all up, she was *sure* of it.

And in every area of her life, not just on a hockey field or a netball court, she felt clumsy, heavy-footed, permanently out of breath. She felt like she was always getting things just a little bit *wrong*. The Girl Least Likely to be Picked was now her persona, her character, the part she played when she was out with her friends. She could never attract the right kind of boy or manage to impress her teachers. Instead she always felt a little bit useless because she was forever telling herself that she couldn't, couldn't, couldn't, can't, can't can't …

Until one day, she got fed up with it. She was sick of playing the role of Girl Least Likely to be Picked. And she had realised, as she watched other girls and women struggling with the same issues, that the only person forcing her to play it was herself. She wanted to know what she could do, as opposed to what she couldn't. Because she was sure that there had to be *something*, even if it was only aqua aerobics with the old ladies at the local leisure centre.

So one day she decided, on a whim, to run a marathon. Because why not? Because what was the worst that could happen? Sure, right at that moment she couldn't run for a bus … but she reminded herself that she was supposed to be focusing on what she *could* do, not what she couldn't. She *could* download a Couch to 5k app. And then she *could* download a Couch to 10k app. And then she *could* print off a marathon training plan, and work on that. And then, just six short months later, she found herself crossing the finish line of the London Marathon, and she realised she *could* run 26.2 miles, without stopping. (Well OK. She had to stop a couple of times to use the loo, but she had her period, so we'll forgive her.)

A year later, this girl – now very much a woman – did her next marathon … in her knickers and bra, to prove to other women all the things they *could* do with their beautiful, bumpy, varied bodies. People turned up with banners to cheer her on. And then afterwards, Little Mix invited her to feature in their music video for the song 'Strip', to empower more females to feel positive about their body. She went from being the Girl Least Likely to be Picked to the Woman Everyone Wanted to Hang with Because She Believed People Were People Not Sweets to be Chosen or Ignored Like Pick 'n' Mix. And as she shook her size 18 thighs and arse, she laughed! But at the same time, she thought sadly of the little girl she had once been, the one who thought only about what she wasn't. She wanted to say to that little girl: 'You – you may have been told you can't do a handstand or play netball. You may think you can't run or dive into a pool. But you can, you absolutely can. And let me tell you something: you are stronger than you will ever know.'

And how do I know this?

BECAUSE THIS WOMAN IS ME.

my exercise wishes

When it comes to exercise, I wish that when I was growing up I hadn't learnt to focus on the losses – be it of a competitive nature, or regarding the inches around my waist – but had been taught about the gains: the powerful hormones called endorphins that surge through your body and make you feel as if you are flying. The clarity that exercise can bring, cutting through the fog in your brain like a knife.

I wish I hadn't been told that exercise was about shrinking bits of myself I had mistakenly assumed other people didn't like. I wish that my friends and I hadn't come to see exercise as a sort of punishment to be endured as part of our legal requirement to adhere to the national curriculum – a weekly ritual in which we were forced to measure all the ways we were slower, weaker, less agile than one another. I wish that I'd known that exercise was not about making myself smaller, about trying to take up less space, but that it was actually a way of making myself bigger, brighter, *even* more brilliant!

I wish that I had known exercise is for everyone. It is not owned by a club whose members are exclusively made up of Olympic athletes and Instagram influencers that can do 60 squats and 20 wall climbs before they've even opened their eyes and properly woken up. If only someone had told me that exercise is doing the thing you think you can't, over and over again, that it is the quickest and easiest way to feel as if you are achieving the impossible – that my PE teacher had said that it was really only about getting your blood pumping, your heart rate thumping, nothing more, nothing less. I wish I had been told that doing exercise is about remembering that you are alive, that you are here, that you are everything you need to be right at this very moment as your body keeps you going against all the odds. It can be hard, but it is never, ever harder than the days when you feel that you can't move at all.

And most importantly, I wish I had realised that though sport for some people is about being the fastest, or the strongest, more often than not, it's simply about realising you and your body – no matter the shape and size – are much stronger than you think.

Make exercise something you actually want to do.

Of course, when your ovaries are suddenly performing the menstrual equivalent of a thrash metal concert, and your boobs feel as if they are being repeatedly walloped every time you move, it can be difficult to want to do any sport at all. Maybe you're feeling tired. Perhaps you've got homework to do and can't find the time. Or maybe you just don't want to squeeze yourself into those gross gym knickers that some schools still insist on handing out. But the ability to move that miraculous, beautiful body of yours is one of the greatest gifts you will ever give yourself. Give exercise 20 minutes of your time and it will give you back even more – moving when you are tired is the best way to perk yourself up and make yourself feel better about your body.

So here are my top tips for making exercise something you actually *want* to do, rather than something you feel you have to.

Remember that most of us start our lives completely and utterly in love with exercise.

We're just not aware that that's what it is. As kids, it's something we did without even *thinking* of it as exercise – instead, it's that fun thing you get up to with your mates, that involves jumping around and goofing about and generally just getting out there in some fresh air. The desire to move is strong in children, but something happens along the way. Something changes.

The most obvious thing that changes is the body itself. Once we go through puberty we can start to feel like Jabba the Hutt in a pair of tracksuit bottoms, even though nothing – absolutely NOTHING – could be further from the truth. (I know that the truth doesn't matter when you are going through puberty – just what you *feel* is the truth, which can be every bit as powerful.) But I think there is something else at play here, too, and it's that almost as soon as we learn how to move, our parents try to stop us – initially so that we don't tumble down a flight of stairs or into the path of oncoming traffic, but later because we are getting under their feet and in their way. So subconsciously, we start to see movement as a bad thing. It feels like another way in which we are taking up too much space. Then there's the aforementioned PE kit you get at school, which can make you feel self-conscious. That's normal. But darling – you need to own your body. It's keeping you *alive*, goddamit.

Move it around as much as you like. There's enough space for all of us, I promise.

Think of exercise as something that makes you feel good, rather than something that makes you look good.

More often than not, movement is packaged up and presented as the ultimate way to achieve physical perfection: do lots of exercise and you too can have rock-hard abs, a tight bum and the thigh gap of a Victoria's Secret model! When we think of exercise, we think of all the ways in which we don't match up physically … and so unless we are one of those rare genetic creatures built like an athlete or a supermodel, the thought of doing exercise gives us the fear.

If much of the motivation to do exercise is rooted in disliking our bodies, is it really a surprise then, that so many of us dread it and put it off and then eventually stop doing it at all? But when you stop doing exercise for the losses – the way it might make you slimmer and smaller – and start doing it for the gains – the mental clarity it gives you, the time to think, the rush of endorphins – then suddenly, exercise becomes something to look forward to. It becomes about improving *your* view of you, rather than ludicrously trying to improve everyone else's.

Find a sport that suits you.

So many people are put off sport by its inherently competitive nature. Life is hard enough, without also having to battle it out on the hockey pitch or netball court with your mates for an hour or two each week. If team sports are not your bag, then go it alone! I go for jogs with nothing more than a podcast for company. That way, I get the things out of exercise I want, and can leave behind all the things I don't. But it may be completely different for you. You might hate the idea of running for miles alone; the thing you like about exercise might be the social nature of netball or football or run club. The point is there should be something that you can at least try and get into.

If you like outdoor sports you could try:

* Cold-water swimming (yasss!)
* Football
* Tennis
* Skateboarding
* Hiking
* Rowing
* My personal favourite, beach rounders

If you like exercising alone you could try:

* *Running*
* *Cycling*
* *Swimming*
* *Online yoga or exercise videos so you can exercise from the comfort of your own bedroom*

If you like going to classes you could try:

* *Dance*
* *Yoga*
* *Spinning*
* *Pilates*
* *Karate*
* *Judo*

And by the way, when you're in those classes, move the way you want to, not the way you think you should. Remember, everybody is too focused on themselves to notice what you are doing! (Which is a shame, because what you are doing is totally ace.)

It doesn't matter how 'well' you do. The only thing that matters is that you are doing it at all.

When I did my first marathon, people used to ask me what my time was. To which I would almost always reply: 'What was *your* time?' Inevitably, the person would shake their head. 'Oh no, I've never done a marathon,' they would say. 'Well exactly,' I would smile.

In reality, it took me almost six hours. I saw it this way: us lot at the back were the real elite athletes. While the likes of Mo Farah had probably been at home with their feet up for the last three hours, we had spent that time pushing on, pounding the streets as we attempted to get to the finish line. And that was something to be proud of, not embarrassed about.

Remember that exercise is one of the many things scientifically proven to help your mental health.

Not only do the endorphins we release when we exercise make us feel better, but activity also helps us to get out of our heads in a healthy way. Whenever I feel a bit down, I know I immediately have to get out of the house and move around – even if it is absolutely the last thing I want to do. *Especially* because it is the last thing I want to do.

The way I see it, most mental health issues *want* you inside and isolated in your bedroom, so getting up and out is the quickest and easiest way to prove the negative voice in your head wrong. (And it is also, crucially, the quickest and easiest way to create space between you and any irritating members of your family.) Sure, exercise is not going to cure any mental illness you have. But approached in the right way, it's certainly not going to make it any worse. And if you don't believe me, just try it. What's the worst that can happen? Your lovely cosy bedroom and duvet will still be there when it's all over. And they will feel even more welcoming than before.

Remember that everyone feels exactly the same as you do about exercise.

Before I began exercising regularly, I foolishly believed that everyone who engaged in intense physical activity sprang out of bed every morning, desperate to pull on a pair of leggings and lace up a pair of trainers. In comparison, I felt lazy. What was wrong with me? Why didn't I have that same sense of enthusiasm for working out? But now I have realised: nobody wants to go and do exercise. The difference between those who do and those who don't, is that the people who do know they will never regret doing exercise. Keep that in mind, and getting out of the house suddenly becomes a whole lot easier.

You can do a handstand, whatever your body shape.

I really wanted to put this here, to show that even if other people think you can't do something, you *still* can. You can do whatever you want. And so it was that a year ago, I did my first handstand. I did my first handstand, despite what that gymnastics teacher said all those decades ago. So take *that*, Mrs Carter.

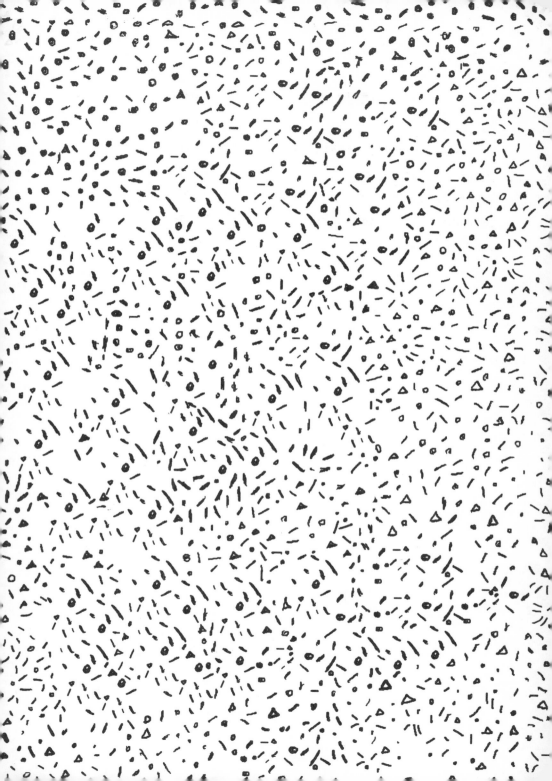

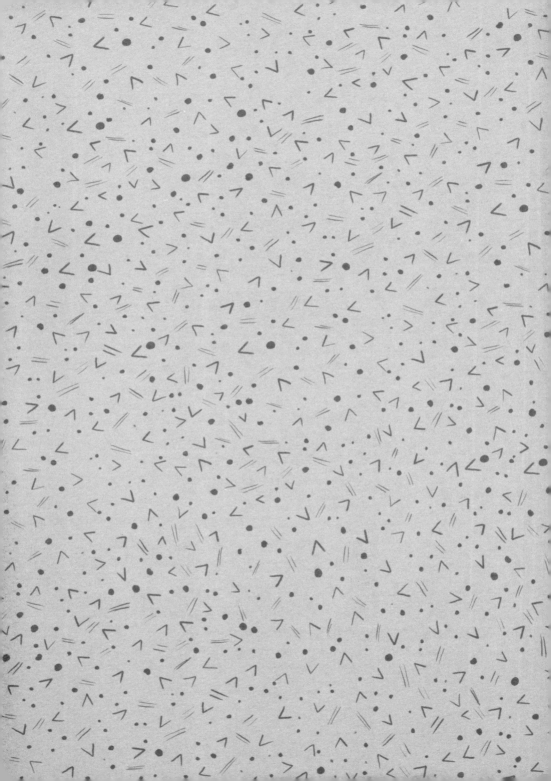

Six

You Are Miss Right

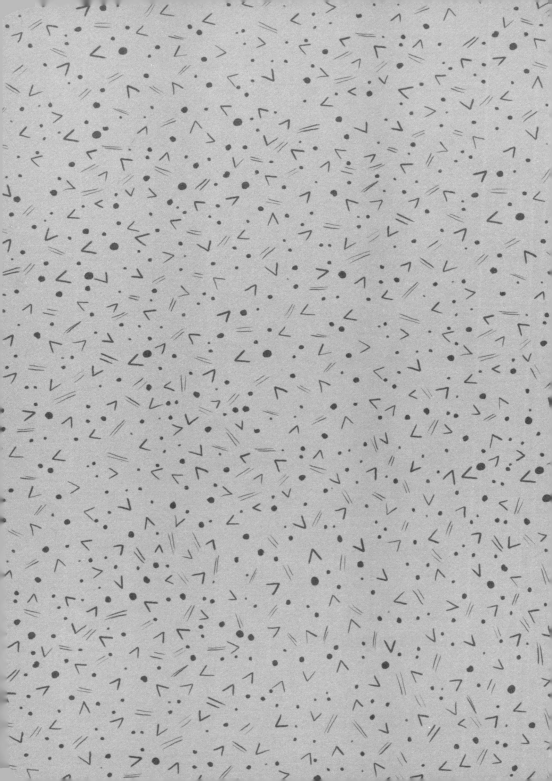

I'm going to write something so embarrassing now that I need you to promise me in advance that you won't judge me for it.

I know, I know. You're not the judgey type at all. And by now I feel like we are friends, so I probably shouldn't worry. But I still feel completely mortified by what I am about to write, so go easy on me.

OK.

Right.

Here goes.

Are you ready?

Reader, I thought that if I married someone, my life would be complete.

I thought that if I got a boyfriend, all my problems would be solved, and all my worries would go away.

In short, I thought that the only thing that could save me from all my problems was … a *man*.

Now do you see why I was worried? I mean, such a notion seems laughable in this day and age, where girls are brought up with concepts such as independence, self-sufficiency, and the ability to step over a puddle without a dashing gentleman throwing down his cloak to help them on their way. But back when I was a kid, I kept on being told the same story over and over again. The characters and the locations may have been interchangeable, but the plot remained the same: girl finds herself in peril, usually, though not exclusively, due to the behaviour of some evil female step-relation, and the only way she can escape the peril is by being saved by a handsome prince.

There was the girl whose evil stepmother was so jealous of her beauty that she poisoned her, with only a handsome prince having the power to bring her back round to consciousness.

There was the girl who was forced to spend her days dusting and cleaning by her wicked step-mother and hideous stepsisters, only to be saved from her life of domestic drudgery by a handsome prince.

There was the mermaid who freaking hated being a mermaid, and was totally in love with a human she **had never even spoken to**, and so she found a nasty sea witch who would give her legs in exchange for her beautiful voice. Only the love of a handsome prince could return it to her. (Ladies: this one REALLY sucks. Never, ever give up your voice for a man.)

There was the great beauty who was held hostage, essentially, by a grotesque, frightening beast. But her kindness showed him the way and eventually they fell in love and the grotesque, frightening beast turned into a – yep, you guessed it – a handsome prince.

There was the girl with really swishy hair who had been locked away by an ogre in a tower. Eventually she throws her swishy plaited hair out of the tower window and – would you look at that? – a handsome prince comes along to climb up it and save her. Hooray for swishy sex hair! Hooray for handsome princes!

**There was the girl** who was cursed by an evil fairy to prick her finger and fall into a magical sleep on the occasion of her 16th birthday. Only one person can save her from eternal slumber: yep, a handsome prince, who wakes her up by kissing her! (Er, excuse me guys, but in what way is this, like, even **consensual**.)

And everyone lived happily ever after, and so on and so on and so on.

THE END

Except, well … I mean, perhaps we need to have a little chat about this?

handsome toe rags and mr right

I went through most of my teens expecting that any minute now, my Handsome Prince was going to come and save me. Except that he didn't. And sometimes, he actually made things worse. I was so desperate to be saved by a Handsome Prince that sometimes I threw myself at Handsome Toe Rags, who look similar but are not at all the same. Handsome Toe Rags complicated my life instead of making it easier, and one of them gave me a year-long headache. Where was *that* particular story arc in the fairy tales I had been told as a child?

As I got older, people stopped talking to me about Handsome Princes, and started referring to someone called Mr Right. Mr Right seemed to me to be a bit like Father Christmas – in that he was spoken of in hushed, reverential tones, but didn't actually appear to exist. Still, I fantasised about the idea of Mr Right filling my stocking. Plus, this was a story I had been told so often that I could not bear to entertain the idea that none of it was true. I was determined to prove that the foundations I had built my life on were made up of more than a pack of lies and fabrications. So I pushed on in my quest to find Mr Right, this magical, (almost) mythical man who was going to sort out all my wrongs.

I eventually met my soon-to-be husband, Harry, and decided that he was going to be my Mr Quite Right. But the rescue was not quite what I had expected. It didn't seem to involve wicked step relations, towers, castles, princess dresses or eternal slumbers from which I needed to be woken (unless you count hangovers, which I don't). There were no fireworks, no diamond rings (well, not immediately) and no lavish weddings like the ones I had read about in the fairy tales. Instead we had a hurried wedding where everyone got drunk, including my new husband, who made a quick speech about how very fond he was of me and then returned to his quest to find more champagne. And while I love him very much, and am incredibly content with him, he did not save me. I still ended up experiencing depression and entering rehab. And it was there that I realised the one crucial truth that *would* begin to right all my wrongs: the only person who could save me from my problems had been there all along.

The only person who could save me was me.

I mean, doh!

fearless fairy tales

So instead of growing up with bedtime stories of handsome princes, helpless heroines and happily ever afters, what if we were told some realistic feminist fairy tales instead? Here are some to get us started ...

The one where the girl discovered that a relationship is part of you, but it should never ever be all of you.

In this story, our protagonist creates for herself a rich and fulfilling life made up of many varied hobbies and interests. She reads. She goes to the movies. She attends art exhibitions (or something similarly cultured). She gets massively into cross-stitching, and skateboarding, and also ballroom dancing, because as I said, this girl has many varied hobbies and interests. She wakes up in the morning and thinks: 'Gosh! Aren't I fortunate to have such a rich and fulfilling life made up of my many varied hobbies and interests?! I hope that one day I can share it with someone! Anyway, what shall I do today? Oh, I know, I promised a good friend that I would knit her a hat! I better get going on the pattern so that I can at least go to five-a-side football tonight knowing I have made a start on it!'

Will our heroine ever meet her handsome prince? Let's get back to her on that – she's yet to decide if she prefers princes to princesses, if indeed there even is a choice to be made. But when she does choose a partner, she will make sure it is someone who will nurture her and help her to flourish as she goes about her rich and fulfilling life made up of many varied hobbies and interests, which will hopefully now include loads more because of her new mate. Our heroine ain't looking for someone to complete her because, guess what? She's already totally complete! Hooray! Let's throw a party to celebrate!

The one where the girl learnt that wanting a boyfriend doesn't make her a substandard member of the sisterhood.

Once upon a time there was a girl who dreamed of many things. She dreamed of having a successful career. She dreamed of travelling the world. She dreamed of sky diving, and bungee jumping, too. She dreamed of one day seeing Arsenal win the Premiership, and she dreamed of the day when her parents would stop doing that really irritating *thing* that only they could do (it was difficult for this girl to describe, in words, what this thing was, and sometimes she wondered if it were more of a simple chemical reaction caused by them walking into a room than something they actually *meant* to do). But she also dreamed of something else, something she felt she couldn't admit to in class or at sleepovers. For this girl dreamed of getting married, and she dreamed of having lots of babies, too.

This dream made her feel weak. It made her feel that she was somehow failing as a girl. What right did she have to desire such basic things when women had died for her right to vote? How could she hanker after a life of domestic bliss when women had literally fought dinosaurs to ensure she didn't have to struggle in the workplace? Was she a bad feminist? Was she a feminist at all? Should she shut up about these desires in case her friends thought that simply by having them, she was letting them down? As she got older, this sense of inadequacy only intensified. When she walked past people pushing prams, her ovaries seemed to scream at her. At night, she would creep up to her bedroom and secretly watch episodes of *Don't Tell the Bride* and *Say Yes to the Dress*, weeping happy tears. She read all the Bridget Jones books, over and over again, wincing at the identification she felt. Why couldn't she just be happy with her high-flying career, and her twice-weekly cocktail nights with the girls?

But one day, her fairy godmother appeared to her, in the form of a kind and knowledgeable woman at work. Her Fairy Godmother took her aside, and over a cup of tea and a slice of cake she told her many things. She told her that she shouldn't feel bad for wanting a boyfriend, that this was a very normal thing, that, indeed, a yearning for companionship was the most normal thing in the world. She told her that if she wanted to go off and have babies with a nice man, and never work again, then she would not be letting down her female friends. She said that the beauty of feminism was that it was about allowing women to have a choice, and that choice didn't have to be smashing through corporate glass ceilings with a toddler in each arm. That staying at home looking after children was a job in itself – but if she decided she didn't like that job, she wouldn't be letting her kids down if she decided to go back to her old one, and put them in childcare. In childcare, said the Fairy Godmother, they are just as happy because they get to muck about with their mates all day. 'So in conclusion,' announced her Fairy Godmother, 'you go do what you want to do, and don't let anybody tell you otherwise. It's your life – you live it the way you want to.'

So she did, and she discovered that really, this was the only way to get your happily ever after. By choosing the path you most like the look of, and not worrying about the fact that it looks different to all the others.

Different is what makes you you. Different is what we all do best.

The one where the girl learnt that heartache was the worst feeling in the world.

In this story, there is no happy ending – just an endless sense of the misery that is heartbreak. I know, I know. It hardly sounds like an uplifting read. It's like watching Baz Luhrmann's version of *Romeo and Juliet*, but with no Leonardo DiCaprio to cheer you up. But I promise you that once you've heard this story – once you have *lived* this story – you will be able to take on anything the world throws at you.

Heartbreak is awful. Heartbreak is worse than awful. Heartbreak is the thing that makes you wonder if you can go on, the thing that makes you feel as if you are existing in a tracing paper version of the world, while everyone else seems to be in the real one. Heartbreak is a blind drawn on a summer's day. It is waking up and thinking for a split second that everything is OK, and then remembering that it absolutely isn't. Heartbreak is one minute knowing someone intimately, the next only being able to see them on Instagram. As if they were a stranger. As if they were Kim freaking Kardashian. Heartbreak is an actual physical pain in your chest, and often your stomach, too. Heartbreak is only being able to hear the sadness in songs, the sadness in stories, no matter how uplifting they might be. Heartbreak is horrible. It is the thing I wouldn't wish upon my worst enemy. But it happens to almost everyone, and if you breathe into it, if you allow it, if you let it go through you, it will probably be your happy beginning. It will be the start of realising that the person who was careless enough to break your heart wasn't good enough for your heart anyway. The start of the next thing. The start of the better thing. The start of something, and the joyous excitement of not knowing what that something might be.

The one where the girl discovered that friendships are as important as romantic relationships.

Now you already know how this story goes. You know how it goes because you are living it right now. We are *all* living it right now, regardless of our age or gender.

In many ways, friendships are the most important love stories of all time and, certainly, they are the most enduring.

You had friends before you had boyfriends or girlfriends,
and you will have friends after you have boyfriends and
girlfriends. You have friends right now that will be your friends
for 40 years, long after a load of your romantic relationships
have bitten the dust. There are people in your life who will
talk you through first dates and last dates and console you
when you get drunk and think you've made a fool of yourself
(you haven't). There are people in your life right now with
whom it truly is possible to experience *anything*. So you want
to nurture your relationships with those people, and not
take them for granted (though sometimes this will happen,
because: life! But don't worry – a really good friend will
understand, and when you make up it will be like nothing
ever happened). Those friends will be with you through thick
and thin. They will be with you through bad times, and good
times. Sometimes they will disappear to deal with their own
things, but they will always, always be there with you in spirit,
thinking about what you are up to and meaning to check
in with you but not quite managing to because their daily
schedules are crazy with schoolwork, netball practice and
everything in between. The light of your friendship, just the
knowledge that it even exists, will help them through.

Your friends won't make you feel giddy with love, but they will
be there to help you when you aren't. Your friends won't make
your heart flip, but they will pick it up should someone treat
it carelessly and allow it to crack into a thousand tiny pieces.

They will pick it up, and they will methodically and carefully put it back together again. They won't stop until every last piece is back where it should be. And then they'll do exactly the same should it happen again.

Your friends, your friends are everything. They are a love that is unconditional. They are the thing that gets us through. Sometimes, there may be falling outs – but they will rarely last longer than a turn around the moon. And then you'll be there together again, having seen the worst of each other, but still only being able to see the best.

Thank God for friends.

The one where the girl found out she didn't have to play silly games.

There once was a girl who was really, really out there, in the best way possible. While some people worried about being 'Less Than', she worried about being 'Too Much'. She was loud. She was laughter. She was lovely. The thing she absolutely *wasn't* was a wallflower – and this wasn't normally a problem, except for when it came to dating.

Here, her out-there-ness seemed to work against her. Whereas in most areas of her life it was what made her *her*, the thing that people celebrated, in matters of the heart, it seemed to make her a bit of a failure. This was because everyone knew that if you liked someone, the only way to make them like you back was by playing hard to get. Except this girl could no more play hard to get than she could Mozart's Fifth Symphony on the piano. Playing hard to get came about as naturally to her as Mandarin – which was to say, not naturally at all. If she liked someone romantically, she always sent the first WhatsApp, and sometimes she sent two or three. As she watched the grey tick go from one to two and then blue, only for no reply to be immediately forthcoming, she felt as if her world was falling in on her head. Was she too much? Should she tone herself down? Did she need to take acting classes in how to be the Cool Girl?

Whenever she liked someone, she seemed to mess it up simply by being *her*. In the grown-up world of dating, her natural enthusiasm for life was seen as a bad thing, not a good thing. She tried to be quiet, and wait for them to get in touch with her. She did her very best to appear mysterious, whatever that meant. But she was always left with the impression that she wasn't being herself, and did she really want to go out with someone who liked her best when she wasn't being herself? No. No she didn't.

And she hated playing games. Game-playing was the kind of thing she had done in the playground as a child. It hardly struck her as the foundation of a good relationship. Did she want to spend her life having to go cold on someone every time she wanted to get their attention? Did she want to spend her life having someone else go cold on *her* every time they wanted to get her attention? That sounded like a funny kind of love to her. It sounded kind of cruel.

And this girl, she thought that relationships should be about abundance, not punishment. She thought that she didn't want love to feel like it was always about to leave her. She thought that love was probably kind of precious, and when she loved someone, she didn't want them to treat her love like it was a game of Snakes and Ladders. Her love was worth more than that. So she decided that in future, she would refuse to play games, because by playing games, she wasn't being true to herself – and the only people she wanted in her life were the ones who wanted her to be true to herself. So she stood her ground. She didn't falter. She continued to be fearlessly, unapologetically her.

And she found, over time, that the people she attracted into her life were also fearlessly, unapologetically them. Like her, they weren't sending out promises they could never keep. They didn't have to.

Because together, the only promise they needed was the promise to always be themselves. And in the end, that is the most gorgeous thing we can give someone. In love, it is really the only thing.

The one where the girl does meet a handsome prince, and they don't fall in love, but they do end up changing the world together, which is kind of better.

I like this story best, because it is about me. Dear reader, I have met actual, real-life handsome princes. On several occasions. In fact, I encounter them quite regularly in my job. Yep, I know Prince Harry and Prince William. And while we haven't fallen in love, we have done something a whole lot better: we have got together to try and make the world a happier place, which in my opinion is a whole lot more fun. In 2017, Prince Harry and I sat down in a living room at Kensington Palace and he told me all about his mental health issues for my podcast, *Mad World*. It was the first time a member of the royal family had spoken so candidly about this stuff, and it was an honour to play a small part in changing the way that mental health is viewed in this country.

The moral of this story? Handsome princes are not just there to fall in love with. Members of the opposite sex can also make great friends and work buddies. It is simply not true that you can't be mates with boys, and that there will always be some secret, sexual agenda. Boys are not the enemy! They're just humans, like you, trying to deal with their own problems – and more often than not, they're dealing with their own problems really badly, due to that same awful social conditioning that says girls are weak and boys don't cry. Together, you can bust those myths.

The one where the girl learnt what love actually is.

Once upon a time there was a girl whose first boyfriend was as handsome as any prince. He had piercing blue eyes, jet-black hair, and cheekbones so sharp you could grate cheese on them. He was six foot three, and clever, and funny, and sporty, and popular, and the girl could not believe her luck. She was in love, or so she thought, because that was what love was, wasn't it? It was getting the guy, the guy that everyone else wanted. It was being the couple from the high-school movie that everyone wanted to be. It was candlelit dinners that looked great on Instagram, and trips to photogenic bridges that you could lock your love to.

Except that sometimes, it didn't feel very much like love. Sometimes, it was a funny kind of love that felt more like hate. He started to criticise the way she looked, and began to put her down. He mentioned other girls, and how attractive they were, and how much better it would be if she was more like them. Soon, everything she did seemed to make him cross. She felt that she couldn't do right for doing wrong.

They argued all the time, and she told herself that this was OK, that this was just passionate love. He would break up with her, and then come running back a few days later, and she told herself that this was simply a sign that he couldn't live without her – which was good, wasn't it, because she felt as if she couldn't live without him. She put up with his cruelty, because really he was just trying to help her, to improve her and make her better. Without him, she was nothing.

Um.

Er.

Hang on one second.

This doesn't sound right, does it?

I know this story well, because I've been that girl. My first boyfriend was a giant douchebag, the kind of boy who was really, really good at finding girls with zero self-esteem; with him it was easier to spin hate and make it look like love. It was a hideous experience, but it taught me a lot about what *not* to put up with in a man. Be warned: if any of what you have just read feels familiar, EXIT THAT RELATIONSHIP AT ONCE. Because none of it is love. It's just two really unwell people doing a twisted

dance of dysfunction. And the sooner you stop doing that dance, the sooner you can start finding out what love *really* is.

Here's what I have discovered love to be since I managed to get out of that toxic relationship …

Love is kind. Always, it is kind.

Love doesn't pressurise you into doing something you don't want to. It understands that thing is not for you right now, respects you for communicating that, and then gets on with loving you.

Love is not always explosive. In fact, sometimes it is kind of the opposite.

Love doesn't try to change you.

Love doesn't *want* to change you.

Love shouldn't tear you apart, contrary to what the famous Joy Division song says.

Love sometimes smells. Sorry.

And love is sometimes *really* annoying. Sorry again.

Love will set you free to explore the things you want to, and develop the interests you need to.

Love doesn't look like it does in the movies. Sometimes love is more mundane than that.

Love is already there. It is in you. Your goal in life is to nurture that love, and only give it to people who are grateful for it.

There are plenty of them out there. I promise.

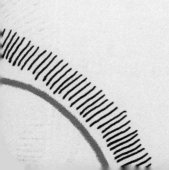

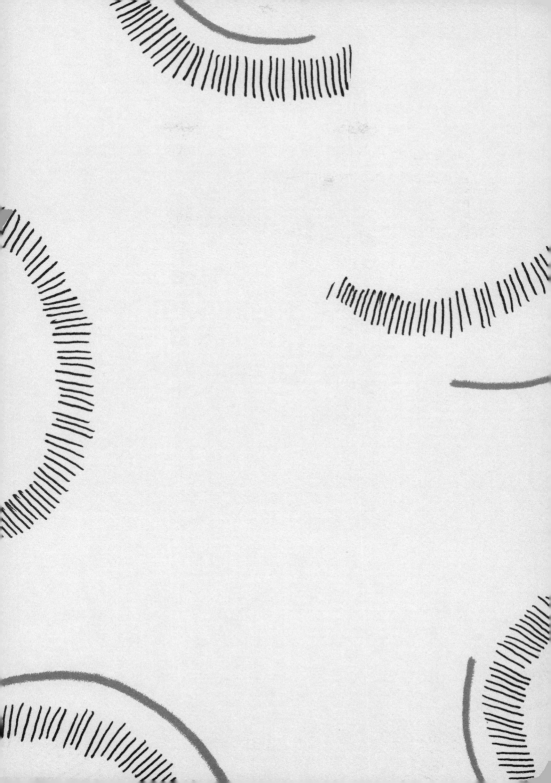

Seven

You Are So Much More Than A Grade Or A Number

At school, I didn't just think I was the Girl Least Likely to be Picked.

I also felt like the Girl Most Likely to Amount to Not Very Much Professionally. The Girl Most Likely to be Vaguely Capable of Working in a Mediocre Company Doing a Mediocre Job for the Rest of Her Mediocre Life. I thought I was so middle-of-the-road, people barely noticed me as they passed by to more interesting destinations: the Girl Most Likely to be Expelled, for example, or the Girl Most Likely to Become Prime Minister.

To give you an idea of just how mediocre I was, I will now relive the only time I ever won anything at school for you. Picture the scene: it was the end of the summer term, and though the long holidays stretched gloriously ahead of us, first I had to get through the long prize giving. You know the kind of thing I am talking about: an end of term 'extravaganza' that is really more like the world's most rubbish awards ceremony – no sequins, no goodie bags, no tearful speeches, just the same students sashaying to the stage to exchange smug smiles with the head teacher, who would then turn to the remainder of the school with a look that said we could only dream of being quite so successful.

You know the look.

Every year, the same handful of students seemed to win the same handful of prizes, the rest of us forced to bow down to their greatness if we ever wanted to be released into the safety of the summer holidays. Sensing the unfairness of this, the school offered a consolation prize, a sort of booby prize, as a nod to the other 293 students in the school who also happened to be in the main hall at the time. The Progress Cup was a sad-looking thing, more of a mug really than a cup. It was the prize absolutely nobody wanted to win, on account of the patronising speech the head teacher always gave before handing it out, making it sound like the recipient was the kind of person who needed to be congratulated every time they managed to tie their shoelaces. It was a consolation prize – and for a girl on the cusp of adulthood, this felt like no prize at all.

At this particular assembly, the head teacher really went for it with her Progress Cup speech. 'This year's winner does not find academia easy,' she announced, as if she was talking about someone who could barely write their name. 'The winner has struggled to get good grades, and not always been very good at concentrating.' I cringed on the 'winner's' behalf, just as the rest of my row appeared to be, judging by all the wincing they were doing. 'Focus has been a problem,' continued the head teacher. 'But this year, she has really shown the power of potential, moving her grades up from Ds and Es to solid Bs and Cs, and she shows us what is possible if we buckle down and do what we are told …' I felt sorry for the girl who was about to be humiliated in front of the entire school … and then …

'And the winner is, Bryony Gordon!'

Oh God.

Of course.

It had to be me, didn't it?

Here is a list of the only things at which I excelled in at secondary school:

▶ *Masturbation*

▶ *Daydreaming*

▶ *Playing my Gameboy*

▶ *Drawing really elaborate flowers on my notebooks*

▶ *Sulking*

And ...

▶ *Eating raw frankfurters*

(Don't ask. OK, do. For some reason – and I have no idea how
I discovered this – I preferred the taste of raw frankfurters to
cooked ones. Sometimes I would go into the fridge and eat
a whole packet, because I thought they were so delicious. I
wouldn't advise this because a) it might make you sick and b)
well, who needs a B? A is enough. A is all you need.)

That's quite a lot of things to excel at, of course. But none of
them seemed to be *useful* things to excel at – not in the all-
important world of academia, that is. Masturbation is a very
important life skill, but I didn't think it was going to wash
with my teachers, who were more concerned with whether or
not I could play an instrument other than the triangle (or my
clitoris). Daydreaming is great, but I never seemed to be able to
transfer those daydreams onto pages, into stories that excited
my English teacher. My skills at Tetris and Super Mario were
impressive, but they were hardly going to help when it came to
algebra. Drawing elaborate doodles was as lovely a way to pass
the time as any in French class, but it wasn't actually helping me
learn any French. Sulking? Meh. Eating raw frankfurters? Double
meh. I felt, as a young girl, fundamentally a bit useless, because
there was no one subject I excelled at, no one subject I was
even vaguely good at – and the message I got from my parents

and teachers and *everyone* was that if I didn't excel at school, I wouldn't excel anywhere. Ever. My abilities at the age of 11 and 12 were, it felt, the only abilities I would have for the rest of my life. So that on the one hand, while I was always being told that I was 'developing' physically, the same could not be said for me academically. On that front, I felt as fully formed as I would ever be, and that the way I was at school was going to be a pretty adequate reflection of the way I would be for the rest of my life. Fair to middling. Fine. OK. Just not very memorable. The kind of person who goes nowhere very, very slowly.

None of my so-called life skills, or my grades at school, led me to believe that things would turn out as they did. As they have done. There was not a single flicker or sign that what was going to happen was going to happen. Nobody voted me the Girl Most Likely to Have a Number One Bestselling Book, or the Girl Most Likely to Get Invited to Hang with Prince Harry and Meghan Markle. Nobody predicted *this*, least of all me. If you had told me at 12 that I would end up with awards on my mantelpiece and a column on a national newspaper, I would have laughed in your face. I would have laughed in your face, and then told you it's mean to play jokes on people.

This isn't an attempt at a humble brag. And in fact, while we are here, please can we do away with the phrase 'humble brag'? Talking about your achievements, however small, is something that should be encouraged – people don't do enough of it. If you're proud of something you've done, be proud! Do not be tempted to use the word 'only' or 'just' when talking about a thing you have accomplished. You haven't *only* run 5k in cross country – you've *run* 5k in cross country. And you haven't *just* got your grade 4 in guitar – you've *got* your grade 4 in guitar. Light up when talking about what you have done – don't make it sound like a trip to the corner shop (although sometimes, when you are down, that can be a massive achievement too).

What I'm trying to say is: don't do yourself down. Every time you minimise your achievements, or ignore them, a little bit of your self-esteem dies. If you feel a sense of joy about what you have done in life, everyone else will feel that joy too.

lessons we should be taught at school

Now obviously, I am the world's worst teacher – or at the very least, the world's most irresponsible. I barely have any qualifications other than a handful of fair-to-middling GCSEs and A levels (I don't have a degree, having dropped out of university after a term). But there are quite a lot of lessons I would like to teach you, despite all of this. Think of me as the slightly mad supply teacher, who has only been brought in because a sick bug has swept the local area and I am the only one who seems to be immune to it. I'm clearly way too much fun to be allowed to stay, but while I'm here, I plan to make a bigger impact on you than that dreary physics teacher who you suspect spends most of his spare time playing *Minecraft* (not that there's anything wrong with that, of course).

Here are the key lessons we will be going through while I am here:

Lesson 1: Grades matter ... but they are not the only thing that matters.

Here's the kind of school report your parents won't thank me for giving you:

It's all going to be OK.

Really, truly, whatever grades you get, it is probably going to be OK.

I know, I know. It's hardly the old failsafe 'panic method', which has been used on kids for generations, and basically involves telling you that your life will be over if you don't get straight As – that you will wind up destitute and on the streets, bringing great shame upon your family's good name. But calm down, guys! It's just an essay about *Lord of the Flies*, not the Paris Climate Change Accord.

I remember my mum and dad pulling the panic method on me, which might have worked had they themselves been able to tell me how they did in their A levels, or if indeed they had actually done A levels at all (their memories seemed to be terribly sketchy for people who were obsessed with the importance of learning).

But look, 'it's going to be OK' is a far more accurate prediction of the future than 'the world is going to end', at least when it comes to exam grades. In fact, when it comes to most things. And I know 'it's going to be OK' is easily said when you have the benefit of hindsight … but I promise you that it's true. I promise you that statistically, things are far more likely to be OK than not – that an asteroid is not heading for you if you happen not to get an A or a B or even a C in your exams. And I think it is really important that I say this, because sometimes, the weight of expectation at school can feel crushing. I made myself so ill with stress in the run up to my A levels that I was put on anti-depressants and signed off school for two weeks – meaning I just stressed myself out even more. And a bit of stress is important, believe it or not. A bit of stress will help you reach a coursework deadline, and knuckle down to revise when you most need to. A lot of stress, however, is not going to do you any favours. All the A grades in the world don't mean anything if you have to make yourself ill to get them.

Your grades are important, of course they are. If you want to be a doctor, you probably want to knuckle down and work hard at sciences. But your grades are not the only things that are important. Ditto: exam and test results. They matter, in much the same way that it matters to you once every four years that England do well in the World Cup. At the time it all seems terribly important, but believe me when I say that there will be long, long periods when you don't think about them at all.

Lesson conclusion:

If you're freaking out about not doing well at school, I totally get it. Right now, I'm freaking out about nobody buying this book. A helpful thing to do at times like these is take a deep breath, go for a walk, and make a list of things that are important to you other than your grades (or book sales). You'll find that more often than not, these are the everyday things that give you joy; not a certificate or an award for doing well academically. For example, other things that make me happy and are incredibly important to me include ...

▶ *My family*

▶ *Katie and Charlotte, my daughter's guinea pigs. They are boys, but she insisted on these names, so that they could be gender fluid*

▶ The common up the road that I can run around when I am feeling particularly mad

▶ Hot baths

▶ My sense of humour

▶ Netflix nights on the sofa

▶ That feeling you get when you wake up on a Saturday morning and realise you don't have to get ready for anything or anyone other than you

Lesson 2: Being rubbish at maths or English doesn't make you rubbish at being a human being.

I know this may be a hard concept to grasp as you walk down the school corridors, trying to avoid the eyes of the bully in the year above and the texts from your mum asking if you have yet cleaned your bedroom, but: what if you are totally fine as you are? I know, I know. It's a radical thought. But just because you're having a hard time at school, or dealing with some issues with friends, it doesn't mean you are a failure as a human being. Being rubbish at maths doesn't automatically mean you are rubbish at life. What it means is that you might need to do a bit more work on it, but if it still doesn't work out for you, don't worry. There are plenty of careers out there that don't involve algebra or equations. Phew!

You don't have to excel at every subject. You don't even have to excel at *any* subject. Because what if the subject you really excel at right now is being you? Nobody else is you. Literally, nobody else on the planet can beat you at that. And just because you can't immediately see something right now that you are passionate about and enjoy doing, it doesn't mean that this will be true for the rest of your life.

The problem with rankings and grades is that they are just singular numbers and letters, and taken out of context they don't really stand for anything at all. I mean, Hitler probably did well at school, but I'm pretty sure I wouldn't have wanted to be his friend. Grades tell you how good someone is in exams, or at homework, but they don't tell you much else. They don't tell you the really important stuff. They don't tell you if someone is loyal, or kind, or if they're going to stick up for you even when to do so feels really hard. They don't tell you that someone dances hilariously, tells great jokes, or makes a mean cupcake. Think about it. When you meet people, do you decide whether you like them or not based on how they are doing in French? OK, maybe if you're bad at French and need someone to help you, then you might. But otherwise, you decide who you like based on *them*, not their exam results. On their hobbies and interests and personality. On the way they make you feel. That – that is worth more than any certificate that you can be awarded by any exam board.

Lesson conclusion:

It's really important to be able to apply yourself in life, but if that thing doesn't happen to be on the national curriculum, it doesn't mean you are doing life wrong. And it's OK to enjoy a subject, but not excel at it. I really loved all the experiments in science, but I was never very good at doing them.

I adored all the reading in English, but I loathed writing essays. Ask yourself what success means to you. Is it really straight As? Or is it getting through the school day because you've found little bits of joy in the unexpected?

Try not to let your feelings about life be dictated by rankings and grades. They are fleeting, ever changing, and fail to tell you the whole story. An exam reflects what was going on for a particular period at a particular time on a particular day. It is not something that you have to carry through life like a ball and chain. And sure, doing well in exams is great – it is something to be celebrated, in fact, an accomplishment you should rightly be proud of yourself for. But the stuff that is going to get you through the really hard times in life is not what you got in your GCSEs, or what you learnt in geography.

It's you. Brilliant, glorious YOU.

Lesson 3: A bit of self-belief goes a very long way.

My mum told me lots of things when I was growing up: that I was difficult, that I was messy, that I didn't listen to her enough and should try brushing my hair from time to time. She told me she would ground me if I didn't do well at school, and that she would like it if I could. Just. Give. Her. Some. SPACE. But she also told me this, day after day after day:

She told me I was special.

That one day, I would do amazing things.

It was probably just that I was special to her. But it was enough. It was enough to plant in me the belief that I could do something if I wanted to. That I could take on the world, and that taking on the world was a version of winning all in itself, whatever the outcome of it happened to be. My grades, which were as you have seen distinctly average, were not what got me where I am today. Her belief in me was. And when you are young, I think that is all you really need. It's someone who loves you regardless of what you do. It's someone who is there for you unconditionally, who doesn't care how many times you screw up. There is an amazing video on YouTube of the late great poet and author Maya Angelou, where she talks

191

about what her mother's love did for her: she says that it liberated her to go out and do what she had to, knowing all the time that her mother was there for her when things went wrong, as they inevitably would.

This is what people mean when they say that love sets you free. Great love lets you be you, without judgement or commentary, and it doesn't say 'I told you so' when things go awry.

Having someone believe in you is a much greater thing to have in life than a string of A*s – anyone with a string of A*s will tell you that. It is something to hold on to, and look after, like a particularly wonderful Tamagotchi, or a pet guinea pig.

What if you feel like nobody believes in you? Well for a start, I promise you that somebody does. It may not feel like it's your mum and dad, but that's *their* problem, not yours. That's some age-old stuff that they really need to deal with, and has absolutely nothing to do with you. What I'm trying to say is this: your parents probably do believe in you, deep down. They're just also dealing with their own rubbish – and remember, rubbish that is in your own head often appears bigger than it does from someone else's head. In most cases, a parent who claims not to believe in their child is usually struggling to believe in themselves.

Find someone else who believes in you. It may be an aunt. It may be a teacher. It may be someone who works in the local corner shop and thinks you're a great kid. It could be a friend. It could even be an enemy (quite often, enemies are the ones who believe in you most, their belief manifesting itself in feeling threatened). It could be me. I believe in you. I believe in you, as I sit here right now in my underwear, writing at my desk that it is actually a dressing

table, and letting you know that perfect is not a state that
will be reached when you finally get an A in English.

Perfect is you, right now, whatever your grades happen to be.

Lesson conclusion:
You're great, you are. So don't ever forget it, kiddo.

Lesson 4: Failure is not the end. Sometimes, it's only the beginning.

When I was ten, a man called John Major became Prime Minister. John Major, now Sir John Major KG CH (whatever those letters even mean) left school at 16, with only three O levels to his name (O levels being a really, really old version of GCSEs). He later took three more, but six is hardly Head Boy territory. I mean, it's not even detention territory.

Thomas Edison's teachers told him he was 'too stupid to learn anything'. He went on to create the light bulb.

Carey Mulligan was rejected from every single drama school she applied to. She has been nominated for an Oscar.

Jo Malone left school at 13 to look after her mother when she had a stroke. Malone now has a multi-million pound beauty business, founded because she used to love the smell that came from grating soap as a child.

Saul Bellow, who won the Pulitzer Prize and the Nobel Prize for Literature, was described by one of his professors as 'a dud' who showed no signs of literary greatness.

Bill Gates is a university drop out.

Chris Pratt was homeless as a teen.

Richard Branson left school with not a single qualification to his name.

As a child, Maya Angelou was mute.

Albert Einstein did not develop 'normally'.

And for every supposed failure who has gone on to be a success, there are a trillion more wonderful, happy, thriving people who were simply fair to middling when they were in education. Just look at Charles Darwin, considered 'average' as a student. Oh, how he had the last laugh.

Lesson conclusion:

Failure is not the end. For most people, it is just the beginning. Without wanting to sound like one of those cheesy Instagrammable quotes: you can choose to be defined by failure, or you can choose to define it. Remember, when nobody has any expectations of you, least of all yourself, you are free to thrive. You are also free to prove people wrong. Negatives can always, always be turned into positives. In fact, that's the best damn thing you will ever do with them.

Lesson 5: When you're top of the class, it can feel like there's a long way to fall.

This is for those of you who are killing it at school, the ones who are super bright and excel at things. I feel for you, I really do. I feel for you, because there is pressure in always being good, too. There is pressure in not letting your family down, or your school, who may feel that their position in the league table is entirely dependent on you continuing to do well. The view at the top may be lovely, but those who manage to get there know that there is way further to fall. It can be tough being bright, and feeling like you only matter because of your grades – that there is nothing else to you than your brilliant ability to pass exams. Maybe sometimes you just want to let loose. Maybe sometimes you don't want to always be seen as the studious one. Maybe sometimes you don't want to have to answer everyone's questions about how to write the perfect essay or solve a quadratic equation. Maybe you just want to be *you*, free of the expectation and the pressure and the belief that everything in your life is perfect. That's OK. Go fail an exam from time to time, and let everyone know that you're human, too.

The world won't end, I promise.

Lesson conclusion:

Sweetheart: your best is always the best, however that looks.

After all the exams and essays, all the tests and tutorials, this is the only thing you have to remember, really.

Eight

You Are Not A Snowflake

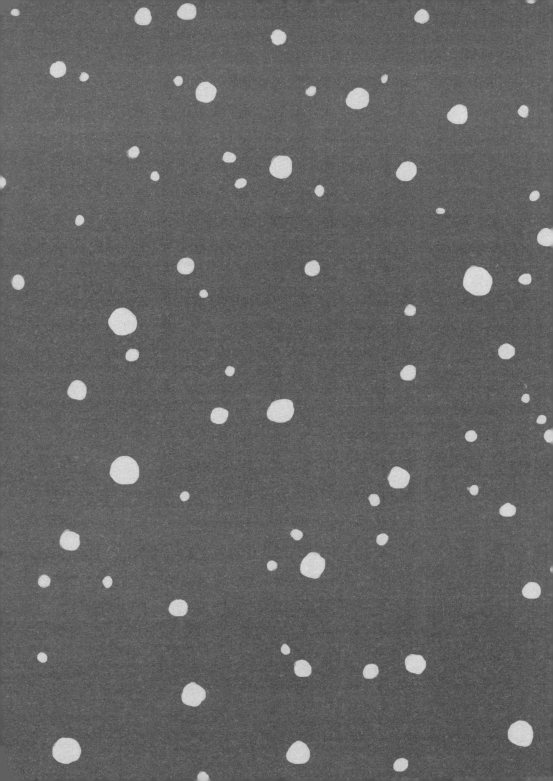

You are not a snowflake.

Seriously, you are not.

Are you shaped like a hexagon? Are you ice-cold to touch? Do you tend to melt when the temperature goes above two degrees?

No?

Then you are definitely not a snowflake.

Snowflakes, for example, cannot read books. They can't laugh, or cry. They can't play sport, communicate through language, or start YouTube channels. They can't be there for their friends, or stick up for one another should another snowflake start behaving badly. Snowflakes cannot dance. Snowflakes cannot sing. Snowflakes cannot shout or scream or feel. Snowflakes don't get to experience the dizzying, complicated, life-affirming range of emotions that humans do.

So no, you are not a snowflake. You are far more impressive than a snowflake. You are a glorious, gorgeous person with an incredible, breathtaking brain that will, during the course of your life, take you to the most beautiful, incredible, terrifying places … sometimes, without you even having to leave your bedroom.

You are not a snowflake. You are: kick-ass; complex; nuanced; fascinating; awe-inspiring. But a snowflake?

No way.

You may have guessed by now that I really don't dig the term 'snowflake' – unless of course it is applied to actual snow, in which case it is just fine. But the use of the word 'snowflake' as a label for the younger generation undermines all the young people who are bravely speaking out and expressing their feelings in an attempt to help groups who have previously been ignored. And it makes my blood boil. Here are just a few of the headlines I have seen in the news recently:

'SNOWFLAKES ARE THE MOST STRESSED GENERATION'

'IS THE SNOWFLAKE GENERATION TOO SELF-OBSESSED?'

'SNOWFLAKE KIDS GET LESSONS IN CHILLING'

(above a front page story in a daily newspaper about a school offering children mindfulness and meditation)

the monsters in my head

Well, all this nonsense about snowflakes isn't only insulting, it is also *dangerous*. It is dangerous, because it makes people feel that they shouldn't give voice to their feelings. And when you feel you can't give voice to your feelings, the results can be catastrophic.

I know this, personally. I know this, because I grew up during a time when nobody spoke about the stuff inside their heads. So when, at the age of 12, I suddenly became convinced that I was going to die of a terrible, infectious illness, I had no idea that the *actual* illness that would threaten to kill me over the next few years was a mental illness, Obsessive Compulsive Disorder, and the subsequent depression it caused. I just thought I was bad, wrong, on the verge of death. I became so obsessed with germs that I would spend hours by a sink washing my hands until they bled. I found it difficult to leave the house, because I thought that everything I touched in the outside world had the power to infect and kill me. I slept with my toothbrush under my pillow and refused to touch my family. I didn't want to kill them too, with whatever it was I had. I began chanting phrases to keep them alive. I had, as a child, been warned about the monsters that lurked outside. But nobody told me about the one I might find in my own head.

My parents thought that it was just an adolescent phase. The irony was, it could have been. We know now that most mental illnesses are incredibly treatable – it's when they have bedded in that things start to get a bit more complicated. Without treatment, sufferers develop terrible coping mechanisms in an attempt to control what is happening to them – in my case, over the years, bulimia, drug addiction and alcoholism. What could have been an unpleasant but simple case of adolescent OCD snowballed into a lifetime of complex mental illness that didn't just make me miserable – it caused great misery to everyone who loved me, too. And this entirely preventable misery is why I do what I do now. It is why I shout and scream about mental illness, sometimes until I am blue in the face. It is because I don't want my daughter to grow up in the same kind of world that I did, one that stigmatises mental illness and in the process makes it almost impossible to deal with.

And let me tell you now:

Mental illness is absolutely not impossible to deal with, even if it feels so at the time.

Even if you cannot see a way upwards and outwards – I promise you, it is there. I promise you, because I am living proof that is there, as I sit here typing this book for you.

I am sitting here typing this book for you because I don't want you to go through what I did. Because mental illness is sometimes unavoidable, in the same way that many physical illnesses are. But it is never, ever untreatable, in the same way that most physical illnesses aren't. I often use the diabetes analogy when I give talks about mental health: imagine that someone gets a diagnosis of Diabetes Type II today. Imagine that they take their medication, change their diet, start to do exercise – if they do this, they are going to live a reasonably long and healthy life and feel better for it. Now, imagine that they don't do any of this. Imagine that they refuse to take their medication, that they eat only junk food, and that they never leave the sofa. In this case, the patient is likely to end up having his foot amputated, as can actually happen with untreated diabetes. A similar outcome can be expected with mental illness – treat it and you end up with a pretty normal life experiencing the occasional glitch; don't treat it and that's when things can go very, very wrong.

Like many mental health campaigners, I am convinced that the key to good mental health is making young people aware of what that entails. Prevention is better than cure, and it simply doesn't make sound economic sense to wait until people are extremely ill adults to treat them. We know that 50 per cent of mental health issues will be present in a sufferer by the time they are 14, and 75 per cent by the age of 24. Our prisons are full of people who never got the help they needed as a child; people who suffer from poor mental health are more likely to experience bad physical health, too, not to mention unemployment. I don't say this to alarm you. I just say this to make you aware of how very important it is that you take your mental health seriously right now.

Mental health issues are not new. People have been living with them and dying from them from the year dot – they've just never ever felt able to talk about them. This is why I can't stand the 'snowflake' tag. This is why I want to tell everyone who uses it to pipe down and let others speak for a moment. This is why, when some old dude (usually a politician or a right-wing television personality) who last healthily expressed an emotion in 1974 starts talking about how a stiff upper lip never harmed him and one must keep their feelings to themselves, I want to scream:

'Well maybe it never harmed YOU. But what about that quiet boy in the class you never heard from again, or the friend you used to play with from down the street who ended up drinking himself to an early grave? A stiff upper lip may never have harmed you, but that is not to say it didn't harm anyone else.

And perhaps instead of trying to stop other people from feeling, your time might be better spent locating yours.'

Stiff upper lips may have been the order of the day when the biggest killer of young men in this country was the Nazis. But now it is suicide, a different approach is required.

Screw stiff upper lips.

Screw stiff upper lips, and thank God for so-called 'snowflakes'. Because if the absolute worst thing people can think of to describe young folk as is 'sensitive', then frankly, I think we are in pretty good hands.

dealing with all that stuff in your head

Now my rant is out of the way, you may well be wondering what on earth you can do if you are worried about your mental health.

Because it's all well and good standing up and shouting about things, quite another actually *dealing* with these things.

I know, I know. *Believe* me, I know.

I also know what you want from this chapter. What you want is for me to say some words that are suddenly going to make everything OK again. You want me to give you some practical tip that is going to immediately unfog your head and light up the way you view things.

I know you want these things, because I have wanted them too.

When you are desperate, when you are low, when even the brightest things look dark … you want it all to be better. Of course you do. Nobody *wants* to wake up in the morning and immediately feel the heavy weight of the day sitting on their chest. Nobody *wants* to feel despair where they should be feeling hunger for life, or to find panic in a space where they should be feeling calm. Nobody wants to feel so bad that they wish they could disappear under their duvet forever more, even if under their duvet is the place where all the monsters in their head seem to come out to play.

Nobody wants any of this. But sometimes, these things happen. And I hope I don't sound unsympathetic here, because you know that I am not: really, what I am trying to do is make you feel less alone. Because quite a lot of the time, these things happen. A quarter of us will experience a mental health issue this year, and a fifth of us will have suicidal thoughts. And these things happen to you not because you are bad or faulty or a freak. In fact, they happen to you because quite the opposite is true. It is actually the most normal thing in the world to feel weird – even if it doesn't feel so normal at the time. The real weirdos are the ones who claim to feel fine 24/7. So this is the first thing I will say to you:

You are feeling like this because you have a brain, and just like all other organs, brains sometimes play up.

I dream of the day when nobody talks about mental health and physical health, and instead just uses the term health, because what are brains if not part of our physical body? But until that blissful day of stigma-free existence, I would like to tell you all the things that have helped me over the many, many years I have experienced mental illness and somehow, simultaneously, thrived. Because it is possible – it really, truly is. I may not be able to magically make everything better for you. But what I can do is give you lots of seemingly tiny steps that will add up and make a huge difference over time. I can hold your hand, and let you know that I am there for you. That there are plenty of people there for you, even if it might not feel like it right now.

Talking is the only way forward.

Let me make this very clear: nobody has ever, ever got better from a mental illness by not talking about it. Talking about mental illness is the key to getting better. Admitting the stuff in your head may not immediately cure you – in fact, I can guarantee it won't – but it will start you on the path to recovery. This, I promise you.

There are many different mental illnesses out there, from OCD to depression to eating disorders to schizophrenia – but they all work in much the same way. They all work like an abuser, thriving in a culture of silence. In a culture of silence, your mental illness can lie to you and isolate you. It can tell you that you are a freak, and that you are alone, and that nobody will ever understand what you are going through. But this is an outrageous lie. It is simply not true. There are people who understand what you are going through on your street right now. There are people who understand what you are going through, possibly even in your own house right now. I know that from your isolation this can feel completely ludicrous – but the chances are that right round the corner, someone else is stuck in their own isolation, too, feeling terribly alone.

Once we start to give a voice to what is going on in our heads, we prove the mental illness wrong on a very, very basic level.

By speaking our feelings out loud, or even just putting them down in a journal, we can start to see the illness for what it is – an illness, and not a damning indictment of our characters. Finding a sympathetic ear is often the best way to do this – but I know, at first, that can seem hard, so at the back of this book I have listed a heap of absolutely incredible text and phone services that you can use to take that first step. I promise you there is someone out there who will understand you. More than anything, *I* understand you.

You are not making a fuss.

A couple of years ago, I was doing a talk at a big festival in the UK. As is usual, we leave 20 minutes for questions at the end – though when it comes to mental health, we could usually fill double that time. On this particular occasion, a woman stood up and started talking about her 16-year-old daughter, who she said 'claimed' to have depression. The woman thought that her daughter was 'just attention-seeking'. My flabbergasted response was this: 'Well then maybe try giving her some attention?'

A lot of grown-ups dismiss the feelings of young people as 'making a fuss'. There is nothing wrong with 'making a fuss'. 'Making a fuss' is a very good thing if someone actually listens to you as you make that fuss, and then helps you to feel less fussy about the thing that is causing you distress.

Here's another way that we often put down people who need help: often, talking about feelings and emotions is viewed in society as 'self-indulgent'. It is quite the opposite. It is, in many ways, *selfless*.

Dealing with the stuff in your head helps you to free up space so you can be there for others.

Self-indulgence is silencing other people and stopping them from talking about the way they feel because it doesn't fit with your schedule.

Wanting attention is not a negative thing either. Asking for help from your family and friends is not a weakness. It is a strength. It shows that you have resilience, because you want to sort your head out and get on with the rest of your life. Sometimes, our mental illness will lie to us by telling us that our problems are not worthy of other people's attention – that what we are going through is 'nothing'. And something may well be nothing – but then, even if it is, wouldn't you rather raise your concerns and keep them at nothing instead of stewing on them silently until they turn into something really, really big?

Don't let anyone silence you. And that includes yourself.

Give your demon a name.

Thinking of your head in a slightly detached way can be a really brilliant way of getting some space from mental health issues. I know, I know – surely the whole point of mental illness is that it doesn't let you think of your head in a detached way? It throws you into it, makes it harder to leave it. But there are little tricks I have picked up along the way that can help you to get some space from the stuff going on in your head. And one of those is giving your demon a name.

I learned this from a therapist who told me to name my OCD. I call it Jareth the Goblin King, after the character from the children's film *Labyrinth* – he was played by David Bowie in tight silver trousers, and I thought it was an appropriate name given that, like Jareth, my OCD felt evil and yet very, very enticing. Every time I had a moment where Jareth tried to suck me in, I would call him out. 'Get lost, Jareth!' I would shout to nobody in particular as I walked down the street. Sure, I may have *looked* mad, but I didn't care, because actually, doing this made me feel slightly less bonkers. It helps me to see my OCD for exactly what it is: a nasty, horrible illness I happen to have, but that absolutely isn't my fault.

Another thing I like to do is think of my brain as being wired slightly strangely. You know movies where some action hero has to defuse a bomb by cutting the green wire – but absolutely not the red wire? I think of the wires in my brain as being completely mixed up – so that the green wire is where the red wire is, and vice versa. As a result, my thoughts are sometimes a bit off. That doesn't make me a bad person. It just means that, like loads of other people, I was wired a little differently to the original blueprints, and that can sometimes make life feel a little harder.

Go easy on yourself – you can't help how you were wired, any more than you can help what kind of blood type you have.

Beware: social media.

Social media can be a great place to find like-minded people who understand what you are going through. But it can also be a dangerous place where it is quite possible to be sucked into a dark underworld without even noticing. There have, tragically, been reports of people taking their own lives due to content found on Instagram, which has led the media giant to announce it will remove all images that explicitly show methods of self-harm and suicide. This is a start, but there are other things you can do to make yourself safe online.

How can you use the internet so you get the best out of it, as opposed to it getting the best out of you? Well that's the trillion-dollar question, isn't it? If I could answer that one, I probably wouldn't be sitting here in my pants in my bedroom, writing this book. I would instead be doing it in my pants in my giant writing room, that leads off my library, that is part of my mansion that has a walk-in wardrobe, several opulent bathrooms, a cinema, a disco (the disco is key), and indoor and outdoor swimming pools.

Navigating social media can be really hard. It can be fake. It can be dark. Like mental illness, it lies to you rather a lot, with people showing you their best lives but never, ever their worst. There is graphic, horrible stuff on there that nobody needs to see, and I haven't even got to online bullying yet.

But what if it also feels like the only place where you can find people who understand you? What if it feels like a lifeline?

Look, I am not here to lay down rules and regulations. I am not your mum. I hope you feel that I am your friend when I tell you that on a very personal level, I find it much better for my own mental health to stay off social media when I am feeling really, really low. It's not just all the stuff on there, like the endless memes and the women who look like cartoon versions of themselves – it's the looking down and into a screen rather than up and out into the world.

I recently locked my phone away for six days. It was really hard at first, and I was crashing around the place like a raging bull, as if my life was going to end because I couldn't watch what everyone was up to on Insta Stories. Instead – and here's a crazy idea! – I had to go and watch what everyone was up to IN THE REAL WORLD. I know, I know, it will never catch on. Anyway, I felt actual anger for the first couple of days. It sort of scared me. But by the end of it, I was so much fresher. It was like I'd been reborn – until I opened up my phone and got sucked straight back in again. But you know. I *tried*.

Now I'm not suggesting you go off social media entirely – that may feel too hard. But what I would suggest is:

Set limits for yourself.

Read a book. I mean, you *are* reading a book right now, so I am kind of preaching to the converted. You get what I mean.

Make sure you give
yourself regular breaks.

Try not checking your social media
until the evening, if you can.

Go out for a walk without
your phone if possible.

And you really don't need *me* to tell *you* any of this. You know it all, deep down inside.

But, here's my best tip for dealing with social media. It's kind of the same one I would give you for dealing with life, generally. If something makes you feel uncomfortable, if deep down in your incredible intelligent gut something doesn't sit right – then shut it down. Shut it down, take a deep breath, and if it feels possible, talk to someone about it.

Remember that you are not supposed to feel happy all the time.

Happy is good. Happy is great. Happy is … well, happy. We spend a lot of time, as kids, being taught about the importance of happy, but nobody ever teaches us how to be sad. This can end up being really problematic, because sad is also a legitimate feeling that we will all experience at some point in our lives. Until quite recently, I was really scared of sad. I would have done anything to avoid it. But then I realised it's OK to be sad. It doesn't feel great, sure, but if you actually feel it, you'll probably get through it a whole lot quicker than if you try and avoid feeling it. At some point, you are going to have to feel all the feelings your brain wants you to feel … so you may as well get them out of the way now, rather than putting them off until they all come at you at once, threatening to overwhelm you entirely. Embrace sadness, and it's actually a whole lot easier to get to happy.

We don't live in an *Avengers* movie (thank God).

Now you may be thinking 'What has a Marvel movie starring Scarlett Johansson and Chris Hemsworth got to do with any of this? Has this woman gone COMPLETELY LOCO?' Bear with me, here. Let me explain.

When I was suffering from mental illness as a young woman, I often thought this mental illness was actually a sign that I was a bad person. I was bad, bad, bad, and everyone else was good,

good, good. The good girl thing I had been brought up with was so ingrained within me that any deviation from it made me feel like I was probably an evil villain.

Here's the thing: the world is not made up of goodies and baddies. We don't live in the Marvel Universe (more's the pity, because I would totally love to be one of the Guardians of the Galaxy). I have realised now that I was not a bad person … I was just an unwell one, who would sometimes do bad things as a result of being unwell. Life is not binary. It is not black and white. Like you, it is made up of a colour palette so rich that to try and describe it by just one or two of them would be to undermine it entirely. So no, this is not the Marvel Universe. But if you can do battle with mental health issues, you are basically a super hero in my eyes.

Don't trash talk yourself.

THIS ONE IS SO SUPER IMPORTANT I AM GOING TO WRITE IT IN CAPITALS IN THE HOPE THAT THIS SHINES THROUGH. BE KIND TO YOURSELF. HAVE EMPATHY FOR YOUR SELF. TREAT YOURSELF AS YOU WOULD A CUTE PUPPY – EXCEPT PERHAPS WHEN IT COMES TO THE DOG FOOD. IF YOU WOULDN'T TALK TO SOMEONE ELSE THE WAY YOU ARE TALKING TO YOURSELF, CHANGE THE INTERNAL CONVERSATION. I KNOW SOMETIMES IT FEELS THAT IF YOU DO YOURSELF DOWN, THEN NOBODY ELSE CAN. BUT NOBODY ELSE MATTERS AS MUCH AS YOU DO. YOU ARE YOUR NUMBER ONE, AND ALWAYS WILL BE, SO YOU MAY AS

WELL MAKE IT THE KIND OF NUMBER ONE YOU'D ACTUALLY LIKE TO LISTEN TO – RATHER THAN, SAY, BABY SHARK … NO, I WON'T GO THERE AGAIN, I PROMISE. BEATING YOURSELF UP WHEN YOU ARE ALREADY DOWN ONLY MAKES IT HARDER FOR YOU TO GET BACK UP AGAIN. SO DON'T DO IT. LOOK AFTER YOURSELF. YOU ARE PRECIOUS. YOU ARE WORTH BEING LOVELY TO. SO START, AND THEN I CAN STOP WRITING IN CAPITALS!

Medication is nothing to be ashamed of … but is not the only answer.

I am on anti-depressants, and have been, on and off, since I was 17. They work for me, but it is important to say that they are not the *only* thing that works for me. It is really, really crucial that you explore all the available options with your GP, including therapy. I know that child mental health services are severely under-resourced in this country and that it can feel impossible to get help without your parents first having to experience severe distress too. I do a lot of work on this with other mental health campaigners, but this book is not a political manifesto, and nor would you want it to be, I suspect. What I want to say is that it is possible to get through this with the right support.

Organisations such as Young Minds, Place2Be and The Mix are really, really brilliant in terms of providing practical support (their details are at the back of this book). There is a number of peer support groups out there, Mental Health Mates, which I founded, among them (again, details are at the back of this book). And if you do feel unsafe, please go to your local A & E where a team of doctors and nurses can assess you.

On a very basic level, I would ask you to try some simple things too like …

✳ Rest as much as you can

✳ Eat as healthily as you can

✳ Cut out gross, sugary, fizzy stuff (if you can). I know this sounds boring, I know it sounds basic, but these things do really, really help

✱ Try and exercise (if you can). That does not have to be a run – it can be getting up, stretching, or walking to the local park and back

✱ Do not try and deal with the whole day – take each hour as it comes, if you have to

These little things will also help you to feel like you are clawing back some sort of control when it otherwise seems like you have none. You are not alone – you are so not alone, and all the numbers and details of organisations at the back of this book will help you to realise that.

Remember that your courage to speak out helps others too.

People will look back on your generation and see you as trailblazers. As revolutionaries. Mental illness is not new – but talking about it is, and by talking about it, you are holding mental illness accountable. You are letting governments and powerful people know that your generation – YOURS – will not ignore this stuff any more. That they need to buck up and help people – or otherwise, ship out. You are paving the way for other people to get help. You should be proud of the way you and your friends talk about things, not ashamed of it. Because you will help future generations to be able to access the treatment that they deserve. That you deserve.

Remember this: you are as magnificent and intricate and brilliant as a snowflake. But you are not as weak or impermanent as one.

You are changing things. Just by admitting the stuff in your head, you are making a huge difference that will be felt for years to come. So when your head tries to lie to you, when some old fart tries to keep you down, remember this: by speaking out, the so-called snowflake generation are actually saving lives. And to a woman like me who has had to suffer for decades in silence, that is kind of mind-blowing. So thank you. From the bottom of my heart and top of my sometimes hurting head, thank you.

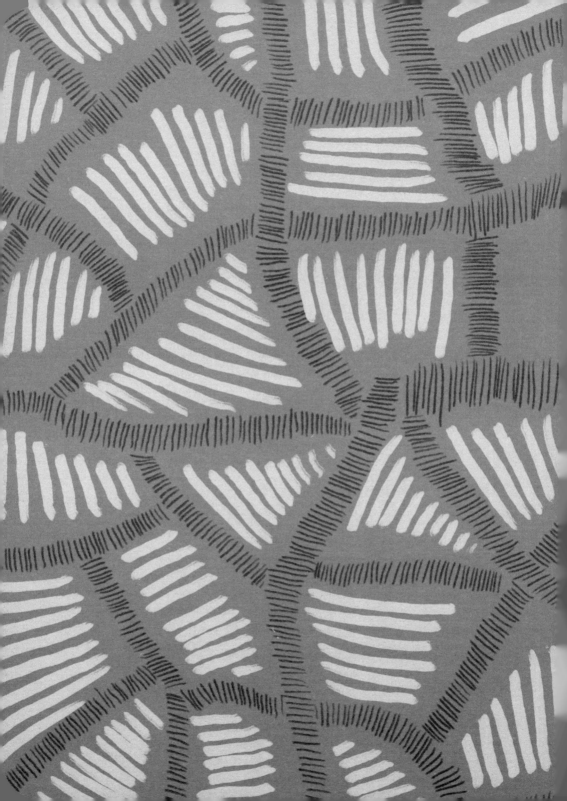

Nine

You Are More Than Your Chaos

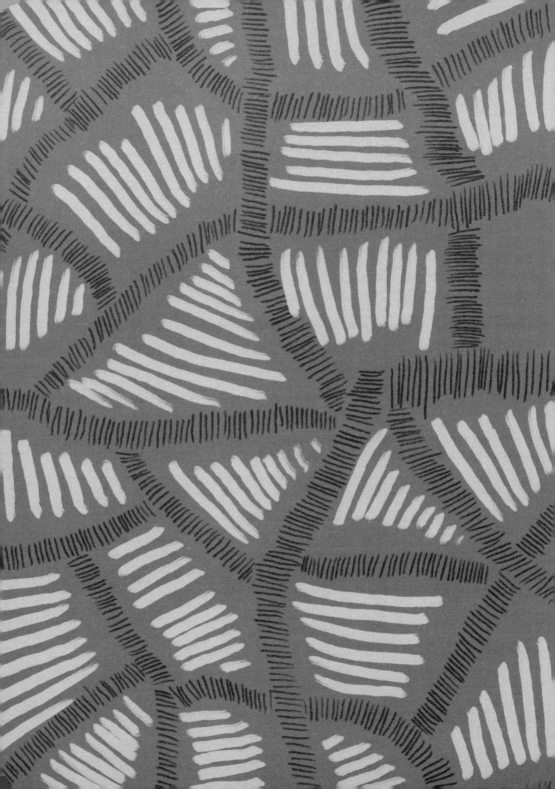

When I was a teenager, I used to do this thing – this quite embarrassing thing, truth be told – which involved listening to a song and imagining I was starring in the music video that would accompany it.

These songs were usually sung by some boy band or hunky pop star and were normally about some romantic drama involving a to-die-for girl whom I always imagined was me. Because, you know, why not? It wasn't as if there was anything else going on in my life. There would be a verse, a bridge and a chorus, during which the video would pan between me – usually walking around some beach looking gorgeous and mysterious, my skin bronzed, my hair tousled, etc. – and Robbie Williams, pining longingly from afar. I would look into the distance at nothing in particular, in a smouldering, sexy way, as girls in music videos do. And then, finally, there would be a dramatic crescendo where I imagined Robbie running across some dunes to sweep me off my feet, my friends magically appearing out of nowhere to look on enviously, perhaps breaking into a coordinated dance routine they somehow all knew by heart.

I *lived* for this imaginary dramatic crescendo.

Reader, when I was a teenager, *this* was what passed for an attempt to elevate my life from the mundane to the magical. And actually, now I come to think about it, it is *still* what occasionally passes as an attempt to lift my life from the mundane to the magical. I tell you this not to try and humiliate myself – I think we can all agree that I have done quite enough of that over the preceding pages. No, I tell you this to stress that I did this (and sometimes still do) because the only thing that really excited me was the idea of excitement itself. Drama. Turmoil. Passion. Adventure. Non-stop action. A topsy-turvy rollercoaster of emotions.

In my bedroom, I tried to ignore the fact that my life was nothing of the sort, mostly revolving as it did around homework, and ferreting away my allowance (so much more grown-up than pocket money) to buy lipstick and nail varnish. I wanted my life to be like one long series of music videos, not one of those dreary public health broadcasts they sometimes showed you at school, telling you about the importance of nutrition and a good night's sleep (yawn). I wanted *my* life to be an endless procession of cinematic crescendos, in which I was cast as the heroine, the powerful protagonist, the woman who saved the world and captured everyone's – EVERYONE'S – hearts in the process. And I thought that drama was the key to this. Drama and gossip – but kind, awestruck gossip about how cool I was. (Hey, guess what? Gossip doesn't work like that!) I thought that to save the day, I first had to create some crazy soap-opera story line from which to save it. There probably needed to be mean girls and mean boys, and then a plucky friend and unexpected love interest to help me triumph over them. There needed to be: tears; shouting matches; prolonged periods of refusing to talk to someone; more tears; more shouting matches; fireworks. And so on and so on.

I should have been careful what I wished for.

Because as I got older, life *did* become one long drama. And it wasn't quite as glamorous as I had perhaps imagined it to be – the reality was a little different to the fantasy, shall we say? My life was *kind* of like a music video, had that music video been put together on a phone in the back garden for a bit of a laugh, with zero production values and before filters had been invented. There were many tears. There were many mean girls, though now I think about them, their meanness was probably only something I imagined – a look I didn't like, or a pout I took personally, because I took *everything* personally. There were plenty of mean boys, real mean boys who genuinely behaved badly, breaking my heart. My plucky friends were many and varied, but their way of helping me to triumph was by worrying about me, telling me to take vitamin supplements, eat more broccoli, and stay in a couple of nights a week so I could get more sleep. And the unexpected love interest? Well he only turned up at the very, *very* last minute, just as the credits were about to roll.

The drama sometimes revealed itself in different plot lines, depending on the episode. Season one: Will our heroine be able to scrape enough money together to pay her rent? Will she be able to hand in the big work project she is supposed to have been working on for weeks, but potentially screwed up by going out with her friends before it is due in? Season two: Will our heroine pluck up the guts to leave the handsome toe rag who isn't treating her well? Will she ever turn up for anything on time? Will she ever get her stuff together and stop having to borrow money off her parents? Is anyone even still watching?

When I was young, I thought that I had to do things to entertain people. I felt, perhaps because of my history of mental illness, that I was duty bound to be a screw-up, and that if this was going to be the case, then I might as well make people laugh as I did it. I may as well take the stuff that made me frown and use it to make other people smile. I had no idea that none of this was true, that people would have hung out with me regardless of my ability to turn my mishaps into comedy gold. That perhaps they would have even *preferred* to hang out with me if I didn't mercilessly mock myself all the time. But I am being hard on myself, and that is something I try not to be now. All I am saying is that I felt I had to be a bit dramatic to get anyone's attention. I had to be crazy, kooky and 'fun', otherwise I would disappear off everybody's radar. Nobody told me that in my desperate quest to be 'fun', I would almost do this *anyway*. And nobody told me that being fun is very, very different to being happy.

Or maybe they did, but I was too busy imagining myself in a music video to listen.

what makes you interesting

You Make You Interesting.

Drama doesn't make you interesting.

You make you interesting.

You, you, YOU.

The fact that you have a crazy boyfriend doesn't make you interesting.

The fact that you might have a crazy girlfriend doesn't make you interesting.

Drinking alcohol and taking drugs doesn't make you interesting – indeed, the opposite is true. It's really tedious, talking to someone who is off their face.

Smoking doesn't make you interesting. It just makes you smell and extremely unhealthy.

Arguing with people doesn't make you interesting.

Not talking to them to try and teach them some sort of lesson doesn't make you interesting.

And as for gossip? Yep, you guessed it: it doesn't make you interesting.

It just makes you someone who can spill other people's secrets. And we can *all* do that.

Taking the bad stuff that has happened to you, and then turning it into some sort of performance piece rather than actually dealing with it: this doesn't make you interesting either.

It just makes me want to jump through this book and give you a big hug.

Breaking rules doesn't make you interesting, no matter how fun it might be at the time. Not bothering to do any work at school doesn't make you interesting – it just makes you a little bit self-destructive (dude, we all have to go to school for a reason, and that reason isn't just to get us out of our parents' hair for a few hours each day).

Your clothes don't make you interesting, and nor does your make-up. The way you do your hair doesn't make you interesting. These are all lovely ways to express your personality, but they are not your personality. And your personality … well, that's what makes you interesting.

You. You make you interesting.

Your opinions on things. Your take on the world. The things that really, truly interest you – these are some of the things that make you interesting.

Being interested in other people makes you interesting. And actually, you don't have to be interesting. You don't owe anyone interesting. You are not a streaming service that people subscribe to for £7.99 a month. You are not a walking, talking YouTube channel. You are a person who is sometimes up and sometimes down and most of the time somewhere in between. You are a person who sometimes needs to be around people, and sometimes needs to be alone, without worrying about whether you are interesting or not.

OF COURSE YOU ARE INTERESTING. YOU'RE **YOU**.

make boredom brilliant

Does this all sound boring? Good. Boring, I have learnt, after lifetime of chaos, is not such a bad thing. It's not something to be feared and avoided at all costs. In fact, sometimes it is absolutely necessary. Boring is where the magic happens. It is where the inspiration strikes. Boring is when your brain gets to settle and have some much-needed time out, so that it can come back at you with stuff to make your life interesting. If you want to live a rich and fulfilled life, boredom is sometimes exactly the thing that you need.

So with that in mind, here is how to make boredom brilliant.

You can sky dive and have a savings account at the same time.

Remember that being sensible does not make you dull. Refusing to give into peer pressure because it doesn't sit right with you doesn't make you dreary – it makes you someone who knows their own mind, which is pretty damn cool if you ask me. Sensible people take risks all the time. They risk being 'left out' because they don't want to go with the flow and prefer to stand their ground. Sensible is not the same as disinteresting, not at all. It is knowing what interests you and what makes you tick

239

and what doesn't. It is taking stock of a situation and making sure that everything is right before you launch yourself into it. Sensible is knowing your mind, and going with it.

Sometimes, most of the time actually, to be sensible is to be brilliantly, beautifully brave.

Giving value to basic life skills is basically the same as valuing yourself.

Learning to budget and cook are not the kind of things you will see depicted in music videos. Mariah Carey has never writhed around putting together a spag bol and doing household chores. These things are not sexy or exciting. They may seem like a waste of time, now, but actually they are important skills that, by learning, will help you give value to your life. There is something really nourishing about being able to cook for yourself, and it is empowering to try and save money – or at least have a plan to save money – so that you don't have to worry about it all the time. Learning to be self-sufficient was one of the most mind-blowing things I ever did for myself. Not having to rely on anyone else makes me feel strong and capable and like I can take on the world. And the bonus? Being sensible about my life actually frees up more time for me to be silly.

Putting off stuff just means it ends up taking up more of your time.

Take it from someone who has spent more time worrying about this book than actually writing it: do your homework and your chores now. Get them out the way. Then you can go and do stuff you actually actively enjoy.

Cherish your privacy.

Ohmigod, did I just write that heading? Has this turned into a self-help book? It has totally turned into a self-help book, hasn't it? I'm so, so *sorry*. But when I talk about 'cherishing your privacy', what I really mean is 'look after your bedroom'. Your bedroom is everything, because it is most likely the only place in the world where you have your own space that others aren't allowed to step into without permission. You can do what you want with this space (within reason), and you should.

Look, I'm not Marie Kondo. My mum used to be scared to come into my bedroom in case she discovered new life forms that would try to eat her. Even now, I have a tendency towards mess and mayhem (this is probably the least surprising news *ever?*). But I find that if I keep things tidy(ish), and take pride in the

place that I live, I actually have more freedom to make a mess
– creatively, at least. When things are calm around me, I can
concentrate on working through the stuff in my head.

Your bedroom is yours. It is the space where you can really *be*.
Love it and look after it and your life will be better for it,
I promise.

You may be growing up, but never forget to treat yourself like a very small child.

Look after yourself. Eat three meals a day. Drink water. Get a
good night's sleep. Exercise to grow yourself, not shrink yourself.
Get some fresh air, even if it's just for a moment. We may not
actually be babies, but we should never, ever stop treating
ourselves like we are.

You are not a performing monkey, put there for other people's entertainment.

The most important thing to you should be your own happiness,
not other people's. Sure, it's not cool to go around making
other people *un*happy. But you are also not obliged to go
around making people laugh all the time, especially if it's at
your expense.

It's OK to be loud, and it's OK to be quiet. It's also OK to be both.

You know I am a huge advocate of talking about stuff. But I also know that you don't always feel like talking about stuff. And that's OK, too. You are not letting people down if you want to stew on something by yourself for a bit, to try and make sense of it. You have every right to be quiet and thoughtful. You are not being moody, or sulky, if you do this. You are just doing what you have to do!

Life is not *Riverdale*, and nor would you want it to be. Endless drama is exhausting. If you can, avoid it in your own life at all costs, and leave it to the programmes playing out on Netflix. This doesn't mean you should avoid the awkward conversations you need to have with friends who have perhaps upset you or treated you badly. Nor do you have to storm off and make a scene. Say the things you have to say calmly and constructively, and then everyone can get on with the more important things in life … like, er, watching *Riverdale*. (Not that I do. OK. Sometimes I do. But only very occasionally. Like, each week when there is a new episode.)

Treat other people's drama as you would their backpack. Don't go near it – unless you have been asked to help **zip it up**. I used to tell myself that if I didn't actually start gossip, then it was OK. But it wasn't, not really. I was still complicit in it, still allowing the drama to play out. Whoever was the subject of the gossip was still going to get hurt. Remember: there's no rule that says you have to get sucked into other people's stuff. If they want to offload on you and use you as a shoulder to cry on so that they can stay afloat, that's fine. But if they want to drag you down with them, that's not.

Don't fall for the myth of FOMO.

Everyone fears missing out. *Everyone.* I do. You do. That person over there does. It is human nature to imagine that around the corner, everyone else is having a better time than you. But they're not. They're wondering what *you* are up to.

The irony is that simply by fearing you are missing out, you will miss out. You will miss out because you will be so busy looking to see what is going on over there that you won't notice what is going on right in front of you. Who cares what's going on where you're not? It doesn't matter. It's really, truly, not important. It has nothing to do with you. Yes, I know it can be hurtful if you haven't been invited to a party. But there will be other parties – better parties, where you actually like the people and won't spend the entirety of it worrying if everyone hates you (they don't, they're just being douchebags). Look at it this way: you're not missing out … people are missing out on you. It's their loss. Now you go focus on all your gains.

Sometimes, most of the time, the drama is only playing out in your head. That is not to undermine the drama. Just because you are actually the only one experiencing it, that doesn't make it any less important. But remember: each and every person in your class and school will have a completely different one playing out in their own heads. You may think that someone is blanking you, but there is every possibility that they are just absorbed in their own stuff. Everyone has their own music video looping through their brains. Your music video will play out perfectly, if you just stop worrying about everybody else's.

Be kind. Mostly, be kind to yourself.

Do this, and you will get a cinematic crescendo beyond your wildest dreams. It may not look the way you want it to, right now. But it will be perfect, I promise. It will be just as it should.

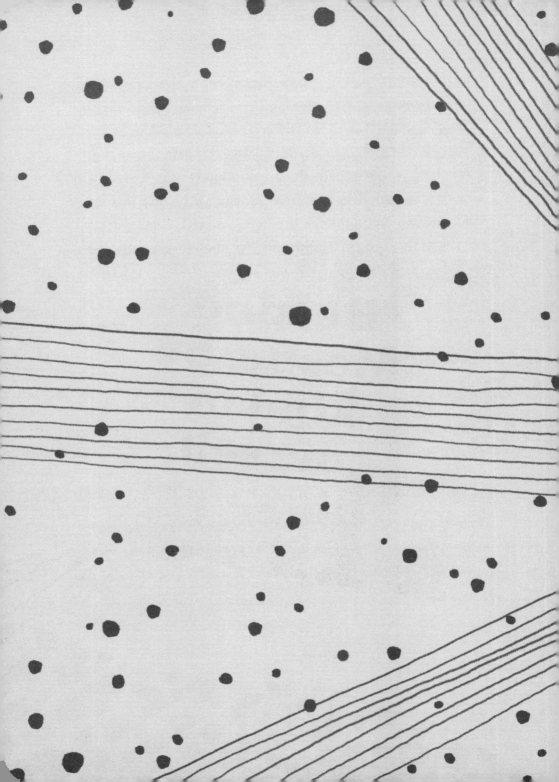

Ten

You Got This

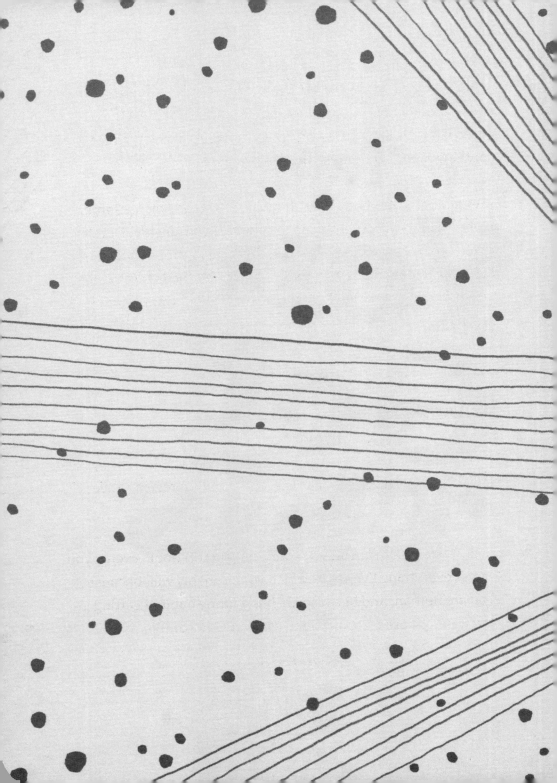

Really, you have.

Even if it feels like you haven't, even if it feels like you've got nothing at all … I promise that you've got *this*.

Remember: everybody feels this way, too. Even Selena Gomez. Even Taylor Swift. Even Michelle Obama. Even Meghan Markle. Even the Queen. At some point in their lives – probably at *lots* of points in their lives – they will all have felt the fear that they are too little or too much, that the world might be about to fall in on them.

But it didn't.

And just like them, you've got this.

If your parents and your teachers tell you that you haven't, you still absolutely *have*. You just need to go out there and prove them wrong.

Even if you ignore absolutely everything in this book, even if you forget everything I've said – which you probably will, because you are human, and because life has a funny habit of getting in the way – please trust me when I say: You've got this.

Because you are lovely.

You are magic.

You are everything you need right now, and forever more.

You?
You
Got
This.

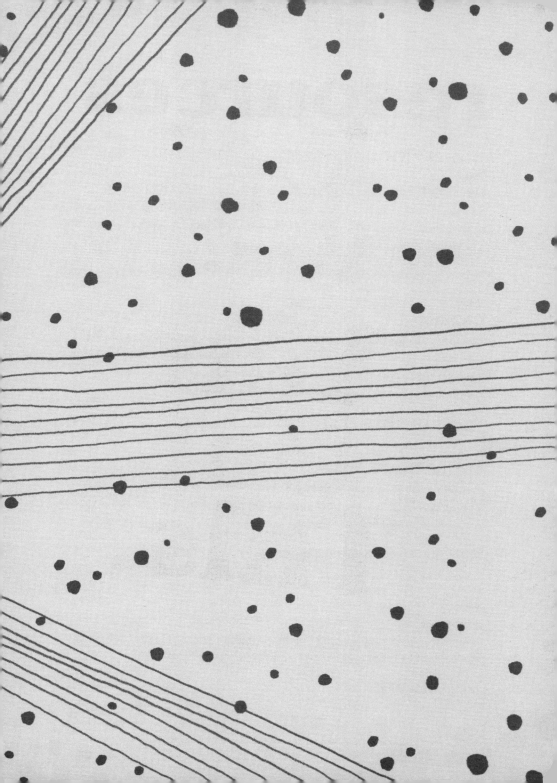

resources

Beat
Beat is the UK's leading charity supporting anyone affected by eating disorders, anorexia, bulimia, or any other difficulties with food, weight and shape. They have lots of downloadable resources, online support groups and a helpline on their website too.

https://www.beateatingdisorders.org.uk

Childline
Childline is a counselling service for children and young people and you can contact them just by giving them a call. They can give information and advice on lots of things from school, family and bullying, to anxiety, mental health and puberty. They have lots of online advice too.

https://www.childline.org.uk

Mental Health Mates
Mental Health Mates is a network of support groups run by people with mental health issues. Members meet regularly to walk and talk about their problems without any judgement.

https://www.mentalhealthmates.co.uk/

Mind
Mind is a leading mental health charity that offers advice and support to anyone experiencing a mental health problem. They have crisis helplines, drop-in centres, and deliver mental health services across the UK.

https://www.mind.org.uk

Place2Be

Place2Be is a leading national children's mental health charity, with the aim of providing therapeutic and mental health support in schools.

https://www.place2be.org.uk/

Shout

Shout will be the UK's first free 24/7 direct messaging service for anyone in a crisis.

www.giveusashout.com

The Mix

The Mix offers free and confidential advice to under 25s on everything from mental health to money, drugs or relationships. You can talk to them over the phone, email or webchat. Plus they have discussion boards and loads of helpful advice on their website.

https://www.themix.org.uk

Young Minds

Young Minds is the UK's leading charity fighting for children and young people's mental health. They even have a free, confidential helpline for parents who might be worried about how a child or young person is feeling.

https://youngminds.org.uk

acknowledgements

I would like to thank Debbie Foy, Laura Horsley and everyone else at Wren & Rook for parenting me through the creation of this book. Thank you also to my agent Nelle Andrew, who listened to my random idea, didn't laugh, and instead went out and made it happen. Nelle, you might be younger than me, but there's no doubt about it: you are my publishing mum.

I'd like to thank my real mum (and dad) for conceiving the miracle that is me, and my sister, Naomi, and brother, Rufus, for living with the miracle that is me. You are all miracles, even if I sometimes find you annoying.

Thank you to the following people for holding my hand from childhood into adulthood: Laura Wilkins, Katie Starmer-Smith, Louise Wilkinson, Olivia Bridges, Nikki Minors, Rosie Thomas. For holding my hand in adulthood, and helping me to see the importance of looking after the child in me: Martha Freud, Giorgina Ramazzotti, Rebecca Priestley, Mika Simmons, Jada Sezer, Helena Marchese, Daisy Le Vay, Fearne Wood and last but certainly by no means least, Holly Beck. A massive thanks to Tertius Richardson and Donna Lancaster. Without your therapeutic work (is that what I call it?!), I am not sure this book would exist at all.

Finally, thank you to Harry, for always allowing me to be me, and Edie, for always being you.